KB271510

READING
HUNTER

READING HUNTER (리딩헌터) 중 · 고급 

지은이 장수용
펴낸이 임준현
펴낸곳 도서출판 넥서스

초판 1쇄 발행 2007년 8월 30일
초판 10쇄 발행 2011년 9월 25일

2판 1쇄 인쇄 2012년 4월 25일
2판 1쇄 발행 2012년 4월 30일

출판신고 2001년 12월 5일 제313-2005-00004호
서울시 은평구 통일로82길 17
Tel (02)330-5500 Fax (02)330-5555
ISBN 978-89-5795-218-4 13740

저자와 출판사의 허락없이 내용의 일부를 인용하거나
발췌하는 것을 금합니다.
저자와의 협의에 따라서 인지는 붙이지 않습니다.

가격은 뒤표지에 있습니다.
잘못 만들어진 책은 구입처에서 바꾸어 드립니다.

www.nexusbook.com
넥서스ACADEMY는 도서출판 넥서스의 수험서 전문 브랜드입니다.

영문독해 교재가 진화한다

READING HUNTER

리딩헌터 중 · 고급

장수용 지음

넥서스 ACADEMY

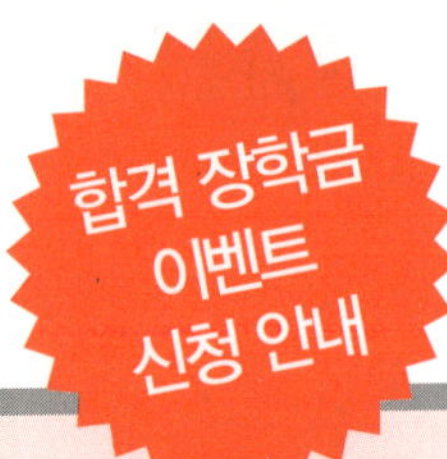

장수용 선생님이 저술한 교재(그래머헌터, 리딩헌터 및 강의용 교재 포함)로 공부하거나 장수용 선생님의 편입 강의를 듣고 대학에 합격한 독자님께 소정의 절차 확인 후 장학금(2만 원)을 드립니다.
naty316@hanmail.net 으로 다음의 양식을 기재하여 교재 구매 후 합격 발표 전에 미리 신청하시면 됩니다.
(장학금 받기 절차는 www.megaut.com 장수용 선생님 메인 페이지의 공지사항에서 확인)

① 이름 :
② 연락처 :
③ 목표 대학 및 학과 :
④ 교재 구매 날짜 :
⑤ 구매 서점 :

들어가기

편입 영어시험에서 독해의 비중은 예전과는 달리 평균적으로 65%의 비중을 차지한다고 해도 과언은 아닌 듯 싶습니다. 소위 말해서 편입 시험에 합격하느냐 못하느냐는 독해에서 결판이 난다고 할 정도이므로, 독해의 고득점 확보는 합격의 최우선 목표가 된 실정입니다.

『READING HUNTER 중·고급』은 편입시험에 등장하는 13개 Chapter의 공략을 통한 점진적인 실력 다지기 이후, 10회분의 Actual TEST를 통한 집중 훈련으로 독해 고득점을 확보할 수 있는 중·고급 독해 교재입니다.

저에 대한 수험생 여러분들의 과분한 사랑에 보답하고자 최선을 다했습니다. 본 교재의 완벽한 공략을 위해서 알찬 강의로써 확실한 도움을 드릴 것을 약속드립니다.

감사의 인사

이 책이 출간되기까지 많은 분들이 도움을 주셨습니다. 부족함이 많은 제자를 받아 주시고 많은 가르침을 주시는 한국외국어대학교 대학원 영어영문학 교수님들, 까다로운 저자의 부탁에 귀찮은 내색 한번 보이지 않으시면서 지극한 정성을 보여 주시는 넥서스 신옥희 상무님, 플랜티 편입 아카데미 전수용 원장님과 박명숙 실장님, 진정한 영어 실력 향상에 모든 열정을 쏟으시는 플랜티 TSE의 허혜영 선생님, 프린서플어학원의 이창훈 선생님, 편입 수험생들에게 양질의 강의를 선보이는 김기원 선생님, 본 교재의 집필에 많은 조언을 해 주신 『Voca Bible』 허민 선생님, 앞으로 많은 활동을 같이 하게 될 『the World Best Columns』의 정득권 선생님, 세상에서 가장 열심히 공부하시는 '편입에 실패란 없다' 카페 회원님들, 그리고 사랑하는 부모님과 누나, 이 모든 분들의 격려와 질책이 있었기에 『READING HUNTER 중·고급』이 완성되었습니다. 이 자리를 빌려 고개 숙여 감사의 인사를 전합니다.

저자 장수용

유형별 총정리

편입시험에 등장하는 독해의 모든 유형을 세분화하여, 어떠한
대학을 응시하든 간에 철저히 편입영어 독해의 훈련 및 적응이
가능하게 구성하였습니다.

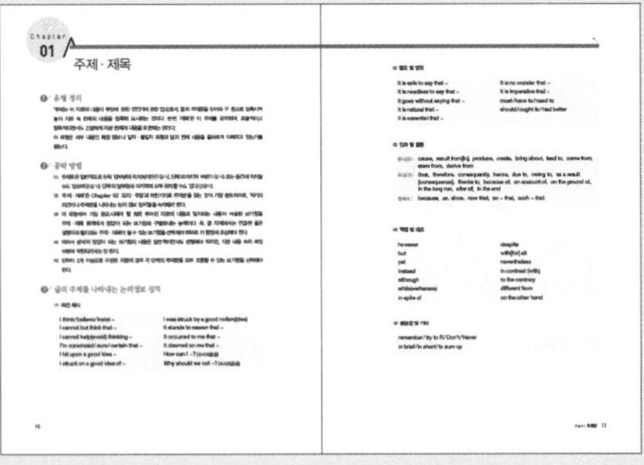

중 · 고급 수준

실제 편입시험에서 출제되었던 상위권 대학 500여 개의 기출문
제들과 편입시험 출제위원급 현직 대학교수님들이 출제하셨던
국내 수험영어 기출문제 중 200여 개를 조화롭게 혼합하여 중 ·
고급 수준의 독해 공략에 만전을 기할 수 있도록 구성하였습니다.

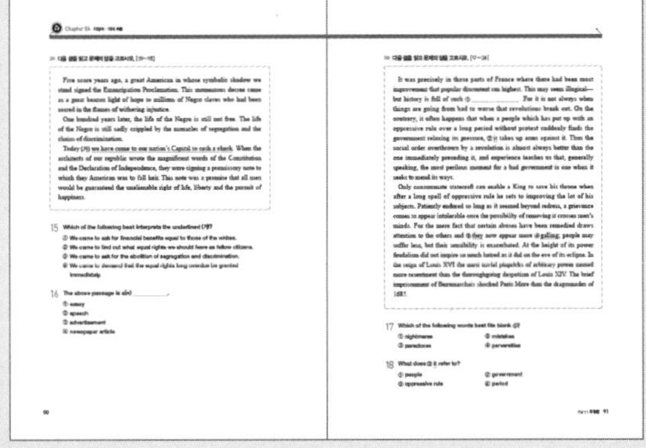

유형별 독해를 통한 체계적인 학습

예컨대, '주제 고르기' 하나만을 물어보는 기본 유형의 문제는 독
해의 비중만으로 보았을 때 20%도 되지 않으며, '주제'와 '특정 정
보'를 동시에 물어보는 것처럼 복합 유형의 문제가 절대적인 비중
을 차지합니다. 본 교재에서는 각각의 단원의 유형과 앞서 다루었
던 유형이 혼합된 복합 유형 문제들을 Part 1에서 다루어 입체적
인 공부가 가능하게 구성하였습니다.

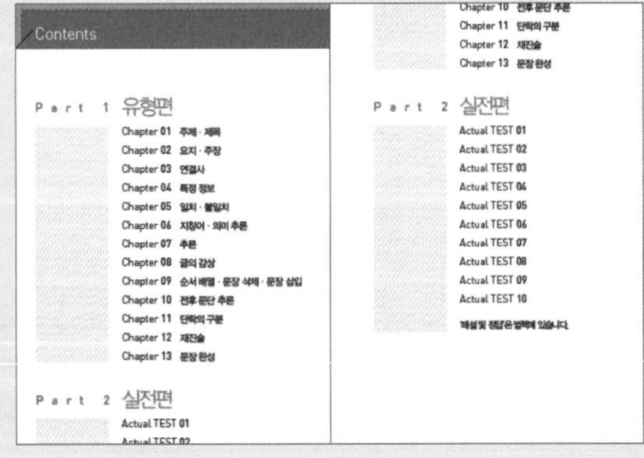

Contents

Part 1 유형편
Chapter 01 주제 · 제목
Chapter 02 요지 · 주장
Chapter 03 연결사
Chapter 04 특정정보
Chapter 05 일치 · 불일치
Chapter 06 지칭어 · 의미 추론
Chapter 07 추론
Chapter 08 글의 감상
Chapter 09 순서 배열 · 문장 삭제 · 문장 삽입
Chapter 10 전후 문단 추론
Chapter 11 단락의 구분
Chapter 12 재진술
Chapter 13 문장 완성

Part 2 실전편
Actual TEST 01
Actual TEST 02

Chapter 10 전후 문단 추론
Chapter 11 단락의 구분
Chapter 12 재진술
Chapter 13 문장 완성

Part 2 실전편
Actual TEST 01
Actual TEST 02
Actual TEST 03
Actual TEST 04
Actual TEST 05
Actual TEST 06
Actual TEST 07
Actual TEST 08
Actual TEST 09
Actual TEST 10

해설 및 정답은 별책에 있습니다.

실전 독해를 통한 집중 훈련

Part 1에서 유형별 독해를 통한 체계적인 훈련을 한 후, Part 2에서는 13개의 유형이 모두 혼합된 독해 실전 모의고사를 통한 집중 훈련을 하게 됩니다. 최근 상향 평준화되는 독해 시험에서 고득점을 노릴 수 있는 최상의 quality를 갖춘 문제들로 구성하였으므로, 확실한 공부를 당부드립니다.

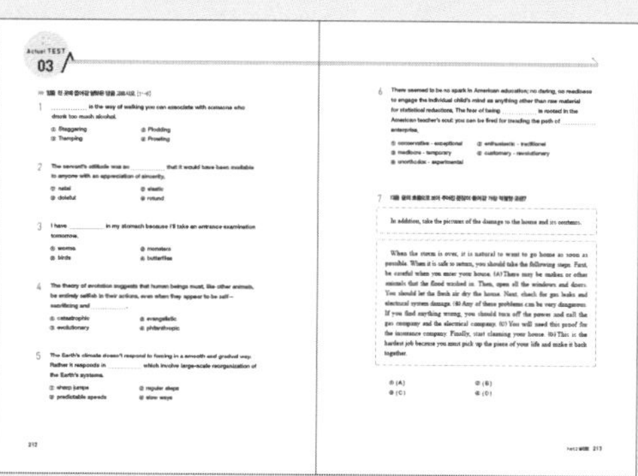

간결하고 명확한 해설

모든 보기항의 해석을 제시하여, 보기항의 정·오답이 되는 근거를 파악하는 연습이 독학생 스스로도 가능하게 했으며, 정답이 되는 이유 또한 제시하여 학습 효과를 높이도록 하였습니다.

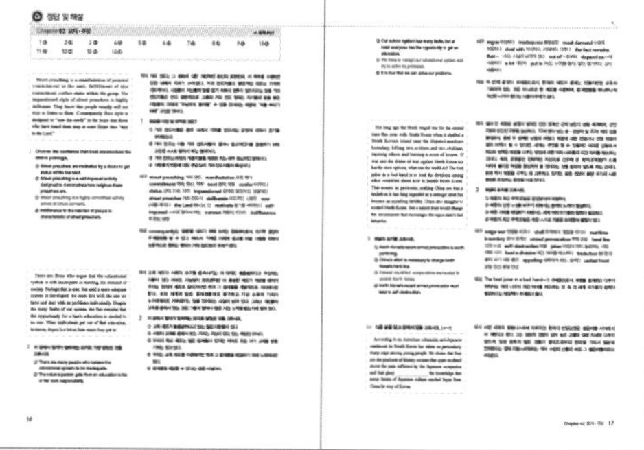

편의를 도모한 어구 정리

사전을 따로 찾아볼 필요 없이 지문에서 쓰인 어휘의 뜻부터 차례대로 정리하여 그 뜻부터 파악할 수 있게 구성하였습니다. 스터디 그룹 등을 통하여 독학을 하시는 분들은 이 어구 정리를 이용하여 스터디도 원활히 진행하실 수 있을 것입니다.

엄선된 중·고급 '문장 완성' 문제

'문장 완성' 또한 독해의 범주 안에서 함께 공부하는 것이 분명 효율적이므로, 약 150여 개의 핵심 문장 완성 문제를 Part 1과 Part 2에 조화롭게 배치하여 학습의 효율성을 높였습니다.

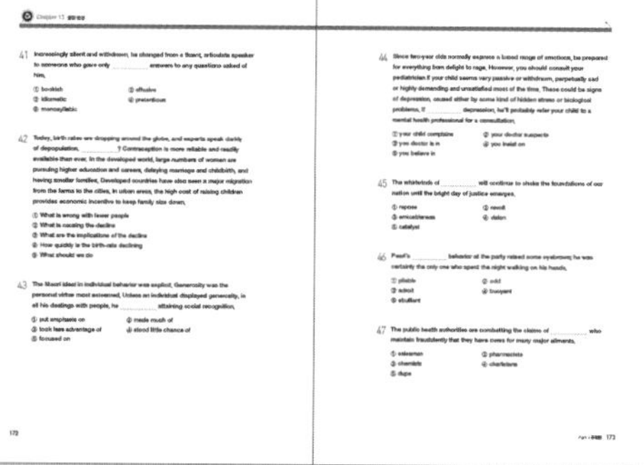

Contents

Part 1 유형편

Chapter 01 주제 · 제목 10

Chapter 02 요지 · 주장 26

Chapter 03 연결사 36

Chapter 04 특정 정보 42

Chapter 05 일치 · 불일치 62

Chapter 06 지칭어 · 의미 추론 83

Chapter 07 추론 97

Chapter 08 글의 감상 117

Chapter 09 순서 배열 · 문장 삭제 · 문장 삽입 129

Chapter 10 전후 문단 추론 138

Chapter 11 단락의 구분 141

Chapter 12 재진술 148

Chapter 13 문장 완성 154

Part 2 실전편

Actual TEST 01 184

Actual TEST 02 198

Actual TEST 03 212

Actual TEST 04 228

Actual TEST 05 242

Actual TEST 06 256

Actual TEST 07 268

Actual TEST 08 284

Actual TEST 09 300

Actual TEST 10 314

'해설 및 정답'은 별책에 있습니다.

Part 1
유형편

주제·제목 | 요지·주장 | 연결사 | 특정 정보 | 일치·불일치 | 지칭어·의미 추론 | 추론 | 글의 감상 | 순서 배열·문장 삭제·문장 삽입 | 전후 문단 추론 | 단락의 구분 | 재진술 | 문장 완성

주제 · 제목

❶ 유형 정의

'주제'는 이 지문의 내용이 무엇에 관한 것인가에 관한 답으로서, 글의 주제문을 단어와 구 등으로 압축시켜 놓아 지문 속 전체의 내용을 정확히 묘사하는 것이다. 반면 '제목'은 이 주제를 요약하여, 포괄적이고 함축적이면서도 간결하게 지문 전체의 내용을 표현하는 것이다.

이 유형은 세부 내용인 특정 정보나 일치 · 불일치 유형과 달리 전체 내용을 올바르게 이해하고 있는가를 묻는다.

❷ 공략 방법

(1) 주제문은 일반적으로 단락 앞부분에 위치하지만(두괄식), 단락의 마지막 부분(미괄식) 또는 중간에 위치할 수도 있으며(중괄식), 단락의 앞부분과 마지막에 모두 위치할 수도 있다(양괄식).

(2) '주제 · 제목'은 Chapter 02 '요지 · 주장'과 마찬가지로 주제문을 찾는 것이 가장 중요하므로, '작가의 의견이나 주제문을 나타내는 논리 정보 장치'들을 숙지해야 한다.

(3) 이 유형에서 가장 중요시해야 할 점은 주어진 지문의 내용과 일치하는 내용이 서술된 보기항을 주제 · 제목 문제에서 정답이 되는 보기항과 구별해내는 능력이다. 즉, 글 자체에서는 언급된 옳은 설명이라 할지라도 주제 · 제목이 될 수 있는 보기항을 선택해야 하므로 이 함정에 조심해야 한다.

(4) 따라서 문제의 정답이 되는 보기항의 내용은 일반적이면서도 분명해야 하지만, 지문 내용 속의 특정 부분에 국한되어서는 안 된다.

(5) 단락이 2개 이상으로 구성된 지문의 경우 각 단락의 주제문을 모두 포함할 수 있는 보기항을 선택해야 한다.

❸ 글의 주제를 나타내는 논리정보 장치

(1) 의견 제시

I think / believe / insist ~	I was struck by a good notion(idea)
I cannot but think that ~	It stands to reason that ~
I cannot help(avoid) thinking ~	It occurred to me that ~
I'm convinced / sure / certain that ~	It dawned on me that ~
I hit upon a good idea ~	How can I ~? (수사의문문)
I struck on a good idea of ~	Why should we not ~? (수사의문문)

(2) **필요 및 당위**

It is safe to say that ~	It is no wonder that ~
It is needless to say that ~	It is imperative that ~
It goes without saying that ~	must / have to / need to
It is natural that ~	should / ought to / had better
It is essential that ~	

(3) **인과 및 결론**

동사(구) : cause, result from[in], produce, create, bring about, lead to, come from, stem from, derive from

부사(구) : thus, therefore, consequently, hence, due to, owing to, as a result [consequence], thanks to, because of, on account of, on the ground of, in the long run, after all, in the end

접속사 : because, as, since, now that, so ~ that, such ~ that

(4) **역접 및 대조**

however	despite
but	with[for] all
yet	nevertheless
instead	in contrast (with)
although	to the contrary
while(=whereas)	different from
in spite of	on the other hand

(5) **명령문 및 기타**

remember / try to R / Don't / Never
in brief / in short / to sum up

When we take the most distant prospect of life, what does it present to us but a chaos of unhappiness, a confused and tumultuous scene of labor and contest, disappointment and defeat? If we view past ages in the reflection of history, what do they offer to our meditation but crimes and calamities? One year is distinguished by a famine, another by an earthquake; kingdoms are made desolate, sometimes by war and sometimes by pestilence; the peace of the world is interrupted at one time by the caprices of a tyrant, at another by the rage of the conqueror. The memory is stored only with vicissitudes of evil; and the happiness, such as it is, of one part of mankind, is found to arise commonly from sanguinary success, from victories which confer upon them the power not so much of improving life by any new enjoyment as of inflicting misery on others and gratifying their own pride by comparative greatness.

1 Which of the following is the best title for the passage?

① Reflections on history
② Suffering humanity
③ A distant view of life
④ Fluctuating failure and success in life

The more complicated our thoughts and emotions, the less effective is language as a tool of expression. This is not a simple matter of style or eloquence, for even the finest speakers and writers, using the most sensitive language, would be incapable of putting certain thoughts into words. For this reason, many people use poetry and music instead of prose. These two forms of communication convey subtle yet powerful meanings that cannot be expressed with ordinary words.

2   **The best title of the passage above is ____________.**

① Uses of Language
② Limitations of Language
③ The Hidden Meanings of Words
④ Words, Poetry, and Music
⑤ Subtle yet Powerful Meanings

>> 다음 글을 읽고 문제의 답을 고르시오. [3~4]

As an editor of a Cairo newspaper, I was given ______________ late one night. Aware that there might not be a place left for it in the next day's edition, I sent it to the printer with the annotation: "space permitting". The following day it appeared in the paper and read: "… may God have mercy on him and may he be with the angels in heaven, space permitting."

3   **Choose the one that best fits into the blank.**

① a benediction
② a religious message
③ an obituary
④ a church bulletin
⑤ an advertisement

4   **Which is the best title of the passage?**

① Space Problems with Newspapers
② Misunderstood Direction
③ Religious Messages in Newspapers
④ Spaces for Annotation
⑤ Advertisement on a Wrong Newspaper

New technology enables monitoring of doctor's prescriptions, with both good and bad consequences: Some medical overseers use it to make sure that doctors choose the medicine that best treats patients' ailments, while others use it to pressure doctors to prescribe not the most effective drug but the cheapest one. Similarly, the existence of digital records tracking patients' medical histories can enhance treatment and promote epidemiological research, but it can also lead to invasion of patients' privacy. Computers can bring new realms into the classroom, but they may divert precious funds from more solely needed educational tools and deepen the divide between rich and poor classrooms. The list of good news-bad news effects goes on and on.

5 **윗글의 제목으로 올바른 것은?**

① The dilemmas in the information age
② The effective use of computers in modern education
③ How to distinguish good news and bad news
④ The impact of public policy on individual privacy

Since 9/11 world technology often has been our crucial but silent partner in helping us to ramp up our law enforcement and national security capabilities. But we also need to right. The marriage of information-gathering technology with information storing technology, manipulated in increasingly sophisticated databases, is beginning to produce the defining privacy challenge of the information age. We are (가) _________________ the verge of an age of a revolution in the capability for the highly detailed, largely automatic, widespread surveillance of our daily lives. Moreover, other powerful new technologies are (나) _______________ the horizon, like sensor technology and nanotechnology. We need to think about these issues broadly while keeping them (다) _______________ overtaking our civil liberties. Who will have access to those data banks, and (라) _______________ what checks-and-balances? In what cases should law enforcement agencies be able to use this information, and what safeguards should apply? There should be a general presumption that Americans can know when their personal information is collected, and to see, check and correct any errors.

6 **Which of the following is the best title for the passage?**

① Civil Liberties
② National Security Capabilities
③ Surveillance of Our Daily Lives
④ Privacy Challenge of the Information Age

7 **Which of the following best fits into the blanks from (가) to (라)?**

① in - on - from - by
② on - in - from - by
③ in - on - for - under
④ on - on - from - under

>>> 다음 글을 읽고 문제의 답을 고르시오. [8~9]

The Constitution embodies the ideology's view of man and of government in its relationship to man. People have both rights and interests: government must respect the former; and it should permit the individualistic pursuit of the latter so long as either national unity or basic rights are not infringed. The polity would be failing if striving individuals were unable to advance their interests within it—or if they were able to be too successful, since every special interest is inherently "activated by some common impulse or passion adverse to the rights of other citizens, or to the permanent and aggregate interest of the community", as James Madison put it in The Federalist Papers. The balance must be found in an elaborate social-political pluralism where no group or interest can get too strong. Underlining the entire constitutional arrangement then as now is the classical liberal distrust of power as a threat to the sovereign individual. The answer to this problem of power: ________________.

8 **The author is talking about __________ .**

① the original of the Constitution

② the American individualism

③ the spirit of the Constitution

④ the social-political pluralism

9 **Choose the one which can be used in the underlined part.**

① raise it and reinforce it

② make it and keep it

③ recognize it and use it

④ disperse it and limit it

The prime ministers of Russia and Ukraine finally reached an agreement Sunday morning. They agreed to resume gas supplies to Europe by early next week. The two leaders have asked the gas providers of their respective countries to prepare by Monday all pertinent documents that need to be signed. The two premiers agreed that Russia would give Ukraine a 20 percent discount on the gas purchase. In exchange, Ukraine will not hike the fees it charged Russia to transport gas onward to European countries.

10 **윗글의 제목으로 가장 적절한 것을 고르시오.**

① Problems with Gas Supplies in Russia and Ukraine

② Russia and Ukraine Agree to Resume Gas Flow

③ The Result of Gas Shutoff in Russia and Ukraine

④ Conditions of Providing Gas for Russia and Ukraine

We must review the threat of flunking and see it as it really is. It is an expression of confidence by both teachers and parents that the students have the ability to learn the material presented to them. However, making it work again would take a dedicated, caring conspiracy between teachers and parents. It would mean facing the tough reality that passing kids who haven't learned the material—while it might save them grief for the short term— dooms them to long-term illiteracy. It would mean that teachers would have to follow through on their threats, and parents would have to stand behind them, knowing their children's best interests are indeed at stake. This means no more doing Scott's assignments for him because he might fail. No more passing Jodi because she is such a nice kid. This is a policy that worked in the past and can work today. A wise teacher, with the support of parents, gave our sons and daughters the opportunity to succeed—or fail. It is time that we returned this choice to all students.

11 윗글의 제목을 고르시오.

① How to Correct Students' Wrongdoings
② Failure as a Positive Teaching Tool
③ Relationship Between Teachers and Parents
④ How to Control Students' Lives

World War II cost the American people more than $300 billion. To finance it, Congress raised income taxes. Also, Congress made employers withhold taxes from workers' paychecks. War bond purchases accounted for nearly two-thirds of government war revenues. The government made it patriotic to buy war bonds. Americans heard and saw daily appeals to buy bonds in newspapers, on the radio, and at the movies. Famous entertainers such as Kate Smith, Jane Froman, Al Johnson, Frank Sinatra, Bob Hope, and Bing Crosby staged bond rallies around the country.

12 **What is the topic of the passage?**

① The contribution of entertainment industry during World War II
② Financial sources of America's expense during the war
③ The origin of government bonds in the American history
④ Economic changes in America after the end of World War II

≫ 다음 글을 읽고 문제의 답을 고르시오. [13~14]

Reid Hilton's new arm is only slightly less remarkable than the Six Million Dollar Man's atomic-powered limb. Hilton, 24, a karate expert who lost his rght arm below the elbow in an accident, will probably not risk smashing bricks with his experimental $40,000 replacement. But the artificial limb should enable him to function like a man with two ① _______________ arms. The controls of the myoelectric arm are directly connected to the nerves in the stump of his severed arm. Unlike most other ② _______________ arms and hands, it is also equipped with feed-back devices that give him a sense of touch.

13 **The best title of this passage would be ___________.**

① Atomic-Powered Arm
② A Karate Expert
③ The Nerves of a Severed Arm
④ Feedback Devices
⑤ The $40,000 Arm

14 **Which of the following pairs best fits into ① and ②?**

① natural - artificial
② natural - aesthetic
③ man-made - aesthetic
④ artificial - aesthetic
⑤ man-made - artificial

>>> **다음 글을 읽고 문제의 답을 고르시오.** [15~16]

The shift from boom to depression came gradually and unevenly to Western Europe in the years around 1300. From the early fourteenth century through much of the fifteenth, a number of related trends—shrinking population, contracting markets, an end to the long process of land reclamation, and a creeping mood of pessimism and retrenchment—resulted in a general economic slump and a deepening of social antagonism. These trends were _______________ universal. They were less marked in northern Italy than elsewhere, and north of the Alps certain localities, profiting from favorable commercial situations or technological advances, became more prosperous than before. At a time when English towns were generally declining, Coventry and a few others grew wealthy from the rise of woolen cloth production.

15 윗글의 제목으로 가장 적합한 것을 고르시오.

① Technological Advances in European Cities in the Late Middle Ages
② General Economic Depression in European Cities in the Late Middle Ages
③ Prosperous European Cities and Markets in the Late Middle Ages
④ Declining European Cities and Shrinking Population in the Late Middle Ages
⑤ Different Economic Situations in European Cities in the Late Middle Ages

16 빈칸에 적합한 단어나 숙어를 고르시오.

① quite ② by no means
③ extremely ④ nevertheless
⑤ not merely

"Most of us are taught to watch money, but not to value time", says Andrea Steenhouse. "As a result, we may not even think about how much irreplaceable time we waste to save a few pennies." Is it worthwhile ________________, searching for picture hangers, when the neighborhood hardware-store owner would point to them immediately? To wait for takeout at the restaurant when delivery is available for a small tip? Rather than dismiss the idea with the words "I can't afford that," it may pay to think twice.

17 Choose the one that best fits into the blank.

① to try to save time while you don't have much to do

② to wander through a giant discount mart

③ to spend lots of money that you have

④ to compare all different kinds of hardware

⑤ to ask a manager of a department store to get quotes

18 Which is the best title for this passage?

① Money Is as Important as Time.

② Picture Hangers Cost You More than You Think.

③ Buy What You Want Whatever It Costs.

④ Don't Save Pennies and Waste Hours.

⑤ Think Twice before You Buy Hardware.

≫ 다음 글을 읽고 문제의 답을 고르시오. [19~21]

Procrastinators are people who have a chronic habit of putting things off, usually until the last minute and sometimes until it is too late altogether. The most common reason that procrastinators themselves give for their habit, which they are usually quite willing to talk about even if not willing to change, is that they are lazy. Other typical excuses are that they are undisciplined, brilliant but disorganized, or very poor at organizing their time.

Some procrastinators, however, almost against their very nature, actually get as far as trying to do something about their problem and seek help. Recent research with such people seems to suggest that their difficulties are much more complex than the procrastinators themselves think. The general conclusions are that such people have a vulnerable sense of self-worth, are particularly fearful of failure, and deliberately put things off precisely so that they never leave themselves time to produce their best work. The reason for their delaying tactics is that, since they do everything at the last moment and under pressure, the procrastinators can retain their illusion of brilliance without ever having to put it to the test.

19 **The first paragraph is mainly concerned with ___________.**

① the undisciplined character of procrastinators

② that disorganization is the procrastinator's main problem

③ procrastinators' willingness to talk a lot

④ the nature of procrastination

20 **The second paragraph is mainly concerned with ___________.**

① that procrastinators always leave everything until the last moment

② research findings regarding procrastinators

③ how some procrastinators never seek help

④ how procrastinators have an illusion of brilliance

21 **The best title of the passage above is ___________.**

① Procrastination: Excuses and Reality

② Disorganization, the True Cause of Procrastination

③ Procrastination: Never Do Today What You Can Put Off Until Tomorrow

④ The Cure for Procrastination

>>> **다음 글을 읽고 문제의 답을 고르시오.** [22~23]

Hurricane Katrina's effect on the city of New Orleans has been _______________. Almost four years after the storm, a quarter of the population has never returned. A third of homes still lie empty, many decked with tarpaulins and with the flood-line still visible. Residential streets are lined with houses with collapsing porches, fallen plasterwork and hopeful For Sale signs. Less than half the city's public transport facilities have been restored, and the wheels on the city's famous street-cars, even the one named Desire, are still rusty.

Most important, though the number of the chronically sick in the city has risen sharply, medical services remain in tatters. Only 57% of the city's medical facilities have reopened, and tens of thousands of records have been lost. In St Bernard Parish, which once had two hospitals, there is now none. Charity Hospital, the main refuge for the poor and uninsured for more than 250 years, is shuttered and surrounded by wire fencing.

22 윗글의 제목은 무엇인가?

① New Orleans: City of Sickness

② People vs. Nature

③ A Ray of Hope in New Orleans

④ A Typical Example of No Preparation

23 빈칸에 들어갈 말로 가장 올바른 것은?

① underestimated by the politicians

② much longer-lasting than most expected

③ influencing the people's state of mind

④ forgotten by the people who moved out

>> 다음 글을 읽고 문제의 답을 고르시오. [24~25]

> The power of poetic composition to create complex new ideas from simpler conventional ideas reveals itself in especially clear form in personification—metaphors through which we understand other things ① ________________ our own terms. Personification permits us to use our knowledge about ourselves to maximal effect, to use insights about ourselves to help us comprehend such things as forces of nature, common events, abstract concepts, and inanimate objects.

24 **The most likely title of this passage would be ____________.**

① Poetic Composition

② Rhetoric

③ Metaphor

④ Metonymy

⑤ Personification

25 **Which of the following best fits into ①?**

① by   ② with

③ in   ④ of

⑤ from

요지 · 주장

❶ 유형 정의

'주제'가 '이 글이 무엇에 관한 것인가에 대한 답'이라면, '요지'는 '이 글을 통해 무엇을 전달하려 하는가에 대한 답'이라고 정의내릴 수 있다. 즉, 글의 중심 사상이 글의 요지가 되는 것이며, 주제문이 가리키는 내용의 중심이 되는 생각을 하나의 문장으로 요약해 놓은 것을 말한다.

❷ 공략 방법

(1) '요지'는 Chapter 01 '주제 · 제목'에서 다룬 바와 같이 글의 지문 속에 있는 주제문을 발견하는 것이 우선순위이다.

(2) 대부분의 영어 글은 두괄식이나 미괄식이지만, 중괄식이나 양괄식을 취하는 경우도 많다. 주제문이 명백히 비춰지지 않는 글의 경우 논리적인 추론을 통하여 필자의 요지와 주장을 추론해야 한다.

(3) Chapter 01 '주제 · 제목'에서 설명했던 것과 마찬가지의 맥락으로서, 요지와 주장은 일반적이면서도 분명해야 한다. 또한 보기항 중 오답은 대개가 문장의 일부분에 그치는 세부 내용들이므로, 전체 내용에 해당되는 것인지 또는 일부분에 그치는지 구별해야 한다.

Street preaching is a manifestation of personal commitment to the sect; fulfillment of this commitment confers status within the group. The impassioned style of street preachers is highly deliberate. They know that people usually will not stop to listen to them. Consequently their style is designed to "sow the seeds" in the hope that those who have heard them may at some future time "turn to the Lord."

1 **Choose the sentence that best summarizes the above passage.**

① Street preachers are motivated by a desire to get status within the sect.

② Street preaching is a self-imposed activity designed to demonstrate how religious these preachers are.

③ Street preaching is a highly committed activity aimed at future converts.

④ Indifference to the reaction of people is characteristic of street preachers.

There are those who argue that the educational system is still inadequate in meeting the demand of society. Perhaps this is true, but until a more adequate system is developed, we must live with the one we have and deal with its problems individually. Despite the many faults of our system, the fact remains that the opportunity for a basic education is denied to no one. What individuals get out of that education, however, depends a lot on how much they put in.

2 **이 글에서 필자가 말하려는 요지로 가장 알맞은 것을 고르시오.**

① There are many people who believe the educational system to be inadequate.

② The value a person gets from an education is his or her own responsibility.

③ Our school system has many faults, but at least everyone has the opportunity to get an education.

④ We have to accept our educational system and try to solve its problems.

⑤ It is true that we can solve our problems.

Not long ago the North waged war for the second time this year with South Korea when it shelled a South Korean island near the disputed maritime boundary, killing two soldiers and two civilians, injuring others and burning a score of houses. If war and the threat of war against North Korea are hardly even options, what can the world do? The best joker in a bad hand is to heal the divisions among other countries about how to handle North Korea. That means, in particular, making China see that a tinderbox it has long regarded as a strategic asset has become an appalling liability. China also struggles to control North Korea. But a united front would change the environment that encourages the rogue state's bad behavior.

3 윗글의 요지를 고르시오.

① North Korea's recent armed provocation is worth punishing.
② China's effort is necessary to change North Korea's hard line.
③ Several countries' cooperations are needed to control North Korea.
④ North Korea's recent armed provocation must lead to self-destruction.

According to an American columnist, anti-Japanese sentiment in South Korea has taken on particularly sharp edge among young people. He claims that they are the products of history courses that spare no detail about the pain inflicted by the Japanese occupation and that glory ________________ the knowledge that many facets of Japanese culture reached Japan from China by way of Korea.

4 **The columnist insists that ____________.**

① South Koreans, especially younger people, do not fully recognize the historical lesson of the Japanese colonial period

② the description of the Japanese colonial period in Korean history courses has many problems

③ it is an indisputable fact that Japanese culture was influenced by Korean culture

④ young Koreans have unfavorable impressions toward the Japanese due to their history education

⑤ Japan and Korea should cooperate with each other in spite of their historical experience

5 **Which one is the most appropriate in the blank?**

① for   ② in

③ to   ④ toward

⑤ against

>>> 다음 글을 읽고 문제의 답을 고르시오. [6~7]

Resilient couples view their marriage as sacred, worthy of sacrifice. "It requires a leap of faith to believe this in our age of divorce, but it's crucial for turning hardship to strength", Wolin says.

The Lafontaines, married 12 years, have taken this leap. "We count on our faith in the marriage and in God much more as the years go by." Alisa says. "When we're struggling with a problem such as too little money, which happens a lot now that we have four kids, faith gives me the confidence to say, 'It will work out.' And it always does."

What if your marriage is so fraught with conflict that you can't appreciate each other? To renew the romance, stir "embers of positive feelings" by focusing on the past, Gottman says.

Jill and Don Ross love to recall how they met. Jill had gone to a restaurant where Don was singing. After hearing a song she loved, Jill clapped exuberantly, "I am very glad you showed up tonight", Don crooned. "Are you married?"

"No", she flirted. "Will you sing at my wedding?"

"I'll sing at _______________ wedding", he replied, surprising even himself.

Seven months later, Don came through on his promise. And they've lived happily ever after.

6   **Which of the following is NOT a correct description of the writer's view?**

① Taking a leap of faith is necessary for a happy marriage.

② Reliving beautiful moments is good for a happy marriage.

③ Faith in God is good for a happy marriage.

④ It is sometimes necessary to renew the romance.

⑤ A problem such as too little money usually causes a divorce.

7   **Fill in the blank with the most appropriate word in the given context.**

① my   ② your

③ her   ④ our

⑤ their

I have chosen the literature we will be reading this quarter hoping that it will inspire you to see literature and America in a new way. Most importantly, I hope these works will cause you to think. Writing at its best is a concentrated form of thinking: writing in your journal with the intent of exploring those aspects of what we see and read will focus your insights and ideas as well as bring new ones. The thoughts that will fill your journal will also motivate our class discussion. Finally, writing regularly in a journal is one more way of becoming more comfortable with writing itself.

8 **Which of the following is the main idea of the passage?**

① In this semester you will discover a New America.

② Although you will not do any written assignments you will be encouraged to think about the reading material.

③ The class discussions will incite you to read American literature.

④ Through reading journalistic writing you will enhance your thought process.

⑤ Writing a journal will enhance your thought process together with your writing skills.

We very rarely consider, however, the process by which we gained our convictions. If we did so, we could hardly fail to see that there was usually little ground for our confidence in them. Here and there, in this department of knowledge or that, some one of us might make a fair claim to have taken some trouble to get correct ideas of, let us say, the situation in Russia, the sources of our food supply, the origin of the constitution, the revision of the tariff, the policy of the Holy Roman Apostolic Church, modern business organization, trade unions, birth control, socialism, the League of Nations, the excess-profits tax, preparedness, advertising in its social bearings; but only a very exceptional person would be entitled to opinions on all these, and on many other questions of equal importance, of which we may know even less. We feel compelled, as self-respecting persons, to take sides when they come up for discussion. We even surprise ourselves by our omniscience. Without taking thought we see in a flash that it is most righteous and expedient to discourage birth control by legislative enactment, or that one who decries intervention in Mexico is clearly wrong, or that big advertising is essential to big business and that big business is the pride of the land. As godlike beings why should we not rejoice in our omniscience?

9   윗글을 가장 잘 요약한 것은?

① In spite of all possible difficulties facing us, we, as godlike beings, have overcome them with confidence.

② We, human beings, are often surprised at our own ability to cope with things successfully in spite of various difficulties and problems.

③ Although we have little reason to trust our convictions on the important issues of life, we delight in forming and expressing such opinions without a moment's thought.

④ Human beings will be punished by God one way or the other for their own overconfidence in competing with God.

Before the introduction of the computer search, library research was a long and tedious task. Now, instead of spending long hours looking through the cards, catalogs and periodical indexes for books and articles on your subject, you can have a computer do the looking for you. All you need to do is give your subject to the computer. This is not as easy as it sounds, however, because you must know exactly what you understand. The computer then searches its memory for books and articles about your subject. It takes less than a second for the computer to complete its search. Finally, it prints a bibliography, a list of authors and titles of the books and articles it has found for your subject.

10 **What is the topic of this paragraph?**

① library research
② computer searches
③ bibliographies
④ looking for books and articles
⑤ the system of a library

11 **What is the main idea of this paragraph?**

① Library research is a long and tedious task.
② A bibliography is a list of authors and titles of books and articles.
③ Library research through a computer is easy.
④ A computer can find books and articles for you.
⑤ A bibliography is important for finding the books you want.

Einstein's theory of relativity is, in essence, a description of the interaction between different perspectives. Sigmund Freud's analytical methods were designed to find details that didn't fit traditional paradigms in order to come up with a completely new point of view. To solve a problem creatively, you must abandon the first approach that comes to mind, which usually stems from past experiences, and reconceptualize the problem. Thus geniuses do not merely solve existing problems; they identify new ones.

12 윗글의 요지로서 가장 적절한 것은?

① Einstein and Freud are real geniuses.

② Geniuses look at problems from all angles.

③ Geniuses usually ignore past experiences.

④ Geniuses try to solve a complicated problem only.

The "broken windows" theory was the brainchild of the criminologists, James Wilson and George Kelling. They argue that crime is the inevitable result of disorder. If a window is broken and left unrepaired, people walking by will conclude that no-one cares and no-one is in charge. Soon, more windows will be broken and the sense of anarchy will spread from the building to the street on which it faces, sending a signal that _________________. In a city, relatively minor problems like graffiti, public disorder and aggressive panhandling are all the equivalent of broken windows, invitations to more serious crimes.

What does this suggest? It says that the criminal—far from being someone who acts for fundamental, intrinsic reasons and who live in his own world—is actually someone acutely sensitive to his environment, who is alert to all kinds of cues, and who is prompted to commit crimes based on his perception of the world around him. That is an incredibly radical—and in some sense unbelievable—idea. It says that behavior is a function of social context.

13 **What is the main idea of the passage?**

① Most break-ins in the city occur through windows.

② An individual's crime behavior is deeply influenced by the environment.

③ Minor offenders may become serious criminals in the long run.

④ Criminals are born to disturb the public peace.

⑤ Pedestrians are irresistibly affected by the condition of street-side windows.

14 **Which of the following best fits into blank?**

① anything goes here

② the police are around

③ the windows need fixing

④ someone is in charge here

⑤ it will collapse soon

연결사

❶ 유형 정의

연결사는 문장과 문장의 연결을 논리적으로 응집시키는 연결어구이며, 연결사 선택 문제는 특정 연결사를
생략한 채 주어진 문장들 간의 응집성을 완성시키기 위해 올바른 연결사를 선택하는 문제 유형이다.

❷ 공략 방법

(1) 연결사 자체가 글의 전개 방식을 자연스럽게 해 주는 장치이니, 글의 논리적 흐름을 살펴야 한다.

(2) 단락의 전개 방식을 자연스럽게 해 주는 '주요 연결사'들을 숙지해야 한다.

❸ 주요 연결사

(1) 열거

> many, several, various, diverse, different, two, some, others, the first, the
> second, the third, … the last, one, another, the next, … the final, the most
> important (essential, necessary, chief) ~, the primary ~

(2) 대조 · 역접

> however, but, yet, instead, although, while(=whereas), in spite of, despite,
> with[for] all, nevertheless, in contrast (with), to the contrary, on the other hand,
> meantime, meanwhile, by the way

(3) 양보

> although, even if, even when, despite, as, granting, admitting

(4) 예시

> for example, for instance, such as

(5) **첨가**

besides, in addition, furthermore, as well, also, too, moreover

(6) **인과**

so, thus, therefore, hence, consequently, accordingly, as a result, as a
consequence

(7) **결론 · 요약**

after all, in conclusion, in the long run, in the end, ultimately, eventually, in short,
in brief

(8) **부연**

that is (to say), in other words, namely, as it were, so to speak, in deed, or

>>> 다음 글을 읽고 문제의 답을 고르시오. [1~2]

Repetition of words and structures can be very effective. We are usually told at school not to begin all our sentences in the same way (and especially not to begin all our sentences with 'I'), and it is certainly true that careless repetitions can be monotonous. ________________, when important words or phrases are repeated deliberately it can help to strengthen the impression that the writer wants to make. Which sounds better: 'I came, I saw, I conquered' or 'I came, saw and conquered?'

1 문맥상 빈칸에 적절한 것을 고르시오.

① For instance   ② As a result

③ However   ④ In other words

⑤ Whereas

2 이 글의 제목으로 가장 적절한 것을 고르시오.

① Repetition of Words and Structures

② Sentence with 'I'

③ Careless Repetitions

④ Deliberate Repetitions

⑤ Strong Impression

Looking first at vocabulary differences, English has ①many words for someone who is not generous with money. Different contexts will require different uses. These words, while expressing basically the same meaning, are not functionally equivalent. ② ______________ words have connotative as well as denotative meanings.

3 Choose the one that is not an example of ①.

① frugal   ② sparing
③ thrifty   ④ stingy
⑤ meticulous

4 Which of the following best fits into ②?

① For example   ② In other words
③ However   ④ Whereas
⑤ In addition

>>> 다음 글을 읽고 문제의 답을 고르시오. [5~6]

Television's variety becomes a narcotic, not a stimulus. Its serial, kaleidoscopic exposures force us to follow its lead. The viewer is on a perpetual guided tour: 30 minutes at the museum, 30 at the cathedral, 30 for a drink, then back on the bus to the next attraction—except on television, typically, the spans allotted are on the order of minutes or seconds, and the chosen delights are more often car crashes and people killing on another. ① ________________, a lot of television usurps one of the most precious of all human gifts, the ability to focus your attention yourself, rather than just passively surrender it.

5 **The best title of this passage is ____________.**

① Television and a guided tour: Similarities and differences

② Attractions on television

③ Pitfalls of television

④ Kaleidescope of TV

⑤ How to break free of TV

6 **The expression that is most appropriate for ① is "____________".**

① In short

② In contrast

③ Likewise

④ In a similar vein

⑤ For instance

I don't deny that the feeling of success makes it easier to enjoy life. A painter, ① _______________, who has been obscure throughout his youth, is likely to become happier if his talent wins recognition. Nor do I deny that money, up to a certain point, is very capable of increasing happiness; beyond that point, I do not think it does so. What I do maintain is that success can only be one ingredient in happiness; and is too dearly purchased if all the other ingredients have been sacrificed to obtain it.

7 Which of the following best fits into ①?

① let us say

② whereas

③ otherwise

④ in contrast

⑤ paradoxically

8 Choose the best title of the above passage.

① Worthlessness of Money

② An Important Requirement of Success

③ The Extent of Success

④ The Inevitable Aim of Life

⑤ The Cost of Success

특정 정보

❶ 유형 정의

주어진 지문의 내용을 바탕으로 하여, 출제 교수가 구체적인 세부 정보를 문제화한 후 문제에서 요구하는
정보를 지문의 내용 안에서 파악해야 하는 유형이다. 즉, 문제에서 요구하는 조건에 합당한 특정 정보를
주어진 지문에서 옳게 추출한 보기항을 선택하는 유형이다.

❷ 공략 방법

(1) 어떠한 특정 정보 추출을 요구하는지 알아야 하므로, 문제부터 반드시 봐야 한다.

(2) CBT TOEFL이나 TOEIC의 경우는 문제만 읽은 후 지문만 훑어나가도 문제에서 요구하는 쟁점을
발견하여 문제를 쉽게 풀 수 있지만, 국내 수험 영어인 '고시'와 '편입' 영어 문제는 이 방법이 통하지
않는다. 즉, Skip과 Scanning을 통해서 문제 해결을 할 수 있다는 것은 결과적인 측면일 뿐, 실제
시험에서는 통하지 않으므로, 순서대로 지문을 읽으면서 머릿속에 기억된 질문에서 요구한 특정 정보를
골라내야 된다.

(3) Chapter 05 '일치 · 불일치' 유형과 마찬가지로 주어진 지문에 있는 내용과 동일한 문장 그대로
보기항에 진술되는 경우는 드물며, 거의 대개가 재진술되어 있는 점을 조심해야 한다.

(4) 보기항에 있는 오답들의 내용이 지문의 내용과는 일치할지라도 주어진 문제의 조건과 상반되지 않는지
조심해야 한다.

(5) 수험 영어는 수험생의 상식을 요구하는 것이 아닌, 주어진 글 안의 내용을 얼마나 신속하고 정확하게
파악하느냐의 사고 능력 테스트이다. 따라서 주어진 지문의 내용을 벗어나는 상식을 동원해서는 안 된다.
상식적인 면에서 동전은 두 면이지만, 작가가 동전은 세 개의 면이라고 한다면 그 글에서는 '동전의 면은
3개이다'가 진리가 된다.

Professor Iyengar of Columbia University conducted an experiment in which she set up a tasting booth with a variety of exotic gourmet jams at an upscale grocery store. Sometimes the booth had six different jams, and sometimes twenty-four different jams on display. She wanted to see whether the number of jam choices made any difference in the number of jams sold. Conventional economic wisdom, of course, says that the more choices consumers have, the more likely they are to buy, because it is easier for consumers to find the jam that perfectly fits their needs. But Iyengar found the opposite to be true. Thirty percent of those who stopped by the six-choice booth ended up buying some jam, while only three percent of those who stopped by the bigger booth bought anything. Why is that? For buying jam is a snap decision. You say to yourself, instinctively, "I want that one." And if you are given too many choices, if you are forced to consider much more than your unconscious mind is comfortable with, you get paralyzed. Snap judgements can be made in a snap because they are frugal, and if we want to protect our snap judgements, we have to take steps to protect that frugality.

1 **Which of the following is the major finding by Professor Iyengar?**

① Snap judgements require fewer choices to choose from.

② Large upscale stores are bound to dominate the market.

③ Conventional economic wisdom has withstood the test of time.

④ Consumers are easily pleased with a wide range of selection.

⑤ Buyers' unconscious mind weighs each and every option carefully.

Then I grasped the child's head with my left hand and tried to get the wooden tongue depressor between her teeth. She fought, with teeth clenched, desperately! But now I also had grown furious—at a child. I tried to hold myself down but I couldn't. Now I know how to expose a throat for inspection.

2 이 글에서 "I"의 직업은?

① surgeon ② athlete

③ physician ④ therapeutist

Chimpanzees, our close relatives, are sometimes compared to politicians: they engage in power plays; they use diplomacy; they assign perks to various positions in a complicated social hierarchy. Blue monkeys, which seem calmer and less prone to form coalitions, appear to be more egalitarian. And yet my study of the group dynamics of territorial battles, and how these may figure into the way a group later splits into smaller new groups, has revealed unexpected complexity in blue monkey social structure. As in some human political organizations, those on top may depend more on those at the bottom than first meets the eye.

The feeding territories over which blue monkeys battle are often so specific that a person could draw lines to demarcate them: this tree belongs to this group, the next tree over doesn't. Groups can coexist peacefully very near one another as long as each stays on its side of these imaginary lines.

3 According to the passage, blue monkeys of different groups can live together as long as ____________.

① they don't cross their territorial boundary

② they share the same feeding grounds

③ they follow the leader's instructions

④ they face the predator's staying around

⑤ they don't touch the other group members

During the first few years of life, when babies' cells continue to undergo "programming," exposure to certain toxic chemicals can disrupt the delicate process. Bisphenol A (known as BPA), a compound in hard, clear polycarbonate plastics that mimics the effects of estrogen, has raised particular concern because it interferes with hormone levels and cell signaling systems. In August, several dozen scientists issued a review of 700 studies on BPA, warning that the levels most people are exposed to put them at elevated risk of cancer. Infants, the report said, are most vulnerable to BPA.

"Plastic bottles and plates that are boiled or put in the microwave or dishwasher are especially problematic because heating them repeatedly causes high amounts of BPA to leach out," says Retha Newbold, a reproductive biologist at the National Institute of Environmental Health Sciences in Triangle Park, N.C. Once small cracks form in the surface, a product should be discarded. She recommends that parents, to be on the safe side, switch to glass bottles or those with disposable liners that don't contain BPA. And they should use microwave-safe paper plates or glass dishes covered with a paper towel rather than plastic wrap.

4 **The best title of the above passage would be ____________.**

① The Problem with Plastic
② New Reasons to Watch What You Eat
③ The Influence of Chemicals on Human Beings
④ Some Factors to Increase Cancers in Babies
⑤ The Side Effects of Modern Kitchenwares

5 **According to the passage, it would be safer for the parents ____________.**

① to feed the babies only with organic food
② to breast-feed their babies
③ to check their babies regularly
④ to use glass bottles
⑤ to sanitize the bottles in the boiling water

Toto is an American rock band founded in 1977 by some of the most popular and experienced session musicians of the era. The band enjoyed great commercial success in the late 1970s and 1980s, beginning with the band's self-titled debut released in 1978. With the release of 1982's critically acclaimed and commercially successful Toto IV, Toto became one of the best-selling music groups of their era. They are best known for the Top 3 hits "Hold the Line," "Rosanna," and "Africa". Although their popularity in the United States diminished in the 1990s and 2000s, they continued to sell out arenas constantly internationally, playing only a number of shows in the USA.

Toto is known for a musical style that combines elements of pop, rock, soul, funk, progressive rock, hard rock, R&B and jazz. Although they were mostly associated with the soft rock genre, Toto's broad array of musical styles helps them appeal to a variety of listeners.

6 According to the passage, what is not mentioned about Toto?

① It consists of professional performing musicians.

② Its music made a good profit, but was not welcomed by music critics.

③ Its revenues were higher in 1980s than in 2000s.

④ Their music seems to be fusion styles.

⑤ Its concert in America has been diminishing.

A powerful tide is surging across much of the world today, creating a new, often bizarre environment in which to work, play, marry, raise children, or retire. In this bewildering context, businessmen swim against highly erratic economic currents; politicians see their ratings bob wildly up and down; universities, hospitals, and other institutions battle desperately against inflation. Value systems splinter and crash, while the lifeboats of family, church, and state are hurled madly about.

Looking at these violent changes, we can regard them as isolated evidences of instability, breakdown, and disaster. Yet, if we stand back for a longer view, several things become apparent that otherwise go unnoticed.

To begin with, many of today's changes are not independent of one another. Nor are they random. For example, the crack-up of the nuclear family, the global energy crisis, the spread of cults and cable television, the rise of flextime and new fringe-benefit packages, the emergence of separatist movements from Quebec to Corsica, may all seem like isolated events. Yet precisely the reverse is true. These and many other seemingly unrelated events or trends are interconnected. They are, in fact, parts of a much larger phenomenon: the death of industrialism and the rise of a new civilization.

7 **Which of the following best characterizes the above passage?**

① informative　　　　② augmentative

③ romantic　　　　④ sarcastic

⑤ dramatic

8 **Which of the following is true according to the above passage?**

① Businessmen work in a steady environment.

② Hospitals struggle to overcome inflation.

③ All institutions need not worry about inflation.

④ Politicians do not care whether their ratings change rapidly.

⑤ People are eager to find a lifeboat in the economic crisis.

9 **The author believes that the changes mentioned in the first paragraph**

_______________.

① are independent pieces of evidence of instability

② are interrelated parts of a much larger phenomenon

③ can never be noticed though they are closely examined

④ help people realize the rise of a new civilization

⑤ are independent of one another

There was a time when Bernie, 19, doubted that she could even finish high school, still less go to college. As a sophomore, she became pregnant and briefly thought about dropping out. But since transferring to the Academy of Urban Planning, she has passed all five of the required state exams for graduation. She is retaking one exam in the hopes of getting a diploma with the state's highest distinction. Her personal turnaround mirrors that of the school she now attends. The academy is housed in the same building that five years ago was known as Bushwick High School. Bushwick had one of the lowest four-year graduation rates of any school in New York—a dismal 23 percent. And violence plagued the school's hallways. Then, five years ago, New York Mayor Michael Bloomberg took control of the city's school districts, launching a flurry of reforms that led to Bushwick's division into four smaller schools.

10 **According to the passage, Bernie _______________.**

① passed the college entrance examination

② gave up the high school diploma

③ is thinking of transferring to another school

④ is taking one exam again to get a better score

It happens to most of us: a sleepless night in a hotel room just before a big presentation. You need to sleep. But no matter how hard you try, you just can't get to sleep. Whether we're traveling two hours by car or 14 hours by plane, the evil sleep monster can visit us at any time. Sleeplessness, called "insomnia" causes us frustration at night and makes us miserable the next day. We're not at the top of our game for the big meeting and our lack of concentration makes us dangerous drivers to boot.

How do we prevent sleeplessness on the road? People say that there are a number of theories about napping before travel and after arrival to help beat jet lag. I've been told to stay up very late the night before an international trip so that I'll be able to sleep on the plane. Usually, I end up staying up late and not sleeping a minute on the plane only to arrive at my destination crabby and miserable. Other people suggest a short nap upon arrival be followed by a shower and a brisk walk. But honestly, after traveling quite a bit, I've determined that you should sleep as often as your body—and your schedule—allows.

11 **According to the passage, which of the following can be caused by insomnia?**

① Frequent headaches and indigestion

② Overuse of sleeping pills and aids for treatment

③ Inability to walk briskly the following day

④ Frequent waking during sleep at night

⑤ Lack of good performance and concentration

12 **Which of the following does the writer suggest to overcome jet lag?**

① Not going to sleep during travel

② Napping before travel and after arrival

③ Staying up very late the night before travel

④ Taking a short nap upon arrival followed by a shower

⑤ Trying to sleep as often as you can wherever you travel

>>> **다음 글을 읽고 문제의 답을 고르시오.** [13~14]

Fluency shaping therapy, also known as "speak more fluently", "prolonged speech" or "connected speech", trains stutterers to speak fluently by controlling their breathing, phonation, and articulation (lips, jaw, and tongue). It is based on operant conditioning techniques. Stutterers are trained to reduce their speaking rate by stretching vowels and consonants, and using other fluency techniques such as continuous airflow and soft speech contacts. After the stutterer masters these fluency skills, the speaking rate and intonation are increased gradually. This more normal-sounding, fluent speech is then transferred to daily life outside the speech clinic, _________________ lack of speech naturalness at the end of treatment remains a frequent criticism. Fluency shaping approaches are often taught in intensive group therapy programs, which may take two to three weeks to complete, but more recently the Camperdown program, using a much shorter schedule, has been shown to be effective.

13 According the passage, which of the following is not described as the treatment of stutter?

① vocalization   ② controlling breath
③ getting rid of anxiety   ④ slowly speaking
⑤ pronunciation correction

14 Which of the following would be the best for the blank?

① because   ② so
③ as well as   ④ though
⑤ despite

Bees make honey to survive. It is their only essential food. If there are 60,000 bees in a hive about one third of them will be involved in gathering nectar. When the bees arrive at the hive carrying nectar they give this to the house bees. The house bees move the nectar around with their mandibles, exposing it to the warm dry air of the hive. When it is first gathered the nectar contains sugar and minerals mixed with about 80% water. After ten to twenty minutes, when much of the excess water has evaporated, the house bees put the nectar in a cell in the honeycomb where evaporation continues. After three days, the honey in the cells contains about 20% water. At this stage, the bees cover the cells with lids which they make out of beeswax.

15 **What is the main difference between nectar and honey?**

① The proportion of water in the substance

② The proportion of sugar to minerals in the substance

③ The type of plan from which the substance is gathered

④ The type of bee which processes the substance

In its breakneck quest for economic growth, the world's most populous nation has created no shortage of environmental disasters—just as other countries did when they, too, industrialized. But the Chinese people are growing impatient with the costs of unchecked development. Around the country, citizens are volunteering for cleanup projects. A small, courageous network of NGOs is naming and shaming the worst polluters. The huge number of pollution-related protests—an estimated 50,000 took place in 2005—unambiguously demonstrates grass-roots resentment of the ecological burden of industrialization. So did a survey by the Pew Global Attitudes Project about a year ago, which found that some 80% of Chinese felt protecting the environment should be a priority—a stark contrast to the global perception of the Chinese as a people in feckless pursuit of wealth.

16 **According to the passage, the Chinese were perceived as a people who ___________ by other people.**

① had a respectful tradition
② didn't care about the neighbors
③ would do anything for money
④ were for global pollution
⑤ didn't hesitate to spend as much as they can

If you already feel inside you the urge of self-expression, then the first thing that you have to do is to study the means of expressing yourself. You will have to study very carefully the English language and especially its grammar. Although most people do not understand the art of good writing, they unconsciously assimilate more easily ideas which are expressed in correct English. It should be pointed out also that good English is not necessarily flowery English, and the simple phrase—which looks so easy to write—is often the most difficult to construct. I can not stress too strongly the desirability of writing your sentences word by word and not phrase by phrase. Many writers fail to get their ideas across to the public solely because they use expressions whose meaning has been killed by repetition.

17 Choose the best title for the passage above.

① Self-expression, an Essential to Writing

② The Art of Writing

③ Dependence of English upon Grammar

④ The Curse of Repetition

⑤ Flowery English: Its Value

18 Writing phrase by phrase is ____________.

① undesirable

② indispensable

③ important

④ easily assimilated

⑤ economical

Melina Kanakaredes is the star of "Providence", the highest rated new drama on America's NBC network since "ER". As Dr. Sydney Hansen, she plays a LosAngeles plastic surgeon who gives up her practice and moves back home to be with her family.

There is a very thin line between the actress and the character she plays, for Kanakaredes's own family has always been closeknit. She is fiercely proud of her Greek heritage—her maternal grandparents emigrated from Greece and opened a chocolate shop in Ohio.

Family loyalty was tested early in her career when she was told to change her name. But keeping her name was a way of honoring the culture she loves. As she puts it, "I always felt if I ever became known for my acting, I wanted it to be Melina Kanakaredes who got there, not some other girl with some other name".

19 **Dr. Sydney Hansen's family ______________.**

① is an extended one

② are very supportive of each other

③ is of Greek heritage

④ do not care about the other members

⑤ runs a candy shop in Ohio

20 **Kanakaredes, when asked to change her name, insisted on keeping it because**

______________.

① she believed her own name to be attractive

② changing one's name into a foreign one would be to betray his or her country

③ changing one's name would not affect his or her success

④ she respected the Greek culture

⑤ she didn't like the names offered to her

21 **Which of the following statements is NOT true of Kanakaredes?**

① She is an actress playing in the NBC drama "Providence".

② Her Greek grandparents ran a candy store in Ohio.

③ Her mother-in-law is a Greek immigrant.

④ She is a medical doctor on "Providence".

⑤ She wanted to succeed as an actress with her own name.

>>> 다음 글을 읽고 문제의 답을 고르시오. [22~23]

Let us begin with some lexicography: the words embryo, fetus, and baby. Embryo is a product of conception more organized than just a cluster of cells but not yet recognizable as a member of the species. A fetus is a further stage of the organism but one not yet born. There is no precise, objectively specifiable moment at which a cluster of cells becomes an embryo and the embryo a fetus.

But there are certain relatively clear cases. The embryo, for example, turns into a fetus—a recognizable form of the human species—at some time between eight and twelve weeks. The fetus at this point cannot exist outside the woman's body until, at the very least, several weeks later. An embryo then is not recognizable as a form of the species and cannot have an existence separate from the mother's body. Once the fetus is born, it is called a baby.

Defenders of the morality of abortion are usually defenders of early abortion: of the embryo or of a fetus well before it is viable outside the womb, usually in the first trimester. That is, they are defenders of the morality of removing from a group of cells that is not an independent, viable, and recognizable human being.

Opponents of abortion use the word baby to refer to the cluster of cells, the embryo, and the fetus alike. The very choice of the word baby imposes the idea of an independently existing human being. Whereas cluster of cells, embryo, and fetus keep discussion in the medical domain, baby moves the discussion to the moral domain.

22 Which of the following statements is true of an embryo?

① It is recognizable as a member of the species.

② It is the final stage of pregnancy.

③ It is not viable outside the woman's body.

④ It turns into a cluster of cells around the eighth week.

⑤ It is a later stage than the fetus.

23 Pro-life advocates use the word baby rather than embryo or fetus because

_______________.

① the latter words are not the ones used in everyday conversation

② they want to treat the issue of abortion in terms of morality

③ the terms embryo and fetus are only used in a medical context

④ the former word is easier for people to understand

⑤ the issue of abortion is not properly understood

>> 다음 글을 읽고 문제의 답을 고르시오. [24~26]

The social settings in which people live have been created by individuals throughout the course of history. The family, universities, and government, for example, are the historical products of our forebears. Although these institutions often seem to be natural and unchanging, we should never lose sight of the fact that they are products of human history.

Social settings also are recreated and reaffirmed by individual action. In obeying the wishes of our parents, following the assignments of our professors, and accepting the decisions of our political leaders, we are reaffirming the existence of the institutions they represent. If you doubt that we daily reconstruct these settings, consider what would happen if a large number of people ceased accepting the dictates of the authority figures in these social settings.

Families as we know them would disappear if children refused to accept parental decisions. Universities would be radically difficult places if students did not recognize the authority of professors. The political sphere would be drastically altered were we to reject the authority of our political leaders.

24 Which of the following can be the main idea of the passage?

① We should follow the dictates of the authority figure.

② A family is the most crucial constitutional factor of a society.

③ Obeying the wishes of our parents is significant.

④ Social settings play an important part in maintaining our daily life.

⑤ Throughout history, social settings are one and the same.

25 If you doubt the value of social settings, the society in which we live will

______________.

① continue to progress slowly

② be more opulent

③ collapse with rapidity

④ not change

⑤ be more prosperous

26 Which of the following is not true of the social settings in which people live?

① They are the products of human history.

② They are natural and immutable all the time.

③ They are recreated and reaffirmed day in and day out.

④ They would crumble if we were to reject their authority.

⑤ They are daily reconstructed by the members of a society.

》》 다음 글을 읽고 문제의 답을 고르시오. [27~28]

Alzheimer's disease, a progressive and irreversible failure of the brain is the common form of dementia, accounting for up to 70% of cases. Early symptoms include confusion, personality changes, apathy, withdrawal, and declining ability to do everyday tasks. A diagnosis of Alzheimer's disease is not a death sentence. Treatments now available can slow down the disease and for some people, improve their ability to perform everyday functions. With the onset of Alzheimer's disease it is possible to live a fulfilling life and benefit from existing treatments if it is diagnosed early.

27 **According to the paragraph, the early symptoms of Alzheimers are all but one of the following choices.**

① declining ability to do everyday tasks
② confusion and personality changes
③ apathy
④ withdrawal
⑤ frequent headaches

28 **The main point stressed in this paragraph is ___________.**

① Once diagnosed with Alzheimer's, death comes quickly to sufferers
② Early detection is the key and drugs are available for patients to live a longer rewarding life with the disease
③ Alzheimer's accounts for only 7% of the cases of dementia
④ Drugs can stop the disease thus allowing a person to live without any difficulties
⑤ Operations are also available to stop the onset of the disease

E-learning(online learning) advocates contend that the Internet allows higher education institutions to seek out top experts in their fields to teach courses online to students globally. E-learning allows busy professionals to finish degrees, earn advanced degrees or take technology-related courses that help their jobs without putting careers on hold. E-learning also pushes higher education away from the age-old textbook-driven approach to teaching, which can be more ① _______________ than interactive. Students who sign ② _______________ for e-learning courses log on to password-protected Web sites to participate in online lectures and chats, and to get assignments and take part in discussions.

29 **Which is NOT mentioned as merits of e-learning in the passage?**

① E-learning allows colleges to offer top experts' teachings to students.

② E-learning allows students to take advantage of breaks in their schedule.

③ E-learning helps busy professionals earn advanced degrees without quitting their jobs.

④ E-learning pushes colleges away from traditional teaching methods.

⑤ E-learning allows students interactively to participate in online lectures and chats.

30 **Choose the one to fill in the blank ①.**

① ardent   ② update
③ old-fashioned   ④ static
⑤ cutting-edge

31 **Choose the one to fill in the blank ②.**

① up   ② off
③ out   ④ over
⑤ away

John Milton was a failure. In writing Paradise Lost, his aim was to "justify the ways of God to men." Inevitably, he fell short and wrote only a monumental poem. Beethoven, whose music was conceived to transcend fate, was a failure, as was Socrates, whose ambition was to make people happy by making them reasonable and just. The surest, noblest way to fail is to set one's standards titanically high.

The flip side of that proposition also seems true. The surest way to succeed is to keep one's striving low. Many people, by external standards, will be "successes." They will own homes, eat in better restaurants, dress well and, in some instances, perform socially useful work. Yet fewer people are putting themselves on the line, making as much of their minds and talents as they might. Frequently, success is what people settle for when they can't think of something noble enough to be worth failing at.

32 **Why were the famous like John Milton regarded as failures, according to the above passage?**

① because they had extremely high aims
② because they had a strong religious inclination
③ because they were essentially lacking in capabilities
④ because they had illogical ends

There are three major kinds of sleep disorders: You cannot sleep, you must always sleep, or your breathing affects your sleep. The first kind, insomnia, means that you cannot sleep well. You may have a hard time falling asleep or you keep waking up. During the day, you may feel sleepy or stressed. You may have a hard time concentrating. The second kind, narcolepsy, is called sleeping sickness. You cannot control yourself when you fall asleep, even during the day. The third kind is called sleep apnea. It is a problem breathing while sleeping. Usually your throat starts to close. This may be because of drinking alcohol or being too heavy. The muscles do not have enough control. Other times, the brain does not send the signal to breathe. Then you wake up.

33 **How does narcolepsy differ from apnea?**

① Apnea is similar to narcolepsy but more severe.

② Alcohol is used to treat apnea but not narcolepsy.

③ Apnea involves breathing, but narcolepsy does not.

④ Apnea and narcolepsy only happen during the daytime.

05

일치 · 불일치

❶ 유형 정의

문제의 보기항에 진술되어 있는 내용과 본문의 내용을 비추어 볼 때, 상호간에 그 내용이 일치하느냐 또는 일치하지 않느냐를 판단하여 글의 구체적인 세부 내용을 올바르게 이해했는지를 판단하는 유형이다. 이는 전 세계 어느 시험에서도 등장하지 않는 유형으로서, 그동안 '고시'에서 발달되어 온 유형이지만 편입에서도 그 문항 수가 점차 증가하고 있다.

❷ 공략 방법

(1) 문제 자체에 어떠한 조건도 제시되어 있지 않으며, 특정 논리 정보 장치와 결합된 문장만 문제의 쟁점이 되는 것이 아니므로, 지문 내용의 정확한 이해를 필요로 한다.

(2) 보기항의 진술된 내용들은 지문의 전개 내용과 순서가 일반적으로 일치한다. 따라서 시간적으로 여유가 있는 대학에 응시할 경우에는 보기항을 먼저 읽는 것도 하나의 방법이 된다.

(3) 지문 속에 있는 특정 내용을 다시 보기항에 진술하지만, 그 내용 그대로 복원시키는 경우는 드물다. 즉 재진술되는 경우가 대부분이므로, 특정 어구가 '동의어'로 전환되었는지, 또는 '태'의 전환에 대해서 유의해야 한다.

Any man who desires, as I do, a fundamental change in the structure of society is forced sooner or later to ask himself the question: what is it that makes one social system seem to him good and another bad? This is undoubtedly very largely a matter of individual caprice. In history, for example, some prefer one epoch, some another. Some admire the polished and civilized ages, others the rude virtues of more barbarous times. One does not wish to think that one's political opinions result from mere fanciful references of this sort, yet I believe that an enormous proportion of political opinion comes from some untested, unexamined, almost unconscious love for a certain type of society actual or imagined. I think it is possible to arrive at something less subjective than such tastes and fancies, and I think the advocate of fundamental change, more obviously than anyone else, needs to find ways of judging a social system which do not embody merely his individual tastes.

1 **According to the passage, which of the following is true?**

① The writer is one of those who oppose the change of the social structure.

② In history a refined age and a barbarous age take turns in coming without fail.

③ People's political opinions generally come from a meticulous investigation of social problems.

④ An age with much rude virtues is very likely to be followed by an age of drastic social change.

⑤ The proponents for the social change should have more objective ways of assessing a social system.

>>> 다음 글을 읽고 문제의 답을 고르시오. [2~3]

Certain individuals have a biological predisposition to addiction. The most serious problem that young people face if they use alcohol or other drugs is the possibility of becoming addicted. Although not everyone who drinks or uses drugs becomes addicted, there is no way to tell who will be ________________ or to what extent the use of alcohol or other drugs will impair their success in life. Some people have a biological predisposition to addiction, especially if any of their relatives are alcoholic. Children of alcoholics have a four to ten times greater risk of becoming alcoholics than children of non-alcoholics. Parents should advise children of any family history of alcoholism or other drug addictions and alert them to the risks of becoming addicted.

2 밑줄 친 곳에 들어갈 단어로 가장 알맞은 것은?

① profitable   ② proficient
③ diffused   ④ convergent
⑤ vulnerable

3 윗글의 내용과 거리가 먼 것은?

① Children with an alcoholic cousin have a greater risk of getting addicted to alcohol than children without one.
② Young people may use alcohol and other drugs because they are not properly informed of alcoholism in their family history.
③ Impaired judgement may lead to regrettable or even dangerous situations that may range from the destruction of property to communicative disorders.
④ Alcohol and other drugs have a fatal effect on children's life.
⑤ One of the reasons why children should not take alcohol or other drugs is the high possibility of getting addicted.

The brain of Albert Einstein has clear differences from an average person's gray matter, according to a California researcher. But any possible link between these differences and his great intelligence is still unknown, she added. To investigate whether the brain of a genius might show special features, Dr. Dahlia W. Zaidel of the University of California, Los Angeles, examined two slides made from the physicist's brain shortly after his death in 1955 at age 76. The slides contained samples of Einstein's hippocampus, a part of the brain responsible for memory and word associations. Zaidel compared Einstein's brain with tissue from 10 individuals of ordinary intelligence who ranged in age from 22 to 84 at the time of death. The neurons on the left side of the Nobel Prize winner's hippocampus were consistently larger than those on the right. Zaidel said these findings were 'markedly different' from those seen in the brains of individuals with normal intelligence. She presented her findings Monday at the Society for Neuroscience's annual meeting in San Diego, California.

4 윗글의 중심 소재는?

① Einstein's gray matter

② age differences and neurons

③ the future of neuroscience

④ Nobel Prize winners

⑤ the past of neuroscience

5 윗글의 내용과 다른 것은?

① Einstein's brain is different from those of other individuals.

② Dr. Zaidel compared Einstein's brain with tissue from 10 individuals of various age.

③ Einstein's intelligence is closely related to the texture and hardness of his brain.

④ Slides of Einstein's brain were made just after his death.

⑤ Dr. Zaidel gave a talk on her results at a certain neuroscience conference.

The problem for leaders comes when people who want to be chosen for a task besiege the leader. Do you remember when you were a kid and you were choosing up sides for a game? The two people who did the choosing, usually the two best athletes who functioned as team captains, had to make quick decisions about whom they wanted for their sides. Not only did they choose on the basis of athletic skills, but they also took into account factors such as trust (whether they had previous playing experience with one person over another), and such convoluted factors as whether, in order to get player A (who was great) you had to pick player B, player A's best friend (who was pretty awful). Finally, after sides were chosen up, the captain then had to find something for each person to do. Choosing up sides and assigning positions in a game is a simple leadership experience compared to delegating authority in a large organizational situation. In a sense, delegating authority is something like choosing up sides with someone standing to one side who has both veto and insistence power.

6 윗글의 내용과 일치하지 않는 것을 고르시오.

① Choosing up sides in a game is a kind of leadership experience.

② Sometimes the captain picks up a poor player in order to get an excellent player.

③ Assigning the position for each player is another important task for the captain.

④ Delegating authority in a group can't be done as you choose up sides in a game.

Comparative psychology has identified a number of symptoms that may help to distinguish intelligent, conscious imitation from automatic copying. In the first case, the solution comes instantly in the form of insight not requiring repetition. Such a solution pertains to all characteristics of intellectual action. It involves understanding the field structure and relations between objects. On the contrary, automatic drill imitation is carried out through repeating trial-and-error series, which show no sign of conscious comprehension and do not include understanding the field structure. In this sense, it can be said that animals are unteachable.

In the child's development, on the contrary, imitation and instruction play a major role. They bring out the human qualities of the mind and lead the child to new developmental levels. In learning to speak, as in learning school subjects, imitation is indispensible. What the child can do in cooperation today he can do alone tomorrow. Therefore the only good kind of instruction is that which marches ahead of development and leads it.

7　**본문의 내용과 가장 잘 부합할 수 있는 것은?**

① Children are good at automatic copying.
② Automatic drill imitation is a process of conscious comprehension.
③ Imitation may involve intellectual action.
④ Instruction is not effective when learning to speak.
⑤ Children should first learn to do things alone.

8　**본문에서 제시되고 있는 모방의 역할을 가장 잘 설명한 것은?**

① 모방이 인성 교육과 학습에 중요한 이유는 아이들이 어른들의 행위를 따라함으로써 협동 정신을 기를 수 있기 때문이다.
② 모방은 아이들의 학습 과정에서 개별적으로 배운 내용을 차후에 보다 강화해 주는 중요한 보조역할을 한다.
③ 근본적으로 모방은 효율적인 학습에 방해가 되기 때문에 학습 과정에서 배제되어야 하지만 때로는 효과적인 문제 해결 방법을 제시해 준다.
④ 모방의 중요한 학습 기능은 아이들이 먼저 어른들이 하는 것을 따라 한 후에 혼자 그 일을 독자적으로 할 수 있다는 데에 있다.
⑤ 동물들은 모방을 할 수 없기 때문에 학습을 할 수 없는 반면에, 인간은 기계적인 모방을 통해 시행착오를 반복하면서 학습을 하게 된다.

>>> 다음 글을 읽고 문제의 답을 고르시오. [9~10]

Plato advocates the opinion that a just man—that means in this connection, a man who obeys the law—and only a just man, is happy; whereas an unjust man—a man who violates the law—is unhappy. Plato says, that "the most just life is the most pleasant." Plato, ________________, admits that perhaps in one case or another the just man may be unhappy and the unjust man happy. But, asserts the Philosopher, it is absolutely necessary that the individuals, subject to the legal order, believe in the truth of the statement that only the just man is happy, even if it should not be true; for otherwise nobody would obey the law. Consequently the government has, according to Plato, the right to spread among the people by means of propaganda the doctrine that the just is happy and the unjust unhappy, even if this doctrine be a lie. If this is a lie, says Plato, it is a very useful lie, for it guarantees obedience to the law. "Could a lawgiver, who was worth his salt, find any more useful lie than this, or one more effective in persuading all men to act justly in all things willingly and without constraint? ... If I were a legislator, I should endeavor to compel the poets and all the citizens to speak in this sense." The government, then, is fully justified in making use of a useful lie. Plato places justice—and that means here, what the government considers to be justice, namely, lawfulness—above truth; but there is no sufficient reason not to place truth above lawfulness and to repudiate as immoral a governmental propaganda based on lies, even if it serves a good purpose.

9   **Which of the following statements is true according to the passage?**

① Plato believes that it is not possible for the unjust man to be happy.
② Plato has sufficient reason to place truth above lawfulness.
③ Plato says that the government should not lie in any case.
④ Obedience to the law brings us a happy life, thinks Plato.

10   **밑줄 친 부분에 들어갈 가장 알맞은 것은?**

① therefore   ② however
③ by the way   ④ accidentally

Like a perilous boat in a storm, the island of Samoa has been being tossed by the waves—the waves of capital and democracy, both of which most of the Samoans are unfamiliar with. Traditionally, the land was owned by the *Matais* (family chiefs) and the *Matais* elected parliament and administered justice. But the tradition of communal land ownership has stultified individual incentive and has resulted in neglect of the land. The system of permitting only the nation's 15,000 *Matais* to elect 45 of the 47 MPs has destroyed political involvement. As a result, many young Samoans are leaving for New Zealand—and the money the emigrants send home—creates a false economy and results in thousands of Samoan families ignoring the land and living off the earnings of their expatriate children.

11 **Choose the best title of the above passage.**

① A promising future of Samoa and its young people
② The exodus of young Samoans to New Zealand
③ The Samoan economy: yesterday and today
④ The traditional economic and political system of Samoa
⑤ The changing roles of the family chiefs in the Samoan society

12 **According to the passage, which of the following is true?**

① In Samoa land is owned by individuals.
② Most Samoans are familiar with modern concepts such as capital and democracy.
③ The Matais represented absolute authority in the village he lived in.
④ There is universal suffrage in Samoa.
⑤ Despite problems, economy is healthy and progressing in Samoa.

A combination of global warming and the climatic phenomenon known as El Niño will make the next 12 months exceptionally warm. El Niño is an occasional warming of the Pacific Ocean which has an effect on weather worldwide. The last El Niño made 1998 the warmest year on record.

This year could be warmer than 1998. Weather experts fear that the predicted weather conditions could spark such anomalies as droughts in tropical countries and deluges in areas with dry climates.

Many European ski resorts had to postpone their ski season this winter due to unseasonably warm weather. Much of the American Midwest and East Coast is also going through an unusually warm winter.

13 **Which of the following is true according to the passage?**

① This year will be warmest on record.

② This year it will not rain in areas with dry climates.

③ El Niño warmed the Pacific Ocean every year in the 1990s.

④ Many European ski resorts postponed their ski season this winter because of heavy rain.

A newspaper in North Carolina fired a photographer for changing the color of the sky in a picture of fire fighters. In 2003, a California newspaper fired a photographer for combining two pictures from Iraq into one. In 2004, the re-election campaign for President Bush altered a video by inserting faces into a crowd of soldiers listening to him to make the audience look larger. Some of these episodes were serious attempts to mislead the public, and some were relatively trivial. All of them undermine the public's trust in the reality of news photographs.

Actually, that's good. The public tends to assign too much 'reality' to what they see in photographs anyway. We should approach all news photos as somewhat unreal. What does it mean for a photograph to be true? That it captures what we would perceive if we were standing where the camera was? That is nonsense.

14 윗글의 내용과 일치하지 않는 것은?

① Some photographers are known to have altered their photos.

② Some altering does not have much effect.

③ Bush's camp wanted to make it look as if many soldiers listened to him.

④ The public is clever enough not to believe what they see in photos.

>>> 다음 글을 읽고 문제의 답을 고르시오. [15~16]

Sticky clay and dry sand are more familiar on the end of a spade than on the dinner table. Yet these are the basic ingredients in the manufacture of the pottery plates we eat from and the glass jars and bottles in which we buy preserved goods and drinks. Glass and ceramic materials share some useful qualities: they resist the flow of heat and electricity, and they have a hard, nonreactive surface. But they are different in other ways. Light passes through glass but not ceramics, and ceramics stay strong when they are heated. In their most basic forms glass and ceramic objects are brittle, but special additives and manufacturing methods make both materials much ① ________________. Glass and ceramics are ancient materials. The Egyptians made decorative glass beads more than 5,000 years ago, and pottery is even older.

15 **Which of the following best fits into ①?**

① fancier   ② more colorful

③ thicker   ④ sturdier

⑤ more profitable

16 **From what is stated or inferred, which of the following is NOT true?**

① Ceramics and glass have a long history of use.

② Glass cannot resist heat as well as ceramics do.

③ Translucency is a common property of ceramics and glass.

④ Glass and ceramics do not conduct electricity.

⑤ Clay and sand are used in making glass and ceramics.

Two hunters got a pilot to fly them into the far north for elk hunting. They were quite successful in their venture and bagged six big bucks. The pilot came back, as arranged, to pick them up. They started loading their gear into the plane, including the six elk. But the pilot objected and he said, "The plane can only take four of your elk; you will have to leave two behind." They argued with him; the year before they had shot six and the pilot had allowed them to put all aboard. The plane was the same model and capacity.

Reluctantly, the pilot finally permitted them to put all six aboard. But when they attempted to take off and leave the valley, the little plane could not make it and they crashed into the wilderness. Climbing out of the wreckage, one hunter said to the other, "Do you know where we are?" "I think so," replied the other hunter. "I think this is about the same place where we landed last year!"

17 윗글의 내용과 일치하지 않는 것은?

① The plane this year was not the same plane the year before.

② The number of the elk hunted this year was six.

③ The plane they were aboard the year before had a safe take-off.

④ The pilot was worried about loading all the elk on the plane.

Can hell really be worse than what we've seen and read about Rwanda? The world must stop such madness. A Rwandan colleague tried to explain to me the legacy of hatred between the Hutu and Tutsi. I don't ever want to understand what it takes to murder men, women and children solely because of their tribal ties or skin appearance. How many Hutu were murdered by mistake by their fellow Hutu? And how many Tutsi by fellow Tutsi? As an African, I tell you there is no excuse. When a country descends into the mire of mindless atrocities, doesn't it automatically suspend the right of self-determination? We must act forcefully to stop such killing by moving in and separating tribes or by disarming both sides. It's not enough for the media to continue reporting on atrocities like this. Those images of bodies floating down the river will remain with me the rest of my life.

18 윗글의 내용과 일치하는 것은?

① Certain religious problem might have resulted in a massacre.

② Disarmament may not be useful as an inhibition against a massacre.

③ The press wasn't effective on the check against a massacre.

④ The Hutu must have slain even their own tribes.

If the current rate of divorce in America continues, at least half of the children under eighteen will experience the divorce of their parents. Divorce is a traumatic experience for parents and children. It can provoke aberrant behavior _________________ both parents and children when emotional resources to deal with aberrance are completely drained. My own experiences as a family law practitioner have convinced me that it is a rare child whose moral development will be untouched by the experience.

19 Which is not true of the above passage?

① The divorce rate in America is extremely high.

② More than half of the children under eighteen will live in broken homes.

③ Divorce is a disturbing experience for both children and parents.

④ Divorce makes both children and parents slip morally or mentally from the right path.

⑤ On some occasions, children are not affected by the experience of their parent's divorce.

20 Which best fills the blank?

① thanks to   ② on the part of

③ irrespective of   ④ regardless of

⑤ by virtue of

Three guys were fishing in a lake one day, when an angel appeared in the boat. When the three astonished men had settled down enough to speak, the first guy asked the angel humbly, "I've suffered from back pain ever since I took shrapnel in the Vietnam War. Could you help me?" "Of course," the angel said, and when he touched the man's back, the man felt relief for the first time in years.

The second guy who wore very thick glasses had a hard time reading and driving. He asked if the angel could do anything about his poor eyesight. The angel smiled, removed the man's glasses and tossed them into the lake. When they hit the water, the man's eyes cleared and he could see everything distinctly.

When the angel turned to the third guy, the guy put his hands out defensively—"Please do not touch me!" he cried, "I'm on a disability pension."

21 Which of the following is true according to the passage?

① Not all the three men believed that the angel could heal anyone.
② The angel threw the shrapnel and the glasses into the lake.
③ One man did not have a driver's license.
④ One man wanted to remain handicapped.

American surface informality often confuses the foreigner because he interprets it to mean no formality at all. He does not understand the point at which informality stops. A teacher, though friendly, pleasant, and informal in class, expects students to study hard, and he grades each student's work critically and carefully. He also expects to be treated with respect. Though students are free to ask questions about statements made by the teacher, they are not expected to contradict him.

22 **Which of the following is true according to the passage?**

① American students are free to contradict their teachers.

② American teachers are generous in grading their students' work.

③ American teachers are so strict that students often disobey them.

④ Americans, though apparently informal, know the limits of informality.

>>> **다음 글을 읽고 문제의 답을 고르시오.** [23~24]

The great English author Charles Dickens was a life-long champion of social justice. In fact, his own childhood foreshadowed the lives of the characters in his novels. Poverty forced Dickens at the age of twelve to quit school and work in a shoe polish factory. He never forgot that experience. Images of poverty appear in many of his novels.

Dickens began his literary career by writing articles for newspapers. He often used the pseudonym "Boz". When he was twenty-four years old, several of these articles were published in one volume called Sketches by Boz.

Dickens' first publications were humorous. However, as his fame grew, he began to write more about social problems. Dickens' novel Oliver Twist dealt with cruelty toward orphaned children. Dickens used Oliver's story to allude to the social system in England. He used the slang of poor people and even criminals in some of the dialogues he wrote.

A London newspaper first published Oliver Twist in serialized form. People waited eagerly for each episode to appear. In addition to entertaining readers, however, Oliver's story made the public aware of the need to protect orphaned children.

Dickens' work often appears in anthologies of great literature. His compassion for poor people inspired many of ① ______________ English to work for improvements in the quality of life of ② ______________ poor.

23 **Which of the following best fits into ① ____________ and ② ____________ ?**

① the - the ② an - a

③ the - a ④ an - the

⑤ some - some

24 **According to the passage which of the following statements is true?**

① Images of poverty appear in none of Dickens' novels.

② Oliver Twist's story praises the social system in England.

③ The episodes of Oliver Twist were first published in several newspapers.

④ Dickens often used his pen name in his newspaper articles.

⑤ Dickens began to write newspaper articles after he became famous.

Woe to the patient waiting for someone to offer up a spare organ for transplantation. Demand so far exceeds supply these days that in America alone around 17 people die every day while languishing in the queue. Nor do problems end there. Even the lucky ones, who do get their desired replacement part, face a lifetime on immunosuppressant drugs, to stop the alien tissue being rejected by their own immune systems.

David Sachs and Benedict Cosimi, of Harvard Medical School, have been working for some time to find a way around these problems. Their goal has been to _______________ the body into thinking that a foreign organ is really a native one, so that its immune system refrains from rejecting the foreigner. In this week's New England Journal of Medicine they report a small but promising study that, if confirmed on a grander scale, may deal with the issue once and for all and usher in a world in which immunosuppressant drugs are unnecessary and organs no longer need be matched to patients. That would make the lives of transplant patients easier and longer, and might also increase the useful supply of organs available for transplant.

25 The best title of the passage would be ____________.

① the Lack of Spare Organs for Transplantation

② the Problem of Immunosuppressant Drugs

③ Immune Systems Blocking Foreign Organs

④ Induce Immune System to Believe Foreign Organs Native

26 According to the passage, which of the following is not true?

① In America, less than 20 people are dying everyday due to transplant problems.

② Foreign organ is difficult to harmonize with a native one.

③ David Sachs and Benedict Cosimi put strong confidence in their experiment.

④ If receiving an organ transplant, the patient can be completely cured.

27 Which of the following best fills in the blank?

① restrain   ② trick   ③ immune   ④ turn

>>> **다음 글을 읽고 문제의 답을 고르시오.** [28~29]

Speakers of a second language are often well advised not to try to sound too much like a native. A foreign accent will often allow as yet imperfectly learned rules of etiquette to be excused as such, ①________________ a speaker who has mastered the phonology of a language is assumed to have also mastered all other aspects of its use, and violations are more likely to be interpreted as rudeness. Additional consequences of perfecting pronunciation in a second language may be suspicion or resentment from native speakers if they do not welcome new members, or feelings from the primary speech community that one is disloyal to it.

28 **Which of the following best fits into ①?**

① when　　　　　② so that

③ while　　　　　④ or

⑤ because

29 **Which of the following statements is TRUE?**

① Speakers of a second language should learn a foreign accent.

② A speaker with native-like pronunciation in a second language is expected to be perfect in all other aspects of its use.

③ Speakers of a second language are not welcomed by all native speakers when they sound too much like a native.

④ As long as one masters pronunciation in learning a second language, he or she need not care about rules of etiquettes in its use.

⑤ Proving phonological incompetence in a second language does not have any practical benefits.

Clara Louise Mass was a nurse who contributed to the research on yellow fever at the turn of the century. She was working as a civilian nurse in Cuba, where army Majors William Gorge and Walter Reed were conducting experiments to isolate the cause of the disease. Tests ruled out dirt and poor sanitation as causes of yellow fever, and mosquito was the suspected carrier. Clara Mass was among the group who volunteered to be bitten by the insect. She contracted the disease and died on August 24, 1901. She was the only woman to participate in the experiment and among the few volunteers to die from it. With her death, the study ended; the results of the experiment provided conclusive evidence that mosquitoes were the source of the disease.

30 윗글의 내용과 일치하지 않는 것은?

① William Gorge and Walter Reed had previously looked for the cause of yellow fever by conducting experiments.

② People do not contract yellow fever when they are situated in the dirty unsanitary condition.

③ In many cases, volunteers who participated in the insect biting experiment did not show lethal condition.

④ Clara Mass served as a nurse and discovered the sources of yellow fever through immunization process.

I am not inclined to accept that those who give orders directly are really insecure and powerless, any more than I want to accept that judgment of those who give indirect orders. The conclusion to be drawn is that ways of talking should not be taken as obvious evidence of inner psychological states like insecurity or lack of confidence. Considering many influences on conversational style, individuals have a wide range of ways of getting things done and expressing their emotional states. Personality characteristics like insecurity cannot be linked to ways of speaking in an automatic, self-evident way.

31 **Which of the following is correct according to the passage?**

① Those who give indirect speech are judgemental.

② Ways of talking are the indexes of personality.

③ There are many factors influencing the manners of speech.

④ Conversational styles have power over individual traits.

지칭어 · 의미 추론

❶ 유형 정의

'지칭어 추론'은 지문의 내용 중 지시대명사, 인칭대명사, 지시형용사, 인칭대명사의 소유격에 밑줄을 그어놓고 그것들이 가리키는 바가 무엇인지를 파악하는 유형이다. 또한 '의미 추론'은 특정 표현이나 특정 문장에 밑줄을 그어놓고 그 부분에 내포된 내용을 추론해 내는 문제 유형이다. 최근 몇 년간 편입시험에서 갑자기 증가하고 있는 유형이라는 점을 꼭 참고하기 바란다.

❷ 공략 방법

(1) '지칭어 추론'의 경우 바로 앞에서 언급된 대상을 지시하는 경우가 거의 대부분이며, 간혹 뒤 문장의 대상을 가리키기도 한다. 또한 대명사가 가리키는 대상의 수와 성을 살펴보는 기본적 문법 지식이 중요하다.

(2) '의미 추론'의 경우 특정 표현이나 추상적인 문장에 밑줄을 그어 놓으므로 모르는 표현이 포함된 문장이 나오면 당황할 수도 있지만, 대개가 문맥을 통한 글의 전개 과정에 따라 그 의미를 유추할 수 있으니 글의 전체 맥락을 놓쳐서는 안 된다.

>>> 다음 글을 읽고 문제의 답을 고르시오. [1~3]

For decades schools have been assigning students to different sections on the basis of academic performance. Many of (1)<u>them</u> don't stop at that. They make students wear different colored blazers and ties to differentiate the (2)<u>'achievers'</u> from 'nonachievers'. Such demarcations invariably translate into discrimination with regard to teachers, with the best teachers reserved for sections with first divisioners. Schooling is, however, not just about academic excellence, but overall personality development. It's the school's duty to help (3)<u>a child</u> discover (4)<u>his</u> latent talents and nurture them. But if schools ① _______________ some of their students at the outset, (5)<u>they</u> cannot realize their potential. A healthy intermingling of students with different aptitudes, capabilities and attainment levels could help everyone perform better.

1 **Choose the statement that the above passage says or implies.**

① Schools have been traditionally avoiding segregation of students on the basis of academic performance.

② Segregating students on the basis of academic performance help everyone perform better.

③ Schooling is above all about academic excellence.

④ Academic excellence is more significant than personality development in schooling.

⑤ An intermingling of students with different aptitudes, capabilities and attainment levels could help everyone perform better.

2 **Choose the most appropriate expression for the underlined blank ①.**

① include   ② write off

③ help   ④ intermingle with

⑤ exterminate

3 **Among (1), (2), (3), (4) and (5), which one differs from the others in what they refer to?**

① (1)   ② (2)   ③ (3)   ④ (4)   ⑤ (5)

On a tour of an old European castle, a young American visitor becomes very nervous. Finally the elderly guide, noticing how jumpy she is, tries to reassure her. "Don't worry," <u>he</u> tells her. "I've never seen a ghost in all the time I've been here." "And how long is that?" asks the tourist. "About 400 years."

4 **Who does the underlined 'he' refer to?**

① the ghost   ② the tourist

③ the author   ④ the castle owner

<u>This impulse</u> is inspired by a genuine love of knowledge. You may see this impulse in a moderately pure form; for example, a cat has been brought to a strange room, and proceeds to smell every corner and every piece of furniture. This impulse grows weaker with advancing years, until at last what is unfamiliar inspires only disgust, with no desire for closer acquaintance.

5 **What does the underlined 'This impulse' refer to?**

① curiosity   ② yearning

③ ambition   ④ culture

>>> 다음 글을 읽고 문제의 답을 고르시오. [6~10]

A thousand years ago, when the earth was reassuringly flat and the universe revolved around it, the ordinary person had no last name, ①let alone any claim to individualism. The self was subordinated to church and king. Then came the Renaissance explosion of scientific discovery and humanist insight and, as both cause and effect, the rise of individual self-consciousness. All at once, it seemed, humanity had replaced God at the center of earthly life. And perhaps more than any great war or invention or feat of navigation, this upheaval marked the beginning of our modern era. There are now 20 times as many people in the world as there were in the year 1000. Most have last names, and many of us have a personal identity or reasonable expectation of acquiring one. This special ②issue examines the transformation of identity through different lenses and concludes with reflections on how hard ③it is, in a time of gathering global conformity, to find one's own way.

6 **The best title of this passage is ____________.**

① Identification of humanity

② Divinity over individualism

③ Importance of the Renaissance in the human history

④ How individual identity was acquired

⑤ Relationship between God and humanism

7 **What does the underlined ① mean?**

① to say nothing of any claim to individualism

② but for empty claims to individualism

③ at the same time no claim to individualism

④ nor any claim at all to individualism

⑤ in the end no claim at all to individualism

8 **According to the passage, before the Renaissance ___________.**

① individualism was respected

② people did not have their own personal names

③ people acquired personal identity

④ church and king dominated individuals

⑤ humanism enhanced individual self-consciousness

9 **밑줄 친 ② issue의 뜻은?**

① 결과

② (출판물의) …호

③ 문제점

④ 논문

⑤ 논쟁

10 **What does the underlined ③ it refer to?**

① this special issue

② transformation of identity

③ a personal identity

④ reasonable expectation of acquiring one

⑤ to find one's own way

In the days of my grandfather, the word "marriage" meant only one thing: the union of one man and one woman until "death do they part". Marriage was traditionally looked upon as something permanent, a sacred bond between man and woman for the purpose of raising a family. ① _______________, marriage today can mean different things to different people. And to some people it doesn't mean much at all. There are a number of alternatives to the traditional marriage, none of which was acceptable fifty years ago. There are homosexual marriages, group marriages, communal living arrangements, and swingers' group, each of these being different from others in the number and type of relationships desired. The word ②"relationship" is often used today when talking about marriage.

11 The expression that is most appropriate for ① is "__________".

① Likewise
② In comparison
③ By and large
④ In the same vein
⑤ Consequently

12 The main topic of the passage is __________.

① Marriage, past and today
② Types of marriage today
③ Marriage and relationship
④ The true meaning of marriage
⑤ The sacredness of marriage

13 Which of the following is NOT associated with the meaning of the underlined "relationship" in ②?

① casualness
② freedom
③ consumerism
④ responsibility
⑤ temporariness

> "Awhile" is a word we frequently use. "(가)This will take awhile," says the man who repairs your car or watch. What does he mean? minutes, hours, days? What is important about "awhile" as far as communication is concerned is that the interpretation is contextual. "Awhile" means different things in different situations, and with different people. (나)It may be well to remember (다)this: our concept of time depends on our cultural way of evaluating (라)it.

14 윗글에서 밑줄 친 부분이 지칭하는 것을 잘못 연결한 것은?

① (가) - repairing your car or watch
② (나) - to remember this
③ (다) - our concept of time depends on our cultural way of evaluating it
④ (라) - the concept of time

>>> 다음 글을 읽고 문제의 답을 고르시오. [15~16]

Five score years ago, a great American in whose symbolic shadow we stand signed the Emancipation Proclamation. This momentous decree came as a great beacon light of hope to millions of Negro slaves who had been seared in the flames of withering injustice.

One hundred years later, the life of the Negro is still not free. The life of the Negro is still sadly crippled by the manacles of segregation and the chains of discrimination.

Today (가) <u>we have come to our nation's Capital to cash a check</u>. When the architects of our republic wrote the magnificent words of the Constitution and the Declaration of Independence, they were signing a promissory note to which they American was to fall heir. This note was a promise that all men would be guaranteed the unalienable right of life, liberty and the pursuit of happiness.

15 **Which of the following best interprets the underlined (가)?**

① We came to ask for financial benefits equal to those of the whites.

② We came to find out what equal rights we should have as fellow citizens.

③ We came to ask for the abolition of segregation and discrimination.

④ We came to demand that the equal rights long overdue be granted immediately.

16 **The above passage is a(n) ____________.**

① essay

② speech

③ advertisement

④ newspaper article

It was precisely in those parts of France where there had been most improvement that popular discontent ran highest. This may seem illogical—but history is full of such ① ______________ . For it is not always when things are going from bad to worse that revolutions break out. On the contrary, it often happens that when a people which has put up with an oppressive rule over a long period without protest suddenly finds the government relaxing its pressure, ②it takes up arms against it. Thus the social order overthrown by a revolution is almost always better than the one immediately preceding it, and experience teaches us that, generally speaking, the most perilous moment for a bad government is one when it seeks to mend its ways.

Only consummate statecraft can enable a King to save his throne when after a long spell of oppressive rule he sets to improving the lot of his subjects. Patiently endured so long as it seemed beyond redress, a grievance comes to appear intolerable once the possibility of removing it crosses men's minds. For the mere fact that certain abuses have been remedied draws attention to the others and ③they now appear more ④galling; people may suffer less, but their sensibility is exacerbated. At the height of its power feudalism did not inspire so much hatred as it did on the eve of its eclipse. In the reign of Louis XVI the most trivial pinpricks of arbitrary power caused more resentment than the thoroughgoing despotism of Louis XIV. The brief imprisonment of Beaumarchais shocked Paris More than the dragonnades of 1685.

17 **Which of the following words best fits blank ①?**

① nightmares   ② mistakes

③ paradoxes   ④ perversities

18 **What does ② it refer to?**

① people   ② government

③ oppressive rule   ④ period

19 **What does ③ they refer to?**

① men's mind   ② certain abuses

③ other abuses   ④ crosses

20 **What view of history is the author trying to get across in the first paragraph?**

① The safest way to rule a country is to rule it with an iron fist.

② The masses are always an ignorant lot, who can never recognize and properly honor a good king when they have one.

③ It is always the best societies that are demolished by violent revolutionary upheavals.

④ People often endure dire tyrannies but are liable to explode when they begin to taste snatches of freedom.

21 **Which of the following is NOT implied about Louis XVI in the second paragraph?**

① He was not a very able statesman.

② He was much less despotic than Louis XIV.

③ He was not guilty of exercising arbitrary power.

④ He tried to improve the lot of his subjects.

22 **Which of the following reflects the author's opinion about the cause of the French Revolution?**

① The French Revolution erupted because Louis XVI was an inhuman despot.

② The French Revolution erupted because Louis XVI drew attention to the abuses by removing some of them.

③ The French Revolution erupted because the French had a tendency to anarchy.

④ The French Revolution erupted because France remained feudalistic, long after other countries have ceased to be so.

23 **Which of the following is closest in meaning to ④ galling?**

① vexing   ② inspiriting

③ galvanizing   ④ injurious

24 **Which of the following is 'the dragonnades of 1685' most likely to have been?**

① a large-scale violation of religious liberty

② a large-scale civic project

③ a large-scale operatic performance

④ a large-scale financial venture that failed

>> 다음 글을 읽고 문제의 답을 고르시오. [25~26]

Racism is so extreme and so pervasive in our American society that no black individual lives in an atmosphere of freedom. The world of physical phenomena is dominated by fear and greed. It consists of pitting <u>the vicious and the avaricious</u> against the naive, the hunted, the innocent, and the victimized. Power belongs to the strong, and the strong are BIG in more ways than one. No one is more victimized in this white male American society than the black female.

25 **Whom does the underlined part refer to?**

① black and white males

② black females

③ black males

④ white males

⑤ white females

26 **Who does the author say is most victimized in American society?**

① black males

② white males

③ black and white females

④ white females

⑤ black females

>>> 다음 글을 읽고 문제의 답을 고르시오. [27~30]

Plagiarism refers to a form of cheating that has been defined as the false assumption of authorship: the wrongful act of taking the product of another person's mind, and presenting it as one's own. Plagiarism, then, constitutes intellectual theft and often carries severe penalties, ranging from failure in a course to expulsion from school.

Plagiarism in student writing is often unintentional, as when an elementary school pupil, assigned to do a report on a certain topic, goes home and copies down, word for word, everything on the subject in an encyclopedia. Unfortunately, some students continue to use such "research methods" in high school and ① ________________ in college without realizing that these practices constitute plagiarism. At all times during research and writing, guard against the possibility of ② <u>inadvertent</u> plagiarism by keeping careful notes that distinguish between your musings and thoughts and the material you gather from others. A writer who fails to give appropriate acknowledgment when repeating another's wording or particularly apt term is guilty of plagiarism. You may certainly use other persons' words and thoughts in your research paper, but the borrowed material must not appear to be your creation.

27 **Which of the following expressions differs in meaning from the others?**

① the false assumption of authorship

② intellectual theft

③ presenting the product of another person's mind as one's own

④ giving appropriate acknowledgment when presenting another's ideas

⑤ making the borrowed material appear to be one's own creation

28 **Which of the following best fits into ①?**

① even　　　　　　　② thus

③ therefore　　　　　④ however

⑤ otherwise

29 **Which of the following is closest in meaning to ②?**

① unembellished
② unintentional
③ inadmissible
④ inauspicious
⑤ incipient

30 **The best title of this passage would be _____________.**

① the Reasons That You should Not plagiarize
② Expulsion from School
③ the Unenlightened Plagiarists
④ the Form and Extent of Plagiarism
⑤ Hazards of Plagiarism

A laser is not a word in itself but actually it stands for Light Amplification by the Stimulated Emission of Radiation. L indicates Light. (가) <u>It</u> is a kind of beam that utilizes the force of light and directs (나) <u>it</u> for its power. Thus, (다) <u>it</u> is created from light, and the resulting laser light has special properties that are very different and unique from regular light. A laser can be of different types and strengths. It can be very tiny so as to be almost invisible, and can be very large so as to occupy an entire room. (라) <u>It</u> is indeed a very useful and exciting invention, with many beneficial applications and uses.

31 **윗글에서 밑줄 친 It/it이 가리키는 대상이 나머지 셋과 다른 것은?**

① (가)
② (나)
③ (다)
④ (라)

A great Indian Buddhist teacher was invited to Tibet to preach the dharma. The teacher took along with (가)<u>him</u> a man who was quarrelsome and irresponsible, and a bad cook as well. After observing (나)<u>him</u> for quite some time, the Tibetans approached the teacher respectfully and said, "Master, why do you keep this useless cook of yours—he is more a nuisance than a help to you." The teacher smiled and replied, "Ah! You don't understand. I do not keep (다)<u>him</u> as my servant but as my teacher." The Tibetans were surprised and asked "How is that so?" The teacher explained, "You see, his inefficiency and his quarrelsome nature teach me to practice patience and tolerance every day. Therefore, I value (라)<u>him</u>."

32 **Which of the underlined <u>him</u> does not refer to the same person?**

① (가) ② (나)

③ (다) ④ (라)

추론

❶ 유형 정의

'추론'은 지문 내용에 의해 도출되는 결론이다. 지문의 내용에 의해서만 직접적으로 얻어지는 것이 아닌, 지문의 전체 내용과 세부 내용에 관한 것으로부터 함축적이면서도 묵시적으로 얻어지는 것을 말한다. 순수 추론 문제가 어떠한 것일 수 있느냐에 대해서 논란이 많은 만큼 앞서 공부한 Chapter 04 '특정 정보'와 Chapter 05 '일치·불일치'의 문제들에서도 이러한 추론적 이해를 요하고 있다. 따라서 본 Chapter에서는 문제의 질문 자체가 직접적으로 '추론'이란 명제를 제시하고 있는 문제들로 국한한다.

❷ 공략 방법

(1) 추론 문제는 지문 속에서 언급된 정보를 통해 추출할 수 있는 정보에 국한하므로, 지문에서 다루어지는 내용에서 범위를 지나치게 넓혀 나가기보다는 지문에서 얻어진 내용에 근거한 내용과 연결될 수 있는지에 대해 미시적으로 판단해야 한다.

(2) 글 전체의 내용을 담고 있는 주제문을 파악한 후 그 논리적 흐름에 맞게 연결될 수 있는 내용인지 판단해야 한다.

(3) 실제 시험에서 이 문제가 추론 문제이냐 아니냐는 질문만 보고서는 알 수 없다. 즉 결과적인 측면이 강하며, 앞서 다룬 '특정 정보'와 '일치·불일치'의 문제 유형 또한 상당수의 문제들이 추론 문제라고 생각해도 좋다.

>>> **다음 글을 읽고 문제의 답을 고르시오.** [1~3]

Numerous public opinion surveys have consistently shown that the public prefers wind and other renewable energy forms over conventional sources of generation. Wind energy is a free, renewable resource, so no matter how much is used today, there will still be the same supply in the future. Wind energy is also a source of clean, non-polluting, electricity. Unlike conventional power plants, wind plants emit no air pollutants or greenhouse gases. In 1990, California's wind power plants offset the emission of more than 2.5 billion pounds of carbon dioxide, and 15 million pounds of other pollutants that would have <u>otherwise</u> been produced. It would take a forest of 90 million to 175 million trees to provide the same air quality.

1 이 글은 다음 중 어느 질문에 답하고 있는가?

① How is the energy in the wind captured?
② Are there good wind resources in the United States?
③ Are there environmental problems facing wind power?
④ What are the advantages of wind-generated electricity?
⑤ What are the economic obstacles to greater wind power usage?

2 밑줄 친 otherwise의 뜻으로 가장 알맞은 것은?

① 풍력 발전을 많이 사용했더라면
② 나무를 심어 숲을 조성하지 않았더라면
③ 풍력이 아닌 재래식 발전을 이용했더라면
④ 많은 사람들이 풍력 발전을 좋아하지 않았더라면
⑤ 이산화탄소 등의 공해 물질을 규제하지 않았더라면

3 Which of the following does NOT describe wind energy?

① free
② clean
③ conventional
④ renewable
⑤ non-polluting

Another tendency which worries me is the growing gulf between students and the rest of the society in which they live. This gulf is sometimes called a generation gap. It is no such thing. The gap exists between students and almost every other group—young or old—in the society; in fact, whether one looks at opinions on Viet Nam, poverty, law and order, or civil liberties, the gap is nowhere greater than it is between college students and their fellow young people who have not gone to college. My anxiety on this score is not relieved by the fact that I share the attitudes of students on many of the issues involved. The gap still exists and it is still unhealthy.

4 Where is the greatest gap according to the above passage?

① It is between young people and old people.

② It is between college students and the rest of the society.

③ It is between college students and other young people.

④ It is between college students and the author.

⑤ It is between old people and young people who have not gone to college.

5 Which of the following cannot be inferred from the above passage?

① The author agrees with college students on many of social issues.

② The gap between college students and the rest of the society worries the author.

③ One of the social issues involved is about Viet Nam.

④ The author does not think that the gulf can be called a generation gap.

⑤ The author thinks that quite a few groups agree with college students.

>>> 다음 글을 읽고 문제의 답을 고르시오. [6~7]

If Italian children can read Dante's Divine Comedy or English children can read Milton in school, why should 'secularist' Indians be ambivalent about teaching the Mahabharata? It's true that the Mahabharata has lots of gods, and in particular the elusive Krishna. But so do Dante and Milton deal with God. As a secular Indian, I appreciate the 'wall' that our founding fathers built between religion and education. But what does one do when our literary classics are 'semi-religious'? If our kids don't read Sanskrit classics in a secular environment they will grow up impoverished. Something has gone terribly wrong in the way our schools bring up deracinated children, who know ① ________________ about their own culture but a great deal about the West. "Every writer needs an address", wrote the Yiddish writer, Isaac Bashevis Singer. That is a fine way of saying that all human beings need local roots, an identity, and a link with a unique identifiable past.

6 **Choose the statement that the above passage does not say or imply.**

① Isaac Bashevis Singer wrote, "Every writer needs an address".

② If Indian kids don't read Sanskrit classics in a secular environment they will grow up impoverished.

③ 'Secularist' Indians are ambivalent about teaching the Mahabharata.

④ Indian literary classics such as the Mahabharata are 'semireligious'.

⑤ Indian schools strongly encourage students to read Indian literary classics such as the Mahabharata.

7 **Choose the most appropriate expression for the underlined blank ①.**

① much   ② enormously

③ little   ④ well

⑤ wisely

I thought it might be feasible to park a car parallel to a space on the street. Then, by pressing a button, I could raise the four tires off the ground slightly, while dropping two special wheels perpendicular to the curb. It would then be child's play to roll into the narrowest of parking spaces. I visited Ed Greene who runs the Ford agency in order to elicit his reaction. After a perfunctory glance at my plans, to my chagrin Ed snorted that my idea was inane, but I decided that he was just jealous of my brilliance. Tomorrow I am going to start on a computer that will enable me to measure the intelligence of perverse automobile dealers who like to deride the efforts of a junior genius.

8 **The author is most likely to be ___________.**

① a mechanic

② a computer analyst

③ an inventor

④ a teacher

⑤ a traffic warden

Advice, as it always gives a temporary appearance of superiority, can never be very grateful, even when it is most necessary or most judicious. Vanity is so frequently the apparent motive of advice that we, for the most part, summon our powers to oppose it without any very accurate inquiry whether it is right. It is sufficient that another is growing great in his own eyes, at our expense, and assumes authority over us without our permission; for many would contentedly suffer the consequences of their own mistakes rather than the insolence of him who triumphs as their deliverer.

9 윗글의 '조언'에 대한 설명으로 추론할 수 있는 것은?

① The motive of advice consists of many lies.

② A person who is given advice has a tendency to receive it blindly.

③ The person that listens to another's advice usually tends not to follow it because of listener's superiority.

④ Even reasonable advice may not be followed.

Asia has long been the home of ① _______________ smokers. To millions of them, cigarettes are the stuff of daily social intercourse. Nothing is done without them—no task unrewarded, no meal concluded. Everybody knows that Asia is supposed to be the last great frontier of the tobacco industry, a place where vast numbers continue to expose themselves to the risks of lung cancer, cardiovascular disease, emphysema and other smoking-related illnesses. And yet, across the region, an Asian antismoking movement is quietly but inexorably gathering strength. It isn't large yet, but it is starting to have a dramatic impact—from fresh legal wins in unlikely quarters to tough bans—on smoking in public places. The Framework Convention on Tobacco Control (FCTC)—a treaty sponsored by the World Health Organization (WHO)—became binding law on Feb. 27 in the first 40 countries to ratify it. A third of these countries are in Asia, and more Asian nations are expected to adopt the treaty's tough antismoking provisions over the coming months.

10 **Choose the most appropriate word for the blank ①.**

① vicious ② offensive

③ sneaking ④ secret

⑤ inveterate

11 **Which can be inferred from the passage?**

① Smoking brings Asian nations to an economic crisis.

② Smoking-related illnesses were eradicated in Asia.

③ Antismoking movements cost Asian nations lots of money.

④ Asian nations are beginning to recognize that the situation must be addressed.

⑤ To secure the passage of legislation to support antismoking movements in Asia is almost impossible.

12 **Choose the best title of the above passage.**

① Why Become Asians the Slave of Cigarettes?

② Asia's Irreversible Hurt: Smoking

③ Can Asia Kick the Habit?

④ Tobaccos and Anti-smoking Movements

⑤ Smoking's Side Effects

>>> 다음 글을 읽고 문제의 답을 고르시오. [13~14]

A hearing-impaired person, I lip-read to communicate. When I held a job as a junior electronics-maintenance technician, a coworker and I were sent out on a service call. She was becoming tense because so many things had been going wrong that day. Finally, after trying unsuccessfully to find a vacant spot in a crowded parking lot, she said, "I'm so upset, I could swear!", "Go ahead", I replied. "________________"

13 **Which of the following best describes the narrator?**

① (S)he is a blind person and has to be constantly told which way to go.

② (S)he is a deaf person and watches the movement of the others' lips to understand them.

③ (S)he was too young a technician to be sent out on a service call.

④ (S)he and her(his) co-worker had had a wonderful day that day.

⑤ Her(his) co-worker was so happy that she had to shout "hurrah".

14 **Which of the following best fits into blank?**

① Calm down.

② You are a truly patient lady.

③ I won't look.

④ Let's get out of here quick.

⑤ I will keep my fingers crossed.

Thunderstorms are particularly prevalent during the summer months in areas close to the warm waters of the Gulf of Mexico. Large cities also act as heat sources, producing convection currents in the air, which carry ocean moisture <u>aloft</u>, along with salt particles and pollutants which are condensation nuclei encouraging cloud formation. The towering cumulonimbus clouds thus formed turn from cottony white to threatening gray and black as the moisture and energy build up. Eventually, the electrical discharge we know as lightning takes place. Every year an estimated 10,000 forest fires are touched off by lightning and other thunderstorm phenomena.

15 **What is this passage primarily concerned with?**

① the condensation of salt particles
② the formation of cottony white clouds
③ the destruction of forests by lightning
④ the causes and effects of thunderstorm

16 **Which of the following can be inferred from this passage?**

① Thunderstorms are a major threat to cumulonimbus.
② Without pollution there would be no condensation of nuclei.
③ Thunderstorms are inescapable during the summer months.
④ Thunderstorms are made by a combination of heat and moisture.

17 **Which of the following can best replace the underlined word, <u>aloft</u>?**

① particles
② discharges
③ into the air
④ over the cities

>>> 다음 글을 읽고 문제의 답을 고르시오. [18~20]

When I was eighteen I wanted something to do. I had tried tutoring for two years and hated it and could not earn my bread that way at the cost of my health; I tried story-writing and got five dollars for stories that now bring a hundred; I had thought seriously of going on the stage, but certain highly respectable relatives were so shocked at the mere idea that I relinquished my dramatic aspirations.

"What shall I do?" was still the question that hounded me. I was ready to work, eager to be independent, and too proud to endure patronage. But the right task seemed hard to find, and my bottled energies were fermenting in a way that threatened an explosion.

18 **Which one best expresses the author's attitude toward work?**

① Jobs are plentiful if you know where to look.

② It is difficult to find a job that pays well and is rewarding.

③ It is better to work at any job than not to work at all.

④ Work is to be avoided at all costs.

19 **The author implies that writing is a job that is ____________.**

① rewarding

② humiliating

③ unprofitable

④ stimulating

20 **According to the author, her energy was like ____________.**

① a bottle

② a stew that is cooking

③ a sewing job

④ a bomb that might go off

One of the side-effects of the second world war was the most momentous social change of the past half-century. As men marched off to fight, women put aside their grooming magazines and gardening gloves and took their husbands' places in factories and on the farms. They never looked back. Many people worry about the impact on family life of their entry into the labour force, but most now take it for granted that women have as much to offer at work as men do.

①Another change as large as that one is now under way. In a further half-century it will seem just as absurd that western societies today are content to press another potentially productive set of workers to stay at home sipping tea and potting begonias? and to pay them for it, to boot.

The question of how to deal with the growing number of retired people has recently been seen as chiefly ②a financial puzzle: how to pay for the leisure of those ageing layabouts. When Bismarck first introduced state pensions in the 1880s, they kicked in at the age of 70, about 20 years more than the typical life span. Nowadays state and company pension schemes kick in at or before 65, almost 20 years less. But ③the issue is more than just a ______________ one: ④it raises social as well as economic questions, and ⑤its resolution will involve governments, employers and people.

21 **Fill in the blank with the most suitable word.**

① warlike   ② moral

③ financial   ④ strained

⑤ compromising

22 **Among ①, ②, ③, ④, and ⑤, which one differs from the others in what they refer to?**

① Another change   ② a financial puzzle

③ the issue   ④ it

⑤ its

23 **Which of the following statements cannot be inferred from the passage?**

① It is not desirable that retired people will take only household affairs.

② The authorities may make a considerable budget for the retired people that need amusement facilities.

③ It seems as though the average span of human life is less than 80.

④ A number of retired people are the problem not only with the general public but with the government.

⑤ In the nineteenth century, the seventies could receive a pension.

More than 28 million Americans have at least some hearing loss (many of them members of Generation iPod). Yet only one in five who could use a hearing aid wears one. For many, it's an aesthetic issue: They don't like the traditional devices' looks. Now some new gadgets may change that. Modern models come in novel shapes (triangles, teardrops) and colors (sporty green, deep red), with customizable volume settings, rechargeable batteries, even Bluetooth technology.

24 **윗글을 통해 유추할 수 <u>없는</u> 것은?**

① Less than 28 million Americans wear a hearing aid.

② As much as 20% of Americans wear a traditional hearing aid.

③ Future hearing aids will look more stylish than traditional ones.

④ iPod might have been one of the causes of Americans' hearing loss.

Private secretary. Female between 20-25. College degree preferably in English or Accounting. Prior job experience not mandatory. Must type at least 30 words/minute and have working knowledge of computers (word processing). Hours flexible but must be willing to relocate and travel extensively. Starting salary at $2,000/month and open to negotiation. Submit résumé(with photo) and college transcripts to the following address.

25 윗글의 성격으로 가장 알맞은 것은?

① local obituary ② product advertisement
③ personal résumé ④ wanted advertisement

26 윗글의 내용으로 보아 상대적으로 가장 유리한 입장에 있는 사람은?

① a man double majoring in English and history in college
② a 21 year old single woman who types 40 words/minute
③ a retired male executive returning to the job market
④ a divorced mother in her late 20s with two young children

As a high school soccer coach, I'm aware that student athletes tend to focus too much on sports. A fellow coach, Bob, was talking about one such player, who called him at home one night. When his wife informed the kid that Bob wasn't home, he became frantic and said he had to speak to the coach right away. "Just calm down, and I'll have him call you as soon as he gets home," the coach's wife told him. "What's your number?" The flustered kid replied, "Three."

27 What does the Three of the last sentence imply?

① his phone number
② his uniform number
③ his room number
④ the number of his team members

Health experts searching for the cause of a frightening outbreak of a deadly flu-like illness in Asia say the culprit is probably a virus, and they are encouraged that some victims appear to _______________. More than 150 people have fallen ill, mostly in Hong Kong and Vietnam, over the past three weeks. And experts suspect that another 300 people in China's Guangdong province had the same disease beginning in mid-November. While experts are unsure precisely what is causing the outbreak, several say their biggest fear is that it is a new and lethal form of influenza.

28 **Which of the following statements CANNOT be inferred from the passage?**

① The recently found disease is deadly and infectious.

② At least, 450 people are suffering from this disease.

③ Experts are sure of finding a cure for this disease soon.

④ This disease is epidemic mainly in the southeast Asia.

⑤ This disease is a sort of influenza.

29 **Which of the following is most appropriate for the blank?**

① be getting better

② be growing

③ be in a critical condition

④ develop complications

⑤ lose weight

He opens a drawer, pulling out a few stacks of paper. Here, he says, are this week's scheduled movements of every famous passenger of a major limousine company in Los Angeles. Here are passenger manifests of every flight on American Airlines. "I get the full printout," he says. "If they fly any coastal flight, I know it. I can also find anybody in the world within 24 hours." He says he has law enforcement officers on his payroll and can have a license plate checked in an hour.

30 **What would be the man's occupation?**

① lawyer ② policeman

③ paparazzi ④ limousine driver

>> 다음 글을 읽고 문제의 답을 고르시오. [31~32]

Fog, tiny droplets of water vapor, is the villain of the airports. In an effort to eliminate dense fog from airports, weathermen utilize giant fans, nylon string, and chemicals dropped from planes or shot upwards from strange machine on the ground. Nothing works as well, though, as a new weapon in the fight against fog: the helicopter. Researchers believe that if warm dry air above the fog could somehow be driven down into the humid blanket of fog, the droplets would evaporate, thus clearing the air. In a recent experiment to test their theory the researchers had a helicopter descend into the fog above barely visible Smith Mountain Airport near Roanoke, Virginia. The blades of the helicopter caused the air to circulate downwards and an enormous hole in the cloud opened above the airport. Weathermen predict that with larger, more expensive helicopters they will be able to make the thickest fog vanish.

31 **윗글의 제목을 고르시오.**

① Why can Helicopter be Defeated?
② How is Fog Formed and not Seen?
③ The Enemy of the Airport: Fog
④ the Secret to Clearing Fog

32 **이 글을 통해 유추할 수 없는 것을 고르시오.**

① In order to clear fog, helicopters fly upwards above it.
② Some actions that airports have ever taken to eliminate fog have been in vain.
③ Fog has obstructed the view of Smith Mountain Airport.
④ The size of a helicopter seems to affect elimination of fog.

>> **다음 글을 읽고 문제의 답을 고르시오. [33~36]**

The Indo-European family of languages is the world's largest, embracing most of the languages of Europe, America, and much of Asia. Who were the original Indo-Europeans and when and where did they live? Since they left no written documents, which are, after all, the basis of history, the answers to these questions can be best obtained by attempting to reconstruct their languages. If we may assume that a word that is similar in most of the Indo-European languages designates a concept that existed in the original Indo-European society and that, ① ________________, a word that varies in most Indo-European languages designates a concept not discovered until later, we may then draw certain tentative conclusions.

It would appear that the Indo-Europeans lived in a cold northern region; that it was not near the waters, but among forests; that they raised such domestic animals as the sheep, the dog, the cow, and the horse; that among wild animals they knew the bear and the wolf; that it was the use of the horse and chariot that enabled them to overrun such an enormous expanse of territory.

33 **The best title of this passage would be:**

① Languages of the World
② Language and History
③ The Origin of Language
④ The Origin of the Indo-European Languages
⑤ The Historical Linguistics of the Indo-European Languages

34 **Choose the one concept that would probably have existed in the original Indo-European society.**

① whale
② needle-leaf tree
③ tropical fruit
④ dinosaur
⑤ book

35 **If a number of related languages had many similar words for concepts such as 'fish', 'shell', and 'sea' and relatively few words for 'mountain' and 'forest', one could assume that the speakers of the original parent language:**

① preferred the sea to the mountain
② preferred the mountain to the sea
③ enjoyed fishing
④ enjoyed mountain-climbing
⑤ lived by the sea

36 **Which of the following best fits into ①?**

① therefore
② say
③ accordingly
④ by the way
⑤ on the other hand

»» 다음 글을 읽고 문제의 답을 고르시오. [37~38]

Whereas family relationships usually constitute a child's first experience with group life, peer-group interactions soon begin to make their powerful socializing effects felt. From play group to teenage clique, the peer group affords young people many significant learning experiences—how to achieve status in a circle of friends. Peers are equals in a way parents and their children or teachers and their students are not. A parent or teacher sometimes can force young children to obey rules they neither understand nor like, but peers do not have formal authority to do this; thus the true meaning of exchange, cooperation, and equity can be learned more easily in the peer setting. Peer groups increase in importance as the child grows up and reach maximum influence in adolescence, by which time they sometimes dictate much of a young person's behavior both in and out of school.

37 According to the passage, which of the following would feel the importance of a peer group the most?

① toddlers ② elementary school students
③ kindergarteners ④ high school students
⑤ adults

38 Which of the following best expresses the main idea of the passage?

① Children learn about cooperation in their peer groups.
② Peer groups are powerful influences in children's lives.
③ Parents can force children to do things that a peer group cannot.
④ Parents have greater influences on children than their teachers do.
⑤ Relationships in and out of school provide learning opportunities for children.

At this point, we enter a world that is truly surreal, defying comment. The rules of the game must be strictly observed in civilized society: assassinations, terrorism, torture, and aggression are crimes that must be harshly punished when the targets are people who matter; they are not even worth mentioning, or laudable acts of self-defense, if the chief mafia don himself conducts the crimes in the name of the Free World. So self-evident are these truths that close to 100 of reporting and commentary on Bush's attack upheld them, even descending to the level of citing US attempts to assassinate foreign leaders in justification of the US attack on Iraq. Any totalitarian state would be proud to have an intellectual class capable of such a performance.

39 **What does the author imply with regard to the recent US attack on Iraq?**

① It was unavoidable as an act of self-defense.

② It goes without saying that it must be upheld.

③ It would only be welcomed in the totalitarian states.

④ It would be justified by the intellectuals.

40 **What kind of world do we enter according to the author?**

① untrue world

② imaginary world

③ surprising world

④ strange world

41 **What is not implied in the reading above?**

① The U.S.A recently became a totalitarian state.

② Terrorism must not be exercised in civilized society.

③ There is no good reason to justify the US attack.

④ It is surprising that the attack was largely upheld in U.S.A.

A recent study reported in the journal Diabetologia may shed some light on one of the causes of type 1 diabetes. Some experts speculate that exposure to certain viruses may trigger type 1 diabetes in people who are genetically susceptible to diabetes. Such viruses may cause the immune system to mistakenly attack the pancreas and destroy cells that produce insulin.

In the largest study of its kind to date, a group of British researchers examined more than 4000 people under age 30 who were diagnosed with type 1 diabetes in Yorkshire, United Kingdom, between 1978 and 2002. The team discovered that new cases of type 1 diabetes occurred in batches within confined sections of Yorkshire, specifically among youths between 10 and 19. The study's findings suggest that perhaps a virus, which people encounter on an irregular basis, may be responsible for this serious autoimmune disease rather than consistent environmental factors such as diet.

42 What's the most appropriate title of this passage?

① Who Is Most Vulnerable to Diabetes Virus?

② Why Is Teens Exposed to Virus?

③ Virus Causing Type 1 Diabetes

④ Protect Your Pancreas from Destroying Insulin.

⑤ Don't be Exposed to Autoimmune Disease.

43 What cannot be inferred as to Type 1 diabetes from the passage?

① Pancreas' damage causes insulin not to be produced.

② Type 1 diabetes may be one of the autoimmune diseases.

③ Type 1 diabetes occurs because of irregular exposure to virus.

④ Type 1 diabetes is due to genetical factors.

⑤ Type 1 diabetes occurs mostly to adults.

글의 감상

❶ 유형 정의

작가의 태도와 글의 심정, 목적 등을 묻는 문제들 또한 글의 전체 내용에 대한 사고를 요하는 문제들이다. 필자가 서술한 글에 대한 주제와 내용에 관해서 자신의 감정이나 느낌을 표출하는 경우가 있는데, 이에 대한 독자의 이해도를 측정하는 문제 유형이다.

❷ 공략 방법

(1) 작가의 감정이나 논조를 나타내는 '단어'를 찾는 데 주력해야 한다. 따라서 감정과 논조를 나타내는 중요 어휘에 대한 정리가 급선무이다.

(2) 글 전체의 핵심 내용을 파악하고 이에 맞는 저자의 태도와 감정 등이 무엇인지 느껴야 한다.

(3) 글의 종류나 글의 전개 방식, 문제 유형들 또한 이 유형에 포함된다는 점도 참고해야 한다.

❸ 감정 · 논조를 나타내는 데 쓰이는 중요 어휘

advisory 권고하는, 조언하는

alarmed 놀란, 걱정하는

aloof 냉담한

ambiguous 애매모호한(vague, obscure)

apathetic 냉담한

attentive 주의 깊은(cautious)

benign 인자한

benevolent 인자한

bitter 통렬한

boredom 지루함(tedium)

chivalrous 용기 있는, 예의 바른

colloquial 담화체의

complimentary 칭찬하는

confused 혼란스러운

considerate 이해심이 있는(thoughtful)

contemptuous 경멸하는

critical 비판하는

crusty 퉁명스러운(touchy)

detachment 무심함, 냉정함

didactic 교훈적인

disinterested 사심 없는, 공정한

doleful 슬픈(woeful)

envious 시기심 어린

exaggerated 과장된

expository 설명적인(explicative)

fastidious 까다로운(particular)

generous 관대한(liberal)

hedonist 쾌락주의자

humble 겸손한, 비천한

humorous 재미있는

indifferent 질투하는

informative 정열적인, 열렬한

instructive 무관심한

ironical 정보를 전달하는

modest 교훈적인

negative 부정적인

neutral 중립적인

objective 객관적인

obstinate 완고한(stubborn, inflexible)

obvious 명백한, 분명한

optimistic 낙관적인

ordinary 평범한

persuasive 설득적인

pessimistic 염세적인

positive 긍정적인

questioning 호기심 많은

reluctant 주저하는

resentful 분노하는

scholarly 학구적인, 유식한

sarcastic 비꼬는(sneering, satirical)

sceptic 회의론자

sophisticated 세련된, 복잡한

sympathetic 동정하는

tenacious 완강한(determined, stubborn)

timid 소심한(cowardly, timorous)

whimsical 변덕스러운(capricious, fickle)

Religion is an important part of any society's culture and can have a significant impact on business operations. McDonald's and Coca-Cola unfortunately offended Muslims by putting the Saudi Arabian flag on their packaging. The flag's design contains a passage from the Koran, and Muslims feel their Holy Writ should never be wadded up and thrown away. Consider the tragedies in Bosnia and the Middle east, where clashes between religious communities have hurt these economics. In Islamic countries, dawn-to-dusk fasting during the month of Ramadan causes workers' output to drop considerably. Also, the requirement to pray five times daily can affect output. For example, an American manager in Islamic Pakistan toured a new plant under his control in full operation. He went to his office to make some preliminary forecasts of production. As he was working, suddenly all the machinery in the plant stopped. He rushed out expecting a possible power failure and instead found his production workers on their prayer rugs. He returned to his office and proceeded to lower his production estimates.

1 Why were the Muslims offended?

① The packaging was thrown away.

② The packaging was kept because of the sacred Holy Writ.

③ The packaging had become worthless.

④ The packaging was too expensive.

2 How does religion affect business according to the paragraph?

① The Holy Writ must be commercialized.

② The Holy wars can devastate the economy.

③ The religious practices can affect power outages in plants.

④ Not being familar with the local religion can cause a foreign employer to underestimate production.

3 Where would you find this paragraph?

① Travel advisory   ② Tourist brochures

③ Terror watch   ④ Business texts

》》 다음 글을 읽고 문제의 답을 고르시오. [4~5]

The eye accepted what the mind could not: a sudden burst of white and yellow fire, then white trails streaming up and out from the fireball to form a twisted Y against a pure heaven, and the metal turning to rags, dragging white ribbons into the ocean. A terrible beauty exploded like a primal event of physics—the birth of a universe; the death of a star; a fierce, enigmatic violence out of the blue. The mind recoiled in sheer surprise. Then it filled with horror.

4 **The above passage can best be characterized as describing an explosion of ____________.**

① a grenade   ② a star
③ a cracker   ④ a rocket
⑤ a balloon

5 **Which is the writer's feeling about the accident?**

① anger   ② playfulness
③ shock   ④ melancholy
⑤ frustration

People were sitting on the sidewalk in the dawn. They were like failed sectarian suicides. Others would come to help them. Within a year there were fires on the ridges, deranged chanting, and numberless deaths. The screams of the murdered. By day the dead impaled on spikes along the road. What had they done? Kurtz thought that in the history of the world it might even be that there was more punishment than crime but he took small comfort from it.

6 **What is the overall tone of the paragraph?**

① analytic   ② persuasive

③ pessimistic   ④ humorous

7 **Which of the following CANNOT be inferred from the passage?**

① Kurtz seems to feel sympathetic for the dead.
② Something happened and lots of people died.
③ Some miracle will come to save these people.
④ The world became barren after the accident.

"I didn't realize that we had got so far away," said Gladys, uneasily. "It is growing cooler," said Irma. She looked up at the sky. "I hope it isn't going to get windy now," she murmured. The girls put their strength into paddling, and the canoe skimmed across the darkening water.

"There's a squall coming!" cried Gladys. A cold wind blew across the lake, and the waves slapped against the canoe. The girls paddled in strained, tense silence. Just as they rounded a curve in the lake a gust of wind hit the canoe, the waves flung it aside, and as it tipped, the two girls were thrown into the water. The canoe was tossed away from them by the waves.

8 윗글의 등장인물들의 심경 변화를 잘 나타낸 것을 고르시오.

① calm → lonely

② anxious → disappointed

③ angry → regretful

④ worried → horrified

⑤ regretful → horrified

>>> 다음 글을 읽고 문제의 답을 고르시오. [9~10]

My musical director wasn't happy with the performance of one of our percussionists. Repeated attempts to get the drummer to improve failed. Finally, in front of the orchestra, the director said in frustration, "When a musician just can't handle his instrument, they take it away, give him two sticks and make him a drummer!"

A whisper was heard from the percussion section: "And if he can't handle that, they will take away one of his sticks and make him a conductor."

9 The above passage is _____________.

① informative   ② funny

③ critical   ④ suggestive

⑤ advisory

10 What the director said means _____________.

① he wouldn't conduct any longer

② the orchestra needs more members

③ the drum is the most important musical instrument

④ the drummer is the worst musician

⑤ the conductor is responsible for the orchestra

It is a ① ________________ sensation, this double-consciousness, this sense of always looking at one's self through the eyes of others, of measuring one's soul by the tape of a world that looks on in amused ② ________________ and pity. One ever feels his twoness—an America, a Negro; two souls, two thoughts, two unreconciled strivings.

The history of the American Negro is the history of this strife, this longing to merge his double self into a better and true self. In this merging he wishes neither of the older selves to be lost. He would not Africanize America, for America has too much to teach the world and Africa. He would not bleach his Negro soul in a flood of white Americanism, for he knows that Negro blood has a message for the world. He simply wishes to make it possible for a man to be both a Negro and an American, without being ③ ________________ and spat upon by his fellows, without having the doors of opportunity closed roughly in his face.

11 **Which of the following best fits into ①, ②, and ③?**

① peculiar - contempt - cursed

② odd - pathetic - disguised

③ obvious - woe - censured

④ appropriate - contempt - disclosed

⑤ naked - indignance - eschewed

12 **The author thinks that Negroes should be treated as ___________.**

① proteges　　　　　　② the ordinary

③ the privileged　　　　④ the execrable

⑤ condemned criminals

13 **What is the tone of the above passage?**

① critical　　　　　　② depressing

③ informational　　　　④ implying

⑤ ironical

>>> 다음 글을 읽고 문제의 답을 고르시오. [14~15]

A melon farmer had noticed that thieves were stealing his crop from the fields at night. Desperate to save what was left to sell at market, he put up a sign with a skull and cross-bones that read, "One of these melons is poisoned." Sure enough, for two nights not one melon was stolen. But after the third night, he noticed that his sign had been altered. It now read, "Two of these melons are poisoned."

14 **Which is the best title for the above passage?**
① Food Poisoning
② Outwitting
③ Melon Farmer
④ Fruit Stealing
⑤ Melon Harvest

15 **In which section of newspapers or magazines do you expect this passage to appear?**
① Editorial
② Advertisement
③ Humor
④ Economy
⑤ Domestic

I once had the misperception that those who are educated in disciplines such as political science, public policy, or pre-law are more likely to be prepared for a graduate education in law than most other students. Now I believe that a student coming from a more (가)<u>nontraditional background</u> can contribute in many ways to society as a lawyer.

In a world where technology is the dominant means of progress and is advancing at such a breakneck pace, it can be a great advantage to society to have knowledgable people working with laws (나)<u>concern</u> technology. I not only believe that I am qualified to perform (다)<u>this service</u> to society as a lawyer, but I am convinced that USC law school possesses the quality of education and diversity in student body that can best help me fulfill these goals.

16 The above passage is a part of ___________.

① a chronological report on technological advance

② a critical essay on the law school

③ a graduate admission essay

④ an itinerary column

⑤ jurisdictional statement

17 What field would belong to the "nontraditional background" in (가)?

① political science   ② social science

③ public administration   ④ computer science

⑤ pre-law

18 Which one is the most appropriate form for "concern" in (나)?

① concern   ② concerning

③ concerned   ④ to concern

⑤ be concerned

19 **What would "this service" in (다) mean?**

① to practice legal service in the field of technology

② to take part in scientific progress

③ to help those who need free legal aid

④ to influence the reform of law school

⑤ to assist the lawyers who need technical knowledge

>>> 다음 글을 읽고 문제의 답을 고르시오. [20~21]

Compulsory schooling was begun in the United States in the 19th century as a way of transmitting and maintaining Anglo-American culture and language. Educators believed that proficiency in two languages was not passionate, so educational policymakers declared that students should ________________. Also, the ability to speak English was made a condition for American citizenship in 1906, and in 1915 and English-literacy requirement was added. The justification provided for these measures was a peculiar doctrine about the connection between language and political thought, which held that speaking a foreign language was inimical to grasping the fundamental concepts of democratic society.

20 **윗글의 어조로 가장 적절한 것은?**

① Critical

② Factual

③ Humorous

④ Pessimistic

⑤ Ambitious

21 **빈칸에 들어갈 말로 가장 적절한 것은?**

① not speak English

② learn English only

③ learn two languages

④ go to public schools

⑤ use their native tongue

In a large metropolitan airport, that is, an air terminal at the edge of a major city, it is not unusual to have many landings and take-offs during a 24-hour period. The heavy air traffic is under the control of a group of people known as air traffic controllers, who direct the flow of air traffic into and out of the airport. The air traffic control group works in the control tower, which is located at the highest point in the airport terminal complex, permitting the controllers to have maximum vision of all the aircraft arriving and departing the airport. When the weather limits the visibility around the runways, many computerized navigational aids are used to permit a safe landing. All of the procedures used for handling traffic under good and poor weather conditions are established by a governmental aviation administration under the department of transportation.

22 Under poor weather conditions an airport will ___________.

① postpone all flights

② plan emergency landings only

③ substitute the judgment of machines for that of men and women

④ turn on all lights

⑤ divert all flights

23 The tone of the passage is best described as ___________.

① argumentative

② factual

③ emotional

④ biased

⑤ sarcastic

>> 다음 글을 읽고 문제의 답을 고르시오. [24~25]

Journalism tends to focus on the poor when the poor make news, usually dramatic news like a tenement fire or a march on Washington. But the poor are poor all the time. It is not journalism's ordinary business to deal with the unstartling normalities of life. Reporters need a story, something shapely and elegant. Poverty is disorderly, anticlimactic and endless. If one wants truth about the poor, one must look ① "where the ball is" not in a ball game.

24 As for the role of journalism in revealing the truth, the author is ____________.

① supportive

② critical

③ enthusiastic

④ neither critical nor supportive

⑤ critical as well as supportive

25 The one that is NOT related to the underlined "where the ball is" in ① is

____________.

① something shapely and elegant

② something climactic

③ celebrities

④ daily routines

⑤ a tenement fire

Chapter 09

순서 배열 · 문장 삭제 · 문장 삽입

❶ 유형 정의

글의 논리적인 전개 과정에 따라 문장과 문장 간의 논리적 배열이 옳게 되었는지(순서 배열), 글의 흐름, 작가의 주장과 이를 뒷받침하는 부연 설명 및 기타 논리 전개에 위배되는 글이 있는지를 판단하고(문장 삭제), 문단의 일관성을 유지하기 위해 특정 문장이 어디에 옳게 위치해야 되는지에 대한 판단(문장 삽입)을 요하는 유형이다. 인하대, 중앙대, 가톨릭대 등 몇몇 대학에서 1 문제 정도를 제외하고는 등장하지 않는 유형이다.

❷ 공략 방법

(1) 순서 배열 유형은 문장과 문장의 선후 관계를 연결시켜 주는 논리 정보 장치, 시간 통제 부사 등과 같은 연결어구 등을 주의해야 한다. 이러한 연결어구가 드러나지 않는 경우에는 정확한 해석에 따른 논리 흐름을 파악해야 한다.

(2) 문장 삭제 유형은 주제문과 그 주제문을 뒷받침해 주는 문장들과의 통일성에 위배되지는 않았는지 글 전체의 흐름을 신경 써야 한다. 즉, 글 전체의 흐름과 논리적으로 위배되는 문장을 고르면 된다.

(3) 문장 삽입 유형은 순서 배열과 마찬가지로 문장 간의 선후 관계 연결의 일관성을 유념하면서, 주어진 문장에 있는 연결어구, 지시어 등을 살펴본다. 또는 주어진 문장과는 상관없이, 지문에 있는 문장들 간에 흐름이 어색한 내용을 발견한다면 그 부분에 주어진 문장이 삽입되어야 한다.

1   Rearrange the following sentences to make a coherent paragraph.

A. One of these was Albert Einstein.

B. There have been only a few scientists whose work has changed man's total view of the world.

C. These theories dealt with everything from the inside of an atom to the farthest regions of the universe.

D. During the first half of this century Einstein set forth a number of theories about the physical world.

① D - C - B - A

② B - D - C - A

③ B - A - D - C

④ B - D - A - C

⑤ A - B - D - C

2   Rearrange the following sentences to make a coherent paragraph.

A. There is a big difference between a liberal and a reactionary.

B. On the other hand, a person may look back or want to return to the way things used to be.

C. This person doesn't like progress and resents change.

D. The person who favors new ideas, tries to change, and looks for new ways is freer or more liberated.

① D - B - A - C

② A - D - B - C

③ A - C - B - D

④ D - C - B - A

⑤ A - C - D - B

3 다음 주어진 문장에 이어질 글의 순서로 가장 적합한 것은?

> Although industrial countries have made great advances in health care, today their health care systems are experiencing some serious problems.
>
> 가. In the United States, for example, nearly \$2 billion is spent every day for healthy care, and this amount is increasing at an annual rate of 12 percent.
>
> 나. As a result of these increasing costs, access to good health care is being reduced rather than expanded.
>
> 다. By far the most urgent of these problems is financial: medical costs are rising faster than prices in most other areas of the economy.

① 가 – 나 – 다   ② 가 – 다 – 나
③ 다 – 가 – 나   ④ 다 – 나 – 가

4 글의 흐름상 가장 자연스럽게 배열한 것은?

> (1) Knowledge is the stuff from which new ideas are made.
>
> (2) Their knowledge just sat in their crania because they didn't think about what they knew in any new ways.
>
> (3) We've all known people who knew lots of facts and nothing creative happened.
>
> (4) Nonetheless, knowledge alone won't make a person creative.
>
> (5) The real key to being creative lies in what you do with your knowledge.

① (1) - (2) - (3) - (4) - (5)   ② (1) - (3) - (4) - (2) - (5)
③ (1) - (3) - (2) - (4) - (5)   ④ (1) - (4) - (3) - (2) - (5)
⑤ (1) - (4) - (2) - (3) - (5)

5 **Which of the following is the most appropriate location for the following sentence?**

> Nonetheless, telecommuting could one day be the norm, not the exception.

It seems that more of us will be telecommuting. [A] Some jobs clearly just can't be performed remotely; a hospital nurse, for example, won't ever be able to work from home, while a hospital accountant could. [B] A report by the Reason Foundation found that telecommuters outnumbered actual mass-transit commuters in 27 of the 50 largest U.S. metropolitan areas. [C] Two thirds of Fortune 1,000 companies now have telecommuting programs, while 60 percent of companies that don't have such programs are considering the idea. [D] As wireless and other telecommunications technologies become more sophisticated, the advantages of athome employment will only grow. [E] It absolutely is the wave of the future.

① [A]   ② [B]
③ [C]   ④ [D]
⑤ [E]

(1) These might include a house or houses, land, antiques, or other valuable goods.

(2) An interesting historical example of a wealth tax from England is the Window Tax that was in force from 1696 to 1857.

(3) Many countries use wealth tax base. Taxes on wealth can take many forms, but they usually involve taxing a person's possessions.

(4) That is why some old English houses have bricked-up windows, which can still be seen.

(5) A person was taxed if he had over ten windows in his house.

6 **Put the above sentences in the best order.**

① (2) - (3) - (1) - (5) - (4)

② (2) - (1) - (3) - (5) - (4)

③ (3) - (1) - (2) - (4) - (5)

④ (2) - (5) - (4) - (1) - (3)

⑤ (3) - (1) - (2) - (5) - (4)

7 **Why did some English people have their windows bricked-up?**

① Because they did not want to pay income tax.

② Because they wanted to pay less tax.

③ Because they wanted to protect their houses from burglary.

④ Because they did not want to allow tax-officials to enter their houses.

⑤ Because their windows were broken.

8 **Choose the place that the given sentence is to be inserted to in the following article.**

> For example, if the mother eats cabbage or garlic, many babies will refuse her milk.

> Most doctors now agree that mother's milk is better for babies than artificial milk. [A] However, artificial milk has one advantage. It always tastes the same for the baby. [B] Mother's milk, on the other hand, can change flavor. [C] Certain foods may give the milk a strange taste. [D] Doctors have also discovered that babies may also refuse their mothers' milk after she has exercised a lot, After exercise, in fact, the milk may have an unpleasant, sour taste.

① [A]　　　　　　　② [B]
③ [C]　　　　　　　④ [D]

9　Choose the place that the given sentence is to be inserted to in the following article.

However, the people who enjoy others' private lives do not always like it when people watch them!

[A] Most people agree that it is fun to watch people. [B] Many people also enjoy learning about the rich and the famous. They spend millions of dollars yearly on newspapers and magazines that tell about the private lives of rich and famous people. [C] This information makes these famous people real to the readers. [D] In other words, many who enjoy stealing glance at others worry about their right to a private life.

① [A]　　　　　　　② [B]
③ [C]　　　　　　　④ [D]

10 다음 글에서 전체 흐름과 관계가 없는 문장은?

On the other hand, some scientist argue that the extinction issue is being exaggerated, and that people are "crying wolf" by depicting the loss of species as more alarming than it really is.

[A] In addition, many people point to the fact that the world is already lacking in resources, food, and adequate health care. [B] Concerned more with economic survival, they ask whether it is, in fact, realistic to make a fuss over species that may become extinct many years from now, when people have families to feed tomorrow.

[C] They see saving endangered species as somewhat contradictory as it interferes with of opposes human goals. [D] These people disagree with a law that puts man's own survival above the continuance of lower forms of life.

① [A]　　　　　　　　　② [B]
③ [C]　　　　　　　　　④ [D]

11 아래 글들을 문맥에 맞게 올바른 순서로 연결한 것은?

(가)　The genre of literature ranges from personal ones such as poetry, literary essay to impersonal ones like drama, epic and novel.

(나)　A literary work therefore possesses greatness by virtue of the power it is able to exert over the imaginative life of attentive readers.

(다)　Out of two types, it can be a simple expression of a private emotion. But in many cases its vision is expanded into the common accumulative experience of human being.

(라)　But however general and grand in scope a single play, or novel may be, its full realization cannot be achieved without the active and pleasurable participation of the reader.

① (가) – (나) – (다) – (라)
② (가) – (다) – (라) – (나)
③ (가) – (나) – (라) – (다)
④ (가) – (라) – (나) – (다)

12 글의 흐름상 제시문 다음에 이어질 내용을 바른 순서대로 배열한 것은?

> One important change that occurs at night time is increased levels of the 'darkness hormone' melatonin, which helps us fall asleep. Most adults start to produce melatonin at about 10 pm.

[I]   This delay in melatonin production might be caused by the behaviour of teenagers.

[II]   This stimulates the brain and exposes the teenagers to bright lights which could cause the later release of melatonin.

[III]   However, researchers discovered that teenagers usually began to produce the hormone at 1 a.m.

[IV]   For instance, when they stay up late, they often play computer games or watch television.

① [I] – [IV] – [II] – [III]
② [III] – [I] – [IV] – [II]
③ [III] – [IV] – [I] – [II]
④ [I] – [III] – [IV] – [II]

전후 문단 추론

❶ 유형 정의

주어진 지문의 앞부분이나 뒷부분에 나올 내용을 묻는 유형이다. 즉, 단락과 단락 사이의 주제를 연결하는 추론 문제이다.

❷ 공략 방법

(1) 주어진 지문 앞에 나온 내용을 추론하는 경우, '첫 문장'에 거의 그 단서가 있다. 대개는 논리 정보 장치가 있어서 '순접'이냐 '역접'이냐를 쉽게 파악할 수도 있지만, 그러한 논리 정보 장치가 없을 경우에는 지문의 주제를 먼저 파악하여야 한다.

(2) 주어진 지문 후에 나올 내용을 추론하는 경우, '마지막 문장'에 그 단서가 포함되어 있다. 즉 보기항에 언급되어 있는 내용 중에서 마지막 문장과 논리적 연결이 될 수 있는지를 확인해야 한다.

Although the three currents which have been discussed so far in twentieth century painting may be founded in sculpture as well, the parallelism should not be overstressed. Whereas painting has been richer and more adventurous, its leadership as an art form has not remained unchallenged, and sculpture has often followed different paths.

1 **The paragraphs that preceded the passage most probably deal with**

____________.

① movements in modern painting
② nineteenth-century art
③ the development of painting techniques
④ current approaches to art history

2 **According to the passage, why are the similarities between painting and sculpture of limited importance?**

① The inspiration for painting rarely comes from sculpture.
② Painters are frequently very critical of sculptors.
③ Sculptor's working methods are basically different from those of painters.
④ Trends in sculpture often develop independently of trends in painting.

》》 다음 글을 읽고 문제의 답을 고르시오. [3~5]

Today, once more, egos are breaking like eggshells against the wall. Now, however, _______________ is associated with the fracture of the family rather than the economy. As millions of men and women clamber out of the strewn wreckage of their marriages, they, too, suffer agonies of self-blame. And once more, much of _______________ is misplaced. When a tiny minority is involved, the crack-up of their families may reflect individual failures. But when divorce, separation, and other forms of familial disaster overtake millions at once in many countries, it is absurd to think the causes are purely personal.

3 **Which of the following topics is most likely to precede this passage?**

① Massive Ego's Shattering

② Causes of Ego's Loss

③ Development of Economic System

④ Change of the Status of Men and Women

⑤ Causes of Social Changes

4 **The author believes that _______________.**

① egos are not fragile unlike eggshells that are easily breakable

② economic depression helps people to maintain their families

③ people belonging to the minority group are not responsible for their failure

④ the causes of family fracture are not only personal but also social

⑤ people need not feel guilty about their economic failure

5 **빈칸에 공통적으로 들어갈 단어는?**

① the guilt

② the result

③ the benevolence

④ the shivering

⑤ the sibling

Chapter 11

단락의 구분

❶ 유형 정의

본래는 두 개 이상의 단락으로 구분되어 있는 글을 마치 하나의 단락으로 구성된 것처럼 두 단락을 합쳐 놓은 채, 두 개의 단락이 시작되는 문장을 선택하라는 문제 유형이다. 성균관대에서만 출제가 되며, 매해 1~2문제가 꾸준히 출제 되고 있다.

❷ 공략 방법

(1) 각 단락은 다른 단락과 구분되는 소주제를 개별적으로 가지고 있다. 따라서 그 소주제를 구분할 수 있어야 한다.

(2) 단순히 대조나 양보, 역접의 연결사가 포함된 문장이라고 해서, 새로운 단락이 시작되는 것은 아니므로, 이러한 연결사가 포함된 문장이 새로운 단락의 첫 문장이라고 오인해서는 안 된다.

(3) 두 번째의 단락이 시작되는 문장으로 간주되는 내용이 마지막 문장까지 포괄적으로 포함된다면 그 문장이 두 번째 단락으로 시작되는 문장이라고 생각해도 좋다.

>>> 다음 글을 읽고 문제의 답을 고르시오. [1~3]

The children scrambled hastily. With prodigious clatter they arranged themselves at table. The babe sat with his feet dangling high from a precarious infant chair and gorged his small stomach. (가) Jimmie forced, with feverish rapidity, the grease-enveloped pieces between his wounded lips. (나) Maggie, with side glances of fear of interruption, ate like a small pursued tigress. (다) The mother sat blinking at them. (라) She delivered reproaches, swallowed potatoes and drank from a yellow-brown bottle. (마) After a time her mood changed and she wept as she carried little Tommie into another room and laid him to sleep with his fists doubled in an old quilt of faded red and green grandeur. Then she came and moaned by the stove. She rocked to and fro upon a chair, shedding tears and crooning miserably to the two children about their "poor mother" and "your father, damn soul."

1 The best title of the passage would be ___________.

① Maggie: A Girl of the Street
② The Beast-like Family
③ Domestic Violence
④ A Mother's Solitude
⑤ Weighty Meal

2 According to the passage, which of the following is not true?

① It seems that Maggie didn't feel empty.
② The relationship among the family might not be good.
③ The mother's attitude is somewhat hostile.
④ The mother complains to her children about her husband.
⑤ The characters are described as wild beasts.

3 When the above passage can be divided into two paragraphs, which would be the best boundary?

① (가)　　　　② (나)
③ (다)　　　　④ (라)
⑤ (마)

The sheer loathsomeness of nausea and vomiting does seem to serve a biological purpose. The benefit of vomiting after eating something poisonous or tainted is obvious: the toxin is expelled. And the dreadfulness of the accompanying nausea deters you from ever wanting to eat anything like it again. (1)This explains why pills, chemotherapy, and general anesthetics so often cause nausea and vomiting: they are poisonous-albeit controlled onesand the body is designed to reject them. (2)Why other things cause nausea and vomiting is more difficult to explain, but scientists are beginning to see some sense in nature's design. (3)You'd think that pregnancy sickness, for example, would be evolutionarily disadvantageous, since a growing embryo needs nutrition. (4)In a famous 1992 paper, however, the evolutionary biologist Margie Profet made a compelling case that pregnancy sickness is actually protective. (5)She pointed out that natural foods that are safe for adults commonly turn out to be unsafe for embryos. All plants produce toxins, and in order to be able to eat them we have evolved elaborate detoxification systems. But these systems don't eliminate harmful chemicals completely, and embryos can be sensitive to even tiny amounts.

4   When the above passage can be divided into two paragraphs, which would be the best boundary?

① (1)   ② (2)   ③ (3)   ④ (4)   ⑤ (5)

5   Which would be the main theme of the passage?
① Positive Effects of Nausea and Vomiting
② Evolutionary Explanation of Nature's Design
③ Several Causes of Nausea and Vomiting
④ Some Merits of Natural Food
⑤ The Birth of Immune System

6 **What is the function of pregnancy sickness?**

① To prevent the pregnant women from overworking

② To control the weight of the embryos

③ To protect the embryos from the poisons

④ To inform the abnormal status of the body

⑤ To supply the mother with the nutrition she needs

7 **What makes the grown-ups tolerate the poisons that plants produce?**

① general anesthetics

② pregnancy sickness

③ nausea and vomiting

④ natural foods

⑤ detoxification system

The new music was built out of materials already in existence: blues, rock'n'roll, folk music. But although the forms remained, something wholly new and original was made out of these older elements—more original, perhaps, than even (가)<u>the new musicians</u> themselves yet realize. The transformation took place in 1966~68. Up to that time, the blues had been an essentially black medium. As made famous by Elvis Presley, rock'n'roll which was (나)<u>a blues derivative</u> was rhythmic, raunchy, teenage dance music. (1) Folk music, with such singers as Joan Baez, was popular among college students. (2) The three forms remained musically and culturally distinct, and even as late as 1965, none of them were expressing any radically new states of consciousness. (3) In 1966~68 there was a spontaneous transformation. (4) In the U.S., it originated with youthful rock groups playing in the Bay Area. (5) In England, it was led by the Beatles, who were already established as an extremely fine and highly individual rock group. What happened were these. First, the separate musical traditions were brought together. Bob Dylan and the Jefferson Airplane played folk rock, folk ideas with a rock beat. White rock groups began experimenting with the blues. Of course, white musicians had always played the blues, but essentially as imitators of the Negro style; now it began to be the white bands' own music, and all of the groups moved towards a broader synthesis and (다).

8 The main theme of the passage is "____________".

① How the new music diverged from the existing three forms of music
② The three different forms of music
③ The originality of the new music
④ Difficulties in characterizing the new music
⑤ How the new music came into being

9 Who does not belong to "the new musicians" in (가)?

① The Bay Area rock groups

② The Beatles

③ Elvis Presley

④ Jefferson Airplane

⑤ Bob Dylan

10 What is most likely the topic of the paragraph following this one?

① A more detailed elaboration of the synthesis in music.

② How the U.S. and England led to the revolution in music.

③ How quickly the traditional forms of music became out-moded.

④ Another feature of the new music.

⑤ How folk ideas combined with rock beat.

11 "A blues derivative" in (나) is a form of music that is ____________ the blues.

① distinct from

② developed from

③ scornful of

④ similar to

⑤ derogatory to

12 Which of the following is most appropriate for the blank (다)?

① distinctiveness

② ramification

③ divergence

④ eruption

⑤ eclecticism

13 If we divide the passage into two paragraphs, where does the second paragraph begin?

① (1)   ② (2)   ③ (3)   ④ (4)   ⑤ (5)

The term "hot dog" was <u>coined</u> in 1901 at the New York Polo Grounds. (1) One cold April day, concessionaire Harry Stevens was losing money with ice cream and ice cold soda. (2) He sent his salesmen out to buy up all the dachshund sausages they could find, along with an equal number of rolls. (3) In less than an hour his vendors were hawking hot dogs from portable hot water tanks with "They're red hot! Get your dachshund sausages while they're red hot!" (4) In the press box, sports cartoonist Tad Dorgan was nearing his deadline and desperate for an idea. (5) Hearing the vendors, he hastily drew a cartoon of barking dachshund sausages nestled warmly in rolls. Not sure of how to spell "dachshund" he simply wrote "hot dog"! The cartoon was a sensation. People began to use the term "hot dog".

14 Why did the sports cartoonist write "hot dog" according to the passage?

① Because the name of the sausages was the same as that of a dog.

② Because the sausages were made of dog meat.

③ Because the sausages looked like a dog.

④ Because the vendors were calling the sausages "hot dog".

⑤ Because the sausages were sold in rolls.

15 Which of the following is closest in meaning to the underlined word "coined"?

① cooked ② moneyed

③ spelled ④ invented

⑤ used

16 When the above passage can be divided into two paragraphs, which would be the best boundary?

① (1) ② (2) ③ (3) ④ (4) ⑤ (5)

재진술

❶ 유형 정의

paraphrasing(재정의) 출제 패턴은 세 가지로 분류할 수 있다.

첫째, 구문 이해

둘째, 관용 표현 이해

셋째, 추론

'구문 이해'의 문제는 물주 구문, 양보 구문, 인과 구문, 강조 구문, 시간 구문, 특수 구문 등에 대한 이해를 물어보는 패턴이다.

'관용 표현 이해'의 문제는 관용 표현의 의미에 따라 문맥의 변화를 물어보는 패턴이다.

'추론 문제'는 제시된 지문을 통해 주제에서 벗어나지 않는 범위 내에서 얻을 수 있는 내용을 찾아내는 패턴이다.

❷ 공략 방법

(1) 세부적인 영문법에 집중하기보다는 먼저 구문에 대해 거시적으로 판단을 해야 한다.

(2) 글의 논리 관계를 결정짓는 논리 정보 장치를 통해 인과, 시간 전후, 양보, 대조, 비교, 강조의 글 흐름을 잘 판단해야 한다.

(3) 아무리 상식적으로 옳은 설명이라 할지라도 지문 내의 특정 부분이나 글에서 직·간접적으로 추론될 수 있어야 한다. 즉, 이글의 요지에서 벗어나는 내용은 재진술되어 추론될 수 없다.

1 The student revolt is not only a thorn in the side of the president's newly established government, but has international implications as well.

① This revolt affects the students.
② This revolt affects national and international affairs.
③ This revolt affects the students and international affairs.
④ This revolt affects the side of the president's body.

2 It wasn't long before different ideas about how the United States government should be run caused people to take sides.

① Before long people was divided as a result of difference in opinions about the system of government.
② The difference of opinion about the system of government was not serious.
③ People agreed on the system of government unanimously.
④ Soon people took part in the discussion of how the government should be run.

3 Language is a necessary tool in the sharing transference of ideas, but can also be an impediment to understanding when confused by dialects and localized idioms.

① Language must have its drawbacks.
② Dialects and localized idioms are the main impediment to sharing the transference of ideas.
③ Language is unnecessarily impaired by idiomatic changes.
④ Comprehension can be blurred by local linguistic differences.

4 What is most obvious in this book are all these details of daily living which make Mrs. Richards anything but common.

① Mrs. Richards is quite ordinary.
② Mrs. Richards is an unusual person.
③ Mrs. Richards is very obvious.
④ Mrs. Richards is anything she wants to be.

5   **He has seen his best days.**

① He was once prosperous, but has now declined.
② He has been quite well up to now.
③ He has never been so well off.
④ He has been living in the memory of his former prosperity.

6   **Long before the genetic basis of heredity was understood, farmers bred animals and plants to enhance desirable traits. In a sense the first genetic engineers, they recognized that selecting superior parents produced improved offspring. Since domestication, cattle have been bred for strength at the plow, for fighting spirit and, as early as 1,700, for more milk or beef.**

① Farmers understood the genetic basis of heredity long after the first genetic engineers.
② Farmers are, so to speak, the forerunners of the present-day genetic engineers.
③ Farmers grew animals and plants to get more domesticated ones.
④ Farmers selected superior parents in order to produce more domesticated offspring.

7   **Since Einstein didn't begin to talk until he was three years old, no one realized that he was a latent genius.**

① Even though he was a genius, it wasn't noticeable because he was late in beginning to talk.
② He talked late, so he must not have been a genius.
③ Geniuses begin talking when they are three years old.
④ No one knows when a genius will begin to talk.

8 The medical journal reported that heart attack victims who recover are approximately five times as likely as to die within the next five years as those people without a history of heart disease.

① People who have had a heart disease will die in five years.
② People who have had a heart disease are less likely to die than people without a history of heart disease.
③ People who have had a heart disease are more likely to die in the near future than others.
④ People who have had a heart disease are likely to recover soon.

9 The ancient notion that there is a single, true meaning for a word has been replaced by the concept that words are essentially nothing more than conventional symbols whose use and pronunciation may vary even from person to person.

① The ancients were able to devise fool-proof meanings for words.
② The concept of one single true meaning for a word is unalterable.
③ Language is a tool that is best used by neophytes.
④ The pronunciation of words and their meanings change with the times and usage.

10 It must be clearly understood that the "fittest" which survive are not necessarily best or highest on any absolute standard, but simply fittest for the given conditions.

① Only the best survive.
② The best can never be the fittest.
③ On some occasions the best do not survive.
④ The fittest are always the best.

11 **The characters in this book are fictional, and any resemblance to living people is purely coincidental.**

① It is only a coincidence if any of the fictitious characters in this book resemble actual people.
② Living persons were used as models for the fictional characters in this book.
③ Coincidences in fiction books are always pure when characters are involved.
④ The people in this book were designed to resemble living persons.

12 **In order to live a religious and moral life worth the name, they feel it is necessary to come out in some degree from the competitive world.**

① To live a religious and moral life, they should start from the ordinary routine lives.
② Religion and morality are indispensible for their lives in the world.
③ If being competitive, some people that have a religious belief may deviate from routine lives.
④ Life is so complicated that they cannot catch up with the harsh realities of the world.

13 **During the periods of physical stress the human body uses up more vitamins than it usually does.**

① Only when the human body needs vitamin, is it the periods of physical stress.
② Vitamin's requirement rises when the physical demands on the human body are usually high.
③ Vitamin is very good for the human body.
④ Whenever the human body needs vitamin, he feels physical stress high.

14   **It is unlikely that the results of the elections will be made public until tomorrow morning.**

① Tomorrow morning is probably the earliest that anyone will know the results of the elections.
② Before tomorrow morning we will probably know the results of the elections.
③ The results of the elections will most likely be made known before tomorrow morning.
④ We will probably not be told the results of the elections tomorrow morning.

15   **The world seldom asks how a man acquired his property. The only question is, has he got it?**

① How a man acquired his money should be nobody's business but his own.
② The world assumes that a rich man must be a good man.
③ A man who has money is usually accepted in any society, even though he may be suspected of dishonesty.
④ The world automatically assumes a rich man to be a crook.

문장 완성

❶ 유형 정의

특정 어휘나 어구 또는 문장을 삭제하여 빈칸을 만든 후, 불완전한 문장을 제시하여 보기항 중 올바른 어휘나 어구 또는 문장을 선택하여 완전한 문장을 완성하는 유형이다. 과거 GRE, SAT에서 도입된 이후, 국내에서는 고시와 대학원에서 그 유래를 찾아볼 수 있으며, 모든 편입 영어 시험에서도 반드시 출제되는 유형이다. 이 유형은 크게 세 가지로 분류할 수 있다.

첫째, 어휘 위주의 문장 완성

둘째, 논리력 위주의 문장 완성

셋째, 2어 문장 완성

❷ 공략 방법

(1) 어휘 위주의 문장 완성이 70% 이상을 차지할 정도로, 이 유형은 어휘력이 가히 절대적이라 할 수 있다. 따라서 본격적인 문장 완성을 공략하기 이전에, 기본적으로 실전 수준의 어휘 교재를 일독 정도를 하는 것이 바람직하다.

(2) 원칙적으로 수험생의 추론 능력을 측정하는 유형이므로 문장 간의 논리 흐름을 통제하는 논리정보 장치를 숙지하여야 한다.

(3) 예시, 열거, 진술부연, 인과, 통념비판, 대조, 양보라는 글의 전개 방식에 따른 접근 방법보다는 글의 핵심어와 동의 관계로 문장이 진행되는 순접이냐, 아니면 그 핵심어와 반의 관계로 진행되는 역접이냐에 초점을 맞추는 것이 가장 바람직하다.

❸ **논리정보 장치** [출처 – 문장 완성 뽀개기 700제(넥서스)]

(1) **의견 제시**

additionally 게다가, 더구나   last but not least 덜 중요하진 않지만 마지막으로

again 또   likewise 유사하게

also 또한   moreover 게다가, 더구나

and (then) 그리고   neither ~ nor 둘 다 ~ 아니다

as well as ~ 외에도   next 다음으로

at the same time 동시에, 또한   not only A but also B(=B as well as A) A뿐 아니라 B도

besides 게다가   not to mention ~은 말할 필요도 없고,

between A and B A와 B사이에   on top of that 게다가

both ~ and 둘 다   or 즉

either ~ or 둘 중 어떤 것   plus 그 외에

further 게다가, 더 나아가   similarly 유사하게

furthermore 게다가   together with ~와 함께, ~와 더불어

in addition (to) ~ 외에도   what's more 게다가

indeed 실로, 사실상

(2) **동의** / AGREEMENT

according to ~에 따르면

in accordance(=in agreement / conformity) ~에 일치하여

(3) **상황** / CIRCUMSTANCES

from the standpoint / viewpoint of ~의 관점에서

in my opinion 내 견해로는

in the midst of ~의 와중에

(4) **대조 / CONTRAST**

after (all) ～에도 불구하고
alternatively 양자택일로
although ～에도 불구하고
as opposed to ～과 반대로
at the same time 동시에, 또한
but / yet 그러나
conversely 반대로
despite ～에도 불구하고
even though ～라 할지라도
for all that 그에도 불구하고
however 그러나
in contrast 대조적으로

in face of / in spite of / nevertheless /
nonetheless / notwithstanding ～에도
불구하고
on the contrary 반면에, 반대로
on the other hand 반면에 또 다른 한편으로는
still 그러나, 여전히 *cf.* 고요한, 정지한
though ～에도 불구하고
unlike ～와 달리
whereas 반면에, ～에 반해서
while 반면에
that is not so. 사실은 그렇지 않다.

(5) **비교 / COMPARISON**

comparing 비교해 보면
likewise 비슷하게
in comparison 비교해 보면

in the same way 비슷하게
similarly 유사하게

(6) **매개 / INTERMEDIATING**

by ～으로
by means of ～을 통해

this way 이런 식으로
through (which) ～을 통해

(7) 강조 / EMPHASIS

above all 무엇보다도

a key feature 주요 특징

a major concern 주요 관심사

definitely(=doubtlessly) 분명히

especially significant 특히 중요한

in any event 좌우간, 여하튼간에

indeed 실로, 사실상

in especial 특히

in fact 사실상

in particular 특히

more / more important(ly) 보다 중요하게도

naturally 당연히

particularly 특히

positively 분명히

primarily 일차적으로

principally 주로, 대개

specifically 구체적으로

the basic cause 기본적 대의

the chief factor 주요 요인

the key point 핵심

the main reason 중요 이유

unquestionably / undoubtedly / without doubt 의심의 여지없이

(8) 사건의 순서 / SEQUENCE OF EVENTS

first 첫째

second 둘째

third 셋째

subsequently 그 뒤, 계속되는

following 이어지는, 뒤따르는

then 그런 후에

next 다음으로

later 나중에

after that 그 후에

finally 마지막으로

at the same time 동시에, 또한

(9) 시간 관련 / TIME RELATIONSHIP

after a while 잠시 후에
afterward(s) 나중에
as time goes by 시간이 흐름에 따라
at last 마침내
at present 현재로선
at this point 지금
at the same time / simultaneously 동시에
during ~동안에
here 지금
immediately 즉시, 당장
in the meantime / meanwhile 한편
lately / recently / currently / nowadays 최근에
later 나중에, 그 후에
meanwhile 한편
now / at the moment 지금

nowadays 현재는, 요즘에
presently 현재
shortly (after) ~한 직후
now 지금(과거 사실과 대비)
since ~한 이래
soon 곧
temporarily 일시적으로
then 그때
thereafter 그 후로
throughout ~전반에 거쳐
thereupon 그 후로
until ~할 때까지
up until now 지금까지
while ~동안에
yet 아직

(10) 목적 / PURPOSE

for this reason 이런 이유 때문에
for your information 정보를 주기 위해
in an effort to ~할 노력으로
in order to ~하기 위해

to the purpose of ~의 목적으로
to this end 이런 목적으로
with this in mind 이를 명심하고
with this purpose 이런 목적으로

(11) 인과관계 설명 / EXPLANATION OF CAUSE OR CONSEQUENCE

as ~함에 따라, ~해서
because ~때문에
due to(=owing to, on account of, thanks to, on the ground of) ~때문에
for 왜냐하면, ~해서
* 간접적 이유로 뒤에 S+V가 온다.
in order that ~하기 위해

now that ~이니까, ~이므로
since ~이니까, ~이므로
so A that B A해서 그 결과 B하게 되다
that is because 그건 ~ 때문이다
that is why 그건 ~ 이유 때문이다
cause / result in / lead to / create / make ~을 야기하다 / 초래하다

⑿ **결과** / RESULT

accordingly 따라서

as a consequence 그 결과

as a result 그 결과

consequently 결과적으로

for this reason 이런 이유 때문에

hence 그래서

in short 간단히 말해

in consequence 따라서

so ~ that(=such ~ that) 너무 ~ 해서 ~ 하다

then 그래서, 그때

thereby / therefore / thus 따라서, 그래서

truly 실로

⒀ **반복, 재언급** / REITERATION, REFORMULATION

in other words 달리 말하자면

in short(=briefly) 간단히 말하면

more simply 더 간단히 말하면

namely(=viz) 즉, 바꿔 말하면

rather 차라리

so to speak 말하자면

that is / that is to say 즉

to make a long story short 간단히 말하면

to put it another way 달리 표현하자면

⒁ **조건** / CONDITION

as long as ～하는 한

even if ～라 할지라도

if ～라면

if not ～아니라면

in case of(that) ～의 경우에

in the event of(that) ～의 경우에

only if 단지 ～라면

otherwise 그렇지 않으면, 그 반대의 경우라면

provided / providing (that) ～라면

suppose ～라 가정해 보자

whether or not ～이든 아니든

⒂ **예외, 제외** / EXCEPTION, EXCLUSION

apart / aside from ～은 별도로 하고, 치워 두고

but / except for / excepting / secluding /
save for / saving ～외에는, ～을 제외하고

unless ～가 아니라면

⒃ **예 / EXAMPLE**

for example 예를 들면

for instance 예를 들면

in another case 다른 경우라면

including ~을 포함하여

in particular 특히

in this case 이 경우

in this manner 이런 식으로

namely/that is 즉

such as ~와 같은 것

take the case of ~의 경우를 들어보자

to illustrate 예를 들면

⒄ **대체 / SUBSTITUTION**

in place of ~ 대신에

instead of ~ 대신에

or 혹은

rather 차라리

⒅ **도입 / INTRODUCTION**

in/with reference to ~에 관하여

(at) first 먼저

by the way 그런데

concerning/in the first place ~에 관하여

first of all 먼저, 무엇보다도

initially 우선

on the one hand 한편으로

(↔ on the other hand 또 한편으로는)

regarding ~에 관해

speaking of ~에 대해 말하자면

to begin/start with 우선, 먼저

⒆ **증거, 확실성 / CERTAINTY, EVIDENCE**

certainly 분명히

doubtlessly 의심의 여지없이

distinctly 분명히

evidently 분명히

explicitly 분명히

indeed 실로, 사실상

naturally 당연히

needless to say ~은 말할 필요도 없고

obviously 분명히

of course 물론

undoubtedly 의심의 여지없이

unquestionably 의론의 여지없이

without question 의심의 여지없이

without a doubt 의심의 여지없이

⒇ **결론, 요약** / CONCLUSION, SUMMARY

all things considered 모든 것을 고려해 보면

at last / finally / eventually / in the end / in
the long run / after all 결국, 마침내

in brief / in short / briefly 간단히 말해

in conclusion 결론적으로

in summary 요약하자면

last(ly) 마지막으로

on the whole(=as a whole) 대체로,
일반적으로

thus 고로

to conclude 결론짓자면

to sum up / to summarize 요약하자면

㉑ **고백** / CONCESSION

after all ～에도 불구하고

although ～이지만

granted that / admitting ～은 인정하지만

1. "I'd like to open a checking account with this paycheck. Do I have to ____________ it by signing on the back?"

① entitle
② endorse
③ guarantee
④ invalidate

2. Far too many people are ____________ the government for help, and steps need to be taken to create jobs to make them independent.

① wiping out
② tearing up
③ relying on
④ stamping out

3. "Tom, what I told you is so confidential. I want you to keep it under your ____________ ."

① hat
② eyes
③ nose
④ feet

4. Barbara Walters distinguished herself as a journalist by asking famous people the kinds of ____________ questions that other reporters shied away from.

① gentle
② pointed
③ vague
④ indirect
⑤ gross

5. When one member of the pair is ____________, couples who hope to become parents often seek to adopt a child.

① incapable
② industrious
③ infatuated
④ incisive
⑤ infertile

6   The management is not responsible for any valuables not ____________ in safety deposit boxes provided at the front office.

① existed   ② secured
③ obtained   ④ acquired
⑤ achieved

7   Hyenas have an undeserved reputation as thieves and scavengers that ____________ the leavings of the larger predator.

① subsist on   ② succumb to
③ suffer from   ④ are subdivided into
⑤ are subsumed under

8   Bacteria are becoming immune to antibiotics used in farming and may now be ____________ to similar drugs to treat illnesses.

① strange   ② tolerant
③ resistant   ④ vulnerable

9   The country saw the number of divorces fall for the first in 16 years last year as Koreans became more ____________ going their separate ways.

① eager in   ② satisfied with
③ supportive in   ④ cautious about
⑤ enthusiastic about

10   The author was too ____________ a figure for us to get any detailed information.

① prominent   ② obscure
③ notorious   ④ sluggish
⑤ skillful

11   In these days of eco-realism, too many environmentalists, scientists and politicians tend to shift focus swiftly from one issue to another, pronouncing the first solved and considering the second fresher, more mediagenic. ____________. Today, the breakdown of stratospheric ozone—a problem recently declared fixed—is being ignored, while the newer controversy of 'climate change' launches a thousand conferences. But in fact, the peril of ozone depletion, which is caused by humankind's release of chlorofluorocarbons(CFCs) and other chemicals into the atmosphere, is demonstrably worse than conventional environmental wisdom holds.

① Ozone depletion is a case in point
② Depleted ozone may begin recovery
③ Ozone depletion causes climate change
④ The ozone layer is torn worse than ever
⑤ The ozone layer filters out the sun's UV rays

12   It is a paradox that while state-funded child care and extremely long and cushy maternity benefits make it easy to be a working mother in Sweden, such benefits also have the effect of ____________ female employment in the most profitable and powerful jobs.

① punishing   ② endorsing
③ dampening   ④ augmenting
⑤ guaranteeing

13   The Cabinet member's resignation was not a total ____________ : rumors of his imminent departure had been making the rounds in Washington for a week.

① withdrawal   ② success
③ shock   ④ eclipse
⑤ pretense

14 With similar programs now widely available in inexpensive, easy-to-use
consumer versions, just about anyone with ______________ computer skills can
cut, paste, erase, combine and retouch photographs.

① solitary   ② complimentary
③ snobbish   ④ sedentary
⑤ rudimentary

15 Because of the trauma they have experience, survivors of a major catastrophe
are likely to exhibit ______________ of behavior and may require the aid of
competent therapist.

① concessions   ② diminutions
③ aberrations   ④ restrictions
⑤ altercations

16 Speciesism is a prejudice or attitude of bias in favor of the interests of
members of one's own species and against those of members of other
species. Speciesism is wrong for the same reason racism and sexism are
wrong—because all beings' interests should count equally. This is often
called the principle of quality. All the arguments to prove human ______________
cannot shatter this hard fact: in suffering, the animals are our equals. For
any individual who can suffer, the degree of suffering, not the species of the
sufferer is what should count.

① superiority   ② genetics
③ nature   ④ suffering
⑤ cruelness

17 Most Americans are accustomed to thinking of lie detectors as foolproof—as machines that can separate the guilty from the innocent. But in fact, nothing could be further from the truth. Lie detectors can and do ___________.

① keep playing
② get repaired
③ produce the desired results
④ prove successful
⑤ make mistakes

18 Reviews on caffeine and conception ___________. One study of 2,817 women found no effect of caffeine on their chances of conceiving, while another of 1,909 women linked more than 300 milligrams of caffeine daily to a delay in conception

① conflict
② explode
③ step up
④ manifest themselves

19 The candidate's speech was filled with empty promises, ___________ and cliches.

① threats
② ingenuity
③ platitudes
④ anger
⑤ candor

20 The ___________ faces of the released prisoners showed how poorly they had been cared for.

① grateful
② exuberant
③ jubilant
④ plump
⑤ haggard

21 Though he was theoretically a skilled craftsman, I found his work ____________ and lacking in polish.

① impeccable
② coarse
③ capable
④ functional
⑤ distinguished

22 ____________ foods may be preserved for a long period of time as they have been freed of moisture.

① Frozen
② Seasoned
③ Jellied
④ Desiccated
⑤ Canned

23 Our sense of humour is one of our most valuable faculties. Thinkers simple and profound point out that the ability to see the funny side of things and to laugh at ourselves and our troubles is an asset of great importance. It can help us fight off adversity, get greater joy out of living, and ____________.

① believe in what other people say
② fall in love with a charming lady
③ maintain our sanity
④ make a lot of money
⑤ look on the dark side of things

24 Critics who have spoken out on these issues have been jailed or silenced by authoritarian governments, and international investors have been prepared to turn a blind eye to the ____________ violations which have caused political instability.

① animal abuse
② child abuse
③ international trade
④ peace talks
⑤ human right

25 He is most generous about forgiving a slight, an insult, and an injury. Never does he harbor resentment, store up petty grudges, or waste energy or thought on means of revenge or retaliation. He's much too ____________ a person.

① urbane
② intrepid
③ versatile
④ adventurous
⑤ magnanimous

26 Many novels by the Bronte sisters and other nineteenth-century female authors were initially published under masculine ____________ in the belief that works by male authors would meet more favorable reception.

① monikers
② aliases
③ rubrics
④ criteria
⑤ pseudonyms

27 Someone once told me I was lucky to be ____________ because I have the best of both worlds. In some ways this is true. I have a huge family that is filled with diversity and is as colorful as a box of Crayons.

① exclusive
② limited
③ biracial
④ cowardly
⑤ arrogant

28 When a couple gets divorced, the court may require the man to pay his former wife a monthly sum of money called ____________. Its amount depends on the husband's income, the wife's needs, and the length of the marriage.

① optimism
② honeymoon
③ elope
④ alimony
⑤ veil

29 Much of the art of being a good teacher or healer consists in staying just one step ahead of your patients or pupils. If you are not ahead, it is unlikely that you will be able to lead them anywhere, but if you are two steps ahead, it is likely that ______________ .

① they will be healed without fail
② they will lead you
③ they will love you
④ you will not catch them
⑤ you will lose them

30 다음 빈칸에 공통으로 들어갈 적절한 단어는?

- I'll finish using the computer in a minute. Just keep your ______________ on, and you'll get your turn.

- Jack invested a lot of money in stocks and lost his ______________

- Mike is such a stuffeed ______________ He always wears a tie, and he even etas chicken with a knife and fork.

① hat
③ pants
⑤ jacket
② shirt
④ socks

>>> 밑줄 친 곳에 들어갈 알맞은 답을 고르시오. [31~67]

31 How could high school girls understand their place in American history if their textbooks told them that, from ______________ America to the present, women have had equal opportunity for upward mobility and political participation?

① colonial
③ primitive
⑤ savage
② obsolete
④ prehistoric

32 She accepted his proposal with alarming ___________ ; she had the "yes" out of her mouth before he finished popping the question.

① enthusiasm
② reserve
③ celerity
④ acerbity
⑤ payola

33 The children were so excited about their vacation trip that they became ___________ and had to be calmed down.

① lanky
② staid
③ boisterous
④ forthright

34 As they helped the community recover from a natural calamity, remarkably ___________ rescue crew worked around the clock with an energy that never seemed to wane.

① chubby
② obsequious
③ indefatigable
④ trenchant
⑤ nominal

35 Sophists are someone who will win an argument by forcing their adversaries to defend it on the sophists' own ___________ .

① qualms
② grounds
③ compromise
④ encouragement

36 In the 1920s Hollywood became a magnet for men and women on the cutting edge—___________ artists genuinely excited by the possibilities of the up-and-coming film medium.

① irritable
② innovative
③ untalented
④ sagacious
⑤ coarse

37 I think that having learned our letters we should read the best that is in literature. However, even the college-bred and so-called liberally educated men here and elsewhere have really little or no acquaintance with the recorded wisdom of mankind, ____________.

① the best-sellers   ② the novel films
③ the TV documentaries   ④ the soap opera
⑤ the ancient classics

38 Many people, out of anxiety, became unable to contemplate their true situation and with it to plan accordingly. Anxiety, and the wish to ____________ it by clinging to each other, and to reduce its sting by continuing as much as possible with their usual way of life incapacitated many.

① contradict   ② counteract
③ frustrate   ④ encourage
⑤ deprecate

39 The hypothesis may explain why college graduates appear less ____________ to memory loss than people with only an elementary school education: Learning strengthens the brain.

① vulnerable   ② vigilant
③ indignant   ④ pertinent
⑤ unsusceptible

40 Peter has a bad habit of making ____________ remarks that wander so far off topic that we forget the gist of what he is saying.

① awkward   ② sagacious
③ digressive   ④ telling
⑤ tentative

41 Increasingly silent and withdrawn, he changed from a fluent, articulate speaker to someone who gave only ______________ answers to any questions asked of him.

① bookish
② effusive
③ idiomatic
④ pretentious
⑤ monosyllabic

42 Today, birth rates are dropping around the globe, and experts speak darkly of depopulation. ______________? Contraception is more reliable and readily available than ever. In the developed world, large numbers of women are pursuing higher education and careers, delaying marriage and childbirth, and having smaller families. Developed countries have also seen a major migration from the farms to the cities. In urban areas, the high cost of raising children provides economic incentive to keep family size down.

① What is wrong with fewer people
② What is causing the decline
③ What are the implications of the decline
④ How quickly is the birth-rate declining
⑤ What should we do

43 The Maori ideal in individual behavior was explicit. Generosity was the personal virtue most esteemed. Unless an individual displayed generosity, in all his dealings with people, he ______________ attaining social recognition.

① put emphasis on
② made much of
③ took less advantage of
④ stood little chance of
⑤ focused on

44 Since two-year olds normally express a broad range of emotions, be prepared for everything from delight to rage. However, you should consult your pediatrician if your child seems very passive or withdrawn, perpetually sad or highly demanding and unsatisfied most of the time. These could be signs of depression, caused either by some kind of hidden stress or biological problems. If ______________ depression, he'll probably refer your child to a mental health professional for a consultation.

① your child complains
② your doctor suspects
③ you doctor is in
④ you insist on
⑤ you believe in

45 The whirlwinds of ______________ will continue to shake the foundations of our nation until the bright day of justice emerges.

① repose
② revolt
③ amicableness
④ vision
⑤ catalyst

46 Pearl's ______________ behavior at the party raised some eyebrows; he was certainly the only one who spent the night walking on his hands.

① pliable
② odd
③ adroit
④ buoyant
⑤ ebullient

47 The public health authorities are combatting the claims of ______________ who maintain fraudulently that they have cures for many major ailments.

① salesman
② pharmacists
③ chemists
④ charlatans
⑤ dupe

48 The name of the housing developing is a ___________ : although it is called "Forest Hills", it is located in a treeless valley.

① dilution   ② misnomer
③ benevolence   ④ stalemate
⑤ malediction

49 Despite strong ___________ from public safety officials, most Californians were inadequately prepared for a moderate preparation to large earthquake.

① calamity   ② admonitions
③ observations   ④ recovery
⑤ execration

50 Before we spend a lot of money on this project, I would like to see ___________ , rather than theoretical, evidence that it is effective.

① empirical   ② erroneous
③ conventional   ④ deficient
⑤ marvelous

51 Some people like to dream about things that are not possible. They plan wonderful vacations, but they have no money. They think of getting married to someone they do not even know. These people, we say, are ___________ .

① building a solid future   ② telling telltales
③ building castles in the air   ④ making a plain living
⑤ making a new life for themselves

52 Many children believe that their parents are ___________ and are shocked to learn that they can make mistakes.

① humble   ② flawless
③ insolent   ④ indolent
⑤ ludicrous

53 While admitting his client's guilt, the lawyer argued that circumstances warranted his plea for ___________ .

① leniency   ② innocence

③ conviction   ④ confidence

54 Suspicious of too powerful a President, Americans are ___________ when a President does not act decisively.

① unified   ② indifferent

③ content   ④ uneasy

⑤ adamant

55 In the thirteenth century, Roger Bacon discovered the main substances in gunpowder. The list of substances included charcoal, sulfur and a chemical compound called "saltpeter". But because Bacon ___________, he wrote the list in secret signs the people were not able to understand until 500 years later.

① intended that his discovery should never be known to anyone

② wished that his discovery should be admired all over the world

③ expected that his discovery would be used openly

④ hoped that his discovery could be used immediately

⑤ feared that his discovery might be used harmfully

56 Punctuality is important, and people who are consistently late for appointments are thought to be ___________.

① diligent   ② friendly

③ practical   ④ inconsiderate

57 A foolish consistency is the hobgoblin of little minds, adored by little statesmen and philosophers and divines. With consistency a great soul ___________.

① has surely something to do
② is undoubtedly concerned
③ has simply nothing to do
④ is greatly satisfied
⑤ is well acquainted

58 Our ordinary ways of talking about the world may conceal and ___________ as well as reveal and clarify.

① hinder
② avoid
③ scrutinize
④ obscure
⑤ celebrate

59 A ___________ is a period of time especially at night, when you remain quiet and watchful in one place. You do this, for example, because you are looking after a sick person, praying, or making a political protest.

① fasting
② transition
③ chronicle
④ quarantine
⑤ vigil

60 It is not wise to invent in stocks and shares when shares prices are ___________ so violently.

① moving
② hesitating
③ fluctuating
④ undulating
⑤ exasperating

61 The public politician and the private person were ___________ : this mayor was no more and no less than she appeared to be.

① impervious
② invincible
③ inscrutable
④ indivisible
⑤ indiscriminate

62 Today's children often combine a deceptive ___________ of speech with a shocking lack of firsthand experience, and much of their seemingly sophisticated patter is "tube-talk", a playback of television situation comedies and commercials.

① impediment ② precision
③ impetuosity ④ precocity
⑤ inhibition

63 A : The pedestrian crossing is too far, why don't we just cross over here?
B : No way! You can be heavily fined for ___________.

① trespassing ② soliciting
③ speeding ④ jaywalking
⑤ overpassing

64 There are some people who believe that the name given to an infant exerts a powerful influence on its later life. But I wonder how many instances they know of a name's being a pointer to the ___________ career of the child who bore it. I have known some Christians in their teens, and I confess I could see few sings that the name had played any part in the molding of their characters.

① malicious ② prodigious
③ frivolous ④ congruent
⑤ subsequent

65 You shouldn't listen to other people's private conversations; it isn't polite to ___________.

① earshot ② saunter
③ eavesdrop ④ utter

66 Your ____________ remarks spoil the effect of your speech; try not to stray from your subject.

① praised   ② antique

③ feeble   ④ disingenuous

⑤ digressive

67 Some people argue against capital punishment because there used to be so much racial prejudice against blacks, and it was mostly blacks who were executed. It is no doubt that capital punishment was used unjustly in many cases, but today racial prejudice is not as great. Capital punishment could be given to all those who deserve such a sentence. Only 17 out of 47 men executed since 1947 were black. As a black American, I do not think the racial prejudice argument is ____________ any more.

① valid   ② trivial

③ ethical   ④ reckless

⑤ irrelevant

68 밑줄 친 부분에 공통으로 들어갈 숙어는?

- Half through the chapter I stopped. I could not ____________ a single word.
- The people in the neighborhood of the university have difficulty to ____________ students to add to the income.
- It was really easy to ____________ you ____________. You must be foolish.

① take in   ② figure out

③ pick up   ④ get through

69 The lady got in ___________ with her boss because she didn't finish an important project by the deadline.

① a nutshell ② the dark
③ the same boat ④ the long run
⑤ hot water

70 Space scientists view space exploration as a sort of ___________ to future achievements like permanent space stations that could monitor the weather and provide new sources of energy.

① steppingstone ② diversion
③ unexpectedness ④ deadlock
⑤ premium

71 Even when his reputation was in ___________, almost everyone was willing to admit that he had genius.

① humidity ② retaliation
③ rebuttal ④ prestige
⑤ eclipse

72 The text brims with details, but there are no overarching theses to ___________ them.

① specify ② exaggerate
③ confound ④ unify
⑤ modify

73 Lovejoy, the hero of Jonathan Gash's mystery novels, is an antique dealer who gives the reader advice on how to tell ＿＿＿＿＿＿ antiques from the real thing.

① priceless ② spurious
③ classical ④ authentic
⑤ antiquated

74 Numerous studies have discovered that people who choose to represent themselves in court on the whole exercise pretty good judgment—they seem to have a ＿＿＿＿＿＿ sense of when they need a lawyer and when they don't.

① faulty ② whimsical
③ reliable ④ transient
⑤ drastic

75 Scientists will discover many subtle genetic factors in the makeup of human beings, and those discoveries will challenge the basic concept of equality on which our society is based. Once we can say that there are differences between people that are easily demonstrable at the genetic level, then society will have to come to grips with understanding ＿＿＿＿＿＿—and we are not prepared for that.

① equality ② scientific discoveries
③ science ④ diversity
⑤ competition among human beings

76 That is partly why changes in institutional stockholding can make markets highly ＿＿＿＿＿＿ and therefore risky for smaller investors.

① volatile ② vociferous
③ mawkish ④ imbecile
⑤ droll

77 The point of my keeping a notebook has never been, nor is it now, to have an accurate factual record of what I have been doing or thinking. That would be a different impulse entirely, an instinct for ___________ which I sometimes envy but do not possess.

① severity
② reality
③ punctuality
④ histrionics
⑤ relativity

78 He had no love for Montpelier last time, and it is unkind to require him to make such a ___________ journey.

① strenuous
② insatiable
③ infallible
④ chaste
⑤ platonic

79 In discussing Rothko's art, Breslin is ___________ in keeping to the facts and resisting the ___________ of fanciful interpretation.

① scrupulous - temptations
② meticulous - integrity
③ ungainly - reward
④ uninterested - echo
⑤ inept - bias

80 This is an age of ___________, with interruptions by telephone, by friends, by noise, by scares and by our own flightiness. Increasingly, work must be done under conditions which are ___________ to concentration.

① concentration - harmful
② concentration - hospitable
③ stress - friendly
④ distraction - favorable
⑤ distraction - hostile

81 Deeply ___________ by the insult to his dignity, he maintained that no true gentleman would accept such an ___________ calmly.

① mortified - opportunity
② incensed - affront
③ puzzled - honor
④ shamed - iconoclasm
⑤ gratified - admonition

Part 2
실전편

Actual TEST 01 | Actual TEST 02 | Actual TEST 03 | Actual TEST 04 | Actual TEST 05 | Actual TEST 06 | Actual TEST 07 | Actual TEST 08 | Actual TEST 09 | Actual TEST 10

>>> 밑줄 친 곳에 들어갈 알맞은 답을 고르시오. [1~6]

1 If he didn't have ______________ in the decision making, it would be impossible to draw any conclusions.

① initiative
② antipathy
③ malignancy
④ reluctance
⑤ tarnish

2 The crisis is not ____________; it will not affect us for years to come.

① specious
② fleeting
③ imminent
④ meaningless
⑤ venomous

3 To help her psychology students understand the power of social ____________, Ms. Ewalt had her class participate in an experiment: on a regularly scheduled basis, each member of the class spent two days being shunned by others—no communication, no sharing of a lunchroom table.

① nexus
② mandate
③ mishap
④ ostracism

4 Despite the poem's archaic and tortuous language, the thrust of the poet's argument is surprisingly ____________.

① vapid
② dated
③ blunted
④ intelligible
⑤ paradoxical

5   I don't mean to suggest that we should seek to eliminate fear altogether from human life. Were this humanly possible, it would not be practically ______________. Fear is the elemental alarm system of the human organism which warns of approaching dangers and without which man could not have survived in either the primitive or modern world. Fear, moreover, is a powerfully creative force.

① desirable   ② repentable
③ lamentable   ④ potential

6   A third revolution was the tremendous growth in industrial chemistry, and in our ability to make chemicals in ______________ quantities, very cheaply, for all kinds of purposes. But these have upset the little understood ______________ balance, and polluted and poisoned our waters.

① adequate - metaphysical   ② vast - ecological
③ lucrative - environmental   ④ substantial - biological
⑤ excessive - economic

>>> 다음 글을 읽고 문제의 답을 고르시오.

> Most women are employed in traditional fields for females, such as clerical sales, education, and service. However, a growing number choose a career that necessitates spending many hours away from home. These women are engineers, politicians, doctors, lawyers, and scientists, and a few have begun to occupy executive positions in business, government, and banking, breaking through the so-called <u>glass ceiling</u>.

7   What would be the meaning of the expression <u>glass ceiling</u>?
① ceiling made of glass
② invisible barrier to the women promotion
③ invisible helping hand for the promotion
④ ceiling shining too bright to look at with the naked eye

>>> 다음 글을 읽고 문제의 답을 고르시오. [8~10]

Indeed, there has been lots of surprisingly good news in general about caffeine and coffee. You would naturally assume that an addictive drug like caffeine must surely be bad for you, and initial studies suggested it might lead to bladder cancer, high blood pressure and other ills. More recent research has not only refuted most of those claims but also come up with some significant benefits. Caffeine appears to have some protective effect against liver damage, Parkinson's disease, diabetes, Alzheimer's, gallstones, depression and maybe even some forms of cancer. The only proven medical downside appears to be a temporary elevation in blood pressure, which is a problem only if you already suffer from hypertension. Some studies have also suggested a higher risk of miscarriage in pregnant women and of benign breast cysts, but those results are highly controversial.

While most of the findings about the effects of caffeine remain open to further testing, caffeine's boosting your brainpower has been proved beyond any reasonable doubt. "As a research psychologist," says Harris Lieberman, "I use the word intelligence as an inherent trait." Caffeine can't change that, Liberman says. But what it can do, he says, is heighten your mental performance.

8   **최근 연구에 의해 카페인이 예방할 수 있는 병으로 추정되는 것이 아닌 것은?**

① diabetes

② bladder cancer

③ Alzheimer's

④ gallstones

⑤ Parkinson's disease

9   **유일하게 입증된 것으로 보이는 카페인의 의학적 문제점은?**

① a temporary elevation in blood pressure

② a higher risk of hypertension

③ miscarriage in pregnant women

④ a high risk of benign breast cysts

⑤ leading to bladder cancer

10   **신빙성 있게 증명된 카페인의 이로운 점은?**

① improving your overall health

② enhancing your intelligence

③ boosting your brainpower

④ cultivating your inherent traits

⑤ having some protective effect against liver damage

》》 다음 글을 읽고 문제의 답을 고르시오. [11~12]

With 950 million people, India ranks second to China (1.2 billion) among the most populous countries. But since China launched a draconian birth control program in 1971, India has been closing the gap. Indians have reduced their own fertility but not nearly as much as the Chinese have. If current growth rates continue, India's population will pass China's around the year 2028 at about 1.7 billion.

Should that happen, it won't be the fault of the enlightened women of Kerala, a state in southern India. While India as a whole adds almost 20 million people a year, Kerala's population is virtually stable. The reason is no mystery: close to two-thirds of Kerala women practice birth control, compared with about 40% in the entire nation.

The difference lies in the emphasis put on health programs. And an educational tradition and matrilineal customs in parts of Kerala help girls and boys get equally good schooling. While one in three Indian women is literate, 90% of those in Kerala can read and write.

Higher literacy rates foster family planning. "Unlike our parents, we know that we can do more for our children if we have fewer of them," says Laila Cherian. She has limited herself to three children—one below the national average of four. That kind of restraint will keep Kerala from putting added pressure on world food supplies.

11 **The best title of this passage is ___________ .**

① Effects of female education on birth control

② A comparison of the birth control policies between China and India

③ High population growth rates in China and India

④ Population explosion in India

⑤ Learning about birth control

12 **According to this passage, which is correct?**

① China is implementing more effective birth control policies than India.

② India's population will be reduced around the year 2028.

③ Birth control rates in Kerala is lower than India's average birth control rates.

④ High literacy rates have little bearing on birth control.

⑤ In India, boys and girls have equal educational opportunities.

>> 다음 글을 읽고 문제의 답을 고르시오. [13~14]

Seldom, if ever, has a highly authoritarian political system, deploying military means sufficient to destroy life on earth, ①dismantle so peacefully. Never has an empire disintegrated with so little bloodshed. Although huge difficulties remained for the successor states, the way Soviet communism came to an end was one of the great success stories of 20th century politics.

13 **Why was, according to the above passage, the way Soviet communism came to an end "one of the great success stories of 20th century politics"?**

① Because it was a highly authoritarian political system.

② Because it has disintegrated with so little bloodshed.

③ Because there still remained huge difficulties for the successor states.

④ Because it has deployed military means sufficient to destroy life on earth.

⑤ Because it should disappear eventually.

14 **Choose the grammatically correct form of the underlined ①.**

① has been dismantled   ② has dismantled

③ to dismantle   ④ to have dismantled

⑤ been dismantled

>> 다음 글을 읽고 문제의 답을 고르시오. [15~19]

James Burton noticed that four times out of five Mary is depicted holding the infant Jesus against her left breast. The Madonna led him to investigate on which side women hold their babies and why. First he noticed that modern mothers, more than 85%, tend to hold their baby on the left. Then (가)an apparently contradictory phenomenon was observed. A large number of mothers who brought their premature babies to follow-up clinic were seen to hold their babies against their right side.

So 115 mothers who had been separated from their babies for 24 hours after birth were observed for (나)holding response. The experimenters presented the baby directly to the midline of the mother's body. 53% of them placed the baby on the left and 47% on the right. Incidentally it was also noted that the mothers of the group who had held their baby on the left had already had a baby from which they had not been separated after birth. The experiment suggests that the time immediately after birth is a critical period when the stimulus of holding the baby releases a certain maternal response, for instance, the feeling that the baby is better off on her left.

Left-handed holding enables the baby to hear the heartbeat. In order to discover whether hearing the heart has a beneficial effect on the baby, the sound of a human heartbeat was played to 102 babies for 4 days in a nursery. A controlled group of babies was not exposed to heartbeats. The babies in the beat group gained markedly more weight and cried far less than the babies in the control group.

15 What is the "apparently contradictory phenomenon" in (가)?

① Mothers of premature babies held their babies differently from other women.

② Mothers of premature babies held their babies on the correct side.

③ Mothers of premature babies took their babies to a follow-up clinic.

④ Mothers who were separated from their babies for 24 hours after birth behaved differently from other women.

⑤ The ways in which Mary and the mothers of premature babies held their babies differed.

16 **Why were mothers observed for "holding response" in (나)?**

① To see how mothers of premature babies held their babies.

② To test their reaction to separation from their babies.

③ To see whether separation from the baby after birth affected the way they held the baby.

④ To see how many of them had delivered a normal baby at her first birth.

⑤ To see how they answered the experimenters' questions.

17 **According to the passage, the time just after birth is important. This is when**

__________**.**

① babies must not be separated from their mothers

② the baby's response to the mother is released

③ the baby can hear the mother's heartbeat

④ the mother develops an instinctive tendency to hold the baby on the left

⑤ the baby gains more weight and is assured of safety

18 **In one experiment, 102 babies spend four days __________.**

① hearing the heartbeat of their mothers at home

② listening to the recording of heartbeats

③ not being exposed to heartbeats, live or recorded

④ in the control group

⑤ being held on the left side of their mothers

19 **According to the passage, which is NOT true?**

① Mothers of normal babies tend to hold them on the left.

② Mothers of premature babies do not have the instinct to hold the babies on the left.

③ Babies can hear the heartbeats of their mothers when they are held on the left.

④ Babies who were exposed to the heartbeats were healthier than those who were not.

⑤ Mothers who had a premature baby at her second birth tended to hold their babies on the right.

We had a game in our house called "setting the table" and I was Mother's helper. Forks were to the left of the plate, and knives and spoons were to the right. Placing the cutlery neatly, as I recall, was one of my first duties, and the event was alive with meaning. When a knife or a fork dropped on the floor, that meant a man was unexpectedly coming to dinner. A falling spoon announced the surprise arrival of a female guest. No matter that these visitors never arrived on cue, I had learned a rule of gender identification. Men were straight-edged, ① ______________ pronged and formidable, women were ② ______________ curved and held the food in a rounded well. It made perfect sense, like the division of pink and blue that I saw in babies, an orderly way of viewing the world. Daddy, who was gone all day at work and who loved to putter at home with his pipe, tobacco and tool chest, was knife and fork. Mommy and Grandma, with their ample proportions and pots and pans, were grownup soup spoons, large and capacious. And I was a teaspoon, small and slender, easy to hold and just right for pudding, my favorite dessert.

20 What would be the main topic of this passage?

① Superstition ② Folk myth

③ Setting the table ④ A childhood activity

⑤ Gender identification

21 Which of the following pairs best fits into ① and ②?

① elegantly - bluntly ② sharply - softly

③ delicately - plainly ④ dexterously - poorly

⑤ sufficiently - insufficiently

A. The idols of today are no longer just war heroes and other male figures, but rather female fashion models and movie stars.

B. And woman now have the right to choose their husbands and obtain jobs outside the home.

C. Therefore Japanese businessmen declare that the surest way to make money nowadays is to produce appliances that will relieve women of work.

D. There are even women executives and business owners who lack time for housework.

E. Housewives demand more automation from their kitchens to liberate them from tiresome household chores.

22 윗글의 흐름상 이어질 내용을 바른 순서대로 배열한 것은?

① A-B-D-E-C   ② A-B-C-E-D

③ B-C-A-D-E   ④ B-A-C-D-E

"I am not the first president to take up this cause, but I am determined to be the last." Thus Barack Obama, late in the day, took his quest to reform America's expensive and flawed health-care system to the floor of Congress with a mighty speech that will surely stand as one of the defining moments of his presidency, whether it leads to eventual triumph or disaster. His is a bold ambition indeed; but this week (가) <u>the president looks a bit closer to fulfilling it.</u>

Politics, as everyone knows, is the art of the possible. There have been times over this ill-tempered summer when the idea of tackling a system that costs almost twice as much as any other rich country's, yet yields substandard results and leaves tens of millions of people with no health insurance at all, has seemed simply impossible. Mr Obama has to find a package of policies that is fiscally and politically moderate enough to win over a vital few Republicans to his side (and also prevent the defection of nervous conservative Democrats). But at the same time he has to keep the support of the leftish Democratic Party base, which wants to see a more expansive and costly set of reforms. He may well fail. But on September 9th the president for the first time laid out in some detail what such a plan might look like. Cleverly borrowing good ideas from both sides of the party divide, his proposals at least look like a plausible basis for agreement.

23 The underlined expression in (가) means ____________.

① it appears to be difficult to persuade the opposition party

② his bold ambition may be not convincing but preposterous

③ reforming America's health-care system seems to be not far-fetched

④ reforming America's health-care system seems to be infeasible

24 What is not the key that the writer gives to Obama?

① Keeping conservative Democrats at his arms' length

② Getting over some Republicans to his side

③ Tying up the left-winger of Democrats

④ Not being afraid of failure to reform

Another mass movement in postwar America was from the cities to the suburbs. Almost as many Americans resided in the suburbs as in the cities by 1960. A combination of motives drew people to the suburbs. Some wanted to leave behind the noise and smells of the city. Some white families moved out of urban neighborhoods because African-American families were moving in. People living in row houses and apartments wanted to move into houses that had yards, family rooms, extra closets, and utility rooms. Many also were looking for a place where they could have a measure of political influence, particularly on the education their children received.

25 윗글의 앞에 들어올 수 있는 내용으로 가장 적합한 것을 고르시오.

① Increase of population of the United States and its geographic distribution
② Change of life style in the United States after World War II
③ Need of housing and highway construction
④ Migrating to the Sunbelt, the southern third of the United States

>> 다음 글을 읽고 문제의 답을 고르시오. [26~28]

When I was twenty-eight I started to trip and drop things. What at first seemed my natural clumsiness soon became too pronounced to ① shrug off. I consulted a neurologist, who told me that I had a brain tumor. A battery of tests, increasingly disagreeable, revealed no tumor. About a year and a half later I developed a blurred spot in one eye. I had, at last, the episodes "disseminated in space and time" requisite for a diagnosis: multiple sclerosis. ②I have never been sorry for the doctor's initial misdiagnosis, however. For almost a week, until the negative results of the tests were in, I thought that I was going to die right away. Every day for the past nearly ten years, then, has been a kind of gift. I accept all gifts.

26 **Which of the following can be the best title for the passage?**

① How I Came to Love My Life

② My Favorite Doctor

③ How I Got Recovered

④ My Anger and Frustration at the Terrible Hospital System

⑤ Different Types of Life-style

27 **Which of the following is closest in meaning to the underlined ①?**

① regard as trivial　　② consider very important

③ worry about　　④ repeat the mistakes

⑤ inquire about

28 **What does the underlined sentence ② imply?**

① I blamed those bad doctors who have misdiagnosed my illness.

② I pities those doctors who have misdiagnosed my illness.

③ I felt relieved when I finally knew what my illness was.

④ I was upset because I didn't know what my illness was.

⑤ I felt I was happier when I had not known what my illness was.

When it comes to corporate cliches, fatigued phrases such as "mission critical" or "value added" are among the most annoying. But when it comes to annoying and dangerous, "outside the box" tops the list at least in the opinion of author and consultant Douglas Rushkoff. Rushkoff advises that when companies try to think or act "outside the box" with new packaging, advertising, acquisitions, or even CEOs, that shift in focus often results in a loss of focus. He recalls meeting with the CEO of a home electronics chain who wanted him to help devise a bottoms-up marketing strategy. But Rushkoff quickly realized the company didn't need new marketing as much as it needed better-quality store-brand products. The company had previously outsourced all its design and manufacturing. To some, outsourcing may seem innovative, but in this case, it was cutting the company off from the in-house expertise that built the firm in the first place. "American companies are obsessed with window dressing ... afraid to look at whatever it is they really do and evaluate it from the inside out," says Rushkoff.

29 **"outside the box"에 해당하지 않는 것을 고르시오.**

① new advertising
② window dressing
③ inviting another CEO
④ improving product quality
⑤ devising new marketing strategies

30 **According to Douglas Rushkoff, ___________.**

① "mission critical" is a very annoying cliche among companies
② the companies, above all, should see their reality as it is
③ the companies should develop what are called "value added" methods
④ the CEO of the home electronics chain had better outsource manufacturing
⑤ the CEO of the home electronics chain had better devise a bottoms-up marketing strategy

>>> 밑줄 친 곳에 들어갈 알맞은 답을 고르시오. [1~6]

1 His remarks were filled with ______________ which sounded lofty but presented
nothing new to the audience.

① aphorism　　　　　　② platitudes
③ bombast　　　　　　　④ adages
⑤ symbols

2 Such was Brandon's ______________ that he was frequently described as being
honest in all cases.

① vigilance　　　　　　　② munificence
③ probity　　　　　　　　④ gravity
⑤ eminence

3 Power may be compared to a great river. While kept within its due bounds
it is both beautiful and useful, but when it overflows its bank, it is then too
uncontrolled—it bears down all before it and brings destruction and desolation
wherever it comes ______________.

① Liberty increases the power of men
② Power is like a great river which can do good and bad
③ Liberty is protection against lawless power
④ A great river is powerful
⑤ We should love a great river

4 ____________ is a temporary disruption of one's normal biological rhythms after long-distance travel by airplane through several time zones without sufficient rest en route.

① Motion sickness   ② Airsickness
③ Insomnia   ④ Jetlag
⑤ Nervous breakdown

5 The South provides the North with the equipment to remove mines. It is notable that such ____________ spirit has been realized inside the DMZ, where the most acute military ____________ on the earth is taking place.

① strong - attack   ② cooperative - standoff
③ friendly - raid   ④ fearful - force
⑤ low - zone

6 Having lived in the public eye for years, the ex-mayor cannot believe that from now on he will live in ____________.

① adulation   ② controversy
③ anonymity   ④ agitation
⑤ veneration

7 다음 글의 내용과 일치하지 않는 것은?

Pop art is an art movement that emerged in the mid 1950s in Britain and in the late 1950s in the United States. Pop art challenged tradition by asserting that an artist's use of the mass-produced visual commodities of popular culture is contiguous with the perspective of fine art. Pop removes the material from its context and isolates the object, or combines it with other objects, for contemplation. The concept of pop art refers not so much to the art itself as to the attitudes that led to it. Characterized by themes and techniques drawn from popular mass culture, such as advertising, comic books and mundane cultural objects, pop art is widely interpreted as a reaction to the then-dominant ideas of abstract expressionism, as well as an expansion upon them.

① Pop art is an art movement of the twentieth century.

② Pop art employs images of popular culture which are in use in advertising.

③ Pop art is not a clear separation from the established art.

④ Pop art removes the material from its context because it is associated with art for art's sake.

8 제시문을 시작으로, 다음 글들을 문맥에 맞게 올바른 순서로 연결한 것은?

> Nearly every major city in the world provides some form of public transportation.

I. The most common form of public transportation is the bus which has been in use in major cities since approximately 1900.

II. Also special busses can be chartered for trips to the mountains, to lakes, and to nearby places of historical interests.

III. This is necessary not only to contribute to visitors to the city, but also to provide citizens with low-cost transportation and to help reduce the traffic on streets and highways.

IV. In some cities, the city bus system offers free "mini-bus" service as a convenience to shoppers in the downtown business district.

① III — II — IV — I   ② I — III — II — IV

③ I — IV — III — II   ④ III — I — II — IV

≫ 다음 글을 읽고 문제의 답을 고르시오. [9~10]

The therapeutic value and healing powers of plants were demonstrated to me when I was a boy of about ten. I had developed an acute, persistent abdominal pain that did not respond readily to hospital medication. My mother had taken me to the city's central hospital on several occasions, where different drugs were tried ① _______________ me. In total desperation, she took me to Egya Mensa, a well-known herbalist in my hometown in the western province of Ghana. This man was no stranger to the medical doctors at the hospital. He had earned the reputation of offering excellent help when they were confronted with difficult cases where Western medicine had failed to effect a cure.

9 **What would be the main topic of the passage?**

① A life of E. Mensa, a well-known herbalist
② The limitation of Western medicine
③ The healing powers of herbs
④ The healing effects of acupuncture
⑤ The kinds of medical practitioners

10 **Which of the following best fits into ①?**

① for   ② on
③ at   ④ toward
⑤ to

Right now in the U.S. there are almost 3 million students in special-education classes specifically because they can't read. Most of them are probably dyslexic. But there are other slow readers who are simply overlooked—ignored in crowded classrooms or dismissed as discipline problems. Unless corrective action is taken, their self-confidence often crumbles as they see other students progressing. Even worse, their peers might taunt or ostracize them—a situation that Sean Slattery's mother, Judy, remembers all too well. "Sean cried for four hours every day after kindergarten," she says. "He was so unhappy."

In Asia, research on dyslexia suggests its incidence might be significantly lower than in the West due to the differences in how Asian scripts are processed by the brain. The bad news is that Asians with dyslexia are far more likely than Westerners to go undiagnosed, unaided and branded as lifetime losers. Growing up in Malaysia, Ahmad Fitri Isahak was taunted by friends and felt cold-shouldered by teachers because he failed most of his tests. It was only at the age of 25, while studying computer and software engineering at university in England, that a professor told him he was probably dyslexic. "I was devastated and failed that year," he recalls. But he _________________, finished his degree, and Fitri is now an IT consultant in Kuala Lumpur—a happy ending that he admits is unusual for dyslexics in his homeland. "For now, they are a lost lot," he says.

11 **Choose the one that best fills in the blank.**

    ① got back in the saddle   ② twisted the knife

    ③ burned my boat   ④ played the fox

12 **What is the best title for the passage?**

    ① Serious Problems of the Children Mentality

    ② Ubiquitous Difficult Condition to Read

    ③ Bad Effects and Good Effects for Dyslexia

    ④ Vulnerable Reading Skills

13 **What is the author's purpose in the passage?**

① To explain several bad effects of dyslexia on readers

② To compare reading ability between the West and the East

③ To inform dyslexics of effective cures

④ To analyze the cause of failure for many children to read well

>>> 다음 글을 읽고 문제의 답을 고르시오. [14~15]

This is the reason why it is more correct, as well as more usual, to speak of a University as a place of education than of instruction, though, when knowledge is concerned, instruction would at first sight have seemed the more appropriate work. We are instructed, for instance, in manual exercises, in the fine and useful arts, in trades, and in ways of business; for these are methods, which have little or no effect upon the mind itself, are contained in rules committed to memory, to tradition, or to use, and bear upon an end external to themselves.

But education is a higher word; it implies an action upon our mental nature, and the formation of a character; it is something individual and permanent, and is commonly spoken of in connection with religion and virtue. When, then, we speak of the communication of Knowledge as being Education, we thereby really imply that Knowledge is a state or condition of mind; and since cultivation of mind is surely worth seeking for its own sake, we are thus brought once more to the conclusion, which the word 'Liberal' and the word 'Philosophy' have already suggested, that there is a Knowledge, which is desirable, though nothing come of it, as being of itself a treasure, and a sufficient remuneration of years of labor.

14 **When does 'education' gain higher significance?**

① When it is based on practical knowledge.

② When it aims at the cultivation of mind.

③ When it loses something individual and permanent.

④ When it combines the merits of education and instruction.

⑤ When it successfully achieves a coexistence of manual skills and Liberal studies.

15 **What is the main topic of the above passage?**

① Philosophical knowledge as the goal of education

② The relationship between education and occupation

③ Two ways of using knowledge

④ The difference between manual exercises and useful arts

⑤ The history of universities

>>> 다음 글을 읽고 문제의 답을 고르시오. [16~17]

Each night as the sun goes down and the desert darkens, the neon lights of Las Vegas, Nevada, flare into the sky. Beneath the lurid glow of giant casino signs, water splashes in Roman fountains, runs into acres of swimming pools, and overflows into street gutters.

Las Vegas, ① <u>prodigal</u> playground of the West, illustrates the conflict between man and nature in the River basin. Within just ten years the metropolitan area could be using virtually every drop of Nevada's legal share of the Colorado River's flow. City leaders, expecting the population of 800,000 to double in the next 10 years, are searching far and wide for new water supplies.

16 The author calls Las Vegas "prodigal" in ① because of ____________.

① gamblings at casino   ② flaring neon lights
③ loose morality   ④ an abundant waste of water
⑤ a luxurious mode of living

17 What will put Las Vegas into trouble in a decade?

① floods from Colorado River
② an increase in population
③ booming business
④ an extreme shortage in electricity
⑤ rising crime rate

>>> 다음 글을 읽고 문제의 답을 고르시오. [18~20]

Perhaps most alarming, says Sharon Levy, a pediatrician and director of the Adolescent Substance Abuse Program at Children's Hospital Boston, is that teens bent on defeating drug tests will sometimes switch their drug of choice to an undetectable (or harder to detect) substance that's considerably more hazardous. Inhalants, for example, include numerous types of chemical vapors that typically produce brief, intoxicating effects. "You don't excrete inhalants in your urine," says Levy, but "inhaling is acutely more dangerous than marijuana." Indeed, inhalants can trigger the lethal heart problem known as "sudden sniffing death" in otherwise healthy adolescents, according to the National Institute on Drug Abuse. The tragic case of young David Manlove is an example.

18 **The main theme of the passage ____________.**

① A New Finding about the Inhalants
② Medical Vulnerability to Cheating
③ Drug Abuse Affecting Heart
④ Dangers of Escaping Drug Tests by Inhalants
⑤ Way to Check Children's Drug Abuse

19 **The above passage is ____________**

① expositive ② hostile
③ ambivalent ④ neutral
⑤ chronological

20 **Whom is the above passage warning?**

① people who already have a heart problem
② the manufacturer that products inhalants
③ a pediatrician
④ the family that has a child
⑤ the younger generation

>>> 다음 글을 읽고 문제의 답을 고르시오. [21~24]

As much as puppies or pandas or even children, dolphins are universally beloved. They seem to cavort and frolic at the least provocation, their mouths are fixed in what looks like a state of perpetual merriment, and their behavior and enormous brains suggest an intelligent approaching hat of humans—or even, some might argue, surpassing ㉠it. Dolphins are turning out to be exceedingly clever, but not in the loving, utopian-socialist manner that sentimental dolphin lovers might have hoped.

Researchers who have spent thousands of hours observing the behavior of bottlenose dolphins of the coast of Australia have discovered that the males form social alliances with one another that are far more sophisticated and devious than any seen in animals apart from human beings.

21 The main subject for the passage is the ____________ of dolphins.

  ① rare brutality   ② high intelligence

  ③ beloved nature   ④ living condition

22 Choose the one which might come after this passage.

  ① What is more, females seem to exert choice over the males that seek to herd them, sometimes swimming alongside them in apparent contentment, but at other times working furiously to escape, and often succeeding.

  ② Species like the bottlenose dolphins make most of their decisions by consensus, spending hours dawdling in a protected bay, nuzzling each other and generating an eerie nautical symphony of squeaks, whistles, barks, twangs and clicks.

  ③ The scientists call this effort to control females "herding" but they acknowledge that the word does not convey the aggressiveness of the act.

  ④ They found that one team of male dolphins will recruit the help of another team of males to gang up against a third group, a sort of multilateral battle plan that requires considerable mental calculus to work out.

23 Which is true about the above passage?

  ① Dolphins cannot be aggressive.

  ② Dolphins attack rival groups only for fun.

  ③ Alliances between groups of male dolphins against others require highly intelligent ability.

  ④ Dolphins receive even more spotlight due to their aggression.

24 Which does ㉠ "it" refer to?

  ① the least provocation

  ② a state of perpetual merriment

  ③ their behavior

  ④ the intelligence of humans

Human beings no longer thrive under the water from which their ancestors emerged, but their relationship with the sea remains close. Over half the world's people live within 100 kilometers (62 miles) of the coast; a tenth are within 10km. On land at least, the sea delights the senses and excites the imagination. The sight and smell of the sea inspire courage and adventure, fear and romance. Though the waves may be rippling or mountainous, the waters angry or calm, the ocean itself is eternal. Its moods pass. Its tides keep to a rhythm. It is unchanging.

Or so it has long seemed. Appearances (가), though. Large parts of the sea may indeed remain unchanged, but in others, especially in the surface and coastal waters where 90% of marine life is to be found, the impact of man's activities is increasingly plain. This should hardly be a surprise. Man has changed the landscape and the atmosphere. It would be odd if the seas, which he has for centuries used for food, for transport, for dumping rubbish and, more recently, for recreation, had not also been affected.

25 **What is the main idea of the passage above?**

① The sea has been affected greatly by man's activities.

② People like to live in areas close to the sea.

③ We cannot live without the help of the sea.

④ There have been various works of literature on the sea.

26 **Which of the following best fills in the blank (가) of the passage above?**

① abound   ② build

③ deceive   ④ lead

27 글의 흐름상 필요 없는 문장을 고르시오.

Think of 'weight control' as 'fat control' and it will fit in well with your other good health habits. For most of us, the problem and the solution are personal, not medical. ① Excess weight is very seldom due to thyroid disease or other specific illness. ② It slows you down, makes you less effective in personal encounters, and lowers your self-image. ③ Like the other habits that change your health, management of this problem begins with the recognition that it is a problem. ④ Weight control requires your continued attention and you must have lifelong vigilance about it.

>>> 다음 글을 읽고 문제의 답을 고르시오.

In southern Africa there is a very special snake called the "spitting cobra." This unusual snake is as dangerous as it is beautiful. However, unlike many other dangerous snakes, the spitting cobra usually does not bother to bite its enemies. When an enemy gets near, a spitting cobra raises up its head. Then it seems to spit right at its enemy's eyes. The cobra's deadly venom is squirted through two tiny holes in its fangs, or teeth. If that poison lands in the eyes, it can cause someone to go blind almost immediately. Oddly enough, the poison is completely harmless if it lands on the skin. Even more surprising is the cobra's aim. Spitting cobras have been known to hit an enemy's eyes from as far away as six feet.

28 Which of the following would be useful if you were near spitting cobras?

① mittens
② long pants
③ sunglasses
④ heavy boots

Perhaps the greatest discovery that man has ever made, greater than the steam engine, the millstone, the wheel, or the button, was made by the Plato more than twenty-three hundred years ago. It is a perpetual discovery which needs to be made over and over again by generations and by individuals. By means of the analytical method of his master Socrates, Plato discovered the difference between things that are permanent and things which are merely transitory. He called these permanent things Ideas. Never has civilized man forgotten Plato's discovery without disaster, and never has he remembered it without a renaissance of the spirit.

29 Choose the best title of the above passage.

① Disaster which counteracts humans' spirit

② A philosopher's ambition

③ A temporary idea's futility

④ The key to checking disaster

⑤ A lofty ideal: something men should not forget

30 In the passage above, what does the underlined sentence imply?

① Humanistic spirit can be destroyed by civilized men, and it can be aided by civilized men.

② Plato is great, so that men endlessly must be reminded of his philosophy.

③ Ideas can guarantee development, but in our ignoring them, catastrophe can arise.

④ To check disaster, we must remember the Renaissance's philosophy.

⑤ The civilized must ignore Plato's ideas, and disaster must be inevitable.

>>> 밑줄 친 곳에 들어갈 알맞은 답을 고르시오. [1~6]

1 ____________ is the way of walking you can associate with someone who drank too much alcohol.

① Staggering ② Plodding
③ Tramping ④ Prowling

2 The servant's attitude was so ____________ that it would have been available to anyone with an appreciation of sincerity.

① natal ② elastic
③ doleful ④ rotund

3 I have ____________ in my stomach because I'll take an entrance examination tomorrow.

① worms ② monsters
③ birds ④ butterflies

4 The theory of evolution suggests that human beings must, like other animals, be entirely selfish in their actions, even when they appear to be self-sacrificing and ____________.

① catastrophic ② evangelistic
③ evolutionary ④ philanthropic

5 The Earth's climate doesn't respond to forcing in a smooth and gradual way. Rather it responds in ____________ which involve large-scale reorganization of the Earth's systems.

① sharp jumps ② regular steps
③ predictable speeds ④ slow ways

6   There seemed to be no spark in American education; no daring, no readiness to engage the individual child's mind as anything other than raw material for statistical reductions. The fear of being ____________ is rooted in the American teacher's soul: you can be fired for treading the path of ____________ enterprise.

① conservative - exceptional   ② enthusiastic - traditional
③ mediocre - temporary   ④ customary - revolutionary
⑤ unorthodox - experimental

7   다음 글의 흐름으로 보아 주어진 문장이 들어갈 가장 적절한 곳은?

In addition, take the pictures of the damage to the house and its contents.

When the storm is over, it is natural to want to go home as soon as possible. When it is safe to return, you should take the following steps. First, be careful when you enter your house. (A) There may be snakes or other animals that the flood washed in. Then, open all the windows and doors. You should let the fresh air dry the house. Next, check for gas leaks and electrical system damage. (B) Any of these problems can be very dangerous. If you find anything wrong, you should turn off the power and call the gas company and the electrical company. (C) You will need this proof for the insurance company. Finally, start cleaning your house. (D) This is the hardest job because you must pick up the piece of your life and make it back together.

① (A)   ② (B)
③ (C)   ④ (D)

8 다음 글의 흐름으로 보아 주어진 문장이 들어갈 가장 적절한 곳은?

Of all the voices in nature, the cry of the loon is one of the most haunting.

The common loon is an unforgettable bird of the northern wilderness. The name loon probably comes from the Old English word lumme, meaning a lummox or an awkward person. That description would apply only when the bird is on land or ice. [I] There, the loon is awkward, but in water, it swims faster than a fish, using its wings like flippers. Above all, the most unforgettable thing about the loon is its cry. [II] The loon seems to have four kinds of cries. [III] Its laughter is used in situations of alarm, annoyance, or greeting. Its yodel is used during wide circles of flight and invites other loons to call. [IV] The loon's wail is heard at night in early summer but never during flight. And finally, the loon does a kind of talking—simple one-syllable notes used to communicate with a mate or with the flock. The loon's cries are said to become stronger and more frequent at the approach of storms.

① [I] ② [II]

③ [III] ④ [IV]

Almost every college student has experienced prefinals terror—the horrible anxiety that puts your stomach on a roller coaster and your brain in a blender. Few escape those final-exam jitters because everyone knows just how much is riding on that one exam, often more than half of the course grade. Yet therein lies the crux of the problem. Infrequent high-stakes exams don't encourage students to do their best work. More frequent tests given—say, every two or three weeks—would be a much more effective method of discovering how well students are or are not mastering course concepts. With more frequent testing, students would be less anxious when they take exams; thus anxiety would no longer interfere with exam performance. More frequent testing also encourages students to review on a regular basis, something that a one-shot final exam does not do. Lots of tests also mean lots of feedback, and students would know early on in the course what terms or concepts required additional explanation and review. They wouldn't have to wait until the end of the semester to find out that they had misunderstood, or missed altogether, a critical point or theory.

9 **What is the main point of the author's argument?**

① Students need lots of feedback early on in the course.

② Counselling programs must be reinforced to lessen students' anxiety.

③ Frequent tests would be a more effective method than infrequent exams.

④ A new evaluation method needs to be developed other than tests or exams.

>>> 다음 글을 읽고 문제의 답을 고르시오.

One of my friends, a musician, is always upbeat. Nothing gets her down. But when she developed ringing in one ear, I was concerned it might overwhelm even her. When I asked if her condition was especially annoying to a musician, she shook her head. "Not really," she said cheerfully. "The ringing sound is in the key of B flat, so I use it to tune my cello a half-tone lower."

10 윗글의 제목으로서 올바른 것은?

① Optimistic Musician

② Annoying Friend

③ Ringing Ear

④ Troublesome Noise

>>> 다음 글을 읽고 문제의 답을 고르시오.

As used in this book, culture has a different and more specialized meaning. It refers to all the accepted and patterned ways of behavior of a given people. It is a body of common understandings. It is the sum total and the organization or arrangement of all the group's ways of thinking, feeling, and acting. It also includes the physical manifestations of the group as exhibited in the objects they make. In this sense, every people—however primitive— has a culture, and no individual can live without culture.

11 이 글의 목적으로 가장 알맞은 것은?

① To categorize a concept

② To define a concept

③ To give examples for a concept

④ To revise a concept

»» 다음 글을 읽고 문제의 답을 고르시오.

Scientists have successfully tested a system that translates brain waves into speech, raising the prospect that people left mute by stroke, Lou Gehrig's disease, and other afflictions will be able to communicate by synthetic voice.

[A] For example, British physicist Stephen Hawking, who is nearly completely paralyzed as a result of Lou Gehrig's disease, takes several minutes to compose a short sentence that is rendered into speech by a computer.

[B] The system was tested on a 26-year-old man left paralyzed by a brain stem stroke, but with his consciousness and cognitive abilities intact.

[C] The condition is known as "locked-in syndrome."

[D] In this condition, communication by eye movement or other limited motion is possible but extremely cumbersome.

12 Choose the best order from [A] through [D] for a paragraph starting with the sentence in the box.

① [B]-[A]-[D]-[C]
② [B]-[C]-[D]-[A]
③ [D]-[A]-[C]-[B]
④ [D]-[B]-[A]-[C]

≫≫ 다음 글을 읽고 문제의 답을 고르시오. [13~16]

Mr. Whitson taught sixth grade science. On the first day of class, he gave us a lecture about a creature called the cattywampus, an ill-adapted nocturnal animal that was wiped out during the Ice Age. He passed around a skull as he talked. We all took notes and later had a quiz.

When he returned my paper, I was shocked. There was a big red X through each of my answers. I had failed. There had to be some mistake! I had written down exactly what Mr. Whitson said. Then I realized that everyone in the class had failed. What had happened?

Very simple, Mr. Whitson explained. He had made up all that stuff about the cattywampus. There had never been any such animal. The information in our notes was, therefore, incorrect. Did we expect credit for incorrect answers?

We should have figured it out, Mr. Whitson said. After all, at the very moment he was passing around the cattywampus skull (in truth, a cat's), hadn't he been telling us that no trace of the animal remained? He had described its amazing night vision, the color of its fur and any number of other facts he couldn't have known. He had given the animal a ridiculous name, and we still hadn't been suspicious. The zeroes on our papers would be recorded in his grade book, he said. And they were.

Mr. Whitson said he hoped we would learn something from this experience. Teachers and textbooks are not infallible. In fact, no one is. He told us not to let our minds go to sleep and to speak up if we ever thought he or the textbook was wrong.

13 **Why did all the students fail in the quiz?**

① Because they answered exactly as their teacher said.

② Because they didn't study hard enough to pass the quiz.

③ Because the questions were too difficult for them to answer.

④ Because they didn't understand the questions.

⑤ Because they intentionally didn't answer the questions.

14 **What did the students actually see when the teacher was passing around a skull?**

① a cat's skull

② an extinct animal's skull

③ an owl's skull

④ a cattywampus skull

⑤ a human skull

15 **Which of the following is true of the cattywampus?**

① It was an animal active mostly at night.

② It became extinct during the Ice Age.

③ It had an amazing night vision.

④ It had very colorful fur.

⑤ It has never existed.

16 **Mr. Whitson hoped that his students ____________.**

① examined the cattywampus skull more closely

② followed him blindly

③ took notes well to pass the quiz

④ learned how to study mathematics

⑤ learned that teachers might not be perfect

>>> 다음 글을 읽고 문제의 답을 고르시오.

Aldous Huxley in his book *Brave New World* painted a picture of a perfectly planned state, from which freedom, difficulty, pain, and insecurity had all disappeared. But too much comfort, too much order, too much pleasure, and a total lack of anxiety had dehumanized the people in it—they had become less than human. Until at last the one rebel in the state cries out to its governor: "I don't want comfort, I want God, I want real danger, I want freedom, I want sin." "In fact," said the governor, "you're claiming the right to be unhappy." Whether or not this is a true picture, there is something in the nature of men which makes them escape from secure situations—e.g., into polar expedition or dangerous mountain climbing.

17 윗글의 요지로서 가장 적절한 것은?

① Material security does not always guarantee happiness to men.
② Human beings prefer, ironically, to be unhappy.
③ Men cannot be made too secure.
④ Men cannot live in a planned state.

With my brow to the glass, I was thus occupied in scrutinizing the mob, when suddenly there came into view a countenance, that of a decrepit old man, some sixty-five or seventy years of age—a countenance which at once arrested and absorbed my whole attention, on account of the absolute idiosyncrasy of its expression. Any thing even remotely resembling that expression I had never seen before. I well remember that my first thought, upon beholding it, was that Retszch, had he viewed it, would have greatly preferred it to his own pictural incarnations of the fiend. As I endeavored, during the brief minute of my original survey, to form some analysis of the meaning conveyed, there arose confusedly and paradoxically within my mind, the ideas of vast mental power, of caution, of penuriousness, of avarice, of coolness, of malice, of blood-thirstiness, of triumph, of merriment, of excessive terror, of extreme despair. I felt singularly aroused, startled, fascinated. Then came a craving desire to keep the man in view—to know more of him. Hurriedly putting on an overcoat, and seizing my hat and cane, I made my way into the street, and pushed through the crowd in the direction which I had seen him take; for he had already disappeared.

18 Which of the following CANNOT be inferred from the passage?

① The old man is malicious and fiendish.

② The narrator feels a voyeuristic desire for the old man.

③ Retszch is a painter who is preoccupied with the representation of the devil.

④ When the narrator first sees the old man, he is inside a building looking out the street.

>>> 다음 글을 읽고 문제의 답을 고르시오.

(A)   They are sure that God intends for them to be happy, and they regard any interference with this attainment of happiness as a violation of their rights.

(B)   Buying a home, taking vacations in Florida, and driving a new car are promoted as ways to achieve happiness.

(C)   The Declaration of Independence includes this pursuit of happiness as a natural right, and the American people are obsessed with this pursuit.

(D)   Commercial advertisements proclaim this much more in America than elsewhere.

19 윗글의 흐름상 이어질 내용을 바른 순서대로 배열한 것은?

① (C)-(D)-(A)-(B)   ② (B)-(C)-(A)-(D)
③ (A)-(B)-(C)-(D)   ④ (B)-(D)-(C)-(A)

An important development in twentieth-century literary criticism was the growth of the New Criticism. The New Critics assumed that the methods devised for reading long poems could be applied to novels. In practice this meant a new emphasis in the reading of fiction on scrupulous textual analysis as a prerequisite for biographical and ideological comment. A novelist's ideas were now significant mainly as components of his or her writing a novel and concentrated on discerning the development of symbolic patterns. By analyzing symbols in this way, the critic could show how the meaning of a symbol accrued as it was repeated in different passages. This permitted a more complete understanding of the symbol to emerge than that which could be discovered through isolated symbol-hunting. One novelist who benefited from this new emphasis on text was D. H. Lawrence, whose work was rescued from hostile critics who had attacked it as mere ideology.

20 According to passage, the New Critics considered the ideas found in a novelist's work to be ______________.

① equally conducive to treatment in poetry or fiction
② important primarily as aspects of the novelist's style
③ ambiguous and therefore stumbling blocks to informed critical judgment
④ most easily analyzed when embodied in a symbol
⑤ open to biographical speculation on the part of a critic

21 The author alludes to D. H. Lawrence in order to give an example of a novelist who ______________.

① sacrificed literary technique to ideology
② wrote both novels and long poems
③ subscribed to the principles of the New Criticism
④ was influenced by New Critical judgment on his work
⑤ was reassessed because of New Critical principles

22 It can be inferred from the passage that the New Critics disliked isolated symbol-hunting because it tended to ___________.

① encourage simplistic critical platitudes
② reduce the role of the critic to that of a literary detective
③ enforce an unnecessary distinction between criticism and symbolism
④ oversimplify the meaning of a symbol
⑤ ignore conventions associated with long poems

>>> 다음 글을 읽고 문제의 답을 고르시오. [23~26]

For the Greeks, beauty was a virtue: a kind of excellence. Persons of beauty were assumed to be what we now have to call—lamely, enviously—whole persons. (1) If it did occur to the Greeks to distinguish between a person's "inside" and "outside", they still expected that inner beauty would be matched by beauty of the other kind. (2) The well-born young Athenians who gathered around Socrates found it quite paradoxical that their hero was so intelligent, so brave, so honorable, so seductive and so ugly. (3) It was principally the influence of Christianity that deprived beauty of the central place it had in classical ideals of human excellence. (4) By limiting excellence to moral virtue only, Christianity set beauty adrift—as an alienated, arbitrary, superficial enchantment. (5) And beauty has continued to lose prestige. For close to two centuries it has become a convention to attribute beauty to only one of the two sexes: the sex which, however fair, is always second. Associating beauty with women had put beauty even further on the defensive, morally.

23 **What is the main theme of the passage?**

① Beauty and morality: Two sides of the same coin

② The Greeks and Christianity

③ Beauty in the Greek and modern times

④ Beauty and woman

⑤ The paradox of beauty

24 **If the passage is divided into two paragraphs, where does the second one begin?**

① (1)　　　② (2)　　　③ (3)　　　④ (4)　　　⑤ (5)

25 **In modern times, "beauty" is most readily associated with ___________ .**

① excellence　　　② wholeness

③ intelligence　　　④ fairness

⑤ bravery

26 **Choose the one that is NOT consistent with the content of the passage.**

① In the classical period, beauty was often associated with the male sex.

② While being associated with sex, beauty came to imply a moral defensiveness.

③ The Greeks believed that the person who had the inside beauty should have the outside beauty as well.

④ In the Greek times, intelligence and bravery were an integral part of beauty.

⑤ Christianity contributed to separating the outside beauty from the inside.

>>> 다음 글을 읽고 문제의 답을 고르시오. [27~28]

(가) Here's a travel guide: if you've had an orthopaedic, chest, abdominal, neurological, ear, nose or throat procedure, wait ten to 14 days before flying, advises lead author Dr Mark Gendreau at Tufts University School of Medicine. An uncomplicated appendectomy or laparoscopic procedure? Schedule your flight at least five days later.

(나) Recent surgery can make air travel a riskier adventure. If you're facing surgery as well as planning a long plane flight, put some time between the two events, says a recent study. Air travel can increase the risk of deep vein thrombosis (potentially lethal blood clots in the deep veins of the legs), and the danger increases if you've recently had an operation—but doctors sometimes fail to warn their patients of the surgery connection, the researchers say.

(다) On board, stay hydrated, avoid caffeine and alcohol, stretch your calves during the flight by walking the aisles or doing seated exercises, and wear compression stockings.

27 Choose the answer that correctly put the above paragraphs into order.

① (다) – (가) – (나)   ② (가) – (나) – (다)
③ (가) – (다) – (나)   ④ (나) – (가) – (다)

28 Which one of the following can be inferred from the passage?

① That who even gets scratch must abstain from getting on a plane.
② The patient who has had a nose operation needs to delay his flight schedule at least three weeks later.
③ If having an operation before long, you had better cancel off your flight schedule.
④ While being in plane, after having an operation, consume much water.

In town for a <u>shopping spree</u>, my grandmother parked on a yellow line and was approached by a policeman who wanted to know why she had stopped there. "Well", Grandmother replied, "everybody else has parked here", "If I jumped into that river down there, Madam, would you do the same?" he asked. "My dear, if I thought I could save your life, then I would", was Grandmother's rapid response. At that, the officer ripped up her ticket and allowed her to drive away.

29 **Which of the following is closest in meaning to "shopping spree"?**

① returning shopped goods for a refund

② shopping contest

③ exhibition where the visitors can make purchases

④ purchasing a large amount of goods in a short time

⑤ getting an advice for shopping

30 **What did the policeman really want to say to the writer's grandmother by asking the question?**

① She would not save his life.

② She was too fragile to jump into the river.

③ She would not blindly repeat other people's action when it was something she didn't want to.

④ Those who parked their cars on a yellow line should jump into the river.

⑤ Had she jumped into the river, he would have ripped up her ticket and allowed her to drive away.

>>> 밑줄 친 곳에 들어갈 알맞은 답을 고르시오. [1~6]

1 A: Do you mean he rejected your requests for an appointment?
   B: Yes, three times he gave me the cold ____________.

   ① stomach   ② ankle
   ③ shoulder   ④ forearm
   ⑤ engine

2 Just about everyone is ____________ at some point. What if every time you met
   a human your hands shook and your forehead sweated?

   ① timid   ② exhausted
   ③ annoyed   ④ injured
   ⑤ volatile

3 The football team won so many games that it became ____________, and the
   worst team in the league snuck up and beat it.

   ① dissolute   ② catholic
   ③ adamant   ④ complacent
   ⑤ rageful

4 In the Roman circus one of the most popular sports was performed by one
   who leaps. This "leaper" rode two horses by vaulting expertly from one animal
   to the other. When people today speak of ____________ conversation, they
   mean a conversation in which the participants flit from one subject to another.

   ① desultory   ② compensatory
   ③ inexorable   ④ obstinate
   ⑤ critical

5 The cells at the surface of the outer skin form a tough, waterproof shield which most germs cannot ____________.

① penetrate
② inflect
③ alienate
④ violate
⑤ transplant

6 Pat is usually so courteous and ____________ that I was completely taken aback by his unaccountably ____________ and surly reply to my question.

① affable - brusque
② equitable - erudite
③ factious - scurrilous
④ narrow-minded - ingenious

>>> 다음 글을 읽고 문제의 답을 고르시오. [7~8]

Human nature does not change, or, at any rate, history is too short for any changes to be perceptible. The earliest known specimens of art and literature are still comprehensible. The fact that we can understand them all and can recognize in some of them an unsurpassed artistic excellence is proof enough (가) ____________ not only men's feelings and instincts, but also their intellectual and imaginative powers, were in the remotest times precisely what they are now. In the fine arts it is only the convention, the form, the incidentals that change: the fundamentals of passion, of intellect and imagination remain unaltered.

7 According to the passage, which of the following is true?

① Human nature doesn't remain rather stationary.
② The ancient works are hard to recognize.
③ Art field's customs are not changeable.
④ Today's intelligence and imagination are similar to those of the past.

8 Which of the following best fits into (가)?

① that
② to
③ for
④ which

다음 글을 읽고 문제의 답을 고르시오. [9~10]

In ancient times, clothing was generally not fitted to the body. People wore whole animal skins, and clothes made from woven material usually consisted of rectangular pieces of cloth draped in some way and secured by a tie. In early Europe, people grew flax or raised sheep for wool. They spun their own thread from the flax and wool and wove it into cloth. They then fashioned the uncut cloth into tunics, sometimes stitched up the sides or down the middle, that tied with rope. They used clothing mainly for warmth and protection, not as a fashion statement.

The 1100s saw clothing production undergoing transition. People began to form guilds, and individuals set up shops as shoemakers, weavers, and tailors. Under the guidance of the weaver's guild, the quality of cloth improved. Tailors began to cut and stitch garments into fitted vests, shirts, and trouser for men. Women's shapeless tunics ㉠_______________ long dresses that were tightly fitted to the upper body. Clothes went from simple coverings for the body to the beginnings of fashionable apparel.

9 Which one is the most appropriate in the blank ㉠ ?

① took over   ② called off

③ put up with   ④ gave way to

⑤ made use of

10 Select the statement which best expresses the main idea of the above passage.

① Clothes have not changed over the centuries.

② The quality of cloth improved before the rise of guilds.

③ Fashion had been an important part of everyone's lives.

④ From its beginning as a simple covering for the body in ancient times, clothing has become a major concern for people.

⑤ Clothing, which for centuries had been loosely draped, began to be fitted and fashionable with the rise of the guild system.

History, like the drama and the novel, grew out of mythology, a primitive form of apprehension and expression in which—as in fairy tales listened to by children or in dreams dreamt by sophisticated adults—the line between fact and fiction was left undrawn. It has, for example, been said of the *Iliad* that anyone who starts reading it as history will find that it is full of ________________ but, equally, anyone who starts reading it as fiction will find that it is full of ______________. All histories resemble the *Iliad* to this extent, that they cannot entirely dispense with the fictional element. The mere selection, arrangement and presentation of facts is a technique belonging to the field of fiction, and popular opinion is right in its insistence that no historian can be "great" if he is not also a great artist.

11 **The best title of the passage would be ___________.**
① Facts and Fictions of History
② Reading Fiction as History
③ Dispensing with the Fictional Elements
④ The Components of Mythology

12 **Which of the following is best for the blanks?**
① art - facts
② facts - art
③ fiction - history
④ history - fiction

>> 다음 글을 읽고 문제의 답을 고르시오. [13~15]

In early 1999 Shpend Ahmeti stared anxiously at the televised scenes of destruction left by Serbian troops in Pristina, Kosovo. Sitting alongside him in a university lounge was Emina Hrustic, his friend from the debating team—and a Serb.

"Was that near your home?" she asked. Ahmeti nodded grimly. "How awful", Hrustic said gently. "I'm worried about your home, too." the dark-eyed Albanian replied. And indeed, when military installations around Hrustic's native city of Novi Sad were bombed by NATO planes soon after, it was to Ahmeti that she looked for comfort. He had grown up filled with suspicion towards Serbs. But that changed after he entered the American University in Bulgaria, where the two were students.

"She knew it wasn't my fault that NATO was bombing her country", Ahmeti told me. "And I knew it wasn't her fault what the Serbian special police were doing in Kosovo."

Ahmeti and Hrustic are typical of the young people who have come together in this remarkable young institution, which offers promise of ethnic reconciliation and a new kind of future for these former Soviet bloc countries.

13 Shpend Ahmeti _____________ .

① is a student of a university in America

② is an Albanian

③ has always been on good terms with Serbs

④ first met Emina Hrustic in Serbia

⑤ lived in Novi Sad before he came to Bulgaria

14 What did Hrustic do when NATO planes bombed her native city?

① She watched television with Ahmeti.

② She blamed Ahmeti for the bombing.

③ She immediately went back to her country.

④ She sought consolation from Ahmeti.

⑤ She discussed the future of Eastern Europe with Ahmeti.

15 **According to the above passage, which of the following statements is NOT true?**

① Ahmeti and Hrustic had a debate about the NATO bombing.

② Ahmeti and Hrustic used to belong to the same debating team.

③ Albania and Serbia used to belong to the soviet bloc.

④ Ahmeti and Hrustic went to the same university.

⑤ The American University in Bulgaria was founded not long ago.

>> 다음 글을 읽고 문제의 답을 고르시오. [16~18]

There is little agreement concerning the way in which kinds of avalanches should be classified. Some classification systems depend on the kind of snow involved, others are concerned with the type of movement, and once scheme includes both, as well as several other criteria. Existing descriptive terms, most of them German, are deeply rooted in avalanche parlance: they are expressive, but they are often untranslatable into other languages and lack precision in their own. Furthermore, <u>as Dr. Quervain has pointed out, avalanches are not only concrete objects capable of being photographed; they are also events</u>. As events, they include, for example, the development of the avalanches through the influences of weather; the incident that starts the snow moving; and the type of movement. The description of the avalanche as an object includes information about the depth, physical consistency, and stratification of the snow, the features of the terrain, and the type and the dimension of the break.

16 **The author suggests that an accurate avalanche classification system would ____________.**

① be more useful in theory than in fact

② be useful only for describing avalanches as objects

③ have to be based on existing descriptive terms

④ have to be approved by numerous authorities

⑤ have to take many factors into account

17 The title below that best expresses the ideas of this passage is ___________.

① Why is it important to be able to classify avalanches?

② What are some criteria for classification of avalanches?

③ How did existing avalanche classifications originate?

④ What are some points on which avalanche classification systems agree?

⑤ What has been the most useful criterion used in avalanche classification?

18 It can be inferred that the author mentions the underlined sentence primarily in order to ___________.

① indicate the temporary nature of an avalanche

② illustrate the imprecision of the terms used in avalanche classification

③ introduce his own avalanche classification system

④ avoid complexity of avalanche classification

⑤ further explain why it is important to classify kinds of avalanches

>>> 다음 글을 읽고 문제의 답을 고르시오. [19~20]

His servant did not come in on time. Like so many philosophers and poets, Tagore was helpless when it came to the less important things in life: his personal wants, his clothes, his breakfast, and tidying up the place. An hour went by and Tagore was getting madder by the minute. He thought of all sorts of punishments for the man, Three hours later Tagore no longer thought of punishment. He'd discharge the man without any further ado, get rid of him, and turn him out. Finally the man showed up. It was midday. Without a word the servant proceeded with his duties as though nothing had happened. He picked up his master's clothes, set to making breakfast, and started cleaning up. Tagore watched this performance with mounting rage. Finally he said it: "Drop everything, and get out."

However, the man continued sweeping, and after another few moments, with quiet dignity he said: "My little girl died last night."

(가) The show must go on.

19 **The best title of the passage would be ____________.**

① Work behind Schedule

② Importance of Work

③ Inevitable Sadness: a Daughter's Death

④ A Man's Confidence in His Master

20 **The underlined phrase in (가) suggests that ____________.**

① don't worry, and we will be happy

② his task will be carried out

③ sweeping and laughing lack harmony

④ his personal matter will continue

» 다음 글을 읽고 문제의 답을 고르시오. [21~22]

The popular image of New York conjures up a jungle of muggers, dope addicts, and hustlers creating an obstacle to course for the city's normal citizens. But the tourist will find that the Big Apple threatens only his budget. New York's menacing streets, while not entirely mythical, fortunately do not approach their notoriety. Common sense and an alert eye must insure the safety of all but the most reckless; steer clear of run-down neighborhoods (especially after dark) and keep to the more tourist's parts of the city and trouble will not find you.

21 **The underlined expression suggests that ____________.**

① it is expensive to travel around in New York

② tourists are easily cheated over prices in New York

③ tourists should keep an eye open for crime in New York

④ New York police is experiencing financial difficulties

⑤ New York is not a good place for business

22 **The main theme of the passage would be that ___________.**

① in New York it is extremely dangerous to hang around

② the violence in New York has been somewhat exaggerated

③ New York needs a new security policy for the safety of tourists and residents

④ the image of New York has recently improved a lot

⑤ New York's security systems have been damaged by financial difficulties

>>> 다음 글을 읽고 문제의 답을 고르시오.

In 1979 when University of Minnesota psychologist Thomas Bouchard read a newspaper account of reuniting of 39-year-old identical twins who had been separated from infancy, he seized the opportunity and flew them to Minneapolis for extensive tests. Bouchard was looking for differences. What "the Jim twins," Jim Lewis and Jim Springer, presented were amazing similarities. Both had married women named Linda, divorced, and married women named Betty. One had a son James Alan, the other a son James Allan. Both had dogs named Toy, chainsmoked Salems, served as sheriff's deputies, drove Chevrolets, chewed their fingernails to the nub, enjoyed stock car racing, had basement workshops, and had built circular white benches around trees in their yards. They also had similar medical histories: Both gained 10 pounds at about the same time and then lost it both suffered what they mistakenly believed were heart attacks, and both began having late-afternoon headaches at age 18. Identical twins Oskar Stohr and Jack Yufe presented equally striking similarities. One was raised by his grandmother in Germany as a Catholic and a Nazi, while the other was raised by his father in the Caribbean as a Jew. Nevertheless, they share traits and habits galore. They like spicy foods and sweet liquors, have a habit of falling asleep in front of the television, flush the toilet before using it, store rubber bands on their wrists, and dip buttered toast in their coffee. Stohr is domineering toward women and yells at his wife, as did Yufe before he was separated.

23 윗글의 요지로 가장 적합한 것을 고르시오.

① Identical twins who were raised separately from infancy provide great opportunities for psychologists to explore differences.
② Identical twins, although separated at birth, have amazing similarities.
③ Religion does not play a significant role in identical twins'traits and habits.
④ Traits and habits of identical twins are influenced by environments to some degree.

>> 다음 글을 읽고 문제의 답을 고르시오.

I. Music is strange stuff. It is clearly different from language. People can, nevertheless, use it to communicate things—especially their emotions. When combined with speech in a song, it is one of most powerful means of communication that humans have. But, biologically speaking, what is it?

II. What are two things that make humans different from all other animals? One is language and the other is music. While other animals can sing—indeed, many birds do so better than a lot of people—birdsong, and the song of animals such as whales, is limited in type. No other animal has developed a musical instrument.

III. If music is truly different from speech, then it ought to come from a distinct part of the brain. That part keeps music separate from other sounds, including language. The evidence suggests that such a part does exist.

24 윗글들을 문맥에 맞게 올바른 순서로 연결한 것은?

① I — II — III
② I — III — II
③ II — I — III
④ II — III — I

>> 다음 글을 읽고 문제의 답을 고르시오.

A study showed that SAT scores for incoming football and basketball players at big-time athletic programs were hundreds of points lower than for the average student admission.

(a) The result is that these athletes find themselves competing in a student body where they are at a considerable disadvantage.

(b) Still, the NCAA insists on using the term "student athlete," claiming that the athlete is and must be treated like all other students.

(c) The leader in this category is The University of Florida, where there is a 346-point gap between its football players and the average student.

(d) This invites the question of transfers. Most students can choose a transfer school.

(e) Not so for student athletes, who do not have this freedom, their current school can prohibit them from enrolling in certain schools.

25 제시문 후에 이어질 내용을 논리 전개 순서대로 나열하시오.

① (a)-(b)-(e)-(c)-(d)　　　② (c)-(a)-(b)-(d)-(e)
③ (b)-(c)-(d)-(e)-(a)　　　④ (d)-(e)-(c)-(a)-(b)

This proverb certainly belongs to one of the most commonly used proverbs in the English language. This should not be surprising since it expresses the only too human idea of discontent, envy, and jealousy in a metaphor which is easily understood. Interestingly enough, the proverb is also literally true, as has been demonstrated in a scientific article based on optical and perceptual laws. Since people are equally dissatisfied with their lot in life, it should not surprise anyone that a modern psychologist has spoken of certain "phenomenon" named after this proverb by which modern individuals continually evaluate supposedly better alternatives for themselves.

26 **이 글의 내용을 속담으로 가장 잘 표현한 것은?**

① Don't put the cart before the horse.
② An apple a day keeps a doctor away.
③ You can't make an omelet without breaking eggs.
④ The grass is always greener on the other side of the fence.

>>> 다음 글을 읽고 문제의 답을 고르시오. [27~30]

An angry child will stamp the ground or box the ears of another child even when neither the ground nor the child attacked is remotely connected with the irritation or frustration.

Of course, this kind of behaviour is so common that everyone feels it to be obvious to constitute no serious scientific problem. That a small boy should pull his sister's hair because it is raining does not appear to the ordinary unreflecting person to be an occasion for solemn scientific inquiry. He is, as we should all say, 'in a bad temper.' Yet it is not, in fact, really obvious either why revenge should be taken on entirely innocent objects, since no good to the aggressor can come of it, or why children being miserable should seek to make others miserable also. It is just a fact of human behaviour that cannot really be deduced from any general principle of reason. But it is, as we shall see, of very great importance for our purpose. It shows how (가) it is possible, at the simplest and most primitive level, for aggression and fighting to spring from an entirely irrelevant and partially hidden cause. Fighting to possess a desired object is straightforward and rational, however disastrous its consequences, compared with fighting that occurs because, in a different and unrelated activity, some frustration has barred the road to pleasure. The importance of (나) this possibility for an understanding of group conflict must already be obvious.

27 **Which of the following would be most likely to precede the passage?**

① A source of fighting among children is a failure or frustration in their own activity.

② Children end in the complete destruction of the objects of common sense.

③ Aggression closely allied to possessiveness is the tendency for children to resent the intrusion of a stranger.

④ Possessiveness is in all its forms a common cause of fighting.

⑤ The reason for the aggression is fundamentally possessiveness.

28 **According to the passage, which of the following is not true?**

① A child's resentfulness is not necessarily connected with frustration or irritation.

② People generally don't consider a child's resentfulness as serious.

③ A child's possessiveness has nothing to do with resentfulness.

④ Fighting to possess an desired object is more rational than another fighting.

⑤ When he doesn't acquire an desired object, a child is apt to use violence.

29 **The underlined "it" (가) means that _____________.**

① human behaviour

② any general principle of reason

③ very great importance for our purpose

④ to spring from an entirely irrelevant and partially hidden cause

⑤ revenge

30 **The underlined "this possibility" (나) means _____________.**

① the fact that some frustration militates against pleasure

② the fact that fighting occurs in an unrelated activity

③ the fact that revenge is surprisingly miserable

④ the fact that fighting for possessiveness may be reasonable

⑤ the fact that group conflict is considerable

>>> 밑줄 친 곳에 들어갈 알맞은 답을 고르시오. [1~5]

1 Businesses would respond to the sales decrease by reducing their own spending and ____________ their employees.

① giving out   ② turning on

③ sack   ④ calling forth

⑤ stimulate

2 One of the American definitions of success is to acquire a high material standard of living. It is not surprising, therefore, that Americans have valued education for its ____________ value.

① reformative   ② ethical

③ vocational   ④ monetary

⑤ depraved

3 The ____________ form looming in the shadows turned out to be a trash can in the light.

① faint   ② mischievous

③ identified   ④ disagreeable

4 In some ways, material possessions are seen not only as ____________ evidence of people's work, but also as their abilities to do work successfully.

① invisible   ② tangible

③ legitimate   ④ invaluable

⑤ of no use

5 Business will account for 80 percent of Internet use and private users just 20 percent, a well-known technologist attending the economic forum here predicted Tuesday. Michael Dell, who runs Dell Corporation, made the forecast at a session on the "Future of the Internet". Microsoft president Bill Gates on Monday ___________ high expectations about trading and banking in cyber-space. "Is everybody going to be shopping, banking there? It's just not realistic, it takes time for these things to happen", he said.

① dampened   ② bolstered
③ illuminated   ④ ensnared
⑤ solidified

>>> 다음 글을 읽고 문제의 답을 고르시오.

I. In Florida, people over 60 ___________ for more than 25 percent of the population.

II. Ms. Popper's vacation in Frankfurt had to be cancelled on ___________ of her husband's illness.

III. Salespeople have to take into ___________ the differences between their customers.

6 빈칸에 공통으로 들어갈 가장 알맞은 어휘를 고르시오.

① account   ② behalf
③ need   ④ regard
⑤ favor

>>> 다음 글을 읽고 문제의 답을 고르시오.

You could find your true reward in teaching.

If you have a desire to help the younger generation, a wish to pass on your specialized knowledge, a way of communication with youth, and the ability to arouse the interest and curiosity of young minds; if you have patience, understanding, tact, a sense of responsibility and preferably a sense of humor, then to you, maths, science or engineering graduates, teaching could be the most rewarding and fulfilling career.

7 **What kind of text is the passage above?**

① An advertisement to the prospective graduates of math and science

② A newspaper article which describes the rewarding experience of teaching math and science to children

③ An exhortation to seriously study math and science at college for pedagogical purposes

④ An essay which describes the personal traits required of a successful teacher

One reason that so many people fail is that they lack confidence in themselves. If you think of yourself as being unworthy of great achievement, you will never achieve greatness. If, on the other hand, you know yourself and understand what your abilities are, and if then you determine to accomplish everything of which you are capable, you will certainly stand a much better chance of success. How may one become inspired to realize all his possibilities or to gain confidence in himself? One of the surest ways is for him to associate with persons who have really achieved greatness. It is impossible, however, for most people to come frequently into the actual presence of the great. The next best thing, perhaps, is for him to spend part of his time in reading about great achievers. Biography is a powerful stimulant to action. But these processes will not avail unless one rids himself of a sense of inferiority and determines to do the best that he possibly can. One of our great philosophers expressed the idea in a single sentence when he said that each individual should hitch his wagon to a star.

8 The title that best expresses the main theme or subject of this selection is

___________.

① The value of biography ② Worthy use of time

③ Outstanding persons ④ A sense of superiority

⑤ Ways of becoming successful

9 According to the writer of the selection, a basic cause of failure is lack of

___________.

① perseverance ② pride

③ thoughtfulness ④ self-confidence

⑤ friendliness

10 The writer advises that, as a start toward greatness, a person should

___________.

① get a college education ② think only of himself

③ read biographies ④ consider himself unworthy

⑤ enter politics

11 The author of the expression "hitch your wagon to a star" was most likely advising people to ___________ .

① travel widely
② study astronomy
③ ignore details
④ determine to do big things
⑤ write great books

>>> 다음 글을 읽고 문제의 답을 고르시오. [12~14]

If you have pain, don't suffer in silence. Surveys have shown that many patients don't tell doctors or nurses about their pain for fear of being labeled cranky or difficult or because they assume that their discomfort will go away. However, such reluctance can backfire. Left uncontrolled, the pain you thought was temporary can trigger a long-term chronic condition. It can also interfere with the healing process and lengthen your recovery time. If your current treatment isn't controlling your pain, say so to your doctor. (a) It often helps to have a family member make the case for you. Learn what pain killers can and can't do. Lots of folks fear they will get hooked on strong medications. In fact, though most patients build up a tolerance to pain drugs, they don't become addicted. Others rely solely on pills and ignore lifestyle changes like losing weight that can alleviate pain in the joints and back.

12 What is the main topic of the passage?

① Effective ways to complain about pain
② Prevention of pain medicine addiction
③ Controlling tolerance to medication
④ Interrelation between pain and healing
⑤ Advice for victims of pain

13 **Which of the following is closest in meaning to (a)?**

① A family member can tell the doctor when you feel better.

② A family member can often be helpful in making a pillow case to reduce your pain.

③ A family member can speak to the doctor in your behalf.

④ A family member can find out about other patients whose cases are similar to yours.

⑤ A family member can inform the doctor of your progress in the healing process.

14 **From what is stated or implied in the passage, which of the following is NOT true?**

① If pain is not treated, it can become a chronic illness.

② Modern pain drugs are so effective that they do not build up a tolerance in patients.

③ Some patients hide their pain from doctors for fear of being considered hypochondriacs.

④ Reduced body weight can reduce the pain in the joints and back.

⑤ For effective pain control patients should take medication and/or make changes in their lifestyle.

>> 다음 글을 읽고 문제의 답을 고르시오.

[1] Not everyone is sold on probiotics. The U.S. Food and Drug Administration is relatively neutral, using the growing popularity of the products as an opportunity to caution manufacturers not to pitch the foods as some sort of panacea for any specific disease. [2] More important, some people should avoid the products altogether. Those with weakened immune systems or who are critically ill would be well advised to stay away from eating live bacteria. [3] The bacteria can battle numerous kinds of allergies— and not just food allergies. [4] Certainly anyone in the hospital would also count.

15 윗글에서 글 전체의 문맥상 어울리지 않는 문장을 고르시오.

① [1]   ② [2]
③ [3]   ④ [4]

>>> 다음 글을 읽고 문제의 답을 고르시오.

The website is quick and simple to use. After looking at Goya and Michelangelo, I turned to someone I didn't know much about, to see how useful the site would be.

[A]   On the website I soon learned that he spent the latter part of his life in extreme poverty. Among the visionary landscapes is one called The Comedy of Death.

[B]   He's an eccentric and unlike anyone else. I've sometimes seen his work in catalogues, but never read about him.

[C]   I chose the draughtsman and print-maker Rodolphe Bresdin, 1822-1885, an artist with a distinctive and busy style which tends to cover the whole of a page with detail.

[D]   In the picture there is a hut on an island, inhabited by two despairing figures, as the text puts it, surrounded by owls and skeletons and bats and devils.

16 윗글의 박스 안에 있는 제시문과 이어질 순서로 가장 올바른 것은?

① [A]-[D]-[C]-[B]
② [A]-[B]-[C]-[D]
③ [C]-[B]-[A]-[D]
④ [C]-[D]-[A]-[B]

Our neighbor is an affluent inventor whose latest brainstorm, a feasible umbrella substitute, has been featured in many magazines. As simply as the eye can discern, it is a hard plastic strip, about the size of a ruler, which fits comfortably into a woman's handbag or a man's suit jacket. If a person is caught in a sudden rainstorm, he swings the plastic open in the shape of a cross. Attached to each arm is a clip-like device. Next, he takes the newspaper he is carrying and slides it under each of the four clips. Now, equipped with a rigid head covering he can sally forth to face the elements. To the consternation of the umbrella manufacturers, it has been enjoying a brisk sale, especially among commuters. If it continues to do well, it could have a pernicious effect upon the umbrella industry.

17 According to the passage, which of the following is true?

① The inventor has been criticized by the press for his absurd idea.

② The new invention has proved too complicated with initial testers.

③ The new invention has proved useless in a sudden weather change.

④ Umbrella manufacturers have been surprised at the success of the new invention.

⑤ The new invention is likely to make a great contribution to the umbrella industry.

18 The underlined expression means ____________.

① he can easily put the parts together

② he can see each individual part of the product

③ he can venture out in the rain

④ he can finally put the product on the market

⑤ he can lower the production costs

>>> 다음 글을 읽고 문제의 답을 고르시오. [19~22]

A married man and woman, who take no greater excursions outside themselves than an occasional turning-on of the radio or an occasional watching together of a movie, are both likely to feel frustrated and confined, and to express ① these obscurely entertained feelings by an everlasting ② wrangle. It is notorious that the business or professional man, who has confined his whole interest to his business or profession, is likely not to survive his retirement for very long. Ennui, expressing itself via heart or kidneys or arteries, drops him in his tracks. The physical organism has no reason to go on continuing. ③ _______________ men devoted to hobbies and similar interests have a way of continuing into great old age, still lively and alert and inquisitive as chipmunks.

19 The best title of the passage is ____________.

① How to survive the retirement long

② Ennui and health

③ Importance of hobbies

④ How to keep balance between family and work

⑤ How to be as inquisitive as chipmunks

20 The one that does NOT belong to the underlined ① is ____________.

① frustration   ② being forlorn

③ a feeling of inferiority   ④ boredom

⑤ a feeling of confinement

21 The one that best interprets the underlined ② is ____________.

① praise   ② encouragement

③ vitality   ④ complaint

⑤ negligence

22 The expression that is most appropriate for ③ is ____________.

① In contrast   ② On the contrary

③ Consequently   ④ In case

⑤ Otherwise

The less expensive ways of going on holidays are to take a camper in which you can stay or to go camping. It is also cheaper when you are travelling abroad to go on a package tour in which your hotel and flight are arranged for you. You can stay in a Bed and Breakfast(also called a B and B) which is usually a private house which takes paying guests and provides them with a room for the night and breakfast for the following morning. In Britain this is usually cheaper than a hotel though in the US it is more expensive. Some people buy timeshares, that is, they become part owners of a holiday home and it is theirs to use a certain time every year.

23 **Which of the following is the best title of the passage above?**

① Where People Stay on Holidays

② Popular Holiday Entertainments

③ When People Leave for Holidays

④ What People Do on Holidays

>> 다음 글을 읽고 문제의 답을 고르시오.

However, prevention policies must consider the role that humans play in wildfires, since, for example, only 5% of forest fires in Europe are not related to human involvement.

Wildfire prevention refers to the preemptive methods of reducing the risk of fires as well as lessening its severity and spread. (가) Effective prevention techniques allow supervising agencies to manage air quality, maintain ecological balances, protect resources, and to limit the effects of future uncontrolled fires. (나) North American firefighting policies may permit naturally-caused fires to burn to maintain their ecological role, so long as the risks of escape onto high-value areas are mitigated. (다) Sources of human-caused fire may include arson, accidental ignition, or the uncontrolled use of fire in land-clearing and agriculture such as the slash-and-burn farming in Southeast Asia. (라) Landholders with flammable investments such as orchards and tree crops may encourage neighboring landowners to reduce fire risks.

24 **Choose the most appropriate place for the above passage.**

① (가) 　　　　　② (나)

③ (다) 　　　　　④ (라)

》》 다음 글을 읽고 문제의 답을 고르시오.

What I should do everyday is take my dog for a walk. Some days we might go to the park. (1) Other days we might go to the woods and let him chase squirrels. (2) If I'm really busy, some of my roommates may keep the house clean, which I really appreciate. (3) Sometimes I feel bad because I'm unable to do this or no one else is. (4) So my dog has to spend the whole day in the house tied up in the backyard. He can't move around very much in those situations and doesn't get as much exercise as he should.

25 윗글의 흐름과 관계없는 문장을 고르시오.

① (1) ② (2)
③ (3) ④ (4)

》》 다음 글을 읽고 문제의 답을 고르시오. [26~27]

Pure pursuit of objective truth has been the great ideal and the great faith of science, and it has brought us magnificent technological rewards. The difficulty is that, from Hiroshima on, the most fundamental of sciences seems to have brought some horrible and terrifying rewards as well. All at once, the morality of the science seems to have (가) run colossally afoul of the grand old morality of respect for life, just as the humane men so often predicted it would. Basic scientists have had to face the fact that nuclear weapons were actually made possible by the most basic and pure and detached studies, and that the lame could not be pushed off onto engineers and technologists, as it could be either with dynamite or the machine gun.

26 윗글의 주제는 무엇인가?

① Benefits and disasters of scientific progress

② Conflict of the morality of science with that of humanity

③ Innocence of scientists as to it use

④ Who to blame for unclear disasters?

⑤ How to prevent scientific findings from being misused?

27 (가) 'run colossally afoul of'가 의미하는 것은 무엇인가?

① been extremely at variance with

② secretly conspired with

③ minimally collided with

④ colorfully patched up

⑤ been roughly in harmony with

>>> 다음 글을 읽고 문제의 답을 고르시오. [28~29]

Under the present system of mass education by large classes too much stress is laid on teaching and too little on active learning. The child is not encouraged to discover things on his own account. He learns to rely on outside help, not on his own powers, thus losing intellectual independence and all capacity to judge for himself. The overtaught child is the father of the newspaper-reading, advertisement-believing, propaganda-swallowing, demagogue-led man—the man who makes modern democracy the farce it is. Moreover, lessons in class leave him mainly unoccupied, and therefore bored. He has to be coerced into learning what does not interest him, and the information acquired mechanically and reluctantly, by dint of brute repetition, is rapidly forgotten.

28 윗글에서 현행 교육제도에 대한 저자의 태도는 어떠한가?

① critical   ② diffident

③ sarcastic   ④ understanding

⑤ optimistic

29 윗글에 따르면, 현행 교육제도 하에서 기대할 수 없는 것은 무엇인가?

① dependence   ② creativity

③ sense of balance   ④ generosity

⑤ modesty

>>> 다음 글을 읽고 문제의 답을 고르시오.

Unjust laws exist: shall we be content to obey them, or shall we endeavor to amend them, and obey them until we have succeeded, or shall we transgress them at once? Men generally, under such a government as this, think that they ought to wait until they have persuaded the majority to alter them. They think that, if they should resist, the remedy would be worse than the evil. But it is the fault of the government itself that the remedy is worse than the evil. It makes it worse. Why is it not more apt to anticipate and provide for reform? Why does it not cherish its wise minority? Why does it cry and resist before it is hurt? Why does it not encourage its citizens to be on the alert to point out its faults, and do better than it would have them? Why does it always crucify Christ, and excommunicate Copernicus and Luther, and pronounce Washington and Franklin rebels?

30 Which of the following is the best title of the passage?

① Reform of Unjust Laws

② Civil Obedience to the Government

③ Injustices of the Government

④ The Government's Struggle to Remove Social Evils

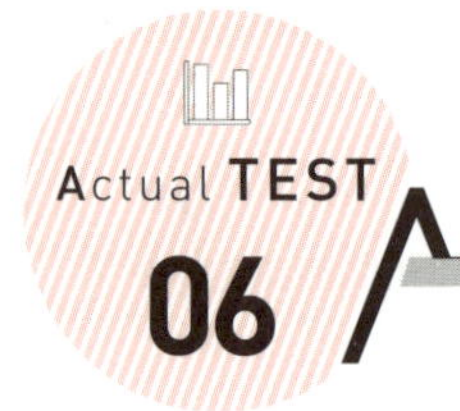

>>> 밑줄 친 곳에 들어갈 알맞은 답을 고르시오. [1~6]

1 As the reputation of books is raised, not by their freedom from defect, but by the greatness of their beauties, so should that of men be prized, not for their ____________ from fault but the size of those virtues they are possessed of.

① exemption
② bulk
③ goodness
④ hatred
⑤ butts

2 Convincing arguments for participatory form of democracy were put forward by Rousseau, an eighteenth-century French philosopher. His influential political theory ____________ the direct experience of political participation.

① hinged on
② had nothing to do with
③ called off
④ kept out
⑤ made up for

3 The ties that bind us together in common activity are so ____________ that they can disappear at any moment.

① tentative
② tenuous
③ restrictive
④ consistent
⑤ tenacious

4 By a strange combination of generosity and greed man protects the weak in asylums and kills the strong in wars. By a strange combination of ingenuity and impotence he multiplies the basic necessities of life far beyond any possible need only to let millions ____________ and unclothed for lack of efficient distribution.

① fall behind
② find shelter
③ go hungry
④ get angry
⑤ be happy

5   The field of American studies began as an amalgam of history and literature during the pre-World War II period. In the post-war period, it gradually incorporated studies of the arts and material culture, expanding later on to encompass popular culture and media, and growing still further with studies that focused on issues of race, ethnicity, and gender. By the end of the 20th century, American studies had also incorporated comparative studies of Canada and Latin America. Indeed a transnational, global perspective on American culture has become one of the leading currents in the filed as we begin the 21st century. Now most scholars agree that the field of American studies ______________, encompassing a wide range of disciplines that, in one way or another, are trying to describe the cultures of the United States.

① began to militate against pluraltiy
② has a shared basis with gender studies
③ is not countenanced
④ is implementing new critical methods
⑤ continues to expand

6   It is an oft-told story, but it does not get any less horrific on repetition. Fifteen years ago, a pedophile enticed seven-year-old Megan Kanka into his home in New Jersey by offering to show her a puppy. He then raped her, killed her and dumped her body in a nearby park. The murderer, who had recently moved into the house across the street from his victim, had twice before been convicted of sexually assaulting a child. Yet Megan's parents had no idea of this. Had they known he was a sex offender, ______________.

① they would have told their daughter to stay away from him
② they would have ordered their daughter to fight him
③ they would have made their daughter make friends with him
④ they would have let the police catch him

>> 다음 글을 읽고 문제의 답을 고르시오. [7~9]

There is nothing so degrading as the constant anxiety about one's livelihood. I have nothing but contempt for people who despise money. They are hypocrites or fools. Money is like a sixth sense without which you cannot make complete use of the other five. Without an adequate income half the possibilities of life are shut off. The only thing to be careful about is that (가) you do not spend more than a shilling for the shilling you earn. You will hear people say that poverty is the best spur to the artist. Such people have never felt the iron of ① it in their flesh. They do not know how mean ② it makes you. ③ it exposes you to endless humiliation. ④ It is what cuts your wings, and eats into your soul like a cancer. ⑤ It is not wealth one asks for, but just enough to preserve one's dignity, to work unhampered, to be generous, frank, and independent. I pity with all my heart the artist, whether he writes or paints, who is entirely dependent upon his art for subsistence.

7 **Which of the following best describes the author's opinion on money?**

① Money is important for a decent life.
② Those who love money excessively are hypocrites.
③ Poverty stimulates the sensitivities of artists most effectively.
④ Human nobility lies in overcoming the obstacles of poverty.
⑤ Most people overestimate the power of money in the modern world.

8 **Which of the following is closest in meaning to (가)?**

① you should stay within your budget
② you should not work solely for money
③ you should spend as little as possible
④ you should not despise doing labor to earn money
⑤ you should strike a balance between poverty and wealth

9 **Of the five occurrences of it in ①~⑤, which does NOT refer to the same thing?**

① ①   ② ②   ③ ③   ④ ④   ⑤ ⑤

If we deduct from nationalism all that (가)it has borrowed or stolen from (나)regionalism, what remains is mostly rubbish. The nation, as distinct from the region, is largely the creation of political manipulators. Almost all nationalist movements are led by ambitious frustrated men determined to hold office. I am not blaming them. I would do the same if I were in their place and wanted power so badly. But nearly always they heavily make use of warm regional feeling, (다)the emotional dynamo of the movement, while being almost untouched by (라)it themselves. Ambition and a love of power can eat like acid into the tissues of (마)regional loyalty.

10 Among (가)~(마), which one differs from the others in its meaning or reference?

① (가)　　　　　　② (나)

③ (다)　　　　　　④ (라)

⑤ (마)

11 According to the passage, which of the following is true?

① There is no such thing as regionalism.

② Regionalism is an invention of power-hungry politicians.

③ Nationalism is really a feeling for one's region.

④ Nationalist movements were initiated by loyal regionalists.

⑤ Nationalism is indispensible for the development of one's region.

>> 다음 글을 읽고 문제의 답을 고르시오. [12~14]

Success in producing mental discipline is the chief merit of traditional higher education. I doubt whether it can be achieved except by compelling or persuading active attention to a prescribed task. It is for this reason chiefly that I do not believe methods such as Madame Montessori's applicable when the age of childhood has been passed. The essence of her method consists in giving a choice of occupations, any one of which is interesting to most children, and all of which are instructive. The child's attention is wholly spontaneous, as in play; it enjoys acquiring knowledge in this way, and does not acquire any knowledge which it does not desire. I am convinced that this is the best method of education with young children: the actual results make it almost impossible to think otherwise. But it is difficult to see how this method can lead to control of attention by the will.

12 Mental discipline of the students can successfully be achieved ____________.

① by applying Montessori's method of education
② by allowing students to choose occupations of their own will
③ by teaching students only prescribed subjects
④ by forcing students to pay heed to a prescribed task

13 Traditional higher education ____________.

① is better in producing mental discipline than Montessori's method
② is applicable only to those who are over the age of childhood
③ makes it difficult for students to have control of attention by the will
④ is based on Madame Montessori's educational method

14 According to the author, Madame Montessori's method of teaching ____________.

① will result in creating a lot of occupations
② is very strict and instructive
③ is not likely to achieve its proposed object
④ can be greatly instrumental to students' obtaining of the control of attention

>>> 다음 글을 읽고 문제의 답을 고르시오.

a. It's obvious that people become violent when they are trying to protect someone or something.

b. When a situation is threatening, not only gang members but also average people act violently.

c. Even people who have never shown any violent tendencies might also commit a violent crime if a loved one is in danger.

d. An obvious example of this is when gang members want to protect their neighborhoods from the "invasion"of members of other gangs.

15 윗글을 문맥에 맞게 올바른 순서로 연결한 것은?

① a - d - b - c
② a - c - b - d
③ b - a - d - c
④ b - d - c - a

>>> 다음 글을 읽고 문제의 답을 고르시오.

[I] Soon after I arrived, I sat on my sunglasses and broke them.

[II] But my worst moments came when I decided to climb up to the high diving tower.

[III] Yesterday at the swimming pool everything seemed to go wrong.

[IV] Later my bathing suit caught on the rough edge of a chair, tearing a hole in the side of the suit.

16 위 문장들을 문맥에 맞도록 가장 잘 배열한 것은?

① [III]–[I]–[II]–[IV]   ② [III]–[I]–[IV]–[II]
③ [I]–[IV]–[III]–[II]   ④ [I]–[IV]–[II]–[III]

>> 다음 글을 읽고 문제의 답을 고르시오. [17~18]

Although Socrates did not work out precise rules for definition, he did employ what came to be known as the 'Socratic method'. To get at the true definition of some term, Socrates would engage in conversation with someone who claimed to understand the term. By careful, probing, and persistent questioning, Socrates would _______________ from his opponent all sorts of definitions and show their inadequacy, until finally a correct version was obtained. Naturally this approach tended to be unnerving and humiliating to those with whom the discussion was carried on and who confidently, sometimes arrogantly, thought they knew it all, especially then a crowd gathered around to hear the philosopher destroy their arguments.

17 밑줄 친 부분에 들어갈 가장 알맞은 것은?

① imply   ② condone

③ prevent   ④ alloy

⑤ elicit

18 윗글의 내용과 일치하는 것은?

① Socrates charmed his opponents in public debates.

② The 'Socratic method' is a kind of mind-reading procedure.

③ Socrates experienced many humiliating moments in his conversations.

④ Socrates tried to obtain true definitions of terms through conversations.

⑤ Socrates perfected the rules for definition.

One of the most notable features of the Blue Mosque in Istanbul is visible from far away: its six minarets. This is very unique, as most mosques have four, two or just one minaret. According to one account, the Sultan directed his architect to make gold (*altin*) minarets, which was misunderstood as six (*alti*) minarets. Whatever the origins of the unique feature, the six minarets caused quite a scandal, as the mosque in Mecca also had six minarets. The problem was solved by adding a seventh minaret to Mecca's mosque.

The main, west entrance is beautifully decorated and should not be missed. However, to preserve the mosque's sanctity, non-worshippers are required to use the north entrance, off the Hippodrome. Hanging from this gate are symbolic chains that encourage everyone, even the sultan on horseback, to bow his or her head upon entering. The interior's high ceiling is lined with about 20,000 blue tiles that give the mosque its popular name.

19 **윗글의 내용과 일치하지 않는 것을 고르시오.**

① Only Moslems are allowed to use the west entrance.

② Both entrances have symbolic chains hung low to make people bow upon entering.

③ The decoration of the main entrance is very beautiful.

④ The minarets of the Blue Mosque are visible from far away.

It it possible to check or monitor all sex offenders? It seems not to be necessarily difficult to. It would not be hard to redesign America's sex laws. Instead of lumping (가)them together on the same list for life, states should assess (나)them individually and include only real threats. Instead of posting everything on the internet, names could be held by the police, who would share them only with (다)those, who need to know. Laws that bar (라)them from living in so many places should be repealed, because there is no evidence that they protect anyone: a predator can always travel. The money that a repeal saves could help pay for monitoring compulsive (마)molesters more intrusively—through ankle bracelets and the like.

In America it may take years to unpick this. However practical and just the case for reform, it must overcome political cowardice, the tabloid media and parents' understandable fears. Other countries, though, have no excuse for committing the same error. Sensible sex laws are better than vengeful ones.

20 **Choose the title of the above passage.**

① Enforcing Rigorous Criminal Law against a Sexual Offense

② When and How to Monitor Law Offenders

③ Unnecessity that Sexual Offenders' Identity be Opened

④ How to Help Pay for Monitoring Sexual Offenders

⑤ Make Punishment Fit the Sexual Crime

21 **Among ①~⑤, which one differs from the others?**

① (가) ② (나)

③ (다) ④ (라)

⑤ (마)

Suppose you saw somebody being shown a pair of cards. On one of them there is a line, and on the other three lines. Of these three, one is obviously longer than the line on the other card, one is shorter, and one the same length. These cards will be shown to a person and he will be asked to point to the line on the second card which is the same length as the one on the first. The victim, having agreed to this seemingly innocent request, is jointed by about half a dozen people and the experimenter seated in a room. Unknown to our victim, none of the other people in the room is a volunteer like himself; they are all in league with the experimenter. A pair of cards, like those I have described, is introduced; and everyone in turn is asked which of the three lines on the second card is equal to the line on the first. They all, without hesitation, pick—as they have been told to pick—the same wrong line. Last of all comes the turn of our volunteer. In many cases the volunteer, (가)_________________, denies the plain evidence of his senses, and agrees.

22 **Which of the following would be the best title for this passage?**

① Distorted Vision under Pressure

② Length Discrimination

③ The Effect of Anonymity

④ Unreliable Experimental Results

⑤ The Pressure to Conform

23 **Which of the following best fits into (가)?**

① pretending to be smart

② tired of false judgment

③ faced with this unanimity

④ forgetting the purpose of the experiment

⑤ embarrassed by the number of cards

>>> 다음 글을 읽고 문제의 답을 고르시오. [24~26]

The theater is one of the richest art forms around. The excitement of opening night can be felt by the people waiting to watch a performance, and by the performance and workers backstage waiting for the curtain to go up. Live theater is thrilling for that reason—no one really knows how well it will go until the play is performed live.

Many people collaborate to bring a play to life. There are playwrights, directors, set designers, costumers, lighting technicians, and, of course, the actors. If the play is a musical, the skills of a songwriter, choreographer, and musicians are also required. The word theater comes from the Greek "theatron", which means "a place for seeing". Although most people think of the theater in terms of a play performed on the stage, theater has taken on much more meaning in the modern world. Theater may come to life on a street corner, or in a classroom. Theater is an art form that changes as it is interpreted in different ways by different people. That is probably why the works of the greatest playwright of all time, William Shakespeare, are still performed and enjoyed today, both in classic and new interpretations.

24 **The best title of the passage might be ____________.**

① Shakespeare and Theater

② Modern Theater: Adventures in Acting

③ The Excitement of the Theater

④ History of Theatrical Productions

25 **According to the above passage, the primary reason that theater is so exciting is that ____________.**

① it is performed live

② it is musical

③ it derives from Greek

④ there are so many people waiting for it

26 **The author's attitude toward theater can best be described as ____________.**

① objective   ② apathetic

③ neutral   ④ admiring

Something had to replace the threat of communism, and at last a workable substitute is at hand: multiculturalism. (가) The Jacobins of the multiculturalist movement, who are described derisively as P.C., or politically correct, are said to have launched a campus reign of terror against those who slip and innocently say "freshman" instead of "freshperson", "Indian" instead of "Native American". (나) But it's silly to mistake verbal purification for genuine social reform. (다) Even after all women are "Ms."and all people are "he or she", women will still earn only 65¢ for every dollar earned by men. (라) Minorities by any other name, such as "people of color", will still bear a hugely disproportionate burden of poverty and discrimination. (마) Disabilities are not just "different abilities" when there are not enough ramps for wheelchairs, signers for the deaf or special classes for ① <u>the "specially" endowed</u>. With all due respect for the new politeness, ② _______________.

27 Where can the passage be divided into two parts?

① (가)　　　② (나)　　　③ (다)　　　④ (라)　　　⑤ (마)

28 The underlined the "specially" endowed in ① includes ___________.

① gifted people　　　② distinguished scientists

③ talented artists　　　④ child prodigies

⑤ mentally retarded people

29 The one that is most appropriate for the blank in ② is ___________.

① the P.C. cause of verbal inoffensiveness should be upheld.

② we should keep watching the language on campus.

③ action should speak louder than fashionable phrases.

④ the P.C. people should be denounced.

⑤ the Jacobins of the multiculturalist deserve more attention.

30 Who does not belong to the group that the P.C. people prefer to call by another name?

① women　　　② homophobic people

③ minorities　　　④ Indians

⑤ handicapped people

>>> 밑줄 친 곳에 들어갈 알맞은 답을 고르시오. [1~5]

1   There is a class of businessmen in the US known as corporate raiders because their business is that of ____________ large corporations.

① taking over
② sneaking into
③ fooling around with
④ infiltrating
⑤ turning down

2   Many westerners find quite ____________ the Korean use of different terms of address when Koreans speak to a superior or an inferior.

① embezzled
② pedantic
③ inquisitive
④ perfunctory
⑤ bewildering

3   We won't let you work shorter hours and get more money. You can't eat your ____________ and have it, too.

① bread
② cake
③ apple
④ pudding
⑤ bread and salt

4   We are far less ready to contemplate our own historical aberrations. Instead, we prefer to project our repressed awareness of wrongdoing on to others, as sacrificial victims or whipping boys. We are markedly reluctant to admit, and work on, our own shortcomings. ____________ is in short supply.

① Power
② Reluctance
③ Resistance
④ Persistence
⑤ Honesty

5   To find their ____________ in the desert landscape during Operation Desert Storm, soldiers relied on hand-held electronic gadgets called Global Positioning System receivers, which can pinpoint a location instantly anywhere on the earth.

     ① bearings   ② groups
     ③ belongings   ④ orders
     ⑤ routines

>>> 다음 글을 읽고 문제의 답을 고르시오.

> I.   Certainly there are plans in ________________ for a response to an attack.
>
> II.   The tree-lined streets of this city wouldn't be out of ________________ in a small town.
>
> III.   Not all engineering failures take ________________ suddenly and dramatically.

6   빈칸에 공통으로 들어갈 가장 알맞은 어휘를 고르시오.
     ① use   ② order
     ③ turn   ④ charge
     ⑤ place

>>> 다음 글을 읽고 문제의 답을 고르시오.

A. Their democratic ideals and system of justice have spread over the world to become the foundation for the laws and government of many nations.

B. Yet no one can fully understand the modern world without knowing some English history.

C. England is a very small country, not much bigger than the state of New York.

D. The English worked out ideas of justice and obedience to law.

7 **Rearrange the following sentences to make a coherent paragraph.**

① A - B - C - D
② C - D - A - B
③ C - A - D - B
④ C - B - D - A
⑤ D - B - C - A

>>> 다음 글을 읽고 문제의 답을 고르시오.

One factor that has affected the price of gold has been the increasingly difficulty in acquiring it. Today, most of the gold left in the ground is in microscopic pieces mixed with rock. To get it, miners must dig up tons of rock to separate the gold. For one ounce of gold—a wedding ring, for example—the mine processes about 30 tons of rock. This is already a costly operation. But the missing and processing of gold is also ruinous to the environment and to the health of people living nearby. Most mines are in poor regions where the people have had little voice in whether there should be mines and how the mines should be run. Large multinational mining companies simply bought the land and opened the mines. However, as people and governments begin to realize the extent of the damage caused by the mines, the situation might change. If the mining companies ever have to pay the full environmental and social costs of mining gold, the price of gold is likely to climb higher.

　윗글의 내용과 일치하지 않는 것은?

① The health of people in mining areas is threatened by the mines today.

② People are starting to be aware of the damages caused by the mines.

③ About 30 tons of rock has to be dug up to acquire an ounce of gold.

④ Mining companies have paid for the environmental damages they caused.

>>> 다음 글을 읽고 문제의 답을 고르시오.

Thousands of years ago, people in Egypt preserved the bodies of their dead and wrapped them in cloth called linen. Today, these mummies can tell scientists about how the Egyptian lived. However, scientists have always had a big problem when they tried to study mummies. If they unwrapped a mummy, they would damage it. Now, scientists have a way to study mummies without unwrapping them. An X-ray machine called a CAT scanner takes pictures of mummies right through their wraps. The first mummies that scientists scanned was a female Egyptian mummy. The scanner took pictures of her from different angles. Then, a computer put all the pictures together to form a complete image.

9　**Which of the following would come after the passage?**

① Additional ways of unwrapping the mummy

② revenge of Egyptian mummies

③ things scientists learned by scanning

④ other machines used by scientists which study mummy

>>> 다음 글을 읽고 문제의 답을 고르시오.

Become the hero or heroine of your own story. Don't feel sad that your favorite show has ended. This city preserves the sets on which popular TV shows and movies had been shot. The beautiful landscapes captured in your favorite movies and TV shows make the romantic plots even more beautiful. Plan a trip to these shooting locations this week and book the right to become the main character of your favorite story!

10 **Which of the following is the main purpose of the passage?**

① to warn   ② to complain

③ to argue   ④ to advertise

Iona sees a hall porter with some sacking, and decides to talk to him.

"Friend, what sort of time is it?" he asks.

"Past nine. What are you standing here for? Move on."

Iona moves on a few steps, doubles up, and abandons himself to his grief. In less than five minutes he straightens himself, holds his head up as if he felt some sharp pain, and gives a tug at the reins he can bear it no longer. "The stables", he thinks, and the little horse, as if it understood, starts off at a trot.

About an hour and a half later Iona is seated by a large dirty stove. Around the stove, on the floor, on the benches people are snoring; the air is thick and suffocatingly hot. Iona looks at the sleepers, scratches himself, and regrets having returned so early.

One of the cabdrivers half gets up, grunts sleepily, and stretches toward a bucket of water.

"Do you want a drink?" Iona asks him.

"Don't I want a drink!"

"That's so? Your good health! But listen, mate—you know, my son is dead… Did you hear? This week, in the hospital… It's a long story."

Iona looks to see what effect his words have, but sees none—the young man has hidden his face and is fast asleep again. The old man sighs and scratches his head. Just as much as the young one wants to drink, the old man wants to talk. Is it nothing to tell?

"I'll go and look after my horse", thinks Iona; "there's always time to sleep. No fear of that!"

He puts on his coat, and goes to the stables to his horse; he thinks of the corn, the hay, the weather. When he is alone, he dares not think of his son; he can speak about him to anyone, but to think of him, and picture him to himself, is unbearably painful.

"Are you tucking in?" Iona asks his horse, looking at its bright eyes, "Go on, tuck in. Though we've not earned our corn, we can eat hay."

Iona is silent for a moment, then continues:

"That's how it is, my old horse. There's no more Kuzma Ionitch. Now let's say, you had a foal, you were the foal's mother, and suddenly, let's say, that foal went and left you to live after him. It would be sad, wouldn't it?"

The little horse munches, listens, and breathes over its master's hand... Iona's feelings are too much for him, and he tells the little horse the whole story.

11 **Iona most probably regrets going to the room with the stove because** ____________.

① his horse has not been fed
② there is no room for him
③ the sleepers are unfriendly to him
④ there is no one who will listen to him

12 **In his encounter with the cabdriver Iona shows** ____________.

① patriotism   ② resignation
③ suspicion   ④ ill will

13 **In this story it is ironic that** ____________.

① the cabdriver wants a drink
② the hall porter tells Iona to move on
③ Iona tells his story to his horse
④ Iona has run out of food for his horse

14 **Iona's grief is strongest when he** ____________.

① is seated by the stove
② realizes that he is dying
③ speaks with the cabdrive
④ is alone

15 The author's purpose in using the present tense is most probably to

______________.

① make the story seem modern
② increase the length of the story
③ heighten the reader's sense of immediacy
④ reinforce the first person point of view

16 The title that best expresses the main idea of the passage is ______________.
① "A Father's Grief"
② "A Horse and Its Master"
③ "A Day in the Life of a Groom"
④ "A Senile Old Man"

17 Iona goes to take care of his horse. He does so most probably to

______________.

① have something to do
② show his great love for his horse
③ remove his feelings of guilt
④ prove that he does not resent the cabdriver's action

18 The tone of the passage is one of ______________.
① gaiety   ② impartiality
③ destruction   ④ sadness

>> 다음 글을 읽고 문제의 답을 고르시오. [19~20]

Writing these novels helped prepare Melville for Moby-Dick(1851), perhaps the greatest novel of American literature. Equally important was the encouragement Hawthorne gave Melville while he was writing it. From the beginning, it is clear that the voyage of the whaling ship Pequod will be a symbolic voyage. It is also clear that Moby-Dick, the great white whale, represents God or fate, _______________ Melville gives the reader a great deal of factual information about whale-hunting in order to make the world of Moby-Dick seem real. Captain Ahab, the central character, is "a grand, ungodly, God-like man". He is torn between his humanity and his desire to destroy the white whale. These two sides—the light and the dark—fight each other in Ahab. The dark side wins. To Ahab, Moby-Dick is part of a "universal mystery" which he hates, because he cannot understand it. When Ahab finds the whale and attacks him, his ship is destroyed. Ahab himself is pulled down into the sea to his death. Melville seems to say that personal identity is only an illusion.

19 **Choose the main idea of the above passage.**

① Men cannot hold sway Nature.

② Men cannot defy God.

③ Evil cannot help repelling good.

④ It is vain that he himself judges his identity.

⑤ Good and evil are inevitably opposite.

20 **Which one is most appropriate for the blank?**

① whereas   ② otherwise

③ for   ④ as though

⑤ meanwhile

The word "hacker" is widely misused. Among hackers themselves, it refers to someone who enjoys tinkering with technology, exploring its boundaries and getting it to do unexpected or unintended tricks, though in general use the word refers to individuals who break into computers for nefarious ends (for whom hackers prefer the terms "malicious hacker" or "cracker"). But a hacker is not necessarily bad and is not necessarily just someone who messes around with computers. Thomas Edison was arguably a hacker, back in the 19th century. Today's technological tinkerers, however, have a far wider range of household gizmos to play with and modify, from cars to cameras. Getting them to do new things, and not merely what the manufacturer had in mind, is an increasingly popular pastime. It even has its own magazine, MAKE, which is filled with projects for the technologically intrepid.

21 Choose the best topic of the above passage.

① Misapplication of the term hacker

② The comparison between a hacker of the past and a hacker of the present

③ The ends of contemporary hackers

④ The household goods which is made by hackers

⑤ How hackers break to pieces household goods

22 According to the passage, which of the following statements is true?

① Thomas Edison was a malicious hacker.

② Hackers are individuals that not only break computers but rebuild other equipment as well.

③ The magazine, MAKE, lets persons know the information that they can illegally rebuild various machines.

④ The hackers of the past is not much similar to those of the present.

⑤ Hackers resort to tricks within the limits of possible supposition.

>>> 다음 글을 읽고 문제의 답을 고르시오. [23~24]

The way we parent our children is undergoing a rapid and profound transformation. Where once mothers did virtually all the caring, today there is greater sharing of that task by dads. Typically, where a mother is working outside the home, fathers now do a third of parental childcare—an eightfold increase in a generation for fathers of pre-school children, according to the Equal Opportunities Commission. This revolution from one-parent to two-parent care in the UK is a direct consequence of women taking a greater role in the workplace and the falling away of gendered roles in our society. These social changes pose important questions. If fathers are now looking after children—including small babies—for lengthy periods of time, fathers need the same skills and knowledge that we have traditionally expected mothers to have. And this means services which support parents should ① ______________ to support fathers as well as mothers. The task now for these family services is to modernize—to support other significant carers in the family, notably fathers, who have, or want to have, a more active role in day-to-day care of their children.

23 **Choose the statement that the above passage does not say or imply.**

① Nowadays in the UK fathers' participation in childcare has greatly increased.

② The revolution from one-parent to two-parent care is taking place in the UK.

③ Fathers nowadays have, or want to have, a more active role in day-to-day care of their children.

④ All fathers in the UK should play a more active role in day-to-day care of their children.

⑤ Once mothers did virtually all the parental childcare.

24 **Choose the most appropriate expression for the underlined blank ①.**

① satisfy   ② enlighten

③ be geared up   ④ be helped

⑤ be focus

Still and her husband, Ed, who has lost nearly 100 pounds, get most of their exercise at work. They visit an onsite fitness center almost daily, meet co-workers outside to walk through beautifully landscaped grounds and take wide, airy stairs instead of elevators. That's exactly what their employer, Sprint Corp, intended when it moved its thousands of employees to a 200-acre campus in suburban Johnson County. Sprint is part of a small but growing movement that encourages business owners to construct or renovate buildings in ways that motivate—or require—employees to get more exercise. The premise is simple: Happier, healthier employees are more productive and reduce health care costs for their companies.

25 이 글의 내용과 일치하는 것을 고르시오.

① Still and Ed are frequent users of elevators at work.
② Sprint Corp. is located in the center of Johnson County.
③ Sprint Corp. put parking garages next to its buildings.
④ Sprint Corp. induces its workers to exercise.

>>> 다음 글을 읽고 문제의 답을 고르시오.

Sociologists reserve the term small group to refer to a group small enough for all members to interact simultaneously, that is, to talk with each other or at least be acquainted with each other. Small groups such as work groups and families are the intermediate link between the individual and the larger society. The intermediate position defines their importance in terms of attitudes, values, and behaviors. For this reason, sociologists are interested in what happens when people get together in small groups, whether it is to share gossip, reach a decision, or even play card games.

26 윗글의 내용과 일치하는 것을 고르시오.

① Sociologists reserve the place for small groups to interact one another.
② Small groups function as a link between the family and the society.
③ Sociologists are interested in attitudes, values, behaviors of small groups.
④ Gossiping and playing games are the best ways to make the members of small groups acquainted with each other.

The authority of government, even such as I am willing to submit to, is still an impure one: to be strictly just, it must have the sanction and consent of the governed. It can have no pure right over my person and property but what I concede to it. The progress from an absolute to a limited monarchy, from a limited monarchy to a democracy, is a progress toward a true respect for the individual. Even the Chinese philosopher was wise enough to regard the individual as the basis of the empire. There will never be a really free and enlightened State until the State comes to recognize the individual as a higher and independent power, from which all its own power and authority are derived, and treats him accordingly. I please myself with imagining a State at least which can afford to be just to all men, and to treat the individual with respect as a neighbor; which even would not think it inconsistent with its own repose if a few were to live aloof from it, not meddling with it, nor embraced by it, who fulfilled all the duties of neighbors and fellow-men.

27 윗글의 요지를 고르시오.

① Individual's challenge to their government is always legitimate.

② The best government is one which esteems the individual's right.

③ The power of government can be justified by democratic leaders.

④ Individuals can hardly be alienated from society.

28 다음 글의 흐름상 필요 없는 문장을 고르시오.

The diversity of ethnic and racial backgrounds of Americans today is the living legacy of immigration. The social forces that cause people to emigrate are complex. ① The most important have been economic: expectations of higher incomes and standards of living in the new land. ② Many come legally, applying for immigrant visas, but others enter illegally. ③ Other factors include dislike of new regimes in their native lands and a desire to reunite families. ④ All these factors push people from their homelands and pull them to other nations such as the United States.

》 다음 글을 읽고 문제의 답을 고르시오.

Alternative medicine is not available under the national health service in some countries, such as Britain.

Medical treatments which are used instead of drugs, surgery, and other officially accepted methods of treatment are known as alternative medicine, or complementary medicine. (가) These more natural methods of treating illness include acupuncture, chiropractic and aromatherapy. (나) Therefore, in such countries, people who use it have to pay for it when they receive their treatment. (다) Since the beginning of the 1980s, alternative medicine has become more and more popular with people. (라) Although it is not officially accepted by the medical profession, some doctors do accept that such methods can be effective in treating some types of illness.

29 제시문이 위치하기에 가장 적합한 곳을 고르시오.

① (가)   ② (나)

③ (다)   ④ (라)

Travel at its best is a solitary experience: to see, to examine, to assess, you have to be alone and unencumbered. Other people can mislead you; they crowd your meandering impressions with their own; if they are companionable they obstruct your view, and if they are boring they corrupt the silence with non-sequiturs, shattering your concentration with "Oh look, it's raining. And You see a lot of trees here." The gist of travelling is not understood by Japanese who, coming across you smiling wistfully at an acre of Mexican buttercups, tend to say things like 'Where is the rest of your team?' It is hard to see clearly or to think straight in the company with other people. Not only do I feel self-conscious, but the perceptions that are necessary to writing are difficult to manage when someone close by is thinking out aloud.

30 According to the passage, Japanese travellers considered the author ____________.

① indifferent ② courageous

③ unreliable ④ cynical

⑤ odd

>>> 밑줄 친 곳에 들어갈 알맞은 답을 고르시오. [1~6]

1 He has had three jobs in the last two years; he never ____________ anything for long.

① sticks down
② thinks over
③ goes with
④ sticks to
⑤ takes after

2 Since the detective believed her to be candid and trustworthy, he refused to consider the possibility that her explanation had been ____________.

① irrelevant
② facetious
③ mistaken
④ insincere
⑤ critical

3 The world of nature is free for our enjoyment, from the glory of a sunrise to the quaintness of a cricket. It is all here, around us, for taking. There is no ____________. Not only free, nature has the priceless advantage of being everywhere.

① serious planning
② danger
③ hurry
④ charge
⑤ obligation whatsoever

4 She was usually a model of ____________, so her sudden burst of temper was atypical.

① veracity
② lucidity
③ facility
④ equanimity
⑤ wrath

5 Legal ______________ initiated by the government necessitate that manufacturers use ______________ in choosing food additives.

① entanglements - knowledge

② devices - intensification

③ talents - decretion

④ proclivities - moderation

⑤ restraints - caution

6 The term stork indicates that the fact that a woman sees a bird of stork is that she will be pregnant. The fact that Caroline saw a stork the week before she became pregnant is merely a coincidence; it should not imply any ______________ whatsoever.

① fortuity   ② catastrophe

③ causality   ④ nemesis

> When I overheard one of my cashiers tell a customer, "We haven't had it for a while, and I doubt we'll be getting it soon," I quickly assured the customer that we would have whatever she wanted by next week. After she left, I read the cashier the riot act. "Never tell the customer that we're out of anything. Tell them we'll have it next week," I instructed her. "Now, what did she want?" The cashier said, "She wanted rain."

7 What would be the writer's occupation?

① customer

② supervisor

③ teacher

④ lawyer

>> 다음 글을 읽고 문제의 답을 고르시오.

It's noon on a sweltering June day, a perfect time for a teenager to listen to tunes and work on a tan. So Hanna Forest, 16, blond and blue-eyed, is trying to brown. But she's not worshiping the sun. She lies on a glass bed in the Coral Reef tanning salon in a suburban strip mall, basking under the ultraviolet. "It takes too long to lay out," says Hanna, a high-school cheerleader in Sycamore, Illinois. "I don't want to be pale. This makes me feel as if I look healthy." But it's the health of so many tanning-bed teens that worries dermatologists, who say the UV rays increase the risk of skin cancer. Now a bill proposed in California would prohibit youths under 18 from using tanning salons without a doctor's prescription. It would be the first such ban in the nation. For now, 27 states, including California, require parental consent for tanners 15 to 17, and turn away those 14 and under. The tanning industry says a ban could do more harm than good because people who tan indoors are less likely to burn outside.

8 이 글의 내용과 가장 일치하는 것을 고르시오.

① Tanning has the same risk of skin disease as burning.

② Tanners under the age of 14 need their parents' consent for using tanning salons.

③ California would be the first state to ban using tanning salons for those under the age of 18.

④ The tanning industry in the US argues that people obsessed with tanning are most at risk.

(가) Although your resume looks impressive, we have no plans to hire new staff in the immediate future.

(나) Allow me to begin by thanking you for your interest in joining our firm.

(다) Your resume, however, will be duly filed for future reference.

(라) Thanks again, and I wish you every success.

9 윗글들을 문맥에 맞게 올바른 순서로 연결한 것은?

① (가) – (다) – (나) – (라)

② (가) – (나) – (라) – (다)

③ (나) – (가) – (다) – (라)

④ (나) – (라) – (가) – (다)

>> 다음 글을 읽고 문제의 답을 고르시오.

Undeterred by this scientific pronouncement, a few weeks later the Wright brothers took their "flyer" to Kitty Hawk, North Carolina, and changed the world.

The idea of a heavier-than-air flying machine was roundly ridiculed by the scientific establishment in the early 1900s. [A] In 1902, the year before Wilbur and Orville Wright took their famous flight, the U.S. Navy's chief engineer declared the very idea to be "absurd." [B] The following year, an eminent professor of mathematics and astronomy at Johns Hopkins University proved to the world that a heavier-than-air craft was "scientifically impossible." [C] Even after photographs circulated of the historic flight, the Wright brothers's hometown newspaper refused to print anything about their revolutionary contraption because, as the editor admitted, "We didn't believe it." [D]

10 윗글의 흐름으로 보아 주어진 문장이 들어갈 가장 적절한 곳은?

① [A]　　　　　　　② [B]
③ [C]　　　　　　　④ [D]

The kind of people who send their kids to Bible camp are appalled. Answers in Genesis, a Christian fundamentalist group, berates Camp Quest for drumming a "hopeless" world view into young minds. But a humanist camp is about indoctrination less than about reassurance that it is all right not to be religious; that it is possible to be moral without believing in the supernatural. (가) Nearly all the kids at Camp Quest say they find it comforting to be surrounded by others who share their lack of belief. Many attend schools where Christianity is taken for granted. (나) Many keep quiet about their atheism. (다) Those who don't are sometimes taunted or told they will burn in hell. (라) Atheists are broadly disliked in America. Only 5% of Americans admit that they would not vote for an otherwise qualified black presidential candidate, but 53% say they would shun an atheist. That makes the godless less popular than Muslims, Mormons or gays. Granted, the proportion of Americans who say they might vote for an atheist has doubled in the past half-century, and the polls are muddied by those who do not know what an atheist is.

11 두 번째 단락이 시작되는 문장을 고르시오.

① (가)   ② (나)

③ (다)   ④ (라)

12 밑줄 친 부분이 가리키는 것은 무엇인가?

① people who don't preach Christianity

② people who suggest that they don't believe in God

③ people who dislike atheists

④ people who vote for black presidential candidates

>> 다음 글을 읽고 문제의 답을 고르시오. [13~15]

Judge Richard Posner, the most prolific federal judge, quotes the Austrian-born economist Joseph Schumpeter. Schumpeter—hardly a sympathetic figure—was an elitist who believed the achievements of capitalism were threatened by the greed and ignorance of the masses. "Democracy", as Posner describes Schumpeter's view, "is conceived of as a method by which members of a self-interested political elite compete for the votes of a basically ignorant and apathetic, as well as determinedly self-interested, electorate."

Is our democracy, then, entirely squalid? Not really, or not so it should bother us. Judge Posner brings to mind Winston Churchill's quip that democracy is the worst system of government except all the others that have been tried over the years. As most people believe, "American democracy", writes Posner, "enables the adult population to punish at least the flagrant mistakes of officialdom, to assure an orderly succession of at least minimally competent officials, to generate feedback to the officials concerning the consequences of their policies, to prevent officials from entirely ignoring the interests of the governed, and to prevent serious misalignments between the government action and public opinion".

13 **Winston Churchill implies that democracy is ____________ tried over the years.**

① an ideal system of government

② as bad as any other system of government

③ as good as any other system of government

④ worse than any other system of government

⑤ better than any other system of government

14 **According to Richard Posner, democracy can ____________.**

① stop the mistakes of bureaucracy

② make the officials more responsible for their policies

③ make the officials do their best for the interests of the governed

④ bring about an ideal cooperation between the government and the people

⑤ guarantee the succession of the social system by the ablest officials possible

15 **Concerning democracy, who differ in opinion?**

① the writer ② most people

③ Richard Posner ④ Winston Churchill

⑤ Joseph Schumpeter

>>> 다음 글을 읽고 문제의 답을 고르시오.

[A] "I'm just waiting around so I can put away the chairs," he added.

[B] After pounding out more songs, one of the tired musicians finally suggested to the music lover that if he left, they could all go home.

[C] "Do whatever you want," said the man.

[D] A colleague's band performed in a park before an audience that gradually dwindled down to one lone man.

16 **윗글들을 문맥에 맞게 올바른 순서로 연결한 것은?**

① [B]-[A]-[C]-[D] ② [B]-[D]-[A]-[C]

③ [D]-[A]-[C]-[B] ④ [D]-[B]-[C]-[A]

In June the high court of the secular government of Turkey upheld a long-standing ban on religious headscarves at universities. Hundreds of women took to the streets. But the controversy isn't new. A former member of the Turkish parliament, Merve Kavakci, was stripped of her citizenship for wearing a hijab to work in 1999 and is now living in the United States. Writing in Foreign Policy, she challenged Westerners and feminists who, like her former government, denounce the hijab: "They're better off honoring a woman's right to choose than trying to impose their prejudices on Muslims."

17 Which is NOT true of Ms. Kavakci?

① She used to be a Turkish.
② She is now an active feminist.
③ She was a member of the Turkish parliament.
④ She was kicked out of Turkey for wearing a hijab.
⑤ She is currently staying in the USA as a Muslim.

In reading, one should notice and fondle details. There is nothing wrong about the moonshine of generalization when it comes after the sunny trifles of the book have been lovingly collected. If one begins with a ready-made generalization, it means that he begins at the wrong end and travels away from the book before he has started to understand it. Nothing is more boring or more unfair to the author than starting to read, say, *Madame Bovary*, with the preconceived notion that it is a denunciation of the bourgeoisie. We should always remember that a literary work is invariably the creation of a new world, so that the first thing we should do is to study that new world as closely as possible, approaching it as something brand new, having no obvious connection with the worlds we already know.

18 **Which of the following best expresses the main idea of the passage?**

① Generalization is based upon what we already know of the world.
② Reading always provides us with the practical information about the world.
③ A close reading is essential in understanding a literary work.
④ *Madame Bovary* deals with the condemnation of the bourgeoisie.

>>> 다음 글을 읽고 문제의 답을 고르시오.

The same nonverbal behavior may have a totally different meaning when it occurs in another context.

Like verbal communication, nonverbal communication exists in a context, and that context determines to a large extent the meanings of any nonverbal behaviors. (1) A wink of the eye to an attractive person on a bus means something completely different from a wink of an eye to signify a lie. (2) Similarly, the meaning of a given bit of nonverbal behavior depends on the verbal behavior it accompanies or is close to in time. (3) Pounding the fist on a table during a speech in support of a politician means something quite different from the same fist pounding in response to news of a friends'death. Of course, even if we know the context in detail, we still might not be able to decipher the meaning of the nonverbal behavior. (4) In attempting to understand and analyze nonverbal communication, however, it is essential that full recognition be taken of the context.

19 **윗글의 흐름으로 보아 주어진 문장이 들어갈 가장 적절한 곳은?**

① (1) ② (2)
③ (3) ④ (4)

>>> 다음 글을 읽고 문제의 답을 고르시오.

A common pattern in many societies provides for a periodic relaxation of the rules of conventional behavior. In some societies this goes to the length of letting down all sex barriers, even to the relaxing of incest taboos. In other societies there may simply be feasting, drinking, or dancing along with some other forms of entertainment. We find a counterpart of such activities in our Halloween parties, masked balls, costume parties, and Mardi Gras. Some societies make provision for ritual teasing and joking, or occasions when buffoonery, ribald tricks or tales, and other such activities are permitted or even encouraged. The jester and the clown are stock characters in many societies. By their uninhibited behavior they provide a vicarious outlet for socially restrained resentments and hostilities.

20 **Which one of the following best summarizes the above passage?**

① People in many societies enjoy life by relaxing rules.

② In some societies sex taboos are relaxed from time to time.

③ People in many societies relax their rules of behavior periodically.

④ Relaxation of morality is not dangerous in some cases.

The absence of risk produces a type of boredom which paralyses in a different way from fear, but almost as much. Risk is a form of danger which provokes a deliberate reaction; that is to say, it doesn't go beyond the soul's resources to the point of crushing the soul beneath a load of fear. The protection of mankind from fear and terror doesn't imply the abolition of risk; it implies, on the contrary, the permanent presence of a certain amount of risk in all aspects of social life; for the absence of risk weakens courage to the point of leaving the soul, if the need should arise, without the slightest inner protection against fear. All that is wanted is for risk to offer itself under such conditions that it is not transformed into a sensation of fatality.

21 **윗글의 내용과 일치하지 않는 것은?**

① A certain amount of risk always exists in all aspects of social life.

② We must protect mankind not only from fear and terror, but also from risk.

③ A type of boredom produced by the absence of risk paralyses nearly as much as fear does.

④ If risk is entirely absent, our courage will become so weak that the soul will not be properly protected against fear.

>> 다음 글을 읽고 문제의 답을 고르시오. [22~23]

The idea that work is good for teenagers, no matter how miserable or time-consuming their jobs, is held with a deep moral conviction comparable to that surrounding the joys of motherhood or the benefits of apple pie. The idea has its origins in images of diligent adolescent apprentices working side by side with caring adult mentors.

Although the workplace has changed, it is still widely held that paid work is a character-building enterprise for young people—even more so than schooling. _________________ studies indicate that the sorts of characters work builds in the current workplace are not exactly what most of us have in mind.

22 윗글의 내용과 일치하는 것을 고르시오.

① It is a myth that paid work is instrumental in teenagers' character-building.
② Education in school now has nothing to be desired.
③ Teenagers in general work under favorable conditions.
④ Young students are recommended to work together with thoughtful adult supervisors.
⑤ Teens usually benefit a lot from their mothers.

23 빈칸에 들어갈 가장 적절한 것을 고르시오.

① Yet
② No doubt
③ In addition
④ Indeed
⑤ Otherwise

Pigeons have been taught to recognize human facial expressions, upsetting long-held beliefs that only humans had evolved the sophisticated nervous systems to perform such a feat. In recent experiments at the University of Iowa, eight trained pigeons were shown photographs of people displaying emotions of happiness, anger, surprise, and disgust. The birds learned to distinguish between these expressions. Not only that, but they were able to correctly identify the same expressions on photographs of unfamiliar faces. Their achievement does not suggest, of course, that the pigeons had any idea what the human expressions meant.

24 From the passage, which of the following can be inferred about pigeons?

① They can understand the same emotions humans can.

② They can always recognize human emotions.

③ They can only identify the expressions of people they are familiar with.

④ They have more sophisticated nervous systems than was once thought.

25 Choose the one which is corresponding to the meaning of the above passage.

① Pigeons had an idea what the humans beings' expressions meant.

② Pigeons could not identify the same expressions on photographs of unfamiliar faces.

③ Pigeons became to distinguish emotions of human beings' facial expressions after they were taught to.

④ Pigeons were able to distinguish emotions of human beings' facial expressions before they learned to.

>>> 다음 글을 읽고 문제의 답을 고르시오. [26~30]

Robert had just moved into the neighborhood where he felt strange and unwanted. He realized that the other boys were probably sizing him up. He could not blame them for their lukewarm reception. He knew that he had to be tested, but proving himself would not be all that easy. (1) He did not want to run with the gangs or get into a legal hassle in order to prove that he was tough. (2) No! He must show what he was made of in (가) a more constructive way. (3) The next day was Sunday. (4) He knew that most of the guys would be down at the schoolyard choosing up sides for the weekly game. (5) Robert knew he could play well and that just might be enough to gain their approval. He arrived early and went through his places.

He wheeled around for a reverse layup, dribbled to the top of the key for a long jumper; and ran through his sky hook. Then the guys came. No one said a word. Everyone just stared and mulled it over. Then the biggest of the group just grinned and shook his head. Robert knew he had made it.

26 **The best theme of the passage is "＿＿＿＿＿＿".**

① How to gain friendship

② How to test courage

③ How to beat out tough guys on the street

④ How to be admitted into a sports team

⑤ How to mull over a tough situation

27 **According to Robert, what is "a more constructive way" in (가)?**

① To run with the guys

② To make friends with the guys

③ To show that he is a good athletic player

④ To subdue the toughest guy of the group

⑤ To get into a legal hassle

28 **According to the passage, what game did Robert play?**

① Boxing
② Basketball
③ Tennis
④ Football
⑤ Baseball

29 **The attitude of the guys toward Robert was ____________.**

① rather friendly
② quite hostile
③ quite indifferent
④ rather inhospitable
⑤ extremely antagonistic

30 **If we divide the passage into three paragraphs, where does the second paragraph begin?**

① (1)　　② (2)　　③ (3)　　④ (4)　　⑤ (5)

>>> 밑줄 친 곳에 들어갈 알맞은 답을 고르시오. [1~6]

1 Although all of the guests at the dinner party were ____________, the food was so poorly prepared that no one ate more than a small portion.

① elegant   ② ravenous
③ invited   ④ forewarned
⑤ surly

2 Judging from the ____________ of new talent on Broadway and the large number of revivals, we may assume that the era of the American musical is over.

① temerity   ② versatility
③ laxity   ④ verbosity
⑤ paucity

3 Again his speech was ____________. He just rattled away, boring everybody to death.

① to the point
② off the record
③ run-of-the-mill
④ straight from the horse's mouth
⑤ off the air

4 Hot milk has long been a standard cure for insomnia because of its ____________ quality.

① malevolent   ② amorphous
③ soporific   ④ plaintive
⑤ desultory

5 Her acceptance speech was ______________, eliciting thunderous applause at
several points.

① tedious   ② well-received
③ cowardly   ④ uninteresting
⑤ poorly written

6 When interest rates fall as quickly as the retired have in recent months, their
income falls, and they will be forced to spend less. ______________________.
They are too old to work, or companies may not consider them employable.
They could take more risk by moving into corporate bonds or equities. But that
strategy incurs the danger of a permanent loss of capital.

① They do not have the option of making up lost income
② They must build a castle in the air
③ They can find a change of occupation
④ They have no choice but to return to a former business
⑤ They should plan to get rich at a single bound

>>> 다음 글을 읽고 문제의 답을 고르시오.

> Although Malthus was disciple of Smith and on a number of basic issues
> sided with the Classical school, he nevertheless holds a special place as the
> consistent defender of the interests of the landed aristocracy, in opposition
> to the Classics(Smith, Ricardo, and their followers), who expressed the
> interests of the industrial bourgeoisie.

7 윗글의 내용과 일치하는 것은?

① Malthus mainly defended the interests of the bourgeoisie.
② Ricardo theoretically represented the views of the landed aristocracy.
③ Smith was one of Malthus' pupils.
④ Malthus learned a lot from Smith.
⑤ Malthus was one of the chief exponents of the Classical school.

>>> 다음 글을 읽고 문제의 답을 고르시오.

Brains in middle age, which, with life spans increased, now stretches from the 40s to late 60s, also get more easily distracted. Start boiling water for pasta, go answer the doorbell and—whoosh—all thoughts of boiling water disappear. Indeed, aging brains, even in the middle years, fall into what's called the default mode, during which period the mind wanders off and begin daydreaming. Given all this, the question arises, can an old brain learn, and then remember what it learns? Put another way, is this a brain that should be in school?

As it happens, yes. While it's tempting to focus on the flaws in older brains, that inducement overlooks how capable they've become. Over the past several years, scientists have looked deeper into how brains age and confirmed that they continue to develop through and beyond middle age.

8 **According to the passage, brains in middle age ____________.**

① are hopeless

② deteriorate rapidly

③ need to be trained

④ start producing new cells

⑤ cease to evolve

Unfortunately, the guarantee is often also a lie.

How can you recognize a quack? Sometimes it's easy because he or she offers something that we know is impossible. (1)A drink to keep you young is an example of this. But many times, these people lie, saying that their product was made because of a recent scientific discovery. (2)This makes it more difficult to know if the person is real or a fraud. Another way to recognize quackery is that many quacks will say their product is good for many different illnesses, not just for one thing. They usually like to offer money-back promises if their treatment doesn't work. (3)Finally, the fraudulent clinic will often be in another country. (4)Laws in the United States will not allow a quack to have a clinic in the United States because the quack doesn't have the proper medical training.

9 윗글의 흐름으로 보아 주어진 문장이 들어갈 가장 적절한 곳은?

① (1)　　　　　　　　② (2)
③ (3)　　　　　　　　④ (4)

>>> 다음 글을 읽고 문제의 답을 고르시오. [10~11]

I have lived through most of this century and I have traveled to the four corners of the globe. I do not think I am stuck in a white U.S.—European viewpoint: I know how it feels to be an ① underdog. I have been in various jails as a political protester, and during those five medieval years when the Germans occupied the country of my youth, Holland, and most of Europe, I was a fugitive and a "terrorist."

10 **Which of the following statements is NOT true?**

① The writer is quite old.

② The writer has traveled various places of the world.

③ The writer was in Holland when he was young.

④ The writer was a runaway in the Middle Ages.

⑤ The writer spent some part of his life in jail.

11 **Which of the following is closest in meaning to ①?**

① loser　　　　　　　② tyrant

③ undergrounder　　④ runaway

⑤ pervert

Maps don't just pinpoint sites and attractions; they influence how their readers experience a region. "They are generalizations," says geographer Mark Monmonier, "that often depict only what those who make them want you to see." In Asia and beyond, a good map—current or historical—can serve ① _________________ both an essential traveler's tool and a rich portrait of the region's past. Early Western explorers, like Macro Polo and Christopher Columbus, used maps derived ② _________________ incredible tales about Asia that were accepted as facts. A widely used 1626 map of China drawn by the Englishman John Speed was based on the writings of Marco Polo, who some historians contend never actually laid ③ _________________ on the place. ④ In Speed's map, China is drawn in the shape of a horse's head, the South China Sea is infested with monsters and the region north of the Great Wall (present-day Mongolia) is noted as a place where "men are seduced by wonderful illusions." The earliest Chinese-made world maps usually portrayed the country as a large, smooth circle surrounded by several smaller satellites.

12 Which of the following is true?

① Map-making has been one of the most empirical businesses from the beginning.

② In Speed's map, the South China Sea is noted as a place where men are seduced by wonderful illusions.

③ Speed's 1626 map of China was based on the actual drawings by Marco Polo of the regions of the country.

④ The maps which explorers like Marco Polo and Christopher Columbus used in their adventures were based on unreliable tales about Asia which no one believed to be true.

⑤ According to Mark Monmonier, the configuration of a map is often decided by what the maker wants the user to see on it.

13 **Which of the following best fits into ① and ②?**

① as - by
② as - from
③ by - to
④ before - to
⑤ for - from

14 **Which of the following best fits into ③?**

① hands
② imagination
③ eyes
④ emphasis
⑤ arms

15 **The underlined part ④ implies __________.**

① The South China Sea was a very dangerous place for travelers because of monsters.
② Speed's map cannot be said to have been the result of first-hand experience.
③ The earliest Chinese map drawers were very interested in the realistic depiction of countries other than China.
④ Northern China was a strange place where men were seduced by wonderful illusions.
⑤ None of the above.

For a week or so after the Storm, when (1) New Orleans wallowed in its filth and misery without help from (2) the United States of America, which (3) it had mistakenly believed (4) it was part of, people helped one another drag the taped-up fridges outside. Rows and rows of white metal boxes cradling generations of maggots began to fill the narrow byways of one of America's oldest cities. Waves of putrefaction rolled over the streets. New Orleans sank into the ① _______________ like a corpse into the embrace of the earth. New Orleans music and art had always been inspired by ① _______________: rotting vegetation, blooming night jasmine, the faint smell of the dead wafting from the city's above-ground cemeteries, rotting crustaceans, transpiration and sex. Now (5) here was all this ① _______________, magnified a thousand times. And here were ② all these metal tombs stretching as far as the eye could see, more numerous than the graves they resembled.

16 **Choose one word most appropriate for the three underlined blank ①.**

① inspiration   ② funk

③ integrity   ④ felicity

⑤ bliss

17 **What does the underlined ② refer to?**

① the city's graves   ② the taped-up fridges

③ rotting crustaceans   ④ blooming night jasmine

⑤ rotting vegetation

18 **Which of the following cannot be inferred from the above passage?**

① The administration might not be concerned about New Orleans' disaster.

② New Orleans was a slum for a long time.

③ Under the condition that there were no supports, the dwellers laid corpses in refrigerators.

④ New Orleans' music presented a gore atmosphere as well as no animation.

⑤ New Orleans didn't yearn for active support of the administration.

19 **Among (1), (2), (3), (4) and (5), which one differs from the others in what they refer to?**

① (1)   ② (2)
③ (3)   ④ (4)
⑤ (5)

Bill Smith said the most common form of HIV worldwide evolved from simian immunodeficiency virus, or SIV, that was in the chimpanzee. SIV genetically converted to HIV either while it was in the chimp or after a human (A) contracted SIV.

The disease did not become a worldwide menace, he said, until people left the isolated areas of Africa and carried the virus around the globe.

The findings are consistent with earlier studies that suggested that HIV originated early in 20th century and then was spread when Africa became less isolated.

Bill Smith said the date when SIV first evolved to HIV makes it "very unlikely" that a polio vaccination campaign in the late 1950s can be blamed for the rise of AIDS. Some researchers have suggested that a polio vaccine made using chimpanzee kidney cells could have transferred HIV into humans between 1957 and 1960.

Although the new research could not eliminate that possibility entirely, Bill Smith said, the fact that HIV originated before the polio vaccine means "you can probably discount (B) the scenario".

20 **The best title of this passage is _____________.**

① Spreading of HIV
② A Polio Vaccine as the source of HIV
③ Africa as the Origin of HIV
④ HIV vs. SIV
⑤ Origin of HIV

21 The underlined "contracted" in (A) is closest in meaning to ____________.

① was immunized against   ② discovered

③ inherited   ④ became infected with

⑤ detected

22 밑줄 친 (B) the scenario가 일컫는 것은?

① HIV가 소아마비 백신을 사용하기 전에 인간에게 전염되었다는 것

② HIV가 아프리카의 개방과 더불어 인간에게 급속히 퍼졌다는 것

③ HIV가 침팬지를 이용한 소아마비 백신을 통해서 인간에게 전염되었다는 것

④ HIV가 침팬지 몸에 있는 SIV를 통해 인간에게 퍼졌다는 것

⑤ HIV가 20세기에 원숭이의 바이러스를 통해 인간에게 발생했다는 것

>> 다음 글을 읽고 문제의 답을 고르시오.

It is estimated that there are nearly 5,000 gangs in the United States with a total of almost 250,000 members.

a. In my opinion, gangs are a direct result of the breakdown of the traditional family.

b. Why are all these young adults choosing to be gang members?

c. In fact, in inner cities, where gangs are most common, 7 percent of all teenagers are gang members.

23 제시문 이후 문장들이 올바른 순서로 배열된 것은?

① a - b - c

② b - c - a

③ a - c - b

④ c - b - a

>>> 다음 글을 읽고 문제의 답을 고르시오.

In the very old time, there lived a king who was a man of exuberant fancy and of an authority so irresistible that, at his will, he turned his varied fancies into facts. He was greatly given to self-communing, and when he and himself agreed upon anything, the thing was done. When everything moved smoothly, his nature was bland and genial; but whenever there was a little hitch, he was blander and more genial still, for nothing pleased him so much as to make the crooked straight, and crush down uneven places.

24 **According to the following passage, which of the following is true about the king?**

① He was generous but incompetent.
② He was so keen to construct new buildings.
③ He was determined and autocratic.
④ He dedicated himself to forgiving wrongdoers.

>>> 다음 글을 읽고 문제의 답을 고르시오.

I am passionate about the game of golf. I have played it most of my life and have spent more time than I should try to figure out what I find so intriguing about getting a small white ball into a small dark hole. I'm sure that part of the reason is the range of emotion a round of golf can bring out and the complex array of personality traits it reveals.

I have often said that I can tell more about how someone is likely to react in a business situation from one round of golf than I can from a hundred hours of meetings. Maybe golf cuts more directly to the psyche than other games and situations. Or maybe it's the venue itself—green grass and rolling hills. It's astonishing how so simple a game can reveal so much.

 윗글의 요지로서 가장 적절한 것은?

① Most businessmen are passionate about the game of golf.
② A golf course is often used for important business meetings.
③ You can get much insight about people from a round of golf.
④ You need lots of mental training to become a good golf player.

>> 다음 글을 읽고 문제의 답을 고르시오.

TV watching not only contributes to making us more violent, primarily by modelling violence as a conflict resolution strategy of first resort—it also serves to make us more frightened of the society we live in. Studies conducted by George Gerbner, founder of the Cultural Environment Movement, show that the more TV one watches, the more violent they believe the world around them to be, and hence, the less likely they are to leave their homes or interact with other people. He calls this the "Mean World Syndrome." Of course, the less people leave their homes, the more they watch TV. Hence, as they become trapped and isolated in front of their TV sets, the meaner they believe the world they no longer interact with to be.

26 **윗글에서 말하는 Mean World Syndrome이란 무엇인가?**

① The more TV people watch, the more violent they tend to become and the meaner they believe the world to be.
② More and more people show the tendency of hating their violent world.
③ The more people stay home, the more they watch TV and the more isolated they are form the world.
④ The more people watch TV, the more violent they believe the world to be and the less they interact with it.

>> 다음 글을 읽고 문제의 답을 고르시오.

"If I were to die first, would you remarry?" the wife asks. "Well," says the husband, "I'm in good health, so why not?" "Would she live in my house?" "It's all paid up, so yes." "Would she drive my car?" "It's new, so yes." "Would she use my golf clubs?" "No, she's left-handed."

27 **Which of the following CANNOT be inferred from the passage?**

① The wife will die soon.

② The wife is right-handed.

③ The husband is having an affair.

④ The husband is healthy.

28 다음 글의 흐름상 필요 없는 문장을 고르시오.

What makes college such a vital force in shaping lives? For us, college not only can prepare you for a career, but also can broaden your horizons in other ways. ① From history classes, you may develop an interest in the French Revolution. ② You may become a regular concert-goer due to a music course. ③ A literature course may help discover the authors you will be reading for most of your life. ④ In many courses, most professors share information primarily via lecture and the text.

A form of diabetes common in overweight adults is increasingly striking overweight children, says a panel convened by the American Diabetes Association. In the past, nearly all cases of childhood diabetes were Type 1, in which the body fails to make insulin. But Type 2, an obesity-related disease in which the body can't respond well to insulin, has surged in children.

The panel recommends: children aged ten or older, more than 20 percent overweight and with a family history of Type 2 diabetes should see a doctor to determine if they need testing.

Overweight children of Asian, African, South Pacific or Hispanic ancestry are at greater risk. The best Prevention: (A) an active lifestyle and healthy weight, says Dr. Alan Moses of Boston's Joslin Diabetes center. "Tell your kids to go and run around."

29 **What does the author imply by (A) "an active lifestyle"?**

① Participating in every event actively
② Going everywhere to listen to ideas about treating Type 1 diabetes
③ Searching for good medical care for Type 2 diabetes
④ Encouraging people with incurable diseases like diabetes
⑤ Getting plenty of exercise and going out for many activities

30 **According to the passage, which of the following statements is true?**

① Type 1 diabetes has not appeared so far in children.
② Type 1 diabetes has increased in children due to the failure of making insulin.
③ Children with Type 2 diabetes are responsive to insulin.
④ Children with Type 2 diabetes are mostly age ten or younger.
⑤ Type 2 diabetes is closely linked to weight problems.

>>> 밑줄 친 곳에 들어갈 알맞은 답을 고르시오. [1~6]

1 Looting is wrong and looters have no legal title to the things they

___________.

① buy   ② steal
③ sell   ④ give
⑤ seek

2 The society was not ___________ and required much help from outside.

① self-centered   ② self-indulgent
③ self-absorbed   ④ self-conscious
⑤ self-sufficient

3 At first I was blamed for damaging Dad's typewriter, but when my sister said
she was responsible, I was ___________.

① expiated   ② exonerated
③ amended   ④ set free
⑤ encroached

4 The economic stability of nations and continents is often affected by the
abundance or ___________ of precipitation.

① dearth   ② allusion
③ force   ④ condensation
⑤ rainfall

5　Knowledge of language results from the interplay of initially given structures of mind, maturational processes, and interaction with the environment. Thus there is no reason to expect that there will be ______________ properties of the knowledge that is acquired.

① invariant　　　　　② minimal
③ pointless　　　　　④ imaginative
⑤ unanimous

6　Johnnie ______________for his girlfriend the entire time she was away at camp; he didn't eat or sleep and just stared at her picture all day.

① pined　　　　　② apologize
③ precipitate　　　　　④ distill
⑤ vie

》》 다음 글을 읽고 문제의 답을 고르시오. [7~9]

Chimps and children, gulls and Greeks—the ethologists go their merry way, comparing bits of human cultural behavior with bits of genetically programmed animal behavior. True, humans are animals; they share certain anatomical features with other animals, and some items of human behavior may seem analogous to the behavior of other animals. But such analogies can seriously mislead if we fail to look at the context of a particular item of behavior. Thus one ethologist compares the presentation of a twig by a cormorant with gift-giving in humans. Yet the cormorant's twig-presentation simply inhibits attack and is comparable to other appeasement rituals found in many species. Human gift-giving differs in form and purpose not only from culture, but within the same culture in various social contexts. Everything significant about it derives from its social context. Thus, ethologists can accomplish little-beyond reminding us that we are animals— until they study humans as cultural beings.

7 **The author is primarily concerned with __________ .**

① demonstrating the usefulness of ethology in discovering the behavioral limits within which humans operate

② objecting to the degradation of humanity implicit in the ethologists' equation of humans and animals

③ pointing out the dangers inherent in comparing highly dissimilar species, such as humans and cormorants, rather than similar ones, such as humans and apes

④ refuting the idea that the appeasement rituals in human cultural behavior can be profitably subjected to ethological analysis

⑤ arguing that the ethologists' assumption that human behavior can be straight forwardly compared with animal behavior is invalid

8 **The author believes that gift-giving in humans ____________.**

① is instinctive behavior

② is analogous to appeasement rituals in other animals

③ is not an appropriate subject of study for ethologists

④ must be considered within its social context to be properly understood

⑤ may be a cultural remnant of behavior originally designed to inhibit attack

9 **The author's attitude toward contemporary ethologists can best be described as ____________.**

① puzzled　　　　　② conciliatory

③ defensive　　　　④ amused

⑤ disparaging

>> 다음 글을 읽고 문제의 답을 고르시오.

Today even the most incorrigible junk food addicts know that fats in any form are bad for their health and girth, but (1) trans fats are doubly bad for the heart. Formed when (2) liquid oils are solidified by adding hydrogen, trans fats boost bad-cholesterol (LDL) and depress good-cholesterol (HDL) levels in the blood. A recent study estimates that processed food and oils account for 80% of Americans' intake of trans fats. Researchers recommend people cut down as much as possible on (3) the fats. Another study concluded that eliminating (4) hydrogenated oils could prevent up to 100,000 premature coronary deaths a year.

10 **밑줄 친 (1)~(4) 중 가리키는 대상이 나머지 셋과 다른 것은?**

① (1)　　　　　② (2)

③ (3)　　　　　④ (4)

>> 다음 글을 읽고 문제의 답을 고르시오.

The bird dipped again slanting his wings for the dive and then swinging them wildly and ineffectually as he followed the flying fish. The old man could see the slight bulge in the water that the big dolphins raised as they followed the escaping fish. The dolphins were cutting through the water below the flight of the fish and would be in the water, driving at speed, when the fish dropped.

"It is a big school of dolphins," he thought. "They are widespread and the flying fish have little chance. The bird has no chance."

11 Which of the following is most likely to be discussed afterwards?

① The bird will catch the flying fish.
② The dolphins will attack the old man.
③ The flying fish will be caught by the dolphins.
④ The wings of the bird will be hurt by the old man.

>> 다음 글을 읽고 문제의 답을 고르시오.

Life moves in circles of power and of vividness, and each circle of life only maintains its orbit upon the subjection of some lower circle. If the lower circles of life are not mastered, there can be no higher circles. In nature, one creature devours another, and this is an essential part of all existence and of all being. It is not something to try to reform, nor something to lament over.

12 다음 글의 제목으로 가장 적절한 것은?

① The ladder of power and vividness in life
② The perpetual motion of life
③ Sacrifice; a tragedy of life
④ The stronger preying on the weak

》》 다음 글을 읽고 문제의 답을 고르시오. [13~14]

> What is good literature, what has educational value, what is refined public information, what is good art, varies with individuals as it does from one generation to another. There doubtlessly would be a contrariety of views concerning Cervantes' *Don Quixote*, Shakespeare's *Venus and Adonis*, or Zola's *Nana*. But a requirement that literature or art conform to some norm prescribed by an official smacks of an ideology foreign to our system.

13 **The writer above is discussing ____________.**
   ① how literature is created   ② censorship
   ③ limits of literature   ④ the importance of literature
   ⑤ vicissitudes of literature

14 **The writer above introduces Shakespeare's *Venus and Adonis* to make the point that ____________.**
   ① people differ on what is considered obscene in literature
   ② people should not be exposed to obscene literature
   ③ modern literature is better written
   ④ what was obscene in the past is obscene now
   ⑤ he introduces the importance of literature

>>> 다음 글을 읽고 문제의 답을 고르시오.

At the age of eighty my mother had her last bad fall, and after that her mind wandered freely through time. Some days she went to weddings and funerals that had taken place half a century earlier. On others, she presided over family dinners cooked on Sunday afternoons for children who were now gray with age.

"Where's Russell?" she asked one day when I came to visit at the nursing home.

"I'm Russell," I said.

"Russell's only this big," she said, holding her hand, palm down, two feet from the floor. That day she was a young country wife with chickens in the backyard and I was a stranger old enough to be her father.

15 **Which of the following is NOT true regarding Russell's mother?**

① She is at the nursing home.

② She remembers her father as a stranger.

③ She has some problem to recognize her son.

④ She wanders free through time after her fall.

In most areas of the world, both the physical landscape and the maps of it are relatively stable. Map revision is usually concerned with man-made features, such as buildings and roads. This is not true of Antarctica. The Antarctic ice sheet is a dynamic entity and cartographers have to contend with big and rapid changes in the physical geography of the continent. For example, earlier this year they faced the dramatic break-up of the Larsen ice shelves in the Antarctic region, which is where the British Antarctic Survey concentrates its mapping activity. Topographic maps are probably changing faster in Antarctica than anywhere else in the world.

16 **What does the break-up of the Larsen ice shelves illustrate?**

① The errors that occur on maps of the Antarctic

② The difficulties in reaching areas in the Antarctic

③ The sort of changes that can occur in the Antarctic

④ The regularity with which map-makers visit the Antarctic

>>> 다음 글을 읽고 문제의 답을 고르시오.

To what use does a kangaroo put its great heavy tail? It leans back and props itself on it, a man does on a shooting stick. Many lizards use their tails that way too. The original monster lizards, almost certainly, swung their tails as weapons, in a carry-over from the tail-swinging technique of fish. And today? Is it true that a crocodile uses its tail as a weapon? Yes. It can knock a man over with one wallop. Do any warm blooded animals do the same sort of thing? Yes again. Take an ant bear. It thwacks with its tail as powerfully as a bear with its forepaw.

※참고   shooting stick 수렵용 지팡이 | ant bear 개미핥기

17 윗글의 내용과 일치하는 것을 고르시오.

① A lizard is the only animal which can use its tail as a shooting stick.

② A kangaroo uses its tail as a tool to recline itself.

③ A monster lizard is good at the technique of transportation.

④ An ant bear like the warm blooded animals uses its tail more than a forepaw.

[I]   Taboos are associated with behavior that is considered undesirable or immoral.

[II]   One clear example of this is the way in which languages reflect cultural taboos.

[III]   We have already seen that language often mirrors its own society's values and beliefs.

[IV]   Consequently, these acts are forbidden and to be avoided.

18 위 문장들을 의미가 가장 잘 통하도록 배열한 것은?

① [I] − [III] − [IV] − [II]

② [I] − [II] − [III] − [IV]

③ [III] − [I] − [IV] − [II]

④ [III] − [II] − [I] − [IV]

》》 다음 글을 읽고 문제의 답을 고르시오. [19~21]

The complete science of 'politics' falls into two parts which may for convenience be called ethics and politics. Aristotle's ethics, no doubt, are social, and his politics are ethical; he does not forget in the Ethics that the individual man is essentially a member of society, nor in the Politics that the good life of the state exists only in the good lives of its citizens. Still, he has no doubt that there is a difference between the two enquiries. About the nature of the relationship between them he is not so clear. At the outset of the Ethics he describes the good of the state as 'greater and more perfect' than that of the individual, and the latter as merely something _________________ which we may have to put up if we cannot attain the former. But his sense of value of the individual life appears to grow as he discusses it, and at the end of the work he speaks as if the state were merely ancillary to the moral life of the individual, supplying the element of compulsion which is needed if man's desires are to be made subservient to his reason.

19 **According to the passage, which of the following statements is true?**

① Aristotle wrote the Ethics, but not the Politics.

② Aristotle didn't distinguish between ethics and politics which constitute social science.

③ Aristotle didn't lucidly specify the nature of the relationship between ethics and politics.

④ Aristotle criticized politicians, in the Politics, for pursuing a policy of conciliation.

⑤ Aristotle was the only scholar who considered ethics and politics are both social.

20 **According to the passage, what does Aristotle think at the end of the Ethics about the relationship between the state and the individual?**

① Man's desires are more important than the state's future.

② The individual must work hard to build up the power of the state.

③ The state must provide the individual with wealth and power.

④ The moral life of the individual is secondary to the good of the state.

⑤ The state is subsidiary to the moral life of the individual.

21 **밑줄 친 부분에 들어갈 가장 알맞은 것은?**

① for 　　　　② with

③ of 　　　　④ under

⑤ to

≫≫ 다음 글을 읽고 문제의 답을 고르시오 [22~24]

The common good is a term that can refer to several different concepts. In the popular meaning, the common good describes a specific "good" that is shared and beneficial for all (or most) members of a given community. This is also how the common good is broadly defined in philosophy, ethics, and political science.

However there is no strict definition of the common good for each situation. The good that is common between person A and person B may not be the same as between person A and person C. (가)＿＿＿＿＿＿＿＿, although there are some things such as the basic requirements for staying alive: food, water, and shelter—that are always good for all people.

The common good is often regarded as a utilitarian ideal, thus representing "the greatest possible good for the greatest possible number of individuals". In the best case scenario, the "greatest possible number of individuals" would mean all sentient beings. This definition of the common good presents it as a quality which is convertible, or reducible, to the sum total of all the private interests of the individual members of a society and interchangeable with them.

22　Choose the main theme of the above passage.

① The basic requirement for the utilitarian ideal

② The common good's relativity

③ How to tell the difference between private and common good

④ The absolute quality of the private interests

23　Which of the following is best for the blank (가)?

① Paradoxically the good may be unuseful.

② The common good can always be absolute.

③ Each group's opinion can be objective.

④ Thus the common good can often change.

24　According to the passage, which of the following is characteristic of common good?

① either absolute or subjective

② either objective or subjective

③ either relative or adaptable

④ neither absolute nor adaptable

>> 다음 글을 읽고 문제의 답을 고르시오. [25~26]

A lot of experimental work is being done to increase our knowledge about insomnia and other sleep-related problems in order to help people who are deprived of sleep. Some of these studies have shown that, although some people have trouble falling asleep, others have an equally difficult time waking up. It is believed that there is a natural cycle which regulates man's body temperature. During the night a person's temperature may drop one or two degrees, and it can be difficult to arouse him in the morning if his body hasn't become hot enough yet. In addition, a person awakened during a period of heavy sleep is irritable and can not think clearly. Finally, some people don't want to get up simply because they don't like the activity that awaits them.

25 **According to the passage, which of the following is NOT true?**

① In our falling asleep, our temperature may fall.

② For men to get up from bed well, some temperature will be needed.

③ Heavy sleep can cause people to be nervous.

④ Potential daily work can cause men to suffer from insomnia.

⑤ Natural phenomenon can affect men's sleeping cycle.

26 **이 글의 주제를 고르시오.**

① Our Increased Knowledge about Insomnia

② Men's Body Temperature

③ The Reasons for Insomnia

④ The Contents of Sleep Research

⑤ The Interrelation between Insomnia and Oversleeping

Christopher Finch, in his semiofficial pictorial history of Disney's work, comments: "The Mickey Mouse who hit the movie houses in the late twenties was not quite the ⓐ ______________ character most of us are familiar with today. He was mischievous, to say the least, and even displayed a ⓑ <u>streak</u> of cruelty." ⓒ ______________ Mickey soon cleaned up his act, leaving to gossip and speculation only his unresolved relationship with Minnie and the status of Morty and Ferdie. Finch continued: "Mickey … had become virtually a national symbol, and as such he was expected to behave properly at all times."

27 **Choose the most appropriate word for blank ⓐ.**

① well-known   ② well-trained

③ well-to-do   ④ well-dressed

⑤ well-behaved

28 **Choose the word closest in meaning to the underlined word ⓑ.**

① steak   ② stream

③ tendency   ④ strength

⑤ toughness

29 **Choose the most appropriate transition word for blank ⓒ.**

① Additionally   ② Therefore

③ But   ④ First

⑤ Moreover

30 **According to the passage, Mickey ______________.**

① has not been shown until the thirties

② has shown no change in character from the beginning

③ has developed its mischievousness later

④ has shown no cruelty in the beginning

⑤ has been influenced by the public opinion

MEMO

MEMO

영문독해 교재가 진화한다

READING
HUNTER

중·고급
정답 및 해설

READING HUNTER (리딩헌터) 중 · 고급
정답 및 해설

지은이 장수용
펴낸이 임준현
펴낸곳 도서출판 넥서스

출판신고 2001년 12월 5일 제313-2005-00004호
서울시 은평구 통일로82길 17
Tel (02)330-5500 Fax (02)330-5555

저자와 출판사의 허락없이 내용의 일부를 인용하거나
발췌하는 것을 금합니다.
저자와의 협의에 따라서 인지는 붙이지 않습니다.

www.nexusbook.com
넥서스ACADEMY는 도서출판 넥서스의 수험서 전문 브랜드입니다.

Part 1
유형편 정답 및 해설

01 주제·제목 | 02 요지 · 주장 | 03 연결사 | 04 특정 정보 | 05 일치 · 불일치 | 06 지칭어 · 의미 추론 | 07 추론 | 08 글의 감상 | 09 순서 배열 · 문장 삭제 · 문장 삽입 | 10 전후 문단 추론 | 11 단락의 구분 | 12 재진술 | 13 문장 완성

1 ②	2 ②	3 ③	4 ②	5 ①	6 ④	7 ④	8 ③	9 ④	10 ②
11 ②	12 ②	13 ⑤	14 ①	15 ⑤	16 ②	17 ②	18 ④	19 ④	20 ②
21 ①	22 ①	23 ②	24 ⑤	25 ③					

When we take the most distant prospect of life, what does it present to us but a chaos of unhappiness, a confused and tumultuous scene of labor and contest, disappointment and defeat? If we view past ages in the reflection of history, what do they offer to our meditation but crimes and calamities? One year is distinguished by a famine, another by an earthquake; kingdoms are made desolate, sometimes by war and sometimes by pestilence; the peace of the world is interrupted at one time by the caprices of a tyrant, at another by the rage of the conqueror. The memory is stored only with vicissitudes of evil; and the happiness, such as it is, of one part of mankind, is found to arise commonly from sanguinary success, from victories which confer upon them the power not so much of improving life by any new enjoyment as of inflicting misery on others and gratifying their own pride by comparative greatness.

1　Which of the following is the best title for the passage?

① Reflections on history
② Suffering humanity
③ A distant view of life
④ Fluctuating failure and success in life

해석 우리가 인생의 먼 미래를 내다볼 때, 불행으로 범벅이 된 혼란, 노동, 경쟁의 혼란스럽고 격정적인 장면들, 실망 그리고 패배를 제외하고 그 무엇을 우리에게 보여주는가? 만약 우리가 역사에 비친 과거를 바라볼 때, 그 과거는 범죄와 재난을 제외하면 그 무엇을 우리에게 생각나게 하는가? 한 해는 기근에 의해서, 또 다른 해에는 지진에 의해서 특징지어진다. 왕국들은 때로는 전쟁에 의하여, 때로는 역병에 의해 황폐화된다. 세계의 평화는 어떤 때는 폭군의 변덕에 의해, 또 어떤 때는 정복자의 광기에 의해 깨진다. 과거에 대한 기억은 오직 이런 저런 악의 변천과 더불어 축적해 간다. 그리고 인류의 한 부분이라고 할 수 있는 변변치 못한 행복은 흔히 피비린내 나는 성공으로부터, 즉 어떤 새로운 즐거움에 의해 삶을 향상시키는 힘이라기보다는, 오히려 남에게 비극을 안겨 주고 상대적인 위대함으로 그들 자신의 자만심을 만족시키는 힘에 의해 주어지는 승리로부터 생겨나는 것으로 여겨진다.

1　이 글의 제목을 고르시오.

① 역사에 대한 조망
② 고통 받는 인류
③ 삶의 조망
④ 삶의 동요하는 실패와 성공(흥망성쇠의 삶)

어구 prospect 전망, 예상　present 증정하다, 선물하다　chaos 혼돈, 무질서　unhappiness 불행, 비참함　confused 혼란스러운, 당황한　tumultuous 떠들썩한, 소란스러운, 거친　labor 노동, 수고, 애씀　contest 경쟁, 싸움, 논쟁　disappointment 실망　defeat 패배, 좌절　reflection 명상, 심사숙고　crime 죄, 범죄　calamity 재난, 불행　distinguish 식별하다, 분간하다　famine 식량 부족, 굶주림　earthquake 지진　kingdom 왕국　desolate 황량한, 황폐한, 고독한　pestilence 페스트, 흑사병　interrupt 가로막다, 저지하다　caprice 변덕　tyrant 폭군, 전제군주　rage 격노; (일시적) 대유행　conqueror 정복자　store 저장하다, 축적하다　vicissitude 변화, 변천, 흥망성쇠　evil 악, 사악　mankind 인류　arise (문제 등이) 일어나다, 발생하다　commonly 일반적으로, 보통으로　sanguinary 피비린내 나는, 잔인한　confer 주다, 수여하다　improve 개선하다　enjoyment 향락, 기쁨　inflict (구타 · 상처 등을) 가하다　misery 고통, 불행　gratify 만족시키다, 기쁘게 하다　comparative 비교의; 상대적인　greatness 위대함; 탁월함　humanity 인간성, 인간, 인류　fluctuating 변동이 있는, 오르내리는

해설 인생을 멀리 전망해 보면 우리 인간들은 끝없는 고통 속에서 살았다는 내용이 주제가 된다.

The more complicated our thoughts and emotions, the less effective is language as a tool of expression. This is not a simple matter of style or eloquence, for even the finest speakers and writers, using the most sensitive language, would be incapable of putting certain thoughts into words. For this reason, many people use poetry and music instead of prose. These two forms of communication convey subtle yet powerful meanings that cannot be expressed with ordinary words.

2 The best title of the passage above is

__________.

① Uses of Language
② Limitations of Language
③ The Hidden Meanings of Words
④ Words, Poetry, and Music
⑤ Subtle yet Powerful Meanings

2 윗글의 가장 적합한 제목을 고르시오.

① 언어의 이용
② 언어의 한계
③ 단어의 숨겨진 의미들
④ 단어, 시, 음악
⑤ 미묘하지만 강력한 의미들

어구 complicated 복잡한, 이해하기 어려운 tool 수단, 도구 matter 문제 eloquence 화술, 웅변, 웅변술, 말을 잘함 sensitive 감각적인, 민감한, 섬세한 put ~ into words ~을 말로 표현하다 prose 산문 convey 전달하다, 알리다 subtle 미세한, 구별하기 어려운

해설 머릿속의 복잡한 생각들을 모두 언어로 표출할 수 없다는 첫 번째와 두 번째 문장이 주제문으로서, 언어의 한계와 제한을 다룬 내용이 주제가 된다.

>>> 다음 글을 읽고 문제의 답을 고르시오. [3~4]

As an editor of a Cairo newspaper, I was given __________ late one night. Aware that there might not be a place left for it in the next day's edition, I sent it to the printer with the annotation: "space permitting". The following day it appeared in the paper and read: "… may God have mercy on him and may he be with the angels in heaven, space permitting."

3 Choose the one that best fits into the blank.

① a benediction
② a religious message
③ an obituary
④ a church bulletin
⑤ an advertisement

4 Which is the best title of the passage?

① Space Problems with Newspapers
② Misunderstood Direction
③ Religious Messages in Newspapers
④ Spaces for Annotation
⑤ Advertisement on a Wrong Newspaper

3 빈칸에 들어갈 알맞은 것을 고르시오.

① 기도 ② 종교 메시지 ③ 사망 기사 ④ 교회 공고 ⑤ 광고

4 이 글의 적합한 제목은 무엇인가?

① 신문의 공간 문제
② 곡해한 지시
③ 신문의 종교 메시지
④ 주석 공간
⑤ 그릇된 신문의 광고

어구 be given 받다 aware that S+V ~을 인식한 edition (초판·재판의) 판, 간행 annotation 주석 permitting 허락되는 한 the following day 다음날 benediction 기도, 축복 obituary 사망 기사, 사망자 약력 bulletin 게시, 공고

해설 3 마지막 문장에서 기원문의 어순을 갖춘 'May+S+본동사' 어순의 문장이 나오는데, 이 문장에서 '신이 가지고 계신 공간이 허락되면 그를(죽은 이를) 함께 천국에 있게 하시니'라는 내용이 나온다. 즉, 사망한 이에 대한 위로의 기사로 인쇄공이 오해했으므로 사망기사가 옳다.

4 "space permitting"을 쓴 편집장의 의도는 신문 공고에 위 사망기사가 등장할 공간이 없다고 생각되어 당부의 목적으로 저 문구를 쓴 것인데, 인쇄공은 종교적 메시지로 오해한 것이 이 글의 핵심이다. 따라서 지시를 잘못 판단했다는 보기 ②가 정답이다.

New technology enables monitoring of doctor's prescriptions, with both good and bad consequences: Some medical overseers use it to make sure that doctors choose the medicine that best treats patients' ailments, while others use it to pressure doctors to prescribe not the most effective drug but the cheapest one. Similarly, the existence of digital records tracking patients' medical histories can enhance treatment and promote epidemiological research, but it can also lead to invasion of patients' privacy. Computers can bring new realms into the classroom, but they may divert precious funds from more solely needed educational tools and deepen the divide between rich and poor classrooms. The list of good news-bad news effects goes on and on.

5 윗글의 제목으로 올바른 것은?

① The dilemmas in the information age
② The effective use of computers in modern education
③ How to distinguish good news and bad news
④ The impact of public policy on individual privacy

해석 새로운 기술은 의사의 처방전을 감시할 수 있도록 하는데, 이는 좋은 결과와 나쁜 결과를 모두 초래한다. 몇몇 의료 감독관들은 그 기술을 이용하여 의사들이 환자들의 질병에 가장 적합한 약을 선택하는지 확인하지만, 다른 의료 감독관들은 그것을 이용하여 가장 효과가 뛰어난 약물이 아닌 가장 저렴한 약물을 처방하도록 의사들을 압박하기도 한다. 마찬가지로, 환자의 병력을 추적하는 디지털 기록의 존재는 치료를 향상시키고 전염병 연구를 증진시킬 수 있지만, 또한 환자의 사생활을 침해할 수도 있다. 컴퓨터는 새로운 영역을 학교 현장에 제공해 주었지만 교육 현장에 필요한 유용한 도구들을 들이는 가격과 이를 맞바꾼 것일 수도 있으며, 교실 내 빈부차를 더욱 악화시킬 수 있다. 좋은 점과 나쁜 점을 동시에 갖는 이러한 예들은 끊임없이 발생한다.

5 윗글의 제목으로 올바른 것은?

① 정보화 시대의 딜레마
② 현대 교육에서 컴퓨터의 효과적인 이용
③ 좋은 소식과 나쁜 소식을 구별하는 방법
④ 개인 사생활에 대한 공공정책의 영향

어구 prescription 처방(전); 명령, 규정; 법규 ailment 질병 pressure A to R A로 하여금 ~하도록 압력을 가하다 epidemiological 전염병(학)의 invasion 침임, 침해 realm 범위, 영역; 왕국 divert 딴 데로 돌리다, 전환시키다, 기분을 전환시키다

해설 이 글은 현대 사회에서 의료계, 교육 분야의 신기술로 인한 장점과 단점을 동시에 다루고 있으므로, 정보화 시대의 딜레마가 제목으로서 합당하다.

>>> 다음 글을 읽고 물음에 답하시오. [6~7]

Since 9/11 world technology often has been our crucial but silent partner in helping us to ramp up our law enforcement and national security capabilities. But we also need to right. The marriage of information-gathering technology with information storing technology, manipulated in increasingly sophisticated databases, is beginning to produce the defining privacy challenge of the information age. We are (가) ＿＿＿＿＿＿ the verge of an age of a revolution in the capability for the highly detailed, largely automatic, widespread surveillance of our daily lives. Moreover, other powerful new technologies are (나) ＿＿＿＿＿＿ the horizon, like sensor technology and nanotechnology. We need to think about these issues broadly while keeping them (다) ＿＿＿＿＿＿ overtaking our civil liberties. Who will have access to those data banks, and (라) ＿＿＿＿＿＿ what checks-and-balances? In what cases should law enforcement agencies be able to use this information, and what safeguards should apply? There should be a general presumption that Americans can know when their personal information is collected, and to see, check and correct any errors.

해석 9/11테러 이후 세계의 기술력은 법 집행과 국가 안보를 책임지는 중요하지만 조용한 동반자였다. 그러나 우리는 바로 잡아야 할 필요가 있다. 정보 수집 기술과 정보 축적 기술의 결합이 점점 더 정교한 데이터베이스 속에서 조작되면서 정보화 시대의 결정적인 사생활 문제를 야기하기 시작했다. 우리는 매우 상세한, 대부분 자동적으로, 만연하게 우리 일상생활을 감시하는 능력을 갖춘 혁명의 시대 직전에 있다. 더욱이 센서 기술과 나노 기술과 같은 다른 강력한 새로운 기술들이 등장하고 있다. 이러한 문제들이 우리의 시민의 자유를 추월하지 못하게 하면서(보다 더 중요시되지 않도록 하면서) 이 문제들을 폭넓게 생각할 필요가 있다. 누가 그리고 어떤 견제와 균형 하에서 데이터 뱅크에 접근할 수 있을까? 어느 경우에 법 집행 기관이 이 정보를 이용할 수 있고, 어떤 보호가 적용될까? 미국인들은 언제 그들의 정보가 수집되는지를 알고, 또는 그것들을 확인·점검하며 어떤 잘못된 점이라도 수정할 수 있어야 한다는 일반적인 추정을 하고 있다.

6 이 글에 알맞은 제목은 다음 중 무엇인가?

① 시민의 자유
② 국가 안보 능력
③ 일상생활의 감시
④ 정보화 시대의 사생활 침해

7 (가)~(라)의 빈칸에 가장 알맞은 것은?

6 Which of the following is the best title for the passage?

① Civil Liberties
② National Security Capabilities
③ Surveillance of Our Daily Lives
④ Privacy Challenge of the Information Age

7 Which of the following best fits into the blanks from (가) to (라)?

① in - on - from - by
② on - in - from - by
③ in - on - for - under
④ on - on - from - under

The Constitution embodies the ideology's view of man and of government in its relationship to man. People have both rights and interests: government must respect the former; and it should permit the individualistic pursuit of the latter so long as either national unity or basic rights are not infringed. The polity would be failing if striving individuals were unable to advance their interests within it—or if they were able to be too successful, since every special interest is inherently "activated by some common impulse or passion adverse to the rights of other citizens, or to the permanent and aggregate interest of the community", as James Madison put it in The Federalist Papers. The balance must be found in an elaborate social-political pluralism where no group or interest can get too strong. Underlining the entire constitutional arrangement then as now is the classical liberal distrust of power as a threat to the sovereign individual. The answer to this problem of power: ______________ .

8 필자는 ______________ 에 대해 이야기하고 있다.

① 헌법의 기원
② 미국인들의 개인주의
③ 헌법의 정신
④ 사회와 정치의 다원주의

9 밑줄 친 부분에 알맞은 것을 고르시오.

① 권력을 증가해서 강화하는 것
② 권력을 만들고 유지하는 것
③ 권력을 인식하고 이용하는 것
④ 권력을 분산시키고 제한하는 것

8 The author is talking about ____________.

① the original of the Constitution
② the American individualism
③ the spirit of the Constitution
④ the social-political pluralism

9 Choose the one which can be used in the underlined part.

① raise it and reinforce it
② make it and keep it
③ recognize it and use it
④ disperse it and limit it

어구 constitution 헌법 embody 포함하다, 구체화하다, 구체적으로 나타내다, 통합하다 interests 이익, 이해(관계) pursuit 추구 so long as ～하는 한 unity 일치, 통일성, 일관성 infringe 위반하다 polity 통치 구조, 국가 조직 strive 노력하다, 애쓰다, 분투하다 inherently 본질적으로 activate 활발하게 하다 adverse 적대적인, 반대의 aggregate 모으다; 합계의 put 표현하다 The Federalist Papers 연방백서 elaborate 정교한, 정성 들인 pluralism 다원주의 underline 강조하다 constitutional arrangement 헌법상의 협정 classical 전형적인, 모범적인, 최고급의 liberal 공정한, 자유주의의 sovereign 주권이 있는 reinforce 강화하다 disperse 분산시키다

해설 **8** 시민들의 권리의 공동체의 이해관계에 대한 조화는 사회와 정치 간의 정교한 다원화에서 이루어진다고 했는데, 이것이 이 글의 주제가 된다. 이는 즉 권력의 집중화를 막고 권력을 분산시키겠다는 것인데, 이것이 헌법의 정신이 된다. 따라서 권력의 분산이라는 내용을 포함하고 있는 '헌법의 정신'이 정답이다.
9 권력의 문제를 해결한다는 내용은 결국 집중화를 막는 것이며, 이는 다시 권력을 분산시키고 제한하는 내용이다.

The prime ministers of Russia and Ukraine finally reached an agreement Sunday morning. They agreed to resume gas supplies to Europe by early next week. The two leaders have asked the gas providers of their respective countries to prepare by Monday all pertinent documents that need to be signed. The two premiers agreed that Russia would give Ukraine a 20 percent discount on the gas purchase. In exchange, Ukraine will not hike the fees it charged Russia to transport gas onward to European countries.

10 윗글의 제목으로 가장 적절한 것을 고르시오.

① Problems with Gas Supplies in Russia and Ukraine
② Russia and Ukraine Agree to Resume Gas Flow
③ The Result of Gas Shutoff in Russia and Ukraine
④ Conditions of Providing Gas for Russia and Ukraine

해석 러시아 수상과 우크라이나 수상은 일요일 아침에 마침내 합의에 도달했다. 다음 달 초까지 유럽에 가스 공급을 다시 시작하기로 동의한 것이다. 그 두 정상은 각 국가의 가스 공급업체들에게 서명을 필요로 하는 모든 관련 문서를 월요일까지 준비하도록 요청했다. 두 수상은 러시아가 우크라이나에게 가스 구입의 20퍼센트를 할인해 주기로 동의했다. 그에 대한 답례로 우크라이나는 유럽 국가들로 가는 가스에 대해 러시아에 부과했던 운송비를 인상하지 않을 것이다.

10 윗글의 제목으로 가장 적절한 것을 고르시오.
① 러시아와 우크라이나의 가스 공급에 대한 문제
② 러시아와 우크라이나가 가스 공급 재계약에 합의하다.
③ 러시아와 우크라이나의 가스 (공급) 중단의 결과
④ 러시아와 우크라이나에 가스를 공급하는 조건

어구 reach an agreement 합의에 도달하다 resume 다시 시작하다; 되찾다; (자리 따위를) 다시 차지하다[점유하다] pertinent 관련 있는; 타당한 premier (영국 · 프랑스 등의) 수상(prime minister); 국무총리; (캐나다 · 오스트레일리아의) 주지사 in exchange 답례로; 그 대신 flow (전기 · 가스의) 공급; 흐름 shutoff 멈춤, 차단, 마감

해설 러시아와 우크라이나가 가스 공급 계약을 맺는 합의를 보았다는 내용이 주제가 된다.

We must review the threat of flunking and see it as it really is. It is an expression of confidence by both teachers and parents that the students have the ability to learn the material presented to them. However, making it work again would take a dedicated, caring conspiracy between teachers and parents. It would mean facing the tough reality that passing kids who haven't learned the material—while it might save them grief for the short term—dooms them to long-term illiteracy. It would mean that teachers would have to follow through on their threats, and parents would have to stand behind them, knowing their children's best interests are indeed at stake. This means no more doing Scott's assignments for him because he might fail. No more passing Jodi because she is such a nice kid. This is a policy that worked in the past and can work today. A wise teacher, with the support of parents, gave our sons and daughters the opportunity to succeed—or fail. It is time that we returned this choice to all students.

11 윗글의 제목을 고르시오.

① How to Correct Students' Wrongdoings
② Failure as a Positive Teaching Tool
③ Relationship Between Teachers and Parents
④ How to Control Students' Lives

World War II cost the American people more than $300 billion. To finance it, Congress raised income taxes. Also, Congress made employers withhold taxes from workers' paychecks. War bond purchases accounted for nearly two-thirds of government war revenues. The government made it patriotic to buy war bonds. Americans heard and saw daily appeals to buy bonds in newspapers, on the radio, and at the movies. Famous entertainers such as Kate Smith, Jane Froman, Al Johnson, Frank Sinatra, Bob Hope, and Bing Crosby staged bond rallies around the country.

12 What is the topic of the passage?

① The contribution of entertainment industry during World War II
② Financial sources of America's expense during the war
③ The origin of government bonds in the American history
④ Economic changes in America after the end of World War II

해석 우리는 낙제의 위협을 재검토하고, 있는 그대로 그것을 보아야 한다. 학생이 주어진 자료를 배울 수 있는 능력이 있다는 것은 교사와 부모 모두가 확신하고 있다. 그러나 이것이 반복해서 효과를 가지려면 교사와 부모가 헌신적으로 세심하게 협력을 해야 한다. 자료를 학습하지 못한 아이를 통과시키는 것은 단기적으로는 아이가 슬퍼하지 않을 수 있지만, 장기적으로는 그 아이를 문맹으로 만들 어려운 운명에 처한다는 것을 의미한다. 그것은 교사들이 학생들에게 위협을 계속 가해야 한다는 것이고, 자식들에게 득이 되는 상태가 풍전등화에 놓인 것을 안다면 부모들은 교사를 지지해야 하는 것을 의미한다. 이것은 더 이상 스콧이 낙제할지도 모르기 때문에 숙제를 대신해 주는 것이 아니며, 조디가 좋은 아이니까 그냥 통과시키는 것도 아니다. 이것은 과거와 현재에 모두 효과적인 방식이다. 과거에는 현명한 교사가 부모의 도움을 받아 우리의 자식들에게 성공하거나 실패할 기회를 주었다. 이제는 우리가 이러한 선택을 모든 학생들에게 돌려주어야 할 때이다.

11 윗글의 제목을 고르시오.

① 학생의 비행을 교정하는 방법　　② 긍정적인 교육 수단으로서의 실패
③ 교사와 부모 간의 관계　　④ 학생들의 생활을 통제하는 방법

어구 **flunk** 실패하다; 낙제점을 따다[매기다]; 단념하다　**as it is** 있는 그대로　**work** 효과가 있다　**dedicated** 일신을 바친, 헌신적인　**caring** 돌보는; 상냥함　**conspiracy** 협력; 공모　**save grief** 슬픔을 덜어 주다　**for the short term** 단기간 동안　**doom** ～의 운명을 정하다　**follow through** ～을 계속하다　**stand behind** ～을 지지하다　**at stake** 성패가 달려 있는; 관련된; 위태로운

해설 이 글은 낙제(flunking=failure) 제도의 장점에 대해 부각하는 내용이 주제가 된다.

해석 2차 세계 대전으로 인해 미국인들은 3천억 달러 이상을 소비했다. 그 비용을 조달하기 위해 의회는 소득세를 증가시켰다. 또한 의회는 고용주들이 직원들의 임금에서 세금을 공제하게 했다. 전시 공채는 정부의 전시 세수입의 거의 2/3를 차지했다. 정부는 전시 공채를 구입하는 것이 국가에 봉사하는 것으로 만들었다. 미국인들은 신문, 라디오, 영화에서 전시 공채를 구입하라고 매일같이 호소하는 내용을 듣고 보았다. 케이트 스미스, 제인 프로먼, 알 존슨, 프랭크 시나트라, 밥 호프와 빙 크로스비와 같은 유명 연예인들은 미국 전역에서 전시 공채 집회에 참여했다.

12 이 글의 주제는 무엇인가?

① 2차 세계 대전 동안 연예계 분야의 공헌
② 전쟁 기간 동안 미국 소비 자원
③ 미국 역사에서 국채의 기원
④ 2차 세계 대전 종식 후 미국의 경제 변화

어구 **finance** ～의 비용을 조달하다　**income taxes** 소득세　**withhold** 공제하다, (승낙 등을) 보류하다　**war bond purchases** 전시 공채　**patriotic** 애국의　**stage** (파업·정치 운동·군사 작전 등을) 계획하다, 해내다, 행하다; 상연하다

해설 첫 문장이 주제문으로서, 3천억 달러라는 전쟁 비용의 자금 충당에 대한 방법·수단이 이 글의 주제가 된다. 이하에서 '노동자의 임금 공제', '전시 공채 구입 유도', '연예인을 통한 홍보'가 수단으로 열거되고 있다.

>>> 다음 글을 읽고 문제의 답을 고르시오. [13~14]

Reid Hilton's new arm is only slightly less remarkable than the Six Million Dollar Man's atomic-powered limb. Hilton, 24, a karate expert who lost his right arm below the elbow in an accident, will probably not risk smashing bricks with his experimental $40,000 replacement. But the artificial limb should enable him to function like a man with two ① _______________ arms. The controls of the myoelectric arm are directly connected to the nerves in the stump of his severed arm. Unlike most other ② _______________ arms and hands, it is also equipped with feed-back devices that give him a sense of touch.

13 The best title of this passage would be

_______________.

① Atomic-Powered Arm
② A Karate Expert
③ The Nerves of a Severed Arm
④ Feedback Devices
⑤ The $40,000 Arm

14 Which of the following pairs best fits into ① and ②?

① natural - artificial
② natural - aesthetic
③ man-made - aesthetic
④ artificial - aesthetic
⑤ man-made - artificial

해석 레이드 힐튼 씨의 새 팔은 육백만 달러 사나이의 원자력 팔보다 아주 약간만 덜 놀라울 뿐이다. 24세의 힐튼은 사고로 오른팔 팔꿈치 아래를 잃은 가라데 전문가이며, 아마도 실험적인 4만 달러나 되는 대체물로 벽돌을 부셔 버릴 위험을 무릅쓰지 않을 것이다. 그러나 인조 팔은 그로 하여금 원래 두 팔이 있는 사람처럼 기능할 수 있게 해야 한다. 보철 장치를 전기로 움직이는 팔을 조종하는 컨트롤 장비들이 그의 잘린 팔의 다른 부분 신경에 직접 연결되어 있다. 대부분의 다른 인공 팔, 손과는 다르게 그의 팔에는 촉각을 전달하는 귀환 장치들이 갖추어져 있다.

13 가장 적절한 제목을 고르시오.

① 원자력 팔
② 가라데 전문가
③ 잘려 나간 팔의 신경들
④ 귀환 장비들
⑤ 4만 달러의 팔

14 ①과 ②에 각각 알맞은 것을 고르시오.

① 자연적인 – 인공의
② 자연적인 – 심미적인
③ 인조의 – 심미적인
④ 인공의 – 심미적인
⑤ 인조의 – 인공의

어구 **slightly** 약간, 조금 **atomic-powered** 원자력의 **limb** 수족, 손발 **karate** 가라데 **elbow** 팔꿈치 **smash** 박살내다, 부딪히다 **brick** 벽돌 **replacement** 교체물, 교체자 **function** 작용하다, 역할을 다하다 **myoelectric** 보철 장치를 전기로 움직이는 **stump** (손이나 발의) 잘리고 남은 부분, 그루터기 **severed** 절단된 **feed-back** 피드백, 귀환(생체(生體) 기구에 있어서 다른 환경에 대한 적응 기능) **artificial** 인공의, 부자연스러운 **aesthetic** 미의, 심미적인 **man-made** 인조의, 인공의, 합성의

해설 13 이 글은 사고를 통해 자신의 팔을 잃은 레이드 힐튼 씨의 4만 달러의 비용이 든 인공 팔의 기능 및 그 구성 장비를 설명하는 내용이 주제가 되므로, '(힐튼 씨의) 4만 달러의 팔'이 제목으로서 합당하다.

14 ①빈칸에는 '인공 팔이 본래의 팔과 같은 기능을 수행한다'는 논리가 적합하며, ②빈칸에는 주절에 '신경까지 전달해 준다는 (특수) 장비'를 설명하므로 (보통의 일반적인) '인공 팔'을 의미한다고 볼 수 있다.

The shift from boom to depression came gradually and unevenly to Western Europe in the years around 1300. From the early fourteenth century through much of the fifteenth, a number of related trends—shrinking population, contracting markets, an end to the long process of land reclamation, and a creeping mood of pessimism and retrenchment—resulted in a general economic slump and a deepening of social antagonism. These trends were _____________ universal. They were less marked in northern Italy than elsewhere, and north of the Alps certain localities, profiting from favorable commercial situations or technological advances, became more prosperous than before. At a time when English towns were generally declining, Coventry and a few others grew wealthy from the rise of woolen cloth production.

15 윗글의 제목으로 가장 적합한 것을 고르시오.

① Technological Advances in European Cities in the Late Middle Ages
② General Economic Depression in European Cities in the Late Middle Ages
③ Prosperous European Cities and Markets in the Late Middle Ages
④ Declining European Cities and Shrinking Population in the Late Middle Ages
⑤ Different Economic Situations in European Cities in the Late Middle Ages

16 빈칸에 적합한 단어나 숙어를 고르시오.

① quite
② by no means
③ extremely
④ nevertheless
⑤ not merely

해석 경기 호황에서 경기 침체의 변화는 1300년쯤에 수년 간 서유럽에서 점진적이고 불균형적으로 발생하였다. 14세기 초반부터 15세기의 상당 기간을 거치며 감소하는 인구, 위축되는 시장, 오랜 토지 개간 과정의 종료와 기어들어오는 비관주의와 후퇴의 분위기 같은 연관성 있는 많은 추세들은 전반적인 경제 침체와 사회적 적대감의 심화를 야기했다. 그러나 이러한 경향들은 결코 보편적인 것이 되지 못했다. 이러한 경향들은 다른 그 어느 지역보다 북부 이탈리아에서는 더 두드러진 특징이 되지 못했고, 알프스 북부의 몇몇 지역들은 순조로운 상업적 상황 또는 기술 발전의 혜택을 받으며 이전보다 더 번창하게 되었다. 영국의 소도시들이 점차적으로 쇠퇴하고 있었을 때, 코번트리(영국 지방 소도시)와 몇몇 다른 지역들은 양모 생산의 증가를 통해 부유해졌다.

15 윗글의 제목으로 가장 적합한 것을 고르시오.

① 중세시대 후기 유럽 도시들의 기술 발전
② 중세시대 후기 유럽 도시들의 보편화된 경제 침체
③ 중세시대 후기의 번창한 유럽 도시들과 시장
④ 중세시대 후기의 쇠퇴하는 유럽 도시들과 위축된 인구
⑤ 중세시대 후기 유럽 도시들의 다양한 경제적 상황

16 빈칸에 적합한 단어나 숙어를 고르시오.

① 매우
② 결코 ~이 아니다
③ 극단적으로
④ 그럼에도 불구하고
⑤ 꼭 ~한 것은 아니다

어구 **shift** 변천, 교체, 임시변통; 이동하다　**unevenly** 고르지 않게, 불균형적으로　**around** 대략　**a number of** 수많은　**related** 관련된　**shrinking** 위축된　**contracting** 수축성 있는, 계약의, 결혼의　**land reclamation** 토지 개간　**creeping** 기어 돌아다니는, 느린　**retrenchment** 축소, 단축　**deepening** 심화　**antagonism** 적대(관계)　**marked** 두드러진　**elsewhere** (어딘가) 다른 곳에서　**locality** 위치, 장소　**profit** 득을 보다, 이윤을 얻다　**favorable** 유리한, 좋은, 호의를 보이는　**prosperous** 번영하는, 번창하는　**woolen cloth** 양모　**quite** 완전히, 아주, 전혀, 매우, 확실히　**by no means** 결코 ~이 아니다　**extremely** 매우, 극단적으로　**not merely** 꼭 ~한 것은 아니다

해설 **15** 첫 문장이 주제문으로서, '서유럽에서 경제의 변화가 일관되지 못했다는 내용'이 주제가 된다. 이하에서 어떤 지역에서는 인구 감소, 시장 위축과 같은 불황을 겪었지만, 알프스 북부 지역에서는 상업과 기술의 발전이 있었다고 설명하므로, 다양한 경제적 상황이 핵심어로서 옳다.
16 앞 문장까지 위치한 지역에서는 경제 침체와 사회적 적대감이 만연했지만, 빈칸이 제시된 다음 문장부터는 알프스 북부 지역과 같은 곳에서 '발전'의 혜택을 이루었다고 했으므로, '이러한 경향(경제 침체와 사회적 적대감)'이 결코 보편적인 것은 아니라는 부정의 내용이 옳다.

"Most of us are taught to watch money, but not to value time", says Andrea Steenhouse. "As a result, we may not even think about how much irreplaceable time we waste to save a few pennies." Is it worthwhile _______________, searching for picture hangers, when the neighborhood hardware-store owner would point to them immediately? To wait for takeout at the restaurant when delivery is available for a small tip? Rather than dismiss the idea with the words "I can't afford that," it may pay to think twice.

17 Choose the one that best fits into the blank.

① to try to save time while you don't have much to do
② to wander through a giant discount mart
③ to spend lots of money that you have
④ to compare all different kinds of hardware
⑤ to ask a manager of a department store to get quotes

18 Which is the best title for this passage?

① Money Is as Important as Time.
② Picture Hangers Cost You More than You Think.
③ Buy What You Want Whatever It Costs.
④ Don't Save Pennies and Waste Hours.
⑤ Think Twice before You Buy Hardware.

해석 앤드리아 스틴하우스는 "우리들 대부분은 돈을 경계하라고 배웠지만, 시간을 소중히 여기라고 배우지는 않는다."라고 말한다. "그 결과 푼돈을 절약하기 위해 우리는 둘도 없는 많은 시간을 낭비하고 있다는 생각조차 하지 못하고 있는 것일 수도 있다." 이웃 철물점의 주인이 그림걸이를 즉시 찾아주는데, 그것들을 찾기 위해 대형 할인매장을 돌아다니는 것이 과연 가치가 있겠는가? 약간의 팁만 지불하면 배달도 가능한데, 레스토랑에서 음식을 사 가지고 가기 위해 요리 시간을 기다리는 것도 (가치가 있겠는가)? "난 그럴 여유 돈이 없어."라는 말로 그런 생각을 무시하기보다는, 두 번 생각하는 것이 이롭겠다.

17 빈칸에 들어갈 알맞은 것은?

① 할 일이 많지 않은 동안에는 시간을 아끼도록 노력하는 것
② 대형 할인매장을 배회하는 것
③ 보유하고 있는 많은 돈을 쓰는 것
④ 다른 모든 종류의 철물을 비교하는 것
⑤ 백화점 매니저에게 견적서를 부탁하는 것

18 이 글의 가장 올바른 제목은?

① 돈은 시간만큼 중요하다.
② 그림걸이는 당신 생각 이상으로 비용이 많이 든다.
③ 비용이 얼마가 들든지 간에 당신이 원하는 물건을 구입하시오.
④ 푼돈을 아끼지 말고 시간을 허비하지 마시오.
⑤ 철물을 구입하기 전에 두 번 생각하시오.

어구 **watch** 경계하다 **value** 존중하다 **as a result** 그 결과 **irreplaceable** 바꿔 놓을 수 없는, 둘도 없는 **a few pennies** 푼돈들 **it is worthwhile to R** ~하는 것이 가치가 있다 **search for** 찾다, 구하다 **hanger** 걸이, 매다는 것 **hardware-store** 철물점 **point to** ~을 가리키다 **takeout** 사 가지고 가는 요리 **be available for** ~을 이용할 수 있다, 유효하다 **dismiss** 무시하다 **pay** 이롭다, 수지가 맞다 **wander through** 배회하다 **giant discount mart** 대형 할인 매장 **quote** 견적서, 인용

해설 **17** 이하의 문장을 보건대, 빈칸이 위치한 문장의 내용은 형태는 긍정일지라도 내용은 완전 부정을 의미하는 '수사의문문'이다. 대형 할인매장에 가서 이것저것 찾아보느라 시간을 낭비하느니, 근처에 위치한 철물점에 가서 그림걸이 정도는 쉽게 구입이 가능하다는 내용이 가장 적합하다.
18 시간을 낭비할 경우가 생긴다면 푼돈 정도는 아끼지 말라는 내용이 이 글의 주제가 된다.

Procrastinators are people who have a chronic habit of putting things off, usually until the last minute and sometimes until it is too late altogether. The most common reason that procrastinators themselves give for their habit, which they are usually quite willing to talk about even if not willing to change, is that they are lazy. Other typical excuses are that they are undisciplined, brilliant but disorganized, or very poor at organizing their time.

Some procrastinators, however, almost against their very nature, actually get as far as trying to do something about their problem and seek help. Recent research with such people seems to suggest that their difficulties are much more complex than the procrastinators themselves think. The general conclusions are that such people have a vulnerable sense of self-worth, are particularly fearful of failure, and deliberately put things off precisely so that they never leave themselves time to produce their best work. The reason for their delaying tactics is that, since they do everything at the last moment and under pressure, the procrastinators can retain their illusion of brilliance without ever having to put it to the test.

19 The first paragraph is mainly concerned with

___________.

① the undisciplined character of procrastinators
② that disorganization is the procrastinator's main problem
③ procrastinators' willingness to talk a lot
④ the nature of procrastination

20 The second paragraph is mainly concerned with ___________.

① that procrastinators always leave everything until the last moment
② research findings regarding procrastinators
③ how some procrastinators never seek help
④ how procrastinators have an illusion of brilliance

21 The best title of the passage above is

___________.

① Procrastination: Excuses and Reality
② Disorganization, the True Cause of Procrastination
③ Procrastination: Never Do Today What You Can Put Off Until Tomorrow
④ The Cure for Procrastination

해석 시간을 미루는 사람들은 대개 마지막 순간까지 또는 정말로 너무나 늦을 때까지 일을 지연시키는 고질적인 습관을 가진 사람들이다. 일을 질질 끄는 사람들이 보통 고칠 마음조차도 없다고 말하는 그 습관에 대해 스스로 얘기하는 가장 흔한 핑계는 그들이 게으르다는 것이다. 다른 일반적인 핑계는 그들이 훈련을 받지 않았으며, 총명하지만 무질서하거나, 또는 시간 계획을 세우는 데 매우 서툴다는 것이다.

그러나 그와 같이 시간을 미루는 이들은 그들의 그러한 성격과는 다르게도, 실제로 그들의 문제에 대해 무엇인가를 해보려고 하기도 하며 도움을 청하기도 한다. 이러한 사람들에 관한 최근의 연구가 시사해 주기를, 그들의 곤란한 사항들은 자신이 생각하는 것보다 훨씬 더 복잡하다. 일반적인 결론은 그와 같은 사람들이 자신의 가치에 대해 상처받기 쉬운 감정을 가지고 있으며, 특히 실패를 무서워하며, 그들은 스스로 최선의 작업을 할 시간을 결코 남겨 두지 않기 위하여 일부러 일을 정확하게 연기한다. 시간 지연 전술의 이유는 시간을 미루는 이들이 마지막 순간에 압박을 받으며 모든 일을 하기 때문에, 그들은 자신들이 총명하다는 것을 검증할 필요가 전혀 없이 총명하다는 망상을 가질 수가 있다는 것이다.

19 첫 단락의 주제는?

① 시간을 지연하는 이들의 훈련받지 못한 특징
② 혼란이 시간을 지연하는 이들의 주된 문제점이라는 사실
③ 시간을 지연하는 이들의 말을 많이 하려는 의지
④ 시간 지연의 특징

20 두 번째 단락의 주제는?

① 시간을 지연하는 이들이 항상 마지막 순간까지 모든 것을 남겨 놓는다는 사실
② 시간을 지연하는 이들에 관한 연구 결과들
③ 몇몇 시간을 지연하는 이들이 결코 도움을 구하려 하지 않는 상태
④ 시간을 지연하는 이들이 총명함이라는 망상을 갖고 있는 상태

21 이 글의 제목은?

① 시간 지연: 핑계들과 현실
② 시간 지연의 주된 원인이 되는 혼란
③ 시간 지연: 오늘 할 수 있는 일을 결코 내일까지 미루지 마시오.
④ 시간 지연의 치료책

어구 procrastinator 시간을 미루는 사람, 일을 질질 끄는 사람 **chronic** 고질적인, 만성적인 **put off** 미루다, 연기하다 **last minute** 마지막 순간 **altogether** 아주, 전부 **lazy** 게으른 **typical** 전형적인, 모범적인 **undisciplined** 훈련받지 않은 **brilliant** 영리한, 화려한 **disorganized** 무질서한, 지리멸렬한 **be poor at** ~에 서툴다 **complex** 복잡한 **vulnerable** 취약한

해설 **19** 시간 지연을 야기하는 이들의 이유가 그들이 훈련을 받지 못했으며, 총명하지만 무질서하고, 시간 계획을 세우는 것이 서툴다는 본질을 설명하므로, 시간 지연의 본질이 첫 단락의 주제로서 옳다.

20 두 번째 단락의 주제는 시간 지연을 야기하는 이들에 대한 성격과 감정, 시간 지연의 이유에 대한 최근 연구 결과를 나타낸다는 것이다.

21 시간을 지체시키는 이유에 관해 시간 지체자들의 입장과 객관적인 연구 결과 모두를 설명하므로, 핑계와 (객관적인 연구를 통해 드러난) 현실이 제목으로서 가장 옳다.

Hurricane Katrina's effect on the city of New Orleans has been _____________. Almost four years after the storm, a quarter of the population has never returned. A third of homes still lie empty, many decked with tarpaulins and with the flood-line still visible. Residential streets are lined with houses with collapsing porches, fallen plasterwork and hopeful For Sale signs. Less than half the city's public transport facilities have been restored, and the wheels on the city's famous street-cars, even the one named Desire, are still rusty.

Most important, though the number of the chronically sick in the city has risen sharply, medical services remain in tatters. Only 57% of the city's medical facilities have reopened, and tens of thousands of records have been lost. In St Bernard Parish, which once had two hospitals, there is now none. Charity Hospital, the main refuge for the poor and uninsured for more than 250 years, is shuttered and surrounded by wire fencing.

22 윗글의 제목은 무엇인가?

① New Orleans: City of Sickness
② People vs. Nature
③ A Ray of Hope in New Orleans
④ A Typical Example of No Preparation

23 빈칸에 들어갈 말로 가장 올바른 것은?

① underestimated by the politicians
② much longer-lasting than most expected
③ influencing the people's state of mind
④ forgotten by the people who moved out

해석 허리케인 카트리나가 뉴올리언스에 미친 영향은 대부분의 사람들이 예상했던 것보다 훨씬 더 오랫동안 지속되고 있다. 태풍이 지나간 지 거의 4년이 지났지만, 인구의 1/4이 그들 원래의 거주지로 복귀하지 못했다. 가구의 1/3이 여전히 빈 상태이고, 많은 집들이 방수포로 뒤덮여 있으며 홍수에 잠겼던 흔적이 선명하다. 거주 구역에는 무너진 현관, 떨어져 나간 벽타일, "팝니다"라고 적힌 희망의 표지판들이 있는 집들이 줄지어 있다. 뉴올리언스의 명물인 전차들 중 절반 미만이 아직도 녹이 슬어 있다.

가장 중요한 것은, 도시 내에서 만성질환에 시달리는 사람의 수가 급격히 증가했음에도 불구하고 의료 서비스가 아직도 잘 시행되지 않는다는 것이다. 도시의 의료 시설 중에서 57%만이 재개장했고, 수만 개의 진료 기록들이 사라졌다. 세인트 버나드 패리시에는, 한때 두 개의 병원이 있었지만, 지금은 한 개도 없다. 250년 이상 가난하고 의료 보험을 못 받은 사람들이 주로 의존하던 곳인 자선 병원은 지금 문이 닫혀 있으며 철책으로 둘러싸여 있다.

22 윗글의 제목은 무엇인가?

① 뉴올리언스: 아픈 도시
② 인간 대 자연
③ 뉴올리언스의 희망의 빛
④ 무방비 상태의 전형적인 예

23 빈칸에 들어갈 말로 가장 올바른 것은?

① 정치인들에 의해 과소평가된
② 대부분의 사람들이 예상했던 것보다 훨씬 더 오래 지속된
③ 사람들의 정신 상태에 영향을 미친
④ 이사를 간 사람들에 의해 잊혀진

어구 **lasting** 지속되는　**empty** 텅 빈; 허기를 느끼는　**deck** 장식하다　**tarpaulin** 방수포　**flood-line** 홍수의 흔적　**visible** 명백한, 분명한　**be lined with** 나란히 세워져 있다　**collapsing** 무너지는　**porch** 현관, 차 대는 곳　**plasterwork** 미장 공사　**facility** 편의 시설; 용이함　**rusty** 녹슨　**chronically** 만성적으로　**tatter** 누더기 옷　**refuge** 피난처　**uninsured** 보험을 받지 못한　**wire fencing** 철책　**typical** 전형적인; 모범의

해설 **22** 뉴올리언스가 카트리나 허리케인의 영향으로 인해 회복되지 못하고 있음을 말하는 것이 이 글의 주제이다.

23 글 전체에서 뉴올리언스의 회복 속도가 너무 느리고 그 전망 또한 좋지 못한 점을 밝히고 있기 때문에 첫 문장의 내용 또한 예상했던 것보다 허리케인의 영향이 훨씬 더 오래 지속된다는 논리가 옳다.

The power of poetic composition to create complex new ideas from simpler conventional ideas reveals itself in especially clear form in personification— metaphors through which we understand other things ① _______________ our own terms. Personification permits us to use our knowledge about ourselves to maximal effect, to use insights about ourselves to help us comprehend such things as forces of nature, common events, abstract concepts, and inanimate objects.

24 The most likely title of this passage would be _______________.

① Poetic Composition
② Rhetoric
③ Metaphor
④ Metonymy
⑤ Personification

25 Which of the following best fits into ①?

① by
② with
③ in
④ of
⑤ from

해석 더 단순한 관습적 생각에서 복잡한 새로운 생각을 창조하는 작시의 힘은 의인화에서 특히나 분명히 드러나는데, 즉 은유를 거쳐서 우리 자신의 말을 통해 다른 것들을 이해하게 된다. 의인화는 우리 자신에 관한 지식을 우리가 최대한으로 효과적으로 사용하게 하며, 자연의 힘, 평범한 일들, 추상적인 개념들, 무생물과 같은 것들을 이해하도록 돕기 위해서, 우리 자신에 관한 통찰력을 이용할 수 있게 한다.

24 이 글의 가장 적절한 제목은?

① 작시   ② 수사법
③ 은유   ④ 환유어법
⑤ 의인화

25 ①에 가장 적절한 것은?

어구 **poetic composition** 작시   **conventional** 전통적인, 관습적인 **personification** 의인, 인격화   **metaphor** 은유, 유사한 것   **term** 말, 기간, 조건   **permit A to R** A가 ~할 것을 허락하다   **to maximal effect** 최대한도로   **insight** 통찰   **comprehend** 이해하다, 포함하다   **abstract** 추상적인; 요약하다   **inanimate object** 무생물   **rhetoric** 수사법 **metonymy** 환유어법

해설 **24** 이 글은 작시의 과정에서 '의인화'에 관한 중요성을 설명하는 글이다. 은유는 의인화의 과정일 뿐이므로 핵심어가 될 수는 없다.
25 term은 전치사 in과 결합한다.

Chapter 02 요지·주장

⇒ 본책 p.27

| 1 ③ | 2 ④ | 3 ③ | 4 ④ | 5 ② | 6 ⑤ | 7 ④ | 8 ⑤ | 9 ③ | 10 ② |
| 11 ④ | 12 ② | 13 ② | 14 ① | | | | | | |

Street preaching is a manifestation of personal commitment to the sect; fulfillment of this commitment confers status within the group. The impassioned style of street preachers is highly deliberate. They know that people usually will not stop to listen to them. Consequently their style is designed to "sow the seeds" in the hope that those who have heard them may at some future time "turn to the Lord."

1 **Choose the sentence that best summarizes the above passage.**

① Street preachers are motivated by a desire to get status within the sect.
② Street preaching is a self-imposed activity designed to demonstrate how religious these preachers are.
③ Street preaching is a highly committed activity aimed at future converts.
④ Indifference to the reaction of people is characteristic of street preachers.

해석 거리 전도는 그 종파에 대한 개인적인 헌신의 표현인데, 이 책무를 수행하면 집단 내에서 지위가 수여된다. 거리 전도자들의 열정적인 태도는 지극히 의도적이다. 사람들이 자신들의 말을 듣기 위해서 멈추지 않으리라는 점을 거리 전도자들은 안다. 결론적으로 그들의 거리 전도 형태는 자기들의 말을 들은 사람들이 미래에 "주님에게 돌아올" 수 있을 것이라는 희망에 "씨를 뿌리기 위해" 고안된 것이다.

1 윗글을 가장 잘 요약한 것은?
① 거리 전도자들은 종파 내에서 지위를 얻으려는 갈망에 의해서 동기를 부여받는다.
② 거리 전도는 이들 거리 전도사들이 얼마나 종교적인지를 증명하기 위해 고안된 스스로 맡아서 하는 행위이다.
③ 거리 전도는 미래의 개종자들을 목표로 하는 매우 헌신적인 행위이다.
④ 사람들의 반응에 대한 무관심이 거리 전도사들의 특징이다.

어구 **street preaching** 거리 전도 **manifestation** 표현, 명시 **commitment** 약속, 헌신, 책무 **sect** 종파, 파벌 **confer** 수여하다 **status** 상태, 지위, 자격 **impassioned** 감격한, 열정적인, 정열적인 **street preacher** 거리 전도사 **deliberate** 의도적인, 신중한 **sow** (씨를) 뿌리다 **the Lord** 하느님, 신 **motivate** 동기를 부여하다 **self-imposed** 스스로 맡아서 하는 **convert** 개종자, 귀의자 **indifference** 무관심, 냉정

해설 consequently는 '결론'을 내리기 위해 쓰이는 접속부사로서, 마지막 문장이 주제문임을 알 수 있다. 따라서 가까운 미래에 종교를 바꿀 이들을 위해서 능동적으로 행하는 행위가 거리 전도임이 주제가 된다.

There are those who argue that the educational system is still inadequate in meeting the demand of society. Perhaps this is true, but until a more adequate system is developed, we must live with the one we have and deal with its problems individually. Despite the many faults of our system, the fact remains that the opportunity for a basic education is denied to no one. What individuals get out of that education, however, depends a lot on how much they put in.

2 **이 글에서 필자가 말하려는 요지로 가장 알맞은 것을 고르시오.**

① There are many people who believe the educational system to be inadequate.
② The value a person gets from an education is his or her own responsibility.

해석 교육 제도가 사회의 요구를 충족시키는 데 아직도 불충분하다고 주장하는 이들이 있다. 아마도 사실일지 모르겠지만 더 충분한 제도가 개발될 때까지 우리는 현재의 제도로 살아가야만 하며 그 문제들을 개별적으로 처리해야만 한다. 우리 체계의 많은 문제점들에도 불구하고 기본 교육의 기회가 누구에게라도 거부되지는 않을 것이라는 사실이 남아 있다. 그러나 개인들이 교육을 통해서 얻는 것은 그들이 얼마나 많은 시간, 노력을 쏟는지에 달려 있다.

2 이 글에서 필자가 말하려는 요지로 알맞은 것을 고르시오.
① 교육 제도가 불충분하다고 믿는 많은 사람들이 있다.
② 사람이 교육을 통해서 얻는 가치는 자신이 갖고 있는 책임인 것이다.
③ 우리의 학교 제도는 많은 문제들이 있지만 적어도 모든 이가 교육을 받을 기회를 갖고 있다.
④ 우리는 교육 제도를 수용해야만 하며 그 문제들을 해결하기 위해 노력해야만 한다.
⑤ 문제들을 해결할 수 있다는 점은 사실이다.

③ Our school system has many faults, but at least everyone has the opportunity to get an education.
④ We have to accept our educational system and try to solve its problems.
⑤ It is true that we can solve our problems.

어구 argue 주장하다 inadequate 불충분한 meet demand 수요에 부응하다 deal with 처리하다, 거래하다, 다루다 the fact remains that ~ ~라는 사실이 남겨져 있다 out of ~로부터 depend on ~에 의존하다 a lot 대단히 put in (시간, 노력)을 쏟다; 넣다, 첨가하다, 심다, 제출하다

해설 두 번째 문장이 주제문으로서, 현재의 제도가 문제는 있을지언정 교육의 기회마저 없는 것은 아니므로 현 제도를 수용하여, 문제점들을 하나하나씩 개선해 나가야 한다는 내용이 주제가 된다.

Not long ago the North waged war for the second time this year with South Korea when it shelled a South Korean island near the disputed maritime boundary, killing two soldiers and two civilians, injuring others and burning a score of houses. If war and the threat of war against North Korea are hardly even options, what can the world do? The best joker in a bad hand is to heal the divisions among other countries about how to handle North Korea. That means, in particular, making China see that a tinderbox it has long regarded as a strategic asset has become an appalling liability. China also struggles to control North Korea. But a united front would change the environment that encourages the rogue state's bad behavior.

3 윗글의 요지를 고르시오.
① North Korea's recent armed provocation is worth punishing.
② China's effort is necessary to change North Korea's hard line.
③ Several countries' cooperations are needed to control North Korea.
④ North Korea's recent armed provocation must lead to self-destruction.

해석 얼마 전 북한은 분쟁이 벌어진 연안 경계선 근처 남한의 섬을 폭격하여, 군인 2명과 민간인 2명을 살상하고, 10여 명이 넘는 중·경상자 및 20여 채의 집을 불태워서, 올해 두 번째로 남한과 싸웠다. 북한에 대한 전쟁이나 전쟁 위협이 결코 비책이 될 수 없다면, 세계는 무엇을 할 수 있을까? 어려운 상황에서 최고의 방책은 북한을 다루는 방법에 대한 여러 나라들의 의견 차이를 해소하는 것이다. 특히, 오랫동안 전략적인 자산으로 간주해 온 화약고(북한)가 소름 끼치게 불리한 책임을 동반하게 될 것이라는 것을 중국이 알도록 하는 것이다. 중국 역시 북한을 다루는 데 고투하고 있지만, 공동 전선이 불량 국가의 나쁜 행동을 조장하는 환경을 바꿀 것이다.

3 윗글의 요지를 고르시오.
① 북한의 최근 무력 도발은 응징받아야 마땅하다.
② 북한의 강경 노선을 바꾸기 위해서는 중국의 노력이 절실하다.
③ 북한 사태를 해결하기 위해서는 세계 여러 국가들의 협력이 필요하다.
④ 북한의 최근 무력 도발은 북한 스스로 자멸을 초래함에 틀림이 없다.

어구 wage war 전쟁을 치르다 shell 포격하다; 껍질을 벗기다 maritime boundary 군사 경계선 joker 비장의 카드; 농담하는 사람; 책략; 사기 heal a division 의견 차이를 해소하다 tinderbox (분쟁의) 불씨; 타기 쉬운 물건 appalling 섬뜩하게 하는, 질색인 united front 공동 전선; 통일 전선 armed provocation 무력 도발 hard line 강경 노선 self-destruction 자멸

해설 The best joker in a bad hand~가 주제문으로서, 북한을 통제하고 다루기 위해서는 여러 나라의 의견 차이를 해소하는 것, 즉 전 세계 국가들의 협력이 필요하다는 해결책이 주제로서 옳다.

>>> **다음 글을 읽고 문제의 답을 고르시오.** [4~5]

According to an American columnist, anti-Japanese sentiment in South Korea has taken on particularly sharp edge among young people. He claims that they are the products of history courses that spare no detail about the pain inflicted by the Japanese occupation and that glory _______________ the knowledge that many facets of Japanese culture reached Japan from China by way of Korea.

해석 어떤 미국의 칼럼니스트에 따르자면 한국의 반일감정은 젊은이들 사이에서 더 격했다고 한다. 그는 일본의 강점이 심어 놓은 고통에 대해 자세히 다루지 않으며, 일본 문화의 많은 점들이 중국으로부터 한국을 거쳐서 일본에 전해졌다는 점에 자랑스러워하는 역사 수업의 산물이 바로 그 젊은이들이라고 주장한다.

4 The columnist insists that __________.

① South Koreans, especially younger people, do not fully recognize the historical lesson of the Japanese colonial period

② the description of the Japanese colonial period in Korean history courses has many problems

③ it is an indisputable fact that Japanese culture was influenced by Korean culture

④ young Koreans have unfavorable impressions toward the Japanese due to their history education

⑤ Japan and Korea should cooperate with each other in spite of their historical experience

5 Which one is the most appropriate in the blank?

① for
② in
③ to
④ toward
⑤ against

---

4 칼럼니스트는 무엇이라 주장하는가?

① 특히나 한국 젊은이들은 일본 식민지 시대의 역사적 교훈을 충분히 이해하고 있지는 못하다.

② 한국의 역사 수업에서 일본 식민지 시대의 설명은 많은 문제점을 갖고 있다.

③ 한국 문화가 일본 문화에 영향을 미친 점은 명백한 사실이다.

④ 젊은 한국인들은 역사 교육을 받은 탓에 일본에 대하여 좋지 않은 인상을 가지고 있다.

⑤ 일본과 한국은 역사의 경험에도 불구하고 상호 협력을 해야만 한다.

5 빈칸에 가장 알맞은 것은?

어구 sentiment 감정, 경향 take on edge 격렬하다, 흥분 상태이다 inflict (고통, 타격) 주다 occupation 점령, 거주, 직업, 점유 glory in ~을 자랑스러워하다, ~에 기뻐하다 facet 양상, 국면 by way of ~을 경유하여 fully 충분히, 완전히 colonial 식민지의 indisputable 명백한 unfavorable 비판적인 due to ~ 때문에 cooperate with ~와 협력하다

해설 4 첫 문장에서 한국의 반일 감정은 젊은이들 사이에서 더 격하다고 했으며, 두 번째 문장에서 일제 강점기가 심어 놓은 고통을 제대로 반영하고 있지 못한 한국의 역사 교육이 원인이 된다고 설명한다.

5 glory는 자동사로서 목적어를 위치시키기 위해서는 전치사 in이 필요하다.
e.g. She didn't like to glory in her past victories.

>>> 다음 글을 읽고 문제의 답을 고르시오. [6~7]

Resilient couples view their marriage as sacred, worthy of sacrifice. "It requires a leap of faith to believe this in our age of divorce, but it's crucial for turning hardship to strength", Wolin says.

The Lafontaines, married 12 years, have taken this leap. "We count on our faith in the marriage and in God much more as the years go by." Alisa says. "When we're struggling with a problem such as too little money, which happens a lot now that we have four kids, faith gives me the confidence to say, 'It will work out.' And it always does."

What if your marriage is so fraught with conflict that you can't appreciate each other? To renew the romance, stir "embers of positive feelings" by focusing on the past, Gottman says.

Jill and Don Ross love to recall how they met. Jill had gone to a restaurant where Don was singing. After hearing a song she loved, Jill clapped exuberantly, "I am very glad you showed up tonight", Don crooned. "Are you married?"

"No", she flirted. "Will you sing at my wedding?"

"I'll sing at __________ wedding", he replied, surprising even himself.

Seven months later, Don came through on his promise. And they've lived happily ever after.

해석 회복력이 빠른 부부들은 그들의 결혼 생활이 희생할 가치가 있는 신성한 것이라고 간주한다. "이혼의 시대에 살면서 갖게 되는 믿음은 믿음의 도약을 필요로 하는 것이지만 역경을 힘으로 바꾸기 위해서는 필수적인 것이다."라고 월린은 말한다.

결혼한 지 12년이 된 라폰텐느 부부도 이러한 도약을 했다. "우리는 시간이 지날수록 우리의 결혼에 대한 믿음과 신에 대한 믿음에 의존한다. 네 명의 자녀들을 키우면서 종종 발생하는 돈 부족과 같은 문제로 싸울 때, 믿음은 '잘 될 것이다'라는 자신감을 부여해 주면 계속해서 모든 일이 실제로 잘 풀린다."라고 알리사는 말한다.

결혼이 갈등으로 가득해서 서로에게 감사할 줄 모른다면 어떻게 될까? 낭만적인 분위기를 새롭게 하기 위해 과거에 집중함으로써 "적극적인 감정의 불씨들"을 섞어 보라고 고트만은 말한다.

질과 돈 로스 부부는 그들이 어떻게 만나게 되었는지를 즐겨 회상한다. 질은 돈이 노래를 부르던 레스토랑에 갔었다. 자신이 좋아하는 노래를 들은 후에 질은 열광적인 박수를 쳤다. "당신이 오늘 와 주셔서 기분이 좋아요, 결혼은 하셨는지요?"라고 돈이 작은 목소리로 물어보았다.

"아니요, 제 결혼식에 오셔서 노래를 불러 주시겠습니까?"라고 그녀가 장난쳤다. "전 우리 결혼식에서 노래를 하겠어요."라고 대답한 돈은 스스로도 놀랐다.

7개월 후에 돈은 약속을 지켰다. 그들은 그 이후에 계속 행복하게 살았다.

6 작가의 견해로 올바르지 못한 내용은?

① 믿음의 도약을 하는 것은 행복한 결혼 생활에 필수적이다.

② 아름다운 순간들을 회상하는 것은 행복한 결혼 생활에 효과적이다.

③ 신에 대한 믿음은 행복한 결혼 생활에 효과적이다.

④ 사랑의 순간을 재개하는 것은 때때로 필수적이다.

⑤ 돈이 너무 부족한 것과 같은 문제는 자주 이혼을 야기한다.

6 Which of the following is NOT a correct description of the writer's view?

① Taking a leap of faith is necessary for a happy marriage.
② Reliving beautiful moments is good for a happy marriage.
③ Faith in God is good for a happy marriage.
④ It is sometimes necessary to renew the romance.
⑤ A problem such as too little money usually causes a divorce.

7 Fill in the blank with the most appropriate word in the given context.

① my
② your
③ her
④ our
⑤ their

---

7 빈칸에 적절한 보기를 고르시오.

① 나의
② 당신의
③ 그녀의
④ 우리의
⑤ 그들의

어구 resilient 탄력이 있는, 원기를 회복하는 sacred 신성한 leap 도약 crucial 중요한 turn A into B A를 B로 바꾸다 hardship 역경 go by 지나가다 struggle with ~과 싸우다 confidence 신뢰 work out 해결되다, 성립하다 be fraught with ~으로 가득 차다 appreciate 감상하다, 이해하다, 감사하다 renew 재개하다, 갱신하다 stir 휘젓다 ember 타다 남은 것, 불씨 focus on ~에 집중하다 clap 박수를 치다 exuberantly 열정적으로 show up 나타나다 croon 중얼거리다 flirt (남녀 간에) 장난치다 come through (약속 등을) 이행하다

해설 **6** 두 번째 단락에서 돈이 부족한 문제 또한 '잘 될 것이다'라는 믿음을 가지게 해 준다고 했으므로 보기 ⑤는 틀린 설명이다.

7 마지막 문장에서 앞서 나온 얘기를 한 '돈'과 그 얘기를 들은 '질'이 그 후 함께 행복하게 살았다는 내용이 나오므로, '우리의 결혼식'이 옳다.

I have chosen the literature we will be reading this quarter hoping that it will inspire you to see literature and America in a new way. Most importantly, I hope these works will cause you to think. Writing at its best is a concentrated form of thinking: writing in your journal with the intent of exploring those aspects of what we see and read will focus your insights and ideas as well as bring new ones. The thoughts that will fill your journal will also motivate our class discussion. Finally, writing regularly in a journal is one more way of becoming more comfortable with writing itself.

8 Which of the following is the main idea of the passage?

① In this semester you will discover a New America.
② Although you will not do any written assignments you will be encouraged to think about the reading material.
③ The class discussions will incite you to read American literature.
④ Through reading journalistic writing you will enhance your thought process.
⑤ Writing a journal will enhance your thought process together with your writing skills.

해석 나는 여러분이 새롭게 문학과 미국을 이해하기를 희망하면서 이번 학기에 읽게 될 문학 작품을 선택했다. 가장 중요한 것은, 이 작품들로 인해 여러분이 사고하기를 바란다는 것이다. 글은 집중된 생각의 형태이며, 일지에 우리가 보고 읽는 모든 것들을 연구하려는 의도를 가지고 써놓은 글은 새로운 생각을 떠올릴 뿐만 아니라 여러분의 통찰력과 생각들에 초점을 맞춰 줄 것이다. 여러분의 일지를 채우게 될 생각들은 더욱이 우리 수업의 토론에 동기를 부여해 줄 것이다. 끝으로 정기적으로 일지를 쓰는 것은 글 쓰는 일 자체에 친숙해져 가는 또 하나의 방법이다.

8 이 글의 주제는?

① 이번 학기에 당신은 새로운 미국을 발견하게 될 것이다.
② 당신이 필기 숙제를 전혀 못 하게 될지라도 독서 자료에 대해서 생각하도록 권유받을 것이다.
③ 수업 토론은 당신으로 하여금 미국 문학을 읽게 하도록 자극할 것이다.
④ 신문, 잡지의 기사를 읽음으로써 당신은 사고 과정을 향상시킬 것이다.
⑤ 일지를 쓰는 것은 작문 실력과 더불어 사고 과정까지도 향상시켜 줄 것이다.

어구 quarter 1/4, (미국의 4학기 중) 학기, 15분 inspire 고무시키다 at one's best 최상의 상태로 concentrated 집중된, 응축된 intent 의향, 목적 explore 탐험하다, 연구하다 insight 통찰력 as well as ~뿐만 아니라 motivate 동기를 부여하다 semester 학기 assignment 할당, 임무 be encouraged to R ~하도록 격려받다, 고무되다 incite 자극 · 선동하다 journalistic 신문의 together with ~와 함께, ~와 더불어

해설 일지 작성을 통해서 통찰력 향상과 작문 실력 향상에 도움이 되게끔 하기 위해 문학 작품을 새 학기의 공부 과정으로 선택하게 되었다는 내용이 이 글의 주제가 된다.

We very rarely consider, however, the process by which we gained our convictions. If we did so, we could hardly fail to see that there was usually little ground for our confidence in them. Here and there, in this department of knowledge or that, someone of us might make a fair claim to have taken some trouble to get correct ideas of, let us say, the situation in Russia, the sources of our food supply, the origin of the constitution, the revision of the tariff, the policy of the Holy Roman Apostolic Church, modern business organization, trade unions, birth control, socialism, the League of Nations, the excess-profits tax, preparedness, advertising in its social bearings; but only a very exceptional person would be entitled to opinions on all these, and on many other questions of equal importance, of which we may know even less. We feel compelled, as self-respecting persons, to take sides when they come up for discussion. We even surprise ourselves by our omniscience. Without taking thought we see in a flash that it is most righteous and expedient to discourage birth control by legislative enactment, or that one who decries intervention in Mexico is clearly wrong, or that big advertising is essential to big business and that big business is the pride of the land. As godlike beings why should we not rejoice in our omniscience?

9 윗글을 가장 잘 요약한 것은?

① In spite of all possible difficulties facing us, we, as godlike beings, have overcome them with confidence.

② We, human beings, are often surprised at our own ability to cope with things successfully in spite of various difficulties and problems.

③ Although we have little reason to trust our convictions on the important issues of life, we delight in forming and expressing such opinions without a moment's thought.

④ Human beings will be punished by God one way or the other for their own overconfidence in competing with God.

해석 그러나 우리는 우리가 신념을 체득하는 과정을 거의 고려하지 않는다. 만일 고려한다면, 우리는 우리 자신의 신념에 대한 근거가 항상 부족하다는 것을 알게 될 것이다. 이 분야 저 분야 등 여기저기에서, 러시아의 상황, 식량 공급원, 헌법의 유래, 관세의 개정, 신성 로마 교황청의 정책, 현대 기업, 노동조합, 산아 제한, 사회주의, 국제연합, 초과 이득세, 군사 비용, 사회 정세에 대한 광고를 옳게 알기 위하여 약간의 어려움을 겪었다는 올바른 주장을 우리들 중 몇몇은 할 수 있을런지도 모른다. 그러나 아주 극히 뛰어난 몇몇 사람만이 이런 몇몇의 문제 전부에 대해서 의견을 제시할지도 모른다. 그럼에도 불구하고 우리들 대부분은 이 모든 것들과 심지어 우리가 잘 알지 못하는 동일한 중요성을 가지고 있는 많은 다른 문제들에 대한 의견을 가지고 있다. 각자 자존심을 갖고 있는 우리로서는 그것들이 논의의 화젯거리가 되면 (자기주장에 대해) 편을 들어야만 한다고 느낀다. 우리는 심지어 우리 자신의 유식함 때문에 놀란다. 생각을 하지 않고서도, 입법정책이 출생을 막는 것이 가장 옳고 합당한 것이며, 멕시코의 개입을 비난하는 사람은 분명히 나쁘며, 대형 광고는 대기업에 필수적이고 대기업은 그 나라의 자존심이라는 것이 가장 옳다는 것을, 단번에 우리는 간파한다. 어찌하여 우리는 신처럼 우리 자신의 전지전능함을 기뻐하지 말아야 하는 것인가?

9 윗글을 가장 잘 요약한 것은?

① 우리에게 직면한 모든 잠재적인 난관들에도 불구하고 우리는 신처럼 확신을 가지고 난관들을 극복해 왔다.

② 인간들인 우리는 여러 난관들과 문제들에도 불구하고 이것들을 성공적으로 대처할 수 있는 우리가 보유한 능력에 종종 놀란다.

③ 우리가 인생의 중요한 문제점들에 대한 우리의 확신을 믿을 근거가 없을지라도 그와 같은 의견을 형성하고 표현하는 것을 순간의 생각조차 없이 즐거워한다.

④ 인간들은 신과 겨루겠다는 지나친 자신감 때문에 이런저런 방식으로 신에게 처벌을 받을 것이다.

어구 rarely 거의 ~않는 conviction 신념, 확신, 유죄 판결 hardly 거의 ~ 는 fail to R ~하지 못하다 confidence 확신, 신용 here and there 여기저기 department (회사·기관의) 부서, (대학의) 학과, (활동의) 분야 make a fair claim that ~라는 옳은 주장을 하다 take trouble to R ~하는 데 어려움을 겪다 constitution 헌법 revision 개정 tariff 관세 holy 신성한 apostolic 로마 교황의 birth control 산아 제한 excess-profit tax 초과 이득세 preparedness 준비, 군사 비용 bearing 태도, 방위, 인내 exceptional 뛰어난, 극히 예외적인 be entitled to R/ to N ~할 권리가 있다 feel compelled to R ~해야 한다고 압박을 느끼다 self respecting 자존심이 강한 take sides 편을 들다 come up for (화젯거리로) 등장하다, 나타나다 omniscience 전지전능, 만능 in a flash 단번에, 순식간에 righteous 옳은 expedient 편리한, 정략적인 discourage 낙담시키다 decry 비난하다 intervention 간섭, 중재 godlike 신과 같은 rejoice in ~을 즐거워하다 overcome 극복하다 cope with 대처하다, 겨루다 delight in ~을 즐거워하다 overconfidence 과신, 자만

해설 인간들은 상당히 중요한 문제들에 대해서도 깊이 생각하지 않고, 마치 신처럼 자신들의 능력을 과대평가하여 즐기는데, 이는 그러할 만한 합당한 이유가 없다는 것이 이 글의 주제가 된다.

Before the introduction of the computer search, library research was a long and tedious task. Now, instead of spending long hours looking through the cards, catalogs and periodical indexes for books and articles on your subject, you can have a computer do the looking for you. All you need to do is give your subject to the computer. This is not as easy as it sounds, however, because you must know exactly what you understand. The computer then searches its memory for books and articles about your subject. It takes less than a second for the computer to complete its search. Finally, it prints a bibliography, a list of authors and titles of the books and articles it has found for your subject.

10 What is the topic of the this paragraph?

① library research
② computer searches
③ bibliographies
④ looking for books and articles
⑤ the system of a library

11 What is the main idea of this paragraph?

① Library research is a long and tedious task.
② A bibliography is a list of authors and titles of books and articles.
③ Library research through a computer is easy.
④ A computer can find books and articles for you.
⑤ A bibliography is important for finding the books you want.

해석 컴퓨터로 검색하는 시스템의 도입이 있기 전에 도서관 검색은 오랜 시간이 걸리고 지루한 일이었다. 지금은 자신의 주제에 대한 책과 논문을 수록한 카드와 목록과 정기 간행물 색인을 찾느라 오랜 시간을 소비하는 대신에, 컴퓨터가 대신 그 일을 한다. 당신이 해야 할 필요가 있는 모든 것은 그저 관련 주제를 입력하는 것이다. 그러나 이 일은 들리는 것처럼 쉽지는 않은데, 왜냐하면 자기가 이해하는 것을 분명히 알고 있어야 하기 때문이다. 그래서 컴퓨터는 당신이 제시한 주제에 관한 책과 논문을 찾기 위해서 자신의 메모리를 찾는다. 컴퓨터가 이 일을 끝내는 시간은 1초가 채 걸리지 않는다. 마침내 컴퓨터는 당신의 주제에 대해 컴퓨터가 찾아낸 서적 목록, 즉 저자들의 목록과 책과 논문의 제목을 인쇄한다.

10 이 글의 주제는?

① 도서관 문헌 검색
② 컴퓨터 검색
③ 관계 서적 목록
④ 책과 논문 검색
⑤ 도서관의 체계

11 이 글의 요지는?

① 도서관 문헌 검색은 시간이 오래 걸리고 지겨운 일이다.
② 도서 문헌은 책과 논문의 저자와 제목의 항목이다.
③ 컴퓨터를 통한 도서관 문헌 검색은 쉽다.
④ 컴퓨터는 당신을 위해 책들과 논문을 찾을 수 있다.
⑤ 도서 문헌은 당신이 원하는 책들을 찾아 주기 위해서 중요하다.

어구 **tedious** 지루한 **look through** 조사하다, ~을 통하여 보다 **catalog** 목록, 일람표, 도서 목록 **periodical** 정기 간행물 **index** 색인 **article** 논문, 품목, 기사, 조항, 논설 **second** 초 **bibliography** (어떤 제목 · 저자에 관한) 저서 목록, 출판 목록, 참고서[문헌] 목록, 인용 문헌

해설 10 도서관에서 컴퓨터로 문헌을 검색할 때에는 지겹고 시간이 오래 걸리는 일이었지만, 컴퓨터가 도입된 이후에는 본인의 주제만 정확하게 이해하고 있다면 검색 결과가 더 빠를 수 있다는 내용이 이 글의 주제가 되므로, 컴퓨터 검색이 옳다.

11 'This is not easy~' 문장을 통해서 컴퓨터를 통한 문헌 검색이 쉬운 일만은 아님을 알 수 있으므로, ③은 정답이 될 수 없다. 위 문제의 일반화된 진술은 ④가 되므로 요지로서 옳다.

Einstein's theory of relativity is, in essence, a description of the interaction between different perspectives. Sigmund Freud's analytical methods were designed to find details that didn't fit traditional paradigms in order to come up with a completely new point of view. To solve a problem creatively, you must abandon the first approach that comes to mind, which usually stems from past experiences, and reconceptualize the problem. Thus geniuses do not merely solve existing problems; they identify new ones.

해석 아인슈타인의 상대성 원리는 본질적으로 서로 다른 사물의 상관관계들 사이의 상호 작용을 설명한 것이다. 지그문트 프로이트의 분석학적인 방법들은 완전히 새로운 관점을 제안하기 위해 전통적인 패러다임에 맞지 않는 세부 사항들을 찾으려고 만들어졌다. 창조적으로 문제를 해결하기 위해서는, 가장 먼저 떠오르는 첫 번째 접근 방법을 버려야 하는데, 그 첫 번째 접근법은 일반적으로 과거의 경험으로부터 나오며, 그 문제를 재개념화할 뿐이기 때문이다. 이와 같이 천재들은 단순히 기존의 문제들을 해결할 뿐만 아니라 그들은 새로운 문제들을 확인하기까지 한다.

12 윗글의 요지로서 가장 적절한 것은?

① Einstein and Freud are real geniuses.
② Geniuses look at problems from all angles.
③ Geniuses usually ignore past experiences.
④ Geniuses try to solve a complicated problem only.

12 윗글의 요지로서 가장 적절한 것은?

① 아인슈타인과 프로이트는 진정한 천재이다.
② 천재들은 모든 견지에서 문제를 바라본다.
③ 천재들은 보통 과거의 경험을 무시한다.
④ 천재들은 복잡한 문제들만 풀려고 노력한다.

어구 **theory of relativity** 상대성 원리   **in essence** 본질에 있어서, 본질적으로   **interaction** 상호 작용[영향], 교호 작용   **perspectives** 원근(화)법; 경치, 조망, 전망; 시각, 견지; 상관관계   **analytical** 분해[분석]의; 분석적[해석적]인   **paradigm** 보기, 범례, 모범   **come up with** ~에 따라 잡다; ~을 제안하다   **point of view** 관점   **come to mind** 생각나다   **reconceptualize** 재개념화하다   **existing** 현존하는, 현재의   **identify** 증명하다, 식별하다   **from all angles** 모든 견지에서

해설 마지막 문장이 주제문으로서, 현존하는 문제뿐만 아니라 새로운 문제들도 해결하는 것이 천재들의 특성이라고 했으므로, 이는 '모든 견지에서 검토한다'는 내용이 요지가 되는 것이다.

>>> 다음 글을 읽고 문제의 답을 고르시오. [13~14]

The "broken windows" theory was the brainchild of the criminologists, James Wilson and George Kelling. They argue that crime is the inevitable result of disorder. If a window is broken and left unrepaired, people walking by will conclude that no-one cares and no-one is in charge. Soon, more windows will be broken and the sense of anarchy will spread from the building to the street on which it faces, sending a signal that _____________. In a city, relatively minor problems like graffiti, public disorder and aggressive panhandling are all the equivalent of broken windows, invitations to more serious crimes.

What does this suggest? It says that the criminal— far from being someone who acts for fundamental, intrinsic reasons and who live in his own world— is actually someone acutely sensitive to his environment, who is alert to all kinds of cues, and who is prompted to commit crimes based on his perception of the world around him. That is an incredibly radical—and in some sense unbelievable— idea. It says that behavior is a function of social context.

해석 '깨진 유리창' 이론은 범죄학자인 제임스 윌슨과 조지 켈링의 창작물이었다. 범죄는 무질서의 불가피한 결과물이라고 그들은 주장한다. 만일 유리가 깨져서 수리되지 않은 채 방치되면, 옆으로 걸어가는 사람들은 누구도 관심을 가지지 않고 책임을 지지 않는다고 결론을 내릴 것이다. 곧 더 많은 창문이 깨질 것이며 건물로부터 마주보고 있는 길거리까지 무질서 의식이 확산되어, 어느 짓이라도 해도 된다는 신호를 보내게 될 것이다. 도시에서 낙서, 질서 위반 및 공격적인 구걸과 같은 비교적 시시한 문제들이 모두 깨진 창문과 같은 것이 되며, 더 심각한 범죄를 유도하게 된다.
이것은 무엇을 암시하는가? 범죄자는 근본적이고 본능적인 이유 때문에 행동을 하고 자신만의 세상에서 사는 사람이 아니라 자신의 환경에 매우 민감한 사람이기 때문에 온갖 종류의 신호에 경계를 하며 자신의 주위에 있는 세상에 대한 생각에 의존하여 범죄를 저지르도록 부추겨지는 사람을 말한다. 그것은 대단히 급진적이고 어느 정도에서는 믿기지 않는 생각이다. 그것은 사회적 상황의 상관관계라고 말한다.

13 이 글의 요지는 무엇인가?

① 도시에서 발생하는 대부분의 주거 침입은 창문을 통해 발생한다.
② 개인의 범죄 행동은 환경에 의해 상당히 영향을 받는다.
③ 경범죄자들은 결국 중범죄자가 될 수 있다.
④ 범죄자들은 대중의 평화를 어지럽히기 위해 태어났다.
⑤ 보행자들은 길거리 구석에 있는 창문의 상태에 따라 불가항력으로 영향을 받는다.

14 빈칸에 가장 알맞은 것은?

① 무엇을 해도 상관없다.
② 경찰이 사방에 있다.
③ 창문을 수리할 필요가 있다.
④ 누군가가 이곳을 책임지고 있다.
⑤ 곧 무너질 것이다.

13 What is the main idea of the passage?

① Most break-ins in the city occur through windows.
② An individual's crime behavior is deeply influenced by the environment.
③ Minor offenders may become serious criminals in the long run.
④ Criminals are born to disturb the public peace.
⑤ Pedestrians are irresistibly affected by the condition of street-side windows.

14 Which of the following best fits into blank?

① anything goes here
② the police are around
③ the windows need fixing
④ someone is in charge here
⑤ it will collapse soon

Chapter 03 연결사
⇨ 본책 p.38

1 ③	2 ①	3 ⑤	4 ②	5 ③	6 ①	7 ①	8 ③

>>> 다음 글을 읽고 문제의 답을 고르시오. [1~2]

Repetition of words and structures can be very effective. We are usually told at school not to begin all our sentences in the same way (and especially not to begin all our sentences with 'I'), and it is certainly true that careless repetitions can be monotonous. ______________, when important words or phrases are repeated deliberately it can help to strengthen the impression that the writer wants to make. Which sounds better: 'I came, I saw, I conquered' or 'I came, saw and conquered?'

1 문맥상 빈칸에 적절한 것을 고르시오.

① For instance
② As a result
③ However
④ In other words
⑤ Whereas

2 이 글의 제목으로 가장 적절한 것을 고르시오.

① Repetition of Words and Structures
② Sentence with 'I'
③ Careless Repetitions
④ Deliberate Repetitions
⑤ Strong Impression

해석 단어와 구문 구조의 반복은 매우 효과적일 수 있다. 모든 문장들을 같은 방식으로 시작하지 말라고 하는데(특히나 '나'로 모든 문장을 시작하지 말라고 말이다), 부주의한 반복은 단조로울 수 있다는 점도 명백히 옳다. 그러나 중요한 단어나 구들이 신중히 반복이 될 때에는 작가가 구현하고자 하는 느낌을 강화시키는 데 도움을 줄 수 있다. '내가 왔다, 내가 보았다, 내가 정복했다.'와 '내가 와서 보았고 정복했다.' 중 어느 것이 더 듣기에 좋은가?

1 문맥상 빈칸에 적절한 것을 고르시오.

① 예컨대
② 결과로서
③ 그러나
④ 즉, 달리 말하자면
⑤ ~임에 반하여[접속사]

2 이 글의 제목으로 가장 적절한 것을 고르시오.

① 단어와 구문 구조의 반복
② 'I'가 포함된 문장
③ 부주의한 반복
④ 신중한 반복
⑤ 강한 인상

어구 **repetition** 반복 **be told to R** ~하라고 듣다, 명령받다 **careless** 부주의한 **monotonous** 단조로운 **deliberately** 신중히 **strengthen** 강화시키다 **impression** 인상, 감명 **in other words** 즉, 달리 말하자면

해설 1 단어나 구를 부주의하게 반복하면 단조로울 수 있는 단점이 있지만, 신중히 반복된다면 강화된 인상을 심어줄 수 있는 장점으로 내용이 전개되므로 however가 옳다. whereas는 접속사이므로 틀리다.
2 단어와 구를 부주의하게 반복하면 단점이 되지만, 신중히 반복하면 장점이 된다는 '단어와 구조의 반복'이 주제로서 옳다.

>>> 다음 글을 읽고 문제의 답을 고르시오. [3~4]

Looking first at vocabulary differences, English has ① many words for someone who is not generous with money. Different contexts will require different uses. These words, while expressing basically the same meaning, are not functionally equivalent. ② ______________ words have connotative as well as denotative meanings.

3 Choose the one that is not an example of ①.

① frugal
② sparing
③ thrifty
④ stingy
⑤ meticulous

해석 우선 어휘 차이에서 바라보면, 영어는 돈에 관대하지 못한 사람에 대한 많은 단어들을 가지고 있다. 다양한 문맥이 다양한 사용을 필요로 할 것이다. 이 단어들이 기본적으로 같은 의미를 표현하는 반면에, 이 단어들은 기능적으로 같지는 않다. 즉, 다시 말하자면 단어는 외연적 의미뿐만 아니라 내포적 의미를 갖는 것이다.

3 ①의 예가 아닌 것을 고르시오.

① 소박한 ② 검소한
③ 검소한 ④ 인색한
⑤ 신중한

4 ②에 맞는 연결사를 고르시오.

① 예컨대 ② 다시 말하자면
③ 그러나 ④ ~일지라도
⑤ 더욱이

4 Which of the following best fits into ②?

① For example
② In other words
③ However
④ Whereas
⑤ In addition

어구 vocabulary 어휘 generous 관대한, 푸짐한 context (글의) 전후 관계 functionally 기능적으로 equivalent 동등한, (역할 따위가) ~에 상당하는 connotative 암시하는, 함축적인 denotative 지시하는, 표시하는 frugal 소박한, 검약한 sparing 검소한 thrifty 검소한, 저축하는, 번영하는 stingy 인색한, 부족한 meticulous 매우 신중한, 소심한 in other words 즉, 달리 말하자면 in addition 더욱이

해설 3 ①~④는 약간의 차이는 있지만 모두 돈의 씀씀이가 많지 않다는 내용이지만 ⑤는 성격을 의미하므로 이질적이다.

4 같은 의미를 표현할지라도 기능에 있어서 차이가 있다는 앞 문장과 단어는 외연적, 내포적 의미를 둘 다 가진다는 내용은 앞 문장을 다시 한번 '강조', '부연' 해주는 것이다.

>>> 다음 글을 읽고 문제의 답을 고르시오. [5~6]

Television's variety becomes a narcotic, not a stimulus. Its serial, kaleidoscopic exposures force us to follow its lead. The viewer is on a perpetual guided tour: 30 minutes at the museum, 30 at the cathedral, 30 for a drink, then back on the bus to the next attraction—except on television, typically, the spans allotted are on the order of minutes or seconds, and the chosen delights are more often car crashes and people killing on another. ① _____________, a lot of television usurps one of the most precious of all human gifts, the ability to focus your attention yourself, rather than just passively surrender it.

5 The best title of this passage is
_____________.

① Television and a guided tour: Similarities and differences
② Attractions on television
③ Pitfalls of television
④ Kaleidescope of TV
⑤ How to break free of TV

6 The expression that is most appropriate for ① is "_____________".

① In short
② In contrast
③ Likewise
④ In a similar vein
⑤ For instance

해석 TV의 다양성은 중독이 되는 것이지 흥분되는 것이 아니다. 그것의 연속적이고 변화무쌍한 모습은 우리가 그것이 이끄는 대로 따르도록 한다. 시청자들은 끊임없는 안내가 있는 여행을 한다. 30분은 박물관, 30분은 성당, 30분은 술 한 잔, 그리고 나서 다른 매력적인 것을 위해 다시 버스에 오른다. 보통 텔레비전상이라는 것을 제외하면, 할당된 시간은 분이나 초에 따르며 선택받은 즐거움은 더 많은 차의 충돌과 다른 사람에게 일어나는 살인 같은 것이다. 한마디로, 많은 텔레비전이 인간의 재능 중에서 가장 가치 있는 것 중의 하나인, 단지 수동적으로 내맡기는 것보다는 스스로 집중할 수 있는 능력을 상실하게 한다는 것이다.

5 이 글의 알맞은 제목은?
① TV와 안내인이 동행하는 여행: 유사점과 차이점들
② TV의 매력들
③ TV의 함정
④ TV의 변화무쌍함
⑤ TV로부터 벗어나는 방법

6 ①에 들어갈 알맞은 것은?
① 한마디로
② 대조해 보건대
③ 마찬가지로
④ 동일한 특징에서
⑤ 예컨대

어구 narcotic 마약 중독 stimulus 자극, 자극제 serial 연속적인 kaleidoscopic 주마등 같은, 변화무쌍한 exposure 모습 perpetual 영속적인 cathedral 성당 attraction 매력 typically 전형적으로 span 범위 allot 배분, 할당하다 usurp 침해하다 rather than ~라기보다는 passively 수동적으로 surrender 내어주다, 포기하다 pitfall 유혹, 함정 kaleidoscope 변화무쌍함, 만화경 in short 한마디로, 즉

해설 5 이 글은 TV의 잡다한 내용들이 사람의 집중도를 떨어뜨린다는 TV의 단점을 다룬 글이다. 따라서 제목 또한 'TV의 함정·위험들'이 옳다.

6 앞 문장까지 TV 안에서 펼쳐지는 내용들을 묘사한 후, 마지막 문장에서 작가의 생각이 담긴 비판이 등장한다. 따라서 '요약'의 기능을 가진 in short가 옳다.

>>> **다음 글을 읽고 문제의 답을 고르시오.** [7~8]

I don't deny that the feeling of success makes it easier to enjoy life. A painter, ① _______________, who has been obscure throughout his youth, is likely to become happier if his talent wins recognition. Nor do I deny that money, up to a certain point, is very capable of increasing happiness; beyond that point, I do not think it does so. What I do maintain is that success can only be one ingredient in happiness; and is too dearly purchased if all the other ingredients have been sacrificed to obtain it.

7 Which of the following best fits into ①?

① let us say
② whereas
③ otherwise
④ in contrast
⑤ paradoxically

8 Choose the best title of the above passage.

① Worthlessness of Money
② An Important Requirement of Success
③ The Extent of Success
④ The Inevitable Aim of Life
⑤ The Cost of Success

해석 나는 성공했다는 기분이 더 쉽게 삶을 즐길 수 있도록 해 준다는 것을 부인하지 않는다. 이를테면 젊은 시절 무명이었던 화가가 그의 재능을 인정받으면 더 행복해질 듯하다. 돈이 어느 정도까지는 행복을 증진시킬 수 있다는 것을 나는 또한 부인하지 않는다. 그러나 그 어느 정도라는 것을 넘어서면 더 이상 그렇지 않다고 생각한다. 내가 주장하는 것은 성공이란 행복에 있어서 한 요소에 불과하며 그것을 얻기 위해 다른 모든 요소가 희생되었다면 그 성공은 너무 비싼 대가를 치르고 산 것이라는 것이다.

7 ①에 알맞은 것은?

① 예컨대
② ~하는 반면에
③ 그렇지 않다면
④ 대조적으로
⑤ 역설적으로

8 윗글의 제목은?

① 돈의 무가치
② 성공의 중요한 조건
③ 성공의 정도
④ 인생의 필연적인 목표
⑤ 성공의 대가

어구 obscure 모호한, 무명의   maintain 주장하다   ingredient 성분, 요소
dearly 비싸게   sacrifice 희생하다

해설 7 앞 문장에 대한 예를 화가를 통해 들어 주므로 예시 표현이 옳다.
8 이 글은 성공은 행복의 한 요소로서 그 정도의 준수를 주장하는 글이다. 따라서 성공의 정도가 제목으로 적합하다.

Chapter 04 특정 정보

⇒ 본책 p.43

1 ①	2 ③	3 ①	4 ①	5 ④	6 ②	7 ①	8 ②	9 ②	10 ④
11 ⑤	12 ⑤	13 ③	14 ④	15 ①	16 ③	17 ②	18 ①	19 ②	20 ④
21 ③	22 ③	23 ②	24 ④	25 ③	26 ②	27 ⑤	28 ②	29 ②	30 ④
31 ①	32 ①	33 ③							

Professor Iyengar of Columbia University conducted an experiment in which she set up a tasting booth with a variety of exotic gourmet jams at an upscale grocery store. Sometimes the booth had six different jams, and sometimes twenty-four different jams on display. She wanted to see whether the number of jam choices made any difference in the number of jams sold. Conventional economic wisdom, of course, says that the more choices consumers have, the more likely they are to buy, because it is easier for consumers to find the jam that perfectly fits their needs. But Iyengar found the opposite to be true. Thirty percent of those who stopped by the six-choice booth ended up buying some jam, while only three percent of those who stopped by the bigger booth bought anything. Why is that? For buying jam is a snap decision. You say to yourself, instinctively, "I want that one." And if you are given too many choices, if you are forced to consider much more than your unconscious mind is comfortable with, you get paralyzed. Snap judgements can be made in a snap because they are frugal, and if we want to protect our snap judgements, we have to take steps to protect that frugality.

1 Which of the following is the major finding by Professor Iyengar?

① Snap judgements require fewer choices to choose from.
② Large upscale stores are bound to dominate the market.
③ Conventional economic wisdom has withstood the test of time.
④ Consumers are easily pleased with a wide range of selection.
⑤ Buyers' unconscious mind weighs each and every option carefully.

해석 콜롬비아 대학의 아인거 교수는 다양한 이국적인 잼을 갖춘 시식대를 고급 식료품 가게에 설치한 실험을 했다. 그 시식대에는 가끔은 6개의 다른 잼을 진열해 놓았고, 가끔은 각기 다른 24개의 잼들이 진열됐다. 그녀는 선택의 폭이 판매되는 잼의 수에 어느 차이를 일으키는지를 파악하기를 원했다. 물론 경제에 대한 통념은 선택의 폭이 클수록, 소비자들은 그들의 욕구에 정확히 부합하는 잼을 더 쉽게 찾기 때문에, 구입할 가능성이 그만큼 더 높아진다는 것이다. 그러나 아인거 교수는 정반대가 옳다는 것을 알았다. 여섯 종류의 시식대에 멈춘 사람들 중 30%가 결국 잼을 산 반면, 더 많은 종류를 갖춘 시식대에 머문 사람들 중에서는 3%만이 잼을 구입했다. 왜 그랬을까? 왜냐하면 잼을 구입하는 것은 빠른 결정을 요하는 행위이기 때문이다. 당신은 자신에게 본능적으로 "나는 저것을 원해."라고 말한다. 그런데 너무 많은 선택이 제시되면, 즉 당신의 무의식적으로 편안하다고 느껴지는 것 이상으로 많은 생각을 해야만 한다면, 당신의 사고는 마비된다. 즉석에서 내리는 판단은 많은 힘이 들지 않기 때문에 곧바로 결정이 내려지며, 만일 우리가 즉석 판단을 지키기 원한다면 그러한 간소함을 지키기 위한 조치를 취해야 한다.

1 아인거 교수가 발견한 주요 내용은 무엇인가?
① 즉석에서 내리는 판단은 선택할 기회의 필요성이 거의 없다.
② 대형 고급 상점은 시장을 지배할 수밖에 없다.
③ 통상적인 경제적 지혜는 시간의 시험을 거역해 왔다.
④ 소비자들은 광범위한 선택에 쉽게 만족한다.
⑤ 소비자들의 무의식적인 생각이 각각의 옵션을 모두 신중히 평가하게 한다.

어구 **set up** 세우다, 똑바로 놓다 **tasting booth** 시식대 **a variety of** 다양한 **exotic** 외래의, 외국산의; 이질적인 **gourmet** 미식가 **upscale** (경제적으로) 풍부한, 높은 수입이 있는, 고소득층에 속하는 **make a difference** 차이가 생기다; 중요하다; 효과가 있다 **economic wisdom** 경제적 통념 **stop by** 들르다; 방문하다 **snap** 급히 행해진, 즉석의, (준비 없이) 불시에 행해진; 덥석 물다 **instinctively** 본능적으로 **paralyzed** 마비된 **in a snap** 즉석에서 **frugal** 검약한, 소박[질박]한, 조리차한 **take a step** 조치를 취하다 **be bound to R** ~하지 않을 수 없다 **dominate** 지배[통치]하다, 위압하다 **withstand** (곤란 등에) 잘 견디다, 버티다; 저항하다

해설 무의식적인 상태에서 이루어지는 즉석 판단은 간소함이 지켜져야 하며, 이 간소함은 결국 '선택이 적어야 함'을 의미한다. 따라서 즉석 판단은 선택권을 거의 필요로 하지 않는다는 ① 설명이 옳다.

> Then I grasped the child's head with my left hand and tried to get the wooden tongue depressor between her teeth. She fought, with teeth clenched, desperately! But now I also had grown furious—at a child. I tried to hold myself down but I couldn't. Now I know how to expose a throat for inspection.

2 이 글에서 "I"의 직업은?

① surgeon
② athlete
③ physician
④ therapeutist

해석 그때 나는 왼손으로 그 아이의 머리를 붙잡고서 나무 혀 누르개를 그 아이의 이 사이로 끼워 넣으려 애썼다. 그 여자아이는 이를 악물고 필사적으로 다투었다. 그러나 이제 나도 아이에게 점점 화가 났다. 나는 자신을 억제하려고 애썼으나 그럴 수 없었다. 지금은 검사를 위해 목구멍을 노출시키는 방법을 알고 있다.

2 이 글에서 "I"의 직업은?

① 외과 의사
② 운동선수
③ 내과 의사
④ 임상 의사

어구 **grasp** 잡다; 이해하다 **tongue depressor** 혀 누르개 **clench** (이를) 악물다; (손·주먹 따위를) 꽉 쥐다 **desperately** 필사적으로 **furious** 성난, 격노한, 화가 치민; 격심한 **hold oneself down** 자제하다; 억누르다 **expose** 까발리다, 노출시키다 **surgeon** 외과 의사 **athlete** 운동선수, 경기자 **physician** 내과 의사 **therapeutist** 임상 의사, 치료사

해설 첫 문장에서 혀 누르개를 이 사이로 끼워 넣었고, 마지막 문장에서 목구멍을 벌리는 법을 안다고 했으므로, 내과 의사로 유추할 수 있다.

> Chimpanzees, our close relatives, are sometimes compared to politicians: they engage in power plays; they use diplomacy; they assign perks to various positions in a complicated social hierarchy. Blue monkeys, which seem calmer and less prone to form coalitions, appear to be more egalitarian. And yet my study of the group dynamics of territorial battles, and how these may figure into the way a group later splits into smaller new groups, has revealed unexpected complexity in blue monkey social structure. As in some human political organizations, those on top may depend more on those at the bottom than first meets the eye. The feeding territories over which blue monkeys battle are often so specific that a person could draw lines to demarcate them: this tree belongs to this group, the next tree over doesn't. Groups can coexist peacefully very near one another as long as each stays on its side of these imaginary lines.

3 According to the passage, blue monkeys of different groups can live together as long as
_____________.

① they don't cross their territorial boundary
② they share the same feeding grounds
③ they follow the leader's instructions
④ they face the predator's staying around
⑤ they don't touch the other group members

해석 우리와 친밀한 인척인(우리와 가까운 종인) 침팬지는 가끔씩 정치인들과 비교된다. 즉, 그들은 권력을 휘두르며, 권모술수를 이용하고, 복잡한 사회 계급 구조 안의 여러 지위에 특권을 부여한다. 더 조용하고 서로 연합하는 경향이 덜한 푸른 원숭이들은 평등주의를 취하는 것으로 보인다. 그러나 영토 분쟁의 집단 역학과 그 집단 역학이 차후에 더 작은 새로운 집단으로 나뉘는 방법에 어떻게 관여하게 됐는지에 대한 나의 연구 결과는 푸른 원숭이의 사회 구조에서 예견할 수 없었던 복잡함을 밝혀냈다. 몇몇 인간의 정치 집단에서처럼, 최고위층 원숭이들은 얼핏 보기보다 더 많이 최하위층 원숭이들에게 의존하는지 모른다. 푸른 원숭이가 싸움을 벌이는 먹이 영역은 종종 너무나 명백하기 때문에 인간은 그 먹이 영역의 경계를 표시하는 선을 그릴 수 있다. 즉, 이 나무는 이 집단의 것이며, 그 옆에 있는 나무는 그렇지 않다는 것이다. 각각의 집단이 이 상상의 자기 쪽 경계선에 머무르는 한, 집단은 서로 매우 가까이에서도 평화롭게 공생할 수 있다.

3 윗글에 따르면, 다른 단체의 푸른 원숭이들이 어떻게 하면 공생할 수 있는가?

① 자신의 먹이 영역을 넘지 않는다.
② 동일한 먹이 영역을 공유한다.
③ 지도자의 지시를 따른다.
④ 약탈 동물의 근처에 맞서고 있다.
⑤ 다른 집단의 원숭이들을 손대지 않는다.

어구 **engage in** (일·사업)에 착수하다 **diplomacy** 권모술수; 외교 **perk** (임직원의) 특전 **hierarchy** 계급 제도 **calm** 차분한 **prone to R** ~하는 경향이 있는 **group dynamics** 집단 역학 **territorial** 영토의

해설 마지막 문장에서 **as long as** ~ 구문을 통해 자신의 경계선 안에 머무른다면 상대방과의 매우 가까운 거리 내에서도 공생할 수 있다고 했다. 따라서 자신의 먹이 영역을 넘지 않는다는 설명이 옳다.

During the first few years of life, when babies' cells continue to undergo "programming," exposure to certain toxic chemicals can disrupt the delicate process. Bisphenol A (known as BPA), a compound in hard, clear polycarbonate plastics that mimics the effects of estrogen, has raised particular concern because it interferes with hormone levels and cell signaling systems. In August, several dozen scientists issued a review of 700 studies on BPA, warning that the levels most people are exposed to put them at elevated risk of cancer. Infants, the report said, are most vulnerable to BPA.

"Plastic bottles and plates that are boiled or put in the microwave or dishwasher are especially problematic because heating them repeatedly causes high amounts of BPA to leach out," says Retha Newbold, a reproductive biologist at the National Institute of Environmental Health Sciences in Triangle Park, N.C. Once small cracks form in the surface, a product should be discarded. She recommends that parents, to be on the safe side, switch to glass bottles or those with disposable liners that don't contain BPA. And they should use microwave-safe paper plates or glass dishes covered with a paper towel rather than plastic wrap.

4 The best title of the above passage would be

　　　　　　.

① The Problem with Plastic
② New Reasons to Watch What You Eat
③ The Influence of Chemicals on Human Beings
④ Some Factors to Increase Cancers in Babies
⑤ The Side Effects of Modern Kitchenwares

5 According to the passage, it would be safer for the parents 　　　　　　.

① to feed the babies only with organic food
② to breast-feed their babies
③ to check their babies regularly
④ to use glass bottles
⑤ to sanitize the bottles in the boiling water

해석 아기의 세포가 계속 "프로그램화"를 경험하는 초기 몇 년 동안, 어떤 유해 화학 물질에 노출되면 그 연약한 성장 과정에 해를 끼칠 수 있다. BPA라고 알려진 비스페놀 A는 에스트로겐의 효과와 유사한 성질을 갖춘 단단하고 투명한 플라스틱 안에 있는 혼합 물질로서, 호르몬 수준과 세포 신호 체계를 방해하기 때문에 특별한 걱정을 야기했다. 8월에 수십 명의 과학자들이 BPA에 관한 700개의 논문을 발표하면서, 대부분의 사람들이 노출된 그(BPA) 수준이 암에 걸릴 위험성을 높여 놓았다고 경고했다. 그 보고 내용은 유아들이 BPA에 가장 취약하다고 전했다.

"플라스틱 병과 접시에 지속적으로 열이 가해지면 상당량의 BPA가 녹아 나오기 때문에 끓이거나 전자레인지, 혹은 세척기에 들어간 것들은 특히 문제가 많다."고 노스캐롤라이나 주 트라이앵글 파크의 미국 국립 환경 보건원의 재생 생물학자인 레타 뉴볼드가 말한다. 작은 금이 표면에 생기게 되면, 그 제품을 버려야만 한다. 그녀는, 안전을 위해서 부모들이 유리병이나 BPA가 없는 일회용 내벽이 있는 병으로 바꾸어야 한다고 조언을 한다. 그리고 부모들은 플라스틱 랩보다는 종이 타월로 덮어서 전자레인지에 안전한 종이 접시나 유리 접시를 사용해야 한다.

4 윗글의 제목은 무엇인가?
① 플라스틱의 문제점
② 당신의 식사를 예의 주시해야 할 새로운 이유들
③ 인간에 대한 화학 물질의 영향력
④ 아기들의 암을 증가시키는 몇 가지 요인들
⑤ 현대 부엌세간의 부작용

5 이 글에 따르면, 부모가 어떻게 하는 것이 더 안전하겠는가?
① 아기에게 유기농 식품만 먹이는 것
② 아기에게 모유를 주는 것
③ 아기를 규칙적으로 확인하는 것
④ 유리병을 사용하는 것
⑤ 끓는 물에 병을 세척하는 것

어구 toxic 독(성)의; 유독한, 중독(성)의　disrupt 붕괴[분열]시키다; 분쇄하다　delicate 연약한, 섬세한; 미묘한　Bisphenol 비스페놀　compound 합성[혼합]물; 화합물, 합성하다　polycarbonate 폴리카보네이트(합성수지의 일종)　mimic 흉내 내다; 흉내 내며 조롱하다　estrogen 에스트로겐　issue (지폐·책 따위를) 발행하다, 출판하다　put A at risk A를 위험에 처하게 하다　vulnerable 취약한　microwave 전자레인지(microwave oven)　dishwasher 접시 닦는 사람[기계]　problematic 문제의; 문제가 되는, 미심쩍은, 불확실한　leach out 걸러지다; 녹다　reproductive biologist 재생 생물학자　crack 갈라진 금, 틈; 날카로운 소리　discard (쓸데없는 것·습관·신앙 따위를) 버리다　be on the safe side 안전하다　switch to ~으로 바뀌다　disposable 사용 후 버릴 수 있는, 일회용의; 처리할 수 있는　liner 안에 대는 것; (마멸 방지용) 입힘쇠, 덧쇠; 정기선(특히 대양 항해의 대형 쾌속선); 정기 항공기　-safe ~에 안전한　kitchenware 부엌세간　feed A with B A에게 B를 (먹이로) 주다　breast-feed 모유로 기르다, 젖을 주다　sanitize 위생적으로 하다

해설 **4** 신체에 해로운 BPA가 플라스틱에 들어 있기 때문에, 플라스틱 용기 사용을 되도록 피하라고 권하는 글이다. 따라서 '플라스틱의 문제점'이 이 글의 제목으로서 옳다.

5 마지막에서 두 번째 문장 '~switch to glass bottles'에서 안전을 위해 유리병으로 바꾸라고 했다.

Toto is an American rock band founded in 1977 by some of the most popular and experienced session musicians of the era. The band enjoyed great commercial success in the late 1970s and 1980s, beginning with the band's self-titled debut released in 1978. With the release of 1982's critically acclaimed and commercially successful Toto IV, Toto became one of the best-selling music groups of their era. They are best known for the Top 3 hits "Hold the Line," "Rosanna," and "Africa". Although their popularity in the United States diminished in the 1990s and 2000s, they continued to sell out arenas constantly internationally, playing only a number of shows in the USA.

Toto is known for a musical style that combines elements of pop, rock, soul, funk, progressive rock, hard rock, R&B and jazz. Although they were mostly associated with the soft rock genre, Toto's broad array of musical styles helps them appeal to a variety of listeners.

6 According to the passage, what is not mentioned about Toto?

① It consists of professional performing musicians.
② Its music made a good profit, but was not welcomed by music critics.
③ Its revenues were higher in 1980s than in 2000s.
④ Their music seems to be fusion styles.
⑤ Its concert in America has been diminishing.

해석 토토는 그 시대에 가장 인기가 많고 노련한 세션 뮤지션들로 1977년에 결성된 미국 록 밴드이다. 그 밴드는 1978년에 발매된 동명의 데뷔 앨범을 시작으로, 1970년대와 1980년대에 엄청난 상업적 성공을 누렸다. 1982년도에 발매된 Toto IV 앨범이 비평가들의 찬사와 상업적 성공을 모두 이루어서, 토토는 그들 세대에서 가장 많은 음반을 판매한 밴드가 되었다. 그들은 세 가지 최고의 히트곡인 Hold the Line, Rosanna와 Africa가 가장 유명하다. 1990년대와 2000년대에 미국에서 인기가 줄었지만, 그들은 전 세계적으로 음반 판매량을 계속 늘렸고, 미국에서는 많은 공연만 했다.
토토는 팝, 소울, 펑크, 프로그레시브 록, 하드 록, 알앤비 및 재즈의 요소를 혼합한 음악 스타일로 유명하다. 그 요소들이 소프트 록 음악과 대개 결합되지만, 토토의 광범위한 음악 스타일은 다양한 음악 애호가들에게 매력으로 다가간다.

6 토토에 관하여 언급되지 않은 것은?

① 토토는 프로 연주가들로 구성됐다.
② 토토의 음악은 상당한 이윤을 냈지만, 음악 비평가들에게 환영받지 못했다.
③ 토토의 이윤은 2000년대보다 1980년대에 더 높았다.
④ 그들의 음악은 퓨전 양식을 갖고 있는 것 같다.
⑤ 미국 내에서의 공연이 줄어들었다.

어구 found 설립하다; 토대를 세우다   experienced 노련한   session musician 세션 음악인(가수의 음반 · 공연 등에 연주해 주는 음악인)   self-titled 자신의 이름을 제목으로 정한   sell out 다 팔아 버리다; 매진되다   arena 공연장; 경기장   fusion 퓨전(재즈에 록 등이 섞인 음악); 용해; 융해

해설 With the release of 1982's critically acclaimed~을 통해 대중뿐만 아니라 비평가들에게도 상당한 찬사를 받았음을 알 수 있다.

>>> 다음 글을 읽고 문제의 답을 고르시오. [7~9]

A powerful tide is surging across much of the world today, creating a new, often bizarre environment in which to work, play, marry, raise children, or retire. In this bewildering context, businessmen swim against highly erratic economic currents; politicians see their ratings bob wildly up and down; universities, hospitals, and other institutions battle desperately against inflation. Value systems splinter and crash, while the lifeboats of family, church, and state are hurled madly about.

Looking at these violent changes, we can regard them as isolated evidences of instability, breakdown, and disaster. Yet, if we stand back for a longer view, several things become apparent that otherwise go unnoticed.

To begin with, many of today's changes are not independent of one another. Nor are they random. For example, the crack-up of the nuclear family, the global energy crisis, the spread of cults and cable television, the rise of flextime and new fringe-benefit packages, the emergence of separatist movements from Quebec to Corsica, may all seem like isolated events. Yet precisely the reverse is true. These and many other seemingly unrelated events or trends are interconnected. They are, in fact, parts of a much larger phenomenon: the death of industrialism and the rise of a new civilization.

7 Which of the following best characterizes the above passage?

① informative ② augmentative
③ romantic ④ sarcastic
⑤ dramatic

8 Which of the following is true according to the above passage?

① Businessmen work in a steady environment.
② Hospitals struggle to overcome inflation.
③ All institutions need not worry about inflation.
④ Politicians do not care whether their ratings change rapidly.
⑤ People are eager to find a lifeboat in the economic crisis.

9 The author believes that the changes mentioned in the first paragraph

____________.

① are independent pieces of evidence of instability
② are interrelated parts of a much larger phenomenon
③ can never be noticed though they are closely examined
④ help people realize the rise of a new civilization
⑤ are independent of one another

해석 오늘날 강력한 풍조가 세상 전역에 물결을 쳐서, 일하고 놀고 결혼하고 아이를 키우거나 은퇴하는 것에 새롭고, 때로는 이상야릇한 분위기를 만들어 내고 있다. 이러한 혼란스러운 상황 속에서 사업가들은 매우 불규칙적인 경제 시류에 역행하고 있다. 정치인들은 그들의 평가가 거칠게 요동치는 것을 보고 있다. 대학들과 병원들과 다른 기관들은 인플레이션에 필사적으로 싸우고 있다. 가치 체계는 가족, 교회, 그리고 정부의 구명보트가 미친 듯이 내동댕이쳐지는 동안 분열되고 파괴된다.

이러한 격렬한 변화를 바라보는 우리는 그것들을 불안정과 붕괴와 재난의 고립된 증거들이라고 간주할 수 있다. 그러나 더 멀리 바라보기 위해 물러서 보면, 그렇지 않았다면 알아채지 못했을 여러 가지 것들이 두드러진다.

우선적으로 오늘날 수많은 변화들이 상호간에 관계가 없는 것이 아니다. 그리고 무작위의 것도 아니다. 예컨대, 핵가족의 분열, 지구 에너지 위기, 종파와 케이블 TV의 확산, 근무 시간 자유 선택과 부가 급부 패키지들의 증가, 퀘벡에서 코르시카로의 분리주의자 운동 출현 등은 모두 고립된 사건들로 보일지도 모른다. 그러나 정확히 그 반대가 사실이다. 이것들과 많은 다른 외관상 상관없는 사건들이나 경향들은 상호 연결되어 있다. 사실상 그것들은 산업주의의 종료와 새로운 문명의 부흥이라는 훨씬 더 커다란 현상의 일부분이다.

7 윗글의 특징은?
① 정보를 제공하는 ② 증가적인 ③ 공상적인
④ 빈정대는 ⑤ 극적인

8 윗글의 내용과 일치하는 것은?
① 직장인들은 안정된 환경에서 일하고 있다.
② 병원들은 인플레이션을 극복하기 위해 애쓰고 있다.
③ 모든 기관들은 인플레이션을 걱정할 필요가 없다.
④ 정치인들은 그들의 평가가 빠르게 변화하든지 어떤지 신경 쓰지 않는다.
⑤ 사람들은 경제 위기 속에서 구명보트를 찾는 데 혈안이 되어 있다.

9 작가가 첫 단락에서 언급된 변화는 어떠한가?
① 불안정한 현상의 독립적인 단면들이다.
② 훨씬 커다란 현상의 상호 관련된 부분들이다.
③ 비록 자세히 관찰된다고 해도 결코 알아낼 수 없다.
④ 사람들이 새로운 문명의 발생을 인식하는 것을 돕는다.
⑤ 각각 독립적인 것이다.

어구 bizarre 기괴한, 별난 bewildering 당혹스러운 swim against currents 시류에 역행하다 rating 등급, 자격 bob (상하로) 움직이다 splinter 쪼개지다 lifeboat 구조선 go unnoticed 무시당하다, 눈에 띄지 않다 to begin with 우선적으로 be independent of ~에 독립하다, ~과 관련이 없다 random 무작위의 nuclear family 핵가족 cult 예배, 숭배, 종파 flextime 근무 시간의 자유 선택 제도 fringe-benefit 부가 급부 emergence 출현 separatist 분리주의자, 이탈자 seemingly 외관상 interconnect 서로 연락하다 in fact 사실상 informative 정보를 제공하는 augmentative (뜻을) 확대하는 sarcastic 빈정거리는 dramatic 극적인 steady 안정적인 struggle to R 노력하다 be eager to R ~을 열망하다 closely 면밀히

해설 7 오늘날 사회에서 급격히 변화하고 있는 풍조에 대해서 설명을 하고 있는 분위기이다.

8 첫 단락 두 번째 문장의 세미콜론 이하에서 '대학들과 병원들과 다른 기관들은 인플레이션에 사적으로 싸우고 있다'고 했다.

9 각각 독립된 것이 아니라 상호 관련되어 있다고 마지막 단락에서 설명하고 있다.

There was a time when Bernie, 19, doubted that she could even finish high school, still less go to college. As a sophomore, she became pregnant and briefly thought about dropping out. But since transferring to the Academy of Urban Planning, she has passed all five of the required state exams for graduation. She is retaking one exam in the hopes of getting a diploma with the state's highest distinction. Her personal turnaround mirrors that of the school she now attends. The academy is housed in the same building that five years ago was known as Bushwick High School. Bushwick had one of the lowest four-year graduation rates of any school in New York—a dismal 23 percent. And violence plagued the school's hallways. Then, five years ago, New York Mayor Michael Bloomberg took control of the city's school districts, launching a flurry of reforms that led to Bushwick's division into four smaller schools.

10 According to the passage, Bernie

______________.

① passed the college entrance examination
② gave up the high school diploma
③ is thinking of transferring to another school
④ is taking one exam again to get a better score

해석 열아홉 살의 버니는 대학 진학은 말할 것도 없고 고등학교를 졸업할 수 있을지 확신하지 못하던 때가 있었다. 2학년이 됐을 때 그녀는 임신을 했으며 학교를 중퇴할 생각을 잠깐 했었다. 그러나 그녀가 Academy of Urban Planning으로 전학을 간 후, 그녀는 주(州)가 주관하는 졸업 시험 5개를 모두 합격했다. 그녀는 주에서 최고 성적으로 졸업장을 받으려는 희망으로 한 과목의 시험을 다시 보고 있다. 그녀 개인의 변화는 현재 다니고 있는 학교의 변화와 유사하다. 그 학교는 5년 전에는 부시윅 고등학교로 알려졌던 바로 그 건물에 입주해 있었다. 부시윅 고등학교는 뉴욕 주의 모든 학교 중에서 4년 내에 졸업하는 학생 비율이 가장 낮은 학교였으며, 그 졸업률이 23%로 비관적이었다. 게다가 학교폭력이 난무했다. 그런데 5년 전에 뉴욕 시장인 마이클 블룸버그가 그 도시의 학군들을 관리하였고, 재빠른 개혁을 착수하여 그 결과로서 부시윅 고등학교를 네 개의 작은 학교로 나누었다.

10 버니는 어떠한 인물인가?

① 대학입학시험에 합격했다.
② 고등학교 졸업을 포기했다.
③ 다른 학교로 편입할 것을 생각하고 있다.
④ 더 좋은 점수를 얻기 위해 시험을 다시 치르고 있다.

어구 **still less** ~은 말할 것도 없고 **sophomore** (4년제 대학 · 고등학교의) 2년생 **briefly** 일시적으로, 잠시 **drop out** 낙오하다, 중퇴하다 **transfer** 전학을 가다; 바꾸다; 옮기다, 이동[운반]하다 **retake** 다시 잡다; 되찾다, 탈환[회복]하다 **diploma** 졸업 증서, 학위 수여증; 면허장 **turnaround** 전회, 선회; (진로 · 방침 · 정세 등의) 180도 전환, 전향 **mirror** 비추다, 반사하다; 반영시키다; 대표하다 **dismal** 음울한, 황량한, 쓸쓸한 **plague** 애태우다, 괴롭히다; 역병(疫病), 전염병 **hallway** 복도(corridor); 현관 **take control of** ~을 관리하다 **district** (행정 · 사법 · 선거 · 교육 등을 위해 나눈) 지역; 지구 **a flurry of** 재빠른; 서두르는 **division** 구분, 부분; 구(區), 부(部), 단(段); 분할, 분배 **take an exam again** 시험을 다시 보다

해설 네 번째 문장에서 현재 진행형(is retaking)을 통해 최고 성적을 받고 고등학교를 졸업하기 위해서 시험을 다시 치르고 있다고 했다. 세 번째 문장에서 과거에 전학을 이미 했기 때문에 ③처럼 현재진행형으로 진학을 갈 생각을 하고 있다는 것은 틀린 설명이다.

It happens to most of us: a sleepless night in a hotel room just before a big presentation. You need to sleep. But no matter how hard you try, you just can't get to sleep. Whether we're traveling two hours by car or 14 hours by plane, the evil sleep monster can visit us at any time. Sleeplessness, called "insomnia" causes us frustration at night and makes us miserable the next day. We're not at the top of our game for the big meeting and our lack of concentration makes us dangerous drivers to boot.

How do we prevent sleeplessness on the road? People say that there are a number of theories about napping before travel and after arrival to help beat jet lag. I've been told to stay up very late the night before an international trip so that I'll be able to sleep on the plane. Usually, I end up staying up late and not sleeping a minute on the plane only to arrive at my destination crabby and miserable. Other people suggest a short nap upon arrival be followed by a shower and a brisk walk. But honestly, after traveling quite a bit, I've determined that you should sleep as often as your body—and your schedule—allows.

11 According to the passage, which of the following can be caused by insomnia?

① Frequent headaches and indigestion
② Overuse of sleeping pills and aids for treatment
③ Inability to walk briskly the following day
④ Frequent waking during sleep at night
⑤ Lack of good performance and concentration

12 Which of the following does the writer suggest to overcome jet lag?

① Not going to sleep during travel
② Napping before travel and after arrival
③ Staying up very late the night before travel
④ Taking a short nap upon arrival followed by a shower
⑤ Trying to sleep as often as you can wherever you travel

해석 중요한 발표를 앞두고 호텔 방안에서 밤새 잠을 못자는 일이 우리들 대부분에게 발생한다. 하지만 잠을 잘 필요가 있다. 그러나 아무리 노력을 해도 잠을 정말로 잘 수가 없다. 우리가 자동차로 2시간을 이동하든 비행기로 14시간을 이동하든, 사악한 잠의 괴물은 언제라도 우리에게 찾아올 수 있다. '불면증'이라고 불리는 잠 못 이룸 증상은 밤에는 우리에게 좌절감을 주고 다음날에는 우리를 비참하게 만든다. 우리는 중요한 회의에서 최선을 다할 수 없게 되며, 게다가 집중력 부족은 우리의 운전을 위험하게 만든다.

어떻게 우리는 여행하면서 불면증을 막을 수 있을까? 여행 전과 여행 후의 낮잠에 관하여 몇 가지 일반적인 방법이 있는데, 이것이 시차를 극복하는 데 도움을 줄 것이라고 사람들은 말한다. 나는 비행기에서 잠을 잘 수 있기 위하여 해외여행을 떠나기 전에 밤늦게까지 자지 말고 있으라는 말을 들었다. 보통 나는 밤늦게까지 자지 않으며, 비행기에서도 단 1분도 자지 못하여 목적지에 도착했을 때에는 시무룩하고 비참한 상태가 된다. 어떤 사람들은 도착하자마자 짧은 낮잠을 잔 다음에 샤워를 하고 활기차게 걸으라고 주장한다. 그러나 솔직히 말해서, 당신의 몸과 스케줄이 허락하는 만큼 자주 잠을 자야 한다는 것을 나는 여행을 많이 해 본 후 확신하게 됐다.

11 이글에 따랐을 때, 불면증에 의해 유발될 수 있는 것은 무엇인가?
① 잦은 두통과 소화 불량
② 수면제 과다 복용과 치료
③ 다음날 활발하게 걷지 못하는 무능력
④ 밤에 잠을 자는 동안 종종 깨어 있는 상태
⑤ 뛰어난 업무력 및 집중력의 부재

12 시차증(時差症)을 극복하기 위해 작가는 무엇을 제안하는가?
① 비행시간 동안 잠을 자지 않는 것
② 비행 전과 도착 후 낮잠을 자는 것
③ 비행 전 밤늦게까지 잠들지 않는 것
④ 도착하자마자 낮잠을 잔 후 샤워를 하는 것
⑤ 당신이 여행을 하는 곳이 어디든지 간에 되도록 자주 잠을 자기 위해 노력하는 것

어구 big presentation 중요한 발표 no matter how 아무리 ~할지라도 get to R ~하게 되다 at any time 언제라도 insomnia 불면증 frustration 짜증 miserable 불쌍한, 비참한, 가련한(pitiable) be at the top of game 최고의 성과를 내다 concentration 집중, 전념 to boot 게다가, 덤으로 on the road 여행 중에 end up 결국 ~을 하다 crabby 심술궂은, 까다로운 nap 낮잠 upon arrival 도착하자마자 A is followed by B A 후에 B가 있다, A 후에 B하다 quite a bit 상당히, 꽤나 overuse 과도한 사용; 지나치게 사용하다 briskly 활발하게 jet lag 시차증(時差症)

해설 11 첫 단락 마지막 문장을 통해 알 수 있다. 불면증에 시달리면 중요한 모임을 위해서 최상의 상태에 있을 수가 없으며, 집중력이 떨어져서 운전 또한 매우 위험할 수 있다고 했다. 따라서 뛰어난 업무력과 집중력이 떨어진다는 ⑤가 옳다.

12 마지막 문장에 언급됐다. 여행을 많이 해 본 작가의 경험을 통해 몸과 스케줄이 허락하는 한 자주 잠을 많이 자야 한다고 말한다. 따라서 여행할 때마다 할 수 있는 한 자주 잠을 자기 위해 노력해야 한다는 설명이 옳다.

Fluency shaping therapy, also known as "speak more fluently", "prolonged speech" or "connected speech", trains stutterers to speak fluently by controlling their breathing, phonation, and articulation (lips, jaw, and tongue). It is based on operant conditioning techniques. Stutterers are trained to reduce their speaking rate by stretching vowels and consonants, and using other fluency techniques such as continuous airflow and soft speech contacts. After the stutterer masters these fluency skills, the speaking rate and intonation are increased gradually. This more normal-sounding, fluent speech is then transferred to daily life outside the speech clinic, _____________ lack of speech naturalness at the end of treatment remains a frequent criticism. Fluency shaping approaches are often taught in intensive group therapy programs, which may take two to three weeks to complete, but more recently the Camperdown program, using a much shorter schedule, has been shown to be effective.

13 According the passage, which of the following is not described as the treatment of stutter?

① vocalization　　② controlling breath
③ getting rid of anxiety　④ slowly speaking
⑤ pronunciation correction

14 Which of the following would be the best for the blank?

① because　　② so
③ as well as　④ though
⑤ despite

해석　유창성 치료법은 '보다 더 유창하게 말하는 방법', '길게 말하기' 혹은 '조리 있는 말하기'라고 알려졌는데, 말을 더듬는 사람에게 호흡, 발성 및 발음(입, 턱, 혀)을 조절하여 유창하게 말할 수 있도록 가르친다. 이 치료법은 조작적 조건 형성법에 기초한다. 말을 더듬는 사람들은 모음 글자와 자음 글자를 늘리면서 지속적으로 숨을 들이마시면서 부드럽게 말을 연결시키는 것과 같은 다른 유창성 훈련을 사용하여 말의 속도를 늦추도록 훈련을 받는다. 이 치료가 끝나고 나면 말의 속도와 발성이 점점 나아진다. 비록 치료가 끝났을 때 부드럽게 말하는 능력이 부족해서 비난을 자주 받는다 하더라도, 더욱 정상적인 소리를 내고 유창한 말을 하는 것은 언어 교정소를 떠나서 일상생활로 이어진다. 유창성 형성법은 단체 집중 치료 내에서 자주 이루어지며 2주에서 3주의 시간이 걸리지만, 훨씬 짧은 기간의 치료를 이용하는 캠퍼다운 프로그램이 더 효과가 뛰어난 것으로 밝혀졌다.

13 이 글에 따랐을 때, 말더듬증의 치료로 언급되지 않은 것은?

① 발성　　　　　　　　② 호흡 조절
③ 걱정 불안 해소　　　④ 천천히 말하기
⑤ 발음 교정

14 다음 중 빈칸에 가장 알맞은 것은?

① ~이기 때문에　　　② 따라서
③ ~뿐만 아니라　　　④ ~일지라도
⑤ ~에도 불구하고

어구　**prolonged speech** 긴 말; 길게 말하기　**phonation** 발성　**operant** 자발적인; 움직이는; 효력이 있는　**operant conditioning technique** 조작적 조건 형성법　**consonant** 자음; 일치하는, 조화하는　**airflow** 공기의 흡입　**vocalization** 발성(법)　**get rid of** ~을 제거하다

해설　**13** 윗글에서 '발성', '호흡조절', '천천히 말하기', '발음 교정'은 모두 말더듬의 치료책으로서 직접 언급됐지만, 걱정 불안 해소는 언급된 바 없는 내용이다.
　14 빈칸 앞뒤로 완전한 문장들이 나오므로 전치사가 아니라 접속사가 필요하다. 일상생활에서 유창한 말이 이어진다는 긍정적인 내용과 치료 후반부에 부드럽게 말하는 능력이 부족해서 종종 비난을 받을 수도 있다는 내용은 '역접-양보'의 논리가 된다.

Bees make honey to survive. It is their only essential food. If there are 60,000 bees in a hive about one third of them will be involved in gathering nectar. When the bees arrive at the hive carrying nectar they give this to the house bees. The house bees move the nectar around with their mandibles, exposing it to the warm dry air of the hive. When it is first gathered the nectar contains sugar and minerals mixed with about 80% water. After ten to twenty minutes, when much of the excess water has evaporated, the house bees put the nectar in a cell in the honeycomb where evaporation continues. After three days, the honey in the cells contains about 20% water. At this stage, the bees cover the cells with lids which they make out of beeswax.

해석　벌들은 생존하기 위하여 꿀을 만든다. 꿀만이 벌의 필수적인 식량이 된다. 벌집 안에 6만 마리의 벌들이 산다면 그 벌의 1/3은 화밀(花蜜)을 모으는 것과 관련이 있을 것이다. 벌이 화밀을 가지고 벌집에 도착할 때, 이 화밀을 집벌에게 넘겨준다. 집벌은 이 화밀을 턱으로 옮겨 벌집의 따뜻하고 건조한 공기로 노출시킨다. 처음 화밀을 모았을 때, 그 화밀은 약 80%의 물에 섞인 설탕과 무기물이 포함되어 있다. 10분에서 20분 후에, 상당히 많은 물이 증발되면, 집벌은 증발이 계속되는 벌집의 구멍 안에 화밀을 넣는다. 3일이 지난 후, 벌집 구멍 안에 있는 꿀은 20%의 물을 포함하게 된다. 이 단계에서 벌들은 그 벌집 구멍 위에 밀랍으로 만든 뚜껑을 덮는다.

15 What is the main difference between nectar and honey?

① The proportion of water in the substance
② The proportion of sugar to minerals in the substance
③ The type of plan from which the substance is gathered
④ The type of bee which processes the substance

15 화밀과 벌꿀의 주된 차이점은 무엇인가?

① 그 화밀 안의 물의 비율
② 그 화밀 안에서 설탕과 미네랄의 비율
③ 화밀이 모이는 식물의 종류
④ 화밀을 처리하는 벌의 종류

어구 hive 벌집(beehive); 꿀벌 떼 be involved in ~과 연관이 있다 nectar 화밀(花蜜); 감미로운 음료 house bee 집벌 mandible (포유동물 · 물고기의) 턱, (특히) 아래턱(jaw) evaporate 증발하다 cell (벌집의) 봉방(蜂房); 세포; 작은 방 honeycomb (꿀)벌집 cover A with B A를 B로 덮다 lid 뚜껑; 단속 make A out of B B를 통해 A를 만들다 beeswax 밀(랍) proportion of A to B A와 B의 비율

해설 화밀은 물이 80%가 포함되지만, 꿀은 화밀의 수분이 증발되면 물이 20%만 남게 되므로, 화밀과 꿀의 주된 차이는 물의 비율이 된다.

In its breakneck quest for economic growth, the world's most populous nation has created no shortage of environmental disasters—just as other countries did when they, too, industrialized. But the Chinese people are growing impatient with the costs of unchecked development. Around the country, citizens are volunteering for cleanup projects. A small, courageous network of NGOs is naming and shaming the worst polluters. The huge number of pollution-related protests—an estimated 50,000 took place in 2005—unambiguously demonstrates grass-roots resentment of the ecological burden of industrialization. So did a survey by the Pew Global Attitudes Project about a year ago, which found that some 80% of Chinese felt protecting the environment should be a priority—a stark contrast to the global perception of the Chinese as a people in feckless pursuit of wealth.

16 According to the passage, the Chinese were perceived as a people who ______________ by other people.

① had a respectful tradition
② didn't care about the neighbors
③ would do anything for money
④ were for global pollution
⑤ didn't hesitate to spend as much as they can

해석 무모하게 경제 성장을 추구하면서, 지구에서 인구가 가장 많은 국가는 다른 산업화된 국가들과 마찬가지로, 적지 않은 환경의 재앙을 일으켰다. 그러나 중국인들은 억제되지 않는 발전에 따른 비용에 인내심을 잃어가고 있다. 중국 전역에 걸쳐서 시민들은 정화 계획에 자발적으로 참여하고 있다. 비정부 기구의 작지만 용감한 네트워크는 최악의 오염원들을 언급하며 망신을 주고 있다. 2005년에 대략 5만 건이 발생한 엄청난 수의 오염 관련 시위가 산업화에 따른 생태계 부담에 대한 대중의 분노를 분명히 증명하고 있다. Pew Global Attitudes Project의 약 1년 전 여론 조사도 마찬가지였으며, 80%의 중국인들이 환경 보호가 우선되어야 한다고 느꼈다는 점을 발견했다. 이것은 중국인들을 무책임하게 부를 추구하는 사람들이라고 세계인들이 인식하는 것과 정반대가 된다.

16 이 글에 따랐을 때, 중국인들은 다른 사람들에 의해 어떠한 민족이라고 인식됐는가?

① 존경받을 만한 전통을 가진
② 이웃을 돌보지 않는
③ 돈을 위해 어느 것이라고 하는
④ 지구의 오염에 책임을 지는
⑤ 할 수 있는 한 많은 돈을 소비하는

어구 breakneck 위험하기 짝이 없는; 가파른 quest 탐색; 연구; 추구 populous 사람 수가 많은 industrialize 산업[공업]화하다 unchecked 저지[억제]되지 않은; 검사받지 않은 name and shame 이름을 밝혀서 공개적으로 망신을 주다 pollution-related 공해와 관련된 protest 항의하다, 이의를 제기하다 take place 발생하다 unambiguously 명백하게 grass-roots 일반 대중; 지표에 가까운 토양 resentment 분개; 원한 burden 짐, 부담 stark contrast 정반대 feckless 무기력한, 연약한; 쓸모없는

해설 마지막 표현인 a stark contrast to the global perception of the Chinese as a people in feckless pursuit of wealth을 통해 앞 문장과 반대되는 내용을 찾아야 한다. 앞 문장에서 중국인들 중 80%가 환경 보호를 우선시해야 한다고 했다. 이 내용과 반대되는 내용이 그동안 중국인들을 바라본 다른 사람들의 인식이 되는 것이다.

>>> 다음 글을 읽고 문제의 답을 고르시오. [17~18]

If you already feel inside you the urge of self-expression, then the first thing that you have to do is to study the means of expressing yourself. You will have to study very carefully the English language and especially its grammar. Although most people do not understand the art of good writing, they unconsciously assimilate more easily ideas which are expressed in correct English. It should be pointed out also that good English is not necessarily flowery English, and the simple phrase—which looks so easy to write—is often the most difficult to construct. I can not stress too strongly the desirability of writing your sentences word by word and not phrase by phrase. Many writers fail to get their ideas across to the public solely because they use expressions whose meaning has been killed by repetition.

17 Choose the best title for the passage above.

① Self-expression, an Essential to Writing
② The Art of Writing
③ Dependence of English upon Grammar
④ The Curse of Repetition
⑤ Flowery English: Its Value

18 Writing phrase by phrase is ___________.

① undesirable
② indispensable
③ important
④ easily assimilated
⑤ economical

해석 당신의 마음속에서 자기표현의 충동을 느낀다면 당신이 해야만 하는 첫 번째 일은 자기 자신을 표현하는 방법을 배우는 것이다. 당신은 매우 조심스럽게 영어, 특히 문법을 공부해야만 할 것이다. 대부분의 사람들이 좋은 문장을 쓰는 방법을 이해하지는 못할지라도 정확한 영어로 표현된 생각들은 무의식적으로 더욱 용이하게 받아들인다. 훌륭한 영어가 반드시 화려한 영어가 아니며, 단순한 어구가 쉽게 쓰인 것처럼 보이지만 작문하기가 가장 어려운 경우도 종종 있다. 작문할 때 어구별이 아니라 단어별로 쓰는 것을 아무리 강조해도 지나치지 않겠다. 많은 작가들이 대중에게 자신의 생각을 전달하는 데에 실패하는데, 그 이유가 반복되어 의미가 죽어버린 표현을 사용하기 때문이다.

17 윗글의 제목을 고르시오.

① 작문의 필수 요소인 자기표현　　② 작문하는 기법
③ 영문법에 대한 의존　　④ 반복에 대한 저주
⑤ 화려한 영어: 그것의 가치

18 구 단위로 작문하는 것은 어떠한가?

① 바람직하지 못한　　② 필수 불가결한
③ 중요한　　④ 쉽게 이해되는
⑤ 경제적인

어구 urge 충동 self-expression 자기표현 means 수단, 재산 art 기술, 예술, 기초 과목, 인공 unconsciously 무의식적으로 assimilate (지식 등을) 이해하다, 흡수하다, 동화시키다 point out 지적하다 flowery (문체 등이) 화려한, 꽃 같은 word by word 단어 단위로 phrase by phrase 구 단위로 repetition 반복, 암송 essential 필수 (요소), 불가결한 요소 curse 저주 undesirable 바람직하지 못한 indispensable 필수 불가결한

해설 **17** 자기표현에 관한 글이 아니라, 문법을 토대로 하여 단계적으로 주의 깊게 써야 한다는 여러 방법들을 제시하고 있다. 따라서 (영어를) 작문하는 방법·기법이 주제로서 옳다.

18 'I can not stress too strongly the desirability of writing your sentences word by word and not phrase by phrase.' 문장에서, 작문을 할 경우 '구 단위가 아니라 단어 단위로' 쓰라고 했으므로, 구 단위의 작문은 바람직하지 못하다는 것을 알 수 있다.

Melina Kanakaredes is the star of "Providence", the highest rated new drama on America's NBC network since "ER". As Dr. Sydney Hansen, she plays a Los Angeles plastic surgeon who gives up her practice and moves back home to be with her family.

There is a very thin line between the actress and the character she plays, for Kanakaredes's own family has always been closeknit. She is fiercely proud of her Greek heritage—her maternal grandparents emigrated from Greece and opened a chocolate shop in Ohio.

Family loyalty was tested early in her career when she was told to change her name. But keeping her name was a way of honoring the culture she loves. As she puts it, "I always felt if I ever became known for my acting, I wanted it to be Melina Kanakaredes who got there, not some other girl with some other name".

19 Dr. Sydney Hansen's family ____________.

① is an extended one
② are very supportive of each other
③ is of Greek heritage
④ do not care about the other members
⑤ runs a candy shop in Ohio

20 Kanakaredes, when asked to change her name, insisted on keeping it because ____________.

① she believed her own name to be attractive
② changing one's name into a foreign one would be to betray his or her country
③ changing one's name would not affect his or her success
④ she respected the Greek culture
⑤ she didn't like the names offered to her

21 Which of the following statements is NOT true of Kanakaredes?

① She is an actress playing in the NBC drama "Providence".
② Her Greek grandparents ran a candy store in Ohio.
③ Her mother-in-law is a Greek immigrant.
④ She is a medical doctor on "Providence".
⑤ She wanted to succeed as an actress with her own name.

해석 멜리나 카나카레데스는 '프로비던스'의 인기 스타인데, 이 작품은 'ER' 이후 NBC 네트워크를 통해 방송되고 있는 미국에서 가장 높은 평가를 받는 새로운 드라마이다. 시드니 한센 박사 역을 맡은 그녀는 병원 업무를 그만두고 가족과 함께 지내기 위해 고향으로 돌아가는 LA의 성형외과 의사를 연기한다.

그 여배우와 그녀가 연기하는 주인공 사이에는 매우 희미한 관계만이 존재하는데, 그 이유는 그녀의 가족이 언제나 단합이 잘 되기 때문이다. 그녀는 자신의 그리스 전통을 매우 자랑스러워하며, 그리스에서 온 외할아버지와 외할머니는 오하이오에 초콜릿 가게를 개업했다.

그녀가 개명을 하라는 말을 들었었던 (배우) 경력 초기에 가족에 대한 충성심이 확인되었다. 그녀의 이름을 그대로 쓰는 것이 그녀가 사랑하는 그 (그리스) 문화를 숭배하는 방법이었다. 그녀가 표현했듯이, "내가 연기 때문에 유명해진다면, 나는 성공한 멜리나 카나케레데스가 되기를 원할 뿐, 다른 이름을 가진 어떤 다른 소녀가 되기를 원하지 않기를 바란다"고 했다.

19 시드니 한센 박사의 가족은 어떠한가?

① 대가족이다.
② 가족 서로를 매우 부양해 준다.
③ 그리스 전통을 잇고 있다.
④ 다른 가족들에 관심을 갖지 않는다.
⑤ 오하이오에 캔디 가게를 운영한다.

20 카나라레데스가 이름을 바꾸라는 요청을 받았을 때 무엇 때문에 자신의 본래 이름을 계속 쓰겠다고 주장했는가?

① 그녀의 이름이 매력적이라고 믿었다.
② 그녀의 이름을 외국 이름으로 바꾼다는 것은 조국을 배신하는 것이 될 수 있다.
③ 그녀의 이름을 바꾸는 것은 자신의 성공에 영향을 미치지 않을 것 같다.
④ 그녀는 그리스 문화를 존경했었다.
⑤ 그녀에게 제안된 이름이 만족스럽지 못해서

21 카나라레데스에 대한 설명으로서 틀린 내용은?

① 그녀는 '프로비던스'라는 NBC 드라마에 출연하는 여배우이다.
② 그녀의 외조부모는 오하이오에 캔디 가게를 운영했다.
③ 그녀의 시어머니는 그리스에서 이주해 오신 분이다.
④ 그녀는 '프로비던스'라는 작품에서 의사 역을 맡고 있다.
⑤ 그녀는 자신의 원래 이름을 가진 여배우로서 성공하기를 원한다.

어구 **rated** 평가받은 **network** 방송망, 회로망, 네트워크 **plastic surgeon** 성형외과 의사 **practice** (의사·변호사 등의) 업무, 영업, 사무소, 진료소, 실행, 연습 **move back** 돌아오다 **thin** 희미한, 빈약한, 얇은 **close-knit** 단합이 잘 된 **fiercely** 지독히, 맹렬히 **heritage** 유산, 상속재산 **maternal** 외조부모 **loyalty** 충성, 충의 **put it** 표현하다 **become known for** ~ 때문에 유명해지다 **get there** 성공을 거두다 **extended family** 대가족 **be supportive of** ~을 돕다 **care about** 걱정하다, 관심을 갖다 **run a shop** 가게를 운영하다 **attractive** 매력적인 **change A into B** A를 B로 바꾸다 **mother-in-law** 장모, 시어머니

해설 **19** Sydney Hansen은 배우인 Melina Kanakaredes가 맡은 배역이다. 질문은 실제 배우의 가족을 물어보는 것이 아닌, 극 중 인물의 가족에 대해 물어보는 것이므로, 첫 단락 두 번째 문장에 소개된 대로 가족 서로를 부양해 준다는 ②가 옳다.

20 세 번째와 두 번째 문장을 통해서 '자신의 이름을 그대로 쓰는 것이 조국인 그리스 문화를 숭배하는 방법이 된다'고 했으므로, '그리스 문화를 존경한 점'이 이름을 계속 쓰게 된 원인으로 볼 수 있다.

21 시어머니에 대한 언급은 전혀 없었다.

Let us begin with some lexicography: the words embryo, fetus, and baby. Embryo is a product of conception more organized than just a cluster of cells but not yet recognizable as a member of the species. A fetus is a further stage of the organism but one not yet born. There is no precise, objectively specifiable moment at which a cluster of cells becomes an embryo and the embryo a fetus.

But there are certain relatively clear cases. The embryo, for example, turns into a fetus—a recognizable form of the human species—at some time between eight and twelve weeks. The fetus at this point cannot exist outside the woman's body until, at the very least, several weeks later. An embryo then is not recognizable as a form of the species and cannot have an existence separate from the mother's body. Once the fetus is born, it is called a baby.

Defenders of the morality of abortion are usually defenders of early abortion: of the embryo or of a fetus well before it is viable outside the womb, usually in the first trimester. That is, they are defenders of the morality of removing from a group of cells that is not an independent, viable, and recognizable human being.

Opponents of abortion use the word baby to refer to the cluster of cells, the embryo, and the fetus alike. The very choice of the word baby imposes the idea of an independently existing human being. Whereas cluster of cells, embryo, and fetus keep discussion in the medical domain, baby moves the discussion to the moral domain.

22 Which of the following statements is true of an embryo?

① It is recognizable as a member of the species.
② It is the final stage of pregnancy.
③ It is not viable outside the woman's body.
④ It turns into a cluster of cells around the eighth week.
⑤ It is a later stage than the fetus.

23 Pro-life advocates use the word baby rather than embryo or fetus because

＿＿＿＿＿＿.

① the latter words are not the ones used in everyday conversation
② they want to treat the issue of abortion in terms of morality
③ the terms embryo and fetus are only used in a medical context
④ the former word is easier for people to understand
⑤ the issue of abortion is not properly understood

해석 embryo, fetus, baby라는 단어들의 사전 편찬으로부터 시작해 보자. Embryo는 단지 세포의 집합체 이상으로 조직된 임신의 결과물이지만, 아직 종의 구성 객체로서 알아볼 수 있을 정도는 아니다. Fetus는 유기체의 다음 단계이지만, 아직 태어나지 않은 존재이다. 세포 집합물이 embryo가 되고 embryo가 fetus가 되는 정밀하고도 객관적으로 구분이 가능한 시기는 없다. 그러나 비교적 명확한 특정 경우는 있다. 예컨대, embryo는 8주에서 12주 사이에 인간의 종으로 인식이 될 수 있는 fetus로 변한다. 이 시점에 fetus는 바로 적어도 몇 주 후가 지날 때까지는 여자의 몸 밖에서 생존할 수 없다. 그때 embryo는 종의 한 형태로 인식이 되지는 않으며, 어머니의 몸과 생존할 수는 없다. 일단 fetus가 태어나면, 그것은 baby라고 불려진다.

낙태의 도덕성을 지지하는 이들은 대체로 초기 낙태를 지지하는 이들인데, 대개는 3개월 이내에, 자궁 밖에서 생존할 수 있기 훨씬 이전인 embryo 또는 fetus에 대한 낙태를 지지한다는 것이다. 다시 말하자면, (모체에서 분리되어) 독립되고 생존할 수 있고 인식이 가능한 인체가 아직 되지 않은 일련의 세포들로부터 떼어놓는 도덕성을 지지하는 이들이다.

낙태를 반대하는 사람들은 세포의 집합체인 embryo와 fetus 모두를 일컫기 위하여 baby라는 단어를 사용한다. baby라는 단어의 바로 그 선택이 독립되어 생존하는 인간이라는 개념을 부여한다. 세포의 집합체, embryo, 그리고 fetus가 의학의 영역에서 계속 토론이 되는 반면, baby라는 단어는 도덕 분야의 토론 대상으로 이동하고 있다.

22 embryo에 대한 설명으로서 옳은 것은?

① 종의 구성객체로서 인식된다.　② 임신의 마지막 단계이다.
③ 모체 밖에서 생존이 불가능하다.　④ 약 8주 동안 세포 집단으로 변한다.
⑤ fetus보다 차후 단계이다.

23 임신 중절 반대를 지지하는 이들이 embryo 혹은 fetus보다 baby라는 단어를 사용하는 이유가 무엇인가?

① embryo나 fetus라는 단어들이 모든 대화에서 사용되는 것들은 아니다.
② 그들이 도덕적 관점에서 낙태의 문제를 다루기를 원한다.
③ embryo와 fetus라는 단어들이 의학 분야에서만 단지 사용된다.
④ baby라는 단어를 사람들이 이해하기 더 수월하다.
⑤ 낙태의 문제가 잘 이해가 되지 않는다.

어구 **begin with** ~부터 시작하다　**embryo** (보통 임신 8주까지의) 태아　**fetus** (임신 3개월이 넘은) 태아　**baby** 아기(나이는 2살 전후까지는 달수로 sixteen months old 따위로 말함)　**conception** 태아, 임신, 개념, 고안　**cluster** 집단, 집합, (과실·꽃 따위의) 송이　**recognizable** 인식이 가능한　**species** 종　**specifiable** 자세한, 구체적인　**relatively** 비교적, 상대적으로　**case** 경우, 사건, 판, 병, 주장　**have an existence** 존재, 생존하다　**separate** 별개의, 분리된　**morality** 도덕성　**abortion** 낙태　**viable** (태아·신생아 등이) 살아갈 수 있는, (계획 등이) 실행 가능한　**human being** 사람　**refer to** 언급하다　**A and B alike** A와 B 모두　**the very** 바로 그　**keep discussion** 계속 토론하다　**domain** 영역, 범위, 소유지　**pregnancy** 임신　**pro-life** 임신 중절 합법화에 반대하는 *

해설 **22** 세포 집단이 embryo가 되고, embryo가 fetus가 된다. fetus 단계에서도 모체 밖에서 생존할 수 없으므로(두 번째 단락 두 번째 문장), fetus 이전 단계인 embryo는 당연히 모체 밖에서 생존할 수 없을 것이다.

23 pro-life의 단어 정의만 알면 쉽게 풀 수 있는 문제이다. 마지막 문장 주절에서, 임신중절을 반대하는 이들(낙태를 반대하는 이들)은 아기라는 단어가 도덕의 분야로 토론의 화제가 이동하고 있다고 설명됐다.

The social settings in which people live have been created by individuals throughout the course of history. The family, universities, and government, for example, are the historical products of our forebears. Although these institutions often seem to be natural and unchanging, we should never lose sight of the fact that they are products of human history.

Social settings also are recreated and reaffirmed by individual action. In obeying the wishes of our parents, following the assignments of our professors, and accepting the decisions of our political leaders, we are reaffirming the existence of the institutions they represent. If you doubt that we daily reconstruct these settings, consider what would happen if a large number of people ceased accepting the dictates of the authority figures in these social settings.

Families as we know them would disappear if children refused to accept parental decisions. Universities would be radically difficult places if students did not recognize the authority of professors. The political sphere would be drastically altered were we to reject the authority of our political leaders.

24 Which of the following can be the main idea of the passage?

① We should follow the dictates of the authority figure.
② A family is the most crucial constitutional factor of a society.
③ Obeying the wishes of our parents is significant.
④ Social settings play an important part in maintaining our daily life.
⑤ Throughout history, social settings are one and the same.

25 If you doubt the value of social settings, the society in which we live will ___________ .

① continue to progress slowly
② be more opulent
③ collapse with rapidity
④ not change
⑤ be more prosperous

26 Which of the following is not true of the social settings in which people live?

① They are the products of human history.
② They are natural and immutable all the time.
③ They are recreated and reaffirmed day in and day out.
④ They would crumble if we were to reject their authority.
⑤ They are daily reconstructed by the members of a society.

해석 사람이 살고 있는 사회적 배경은 역사를 통해 개인이 창조한 것이다. 예컨대 가족, 대학, 정부는 우리 조상들의 역사적 산물이다. 비록 이런 제도가 종종 자연스럽고 변함이 없어 보이지만, 그들이 인간 역사의 산물이라는 사실을 우리는 결코 간과해서는 안 된다.

사회적 배경은 또한 개인의 행위에 의해 재창조되고 재확인된다. 부모님의 기대에 복종하고, 교수님의 숙제를 쫓아서 하고, 정치 지도자들의 결정을 받아들일 때, 우리는 그들이 나타내는 제도의 존재를 재확인하는 것이 된다. 우리가 이런 배경을 매일 다시 쌓아가고 있다는 사실이 의심스럽다면, 또 많은 사람들이 권력자의 지시를 받아들이지 않는다면 무슨 일이 일어날지 생각해 보아라.

아이들이 부모의 결정을 받아들이지 않는다면 우리가 알다시피 가족은 사라지게 될 것이다. 학생들이 교수의 권위를 인정하지 않는다면 대학은 아주 골치 아픈 장소가 될 것이다. 우리가 정치 지도자의 권위를 거부한다면 정치권은 급격히 변하게 될 것이다.

24 이 글의 요지는?
① 우리는 권위자의 명령에 따라야 한다.
② 가족은 사회의 가장 중요한 구성 요소이다.
③ 우리 부모들의 소망에 순종하는 것이 중요하다.
④ 사회적 배경이 우리의 삶을 지탱시켜 주는 중요한 역할을 수행한다.
⑤ 역사를 통해 사회적 배경은 동일했었다.

25 사회적 배경의 가치를 의심한다면 우리가 살고 있는 사회는 어떻게 될 것인가?
① 천천히 발전할 것이다.
② 더 풍요로워질 것이다.
③ 빠르게 붕괴될 것이다.
④ 바뀌지 않을 것이다.
⑤ 더 풍요로워질 것이다.

26 사람들이 살고 있는 사회적 배경에 대한 설명으로서 틀린 것은?
① 사회적 배경은 인간 역사의 산물이다.
② 사회적 배경은 당연한 것이고 언제나 변하지 않는 것이다.
③ 사회적 배경은 언제나 재건되고 재확인된다.
④ 사람들이 사회적 배경의 권위를 무시한다면 사회적 배경은 붕괴될 것이다.
⑤ 사회 구성원들이 매일같이 사회적 배경을 재건한다.

어구 **social settings** 사회적 배경　**forebear** 조상, 선조(ancestor)　**institution** 제도　**unchanging** 불변의　**lose sight of** ~을 놓치다　**recreate** 재창조하다　**reaffirm** 재차 단언(확인)하다　**obey** 복종하다　**assignment** 할당, 임무, 숙제　**reconstruct** 재건하다　**a number of** 많은　**dictate** 지시, 명령　**authority figures** 권위 있는 인물들, 권력자들　**disappear** 사라지다　**parental** 부모의　**radically** 근본적으로, 철저하게, 과격하게　**political sphere** 정치권　**drastically** 철저하게, 과감하게(extremely)　**alter** 변하다　**immutable** 불변의, 변경할 수 없는　**crucial** 중요한(significant)　**one and the same** 동일한　**collapse** 붕괴되다　**opulent** 풍요로운　**with rapidity** 빠르게　**crumble** 붕괴되다

해설 **24** 첫 문장에서 사회적 배경이 개인에 의해 창조되며, 두 번째 단락에서 그 배경들의 예를 제시하여 그 중요성을 가정적으로 설명하고 있다. 따라서 사회적 배경의 중요성을 다룬다는 내용이 이 글의 주제가 된다.

25 두 번째 단락에서 설문의 문제가 포괄적으로 제기되며, 세 번째 단락에서 가족의 소멸 등을 예로 들고 있다.

26 사람들이 언제나 변하지 않는다는 것은 확장 해석이다.

Alzheimer's disease, a progressive and irreversible failure of the brain is the common form of dementia, accounting for up to 70% of cases. Early symptoms include confusion, personality changes, apathy, withdrawal, and declining ability to do everyday tasks. A diagnosis of Alzheimer's disease is not a death sentence. Treatments now available can slow down the disease and for some people, improve their ability to perform everyday functions. With the onset of Alzheimer's disease it is possible to live a fulfilling life and benefit from existing treatments if it is diagnosed early.

27 According to the paragraph, the early symptoms of Alzheimers are all but one of the following choices.

① declining ability to do everyday tasks
② confusion and personality changes
③ apathy
④ withdrawal
⑤ frequent headaches

28 The main point stressed in this paragraph is
____________.

① Once diagnosed with Alzheimer's, death comes quickly to sufferers
② Early detection is the key and drugs are available for patients to live a longer rewarding life with the disease
③ Alzheimer's accounts for only 7% of the cases of dementia
④ Drugs can stop the disease thus allowing a person to live without any difficulties
⑤ Operations are also available to stop the onset of the disease

해석 점진적이고 되돌릴 수 없는 뇌의 감퇴인 알츠하이머병은 치매의 일반적인 형태로, 환자의 70%의 비율을 차지한다. 초기 증상은 혼돈, 성격의 변화, 무감정, 소극성, 그리고 일상 업무의 능력 감퇴가 있다. 알츠하이머병의 진단은 사망 선고는 아니다. 현재 유용한 치료 방법은 병의 진행 속도를 느리게 하고, 일부 사람들의 일상 업무 능력을 향상시키는 것이다. 알츠하이머병의 발병에 있어 빨리 발견되면 만족스러운 삶을 살며, 현존하는 치료법으로 혜택을 받을 수 있다.

27 알츠하이머병의 초기 증상으로서 언급되지 않은 내용은?

① 일상 업무의 능력 감퇴
② 혼돈과 성격의 변화
③ 냉담
④ 소극성
⑤ 빈번한 두통

28 이 글의 요지는 무엇인가?

① 알츠하이머병의 진단을 받는다면 환자에게 죽음이 빨리 닥친다.
② 초기 진단이 중요하며 약물은 질병을 가진 채로 보다 더 오랫동안 고통 받지 않고 살 수 있게 하는 데 유효하다.
③ 알츠하이머병은 치매 질병의 단지 7%만 차지한다.
④ 약물은 알츠하이머병을 막을 수 있으므로, 어려움이 전혀 없이 살 수 있게끔 해 준다.
⑤ 수술은 역시나 질병 발발을 중단시키는 데 유효하다.

어구 disease 질병 progressive 점진적인(advancing) irreversible 돌이킬 수 없는, 회복될 수 없는 failure 감퇴, 실패 dementia 치매 account for 설명하다, 밝히다 up to ~ 정도까지 symptom 징후 confusion 혼돈 apathy 냉담 withdrawal 철회, 소극성 declining 감퇴하는 sentence 선고, 판결 onset 습격, (병의) 발병 fulfilling 만족하는 treatment 치료법 diagnose 진단하다 all but ~을 제외하고서 모두; 거의 headache 두통 detection 발견, 탐지 rewarding 득이 되는 account for ~을 차지하다, 설명하다, 원인이 되다

해설 **27** 두통에 대해서는 언급되지 않았다.
28 알츠하이머가 완치될 수는 없지만, 초기에 발견이 된다면 약물을 통해서 고통을 완화시킴과 동시에 수명 연장이 가능하다는 것이 이 글의 요지로서 옳다.

E-learning(online learning) advocates contend that the Internet allows higher education institutions to seek out top experts in their fields to teach courses online to students globally. E-learning allows busy professionals to finish degrees, earn advanced degrees or take technology-related courses that help their jobs without putting careers on hold. E-learning also pushes higher education away from the age-old textbook-driven approach to teaching, which can be more ① _______________ than interactive. Students who sign ② _______________ for e-learning courses log on to password-protected Web sites to participate in online lectures and chats, and to get assignments and take part in discussions.

29 Which is NOT mentioned as merits of e-learning in the passage?

① E-learning allows colleges to offer top experts' teachings to students.
② E-learning allows students to take advantage of breaks in their schedule.
③ E-learning helps busy professionals earn advanced degrees without quitting their jobs.
④ E-learning pushes colleges away from traditional teaching methods.
⑤ E-learning allows students interactively to participate in online lectures and chats.

30 Choose the one to fill in the blank ①.

① ardent   ② update
③ old-fashioned   ④ static
⑤ cutting-edge

31 Choose the one to fill in the blank ②.

① up   ② off
③ out   ④ over
⑤ away

해석 인터넷 학습 지지자들은 인터넷이 고등 교육기관들로 하여금 온라인을 통해 전 세계 학생들에게 강의하기 위한 최고 전문가들을 찾도록 해 준다고 주장한다. 인터넷 학습은 바쁜 전문가들로 하여금 학위를 끝마칠 수 있으며, 고등 학위를 취득하거나 경력에 지장을 주지 않고서 직업에 도움이 되는 기술 관련 과정을 이수할 수 있게끔 해 준다. 인터넷 학습은 또한 고등교육이 구식 교과서 위주의 교수법에서 벗어나도록 하며, 구식 교육법은 쌍방향의 학습보다 발전이 정적일 수 있다. 인터넷 학습 과정에 등록하는 학생들이 온라인 수업과 채팅에 참여하여 숙제를 받고 토론에 참여하기 위해서 비밀번호로 보안되는 웹 사이트에 로그인을 한다.

29 인터넷 학습의 장점으로서 언급되지 않은 내용은?

① 인터넷 학습은 대학들이 최고 전문가들의 강의를 학생들에게 전할 수 있게끔 해 준다.
② 인터넷 학습은 학생들이 스케줄에 맞추어 휴식을 취할 수 있게끔 해 준다.
③ 인터넷 학습은 바쁜 전문가들이 직장을 그만두지 않고서도 고등학위를 취득할 수 있게끔 해 준다.
④ 인터넷 학습은 대학이 전통 교수법으로부터 벗어나게 해 준다.
⑤ 인터넷 학습은 학생들이 온라인 강의와 대화에 서로 참여할 수 있게 해 준다.

30 ①에 적합한 것은?

① 열렬한   ② 최신식의
③ 구식의   ④ 정적인
⑤ 최첨단의

31 ②에 적절한 것은?

어구 e-learning 인터넷 학습 advocate 지지자, 변호사; 지지하다, 변호하다 contend 주장하다, 싸우다 higher education 고등교육 seek out ~을 찾아내다 teach course 강의하다 online 온라인으로; 온라인 degree 학위, 등급, 정도 take a course ~의 강의를 받다 on hold (일·계획 등이) 보류 상태로, 일시 중단되어 push away 벗어나게 하다. 밀어제치다 -driven ~이 극에 달한 log on 로그온 하다 get an assignment 숙제를 받다 take part in 참여하다 take advantage of ~을 이용하다 ardent 열렬한 update 최신식의 old-fashioned 구식의 static 정적인 cutting-edge 최첨단의, 날카로운; 최첨단, 날카로움

해설 **29** 인터넷 강의를 스케줄에 따라서 '쉬면서 강의를 들을 수 있게 해 준다'는 설명은 언급되지 않았다.

30 비교급 연결사인 more ~ than에 의해서 interactive(서로 영향을 미치는)와 비교되는 단어는 '정적인(static; not moving, changing, or developing)'이 옳다.

31 sign up for는 '가입하다', '계약하다(to put your name on a list for something because you want to take part in it)'라는 뜻을 가졌다.

John Milton was a failure. In writing Paradise Lost, his aim was to "justify the ways of God to men." Inevitably, he fell short and wrote only a monumental poem. Beethoven, whose music was conceived to transcend fate, was a failure, as was Socrates, whose ambition was to make people happy by making them reasonable and just. The surest, noblest way to fail is to set one's standards titanically high.

The flip side of that proposition also seems true. The surest way to succeed is to keep one's striving low. Many people, by external standards, will be "successes." They will own homes, eat in better restaurants, dress well and, in some instances, perform socially useful work. Yet fewer people are putting themselves on the line, making as much of their minds and talents as they might. Frequently, success is what people settle for when they can't think of something noble enough to be worth failing at.

32 Why were the famous like John Milton regarded as failures, according to the above passage?

① because they had extremely high aims
② because they had a strong religious inclination
③ because they were essentially lacking in capabilities
④ because they had illogical ends

해석 존 밀턴은 실패자였다. 〈실낙원〉을 쓸 때에 그의 목표는 '신이 인간을 다루는 방법을 정당화하는 것'이었다. 아니나 다를까, 그의 능력은 그 목표에 미치지 못했으며 단지 기념비적인 시를 썼을 뿐이다. 사람들을 이성적이고 정의롭게 만듦으로써 사람들을 행복하게 하려는 야심을 가졌던 소크라테스가 그러했듯이, 운명을 초월하기 위하여 음악을 구상했던 베토벤도 실패자였다. 실패할 수 있는 가장 확실하고 고상한 방법은 자신의 목표를 어마어마하게 높이 정하는 것이다. 이 명제의 이면 또한 사실인 것 같다. 성공할 수 있는 가장 확실한 방법은 자신의 목표를 낮게 유지하는 것이다. 많은 사람들이 외적 기준에서는 "성공한 사람들"일 것이다. 그들은 집을 가지고 있고 더 나은 식당에서 식사를 하며, 옷을 잘 차려입고, 어떤 경우에는 사회적으로 유용한 일을 수행할 것이다. 그러나 그들의 정신과 재능을 최고로 과대평가하여 이 대열에 끼지 못하고 있는 사람들이 더 많다. 흔히 성공은 사람들이 실패할 만한 가치가 충분할 만큼 고귀한 것을 생각할 수 없을 때, 불만스럽지만 그것으로 만족하는 것이다.

32 윗글에 따르면, 존 밀턴과 같은 저명인사들이 왜 실패한 사람으로서 간주되나?

① 그들이 너무 높은 목표를 가지고 있었기 때문에
② 그들이 강한 종교적 성향이 있었기 때문에
③ 그들이 본래 능력이 부족하기 때문에
④ 그들이 비논리적인 목표를 가졌기 때문에

어구 **fall short** (능력이) 미치지 못하다 **conceive** 구상하다 **titanically** 거대하게, 엄청나게 **flip side** 반대, 이면 **proposition** 명제 **put oneself on the line** 이 대열에 끼다 **make much of** ~을 중시 여기다 **settle for** ~을 불만스럽지만 받아들이다, 만족하다 **fail at** ~에 실패하다, ~을 잡지 못하다

해설 첫 단락에서 목표를 크게 설정하여 실패하게 된 것이라고 설명한다.

There are three major kinds of sleep disorders: You cannot sleep, you must always sleep, or your breathing affects your sleep. The first kind, insomnia, means that you cannot sleep well. You may have a hard time falling asleep or you keep waking up. During the day, you may feel sleepy or stressed. You may have a hard time concentrating. The second kind, narcolepsy, is called sleeping sickness. You cannot control yourself when you fall asleep, even during the day. The third kind is called sleep apnea. It is a problem breathing while sleeping. Usually your throat starts to close. This may be because of drinking alcohol or being too heavy. The muscles do not have enough control. Other times, the brain does not send the signal to breathe. Then you wake up.

33 How does narcolepsy differ from apnea?

① Apnea is similar to narcolepsy but more severe.
② Alcohol is used to treat apnea but not narcolepsy.
③ Apnea involves breathing, but narcolepsy does not.
④ Apnea and narcolepsy only happen during the daytime.

해석 수면 장애는 중요한 세 가지 종류가 있다. 잠을 잘 수 없거나, 계속 잠을 자야만 하거나, 호흡이 수면에 영향을 미치는 경우이다. 첫 번째 종류인 불면증은 당신이 잠을 잘 자지 못하는 것을 의미한다. 당신이 잠을 자는 데 고생을 하거나, 자는 중간에 계속해서 깰지도 모른다. 낮에는 잠이 오거나 압박감을 느낄 수도 있다. 당신이 집중하는 데 고생을 할 수도 있다. 두 번째 종류인 기면증은 수면병이라 일컫는다. 당신은 심지어 낮에도 잠이 드는 것을 통제할 수 없다. 세 번째 종류는 수면성 무호흡이라고 불린다. 수면성 무호흡은 잠을 자는 도중 호흡 장애가 일어나는 것을 일컫는다. 대개 기도가 막히기 시작하며, 이는 술을 마시거나 살이 쪄서 몸이 무거워졌기 때문일 수도 있다. 근육은 이것을 충분히 통제하지 못한다. 어떤 때에는, 뇌가 호흡을 하라는 신호를 보내지 않는다. 그렇게 되면 당신은 잠에서 깨어난다.

33 기면증은 일시 호흡 정지와 어떻게 다른가?

① 일시 호흡 정지는 기면증과 유사하지만, 더욱 심각한 질병이다.
② 알코올이 일시 호흡 정지를 치료하기 위해 이용될 수 있지만, 기면증은 그렇지 않다.
③ 일시 호흡 정지는 호흡과 관련을 맺고 있지만, 기면증은 그렇지 않다.
④ 일시 호흡 정지와 기면증은 낮 시간에 발생할 뿐이다.

어구 **disorder** 장애; 무질서 **insomnia** 불면증 **have a hard time (in) -ing** ~하느라 고생하다 **concentrate** 집중하다 **narcolepsy** 기면(嗜眠)증 **apnea** 일시 호흡 정지; 질식(asphyxia)

해설 일시 호흡 정지는 잠을 자는 도중에 발생하는 호흡 장애이지만, 기면증은 밤과 낮을 가리지 않고 지나치게 졸리는 증상을 말한다.

Chapter 05 일치·불일치

⇨ 본책 p.63

1 ⑤	2 ⑤	3 ③	4 ①	5 ③	6 ④	7 ③	8 ④	9 ④	10 ②
11 ④	12 ③	13 ①	14 ④	15 ④	16 ③	17 ③	18 ④	19 ②	20 ②
21 ④	22 ④	23 ①	24 ④	25 ④	26 ④	27 ②	28 ③	29 ②	30 ④
31 ③									

Any man who desires, as I do, a fundamental change in the structure of society is forced sooner or later to ask himself the question: what is it that makes one social system seem to him good and another bad? This is undoubtedly very largely a matter of individual caprice. In history, for example, some prefer one epoch, some another. Some admire the polished and civilized ages, others the rude virtues of more barbarous times. One does not wish to think that one's political opinions result from mere fanciful references of this sort, yet I believe that an enormous proportion of political opinion comes from some untested, unexamined, almost unconscious love for a certain type of society actual or imagined. I think it is possible to arrive at something less subjective than such tastes and fancies, and I think the advocate of fundamental change, more obviously than anyone else, needs to find ways of judging a social system which do not embody merely his individual tastes.

1 According to the passage, which of the following is true?

① The writer is one of those who oppose the change of the social structure.
② In history a refined age and a barbarous age take turns in coming without fail.
③ People's political opinions generally come from a meticulous investigation of social problems.
④ An age with much rude virtues is very likely to be followed by an age of drastic social change.
⑤ The proponents for the social change should have more objective ways of assessing a social system.

해석 나처럼 사회구조의 근본적인 변화를 갈망하는 사람이라면 누구나 조만간 스스로에게 아래의 질문을 하지 않으면 안 될 것이다. 한 사회체제는 자신에게 좋아 보이고, 다른 사회체제는 나빠 보이는 것은 무엇일까? 이것은 의심할 여지가 없이 상당히 개인의 변덕에 관한 문제이다. 예컨대, 역사에서 어떤 사람들은 한 시대를 좋아하며, 또 어떤 이는 다른 시대를 좋아한다. 어떤 사람들은 세련되고 문명화된 시대들을 찬미하고, 다른 사람들은 야만스러운 시대의 잔인한 가치들을 찬미한다. 사람들은 자신의 정치적 견해들이 이런 종류의 공상적인 견해에서 비롯된 것이라 생각하고 싶지 않아 하지만, 정치적 견해의 상당 비율은 조사되거나 고찰되지 않은, 현실적이든 상상한 것이든 어떤 유형의 사회에 대한 거의 무의식적인 애정에서 비롯된 것이라고 나는 생각한다. 나는 생각하기를, 그와 같은 취향과 공상보다 덜 주관적인 것으로 도달하는 것이 가능하며, 근본적인 변화를 지지하는 이는 다른 그 어느 누구보다 더 분명하게 자신의 개인적 취향을 구체화하지 않는 사회체계를 판단하는 방법을 알아야 할 필요가 있다.

1 윗글의 내용과 일치하는 것은?

① 작가는 사회구조의 변화를 반대하는 이들 중 한명이다.
② 역사에서 세련된 시대와 야만스러운 시대는 틀림없이 교차하며 도래했었다.
③ 사람들의 정치적 견해는 사회문제에 관한 신중한 연구로부터 비롯된 것이다.
④ 매우 무례한 가치의 시대가 있은 뒤에는 급격히 변화하는 시대가 있을 가능성이 매우 높다.
⑤ 사회 변화를 지지하는 이들은 사회 제도를 평가하는 보다 객관적인 방법들을 갖추어야 한다.

어구 fundamental 기초적인, 근본적인 be forced to R ∼하지 않을 수 없다 sooner or later 조만간 undoubtedly 의심할 바 없이 caprice 변덕 polished 세련된 civilized 문명화된 rude 무례한 barbarous 미개의, 야만의 fanciful 공상의 reference 문의, 참조, 관련 enormous 거대한 come from ∼에서 비롯되다 untested 조사되지 않은 unexamined 고찰되지 않은 unconscious 무의식적인 subjective 주관적인 advocate 지지자, 옹호자, 지지; 지지하다, 옹호하다 obviously 틀림없이, 명백하게 embody 구체화하다 merely 단지, 전혀 take turns 교대하다, 번갈아하다 without fail 틀림없이, 완벽하게 meticulous 매우 신중한 A is followed by B A 뒤에 B가 있다 drastic 맹렬한, 철저한 proponent 지지자, 제안자 objective 객관적인 assess 평가하다

해설 마지막 문장을 통해 '덜 주관적인 것에 도달하는 것이 가능하다'고 했으므로, 보다 더 객관적으로 도달하는 것이 가능하다는 내용과 일치한다.

Certain individuals have a biological predisposition to addiction. The most serious problem that young people face if they use alcohol or other drugs is the possibility of becoming addicted. Although not everyone who drinks or uses drugs becomes addicted, there is no way to tell who will be ______________ or to what extent the use of alcohol or other drugs will impair their success in life. Some people have a biological predisposition to addiction, especially if any of their relatives are alcoholic. Children of alcoholics have a four to ten times greater risk of becoming alcoholics than children of non-alcoholics. Parents should advise children of any family history of alcoholism or other drug addictions and alert them to the risks of becoming addicted.

2 밑줄 친 곳에 들어갈 단어로 가장 알맞은 것은?

① profitable ② proficient
③ diffused ④ convergent
⑤ vulnerable

3 윗글의 내용과 거리가 먼 것은?

① Children with an alcoholic cousin have a greater risk of getting addicted to alcohol than children without one.
② Young people may use alcohol and other drugs because they are not properly informed of alcoholism in their family history.
③ Impaired judgement may lead to regrettable or even dangerous situations that may range from the destruction of property to communicative disorders.
④ Alcohol and other drugs have a fatal effect on children's life.
⑤ One of the reasons why children should not take alcohol or other drugs is the high possibility of getting addicted.

해석 어떤 사람들은 중독에 빠져들 생물학적 경향이 있다. 젊은이들이 술이나 기타 약물을 쓴다면 그들이 직면하게 되는 가장 중대한 문제는 중독에 빠져들 가능성이 있다는 것이다. 비록 술을 마시거나 약물을 복용하는 모든 이가 중독에 빠져드는 것은 아닐지라도 누가 취약해질지 또는 얼마나 많이 술을 마신다거나 다른 약물을 사용하는 것이 그들의 인생에서 성공을 망치게 될 것인지를 알려줄 방법은 없다. 특히나 그들 친척들 중 어느 누구라도 알코올 중독자가 있다면 몇몇 이들은 중독에 빠져들 경향이 있다. 알코올 중독자들의 아이들은 4~10배 정도는 알코올 중독자가 아닌 이들보다 알코올 중독자가 될 위험이 상당히 높다. 부모들은 알코올 중독이나 다른 약물 중독에 대한 가족력을 아이들에게 알려 주어야 하며, 중독성의 위험에 대해서 경계를 시켜야 한다.

2 밑줄 친 곳에 들어갈 단어로 가장 알맞은 것은?

① 이윤이 되는 ② 숙달된, 능란한
③ 확산된 ④ 집중적인
⑤ 취약한

3 윗글의 내용과 거리가 먼 것은?

① 알코올 중독에 빠진 친척이 있는 아이들은 그렇지 않은 아이들보다 알코올 중독에 빠질 위험이 더 높다.
② 젊은이들은 가족사에서 알코올 중독에 대해 잘 알지 못하기 때문에 술과 기타 약물을 복용할 수도 있다.
③ 잘못된 판단이 재산의 파괴에서부터 대화의 장애에 이르기까지 이를 수 있는 유감스럽거나 심지어 위험한 상황을 야기할 수 있다.
④ 술과 기타 약물은 아이들의 인생에 치명적인 영향을 미친다.
⑤ 아이들이 술이나 기타 약물을 복용하지 말아야 하는 이유들 중 하나가 높은 중독 가능성 때문이다.

어구 **predisposition** 경향 **addiction** 중독 **addicted** 중독된 **to what extent** 얼마나 많이(how much) **impair** 손상시키다 **relative** 친척 **alcoholic** 알코올 중독자; 알코올의 **family history** 가족사 **alcoholism** 알코올 중독 **alert A to B** A에게 B를 경계시키다 **diffused** 확산된, 널리 퍼진 **convergent** 집중적인, 한 군데로 모이는 **vulnerable** 취약성의, 상처받기 쉬운 **have a risk of ~ing** ～할 위험성이 있다 **be informed of** ～을 알다 **range from A to B** A에서 B까지 퍼지다[이르다] **have an effect on** ～에 영향을 미치다 **take a drug** 약물을 복용하다

해설 **2** or 이하에서 '인생의 성공을 망치게 된다'는 부정적인 내용이 나오므로, 앞의 빈칸에서도 부정적인 내용을 담고 있는 'vulnerable (취약한)'이 들어가는 것이 옳다.
3 판단의 실수나 대화에 장애가 있다는 내용은 본문에 전혀 언급되지 않았다.

The brain of Albert Einstein has clear differences from an average person's gray matter, according to a California researcher. But any possible link between these differences and his great intelligence is still unknown, she added. To investigate whether the brain of a genius might show special features, Dr. Dahlia W. Zaidel of the University of California, Los Angeles, examined two slides made from the physicist's brain shortly after his death in 1955 at age 76. The slides contained samples of Einstein's hippocampus, a part of the brain responsible for memory and word associations. Zaidel compared Einstein's brain with tissue from 10 individuals of ordinary intelligence who ranged in age from 22 to 84 at the time of death. The neurons on the left side of the Nobel Prize winner's hippocampus were consistently larger than those on the right. Zaidel said these findings were 'markedly different' from those seen in the brains of individuals with normal intelligence. She presented her findings Monday at the Society for Neuroscience's annual meeting in San Diego, California.

4 윗글의 중심 소재는?

① Einstein's gray matter

② age differences and neurons

③ the future of neuroscience

④ Nobel Prize winners

⑤ the past of neuroscience

5 윗글의 내용과 다른 것은?

① Einstein's brain is different from those of other individuals.

② Dr. Zaidel compared Einstein's brain with tissue from 10 individuals of various age.

③ Einstein's intelligence is closely related to the texture and hardness of his brain.

④ Slides of Einstein's brain were made just after his death.

⑤ Dr. Zaidel gave a talk on her results at a certain neuroscience conference.

해석 캘리포니아의 한 연구원에 따르면 아인슈타인의 두뇌는 일반인들의 두뇌와는 분명한 차이가 있다고 한다. 그녀는 덧붙여서 이러한 차이점들과 그의 뛰어난 지능 사이의 어떠한 연결이 아직도 알려지지 않은 상태라고 한다. 천재의 두뇌가 특이한 특징이 있는지를 연구해 보기 위하여 UCLA 대학의 달리아 자이델 박사는 1955년에 76세로 죽었던 물리학자 아인슈타인의 뇌 슬라이드 사진을 연구했다. 그 슬라이드 사진들에는 아인슈타인의 해마상 융기 표본이 포함되어 있었고, 기억과 단어 연상을 담당하는 부분이 있었다. 자이델 박사는 아인슈타인의 두뇌를 평범한 10명의 사람들에게서 추출한 조직과 비교했는데, 그들은 22세에서 84살 사이에 죽었던 이들이었다. 노벨상을 수상했던 아인슈타인의 해마 좌측에 있었던 뉴런들은 우측 뉴런들보다 일관되게 더 컸다. 자이델 박사는 이 연구 결과가 지능이 평범한 이들의 뇌에서 나타나는 것들과 분명히 다르다고 말했다. 그녀는 월요일 캘리포니아 주 샌디에이고에서 열린 신경과학 연례 모임에서 연구 결과를 발표했다.

4 윗글의 중심 소재는?

① 아인슈타인의 두뇌　　② 나이 차이와 신경단위

③ 신경과학의 미래　　④ 노벨 수상자

⑤ 신경과학의 과거

5 윗글의 내용과 다른 것은?

① 아인슈타인의 두뇌는 다른 이들의 두뇌와 다르다.

② 자이델 박사는 아인슈타인의 두뇌와 다양한 나이 또래의 10명의 두뇌 조직을 비교했다.

③ 아인슈타인의 지능은 두뇌의 조직 그리고 견고함과 밀접히 연관되어 있다.

④ 아인슈타인 두뇌의 슬라이드 사진은 그가 죽은 뒤에 바로 만들어졌다.

⑤ 자이델 박사는 신경과학 총회에서 자신의 결과를 발표했었다.

어구 **average person** 일반인　**gray matter** 두뇌, 회백질　**link** 연결, 결합　**unknown** 알려지지 않은　**add** 덧붙이다, 추가 설명을 하다　**feature** 특징　**slide hippocampus** 해마, 해마상 융기　**compare A with B** A와 B를 비교하다　**tissue** 세포조직, 직물　**neuron** 신경단위, 뉴런　**consistently** 일관되게　**finding** 발견물, 연구 결과　**markedly** 현저하게, 뚜렷이　**neuroscience** 신경과학　**annual meeting** 연례 모임　**closely** 면밀히　**be related to** ~과 관련이 있다　**texture** 조직, 직물　**hardness** 견고함

해설 **4** 아인슈타인의 두뇌는 일반인들과 분명한 차이점이 있다는 내용이 이 글의 주제이다. 이하에서 등장하는 'the physicist'나 'the Noble Prize Winner'는 아인슈타인을 언급하는 것이다.

5 여섯 번째 문장에서 '아인슈타인의 해마 좌측에 있었던 뉴런들은 우측 뉴런들보다 일관되게 더 컸다'는 내용이 특징일 뿐, 아인슈타인의 지능이 자신의 두뇌 조직 또는 견고함과 연관되어 있다는 내용은 언급된 바 없는 설명이다.

The problem for leaders comes when people who want to be chosen for a task besiege the leader. Do you remember when you were a kid and you were choosing up sides for a game? The two people who did the choosing, usually the two best athletes who functioned as team captains, had to make quick decisions about whom they wanted for their sides. Not only did they choose on the basis of athletic skills, but they also took into account factors such as trust (whether they had previous playing experience with one person over another), and such convoluted factors as whether, in order to get player A (who was great) you had to pick player B, player A's best friend (who was pretty awful). Finally, after sides were chosen up, the captain then had to find something for each person to do. Choosing up sides and assigning positions in a game is a simple leadership experience compared to delegating authority in a large organizational situation. In a sense, delegating authority is something like choosing up sides with someone standing to one side who has both veto and insistence power.

6 윗글의 내용과 일치하지 않는 것을 고르시오.

① Choosing up sides in a game is a kind of leadership experience.

② Sometimes the captain picks up a poor player in order to get an excellent player.

③ Assigning the position for each player is another important task for the captain.

④ Delegating authority in a group can't be done as you choose up sides in a game.

해석 일을 위하여 선택되어지기를 원하는 사람들이 지도자를 괴롭힐 때 문제가 발생한다. 당신이 아이였고 게임을 하기 위해 편을 갈랐던 때를 기억하는가? 팀을 나누었던 두 사람들은 대개는 팀의 주장을 맡았던 뛰어난 운동선수였으며, 그들은 자기편의 선수가 되기를 원하는 사람들에 대하여 빠른 결정을 내려야만 했다. 그들은 운동 실력을 토대로 뽑았을 뿐만 아니라 신뢰와 같은 요소들(그들이 다른 사람을 상대로 이전에 함께 경기를 한 경험이 있는지), 그리고 (실력이 뛰어난) A라는 사람을 얻기 위하여 A의 가장 친한 친구인 (운동 실력이 매우 나쁜) B를 뽑아야 하는가 하는 매우 복잡한 요소들 또한 고려를 해야만 했다. 마침내 팀을 나눈 후 그 주장은 각각의 사람이 해야 할 일을 찾아야 했다. 게임에서 편을 나누고 역할을 분담하는 것은 대형 조직에서 권한을 위임하는 것과 비교되는 단순한 리더십 경험이다. 어떠한 면에서 권한을 위임하는 것은 거부권과 주장권을 모두 가진 사람이 어느 편에라도 속한 채 편을 가르는 것과 같은 것이 된다.

6 윗글의 내용과 일치하지 않는 것을 고르시오.

① 경기에서 편을 가르는 것은 일종의 리더십 경험이 된다.

② 때로 주장은 훌륭한 선수를 얻기 위하여 실력이 좋지 못한 선수를 뽑기도 한다.

③ 각각의 선수를 위하여 역할을 배정하는 것이 주장에게 또 다른 중요한 임무가 된다.

④ 경기에서 팀을 나눌 때 단체의 권한을 위임하는 것은 가능하지 않다.

어구 besiege (요구 · 질문 따위로) 공세를 퍼붓다, 괴롭히다; 포위하다　function 역할[직분]을 다하다　take into account 고려하다, 참작하다　convoluted 뒤얽힌, 매우 복잡한　assign (임무 · 일 따위를) 부여하다, 주다　delegate (권한 등을) 위임하다　in a sense 어느 면에서는　veto (대통령 · 지사 · 상원 등이나 또는 U.N.안보 이사회 상임 이사국의) 거부권　insistence power 주장권

해설 권한을 위임하는 것은 경기에서처럼 행해질 수 있다고 마지막 문장에서 언급되었으므로 그렇지 않다는 부정 내용은 틀린 설명이다.

Comparative psychology has identified a number of symptoms that may help to distinguish intelligent, conscious imitation from automatic copying. In the first case, the solution comes instantly in the form of insight not requiring repetition. Such a solution pertains to all characteristics of intellectual action. It involves understanding the field structure and relations between objects. On the contrary, automatic drill imitation is carried out through repeating trial-and-error series, which show no sign of conscious comprehension and do not include understanding the field structure. In this sense, it can be said that animals are unteachable.

In the child's development, on the contrary, imitation and instruction play a major role. They bring out the human qualities of the mind and lead the child to new developmental levels. In learning to speak, as in learning school subjects, imitation is indispensible. What the child can do in cooperation today he can do alone tomorrow. Therefore the only good kind of instruction is that which marches ahead of development and leads it.

7 본문의 내용과 가장 잘 부합할 수 있는 것은?

① Children are good at automatic copying
② Automatic drill imitation is a process of conscious comprehension
③ Imitation may involve intellectual action.
④ Instruction is not effective when learning to speak.
⑤ Children should first learn to do things alone.

8 본문에서 제시되고 있는 모방의 역할을 가장 잘 설명한 것은?

① 모방이 인성교육과 학습에 중요한 이유는 아이들이 어른들의 행위를 따라함으로써 협동정신을 기를 수 있기 때문이다.
② 모방은 아이들의 학습 과정에서 개별적으로 배운 내용을 차후에 보다 강화해주는 중요한 보조역할을 한다.
③ 근본적으로 모방은 효율적인 학습에 방해가 되기 때문에 학습 과정에서 배제되어야 하지만 때로는 효과적인 문제 해결 방법을 제시해 준다.
④ 모방의 중요한 학습 기능은 아이들이 먼저 어른들이 하는 것을 따라한 후에 혼자 그 일을 독자적으로 할 수 있다는 데에 있다.
⑤ 동물들은 모방을 할 수 없기 때문에 학습을 할 수 없는 반면에, 인간은 기계적인 모방을 통해 시행착오를 반복하면서 학습을 하게 된다.

해석 비교심리학은 지적이며 의식적인 모방과 자동적인 모방을 구별해 주는 여러 증상들이 있다고 발견했다. 첫 번째의 경우 반복이 필요 없는 통찰의 형태로 즉시 해결이 가능하다. 이러한 해결은 지적인 행동의 전형적인 특징에 속한다. 여기에는 영역 구조와 물체들 사이의 관계에 대한 이해가 포함된다. 이와는 달리 자동 연습 모방은 일련의 시행착오를 반복함으로써 이루어지며, 의식적인 이해의 징후나 영역 구조에 대한 이해가 나타나지 않는다. 이런 의미에서 동물들은 교육이 불가능하다고 전해질 수 있다.
이와는 달리 아이의 발전 과정에서 모방과 교육은 중요한 역할을 한다. 정신의 인간적 특징이 모방과 교육을 통해 나오며 아동을 새로운 발달 단계로 나아가게 한다. 학교 과목을 배울 때처럼 말을 배우는 때에 모방은 필수 불가결하다. 지금 협력을 통해 할 수 있는 일은 아이는 그 이후에야 스스로 할 수 있다. 따라서 유일한 바람직한 교육은 발달 단계보다 먼저 그것이 진행되는 것이다.

7 본문의 내용과 가장 잘 부합할 수 있는 것은?
① 아이들은 자동적인 모방에 익숙하다.
② 자동 모방은 의식적인 이해의 과정이다.
③ 모방은 지적인 행위와 연관되어 있다.
④ 아이들은 처음에 스스로 할 수 있는 것을 배워야 한다.

어구 comparative psychology 비교 심리학   identify 발견하다, 확인하다, 동일시하다   symptom 증상, 징후   distinguish A from B A와 B를 구별하다   conscious 의식적인   imitation 모방, 흉내   instantly 즉시   insight 통찰력   repetition 되풀이, 반복   trial-and-error 시행착오   unteachable 가르칠 수 없는   bring out 나타내다, 발휘하다   indispensable 필수 불가결한   march 행진하다, (상황·사건 등이) 진전하다   ahead of ~의 앞에서   be good at ~에 능숙하다

해설 7 아동의 지능 발달에서 모방 연습이 중요한 역할을 하므로, 모방에도 지적 활동이 포함된다.
8 아이가 모방이라는 협력을 통해 배운 후에 스스로 할 수 있다.

>>> 다음 글을 읽고 문제의 답을 고르시오. [9~10]

Plato advocates the opinion that a just man—that means in this connection, a man who obeys the law—and only a just man, is happy; whereas an unjust man—a man who violates the law—is unhappy. Plato says, that "the most just life is the most pleasant". Plato, ______________, admits that perhaps in one case or another the just man may be unhappy and the unjust man happy. But, asserts the Philosopher, it is absolutely necessary that the individuals, subject to the legal order, believe in the truth of the statement that only the just man is happy, even if it should not be true; for otherwise nobody would obey the law. Consequently the government has, according to Plato, the right to spread among the people by means of propaganda the doctrine that the just is happy and the unjust unhappy, even if this doctrine be a lie. If this is a lie, says Plato, it is a very useful lie, for it guarantees obedience to the law. "Could a lawgiver, who was worth his salt, find any more useful lie than this, or one more effective in persuading all men to act justly in all things willingly and without constraint? … If I were a legislator, I should endeavor to compel the poets and all the citizens to speak in this sense." The government, then, is fully justified in making use of a useful lie. Plato places justice—and that means here, what the government considers to be justice, namely, lawfulness—above truth; but there is no sufficient reason not to place truth above lawfulness and to repudiate as immoral a governmental propaganda based on lies, even if it serves a good purpose.

9 Which of the following statements is true according to the passage?

① Plato believes that it is not possible for the unjust man to be happy.

② Plato has sufficient reason to place truth above lawfulness.

③ Plato says that the government should not lie in any case.

④ Obedience to the law brings us a happy life, thinks Plato.

10 밑줄 친 부분에 들어갈 가장 알맞은 것은?

① therefore　　　　　② however

③ by the way　　　　④ accidentally

해석 플라톤은 정의로운 사람이란 이와 같은 점에서는 법을 준수하는 사람이며 정의로운 사람만이 행복하며, 반면에 정의롭지 못한 사람은 법을 어기는 사람으로서 불행하다는 견해에 찬성한다. 플라톤은 "가장 정의로운 인생이 가장 행복하다"고 말한다. 그러나 플라톤은 아마도 이런저런 경우에 정의로운 사람이 불행할 수 있으며, 정의롭지 않은 사람이 행복할 수도 있다고 인정한다. 그러나 이 철학자는 법질서에 순응하는 정의로운 사람만이 행복하다는 말의 진실을 믿는다는 점이 절대적으로 중요하다고 주장 했다. 그렇지 않다면 법에 복종하는 자는 없을 것이기 때문에 그것이 설사 진실이 아닐지라도 말이다. 플라톤에 따르자면 결론적으로 정부는 대중 선동을 통하여 사람들 사이에서 올바름이 행복이며 부정은 불행이라는 이론을 확산시킬 권리를 가지고 있다고 한다. 설사 이 이론이 거짓일지라도 말이다. 플라톤에 따르면 이것이 만약 거짓이라면 그것은 선의의 거짓말이다. 왜냐하면 이것은 법의 준수를 보장하기 때문이다. 플라톤은 "맡은 바 임무를 충실히 하는 입법자가 이보다 더 유용한 거짓말을 발견하거나, 아니면 모든 이들에게 모든 일을 자발적으로 정의롭게 행동하라고 설득할 수 있는 더 효과적인 방법을 찾아낼 수 있을까? 만일 내가 입법가라면 시인과 모든 시민들에게 이런 뜻으로 이야기하라고 노력했을 것이다."라고 말했다. 그러면 정부는 선의의 거짓말을 이용한다는 점에서 충분히 정당화된다. 플라톤은 정의(여기서 정의의 의미는 정부가 정의라고 생각하는 것, 즉 준법)를 진실 위에 둔다. 그러나 설사 그것이 좋은 목적을 두고 있을지라도 준법 위에 진실을 두지 말고, 거짓에 기반을 둔 정부의 대중 선동을 도덕적이지 못하다고 거부하지 말아야 할 충분한 이유는 없다.

9 윗글의 내용과 일치하는 것은?

① 플라톤은 부당한 사람이 행복해질 가능성은 없다고 믿는다.

② 플라톤은 진실을 합법보다 우선시 할 타당한 근거를 가지고 있다.

③ 플라톤은 정부가 어떠한 경우에도 거짓말을 해서는 안 된다고 말한다.

④ 플라톤은 법에 대한 복종이 우리에게 행복한 삶을 영위하게 해 준다고 생각한다.

10 밑줄 친 부분에 들어갈 가장 알맞은 것은?

① 그러므로　　　　　② 그러나

③ 그런데　　　　　　④ 우연히

어구 advocate 옹호하다　just 공정한, 올바른　in this connection 이 점에 대하여　unjust 부당한　violate 위반하다　assert 주장하다　otherwise 그렇지 않다면　obey 복종하다　by means of ~에 의하여　propaganda 선전, 대중 선동　doctrine 교의, 주의, 학설　useful 유용한　guarantee 보장하다　obedience 복종　lawgiver 입법가　worth one's salt 유능한, 성실한, 칭찬받을 만한　constraint 강제, 압박　endeavor 노력하다, 애쓰다　namely 즉, 다시 말하자면　lawfulness 합법, 적법　repudiate 거부하다, 부인하다　place A above B A를 B보다 우선하다　by the way 그런데, 여담이지만　accidently 우연히

해설 9 플라톤은 '악법도 법이다'라는 명제 하에, 진실보다 준법을 우선시했으므로, 법에 대한 복종이 행복한 삶을 영위하게 해 준다고 생각했다.

10 앞 문장에서는 '가장 올바른 삶이 가장 행복하다'고 했지만, 이어서 '올바른 사람이 불행해질 수도 있다'는 완전한 역접의 내용으로 전개되므로, however가 옳다. by the way는 화제의 전환시 사용되므로, 이 경우에는 적합하지 않다.

>>> 다음 글을 읽고 문제의 답을 고르시오. [11~12]

Like a perilous boat in a storm, the island of Samoa has been being tossed by the waves—the waves of capital and democracy, both of which most of the Samoans are unfamiliar with. Traditionally, the land was owned by the *Matais* (family chiefs) and the *Matais* elected parliament and administered justice. But the tradition of communal land ownership has stultified individual incentive and has resulted in neglect of the land. The system of permitting only the nation's 15,000 *Matais* to elect 45 of the 47 MPs has destroyed political involvement. As a result, many young Samoans are leaving for New Zealand—and the money the emigrants send home—creates a false economy and results in thousands of Samoan families ignoring the land and living off the earnings of their expatriate children.

11 Choose the best title of the above passage.

① A promising future of Samoa and its young people
② The exodus of young Samoans to New Zealand
③ The Samoan economy: yesterday and today
④ The traditional economic and political system of Samoa
⑤ The changing roles of the family chiefs in the Samoan society

12 According to the passage, which of the following is true?

① In Samoa land is owned by individuals.
② Most Samoans are familiar with modern concepts such as capital and democracy.
③ The Matais represented absolute authority in the village he lived in.
④ There is universal suffrage in Samoa.
⑤ Despite problems, economy is healthy and progressing in Samoa.

해석 폭풍우 속 위험한 보트처럼 사모아 섬은 사모아 인들이 친숙하지 못한 자본과 민주주의의 물결에 의해 요동쳐져 왔다. 전통적으로 땅은 마타이스라고 불리는 족장들의 소유였으며 족장들은 의회를 선출하며 법을 집행했다. 그러나 공동 토지 소유의 전통은 개인적인 동기를 무의미하게 하였으며 땅의 방치를 야기했다. 그 국가의 오직 15,000명의 족장들만이 의원 47명 중에서 45명을 선출할 수 있도록 허락하는 체계가 정치 참여를 망쳐 놓았다. 그 결과, 수많은 젊은이들이 뉴질랜드로 떠났으며, 이주민들이 집으로 보낸 돈이 거짓 경제를 만들었고, 땅을 무시하고 이민을 간 아이들의 수익에 의존해 살아가는 수천의 사모아 가족들을 양산해냈다.

11 윗글의 제목을 고르시오.

① 사모아와 젊은이들의 밝은 미래
② 젊은 사모아 인들이 뉴질랜드로 떠나는 대 이동
③ 사모아 경제의 어제와 오늘
④ 사모아의 기존 경제 체계 및 정치 체계
⑤ 사모아 사회에서 가족 족장들의 변화하는 역할

12 이 글의 내용과 일치하는 것은?

① 사모아에서는 개인들이 토지를 소유한다.
② 대부분의 사모아 인들은 자본과 민주주의와 같은 현대 개념들에 친숙하다.
③ 족장은 거주하는 마을에서 절대적인 권력을 나타낸다.
④ 사모아에 광범위한 참정권이 있다.
⑤ 문제가 있음에도 불구하고, 사모아의 경제는 건실하고 발전하고 있다.

어구 **perilous** 위험한, 위험이 많은, 모험적인   **toss** (가볍게) 던지다, (공을) 토스하다; 급히 던져 올리다; (배 따위를) 흔들다; 마음을 뒤흔들다   **communal** 자치 단체의, 공동 사회의; 공공의, 공동의, 공유의   **stultify** 어리석어 보이게 하다, 무의미하게 하다; 망쳐 버리다   **incentive** 격려, 유인, 동기; (생산성 향상을 위한) 장려금   **political involvement** 정치 참여   **live off** ~에 기식하다; ~에게 폐를 끼치다; ~에 의존하여 생활하다   **expatriate** 추방하다; 국적을 버리다, 이주하다(emigrate); 국외로 추방된 (사람), 국적을 버린 (사람)   **exodus** 집단적 (대) 이동[이주]   **suffrage** 투표; 선거권, 참정권

해설 **11** 이 글은 사모아 사람들의 참정권이 없는 '황폐한 정치권'과 개인 토지를 소유할 수 없는 '척박한 소유권'에 대한 문제를 현재시제와 과거시제로 구분하여 분석한 글이다.
12 족장에게만 땅의 소유가 허락되었으며, 47명 중 45명의 의원 선출 권한이 있었기 때문에 막강한 권위를 가지고 있다고 유추가 가능하다.

A combination of global warming and the climatic phenomenon known as El Niño will make the next 12 months exceptionally warm. El Niño is an occasional warming of the Pacific Ocean which has an effect on weather worldwide. The last El Niño made 1998 the warmest year on record.

This year could be warmer than 1998. Weather experts fear that the predicted weather conditions could spark such anomalies as droughts in tropical countries and deluges in areas with dry climates.

Many European ski resorts had to postpone their ski season this winter due to unseasonably warm weather. Much of the American Midwest and East Coast is also going through an unusually warm winter.

13 **Which of the following is true according to the passage?**

① This year will be warmest on record.
② This year it will not rain in areas with dry climates.
③ El Niño warmed the Pacific Ocean every year in the 1990s.
④ Many European ski resorts postponed their ski season this winter because of heavy rain.

해석 지구 온난화와 엘니뇨라고 알려진 기상 현상의 결합으로 앞으로 12개월 동안 날씨는 매우 더울 것이다. 엘니뇨는 태평양이 간헐적으로 따뜻해지는 현상으로 이는 전 세계적으로 날씨에 영향을 미친다. 가장 최근의 1998년 엘니뇨로 인해 그 한 해는 가장 무더운 날씨를 기록했다.
올해는 1998년보다 더 무더울 수도 있다. 기상 전문가들은 예상되는 기상 이변이 발생할 수 있다는 것을 걱정한다.
유럽의 많은 스키장들은 계절에 어울리지 않는 따뜻한 날씨 때문에 올 겨울의 스키 시즌을 미루어야 했었다. 미국 중서부와 동부 해안의 많은 지역들 역시 보통 때와는 다른 따뜻한 겨울을 경험하고 있다.

13 이 글의 내용과 일치하는 것은?

① 올해 가장 기록적인 더위가 찾아올 것 같다.
② 올해 건조한 환경의 지역에서는 비가 내리지 않을 것이다.
③ 엘니뇨는 1990년대 이후 매해 태평양을 따뜻하게 했다.
④ 유럽의 많은 스키장들이 폭우 때문에 스키 시즌을 미루었다.

어구 climatic 기후상의; 풍토적인 known as ~라고 알려진 exceptionally 예외적으로, 특별히 occasional 간헐적인, 이따금씩의 have an effect on ~에 영향을 미치다 on record 기록되어; 기록적인 predicted 예측된 anomaly 변칙, 이례, 이상 deluge 대홍수; 범람시키다 postpone 연기하다; 미루다 unseasonably 계절에 맞지 않게 go through 경험하다

해설 두 번째 단락 첫 문장을 통해 올해가 기존에 가장 1998년보다 더 무더울 수 있을 것이라고 미래의 추측을 하고 있다.

A newspaper in North Carolina fired a photographer for changing the color of the sky in a picture of fire fighters. In 2003, a California newspaper fired a photographer for combining two pictures from Iraq into one. In 2004, the re-election campaign for President Bush altered a video by inserting faces into a crowd of soldiers listening to him to make the audience look larger. Some of these episodes were serious attempts to mislead the public, and some were relatively trivial. All of them undermine the public's trust in the reality of news photographs.

Actually, that's good. The public tends to assign too much 'reality' to what they see in photographs anyway. We should approach all news photos as somewhat unreal. What does it mean for a photograph to be true? That it captures what we would perceive if we were standing where the camera was? That is nonsense.

해석 노스캐롤라이나의 한 신문사에서 소방관들이 나온 사진에 찍힌 하늘 색깔을 바꾸었다는 이유로 사진 기자가 해고됐다. 2003년에 캘리포니아 주의 한 신문사는 이라크에서 찍은 두 개의 사진을 하나로 합쳤다는 이유로 사진 기자를 해고했다. 2004년에 부시 대통령을 위한 재선에서는 부시의 연설을 듣는 군인들의 수를 더 많이 보이게 하기 위해 군인들의 영상에 사람들의 얼굴을 삽입하여 영상을 변경했다. 이러한 에피소드들 중 일부는 대중을 오도하기 위한 위험한 시도였으며, 다른 일부는 사소한 것들이었다. 그러한 시도는 뉴스 사진의 진실성에 대한 대중의 신뢰도를 저해하는 것이다.
실제로, 그것(사진 수정)은 괜찮다. 대중은 어쨌든 사진에서 보는 것들에 너무나 많은 '진실성'을 부과하는 경향이 있다. 우리는 모든 뉴스 사진을 어느 정도 사실과 다른 것으로 접근해야 한다. 사진이 현실이라는 것은 어떤 의미가 되는가? 카메라가 있는 곳에 서 있다면 우리가 감지하게 될 바로 그것을 사진이 포착한다는 뜻인가? 그것은 터무니없는 이야기이다.

14 윗글의 내용과 일치하지 않는 것은?

① 몇몇 사진은 변경된 것으로 알려져 있다.
② 몇몇 변경은 큰 효과를 가지지 못한다.
③ 부시의 (선거 운동) 캠프는 많은 군인들이 그의 말을 경청하는 것처럼 보이기를 원했다.
④ 대중은 사진에서 자신이 본 것을 믿지 않을 만큼 현명하다.

어구 fire 해고하다; 발포하다 combine A into B A를 B로 합치다 alter 변경하다 insert A into B A를 B에 삽입하다 mislead 잘못 안내하다 trivial 시시한 undermine 훼손하다 trust 신뢰성; 진실성 assign A to B A를 B에 할당하다; 지명하다 anyway 어쨌든 nonsense 터무니없는 생각

14 윗글의 내용과 일치하지 않는 것은?

① Some photographers are known to have altered their photos.

② Some altering does not have much effect.

③ Bush's camp wanted to make it look as if many soldiers listened to him.

④ The public is clever enough not to believe what they see in photos.

해설 본문의 경우 사진 속 내용을 그대로 받아들이지 말라고 대중에게 충고를 하는 글이다. 따라서 대중이 사진의 내용을 그대로 믿지 않을 만큼 똑똑하지는 못하다고 보아야 한다.

>>> **다음 글을 읽고 문제의 답을 고르시오.** [15~16]

Sticky clay and dry sand are more familiar on the end of a spade than on the dinner table. Yet these are the basic ingredients in the manufacture of the pottery plates we eat from and the glass jars and bottles in which we buy preserved goods and drinks. Glass and ceramic materials share some useful qualities: they resist the flow of heat and electricity, and they have a hard, nonreactive surface. But they are different in other ways. Light passes through glass but not ceramics, and ceramics stay strong when they are heated. In their most basic forms glass and ceramic objects are brittle, but special additives and manufacturing methods make both materials much ① _____________ . Glass and ceramics are ancient materials. The Egyptians made decorative glass beads more than 5,000 years ago, and pottery is even older.

15 Which of the following best fits into ①?

① fancier ② more colorful

③ thicker ④ sturdier

⑤ more profitable

16 From what is stated or inferred, which of the following is NOT true?

① Ceramics and glass have a long history of use.

② Glass cannot resist heat as well as ceramics do.

③ Translucency is a common property of ceramics and glass.

④ Glass and ceramics do not conduct electricity.

⑤ Clay and sand are used in making glass and ceramics.

해석 끈적이는 진흙과 건조한 모래는 저녁 식사 테이블 위보다는 삽의 끝에 있을 때 더 어울린다. 그러나 이것들은 우리가 먹는 도기 접시와 저장용 식품, 음료수들을 구입하는 유리 항아리와 병의 제조의 기본 성분이 된다. 유리와 세라믹 소재는 몇몇 효용성이 있는 성질을 함께 가지고 있는데, 즉 열과 전기의 흐름에 저항하며, 강하고 반발력이 없는 표면을 갖고 있다. 그러나 다른 면에서는 상이한 점도 있다. 빛이 유리는 통과하지만, 세라믹은 그러하지 못하며, 또한 세라믹은 가열이 될 때에도 내구성이 있다. 가장 기본적인 상태에서 유리와 세라믹 물건은 부서지기 쉽지만, 특별한 첨가제와 제조방식에 의해서 두 소재 모두 훨씬 강해지게 된다. 유리와 세라믹은 오래된 소재이다. 이집트인들은 5,000년 전에 장식용 유리구슬을 만들었으며, 도기의 제조는 그보다 더욱 오래되었다.

15 ①에 알맞은 것은?

① 더 공상적인 ② 더 색채가 풍부한

③ 더 두꺼운 ④ 더 완강한

⑤ 더 이로운

16 윗글과 일치하지 않는 내용은?

① 세라믹과 유리는 오랜 역사에 걸쳐서 이용되어졌다.

② 유리는 세라믹만큼 열에 견디지 못한다.

③ 반투명은 세라믹과 유리의 공통된 특징이다.

④ 유리와 세라믹은 전기를 전도하지 못한다.

⑤ 진흙과 모래는 유리와 세라믹을 만들 때 이용되어진다.

어구 **sticky** 끈적이는, 완고한　**spade** 삽　**ingredient** 성분, 재료　**pottery** 도기, 도기 제조법　**plate** 접시　**jar** 항아리, 단지　**preserved** 보관된, 보관용의　**goods** 상품, 재산　**material** 재료, 요소; 물질의, 중요한　**resist** 저항하다, 견디다　**nonreactive** 무반동의, 반응하지 않는　**pass through** 통과하다, 경험하다, (학위 등을) 수료하다　**brittle** 부서지기 쉬운, 덧없는, 완고한　**decorative** 장식(용)의　**bead** 구슬　**even** [비교급 앞에서] 더욱　**fancy** 공상의, 장식적인, 변종의; 공상하다, 장식하다　**thick** 두꺼운, 뚱뚱한　**sturdy** 억센, 완강한　**profitable** 유리한, 이로운　**translucency** 반투명, 거짓 없음　**conduct** (열 · 전기 · 음파 등을) 전도하다, 인도하다, 지도하다

해설 **15** but이라는 '역접-대조'의 논리 정보 장치에 의해서 'brittle(깨지기 쉽다)'의 반대말인 'sturdy(완강한)'의 비교급 형태가 옳다.

16 'Light passes through glass but not ceramics~' 문장을 통해서, 세라믹은 빛이 통과하지 못한다고 했으므로, 세라믹은 반투명의 특징을 가질 수 없다고 유추할 수 있다.

Two hunters got a pilot to fly them into the far north for elk hunting. They were quite successful in their venture and bagged six big bucks. The pilot came back, as arranged, to pick them up. They started loading their gear into the plane, including the six elk. But the pilot objected and he said, "The plane can only take four of your elk; you will have to leave two behind." They argued with him; the year before they had shot six and the pilot had allowed them to put all aboard. The plane was the same model and capacity.

Reluctantly, the pilot finally permitted them to put all six aboard. But when they attempted to take off and leave the valley, the little plane could not make it and they crashed into the wilderness. Climbing out of the wreckage, one hunter said to the other, "Do you know where we are?" "I think so," replied the other hunter. "I think this is about the same place where we landed last year!"

17 윗글의 내용과 일치하지 않는 것은?

① The plane this year was not the same plane the year before.
② The number of the elk hunted this year was six.
③ The plane they were aboard the year before had a safe take-off.
④ The pilot was worried about loading all the elk on the plane.

해석 두 명의 사냥꾼이 엘크 사냥을 목적으로 극북을 향해 자신들을 태우고 비행할 조종사를 구했다. 그들의 이번 사냥은 꽤 성공적이었고 여섯 마리의 큰 엘크를 잡았다. 예정대로 조종사는 그들을 데려가기 위하여 돌아왔다. 그들은 여섯 마리의 엘크를 포함하여 장비를 싣기 시작했다. 그러나 조종사는 이것을 거부했고, "이 비행기에는 단지 엘크 네 마리만 실을 수 있다. 당신들은 두 마리를 남겨 두어야 한다."고 말했다. 사냥꾼들은 조종사와 다투었고 작년에 그들이 여섯 마리를 잡았을 때에는 조종사가 모두 태웠다고 했다. 비행기는 작년과 동일한 모델이며 동일한 능력을 갖고 있었다.
주저하면서 조종사는 마침내 사냥꾼들에게 여섯 마리 모두 태우는 것을 허락했다. 그러나 그들은 이륙을 한 후 계곡을 떠나려고 시도했을 때, 그 작은 비행기는 실패했으며 황야에 불시착했다. 잔해에서 기어 나온 사냥꾼이 다른 사냥꾼에게 "여기가 어디인지 알겠어?"라고 물었다. "알고 있어. 이곳은 우리가 작년에 착륙한 대략 그 지점인 것 같아!"라고 다른 사냥꾼이 대답했다.

17 윗글의 내용과 일치하지 않는 것은?

① 올해 비행기는 작년 비행기와 같지 않았다.
② 올해 잡은 엘크의 수는 여섯 마리이다.
③ 사냥꾼들이 작년에 탄 비행기는 무사히 이륙했다.
④ 조종사는 엘크를 모두 비행기에 태우는 것을 걱정했다.

어구 **far north** 극북 지역   **elk** 엘크(현존하는 사슴 중 가장 큼)   **venture** 모험; 위험을 무릅쓰다   **bag** (사냥감을) 잡다; 자루에 넣다   **as arranged** 예정대로   **pick up** (차 · 비행기 등에) 태우다; 데려가다   **load** (짐을) 싣다; (총을) 장전하다   **gear** 기구, 도구; 전동 장치   **leave A behind** A를 남겨놓다   **put aboard** (배 · 비행기 등에) 싣다; 태우다   **reluctantly** 주저하며, 마지못해   **take off** 이륙하다   **make it** 성공하다   **crash** 불시착하다; 무너지다   **wreckage** 난파; 파멸   **land** 착륙하다; 상륙하다   **the year before** 작년에

해설 마지막 문장에서 '이곳은 우리가 작년에 착륙한 대략 그 지점인 것 같다.'고 말했기 때문에 작년에도 똑같이 불시착한 것으로 보아야 한다.

Can hell really be worse than what we've seen and read about Rwanda? The world must stop such madness. A Rwandan colleague tried to explain to me the legacy of hatred between the Hutu and Tutsi. I don't ever want to understand what it takes to murder men, women and children solely because of their tribal ties or skin appearance. How many Hutu were murdered by mistake by their fellow Hutu? And how many Tutsi by fellow Tutsi? As an African, I tell you there is no excuse. When a country descends into the mire of mindless atrocities, doesn't it automatically suspend the right of self-determination? We must act forcefully to stop such killing by moving in and separating tribes or by disarming both sides. It's not enough for the media to continue reporting on atrocities like this. Those images of bodies floating down the river will remain with me the rest of my life.

18 윗글의 내용과 일치하는 것은?

① Certain religious problem might have resulted in a massacre.
② Disarmament may not be useful as an inhibition against a massacre.
③ The press wasn't effective on the check against a massacre.
④ The Hutu must have slain even their own tribes.

해석 우리가 르완다에 대해서 보고 읽은 것보다 과연 지옥이 더 나쁠 수 있을까? 세계는 그런 미친 짓을 중단해야 한다. 한 르완다 인 동료는 나에게 후투족과 투치족 간의 증오의 유산을 설명하려고 했다. 단지 부족 간의 유대나 겉모습 때문에 남자, 여자, 아이들이 희생되는 것을 나는 결코 이해하고 싶지 않다. 얼마나 많은 후투 인들이 그들의 동료 후투 인들에 의해서 실수로 죽임을 당했는가? 그리고 얼마나 많은 투치 인들이 동료 투치 인들에 의해서 살해당했는가? 한 사람의 아프리카 인으로서 거기에는 변명의 여지가 없다고 나는 생각한다. 한 나라가 무분별한 잔학 행위의 수렁 속에 빠져들 때 그 나라는 자동으로 자결권을 정지 당하는 것이 아닐까? 우리는 거기에 개입해서 부족들을 분리시키거나 양측의 무장을 해제함으로서 그런 살인 행위를 중단시키기 위해서 강력히 행동해야 한다. 언론 매체들이 이와 같은 잔학 행위에 대해서 보도를 계속하는 것으로는 충분치 않다. 강물을 따라 떠다니는 시체들의 모습은 평생 동안 나에게는 잊혀 지지 않을 것이다.

18 윗글의 내용과 일치하는 것은?

① 어떤 종교 문제가 대학살을 야기했던 것 같다.
② 무장 해제가 대량 학살에 대한 억제책으로서 무용지물인 것 같다.
③ 언론은 대량 학살에 대한 억제책으로서 효과가 없는 것 같다.
④ 후투 인들은 심지어 자신의 종족마저 살해했음에 틀림이 없다.

어구 legacy 유산 hatred 적대감 What it takes to R? ~하기 위해 무엇이 필요한가? tribal ties 부족의 유대 excuse 변명 descend 내려가다 mire 수렁, 진창 mindless 정신 나간 atrocity 만행, 잔학 행위 move in 개입하다 disarm 무장 해제하다 massacre 대학살 check 저지, 억제; 확인; 수표

해설 how many Tutsi by fellow Tutsi?의 질문에 이어지는 문장에서 변명의 여지가 없다고 긍정 답변을 하고 있다. 즉, 투치 인들도 자신들 종족을 학살했었다고 언급된 것이다.

》》》 다음 글을 읽고 문제의 답을 고르시오. [19~20]

If the current rate of divorce in America continues, at least half of the children under eighteen will experience the divorce of their parents. Divorce is a traumatic experience for parents and children. It can provoke aberrant behavior _____________ both parents and children when emotional resources to deal with aberrance are completely drained. My own experiences as a family law practitioner have convinced me that it is a rare child whose moral development will be untouched by the experience.

해석 만일 미국의 현재 이혼율이 지속된다면 18세 미만의 아이들 중 적어도 절반은 자신들의 부모가 이혼하는 것을 경험할 것이다. 이혼은 부모와 아이들에게 치명적인 경험이다. 그것은 이상 행위를 다루어 줄 정서적 수단들이 완전히 고갈되었을 때 부모와 아이들의 편에서 모두 다 일탈행위를 유발시킬 수 있다. 가정 법률 변호사로서 나의 경험으로 그러한 경험이(부모의 이혼이) 아이들의 도덕 성장에 영향을 주지 않는 경우가 없다는 것을 확신하게 되었다.

19 Which is not true of the above passage?

① The divorce rate in America is extremely high.

② More than half of the children under eighteen will live in broken homes.

③ Divorce is a disturbing experience for both children and parents.

④ Divorce makes both children and parents slip morally or mentally from the right path.

⑤ On some occasions, children are not affected by the experience of their parent's divorce.

20 Which best fills the blank?

① thanks to

② on the part of

③ irrespective of

④ regardless of

⑤ by virtue of

19 윗글의 내용과 일치하지 않는 것은?

① 미국의 이혼율은 매우 높다.

② 18세 미만의 아이들 중 절반 이상이 결손가정에서 살게 될 것이다.

③ 이혼은 아이들과 부모 모두에게 괴로운 경험이다.

④ 이혼은 아이들과 부모 모두에게 도덕적으로나 정신적으로 올바른 길에서 탈선하게 한다.

⑤ 몇몇 경우에는 아이들이 부모 이혼의 경험으로부터 영향을 받지 않게 된다.

20 빈칸에 들어갈 말은?

① ~ 덕택에

② ~의 편에서

③ ~에 상관없이

④ ~에 상관없이

⑤ ~ 덕택에

어구 **traumatic** 상처를 남기는 **provoke** ~을 유발시키다 **aberrant** 상식에서 벗어난, 탈선한 **drain** 고갈시키다 **family law practitioner** 가족법 전문 변호사 **disturbing** 교란시키는, 혼란스럽게 하는 **slip** 미끄러지다. 탈선하다 **on some occasions** 몇몇 경우에 **thanks to** ~의 덕택에(by virtue of) **on the part of** ~의 편 · 입장에서 **irrespective of** ~에 상관없이(regardless of)

해설 **19** 현재의 이혼율이 지속된다는 조건이 성립될 경우에나, 미래에 18세 미만의 아이들 중 절반 이상이 결손가정에서 살게 될 것이라고 했을 뿐, 그러한 조건 없이 ②와 같은 추측을 한 것은 아니다.

20 부모와 아이들의 입장을 표명하는 어구인 on the part of(~의 편에서)가 문맥상 옳다.

Three guys were fishing in a lake one day, when an angel appeared in the boat. When the three astonished men had settled down enough to speak, the first guy asked the angel humbly, "I've suffered from back pain ever since I took shrapnel in the Vietnam War. Could you help me?" "Of course," the angel said, and when he touched the man's back, the man felt relief for the first time in years.

The second guy who wore very thick glasses had a hard time reading and driving. He asked if the angel could do anything about his poor eyesight. The angel smiled, removed the man's glasses and tossed them into the lake. When they hit the water, the man's eyes cleared and he could see everything distinctly.

When the angel turned to the third guy, the guy put his hands out defensively—"Please do not touch me!" he cried, "I'm on a disability pension."

해석 어느 날 세 남자가 호수에서 낚시를 하고 있는데, 보트에 천사가 나타났다. 놀란 세 남자가 말할 수 있을 만큼 충분히 진정이 됐을 때, 첫 번째 남자가 공손하게 "베트남 전쟁에서 포탄 파편이 박힌 후 줄곧 허리 통증을 겪고 있습니다. 도와주실 수 있는지요?"라고 천사에게 물어보았다. 천사는 "물론이죠."라고 답을 했고, 천사가 그 남자의 등에 손을 대자 그 남자는 몇 년 만에 처음으로 안도를 느꼈다.

매우 두꺼운 안경을 쓴 두 번째 남자가 독서와 운전을 하는데 어려움을 겪고 있다며, 천사가 자신의 나쁜 시력에 대하여 어떤 조치라도 취할 수 있는지를 물어보았다. 천사는 웃으면서 남자의 안경을 벗기고 그 안경을 호수 속으로 던져 버렸다. 안경이 물에 빠지자 남자의 눈은 좋아졌고 모든 것을 또렷하게 볼 수 있었다.

천사가 세 번째 남자에게 몸을 돌리자, 그 남자는 자신의 손을 방어하듯이 뻗었다. "저를 만지지 마세요. 저는 장애 연금을 받고 있습니다."라고 그가 울부짖었다.

21 Which of the following is true according to the passage?

① Not all the three men believed that the angel could heal anyone.
② The angel threw the shrapnel and the glasses into the lake.
③ One man did not have a driver's license.
④ One man wanted to remain handicapped.

21 윗글의 내용과 일치하는 것은?

① 천사가 누구라도 치료할 수 있다고 세 남자 모두가 믿은 것은 아니었다.
② 천사는 파편과 안경을 호수로 던졌다.
③ 한 남자는 운전면허증이 없었다.
④ 한 남자는 계속 장애 상태로 있기를 원했다.

어구 astonished 놀란 settle down 안정하다; 정착하다 humbly 겸손하게; 초라하게 shrapnel 포탄 파편 thick 두꺼운; 빽빽한 have a hard time (in) -ing ∼하느라 고생하다 eyesight 시력 toss A into B A를 B로 던지다 distinctly 명료[뚜렷]하게 turn to ∼로 돌리다; ∼에게 의존하다 put out 뻗다 disability 무능; 불구 pension 연금; 장려금 handicapped 신체적 장애가 있는

해설 천사가 첫 단락과 두 번째 단락에 나오는 남자의 신체적 문제를 치료했다. 그러나 마지막 단락에 등장하는 남자는 장애 연금을 받고 있기 때문에 천사의 치료를 거부하고 있으므로 계속 장애 상태로 남아 있기를 원한다는 설명은 옳다.

American surface informality often confuses the foreigner because he interprets it to mean no formality at all. He does not understand the point at which informality stops. A teacher, though friendly, pleasant, and informal in class, expects students to study hard, and he grades each student's work critically and carefully. He also expects to be treated with respect. Though students are free to ask questions about statements made by the teacher, they are not expected to contradict him.

22 Which of the following is true according to the passage?

① American students are free to contradict their teachers.
② American teachers are generous in grading their students' work.
③ American teachers are so strict that students often disobey them.
④ Americans, though apparently informal, know the limits of informality.

해석 미국인의 겉으로 격식 없이 행동하는 모습은 외국인들을 종종 혼란스럽게 하는데, 그 이유는 외국인들은 그것을(겉으로 격식 없이 행동하는 모습을) 격식이 전혀 없는 의도라고 해석하기 때문이다. 외국인은 격식 없이 행동하는 것이 어느 정도에서 멈추는지를 이해하지 못한다. 교사가 교실에서 친근하고 즐겁게 해 주면서 격식 없이 대한다 해도, 학생들이 공부를 열심히 하기를 기대하며 각 학생들의 성적을 비평적으로 신중히 매긴다. 또한 그는 존경을 받기를 기대한다. 학생들이 교사의 설명에 대하여 자유롭게 질문을 할 수 있지만, 교사에게 반박할 것으로 기대되지는 않는다.

22 윗글의 내용과 일치하는 것은?

① 미국 학생들은 자유롭게 선생님들에게 반박을 할 수 있다.
② 미국 교사들은 학생들 성적을 매기는 데 관대하다.
③ 미국 교사들은 너무나 엄격하여 학생들은 종종 말을 듣지 않는다.
④ 미국인들은 외관상으로는 격식이 없는 것으로 보이지만, 격식 없음의 제한을 알고 있다.

어구 surface 겉모습, 외관 informality 격식 없음; 비공식 interpret 해석하다 grade 등급[격]을 매기다; 등급, 성적 with respect 존경을 받으며 be free to R 자유롭게 ∼을 하다 statement 설명 contradict 반박하다; 부인하다 generous 관대한 disobey 반항하다 apparently 외관상으로; 명백히

해설 세 번째 문장에서 미국 학생들과 그들의 교사의 관계를 예를 들어 설명하고 있다. 교실 내에서는 즐겁게 해 주는 것과 같이 격식 없는 모습을 보여 주지만, 학생들의 성적 측정에서는 신중히 평가한다고 했기 때문에 이것은 격식 없음의 한계를 스스로 알고 있다는 내용이다.

The great English author Charles Dickens was a life-long champion of social justice. In fact, his own childhood foreshadowed the lives of the characters in his novels. Poverty forced Dickens at the age of twelve to quit school and work in a shoe polish factory. He never forgot that experience. Images of poverty appear in many of his novels.

Dickens began his literary career by writing articles for newspapers. He often used the pseudonym "Boz". When he was twenty-four years old, several of these articles were published in one volume called Sketches by Boz.

Dickens' first publications were humorous. However, as his fame grew, he began to write more about social problems. Dickens' novel Oliver Twist dealt with cruelty toward orphaned children. Dickens used Oliver's story to allude to the social system in England. He used the slang of poor people and even criminals in some of the dialogues he wrote.

A London newspaper first published Oliver Twist in serialized form. People waited eagerly for each episode to appear. In addition to entertaining readers, however, Oliver's story made the public aware of the need to protect orphaned children.

Dickens' work often appears in anthologies of great literature. His compassion for poor people inspired many of ① _______________ English to work for improvements in the quality of life of ② _______________ poor.

23 Which of the following best fits into
① ___________ and ② ___________?

① the - the 　　② an - a
③ the - a 　　④ an - the
⑤ some - some

24 According to the passage which of the following statements is true?

① Images of poverty appear in none of Dickens' novels.
② Oliver Twist's story praises the social system in England.
③ The episodes of Oliver Twist were first published in several newspapers.
④ Dickens often used his pen name in his newspaper articles.
⑤ Dickens began to write newspaper articles after he became famous.

해석 위대한 영국 작가인 찰스 디킨스는 사회 정의를 평생 지지했던 사람이었다. 사실, 그의 유년 시절은 그의 소설에 나오는 인물들의 삶을 미리 보여 주었다. 가난 때문에 디킨스는 20세의 나이에 학교를 그만두고 구두약 공장에서 일을 하지 않을 수 없었다. 그는 결코 이 경험을 잊지 않았다. 가난의 이미지가 그의 수많은 소설 작품들 속에 나타난다.

디킨스는 자신의 작품 경력을 신문 기사를 쓰는 것을 통해서 시작했다. 그는 종종 "Boz"라는 필명을 사용했다. 그가 24살이 되었을 때, 이 기사들 중 다수가 "Boz의 스케치"라고 불리는 책으로 출판되었다.

디킨스의 첫 작품들은 유머러스했다. 그러나 점점 유명해지자 그는 사회 문제에 대해 더 많은 것을 썼다. 디킨스의 소설인 "올리버 트위스트"는 고아들에 대한 잔인성을 다루었다. 디킨스는 올리버의 이야기를 이용하여 영국의 사회 체계를 언급했다. 심지어 그가 쓴 대화에서 범죄자들과 가난한 이들의 속어를 이용했다. 런던의 어떤 신문사에서 처음에 "올리버 트위스트"를 연재 형태로 올렸다. 사람들은 각각의 에피소드가 계속해서 나오기를 열렬히 기다렸다. 그러나 올리버 스토리는 독자를 즐겁게 하는 것 이외에도 애독자들에게 고아들을 보호해 주어야 할 필요성을 알게 해 주었다.

디킨스의 작품은 명작 선집에 자주 들어간다. 가난한 이들에 대한 그의 동정심은 많은 영국인들을 고무시켜 가난한 이들의 삶의 질을 향상시키도록 했다.

23 ①과 ②에 들어갈 적절한 것은?

24 이 글과 일치하는 내용은?

① 가난의 모습이 디킨스의 소설에 등장하지 않는다.
② 올리버 트위스트의 이야기에서 영국의 사회 체제를 칭찬했다.
③ 올리버 트위스트의 에피소드들이 여러 신문에서 처음으로 출간됐다.
④ 디킨스는 신문 기사에 자신의 필명을 종종 사용했다.
⑤ 디킨스는 유명해진 후에 신문 기사를 기고하기 시작했었다.

어구 **life-long** 평생의 　**champion** 옹호자, 투사; 옹호하다, 승리하다; 일류의, 우승의 　**childhood** 유년 시절 　**foreshadow** ~의 전조가 되다, 예시하다 **shoe polish** 구두약 　**literary** 문학의 　**pseudonym** 익명, 필명 **volume** (책의) 권(卷), 책, 부피, 양, 음량 　**cruelty** 잔인함 　**orphaned** 고아가 된 　**allude to** ~을 언급하다 　**slang** 속어 　**serialize** 차례로 나열하다 　**eagerly** 열렬히, 열망하면서

해설 23 영국 사람들을 가리키기 위해서는 'the English'가 옳으며, 'poor'라는 형용사가 전치사 of의 목적어가 되기 위해서는 정관사 'the'와 결합하여 복수 보통명사가 되어야 한다.

24 두 번째 단락 두 번째 문장인 He often used the pseudonym "Boz".를 통해서 디킨스는 자신의 필명을 사용했음을 알 수 있다.

Woe to the patient waiting for someone to offer up a spare organ for transplantation. Demand so far exceeds supply these days that in America alone around 17 people die every day while languishing in the queue. Nor do problems end there. Even the lucky ones, who do get their desired replacement part, face a lifetime on immunosuppressant drugs, to stop the alien tissue being rejected by their own immune systems.

David Sachs and Benedict Cosimi, of Harvard Medical School, have been working for some time to find a way around these problems. Their goal has been to _______________ the body into thinking that a foreign organ is really a native one, so that its immune system refrains from rejecting the foreigner. In this week's New England Journal of Medicine they report a small but promising study that, if confirmed on a grander scale, may deal with the issue once and for all and usher in a world in which immunosuppressant drugs are unnecessary and organs no longer need be matched to patients. That would make the lives of transplant patients easier and longer, and might also increase the useful supply of organs available for transplant.

25 The best title of the passage would be

_______________.

① the Lack of Spare Organs for Transplantation
② the Problem of Immunosuppressant Drugs
③ Immune Systems Blocking Foreign Organs
④ Induce Immune System to Believe Foreign Organs Native

26 According to the passage, which of the following is not true?

① In America, less than 20 people are dying everyday due to transplant problems.
② Foreign organ is difficult to harmonize with a native one.
③ David Sachs and Benedict Cosimi put strong confidence in their experiment.
④ If receiving an organ transplant, the patient can be completely cured.

27 Which of the following best fills in the blank?

① restrain
② trick
③ immune
④ turn

해석 장기 이식을 위해 여분의 장기를 제공해 줄 누군가를 기다리고 있는 환자에 대해 슬픈 마음이 든다. 현재 장기 이식의 수요가 공급을 너무나 초과하고 있기 때문에 미국에서만 매일 거의 17명의 사람이 쇠약해지다가 연이어 죽어가고 있다. 문제는 여기에서 끝이 나지 않는다. 바라던 장기를 얻게 된 사람마저도 신체 내 면역 체계의 외부 조직 거부 현상을 막아내기 위하여 한 평생 면역 억제 약물에 의존해 살아가야 한다.

하버드 대학의 데이비드 샤크와 베네딕트 코시미 교수는 얼마간의 연구를 통해 이 문제에 대한 해결책을 찾아내고 있으며 현재도 진행 중이다. 그들의 목표는 신체로 하여금 (이식받은) 외부 장기가 본래의 장기인 것으로 믿게끔 하는 것이다. 이번 주 뉴잉글랜드 의학 저널에, 상당한 정도로 확증만 된다면 확실한 해결책을 마련하여 면역 억제 약물이 불필요하며 장기가 더 이상 환자와 조화가 되어야 할 필요가 없는 새로운 시대의 도래를 알릴 수 있다는 작지만 전도유망한 연구를 발표했다. 그럴 수 있다면 장기 이식 환자의 삶은 더욱 편안해지고 그들은 더욱 오래 살 수 있을 것이며, 이식을 위해 필요한 효율적인 장기 공급도 또한 증가할 것이다.

25 이 글의 제목을 고르시오.

① 장기 이식을 위한 장기 여분의 부족 현상
② 면역 억제 약물의 문제
③ 외부 장기를 거부하는 면역 체계
④ 면역 체계가 외부 장기를 몸 안에 원래 있던 것으로 믿게끔 유도하라.

26 이 글의 내용과 일치하지 않는 것을 고르시오.

① 미국에서 20명 미만의 사람들이 장기 문제 때문에 매일 사망하고 있다.
② 외부 장기는 몸 안에 있는 본래 장기와 조화되기가 어렵다.
③ 데이비드 샤크와 베네딕트 코시미 교수는 자신들의 연구에 확신을 가지고 있다.
④ 장기 이식 수술을 받으면 환자는 완치될 수 있다.

27 빈칸에 가장 알맞은 것은?

① 제지하다
② 속이다
③ 면역성의
④ 틀다

어구 woe (감탄사) 슬프도다 languish 쇠약해지다 in the queue 줄지어, 계속해서 immunosuppressant 면역 억제제 alien tissue 외부 조직 alien 외부의; 외계의; 외국의 tissue (세포) 조직; 직물; (한 장의) 얇은 천; 뒤범벅, 투성이 immune system 면역 체계 trick A into -ing A를 속여서 ~하게 하다 refrain from ~을 삼가다. ~하지 않다 promising 유망한 once and for all 단호하게, 최종적으로 usher in a world 세상의 선구자가 되다 be matched to ~과 조화가 되다 put confidence in ~을 신뢰하다

해설 25 두 번째 단락의 두 번째 문장이 문제의 해결책으로서 주제문이 된다. 장기가 이식될 때 원래 몸 안에 있는 면역 체계가 그 이식된 외부 장기를 거부하는 현상이 장기 이식 수술의 기존 문제점이었다. 그러나 하버드 대학의 두 교수가 몸 안에 있는 그 면역 체계로 하여금 몸 안에 이식된 외부 장기를 원래 몸 안의 것으로 믿게끔 속일 수 있는 이론을 제시하고 있으며 그 내용이 주제가 된다.

26 기존의 장기 이식 수술의 경우, 장기 이식 수술을 받은 후 한 평생 면역 억제 약물에 의존해 살아가야만 한다고 했으므로, 단순히 수술만 받는다고 해서 완치가 가능한 것은 아니다.

27 so that은 '순접-인과'의 논리이다. 해당 문장에서 면역 체계가 외부 장기를 거부하지 못하게 된다고 했으므로, 몸 안에 원래 있는 장기라고 속이게 하는 논리가 적합하다.

>>> **다음 글을 읽고 문제의 답을 고르시오. [28~29]**

　　Speakers of a second language are often well advised not to try to sound too much like a native. A foreign accent will often allow as yet imperfectly learned rules of etiquette to be excused as such, ① ＿＿＿＿＿＿＿ a speaker who has mastered the phonology of a language is assumed to have also mastered all other aspects of its use, and violations are more likely to be interpreted as rudeness. Additional consequences of perfecting pronunciation in a second language may be suspicion or resentment from native speakers if they do not welcome new members, or feelings from the primary speech community that one is disloyal to it.

28 Which of the following best fits into ①?

① when　　　　② so that
③ while　　　　④ or
⑤ because

29 Which of the following statements is TRUE?

① Speakers of a second language should learn a foreign accent.
② A speaker with native-like pronunciation in a second language is expected to be perfect in all other aspects of its use.
③ Speakers of a second language are not welcomed by all native speakers when they sound too much like a native.
④ As long as one masters pronunciation in learning a second language, he or she need not care about rules of etiquettes in its use.
⑤ Proving phonological incompetence in a second language does not have any practical benefits.

해석 제2 외국어 구사자들은 지나치게 원어민처럼 보이려고 노력하지 말라는 충고를 받는다. 외국 악센트는 완전히 습득하지 못한 그 나라에서 요하는 에티켓들에 대해 변명을 할 수 있지만, 반면 한 언어의 발음을 터득한 언어 구사자는 그 언어를 이용할 수 있는 다른 모든 측면들까지도 터득한 것으로 간주되며, 그것을 위반하면 무례한 것으로 생각될 가능성이 있다. 제2 외국어를 완벽하게 발음하여 생기는 추가적 결과로 인해 원어민들이 새로운 구성원들을 환영하지 않을 경우 그들은 의심과 분노가 생길 수도 있으며, 사람들이 원어민의 공동체 사회에 거역한다는 느낌이 생길 수도 있다.

28 ①에 적합한 표현은?

① ～일 때　　　　　② 그리하여
③ ～하는 반면　　　④ 또는
⑤ ～이기 때문에

29 일치하는 내용은?

① 제2 외국어 구사자들은 외국 악센트를 터득해야만 한다.
② 제2 외국어를 네이티브와 같은 발음으로 구사하는 사람은 그 언어를 이용하는 모든 다른 측면에서 완벽할 것으로 기대가 된다.
③ 제2 외국어 구사자들이 네이티브와 같은 발음을 구사할 때 모든 원어민들에 의해 환영받지 못한다.
④ 사람들이 제2 외국어를 배울 때 발음을 터득한다면 에티켓의 법칙에 대해 관심을 가질 필요가 없다.
⑤ 제2 외국어의 음성학적 불완전함을 증명하는 것은 어떠한 실질적인 이점도 없다.

어구 **second language** 제2 외국어　**sound like** ～처럼 들리다　**as yet** 아직까지, 이제껏　**imperfectly** 불완전하게　**excuse** 용서하다, 변명하다　**master** 터득하다, 정복하다　**phonology** 음성학, 음운론　**be assumed to R** ～으로 가정되다　**violation** 위배, 위반, 폭행　**rudeness** 무례함　**resentment** 분노, 격분　**primary** 최초의, 제1의　**disloyal** 불충한, 불성실한　**-like** ～과 비슷한

해설 **28** 불완전하게 학습된 에티켓들이 용서받을 수 있다는 주절의 내용과, 빈칸 이하의 무례한 것으로 간주될 수 있다는 내용은 '역접-대조'의 관계이므로 while이 옳다.
29 원어민처럼 발음을 하는 사람은 발음뿐만 아니라 모든 다른 면들에 있어서도 완벽해야 한다. 그렇지 않다면 무례함, 의심, 반감을 원어민들에게 살 수 있기 때문이다.

Clara Louise Mass was a nurse who contributed to the research on yellow fever at the turn of the century. She was working as a civilian nurse in Cuba, where army Majors William Gorge and Walter Reed were conducting experiments to isolate the cause of the disease. Tests ruled out dirt and poor sanitation as causes of yellow fever, and mosquito was the suspected carrier. Clara Mass was among the group who volunteered to be bitten by the insect. She contracted the disease and died on August 24, 1901. She was the only woman to participate in the experiment and among the few volunteers to die from it. With her death, the study ended; the results of the experiment provided conclusive evidence that mosquitoes were the source of the disease.

30 윗글의 내용과 일치하지 않는 것은?

① William Gorge and Walter Reed had previously looked for the cause of yellow fever by conducting experiments.

② People do not contract yellow fever when they are situated in the dirty unsanitary condition.

③ In many cases, volunteers who participated in the insect biting experiment did not show lethal condition.

④ Clara Mass served as a nurse and discovered the sources of yellow fever through immunization process.

해석 클라라 루이스 매스는 금세기 초에 황열병의 연구에 기여한 간호사였다. 그녀는 쿠바에서 민간 간호사로 근무했는데, 그곳에서 육군 소령인 윌리엄 조지와 월터 리드가 황열병의 원인을 분리시키려는 실험을 하고 있었다. 그 실험을 통해 황열병의 원인으로서 더럽고 열악한 위생은 배제됐으며, 모기가 매개체로 의심되었다. 클라라 매스는 모기에 물리는 실험에 자원했던 무리 중에 한 사람이었는데 황열병에 걸려서 1901년 8월 24일에 죽었다. 그녀는 실험에 참가한 유일한 여성이었고, 그 병으로 죽은 몇 안 되는 지원자 중의 한 명이었다. 그녀의 죽음으로 그 연구는 끝났다. 그 실험의 결과는 모기가 그 병의 원인이라는 결정적인 증거를 제공했다.

30 윗글의 내용과 일치하지 않는 것은?

① 이전에 윌리엄 조지와 월터 리드는 연구를 통해 황열병의 원인을 찾고 있었다.

② 사람들이 비위생적인 더러운 상태에 있을 때 황열병에 걸리지 않는다.

③ 많은 경우에 있어서, 모기에 물리는 실험에 자발적으로 참여한 사람들이 치사 상태를 보이지는 않았다.

④ 클라라 매스는 간호사로 근무했으며, 면역 절차를 통해 황열병의 원인을 찾아냈다.

어구 **contribute** 기여하다, 공헌하다(to) **yellow fever** 황열병 **conduct** 행하다, 수행하다 **isolate** 고립시키다; 분리해 내다, 추출해 내다 **rule out** 배제하다, 인정하지 않다 **sanitation** 위생 (상태) **carrier** 보균자, 질병을 옮기는 원인, 매개체 **volunteer** 지원[자원]하다 **bitten** 물린(bite의 p.p.) **contract** (질병에) 걸리다, 감염되다 **conclusive** 결정적인 **previously** 사전에, 이전에 **lethal** 치명적인 **serve as** ~의 역할을 하다 **immunization** 면역(법)

해설 그녀가 황열병의 원인을 파악하기 위한 임상 실험에 자발적으로 참여했을 뿐, 그녀가 그 원인을 찾아낸 것은 아니다.

I am not inclined to accept that those who give orders directly are really insecure and powerless, any more than I want to accept that judgment of those who give indirect orders. The conclusion to be drawn is that ways of talking should not be taken as obvious evidence of inner psychological states like insecurity or lack of confidence. Considering many influences on conversational style, individuals have a wide range of ways of getting things done and expressing their emotional states. Personality characteristics like insecurity cannot be linked to ways of speaking in an automatic, self-evident way.

31 Which of the following is correct according to the passage?

① Those who give indirect speech are judgemental.

② Ways of talking are the indexes of personality.

③ There are many factors influencing the manners of speech.

④ Conversational styles have power over individual traits.

해석 나는 직설적으로 명령을 내리는 사람들이 실제로 불안정하고 무기력하다고 인정하고 싶지 않고, 마찬가지로 우회적으로 명령을 내리는 사람들의 판단이 그렇다는 사실을 인정하기 원하지 않는다. 말하는 방법을 불안정감 혹은 자신감 부족과 같은 내면의 심리적 상태의 명백한 증거로 오인하지 말아야 한다는 것이 결론으로 도출된다. 대화 방식에 미치는 많은 영향들을 고려해 볼 때, 개인들은 일을 처리하고 감정 상태를 표현할 수 있는 폭넓은 방법들을 가지고 있다. 불안정감과 같은 개인의 특성을 습관적으로 자명하게 말하는 방법과 연결을 시켜서는 안 된다.

31 이 글의 내용과 일치하는 것은?

① 간접적으로 말하는 사람들은 판단력이 뛰어나다.

② 화법은 성격의 지표이다.

③ 화법에 영향을 미치는 요소는 많다.

④ 화법은 개인의 특성을 지배한다.

어구 **be inclined to R** ~하고 싶다 **give an order** 명령을 내리다 **insecure** 불안정한 **draw** 도출하다; 끌다 **take A as B** A를 B로 오인하다 **link A to B** A를 B에 연결하다 **automatic** 습관적인; 자동적인 **self-evident** 자명한 **have power over** ~을 지배하다

해설 'Considering many influences~' 문장을 통해 개인이 일을 하거나 감정 상태를 표현하는 방법은 광범위하다고 했기 때문에 화법에 영향을 미치는 요소는 많다는 ③이 옳다.

Chapter 06 지칭어 · 의미 추론

⇒ 본책 p.84

1 ⑤	**2** ②	**3** ①	**4** ①	**5** ①	**6** ④	**7** ①	**8** ④	**9** ②	**10** ⑤
11 ②	**12** ①	**13** ④	**14** ④	**15** ④	**16** ②	**17** ③	**18** ①	**19** ③	**20** ④
21 ④	**22** ②	**23** ①	**24** ①	**25** ④	**26** ⑤	**27** ④	**28** ①	**29** ②	**30** ④
31 ②	**32** ①								

>>> **다음 글을 읽고 문제의 답을 고르시오.** [1~3]

For decades schools have been assigning students to different sections on the basis of academic performance. Many of (1) them don't stop at that. They make students wear different colored blazers and ties to differentiate the (2) 'achievers' from 'nonachievers'. Such demarcations invariably translate into discrimination with regard to teachers, with the best teachers reserved for sections with first divisioners. Schooling is, however, not just about academic excellence, but overall personality development. It's the school's duty to help (3) a child discover (4) his latent talents and nurture them. But if schools ① ____________ some of their students at the outset, (5) they cannot realize their potential. A healthy intermingling of students with different aptitudes, capabilities and attainment levels could help everyone perform better.

1 Choose the statement that the above passage says or implies.

① Schools have been traditionally avoiding segregation of students on the basis of academic performance.
② Segregating students on the basis of academic performance help everyone perform better.
③ Schooling is above all about academic excellence.
④ Academic excellence is more significant than personality development in schooling.
⑤ An intermingling of students with different aptitudes, capabilities and attainment levels could help everyone perform better.

2 Choose the most appropriate expression for the underlined blank ①.

① include
② write off
③ help
④ intermingle with
⑤ exterminate

3 Among (1), (2), (3), (4) and (5), which one differs from the others in what they refer to?

① (1)
② (2)
③ (3)
④ (4)
⑤ (5)

해석 수십 년간 학교는 학업 성적을 토대로 학생들을 여러 반으로 나누어 왔다. 많은 학교들이 여기서 멈추지 않는다. 학교들은 '우등생'과 '낙제생'을 구별하기 위하여 학생들로 하여금 상이한 컬러 블레이저코트를 입게 하고 타이를 착용하게 한다. 그러한 구분들은 최고의 교사들을 최고의 학생들이 속한 반에 배치시키면서 교사들에 관해서 한결같이 차별로 표현한다. 그러나 학교 교육이란 것은 뛰어난 학업 성적뿐만 아니라 인성의 모든 발전인 것이다. 아이로 하여금 자신의 잠재된 능력을 계발하게 하고 성숙하게 해 주는 것이 학교의 의무인 것이다. 그러나 학교들이 초기에 학생들 중 일부를 포기해 버린다면 아이들은 잠재력을 깨달을 수 없게 될 수 있다. 다른 적성, 능력, 성취도 수준을 가진 학생들을 혼합시켜 놓는 것이 모든 이가 더 잘 학습을 할 수 있게 해 주는 데 도움을 줄 수 있다.

1 이 글을 읽고 알 수 있는 내용은?

① 학교들은 학업 성적을 토대로 하여 전통적으로 학생들의 차별 대우를 삼가 왔다.
② 학업 성적을 토대로 하여 학생들을 차별하는 것은 모든 이가 더 나은 성적을 올리는 데 도움을 준다.
③ 학교 교육은 무엇보다도 성적 우수성에 주안을 둔다.
④ 성적 우수성은 학교 교육에 있어서 인성 발전보다 더 중요하다.
⑤ 다른 적성, 능력과 성취도를 가진 학생들을 혼합시키는 것이 모든 이가 성적을 더 올리는 데 도움을 준다.

2 ①에 들어갈 알맞은 표현은?

① 포함하다
② 고려하지 않다
③ 돕다
④ 혼합되다
⑤ 말살하다

3 (1)~(5)까지 중에서 가리키는 대상이 다른 하나는?

① 학교들
② 우등생
③ 아이
④ 아이의
⑤ 학생들

어구 **on the basis of** ~을 토대로 하여 **differentiate A from B** A와 B를 차별하다, 구분하다 **achiever** 우등생 **non-achiever** 낙제자 **divisioner** 구분된 사람 **not just A but (also) B** A뿐만 아니라 B도 **latent** 잠재된 **intermingling** 혼합, 뒤섞음 **attainment level** 성취 수준 **segregation** 차별, 분리, 격리 **write off** 가치가 없다고 여기다, 단념하다, 고려하지 않다 **intermingle with** 뒤섞이다

해설 1 마지막 문장에서 '다른 적성, 능력, 성취도 수준을 가진 학생들을 혼합시켜 놓는 것이 모든 이가 더 잘 학습할 수 있게 해 주는 데 도움을 줄 수 있다'고 직접적으로 설명하고 있다.

2 '학생들이 자신의 잠재력을 깨닫지 못한다'는 내용이 주절이므로, 그 조건절 또한 그 원인이 될 수 있는 '학교들이 시작부터 학생들 중 일부를 고려의 대상에 포함시키지 않는다'는 내용이 옳다.

3 우등생이나 아이는 모두 학생들의 개념에 포함되지만, (1)의 them은 앞서 나온 학교들을 지칭한다.

On a tour of an old European castle, a young American visitor becomes very nervous. Finally the elderly guide, noticing how jumpy she is, tries to reassure her. "Don't worry," he tells her. "I've never seen a ghost in all the time I've been here." "And how long is that?" asks the tourist. "About 400 years."

4　Who does the underlined 'he' refer to?

① the ghost
② the tourist
③ the author
④ the castle owner

해석 한 젊은 미국인이 오래된 유럽 성을 관광했을 때 매우 겁을 먹었다. 결국 나이가 많은 노인은 그녀(관광객)가 몹시 불안해하는 것을 보고서는, 그녀를 달래려고 노력했다. 그는 그녀에게 "걱정하지 마세요. 내가 이곳에 있는 동안 결코 귀신을 본 적이 없어요."라고 말했다. 그녀는 "얼마나 오래됐는지요?"라고 물어보았다. "약 400년 정도."

4　밑줄 친 he는 누구를 가리키는 것인가?

① 귀신　　　　　　　　② 관광객
③ 작가　　　　　　　　④ 성 주인

어구 **nervous** 겁을 먹은; 신경질적인; 불안한　**jumpy** (신경질·흥분으로) 실룩거리는; 흥분하기 쉬운　**reassure** 안심시키다; 재보증하다

해설 귀신을 얼마나 못 보았느냐는 질문의 답으로 400년 동안 못 봤다는 얘기는 400년 동안 그 성의 근처에 살았다는 것이다. 이는 본인이 귀신이라고 인정하는 꼴이 된다.

This impulse is inspired by a genuine love of knowledge. You may see this impulse in a moderately pure form; for example, a cat has been brought to a strange room, and proceeds to smell every corner and every piece of furniture. This impulse grows weaker with advancing years, until at last what is unfamiliar inspires only disgust, with no desire for closer acquaintance.

5　What does the underlined 'This impulse' refer to?

① curiosity
② yearning
③ ambition
④ culture

해석 이 충동은 지식에 대한 진정한 사랑으로 고취된다. 당신은 비교적 순수한 형태로 이 충동을 볼 수 있다. 예컨대, 고양이가 이상한 방으로 들어와서는 모든 구석과 가구의 냄새를 계속 맡고 다닌다. 이 충동은 해가 지나면서 점점 약해지며, 마침내 낯선 것은 혐오감만 유발하며, 더 면밀하게 알고 싶은 갈망은 사라진다.

5　밑줄 친 This impulse가 가리키는 것은?

① 호기심　　　　　　　② 열망
③ 야망　　　　　　　　④ 문화

어구 **impulse** (마음의) 충동; 충격; 자극　**inspire** 고무[격려]하다, 발분시키다　**genuine** 진짜의; 진심에서 우러난, 성실한　**moderately** 적당하게, 삼가서, 알맞게　**proceed to R** 계속 ~을 하다　**unfamiliar** 낯선, 익숙하지 못한　**disgust** 싫증, 혐오　**acquaintance** 면식, 친면　**yearning** 그리워[동경]함, 사모; 열망

해설 예를 통해 설명하고 있는 내용이 고양이의 행동이다. 고양이가 낯선 방에 들어가서 구석구석 가구의 냄새를 계속 맡는다는 것은 호기심의 충동으로 볼 수 있다.

>>> 다음 글을 읽고 문제의 답을 고르시오. [6~10]

A thousand years ago, when the earth was reassuringly flat and the universe revolved around it, the ordinary person had no last name, ① let alone any claim to individualism. The self was subordinated to church and king. Then came the Renaissance explosion of scientific discovery and humanist insight and, as both cause and effect, the rise of individual self-consciousness. All at once, it seemed, humanity had replaced God at the center of earthly life. And perhaps more than any great war or invention or feat of navigation, this upheaval marked the beginning of our modern era. There are now 20 times as many people in the world as there were in the year 1000. Most have last names, and many of us have a personal identity or reasonable expectation of acquiring one. This special ② issue examines the transformation of identity through different lenses and concludes with reflections on how hard ③ it is, in a time of gathering global conformity, to find one's own way.

6 The best title of this passage is
_______________.

① Identification of humanity
② Divinity over individualism
③ Importance of the Renaissance in the human history
④ How individual identity was acquired
⑤ Relationship between God and humanism

7 What does the underlined ① mean?

① to say nothing of any claim to individualism
② but for empty claims to individualism
③ at the same time no claim to individualism
④ nor any claim at all to individualism
⑤ in the end no claim at all to individualism

8 According to the passage, before the Renaissance _______________.

① individualism was respected
② people did not have their own personal names
③ people acquired personal identity
④ church and king dominated individuals
⑤ humanism enhanced individual self-consciousness

9 밑줄 친 ② issue의 뜻은?

① 결과
② (출판물의) …호
③ 문제점
④ 논문
⑤ 논쟁

해석 1천 년 전, 지구는 분명 평평하고 우주가 지구 둘레를 돌고 있다고 믿었을 때, 일반인들은 개인주의를 주장하는 것은 말할 것도 없고 성조차 가지고 있지 않았다. 자아는 교회와 왕에 종속되어 있었다. 그 후 과학의 발전과 인본주의 통찰의 르네상스가 도래했으며, 또한 그것의 원인과 결과로서, 개인 자아의식의 상승이 도래했다. 갑자기 인간이 지구 생명체의 중심에서 신을 대신하는 것처럼 보였다. 그리고 아마 그 어떤 대형 전쟁이나 발명 또는 항해의 업적 이상으로, 이 격변이 근대 시대의 출범을 특징지었다. 현대에는 1000년에 있었던 것보다 20배나 많은 사람들이 있다. 대부분의 사람들이 성을 가지고 있으며, 우리들 중 많은 이들이 개인의 주체성, 혹은 무엇인가를 얻고자 하는 합당한 기대 심리를 가지고 있다. 이번 특별호에서는 여러 관점을 통해서 주체성의 변화를 연구하고, 세상화에 순응하는 시대에서 개인의 길을 찾는 것이 얼마나 힘든지에 대한 반영들을 통해서 결론을 내린다.

6 이 글의 제목은?
① 인류의 동정심
② 개인주의를 능가하는 신격화
③ 인류역사에서 르네상스의 중요성
④ 개인의 주체성이 어떻게 획득되었는지
⑤ 신과 인본주의의 관계

7 ①의 의미는?
① 개인주의에 대한 어떠한 주장도 말할 것도 없고
② 개인주의에 대한 공허한 주장들은 별도로 하고
③ 개인주의에 대한 주장이 없는 동시에
④ 개인주의에 대한 주장이 전혀 없었다
⑤ 마침내 개인주의에 대한 어떠한 주장도 없었다

8 르네상스 시대 이전에는 어떠했는가?
① 개인주의 사상이 존중되었다.
② 사람들은 자신의 이름을 갖고 있지 못했다.
③ 사람들은 개인의 주체성을 얻었었다.
④ 교회와 왕이 개인들을 지배했다.
⑤ 인본주의가 개인의 자아의식을 부양시켰다.

9 ② issue의 뜻은?
① 결과
② (출판물의) …호
③ 문제점
④ 논문
⑤ 논쟁

10 ③ it의 뜻은?
① 이 특별호
② 주체성의 변화
③ 개인의 주체성
④ 한 개를 얻고자 하는 타당한 기대
⑤ 자신의 길을 찾는 것

어구 reassuringly 든든하게, 위안을 주며   last name 성   let alone ~은 말할 것도 없고   self 자아   be subordinated to ~에 종속되다   explosion 폭발, 급격한 증가   insight 통찰   self-consciousness 자아의식   all at once 갑자기   earthly 지구의, 세속적인   feat 업적   navigation 항해   upheaval 격변, 동란   identity 주체성, 독자성, 개성, 일치, 동일성   reasonable 이치에 맞는, 온당한   issue 판(版), 호, 논쟁,

10 **What does the underlined** it ③ **refer to?**

① this special issue
② transformation of identity
③ a personal identity
④ reasonable expectation of acquiring one
⑤ to find one's own way

결과, 문제 **lens** 렌즈, 관점 **conclude with** ~을 통해 결론을 내리다 **conformity** 적합, 일치, 유사 **identification** 동정심, 구별, 신분증 **divinity** 신격화 **to say nothing of** ~은 말할 것도 없고 **but for** ~은 별도로 하고 **empty** 텅 빈, 공허한 **at all** 결코[부정문], 과연[의문문], 어쨌거나[기타]

해설 6 과거에는 개인의 주체성은 존재하지 않고, 교회와 왕에게 종속되었지만, 과학의 발전과 르네상스의 도래로 인하여 근대 이후부터 개인의 자아가 구현되었다는 내용이 주제가 된다. 따라서 개인의 주체성의 획득에 대한 방법이 이 글의 주제로서 옳다.

7 let alone은 '~은 말할 것도 없고'의 뜻으로, to say nothing of = not to mention과 동의어구이다.

8 르네상스 이전에는 '개인주의 사상도 없었으며, 개인의 성도 없었고, 개인의 주체성도 없었으며, 인본주의도 없었으며', '자아는 교회와 왕에게 종속되었다'고 설명됐다.

9 issue가 등장하는 문장의 동사 2개가 각각 examine(조사하다), conclude(결론을 내리다)의 뜻을 가졌으므로, 이렇게 조사하고 연구하기 위해서는 '잡지나 간행물 또는 서적'이어야 한다. issue는 '출판물의 호, 판(a magazine or newspaper printed for a particular day, week, or month)'이라는 뜻을 가지고 있다.

10 전치사구인 in a time of gathering global conformity 이하에, 진주어인 to find one's way가 등장한다. 이 to부정사구가 진주어이며, 밑줄 친 it은 가주어이므로 ⑤가 옳다.

In the days of my grandfather, the word "marriage" meant only one thing: the union of one man and one woman until "death do they part". Marriage was traditionally looked upon as something permanent, a sacred bond between man and woman for the purpose of raising a family. ① _______________, marriage today can mean different things to different people. And to some people it doesn't mean much at all. There are a number of alternatives to the traditional marriage, none of which was acceptable fifty years ago. There are homosexual marriages, group marriages, communal living arrangements, and swingers' group, each of these being different from others in the number and type of relationships desired. The word ② "relationship" is often used today when talking about marriage.

해석 나의 할아버지 때 "결혼"이란 단어는 한 가지만을 의미했다. 남자와 여자가 "죽음이 그들을 갈라놓을" 때까지 같이 있는 것이다. 결혼은 전통적으로 영원하고, 가족을 구성하기 위한 남자와 여자 사이의 성스러운 결합으로 간주되었다. 그러나 요즈음은 결혼의 의미가 다양한 사람에게 다양한 것으로 받아들여진다. 어떤 사람에게는 별 의미가 없는 것이기도 하다. 그래서 전통적인 결혼에 대한 많은 대안이 생겼는데, 이들 중 어떤 것도 50년 전만 해도 받아들여지지 않는 것이었다. 동성 결혼, 단체 결혼, 공동체 생활, 상대 바꾸기 등이 있는데, 이러한 것들은 각각 바라는 관계의 수나 형태에서 서로 다르다. 결혼에 대해 얘기할 때 요즘은 종종 "친족관계"라는 말이 사용된다.

11 ①에 적절한 것은?
① 유사하게
② 비교해 보면
③ 대체로
④ 같은 방식으로
⑤ 결과적으로

11 **The expression that is most appropriate for** ① **is "___________".**

① Likewise
② In comparison
③ By and large
④ In the same vein
⑤ Consequently

12 The main topic of the passage is

_______________.

① Marriage, past and today
② Types of marriage today
③ Marriage and relationship
④ The true meaning of marriage
⑤ The sacredness of marriage

13 Which of the following is NOT associated with the meaning of the underlined "relationship" in ②?

① casualness
② freedom
③ consumerism
④ responsibility
⑤ temporariness

12 주제는 무엇인가?

① 과거와 오늘날의 결혼
② 오늘날의 결혼 형태들
③ 결혼과 친족관계
④ 결혼의 진정한 의미
⑤ 결혼의 신성함

13 "관계"라는 표현과 관련이 없는 것은?

① 우연
② 자유
③ 소비자 중심주의
④ 책임
⑤ 일시적인 것

어구 traditionally 전통적으로 look upon A as B A를 B로 간주하다 permanent 영원한 sacred 신성한 bond 결합 alternative 대안 homosexual 동성의 communal 공동사회의 arrangement 배열, 계획, 제도 swinger 부부 교환을 하는 사람 sacredness 신성함 casualness 우연 responsibility 책임 temporariness 일시적인 것

해설 11 이전까지는 과거의 결혼에 대해 설명했지만, ① 이하부터 현재의 결혼에 대해서도 언급하므로 '비교'의 표현이 적합하다.

12 과거와 오늘날 바라보게 되는 결혼의 여러 생각의 차이를 비교·대조한 글이다.

13 '관계'라는 용어는 '오늘날의 결혼'에서 언급된다고 했으므로, 과거의 결혼과 관련된 단어를 선택해서는 안 된다. 과거의 결혼이 한 가정을 이루는 성스러웠던 반면, 현대의 결혼은 '관계'라 불리어질 정도로 책임과는 거리가 멀다.

"Awhile" is a word we frequently use. "(가)This will take awhile," says the man who repairs your car or watch. What does he mean? minutes, hours, days? What is important about "awhile" as far as communication is concerned is that the interpretation is contextual. "Awhile" means different things in different situations, and with different people. (나)It may be well to remember (다)this: our concept of time depends on our cultural way of evaluating (라)it.

해석 우리는 "잠깐"이라는 단어를 자주 쓴다. "이것은 잠깐이면 돼요."라고 당신의 차나 시계를 수리하는 사람이 말한다. 그는 무엇을 의도한 것일까? 몇 분? 몇 시간, 혹은 며칠? 대화와 관련하여 '잠깐'이라는 말에 대해 중요한 것은 그 말의 해석이 그 맥락에 좌우된다는 점이다. '잠깐'이라는 말은 다른 상황들과 사람들에 있어서 다른 의미를 가진다. 다음의 내용을 상기하는 것이 이로울 것이다. 우리의 시간 개념은 시간을 평가하는 우리의 문화적 방법에 좌우된다.

14 윗글에서 밑줄 친 부분이 지칭하는 것을 잘못 연결한 것은?

① (가) - repairing your car or watch
② (나) - to remember this
③ (다) - our concept of time depends on our cultural way of evaluating it
④ (라) - the concept of time

14 윗글에서 밑줄 친 부분이 지칭하는 것을 잘못 연결한 것은?

① (가) – 차나 시계를 수리하는 것
② (나) – 다음의 내용을 상기하는 것
③ (다) – 우리의 시간 개념은 시간을 평가하는 우리의 문화적 방법에 좌우된다.
④ (라) – 시간 개념

어구 awhile 잠깐, 잠시 take awhile (시간이) 잠시 걸리다 as far as ~ is concerned ~에 관한 한 contextual 문맥상의, 전후 관계의 be well to R ~하는 편이 좋다 depends on ~에 좌우되다, ~에 의존하다 evaluate 평가하다, 가치를 검토하다

해설 평가하는 문화적 방법의 대상은 '시간'이어야 한다.

Five score years ago, a great American in whose symbolic shadow we stand signed the Emancipation Proclamation. This momentous decree came as a great beacon light of hope to millions of Negro slaves who had been seared in the flames of withering injustice.

One hundred years later, the life of the Negro is still not free. The life of the Negro is still sadly crippled by the manacles of segregation and the chains of discrimination.

Today (가)we have come to our nation's Capital to cash a check. When the architects of our republic wrote the magnificent words of the Constitution and the Declaration of Independence, they were signing a promissory note to which they American was to fall heir. This note was a promise that all men would be guaranteed the unalienable right of life, liberty and the pursuit of happiness.

15 **Which of the following best interprets the underlined (가)?**

① We came to ask for financial benefits equal to those of the whites.

② We came to find out what equal rights we should have as fellow citizens.

③ We came to ask for the abolition of segregation and discrimination.

④ We came to demand that the equal rights long overdue be granted immediately.

16 **The above passage is a(n) ___________.**

① essay

② speech

③ advertisement

④ newspaper article

해석 100여 년 전, 오늘 우리가 서 있는 상징적 그림자의 주인공인 위대한 미국인(링컨을 말함)은 노예 해방 선언에 서명했습니다. 이 중대한 법령은 사람을 시들어가게 하는 불공평의 불꽃 속에 지친 수백만의 흑인 노예들에게 커다란 희망의 신호 등불로 다가왔습니다.

100년이 지나서도, 흑인들은 여전히 자유롭지 못합니다. 흑인의 삶은 여전히 인종 차별 정책의 족쇄와 차별의 사슬로 인해 자유롭지 못합니다.

오늘 우리는 수표를 현금으로 바꾸기 위해 우리나라의 수도에 왔습니다. 우리 공화국의 건국자들이 위대한 헌법과 독립 선언서를 작성하였을 때, 그들은 모든 미국인들이 물려받게 될 확실한 약속 어음에 서명하였습니다. 이 약속 어음은 모든 사람은 빼앗을 수 없는 삶, 자유, 행복 추구권을 갖는다는 약속이었습니다.

15 **밑줄 친 (가)를 올바르게 해석한 것은?**

① 우리는 백인과 동등한 금융 혜택을 요청하기 위해 왔다.

② 우리가 이웃 시민으로 누려야 하는 평등권이 무엇인지 알기 위해 왔다.

③ 우리는 분리 정책과 차별 대우의 폐지를 요청하기 위해 왔다.

④ 우리는 오랫동안 미뤄온 평등권을 즉시 부여받을 것을 요구하기 위하여 왔다.

16 **윗글은 무엇인가?**

① 에세이 　　　　　　② 연설

③ 광고 　　　　　　　④ 신문기사

어구 **score** (숫자) 20　**Emancipation Proclamation** 노예 해방 선언　**momentous** 중대한, 중요한, 쉽지 않은　**decree** 법령; 포고; 판결　**beacon** 횃불; 등대　**sear** 태우다, 그을리다; 낙인을 찍다; 무감각하게 하다　**wither** 시들다　**injustice** 부정, 불의, 불공평　**cripple** 불구[절름발이]가 되게 하다; 무능케 하다　**manacle** 수갑; 속박, 구속　**segregation** 인종 차별(대우); 인종 차별을 규정한 법률　**discrimination** 차별, 차별 대우　**cash a check** 수표를 현금으로 바꾸다　**architect** 개척자; 건축가　**magnificent** 장대한(grand), 장엄한, 장려한　**Declaration of Independence** 독립 선언문　**promissory note** 약속 어음　**fall heir to** ~을 상속받다　**unalienable** (아무에게서) 빼앗을 수 없는; 양도할 수 없는　**the pursuit of happiness** 행복 추구권　**equal to** ~과 동등한　**abolition** 폐지　**overdue** (지급) 기한이 지난, 미불의(어음 따위); 늦은

해설 **15** 이 문장에서 말하는 수표는 다음 문장에서 약속 어음으로 바꿔 말하게 되는데, 마지막 문장에서 밝히기를, 약속 어음의 약속 내용이 빼앗을 수 없는 삶, 자유, 행복 추구권을 갖는다는 것임을 알 수 있다. 따라서 평등권을 보장해 달라는 요청으로 볼 수 있다.

16 이 글은 흑인들의 평등권을 보장해 달라는 강력한 요청이 담겨 있으므로 연설문으로 보아야 한다. 마틴 루터 킹의 연설문인 "I have a dream."에서 발췌된 글이다.

>>> **다음 글을 읽고 문제의 답을 고르시오.** [17~24]

It was precisely in those parts of France where there had been most improvement that popular discontent ran highest. This may seem illogical—but history is full of such ① ______________. For it is not always when things are going from bad to worse that revolutions break out. On the contrary, it often happens that when a people which has put up with an oppressive rule over a long period without protest suddenly finds the government relaxing its pressure, ②it takes up arms against it. Thus the social order overthrown by a revolution is almost always better than the one immediately preceding it, and experience teaches us that, generally speaking, the most perilous moment for a bad government is one when it seeks to mend its ways.

Only consummate statecraft can enable a King to save his throne when after a long spell of oppressive rule he sets to improving the lot of his subjects. Patiently endured so long as it seemed beyond redress, a grievance comes to appear intolerable once the possibility of removing it crosses men's minds. For the mere fact that certain abuses have been remedied draws attention to the others and ③they now appear more ④galling; people may suffer less, but their sensibility is exacerbated. At the height of its power feudalism did not inspire so much hatred as it did on the eve of its eclipse. In the reign of Louis XVI the most trivial pinpricks of arbitrary power caused more resentment than the thoroughgoing despotism of Louis XIV. The brief imprisonment of Beaumarchais shocked Paris More than the dragonnades of 1685.

17 Which of the following words best fits blank ①?

① nightmares   ② mistakes
③ paradoxes   ④ perversities

18 What does ② it refer to?

① people   ② government
③ oppressive rule   ④ period

19 What does ③ they refer to?

① men's mind   ② certain abuses
③ other abuses   ④ crosses

해석 대중의 불만이 최대치까지 올라갔던 것은 가장 발전했었던 프랑스 지역이었다. 비논리적인 것으로 보일 수도 있지만, 역사는 이와 같은 역설로 가득 차 있다. 상황이 더 악화된다고 항상 혁명이 발생하는 것은 아니기 때문이다. 반대로 저항 없이 오랫동안 잔혹한 지배를 견뎌 왔던 국민들이 정부가 통제를 느슨하게 한다는 것을 갑자기 알게 되었을 때, 국민이 정부에 저항하여 무장 궐기하게 되는 일이 종종 생긴다. 따라서 혁명에 의해 전복당한 사회 체계는 전보다 언제나 더 좋고, 일반적으로 말하자면 나쁜 정부가 최고의 위기에 닥치는 순간이 그들의 방법을 호전시키려 할 때라는 것을 경험이 우리에게 가르쳐 준다.

잔혹한 통치의 긴 시간이 지난 후 국민의 운명을 발전시키기 시작할 때, 단지 완전한 치국책만이 왕이 왕권을 지킬 수 있게 해 준다. 개선될 범위를 벗어난 동안 인내하며 견뎌온 사람의 마음에 그것을 없애 버릴 수 있는 가능성이 떠오른다면 불만의 원인은 참을 수 없게 된다. 특정 악행이 고쳐졌다는 단순한 사실이 다른 악행에 대한 관심을 끌게 되고, 그것들을 이제 더욱 짜증나는 것으로 나타난다. 따라서 사람들은 고생이 줄어들지만 감정은 더욱 악화된다. 힘이 절정에 다다랐을 때에는 봉건 제도가 없어지기 직전의 많은 증오를 야기하지는 않았다. 루이 16세의 지배 때에는 독단적인 권력의 가장 시시한 귀찮음이라도 루이 14세의 철저한 전제정치보다 더 큰 분노를 야기했다. 보마르셰(프랑스 유명 극작가)의 짧은 감금은 1685년도의 용기병 박해보다 더 많이 파리인들을 충격으로 몰아넣었다.

17 ①에 적합한 것은?

① 악몽   ② 실수   ③ 역설   ④ 외고집

18 ② it이 가리키는 것은?

① 민족   ② 정부   ③ 가혹한 지배   ④ 기간

19 ③ they가 가리키는 것은?

① 사람들의 마음   ② 어떤 폐해들
③ 다른 폐해들   ④ 십자가

20 필자가 첫 단락에서 전하고자 하는 내용은?

① 국가를 통치하는 가장 안전한 방법은 철권정치를 통해 지배하는 것이다.
② 대중들은 언제나 무지한 존재들이며, 그들에게 왕이 생겼을 때 왕을 인식하거나 존경할 줄 모른다.
③ 폭력적인 혁명에 의해 파괴되는 것들은 언제나 최상의 사회가 된다.
④ 사람들은 끔찍한 전제정치를 대개는 견디지만, 소량의 자유를 음미하기 시작할 때 폭발하는 경향이 있다.

21 두 번째 단락에서 루이 16세에 대한 설명으로 암시하지 않는 것은?

① 매우 유능한 정치인은 아니었다.
② 그는 루이 14세보다 덜 독재적이었다.
③ 독단적인 권력을 행사한 죄가 없다.
④ 많은 백성들의 삶을 향상시키려고 노력했다.

22 프랑스 대혁명의 원인에 대한 필자의 견해가 반영된 것은?

① 프랑스 대혁명은 루이 16세가 비인간적인 폭군이었기 때문에 발생했다.
② 루이 16세가 폐해들 중 일부를 없앰으로써 폐해들에 주의를 기울였기 때문에 프랑스 대혁명이 발생했다.
③ 프랑스 인들은 무정부주의적 경향이 있어서 프랑스 대혁명이 발생했다.
④ 프랑스 대혁명은 프랑스가 봉건주의적이었기 때문에 발생했는데, 다른 나라들이 그러한 봉건주의적 성향을 버린 후에도 오랫동안 프랑스는 그래 왔다.

20 What view of history is the author trying to get across in the first paragraph?

① The safest way to rule a country is to rule it with an iron fist.
② The masses are always an ignorant lot, who can never recognize and properly honor a good king when they have one.
③ It is always the best societies that are demolished by violent revolutionary upheavals.
④ People often endure dire tyrannies but are liable to explode when they begin to taste snatches of freedom.

21 Which of the following is NOT implied about Louis XVI in the second paragraph?

① He was not a very able statesman.
② He was much less despotic than Louis XIV.
③ He was not guilty of exercising arbitrary power.
④ He tried to improve the lot of his subjects.

22 Which of the following reflects the author's opinion about the cause of the French Revolution?

① The French Revolution erupted because Louis XVI was an inhuman despot.
② The French Revolution erupted because Louis XVI drew attention to the abuses by removing some of them.
③ The French Revolution erupted because the French had a tendency to anarchy.
④ The French Revolution erupted because France remained feudalistic, long after other countries have ceased to be so.

23 Which of the following is closest in meaning to ④ galling?

① vexing   ② inspiriting
③ galvanizing ④ injurious

24 Which of the following is 'the dragonnades of 1685' most likely to have been?

① a large-scale violation of religious liberty
② a large-scale civic project
③ a large-scale operatic performance
④ a large-scale financial venture that failed

23 ④ galling 과 유사한 어휘는?

① 짜증나게 하는   ② 원기를 불어넣는
③ 활기를 불어넣는   ④ 모욕적인

24 1685년도의 용기병 박해란 무엇인가?

① 종교 자유의 중대한 침해
② 대규모 시민 계획
③ 대규모 가극 공연
④ 실패로 끝난 대규모 금융 사업

어구 discontent 불만 illogical 비논리적인 break out 발발하다 put up with 견디다 oppressive 포악한, 억압하는 protest 항의, 저항 take up arms against ～에 대해 무장 궐기 하다 overthrow 전복하다 generally speaking 일반적으로 말하자면 perilous 위험한 mend 수정하다, 개선하다 consummate 완전한 statecraft 치국책 throne 왕권 spell 잠시 동안 subject 백성, 주제, 학과 redress 구제, 교정 grievance 불만, 불평 intolerable 견딜 수 없는, 참을 수 없는 cross 교차하다, 엇갈리다 galling 괴롭히는, 짜증나게 하는 exacerbated 악화된 feudalism 봉건제도 hatred 적대감 on the eve of ～의 직전에, ～에 임박하여 trivial 시시한 pinprick 성가심 Beaumarchais 보마르셰[18세기 극작가] dragonnades 용기병의 박해 paradox 역설 perversity 외고집, 사악함 iron fist 철권정치 the masses 대중들 demolish 파괴하다 upheaval 격변, 대변동 tyranny 폭군, 전제정치 snatch 소량, 잡아챔, 강탈, 잡아채다 despotic 독재적인, 횡포의 arbitrary 독단적인 inhuman 비인간적인 draw attention to 관심을 가지다, 주의하다 anarchy 무정부(주의) vexing 짜증나게 하는, 성가신 galvanizing 활기를 불어넣는 injurious 해가 되는, 모욕적인 operatic 가극의, 과장된

해설 **17** such가 지시형용사로 앞서 나온 내용을 가리키므로 illogical (비논리적인) 단어와 순접 내용인 '역설'이 옳다.

18 문맥상 무장 궐기 하여 정부에 대항할 수 있는 것은 앞에 등장한 '민족(a people)'이 옳다.

19 문맥상 certain abuses와 비교 대상이 필요하므로 other abuses가 옳다.

20 평소에는 이의 없이 폭정에 견뎌 오다가 그 폭정이 느슨해지는 순간 혁명이 발생한다는 내용이 첫 단락의 주제가 된다.

21 루이 16세는 루이 14세보다 상대적으로 정도가 약한 독재를 행사했다고 했으므로, 일단 폭정을 행한 것이 사실이므로 ④는 틀린 설명이다.

22 작가는 루이 14세를 잔인한 군주로 보지만, 루이 16세는 상대적으로 그 정도가 덜한 군주로 보고 있다. 첫 단락에서 탄압이 느슨해지는 순간 혁명이 발생했다고 했으므로 루이 14세보다 그 정도가 덜 했던 루이 16세에 발생하게 된 것이다.

23 galling은 '짜증나게 하는(making you feel upset and angry because of something that is unfair)'의 뜻을 가진다.

24 파리에 충격을 주었다는 내용과 비교가 되기 위해서는 그에 합당한 부정적인 내용이 올바르다. 따라서 종교 자유에 대한 중대한 침해가 추론된다.

Racism is so extreme and so pervasive in our American society that no black individual lives in an atmosphere of freedom. The world of physical phenomena is dominated by fear and greed. It consists of pitting the vicious and the avaricious against the naive, the hunted, the innocent, and the victimized. Power belongs to the strong, and the strong are BIG in more ways than one. No one is more victimized in this white male American society than the black female.

25 Whom does the underlined part refer to?
① black and white males
② black females
③ black males
④ white males
⑤ white females

26 Who does the author say is most victimized in American society?
① black males
② white males
③ black and white females
④ white females
⑤ black females

해석 미국 사회에서 인종 차별은 지나칠 정도로 널리 퍼져 있어서 어떠한 흑인도 자유로운 환경 속에서 살지 못한다. 물리적 현상이 나타나는 세계는 공포와 탐욕에 의해 지배를 당한다. 그 세계는 악하고 욕심이 많은 사람들을 순진한 사람들, 쫓기는 사람들, 죄가 없는 사람들과 희생당한 이들과 대립되는 구조로 구성되어 있다. 권력은 강한 이들의 소유가 되며, 강한 이들은 더 많은 식으로 다른 사람보다 강하다. 백인 남성이 지배하는 미국 사회에서 가장 희생을 당하는 이들은 바로 흑인 여성들이다.

25 밑줄 친 부분이 가리키는 것은?
① 흑인과 백인 남성들　　　② 흑인 여성들
③ 흑인 남성들　　　　　　④ 백인 남성들
⑤ 백인 여성들

26 미국 사회에서 누가 가장 희생을 크게 당하는가?
① 흑인 남성들　　　　　　② 백인 남성들
③ 흑인과 백인 여성들　　　④ 백인 여성들
⑤ 흑인 여성들

어구 **extreme** 극단적인　**pervasive** 만연한　**dominate** 지배하다　**greed** 탐욕　**consist of** ~으로 구성되다　**vicious** 사악한　**avaricious** 탐욕스러운　**naive** 순진한　**innocent** 죄가 없는　**victimized** 희생당한

해설 **25** 'the+형용사'는 '복수 보통명사' 취급을 받는다. 마지막 문장에서 가장 희생당하는 이들은 '백인 남성 사회에서 가장 희생을 크게 당하는 이들이 흑인 여성'이라고 했다. 따라서 가해자는 백인 남성임이 유추가 가능하다.
26 마지막 문장에서 가장 큰 희생을 당하는 이들은 than 이하를 통해 흑인 여성이라고 했다.

Plagiarism refers to a form of cheating that has been defined as the false assumption of authorship: the wrongful act of taking the product of another person's mind, and presenting it as one's own. Plagiarism, then, constitutes intellectual theft and often carries severe penalties, ranging from failure in a course to expulsion from school.

Plagiarism in student writing is often unintentional, as when an elementary school pupil, assigned to do a report on a certain topic, goes home and copies down, word for word, everything on the subject in an encyclopedia. Unfortunately, some students continue to use such "research methods" in high school and ① ＿＿＿＿＿＿ in college without realizing that these practices constitute plagiarism. At all times during research and writing, guard against the possibility of ② inadvertent plagiarism by keeping careful notes that distinguish between your musings and thoughts and the material you gather from others. A writer who fails to give appropriate acknowledgment when repeating another's wording or particularly apt term is guilty of plagiarism. You

해석 표절은 원작의 출처를 잘못 추정하게 하는 행위로 정의내려지는 기만행위의 한 형태이다. 즉, 다른 사람의 생각의 산물을 가져가는 행위이며, 그것을 자신의 것으로 발표하는 행위이다. 그래서 표절은 지능적인 범죄로 여겨지며, 학과 과정의 낙제에서부터 퇴학에 이르기까지 자주 혹독한 처벌을 받게 된다.
특정 주제에 관한 보고서를 쓰는 과제를 부여받은 초등학교 학생들이 집에 가서 백과사전에 있는 그 주제에 관한 모든 것을 그대로 베껴 쓸 때처럼, 학생들의 작문에 있어서 표절은 흔히 고의적인 것은 아니다. 불행하게도 몇몇 학생들은 고등학교에서도 그러한 '조사 방법들'을 계속 사용하며, 심지어 대학에서도 이러한 행동이 이어지게 된다. 연구와 작문을 하는 모든 기간 동안 당신이 심사숙고하고 생각한 것들과 당신이 다른 사람들로부터 얻게 된 자료를 구별해주는 세심한 메모를 계속함으로써 부주의한 표절의 가능성으로부터 (당신 자신을) 보호해야 한다. 다른 사람의 용어나 특히 적절한 용어를 반복할 때 (다른 이의 용어라고) 타당한 시인을 하지 못한 작가는 표절의 죄가 있는 것이다. 당신은 분명히 다른 사람의 말과 생각을 연구 논문에 쓸 수 있지만, 인용된 자료가 당신의 창조물처럼 보이게 하지는 말아야 한다.

may certainly use other persons' words and thoughts in your research paper, but the borrowed material must not appear to be your creation.

27 Which of the following expressions differs in meaning from the others?

① the false assumption of authorship
② intellectual theft
③ presenting the product of another person's mind as one's own
④ giving appropriate acknowledgment when presenting another's ideas
⑤ making the borrowed material appear to be one's own creation

28 Which of the following best fits into ①?

① even
② thus
③ therefore
④ however
⑤ otherwise

29 Which of the following is closest in meaning to ②?

① unembellished
② unintentional
③ inadmissible
④ inauspicious
⑤ incipient

30 The best title of this passage would be
______________.

① the Reasons That You should Not plagiarize
② Expulsion from School
③ the Unenlightened Plagiarists
④ the Form and Extent of Plagiarism
⑤ Hazards of Plagiarism

27 가리키는 내용이 다른 하나는?

① 저작자라고 잘못 추정하는 행위
② 지적인 절도
③ 다른 이의 생각을 자신의 것으로 표현하는 행위
④ 다른 이의 생각을 표현할 때 (인용했다고) 시인하는 표시 행위
⑤ 인용된 자료가 자신의 창조물인 것처럼 보이게 하는 행위

28 ①에 들어갈 것은?

① 심지어   ② 따라서
③ 그러므로   ④ 그러나
⑤ 그렇지 않다면

29 ②와 의미상 가장 가까운 것은?

① 꾸미지 않은   ② 의도적이지 않은
③ 승인하기 힘든   ④ 불길한
⑤ 초기의

30 이 글의 제목은?

① 표절하지 말아야만 하는 이유   ② 퇴학
③ 무지몽매한 표절가들   ④ 표절의 형태와 정도
⑤ 표절의 위협들

어구 plagiarism 표절   refer to 언급하다   cheating 기만, 사기   false assumption 추정   authorship 저작자(임을 증명하는 것), 저술업, 출처   constitute 구성·조직하다, 여겨지다   theft 절도   severe 혹독한   range from A to B A에서 B로 이르다   course 교육 과정, 과목, 강좌   expulsion from school 퇴학   unintentional 의도적이지 않은   assign A to R A가 ~하도록 할당·배분·부여·지명하다   copy down 베끼다, 표절하다   word for word 문자 그대로   encyclopedia 백과사전   guard against (위험 따위에서) 보호하다, 방어하다   inadvertent 부주의한, 태만한   musing 숙고, 묵상, 숙고하는   acknowledgement 시인, 고백, 자백, 승인, 인지   apt 적절한   research paper 연구논문   borrowed 빌린, 인용한   unembellished 가공되지 않은, 꾸밈이 없는   unintentional 의도적이지 않은, 우발적인   inadmissible 허락하기 어려운, 승인하기 힘든   inauspicious 불길한, 상서롭지 않은   incipient 초기의, 시초의   plagiarize 표절하다   plagiarist 표절자

해설 **27** 다른 이의 생각을 전할 때, 그 인용에 대해 시인하는 행위는 원 출처를 밝혀주는 행위이므로, 다른 보기 내용들이 갖고 있는 '표절'의 의미와는 다르다.
28 even은 '예외적인 일까지 강조하는' 강조의 기능도 가지고 있다. 따라서 미성년자들의 학교인 고등학교에서라면 이해가 될 수 있지만, 성인의 학습터인 대학에서도 표절 행위가 있다는 내용으로 강조하는 것이 옳겠다.
29 inadvertent는 '무심코 저지른(not realizing what you are doing)'의 뜻을 가지게 된다.
30 이 글은 첫 단락에서 '표절의 정의'를 설명하며, 두 번째 단락에서 '표절이 될 수 있는 범위와 정도, 그리고 형태'를 설명했다. 이 범위에 가장 근접한 ④가 정답이 되겠다.

A laser is not a word in itself but actually it stands for Light Amplification by the Stimulated Emission of Radiation. L indicates Light. (가)It is a kind of beam that utilizes the force of light and directs (나)it for its power. Thus, (다)it is created from light, and the resulting laser light has special properties that are very different and unique from regular light. A laser can be of different types and strengths. It can be very tiny so as to be almost invisible, and can be very large so as to occupy an entire room. (라)It is indeed a very useful and exciting invention, with many beneficial applications and uses.

31 윗글에서 밑줄 친 It/it이 가리키는 대상이 나머지 셋과 다른 것은?

① (가)　　　　② (나)
③ (다)　　　　④ (라)

해석 레이저는 본래 하나의 단어가 아니라, 실제는 방사선 유도 방출에 의한 빛의 증폭을 상징한다. L은 빛을 가리킨다. 레이저는 빛의 힘을 이용하여 그 힘을 위하여 빛을 유도하는 일종의 광선이다. 따라서 레이저는 빛을 통해 만들어지며, 그 결과로 발생하는 레이저 광선은 보통의 빛과는 다르고 독특한 특성을 가지고 있다. 레이저는 다양한 형태와 힘을 가질 수 있다. 레이저는 거의 눈에 보이지 않을 정도로 매우 작을 수 있으며, 방 전체를 차지할 정도로 매우 클 수도 있다. 레이저는 많은 유익한 응용력과 용도를 가지고 있는 매우 유익하고 흥미로운 발명품이다.

어구 **in itself** 본래; 그 자체로　**stand for** ～을 상징하다, 의미하다　**Light Amplification** 빛의 증폭　**Stimulated Emission** 유도 방출　**direct** 지시하다; 유도하다　**invisible** 눈에 보이지 않는　**so as to R** ～하기 위하여　**occupy** 차지하다; 점령하다　**beneficial** 유익한, 이익을 가져오는　**application** 적용, 응용; 신청

해설 (가), (다), (라)는 모두 레이저를 가리키지만, (나)는 빛을 가리킨다.

A great Indian Buddhist teacher was invited to Tibet to preach the dharma. The teacher took along with (가)him a man who was quarrelsome and irresponsible, and a bad cook as well. After observing (나)him for quite some time, the Tibetans approached the teacher respectfully and said, "Master, why do you keep this useless cook of yours—he is more a nuisance than a help to you." The teacher smiled and replied, "Ah! You don't understand. I do not keep (다)him as my servant but as my teacher." The Tibetans were surprised and asked "How is that so?" The teacher explained, "You see, his inefficiency and his quarrelsome nature teach me to practice patience and tolerance every day. Therefore, I value (라)him."

32 Which of the underlined him does NOT refer to the same person?

① (가)　　　　② (나)
③ (다)　　　　④ (라)

해석 인도의 한 고승이 부처의 가르침에 대해 설교를 하기 위해 티베트로 초대를 받았다. 그 고승은 싸우기 좋아하고, 책임감이 없으며, 요리 실력 또한 마찬가지로 형편없는 한 남자를 데려갔다. 함께 온 사람을 오래 지켜본 후에 티베트 스님들이 고승에게 다가와 예의를 갖춘 후, "선사님, 이 쓸모없는 요리사를 왜 계속 두시는지요? 그는 선생님께 도움을 주기보다는 골칫거리입니다."라고 말했다. 선사는 웃으면서, "아, 여러분들은 이해를 못하시는군요. 나는 그를 내 하인으로서가 아니라 스승으로서 데리고 있는 것입니다."라고 답변했다. 그 티베트 사람들은 놀라서 "어떻게 그러실 수 있습니까?"라고 물었다. 선사는 "여러분들도 아시겠지만, 능력도 없고 싸우기를 좋아하는 그의 성격을 통해 나는 매일 나 자신에게 인내와 관용을 수행하도록 가르치고 있습니다. 그래서 그를 소중히 여기는 것입니다."라고 설명했다.

어구 **preach** 설교하다　**dharma** 달마(선종(禪宗)의 시조); 규범　**along with** ～와 함께　**quarrelsome** 싸우기를[말다툼을] 좋아하는　**irresponsible** 책임이 없는; 무책임한　**as well** 게다가, 뿐만 아니라　**respectfully** 공손히, 삼가서　**useless** 쓸모[소용]없는, 무익한, 헛된　**nuisance** 난처한[성가신, 골치 아픈] 것, 귀찮은 행위　**inefficiency** 무효력, 비능률; 무능　**tolerance** 관용; 내성(耐性)　**value** 소중히 여기다; 가치

해설 along with는 '～와 함께'라는 표현으로서, along with him은 삽입된 전치사구이다. 그 다음 a man을 수식하는 관계사절이 나오고, 그 관계사절의 내용이 '성격이 괴팍한 실력도 부족한 요리사'가 되므로, along with의 목적어인 him은 '고승'이 된다. 나머지 대명사의 him은 모두 요리사를 가리킨다.

1 ④	2 ③	3 ③	4 ③	5 ⑤	6 ⑤	7 ③	8 ③	9 ④	10 ⑤
11 ④	12 ③	13 ②	14 ③	15 ④	16 ④	17 ③	18 ②	19 ③	20 ④
21 ③	22 ②	23 ③	24 ②	25 ④	26 ②	27 ②	28 ③	29 ①	30 ③
31 ④	32 ①	33 ④	34 ②	35 ⑤	36 ⑤	37 ④	38 ②	39 ③	40 ④
41 ①	42 ③	43 ⑤							

>>> 다음 글을 읽고 문제의 답을 고르시오. [1~3]

Numerous public opinion surveys have consistently shown that the public prefers wind and other renewable energy forms over conventional sources of generation. Wind energy is a free, renewable resource, so no matter how much is used today, there will still be the same supply in the future. Wind energy is also a source of clean, non-polluting, electricity. Unlike conventional power plants, wind plants emit no air pollutants or greenhouse gases. In 1990, California's wind power plants offset the emission of more than 2.5 billion pounds of carbon dioxide, and 15 million pounds of other pollutants that would have <u>otherwise</u> been produced. It would take a forest of 90 million to 175 million trees to provide the same air quality.

1 이 글은 다음 중 어느 질문에 답하고 있는가?

① How is the energy in the wind captured?
② Are there good wind resources in the United States?
③ Are there environmental problems facing wind power?
④ What are the advantages of wind-generated electricity?
⑤ What are the economic obstacles to greater wind power usage?

2 밑줄 친 otherwise의 뜻으로 가장 알맞은 것은?

① 풍력 발전을 많이 사용했더라면
② 나무를 심어 숲을 조성하지 않았더라면
③ 풍력이 아닌 재래식 발전을 이용했더라면
④ 많은 사람들이 풍력 발전을 좋아하지 않았더라면
⑤ 이산화탄소 등의 공해 물질을 규제하지 않았더라면

3 Which of the following does NOT describe wind energy?

① free
② clean
③ conventional
④ renewable
⑤ non-polluting

해석 수많은 여론조사는 대중이 바람이나 다른 재생 가능한 에너지를 재래식 발전 자원보다 더 선호한다는 것을 계속적으로 보여주었다. 풍력 에너지는 돈이 들지 않는 재생 가능한 자원이다. 그래서 오늘날 아무리 많이 사용된다 할지라도 미래에도 여전히 똑같은 공급을 받을 수 있다. 풍력 에너지는 또한 깨끗한 무공해 전력 자원이기도 하다. 재래식 발전소와는 달리 풍력 발전소는 대기오염 물질이나 온실효과를 일으키는 기체들을 방출하지 않는다. 1990년 캘리포니아의 풍력 발전소는 그대로 공기 중에 방출되었을 25억 파운드의 이산화탄소와 1,500만 파운드의 다른 오염 물질들의 방출을 막았다. 이와 같은 공기의 질을 제공하기 위해서는 9천만에서 1억 7천 5백만 개의 나무들로 구성된 숲이 필요하다.

1 이 글은 다음 중 어느 질문에 답하고 있는가?

① 풍력 에너지가 어떻게 얻어지는가?
② 미국에 좋은 풍력 자원이 있는가?
③ 환경 문제가 풍력을 직시하고 있는가?
④ 풍력으로 가동되는 전기의 장점들이 있는가?
⑤ 더 강력한 풍력 사용에 대한 경제적인 방해 요소들은 무엇인가?

3 풍력을 묘사하지 못하는 것은?

① 무료의
② 깨끗한
③ 재래식의
④ 재생의
⑤ 오염 물질이 없는

어구 **numerous** 수많은 **survey** 공급 **conventional** 재래식의, 전통적인 **renewable resource** 재생자원 **no matter how** 아무리 ~할지라도 **wind energy** 풍력 **non-polluting** 공해를 일으키지 않는 **offset** 상쇄시키다 **emission** 방출 **carbon dioxide** 이산화탄소

해설 **1** 이 글의 주제는 풍력 에너지의 장점들을 설명한 것이므로, 풍력 가동의 장점이라는 핵심어가 들어간 ④가 옳다.
2 otherwise는 '그렇지 않았다면'이란 뜻을 가진 '대격 부사'의 기능을 가진다. 따라서 앞 내용의 '부정 조건'인 '만일 풍력 발전을 하지 않았다면 = 풍력이 아닌 재래식 발전을 이용했다면'이 옳다.
3 윗글에서 언급된 풍력의 특징은 '비용이 들지 않고, 재생이 가능하며, 깨끗함을 유지하는 무공해' 등으로 설명했지만, 재래식은 상반되는 관계이다.

>>> 다음 글을 읽고 문제의 답을 고르시오. [4~5]

Another tendency which worries me is the growing gulf between students and the rest of the society in which they live. This gulf is sometimes called a generation gap. It is no such thing. The gap exists between students and almost every other group—young or old—in the society; in fact, whether one looks at opinions on Viet Nam, poverty, law and order, or civil liberties, the gap is nowhere greater than it is between college students and their fellow young people who have not gone to college. My anxiety on this score is not relieved by the fact that I share the attitudes of students on many of the issues involved. The gap still exists and it is still unhealthy.

4 Where is the greatest gap according to the above passage?

① It is between young people and old people.
② It is between college students and the rest of the society.
③ It is between college students and other young people.
④ It is between college students and the author.
⑤ It is between old people and young people who have not gone to college.

5 Which of the following cannot be inferred from the above passage?

① The author agrees with college students on many of social issues.
② The gap between college students and the rest of the society worries the author.
③ One of the social issues involved is about Viet Nam.
④ The author does not think that the gulf can be called a generation gap.
⑤ The author thinks that quite a few groups agree with college students.

해석 나를 걱정시키는 또 다른 추세는 학생들과 학생들이 살고 있는 사회의 나머지 사이의 점점 벌어지는 괴리 현상이다. 이 괴리 현상은 가끔은 세대 차이라고 불린다. 그러나 그와 같은 것은 없다(세대차이가 괴리현상이 아닌 것이다). 그와 같은 괴리는 학생들 사이, 혹은 나이를 떠나 사회의 거의 모든 단체 사이에서 존재한다. 사실 사람들이 베트남이나 빈곤, 법과 질서 또는 시민의 자유에 대한 견해들을 바라보든 바라보지 않든 간에 (대학에 진학한) 학생들과 대학에 가지 못한 학생들 사이의 괴리가 가장 크다. 이 점 때문에 관련된 많은 문제들에 대한 학생들의 입장을 내가 공유하고 있다고 해서 내 걱정을 경감시켜 주지 못한다. 괴리는 아직도 존재하며 건전하지 못하다.

4 윗글에 따르면 가장 커다란 괴리는 어디에서 존재하는가?

① 젊은이들과 나이 드신 분들 사이에서
② 대학생들과 사회의 다른 집단들 사이에서
③ 대학생들과 다른 젊은이들 사이에서
④ 대학생과 저자 사이에서
⑤ 나이 드신 분들과 대학에 진학하지 못한 젊은이들 사이에서

5 이 글을 통해서 유추할 수 없는 내용은?

① 작가는 많은 사회 문제에 관하여 대학생들의 의견에 동의한다.
② 대학생들과 사회의 다른 집단들 사이의 괴리는 저자를 걱정시킨다.
③ 관련된 사회 문제들 중 하나는 베트남에 관한 것이 있다.
④ 작가는 괴리가 세대 차이라고 불리어질 수 있다고 생각하지 않는다.
⑤ 작가는 적지 않은 단체들이 대학생들의 의견에 동의한다고 생각한다.

어구 **tendency** 경향, 풍토, 추세 **gulf** 괴리, 차이, 심연 **generation gap** 세대차이 **poverty** 빈곤 **A is nowhere greater than B** A는 B에서 가장 대단하다 **on this score** 이 점 때문에 **relieve** 경감시키다 **unhealthy** 건전하지 못한

해설 **4** 'the gap is nowhere greater than ~' 구문에서 가장 괴리 현상이 벌어지는 것은 '대학에 진학한 학생들과 그렇지 못한 학생들 사이'라고 설명했다. 따라서 '대학생들과 (대학에 가지 못한) 다른 젊은이들 사이'가 옳다.
5 단체와 대학생들 간의 의견 일치에 관한 내용은 언급된 바 없다.

>>> **다음 글을 읽고 문제의 답을 고르시오.** [6~7]

If Italian children can read Dante's Divine Comedy or English children can read Milton in school, why should 'secularist' Indians be ambivalent about teaching the Mahabharata? It's true that the Mahabharata has lots of gods, and in particular the elusive Krishna. But so do Dante and Milton deal with God. As a secular Indian, I appreciate the 'wall' that our founding fathers built between religion and education. But what does one do when our literary classics are 'semi-religious'? If our kids don't read Sanskrit classics in a secular environment they will grow up impoverished. Something has gone terribly wrong in the way our schools bring up deracinated children, who know ① _______________ about their own culture but a great deal about the West. "Every writer needs an address", wrote the Yiddish writer, Isaac Bashevis Singer. That is a fine way of saying that all human beings need local roots, an identity, and a link with a unique identifiable past.

6 Choose the statement that the above passage does not say or imply.

① Isaac Bashevis Singer wrote, "Every writer needs an address".

② If Indian kids don't read Sanskrit classics in a secular environment they will grow up impoverished.

③ 'Secularist' Indians are ambivalent about teaching the Mahabharata.

④ Indian literary classics such as the Mahabharata are 'semireligious'.

⑤ Indian schools strongly encourage students to read Indian literary classics such as the Mahabharata.

7 Choose the most appropriate expression for the underlined blank ①.

① much ② enormously
③ little ④ well
⑤ wisely

해석 이탈리아 아이들이 단테의 『신곡』을 읽을 수 있거나 영국 아이들이 밀튼의 작품을 읽을 수 있다면 왜 '세속주의자'인 인도 사람들이 마하바라타를 가르치는 것에 대해서 부정적 태도를 보이는가? 마하바라타에는 많은 신들이 있으며 특히나 이해하기 어려운 크리슈나 신도 있다. 그러나 단테와 밀튼도 이 신을 다룬다. 세속 인도인으로서 나는 우리의 기초를 세우신 아버지들이 종교와 교육 사이에 만들어 놓으신 '벽'을 높이 평가한다. 그러나 우리의 문학 수업이 '반종교적'일 때 우리는 무엇을 해야 하는가? 우리의 아이들이 세속적인 환경에서 산스크리트 고전을 읽지 못한다면 그들은 (정서가) 메마른 상태로 성장할 것이다. 우리의 학교들이 박탈당한 아이들을 키우는 방식에 있어서 무언가 상당히 잘못되어 왔으며, 그 아이들은 자신들의 (인도의) 문화에 대해서는 거의 모르지만 서부 문화에 대해서는 매우 많은 것을 안다. 이디시어 작가인 아이작 싱어가 기록하기를, "모든 작가는 주소가 필요하다"고 했다. 이러한 점은 모든 인간이 지역적인 뿌리와 정체성과 독특한 신원을 확인할 수 있는 과거와의 연결 장치를 필요로 한다는 사실을 말하고자 하는 좋은 방법이 되는 것이다.

6 윗글에서 언급하지 않은 것은?

① 아이작 싱어는 "모든 작가는 주소가 필요하다"고 기술했다.

② 인도 아이들이 세속적인 환경에서 산스크리트의 고전 작품들을 읽지 못한다면 궁핍하게 성장할 것이다.

③ 세속 인도인들은 마하바라타를 가르치는 것에 대해서 반대 감정이 병존을 한다.

④ 마하바라타와 같은 인도의 고전 작품들은 반종교적이다.

⑤ 인도 학교들은 학생들에게 마하바라타와 같은 인도 문학 작품을 읽도록 강하게 권장한다.

7 ①에 들어갈 것은?

① 많이 ② 대단히
③ 적게 ④ 알맞게
⑤ 현명하게

어구 **Divine Comedy** 『신곡』 **secularist** 세속주의자 **ambivalent** 양립 불가능한, 반대 감정이 교차하는 **lots of** 많은 **in particular** 특별히 **elusive** 이해하기 어려운, 도망가기 쉬운 **deal with** 다루다, 거래하다 **appreciate** 평가하다, 감상하다, 감사하다, 물가가 오르다 **founding** (제도·국가의) 기초를 세운 **semi-religious** 반종교적인 **impoverished** 메마른, 궁핍한 **terribly** 몹시, 끔찍하게 **a great deal** 매우 많은 양 **yiddish** 이디시 말(유대어) **local root** 지역 뿌리 **identity** 정체성 **link** 연결 **identifiable** 동일함을 증명할 수 있는 **enormously** 대단히, 터무니없이

해설 **6** 인도 학교의 현실은 마하바라타와 같은 인도의 문학 작품이 교육에 반영되지 못하여 작가가 마하바라타와 같은 문학 작품을 인도 아이들이 공부해야 한다고 주장하는 글이다. 따라서 인도 학교에서 학생들이 마하바라타와 같은 작품들을 공부한다는 설명은 틀렸다.

7 but이라는 '역접–대조' 접속사에 의해서 서양 문학에 대해서는 많이 알지만 모국인 인도의 문학에 대해서는 잘 모른다는 내용이 적합하다.

I thought it might be feasible to park a car parallel to a space on the street. Then, by pressing a button, I could raise the four tires off the ground slightly, while dropping two special wheels perpendicular to the curb. It would then be child's play to roll into the narrowest of parking spaces. I visited Ed Greene who runs the Ford agency in order to elicit his reaction. After a perfunctory glance at my plans, to my chagrin Ed snorted that my idea was inane, but I decided that he was just jealous of my brilliance. Tomorrow I am going to start on a computer that will enable me to measure the intelligence of perverse automobile dealers who like to deride the efforts of a junior genius.

8 The author is most likely to be ___________.

① a mechanic
② a computer analyst
③ an inventor
④ a teacher
⑤ a traffic warden

해석 나는 도로의 빈 공간에서 자동차를 주차하는 것이 가능하다고 생각했다. 그렇다면, 버튼을 눌러서 네 개의 타이어를 땅에서 약간 뜨게 하여 들어 올리면서, 두 개의 특수 바퀴를 보도 연석에 수직 방향으로 내려놓을 수 있을 것이다. 그렇다면 가장 좁은 주차 공간이라도 아이들의 놀이처럼 차를 굴릴 수 있을 것이다. 나는 포드 자동차 대리점을 운영하는 에드 그린의 반응을 끌어내기 위하여 그에게 방문했었다. 나의 계획에 대해 무성의하게 힐끗 보고 난 후에, 유감스럽게도 그는 나의 생각이 어리석다고 비웃었다. 그러나 나는 그가 나의 훌륭한 생각에 질투를 느꼈다고 결론을 내렸다. 내일 나는 젊은 천재의 노력을 조롱하기 좋아하는 고집이 센 자동차 딜러들의 지능을 측정할 수 있는 컴퓨터에 대한 연구를 시작할 예정이다.

8 이 글의 작가는 누구인가?

① 수리공　　　　　② 컴퓨터 분석가
③ 발명가　　　　　④ 교사
⑤ 교통 감시인

어구 feasible 실행할 수 있는, 가능한　parallel 평행의; 병렬(竝列)의　slightly 약간, 조금　perpendicular 직각을 이루는　elicit (진리·사실 따위를 논리적으로) 이끌어 내다　perfunctory 형식적인, 마지못한　glance 흘긋 봄　to chagrin 유감스럽게도　snort 비웃다; 콧방귀를 뀌다　inane 어리석은　be jealous of ∼을 질투하다　brilliance 훌륭함; 광택　start on ∼을 착수하다　perverse 외고집의, 심술궂은　deride 비웃다　traffic warden 교통 감시인

해설 자동차 주차에 대한 새로운 생각을 만들어 낸 사람이기 때문에 발명가임으로 유추할 수 있다.

Advice, as it always gives a temporary appearance of superiority, can never be very grateful, even when it is most necessary or most judicious. Vanity is so frequently the apparent motive of advice that we, for the most part, summon our powers to oppose it without any very accurate inquiry whether it is right. It is sufficient that another is growing great in his own eyes, at our expense, and assumes authority over us without our permission; for many would contentedly suffer the consequences of their own mistakes rather than the insolence of him who triumphs as their deliverer.

9 윗글의 '조언'에 대한 설명으로 추론할 수 있는 것은?

① The motive of advice consists of many lies.
② A person who is given advice has a tendency to receive it blindly.
③ The person that listens to another's advice usually tends not to follow it because of listener's superiority.
④ Even reasonable advice may not be followed.

해석 충고는 항상 거만함을 일시적으로 보여주기 때문에, 매우 필요하고 아주 슬기로운 충고일지라도 그다지 고마운 것이 되지 못한다. 또한 충고를 하게 되는 원천이 자만으로부터 나올 수 있기에, 우리는 어떠한 충고가 정당한 것인지 아닌지를 정확하게 알아보지도 않고 있는 힘껏 그 충고를 받아들이기를 거부한다. 어떤 사람이 우리를 희생의 대가로 하여 나름대로 위대해지고, 우리의 허락도 없이 우리에게 권위를 행사하게 될 때 그것은 그런 대로 있을 수 있는 일이다. 왜냐하면 많은 사람들이 자신들을 구원하는 사도인 양 기뻐 날뛰는 사람의 오만불손을 참느니보다는 차라리 자신들의 실수로 인해 나타나는 결과들을 만족한 채 참으려 하기 때문이다.

9 윗글의 '조언'에 대한 설명으로 추론할 수 있는 것은?

① 조언의 동기는 많은 거짓으로 구성되어 있다.
② 조언을 받는 사람은 맹목적으로 그 조언을 받아들이는 경향이 있다.
③ 다른 사람의 조언을 듣는 사람은 자신의 우월감 때문에 그 조언을 따르지 않는 경향이 있다.
④ 심지어 타당한 조언이라 할지라도 따르지 않을 수 있다.

어구 temporary 일시적인　judicious 현명한　vanity 자만심, 허영심　summon 소환하다, 호출하다　at one's expense ∼을 희생하여　insolence 무례함　deliverer 구원자, 구조자

해설 첫 문장을 통해 매우 슬기로운 사람들조차도 우월적인 특징을 나타내는 조언을 받아들이지 않는 경향이 있다고 했다.

Asia has long been the home of ① ___________ smokers. To millions of them, cigarettes are the stuff of daily social intercourse. Nothing is done without them—no task unrewarded, no meal concluded. Everybody knows that Asia is supposed to be the last great frontier of the tobacco industry, a place where vast numbers continue to expose themselves to the risks of lung cancer, cardiovascular disease, emphysema and other smoking-related illnesses. And yet, across the region, an Asian antismoking movement is quietly but inexorably gathering strength. It isn't large yet, but it is starting to have a dramatic impact—from fresh legal wins in unlikely quarters to tough bans—on smoking in public places. The Framework Convention on Tobacco Control (FCTC)—a treaty sponsored by the World Health Organization (WHO)—became binding law on Feb. 27 in the first 40 countries to ratify it. A third of these countries are in Asia, and more Asian nations are expected to adopt the treaty's tough antismoking provisions over the coming months.

10 Choose the most appropriate word for the blank ①.

① vicious
② offensive
③ sneaking
④ secret
⑤ inveterate

11 Which can be inferred from the passage?

① Smoking brings Asian nations to an economic crisis.
② Smoking-related illnesses were eradicated in Asia.
③ Antismoking movements cost Asian nations lots of money.
④ Asian nations are beginning to recognize that the situation must be addressed.
⑤ To secure the passage of legislation to support antismoking movements in Asia is almost impossible.

12 Choose the best title of the above passage.

① Why Become Asians the Slave of Cigarettes?
② Asia's Irreversible Hurt: Smoking
③ Can Asia Kick the Habit?
④ Tobaccos and Anti-smoking Movements
⑤ Smoking's Side Effects

해석 아시아는 오랜 기간 동안 상습 흡연자의 안식처였었다. 수백만 명의 흡연자들에게 담배는 일상적인 사교의 도구인 것이다. 담배 없이는 아무것도 되지 않으며, (담배 피우는) 일로 보상받지 못한다면 식사 또한 하지 않는다. 모든 이들이 아시아가 담배 산업의 마지막 보루라고 알고 있으며, 수많은 이들이 폐암과 심장질환, 폐병과 기타 담배 관련 질병의 위험에 노출된 곳이라고 알고 있다. 그러나 아시아를 넘어서 아시아의 금연 운동이 조용하지만 가차 없이 확산되고 있다. 아직은 그 확산 범위가 크지는 않지만 가능성이 그다지 크지 못한 부분에서 신법의 승리에서부터 공공장소에서의 강력한 금지에 이르기까지 강한 효과를 보이기 시작하고 있다. WHO(세계보건기구)가 후원하는 협정인 FCTC(담배구제기본협약)가 이 협정을 비준하는 첫 40개의 국가에서 발효력을 갖는 법이 되었다. 이들 중 1/3이 아시아 국가들인데 더 많은 아시아의 여러 국가들이 이 조약의 강한 금연 규정을 몇 달 이내에 수용할 것으로 기대가 된다.

10 ①에 알맞은 것은?

① 사악한
② 불쾌한
③ 은밀한
④ 비밀스러운
⑤ 상습적인

11 윗글로 알 수 있는 것은?

① 흡연 때문에 아시아 국가들은 경제적인 위기에 처하게 됐다.
② 흡연 관련 질병들은 아시아에서 사라졌다.
③ 금연 운동 때문에 아시아 국가들은 많은 비용을 지출했다.
④ 아시아 국가들은 그 상황(흡연의 만연 상태)이 처리되어야만 한다는 점을 인식하기 시작하고 있다.
⑤ 아시아에서 금연 운동을 지지하는 법안의 통과를 확고히 하는 것이 거의 불가능하다.

12 이 글의 제목을 고르시오.

① 왜 아시아인들은 담배의 노예가 되었는가?
② 아시아의 회복될 수 없는 상처: 흡연
③ 아시아가 그 버릇(흡연)을 없앨 수 있는가?
④ 담배와 금연 운동
⑤ 담배의 부작용

어구 social intercourse 사교 task 일, 임무 unrewarded 보상받지 못한 be supposed to R ~하기로 되어 있다, ~하기로 기대가 되다 lung cancer 폐암 cardiovascular 심장 혈관의 emphysema 폐기종 antismoking 금연 quietly 조용히, 은밀히 inexorably 무자비하게, 가차 없이 have a impact on 영향을 미치다 dramatic 극적인, 극의 fresh legal 새로운 법 win 성공, 승리 unlikely 가능성이 없는 quarter 지역, 1/4, 15분 tough 강한, 곤란한 WHO 세계보건기구 FCTC 담배구제기본협약 sponsor 후원하다 treaty 협약 binding 구속력 있는, 의무를 부과하는 ratify 비준·재가하다 vicious 사악한

해설 **10** 다음 문장에서 수백만 명의 아시아인에게 담배는 사교의 도구가 되었으며, 담배 없이는 아무것도 못한다는 내용은 결국 아시아는 상습적인 흡연자들의 고향이라는 비유적인 표현이 옳다.

11 아시아의 금연 운동이 확산되고 있으며, 이를 지지하는 WTO와 FCTC 등의 협정 비준이 뒤따르고 있다. 따라서 ④의 '그 상황의 처리'는 '금연의 확산 운동'이 재진술된 형태이다.

12 흡연을 상습적으로 하는 수많은 사람들이 사는 아시아에서 금연 운동이 급격히 확산되고 있다는 내용이 주제이므로, '아시아인들의 상습적인 버릇인 흡연을 없앨 수 있겠는가'라고 질문하는 문제 제기의 내용이 제목으로서 타당하다.

>>> **다음 글을 읽고 문제의 답을 고르시오.** [13~14]

A hearing-impaired person, I lip-read to communicate. When I held a job as a junior electronics-maintenance technician, a coworker and I were sent out on a service call. She was becoming tense because so many things had been going wrong that day. Finally, after trying unsuccessfully to find a vacant spot in a crowded parking lot, she said, "I'm so upset, I could swear!", "Go ahead", I replied. "___________"

13 Which of the following best describes the narrator?

① (S)he is a blind person and has to be constantly told which way to go.
② (S)he is a deaf person and watches the movement of the others' lips to understand them.
③ (S)he was too young a technician to be sent out on a service call.
④ (S)he and her(his) co-worker had had a wonderful day that day.
⑤ Her(his) co-worker was so happy that she had to shout "hurrah".

14 Which of the following best fits into blank?

① Calm down.
② You are a truly patient lady.
③ I won't look.
④ Let's get out of here quick.
⑤ I will keep my fingers crossed.

해석 청각 장애인인 나는 대화를 하기 위해 독순술을 한다. 내가 하급 전자 정비기술자로서 일할 때, 동료 직원과 나는 서비스 호출로 파견되었다. 그녀(동료)는 그날 너무 많은 문제가 생겨서 긴장을 하고 있었다. 결국, 꽉 들어찬 주차장에서 빈 공간을 찾으려 했으나 찾지 못하자 그녀가 말하기를 "너무 화가 난다. 욕을 할 것 같아."라고 했다. 나는 "어서 해."라고 대답했다. "나는 안 보겠어."

13 화자에 대한 설명으로서 옳은 것은?

① 맹인이며 어디로 가야 하는지를 항상 물어보아야만 한다.
② 농아이며 다른 이들의 말을 이해하기 위해서 그들의 입술을 본다.
③ 서비스 호출에 내보내기에는 너무 어린 기술자이다.
④ 동료가 그날 좋은 하루를 보냈었다.
⑤ 동료는 너무나 행복하여 '만세'라고 외쳐야만 했다.

14 빈칸에 들어갈 말은?

① 진정하시오.
② 당신은 진정으로 인내심 있는 여자이다.
③ (너의 입술을) 보지 않을 거야.
④ 여기서 빨리 떠나자.
⑤ 너의 행운을 빌어줄게.

어구 **hearing-impaired** 청각 장애의 **lip-read** 독순술을 하다 **electronics-maintenance** 전자 정비 **coworker** 동료 **send out** (사람을) 보내다. 급파하다 **go wrong** 잘못되다. 문제가 있다 **finally** 마침내, 결국 **constantly** 항상, 변함없이 **deaf person** 농아 **hurrah** 만세 **calm down** 진정시키다 **get out of** ~에서 떠나다 **keep one's fingers crossed** 행운을 기원해 주다

해설 **13** lip-read는 '독순술로 이해하다'는 뜻을 가졌다. 첫 문장에서 말하기를, 자신은 청각장애인이므로 독순술(상대방의 입술 움직임을 통해서 상대방 의사를 이해하는 방법)을 한다고 했으므로, ②가 옳은 설명이다.

14 결국 이 글은 위 문제와 마찬가지로, 'lip-read(독순술)'의 사전적 이해가 되어 있느냐를 물어보는 글이다. 동료가 '화가 나서 욕을 할 것 같다'고 하니까, 결코 좋지 못한 의사 표현인 '욕'의 '입술 동작'을 보고 싶지 않다는 화자의 표현이 문맥 전체로 미루어 보건대 가장 옳다.

>>> **다음 글을 읽고 문제의 답을 고르시오.** [15~17]

Thunderstorms are particularly prevalent during the summer months in areas close to the warm waters of the Gulf of Mexico. Large cities also act as heat sources, producing convection currents in the air, which carry ocean moisture aloft, along with salt particles and pollutants which are condensation nuclei encouraging cloud formation. The towering cumulonimbus clouds thus formed turn from cottony white to threatening gray and black as the moisture and energy build up. Eventually, the electrical discharge we know as lightning takes place. Every year an estimated 10,000 forest fires are touched off by lightning and other thunderstorm phenomena.

해석 뇌우는 멕시코만의 따뜻한 바다 근처에 있는 지역에서 여름 기간 동안 특히 빈번하다. 대도시들 또한 열의 원천으로서 작용하여, 공기 속에서 대류를 만들어내는데, 이 더워진 공기는 구름의 형성을 촉진하는 응축 핵인 소금 입자와 오염 물질과 함께 바다의 수증기를 위에서 지니게 된다. 형성되어 높이 솟은 적란운(소나기구름)은 습도와 에너지가 증강할 때, 솜과 같던 하얀색이 위협적인 회색과 검은색으로 변한다. 결국 우리가 번개로 알고 있는 전기 방전이 발생한다. 매해 대략 1만 개의 산불이 번개와 다른 뇌우 현상들에 의해 야기된다.

15 What is this passage primarily concerned with?

① the condensation of salt particles
② the formation of cottony white clouds
③ the destruction of forests by lightning
④ the causes and effects of thunderstorm

16 Which of the following can be inferred from this passage?

① Thunderstorms are a major threat to cumulonimbus.
② Without pollution there would be no condensation of nuclei.
③ Thunderstorms are inescapable during the summer months.
④ Thunderstorms are made by a combination of heat and moisture.

17 Which of the following can best replace the underlined word, aloft?

① particles
② discharges
③ into the air
④ over the cities

15 무엇에 관한 글인가?

① 소금 입자의 응축
② 솜털 같은 흰색 구름의 형성
③ 번개에 의한 숲의 파괴
④ 뇌우의 (발생) 원인과 영향

16 이 글에서 암시하는 것은?

① 뇌우는 적란운에 중대한 위협 요소이다.
② 오염이 없다면 핵 응축 현상은 발생하지 않을 것이다.
③ 뇌우는 여름 몇 달 동안은 불가피하다.
④ 뇌우는 열과 습기가 결합하여 만들어진다.

17 밑줄 친 aloft의 동의어는?

① 입자　　　② 방전　　　③ 공중에서　　　④ 도시 너머로

어구 thunderstorm 뇌우　particularly 특히, 두드러지게　prevalent 유행하는, 널리 퍼지는　gulf 만(灣), 심연　convection (열·공기의) 대류, 환류　aloft 위에, 높이　particle 입자, 미립자, 분자　pollutant 오염 물질　condensation 응축, 농축　nuclei 핵, 세포핵(nucleus의 복수형태)　formation 형성, 구성　towering 높은 치솟은, 큰　cumulonimbus 적란운　cottony 솜 같은, 보드라운　threatening 위협적인, 임박한　gray 회색　build up 쌓아 올리다, 증강하다　eventually 결국, 드디어, 마침내　electrical 전기에 관한, 전기 같은　discharge 양륙, 발포, 방전, 해고　lightening 번개, 전광　take place 발생하다　estimated 견적의, 추측의, 추정된　touch off 발화시키다, 유발하다　phenomena 현상(phenomenon의 복수형태)

해설 **15** 전기 방전이 발생하는 원인을 과정과 함께 설명한 후에, 악영향으로 숲을 태우기도 한다는 '원인과 영향'의 '인과 분석'을 다룬 글이다.

16 세 번째 문장에서 '높이 솟은 적란운은 습도와 에너지가 합쳐질 때 솜처럼 하얀색이던 것이 위협적인 회색과 검은색으로 변한다'고 했으므로 뇌우는 열과 습기의 결합에 의해서 만들어진다고 유추가 가능하다.

17 aloft는 '위에', '높이(high up in the air)'라는 뜻을 가진 부사이므로, 본문에서는 '공중에서'라는 의미가 동의어로서 가장 적합하다.

When I was eighteen I wanted something to do. I had tried tutoring for two years and hated it and could not earn my bread that way at the cost of my health; I tried story-writing and got five dollars for stories that now bring a hundred; I had thought seriously of going on the stage, but certain highly respectable relatives were so shocked at the mere idea that I relinquished my dramatic aspirations.

"What shall I do?" was still the question that hounded me. I was ready to work, eager to be independent, and too proud to endure patronage. But the right task seemed hard to find, and my bottled energies were fermenting in a way that threatened an explosion.

해석 내가 18살이 되었을 때 무엇인가 하기를 원했다. 나는 2년 동안 가정교사 일을 했으며, 그 일이 싫어지자 내 건강을 망가뜨리는 방법으로 생계를 유지할 수는 없었다. 그래서 나는 소설을 시험적으로 써 보았으며 지금이라면 100달러를 받는 글들에 대한 수익으로 5달러를 벌었다. 또 나는 배우가 되는 것을 진지하게 생각해 보았지만, 어떤 매우 존경받는 친척들이 그 단순한 생각에 매우 쇼크를 받아서 연극에 관한 나의 갈망을 포기하게 됐다.

나를 쫓아다니는 질문거리인 "나는 무엇을 해야 하는가?"가 아직도 남겨져 있었다. 나는 일할 준비가 되어 있었고, 독립하기를 갈망했으며, 너무나 자신이 있어서 후원을 받기가 싫었다. 그러나 좋은 일을 찾기가 어려워 보였기에, 나의 갇혀 버린 에너지는 폭발할 것 같이 동요하고 있었다.

18 Which one best expresses the author's attitude toward work?

① Jobs are plentiful if you know where to look.
② It is difficult to find a job that pays well and is rewarding.
③ It is better to work at any job than not to work at all.
④ Work is to be avoided at all costs.

19 The author implies that writing is a job that is

_____________.

① rewarding
② humiliating
③ unprofitable
④ stimulating

20 According to the author, her energy was like

_____________.

① a bottle
② a stew that is cooking
③ a sewing job
④ a bomb that might go off

18 일에 대한 필자의 태도는?

① 당신이 찾아야 할 곳을 안다면 직장은 충분히 많다.
② 수지와 보수가 좋은 직장을 구하기가 어렵다.
③ 일을 전혀 하지 않는 것보다 어느 직장에서라도 일을 하는 것이 더 좋다.
④ 일은 어떠한 희생을 치르고서라도 피해야만 한다.

19 작가는 저술이 어떠한 일이라고 암시하는가?

① 득이 되는
② 굴욕적인
③ 수지가 안 맞는
④ 자극적인

20 작가의 에너지는 무엇과 비슷한가?

① 병
② 스튜 요리
③ 재봉업
④ 폭발할 것 같은 폭탄

어구 try-ing 시험 삼아 ~을 해보다　tutor ~에게 가정교사로서 가르치다; 가정교사　earn one's bread 생활비를 벌다, 생계유지를 하다　go on/come on/ take to the stage 배우가 되다　respectable 존경을 받는　mere 단순한, 전적인, 순전한　relinquish 포기하다, 버리다, 단념하다　dramatic 극적인　aspiration 열망　hound 추적하다, 사냥개로 사냥하다; 사냥개, 비열한 놈　be ready to R ~할 준비가 되다　be eager to R ~하기를 열망하다　endure 견디다, 참다　patronage 후원, 보호　ferment 큰 법석을 떨다, 발효하다　bottled 술 취한, 병에 넣은　threaten ~에 임박해 있다, 위협하다　at all costs 어떠한 희생을 치르고서라도　rewarding 수지가 맞는　humiliating 굴욕적인　unprofitable 수지가 맞지 않는　stimulating 자극적인　go off 폭발하다. (약속 따위가) 불이행으로 끝나다. (음식 등이) 상하다

해설 18 건강을 망가뜨리는 가정교사도 싫어지고, 5달러밖에 벌지 못하는 작가 직업도 싫어지고, 후원을 받지 않고 독립된 일을 하기 원했다는 것은 보수가 좋은 직장을 원한다는 것이다. 그러나 그럴 수 있는 일을 구하기 어렵다고 마지막 문장에서 자신의 생각을 밝히고 있다.

19 'I tried story-writing and got five dollars for stories that now bring a hundred'의 문장을 통해, 현재시제에서는 100달러를 벌 수 있는 일을 과거에는 자신이 5달러를 벌었다고 했으므로, 이는 수지가 맞지 않는 일이라고 작가는 넌지시 암시하고 있는 것이다.

20 마지막 문장에서 취해 버린 에너지가 폭발할 것같이 동요하고 있었다고 했으므로 ④가 옳은 내용이다.

One of the side-effects of the second world war was the most momentous social change of the past half-century. As men marched off to fight, women put aside their grooming magazines and gardening gloves and took their husbands' places in factories and on the farms. They never looked back. Many people worry about the impact on family life of their entry into the labour force, but most now take it for granted that women have as much to offer at work as men do.

①Another change as large as that one is now under way. In a further half-century it will seem just as absurd that western societies today are content to press another potentially productive set of workers to stay at home sipping tea and potting begonias? and to pay them for it, to boot.

The question of how to deal with the growing number of retired people has recently been seen as chiefly ②a financial puzzle: how to pay for the leisure of those ageing layabouts. When Bismarck first introduced state pensions in the 1880s, they kicked in at the age of 70, about 20 years more than the typical life span. Nowadays state and company pension schemes kick in at or before 65, almost 20 years less. But ③the issue is more than just a _______________ one: ④it raises social as well as economic questions, and ⑤its resolution will involve governments, employers and people.

21 Fill in the blank with the most suitable word.

① warlike ② moral
③ financial ④ strained
⑤ compromising

22 Among ①, ②, ③, ④, and ⑤, which one differs from the others in what they refer to?

① Another change ② a financial puzzle
③ the issue ④ it
⑤ its

23 Which of the following statements cannot be inferred from the passage?

① It is not desirable that retired people will take only household affairs.
② The authorities may make a considerable budget for the retired people that need amusement facilities.
③ It seems as though the average span of human life is less than 80.
④ A number of retired people are the problem not only with the general public but with the government.
⑤ In the nineteenth century, the seventies could receive a pension.

해석 2차 대전의 부작용 중 하나는 지난 반세기 동안 가장 중대한 사회적 변화의 하나가 되었다. 남자들이 싸우러 전쟁에 나갔을 때, 여성들은 말 손질용 창고와 정원용 장갑들을 치우고 자신들의 남편이 일했던 공장들과 농장으로 갔다. 그들은 결코 움츠러들지 않았다. 많은 이들은 여성들이 노동력에 편성되어 가정사에 미칠 영향에 대해 걱정했었다. 그러나 대부분의 사람들은 남성처럼 여성들도 많은 일을 제공해야 한다는 점을 당연히 여긴다.

이러한 사실만큼이나 또 다른 변화는 지금도 진행 중이다. 앞으로 반세기 안에 서부 국가들이 오늘날 생산력이 있는 잠재 노동자들로 하여금 집에서 차를 마시고 베고니아 꽃에 물을 주라고 강요하고, 게다가 그들에게 돈을 주는 것에 만족을 한다는 사실은 터무니없을 것이다.

증가하는 퇴직자들의 문제를 다루는 법에 대한 문제가 최근에 상당히 재정적인 어려움으로 다가왔다. 즉 이러한 은퇴한 퇴직자들의 여가를 위해서 어떻게 투자를 할 것이냐에 대해 말이다. 비스마르크가 처음으로 1880년대에 국민연금을 도입했을 때, 그 연금들은 평균 수명보다 대략 20살이 더 많은 70세의 나이에 효력을 발생했다. 요즘에는 연금들은 65세나 그 전에 효력이 발생되는데, 거의 20년이 (평균 수명보다) 적은 연령이다. 그러나 문제는 단순히 경제적인 것 이상이다. 즉 경제적인 것뿐만 아니라 사회적인 문제들을 야기하며, 그 해결책은 정부기관과 고용주와 사람들을 관련시킬 것이다.

21 빈칸에 적절한 것은?
① 호전적인 ② 도덕적인 ③ 재정상의 ④ 긴장된 ⑤ 타협적인

22 지문의 ①~⑤ 중 다른 하나를 가리키는 지칭어는?
① 또 다른 변화 ② 재정적인 곤혹스러움 ③ 문제 ④ 문제 ⑤ 문제의

23 이 글에서 유추할 수 없는 것은?
① 은퇴한 사람들이 단지 가정일만 하게 되는 것은 바람직하지 못하다.
② 당국은 오락 편의시설을 필요로 하는 은퇴한 사람들을 위해서 예산을 편성할 수도 있다.
③ 인간의 평균 수명이 80세가 안 되는 것처럼 보인다.
④ 수많은 은퇴한 사람들은 일반 대중뿐만 아니라 정부의 문제가 되기도 한다.
⑤ 19세기에는 70대의 사람들이 연금을 수령할 수 있었다.

어구 **momentous** 중대한 **put aside** 치우다, 저축하다 **grooming** 말을 손질하는 **magazine** 창고, 잡지 **look back** 주춤거리다, 움츠리다 **entry** 편성 **take it for granted that** ~을 당연시 여기다 **absurd** 불합리한 **be content to R** ~에 만족하다 **begonia** 베고니아 꽃 **to boot** 게다가, 덤으로(in addition) **chiefly** 상당히 **puzzle** 당혹스러움 **layabout** 방랑자 **state pension** 연금 **life span** 평균 수명 **kick in** 기부하다, 지불하다, 효과가 나타나다 **warlike** 호전적인

해설 **21** 바로 다음에 위치한 콜론(:)은 무조건 '순접-진술부연'의 관계를 설명한다. 따라서 콜론 이하의 내용이 '경제적인 것뿐만 아니라 사회적인 문제들'이라고 했으므로 '경제적인' 것과 순접의 내용이 되어야 more than에 의해서 비교가 가능하다. 경제적인 내용을 가리키는 보기는 '재정상의'라는 뜻을 가진 financial이 옳다.

22 나머지는 모두 경제적 요소뿐만 아니라 사회적인 요소까지 포함한 '전반의 문제'를 가리키지만, 경제적인 요소만 설명한 ②가 틀렸다.

23 오늘날의 평균 수명보다 20년 적은 65세의 나이에 연금이 지급되므로 평균 나이는 85세라고 유추가 가능하다. 글의 후반부 Nowadays state and company pension schemes kick in at or before 65, almost 20 years less.의 문장 참고.

More than 28 million Americans have at least some hearing loss (many of them members of Generation iPod). Yet only one in five who could use a hearing aid wears one. For many, it's an aesthetic issue: They don't like the traditional devices' looks. Now some new gadgets may change that. Modern models come in novel shapes (triangles, teardrops) and colors (sporty green, deep red), with customizable volume settings, rechargeable batteries, even Bluetooth technology.

24 윗글을 통해 유추할 수 <u>없는</u> 것은?

① Less than 28 million Americans wear a hearing aid.
② As much as 20% of Americans wear a traditional hearing aid.
③ Future hearing aids will look more stylish than traditional ones.
④ iPod might have been one of the causes of Americans' hearing loss.

해석 2천 8백만 이상의 미국인들은 적어도 약간의 청각 장애를 겪고 있다. (그들 중 다수가 아이팟 세대이다.) 그러나 보청기를 사용해야 하는 5명 중 단 한 명만이 보청기를 착용하고 있다. 그것은 많은 이들에게 미적인 문제이기 때문이다. 그들은 기존 보청기의 외관을 좋아하지 않는다. 이제 몇몇 신식 장비들이 외관을 바꾸고 있는 것 같다. 현대적인 모델들은 삼각형, 눈물방울 모양 등의 새로운 모양과 발랄한 녹색이나 진한 빨간색, 고객 맞춤식 음량 장치와 재충전이 가능한 건전지, 무선 장비까지 갖추어 출시된다.

24 윗글을 통해 유추할 수 <u>없는</u> 것은?

① 2,800만 미만의 미국인들이 보청기를 착용한다.
② 자그마치 20%의 미국인들이 기존의 보청기를 착용한다.
③ 미래의 보청기는 기존의 것보다 더욱 맵시가 있어 보일 것이다.
④ 아이팟은 미국인들의 청각 장애를 유발한 원인들 중 하나가 되었던 것 같다.

어구 **hearing loss** 청각 장애, 청각 손실 **hearing aid** 보청기 **aesthetic** 미(美)의, 미술의; 미학의; 심미적인 **gadget** (기계의) 간단한 장치; 도구, 부속품; 묘안 **novel** 신기한(strange), 새로운(new); 기발한 **sporty** 경쾌한, 발랄한 **customizable** 고객 맞춤식의 **rechargeable** 재충전이 되는

해설 2천 8백만 이상의 미국인들이 청각 장애를 경험하고 있고, 이들 중 5명의 한 명꼴로(즉, 20% 정도) 보청기를 착용하고 있다고 했다. 이는 미국인 전체 중 20%가 보청기를 착용하고 있음을 말하는 것이 아니다.

>>> **다음 글을 읽고 문제의 답을 고르시오. [25~26]**

Private secretary. Female between 20-25. College degree preferably in English or Accounting. Prior job experience not mandatory. Must type at least 30 words/minute and have working knowledge of computers (word processing). Hours flexible but must be willing to relocate and travel extensively. Starting salary at $2,000/month and open to negotiation. Submit résumé(with photo) and college transcripts to the following address.

25 윗글의 성격으로 가장 알맞은 것은?

① local obituary
② product advertisement
③ personal résumé
④ wanted advertisement

26 윗글의 내용으로 보아 상대적으로 가장 유리한 입장에 있는 사람은?

① a man double majoring in English and history in college
② a 21 year old single woman who types 40 words/minute
③ a retired male executive returning to the job market
④ a divorced mother in her late 20s with two young children

해석 개인 비서. 20–25세 사이의 여성. 영어 혹은 회계학 전공은 우대함. 경력이 꼭 필요한 것은 아님. 분당 최소 30단어의 타자 실력과 컴퓨터 실무 지식(워드 프로세서)은 꼭 갖추어야 함. 근무 시간은 유동적이지만 근무지 이동에 기꺼이 수락해야 하고 여행도 광범위하게 다녀야 함. 급료는 월 $2,000에서 시작하고 협상 가능. 사진이 첨부된 이력서와 대학 성적표를 이하의 주소로 제출 바람.

25 윗글의 성격으로 가장 알맞은 것은?

① 지역 사망 기사
② 상품 광고
③ 개인 이력서
④ 모집 광고

26 윗글의 내용으로 보아 상대적으로 가장 유리한 입장에 있는 사람은?

① 대학에서 영어와 역사를 복수 전공하는 남자
② 분당 40단어의 타자를 치는 21살 독신녀
③ 인력 시장으로 돌아온 전직 여성 간부
④ 두 어린아이들이 있는 20대 후반의 이혼녀

어구 **preferably** 차라리; 즐겨, 오히려, 되도록이면 **accounting** 회계(학); 회계 보고; 결산 **mandatory** 지령의; 위탁의, 위임의; 의무적인, 강제적인 **relocate** 다시 배치하다; (주거·공장·주민 등을) 새 장소로 옮기다, 이전시키다 **resume** 이력서; 요약; 다시 시작[계속]하다 **transcript** 성적 증명서; 사본, 등본; (연설 등의) 필기록; 복사 **obituary** (약력을 붙여 신문에 싣는) 사망 기사

해설 **25** 비서와 같은 지위, 영어 혹은 회계학과 같은 전공 등과 같은 내용이 열거되며, 마지막에서 이력서와 성적표 제출 얘기가 나오기 때문에 '(신입 사원) 모집 광고'로 유추할 수 있다.
26 분당 최소 30단어를 칠 수 있고 20–25세의 조건을 필요로 했기 때문에 보기 ②의 여성이 가장 유리한 입장에 있다고 볼 수 있다.

As a high school soccer coach, I'm aware that student athletes tend to focus too much on sports. A fellow coach, Bob, was talking about one such player, who called him at home one night. When his wife informed the kid that Bob wasn't home, he became frantic and said he had to speak to the coach right away. "Just calm down, and I'll have him call you as soon as he gets home," the coach's wife told him. "What's your number?" The flustered kid replied, "Three."

27 What does the <u>Three</u> of the last sentence imply?

① his phone number
② his uniform number
③ his room number
④ the number of his team members

Health experts searching for the cause of a frightening outbreak of a deadly flu-like illness in Asia say the culprit is probably a virus, and they are encouraged that some victims appear to _______________. More than 150 people have fallen ill, mostly in Hong Kong and Vietnam, over the past three weeks. And experts suspect that another 300 people in China's Guangdong province had the same disease beginning in mid-November. While experts are unsure precisely what is causing the outbreak, several say their biggest fear is that it is a new and lethal form of influenza.

28 Which of the following statements CANNOT be inferred from the passage?

① The recently found disease is deadly and infectious.
② At least, 450 people are suffering from this disease.
③ Experts are sure of finding a cure for this disease soon.
④ This disease is epidemic mainly in the southeast Asia.
⑤ This disease is a sort of influenza.

29 Which of the following is most appropriate for the blank?

① be getting better
② be growing
③ be in a critical condition
④ develop complications
⑤ lose weight

해석 학교의 축구 감독으로서, 나는 학생 운동선수들이 운동에 너무 많이 집중하는 경향이 있음을 알고 있다. 동료 감독인 밥은 그와 같은 한 명의 선수에 대해 얘기를 하고 있었다. 그 학생은 밤에 밥의 집에 전화를 했고, 밥(Bob)의 아내가 그가 없다고 하자 그 학생은 무척 흥분을 했다. 그 감독의 부인은 그 학생에게 "진정하세요. 남편이 집에 오자마자 당신에게 전화하라고 할게요."라고 말했다. "번호가 무엇인가요?" 그 허둥거리는 학생이 "3번입니다."라고 답했다.

27 마지막 문장의 **Three**가 암시하는 것은?

① 전화번호
② 유니폼 번호
③ 방 번호
④ 팀 동료의 숫자

어구 focus on ～에 집중하다   frantic 미친 듯 날뛰는, 광란의   right away 곧바로   calm down 진정하다

해설 학생 운동선수들은 운동에 너무 집중한다고 했다. 마지막 문장에서 부인이 학생의 번호가 무엇이냐고 묻자, 3번이라고 대답한 것은 전화번호로 답한 것이 아니라 자신의 등번호(유니폼 번호)를 답한 것으로 보아야 한다.

해석 아시아에서 독감과 비슷한 치명적인 질병의 무서운 출현 원인을 조사했던 건강 전문가들이 그 원인이 아마도 바이러스일 수 있다고 말하며, 몇몇 감염자들은 증세가 호전되리라는 점에 고무되어 있다. 150명 이상의 사람들이 주로 홍콩과 베트남에서 지난 3주 동안 병에 걸렸다. 그리고 전문가들은 중국 광동 지역에서 11월 중순 경에 시작된 똑같은 질병이 있다고 의심한다. 전문가들이 (질병의) 발발을 야기하고 있는 것이 무엇인지 정확히는 확신할 수 없을지라도, 여러 전문가들은 그들이 가장 두려워하는 것은 그 질병이 신종이며 치명적인 독감 형태라고 말한다.

28 이 글을 통해서 유추할 수 없는 내용은?

① 최근에 발견된 질병은 치명적이며 전염성이 있다.
② 적어도 450명이 이 병으로 고통 받고 있다.
③ 전문가들은 곧 이 병의 치료책을 찾으리라 확신한다.
④ 이 질병은 남동 아시아에서 주로 전염된다.
⑤ 이 질병은 독감의 한 종류이다.

29 빈칸에 적절한 보기는?

① 더 나아지고 있다.
② 성장하고 있다.
③ 위험한 상태에 있다.
④ 합병증에 걸리고 있다.
⑤ 몸무게가 줄다.

어구 frightening 무서운   outbreak (소동 · 전쟁 · 유행병 따위의) 발발   flu-like 독감과 유사한   culprit (잘못의) 원인, 피의자   be encouraged that S+V ～에 고무되다   fall ill 병에 걸리다   province 지방, 지역, 범위   lethal 치명적인   influenza 독감   deadly 치명적인   infectious 전염하는(epidemic)   complication 합병증, 복잡

해설 **28** 전문가들은 여전히 이 병의 정확한 원인도 밝혀내지 못했다고 했으므로 치료책을 찾으리라 확신했다는 설명은 틀리다.
29 'are encouraged that ～' 표현에 따라 건강전문가들의 '고무될 만한 사실'이 논리상 옳다. 따라서 그 환자들의 상태가 호전된다는 논리가 적합하다.

He opens a drawer, pulling out a few stacks of paper. Here, he says, are this week's scheduled movements of every famous passenger of a major limousine company in Los Angeles. Here are passenger manifests of every flight on American Airlines. "I get the full printout," he says. "If they fly any coastal flight, I know it. I can also find anybody in the world within 24 hours." He says he has law enforcement officers on his payroll and can have a license plate checked in an hour.

30 What would be the man's occupation?

① lawyer
② policeman
③ paparazzi
④ limousine driver

해석 그는 서랍을 열고 몇 다발의 종이를 꺼낸다. LA의 어느 대형 리무진 회사의 모든 유명 승객들의 주간 스케줄이 여기에 있다고 그는 말한다. 아메리칸 에어라인의 모든 비행 편의 승객 명단이 있다. 그는 "모두 인쇄하여 가지고 있습니다."고 말한다. "만일 그들이 어느 연안 비행기를 타더라도 나는 그것을 알 수 있으며, 전 세계 어디에 있든지 24시간 내에 누구라도 찾을 수 있습니다."라고 그는 말한다. 그는 자신의 급여 지불 대장에 경관이 있으며, 한 시간 내에 차 번호판을 확인할 수 있다고 말한다.

30 남자의 직업은 무엇인가?

① 변호사　　② 경찰관　　③ 파파라치　　④ 리무진 기사

어구 **pull out** 빼내다, 꺼내다; 뽑아내다　**stack** 더미, 퇴적, 꾸러미; 많음　**limousine** 리무진(운전석과 객석 사이에 유리 칸막이가 있는 대형 자동차); (공항과 시내 사이의 여객 송영용) 소형 버스　**passenger manifest** 승객 명단　**printout** 인쇄 출력(인쇄기의 출력)　**law enforcement officer** 경관　**payroll** 임금 대장, (종업원의) 급료 총액; 종업원 명부　**license plate** 번호판

해설 비행사 승객 명단을 얻을 수 있으며, 유명 인사의 일정을 언제든지 알아낼 수 있는 불법을 저지르는 자는 보기 중에서 '파파라치'가 유일하다.

>>> 다음 글을 읽고 문제의 답을 고르시오 [31~32]

Fog, tiny droplets of water vapor, is the villain of the airports. In an effort to eliminate dense fog from airports, weathermen utilize giant fans, nylon string, and chemicals dropped from planes or shot upwards from strange machine on the ground. Nothing works as well, though, as a new weapon in the fight against fog: the helicopter. Researchers believe that if warm dry air above the fog could somehow be driven down into the humid blanket of fog, the droplets would evaporate, thus clearing the air. In a recent experiment to test their theory the researchers had a helicopter descend into the fog above barely visible Smith Mountain Airport near Roanoke, Virginia. The blades of the helicopter caused the air to circulate downwards and an enormous hole in the cloud opened above the airport. Weathermen predict that with larger, more expensive helicopters they will be able to make the thickest fog vanish.

31 윗글의 제목을 고르시오.

① Why can Helicopter be Defeated?
② How is Fog Formed and not Seen?
③ The Enemy of the Airport: Fog
④ The Secret to Clearing Fog

해석 안개는 미세한 물방울인 수증기로서, 공항의 골칫거리이다. 공항의 짙은 안개를 없애기 위해 기상 통보관들은 대형 팬과 나일론 줄을 이용하기도 하며, 비행기에서 화학 물질을 투하하거나, 지상에서 하늘을 향해 신식 장비로 화학 물질을 발사하기도 한다. 그러나 안개와의 싸움에서 헬리콥터만큼 효과가 뛰어난 신식 장비는 없다. 만일 안개 위에 있는 따뜻하고 건조한 공기가 안개의 습기층으로 내려온다면, 그 물방울(안개)은 증발하여 하늘이 맑아질 것이다(안개가 사라질 것이다). 이 이론을 검증하기 위한 최근의 실험에서 연구가들은 버지니아 주의 로노크 근처에 있는 거의 잘 보이지 않는 스미스 마운틴 공항(안개 때문에 시야 확보가 힘든 스미스 마운틴 공항) 위에 있는 안개 속으로 헬리콥터를 하강시켰다. 헬리콥터의 날개 때문에 공기가 밑으로 내려갔으며, 공항 위에 있는 구름에 큰 구멍이 발생했다. 기상 통보관들은 비용은 많이 들지만 대형 헬리콥터를 이용하면 가장 짙은 안개도 사라질 수 있을 것이라 예측하고 있다.

31 윗글의 제목을 고르시오.

① 헬리콥터가 왜 패배를 당하는가?
② 안개가 어떻게 형성이 되고 보이지 않는 것인가?
③ 공항의 적: 안개
④ 안개를 없애는 해결책

32 이 글을 통하여 유추할 수 없는 것을 고르시오.

① 안개를 없애기 위하여, 헬리콥터가 안개 위를 향해 상승한다.
② 안개를 없애기 위해 이제껏 취해진 몇몇 조치들은 소용이 없었다.
③ 안개가 스미스 마운틴 공항의 시야를 막았다.
④ 헬리콥터의 크기가 안개의 제거에 영향을 미치는 것으로 보인다.

① In order to clear fog, helicopters fly upwards above it.
② Some actions that airports have ever taken to eliminate fog have been in vain.
③ Fog has obstructed the view of Smith Mountain Airport.
④ The size of a helicopter seems to affect elimination of fog.

어구 water vapor 물방울 villain 악당, 골칫거리 eliminate 제거하다 upwards 위로, 하늘을 향해 blanket 전면을 덮는 것, 피복(被覆) barely 간신히, 가까스로, 겨우, 거의 ~없다 blade (스크루의) 날개; (풀의) 잎 circulate 순환하다 thick (안개 등이) 짙은; 빽빽한; 혼잡한 secret to -ing ~에 대한 비책 be in vain 헛되이 되다

해설 31 공항에 해를 끼치는 짙은 안개를 없애는 최상의 수단으로 헬기를 사용하는 방법을 묘사한 것이 이 글의 주제이다.
32 'Researchers believe that~'을 통해, '안개 속으로 헬리콥터를 하강시켰다'고 했다. 따라서 안개 위로 헬리콥터가 올라가게 한다는 내용은 정반대 설명이 된다.

>>> **다음 글을 읽고 문제의 답을 고르시오.** [33~36]

The Indo-European family of languages is the world's largest, embracing most of the languages of Europe, America, and much of Asia. Who were the original Indo-Europeans and when and where did they live? Since they left no written documents, which are, after all, the basis of history, the answers to these questions can be best obtained by attempting to reconstruct their languages. If we may assume that a word that is similar in most of the Indo-European languages designates a concept that existed in the original Indo-European society and that, ① _______________, a word that varies in most Indo-European languages designates a concept not discovered until later, we may then draw certain tentative conclusions.

It would appear that the Indo-Europeans lived in a cold northern region; that it was not near the waters, but among forests; that they raised such domestic animals as the sheep, the dog, the cow, and the horse; that among wild animals they knew the bear and the wolf; that it was the use of the horse and chariot that enabled them to overrun such an enormous expanse of territory.

해석 인도유럽어족은 세상에서 가장 크고 유럽, 미국, 그리고 아시아 상당 지역의 언어들 중 대부분을 포함한다. 누가 최초의 인도유럽어족이었으며 그들은 언제 어디서 살았는가? 그들은 물론 역사의 기초가 되는 성문화된 기록들을 남겨놓지 않았기 때문에 이 질문들에 대한 답변은 그들의 언어를 재구성함으로써 얻어질 수 있다. 만일 인도유럽들 중 대부분과 유사한 한 개의 단어가 최초의 인도유럽사회에 존재했었던 하나의 개념을 나타낸다고 짐작하고, 반면에 대부분의 인도유럽어들에서 (뜻이) 가지각색인 하나의 단어가 나중에 발견되었던 하나의 개념을 가리킨다고 짐작한다면 우리는 임시적인 결론을 내릴 수 있을 것이다.
인도유럽어족이 추운 북쪽 지역에서 살았으며, 바다 근처가 아니라 숲에서 살았으며, 양, 개, 소, 말과 같은 가축들을 길렀으며, 야생동물들 중에서 그들이 곰과 늑대를 알았으며, 말과 전차를 사용했다는 사실이 그들로 하여금 거대한 영토 확장을 가능하게 해 줄 수 있었을 것으로 보인다.

33 이 글의 제목은?
① 세상의 언어들
② 언어와 역사
③ 언어의 기원
④ 인도유럽어족 언어의 기원
⑤ 인도유럽어족 언어의 역사언어학

34 최초 인도유럽어족의 사회에 존재했었을 만한 개념은?
① 고래
② 침엽수
③ 열대과실
④ 공룡
⑤ 책

35 만일 많은 관련 언어들이 '물고기', '조개', 그리고 '바다'와 같은 개념을 가지고 있고, '산'과 '숲'과 같은 단어들이 상대적으로 적다면 최초 모국어를 구사한 이들은 어떠했다고 가정하겠는가?
① 산보다 바다를 좋아했다.
② 바다보다 산을 좋아했다.
③ 어획을 즐겼다.
④ 산악 등산을 즐겼다.
⑤ 바다 근처에서 살았다.

36 ①에 들어갈 것은?
① 그러므로
② 말하다
③ 따라서
④ 그런데
⑤ 반면에

33 The best title of this passage would be:
① Languages of the World
② Language and History
③ The Origin of Language
④ The Origin of the Indo-European Languages
⑤ The Historical Linguistics of the Indo-European Languages

34 Choose the one concept that would probably have existed in the original Indo—European society.

① whale
② needle-leaf tree
③ tropical fruit
④ dinosaur
⑤ book

35 If a number of related languages had many similar words for concepts such as 'fish', 'shell', and 'sea' and relatively few words for 'mountain' and 'forest', one could assume that the speakers of the original parent language:

① preferred the sea to the mountain
② preferred the mountain to the sea
③ enjoyed fishing
④ enjoyed mountain-climbing
⑤ lived by the sea

36 Which of the following best fits into ①?

① therefore
② say
③ accordingly
④ by the way
⑤ on the other hand

어구 **indo-european** 인도유럽어족(의)　**embrace** 포함하다, 껴안다　**tentative** 임시의, 주저하는　**waters** 바다　**domestic animal** 가축　**chariot** 전차, (구식) 자동차　**enable A to R** A로 하여금 ~할 수 있게 하다　**overrun** 침략하다, ~의 전반에 걸쳐 퍼지다　**needle-leaf** 침엽수의　**dinosaur** 공룡　**a number of** 많은　**parent language** 모국어　**prefer A to B** A를 B보다 더 좋아하다　**accordingly** 따라서

해설 **33** 두 번째 문장에서 인도유럽어족의 기원에 대한 질문을 제기한 이후 그 이하에서 답변을 하는 Q&A 형식의 글로서, 주제는 인도유럽어족의 기원이 된다.

34 두 번째 단락의 첫 문장에서 '추운 지역'에서 살았다고 했으므로, 침엽수가 있었으리라 유추가 가능하다. 침엽수는 겨울에 잎이 돋는 식물을 말한다.

35 설문에 해당되는 이들은 본문에서 언급된 인도유럽어족들과 정반대의 상황이다. 따라서 숲 근처에서 살았다는 본문의 내용과 반대의 장소가 될 수 있는 '바다 근처'가 옳다.

36 and 앞 문장의 내용에 등장하는 단어는 'that is similar(유사한)'의 개념인 반면, and 이하의 단어는 'that varies(가지각색인)'이므로, '역접-대조'이다. by the way는 '화제를 바꿀 때(used when saying something that is not related to the main subject you were talking about before)' 쓰이므로 본문에서는 적합하지 않으며, '앞 내용과 연관되어 대조'를 이루는 'on the other hand(used to give another opinion or fact that should be considered as well as the one you have just given)'가 옳다.

Whereas family relationships usually constitute a child's first experience with group life, peer-group interactions soon begin to make their powerful socializing effects felt. From play group to teenage clique, the peer group affords young people many significant learning experiences—how to achieve status in a circle of friends. Peers are equals in a way parents and their children or teachers and their students are not. A parent or teacher sometimes can force young children to obey rules they neither understand nor like, but peers do not have formal authority to do this; thus the true meaning of exchange, cooperation, and equity can be learned more easily in the peer setting. Peer groups increase in importance as the child grows up and reach maximum influence in adolescence, by which time they sometimes dictate much of a young person's behavior both in and out of school.

37 According to the passage, which of the following would feel the importance of a peer group the most?

① toddlers
② elementary school students
③ kindergarteners
④ high school students
⑤ adults

해석 가족 관계가 일반적으로 아이의 첫 단체 생활 경험을 만들어 주지만, 얼마 지나지 않아 강력한 사회적 영향력을 느끼게 되는 또래 집단의 상호 관계가 시작된다. 놀이 집단에서 십대 집단에 이르기까지 또래 집단은 어린 아이들에게 어떻게 친구들 무리 안에서 지위를 얻게 되는지와 같은 많은 중요한 학습 경험을 제공한다. 또래들은 부모와 자식, 혹은 교사와 학생(의 관계)과는 다른 방법으로 평등하다. 부모나 교사가 아이들이 이해하지도 못하고 좋아하지도 않는 규율을 따르라고 아이들에게 강요할 수 있지만, 또래들은 이렇게 할 수 있는 공식 권한이 없다. 따라서 교환, 협력 및 평등의 진정한 의미는 또래의 환경 내에서 더 쉽게 학습 가능해진다. 또래 집단은 아이가 커가면서 점점 더 중요해지고 청소년기에 최고의 영향력에 달하여, 그 때쯤에는 때때로 학교 안팎에서 젊은이들의 많은 행동을 지시하게 된다.

37 누가 또래 집단의 중요성을 가장 많이 느낄 것 같은가?

① 유아
② 초등학생
③ 유치원생
④ 고등학생
⑤ 어른

38 이 글의 요지는 무엇인가?

① 아이들은 또래 집단과의 협력에 대해 터득해야 한다.
② 또래 집단은 아동의 삶에서 강력한 영향력이 있는 단체이다.
③ 부모들은 또래 집단이 할 수 없는 것들을 아이들에게 하라고 강요할 수 있다.
④ 부모들은 교사들보다 아이에게 더 큰 영향력을 가지고 있다.
⑤ 학교 내부, 외부의 다양한 관계들은 아이들에게 배움의 기회를 제공한다.

38 Which of the following best expresses the main idea of the passage?

① Children learn about cooperation in their peer groups.
② Peer groups are powerful influences in children's lives.
③ Parents can force children to do things that a peer group cannot.
④ Parents have greater influences on children than their teachers do.
⑤ Relationships in and out of school provide learning opportunities for children.

어구 **peer-group** 또래 집단 **interaction** 상호 작용 **socialize** 사회적[사교적]으로 하다, 사회화하다 **clique** (배타적인) 도당, 파벌 **status** 지위; 신분; 상태 **setting** 환경, 주위 **dictate** 지시하다; 구술하다, (말하여) 받아쓰게 하다 **toddler** 아장아장 걷는 사람. (특히) 걸음마 하는 유아 **kindergartener** (유치원의) 보모; (유치원) 원아

해설 **37** 마지막 문장에서 아이가 다 컸을 때 또래 집단의 중요성이 최고조에 달한다고 했기 때문에 성장한 아이(고등학생)가 또래 집단의 중요성에 대해 가장 많이 느낄 것이다.
38 첫 문장의 아이가 상호 관계(사회생활)의 중요성을 또래 집단을 통해 배우게 된다는 내용이 주제가 되므로, ②의 또래 집단은 아이의 삶 속에서 강력한 영향력을 가진다는 것이 옳다.

>>> **다음 글을 읽고 문제의 답을 고르시오.** [39~41]

At this point, we enter a world that is truly surreal, defying comment. The rules of the game must be strictly observed in civilized society: assassinations, terrorism, torture, and aggression are crimes that must be harshly punished when the targets are people who matter; they are not even worth mentioning, or laudable acts of self-defense, if the chief mafia don himself conducts the crimes in the name of the Free World. So self-evident are these truths that close to 100 of reporting and commentary on Bush's attack upheld them, even descending to the level of citing US attempts to assassinate foreign leaders in justification of the US attack on Iraq. Any totalitarian state would be proud to have an intellectual class capable of such a performance.

39 What does the author imply with regard to the recent US attack on Iraq?

① It was unavoidable as an act of self-defense.
② It goes without saying that it must be upheld.
③ It would only be welcomed in the totalitarian states.
④ It would be justified by the intellectuals.

40 What kind of world do we enter according to the author?

① untrue world　　② imaginary world
③ surprising world　　④ strange world

41 What is not implied in the reading above?

① The U.S.A recently became a totalitarian state.
② Terrorism must not be exercised in civilized society.
③ There is no good reason to justify the US attack.
④ It is surprising that the attack was largely upheld in U.S.A.

해석 이 시점에서 우리는 정말 현실적이고 설명하기 힘든 세상으로 진입했다. 문명화된 사회에서 게임의 법칙은 엄격히 준수되어야만 한다. 즉, 암살, 테러, 고문, 침략과 같은 행동들은 그 대상이 되는 이들이 중요한 인물일 때에는 엄중하게 처벌해야만 하는 범죄이다. 설사 마피아 조직의 두목이 자유세계라는 명목으로 이런 일을 직접 범했다 할지라도 이러한 행동들은 심지어 언급할 가치가 없으며 자기방어라고 칭찬받을 일도 아니다. 이러한 사실들은 너무나 자명해서, 부시가 이라크를 공격한 것을 지지하기 위해 100편이 넘는 보고서와 논평을 써서 그 행동을 지지하고, 심지어 미국이 외국의 지도자들을 암살하려고 시도했다는 것을 예로 들 정도로 전락했다. 어느 전제주의 국가라도 그런 일을 할 지식인 계급이 있다면 자신의 행동에 자부심을 느낄 것이다.

39 필자가 최근 미국의 이라크 공격에 관해 암시하는 내용은?
① 자기방어 조치로서 불가피했다.
② 지지받아야 하는 것은 말할 필요조차 없다(당연하다).
③ 전제국가들에서만 단지 환영받을 것이다.
④ 지식인들이 정당화할 것이다.

40 필자에 따르면 우리가 진입한 세상은 어떠한 유형인가?
① 거짓된 세상　　② 상상의 세상
③ 놀라운 세상　　④ 이상한 세상

41 윗글에서 암시하지 않는 것은?
① 미국은 최근에 전제국가가 되었다.
② 테러는 문명화된 국가에서 일어나서는 안 된다.
③ 미국의 공격을 정당화할 근거가 없다.
④ (미국의) 공격이 미국에서 상당히 지지받는다는 점은 놀랍다.

어구 **surreal** 현실적인, 이상한 **defy** 도전하다, ~하기 어렵다 **assassination** 암살 **torture** 고문 **aggression** 공격, 침략 **harshly** 거칠게, 엄하게 **matter** 문제가 되다, 중요하다 **laudable** 칭찬할 만한 **don** 명사. ~님, ~씨 **in the name of** ~의 이름으로, ~을 대신하여 **self-evident** 자명한 **commentary** 논평, 해설 **uphold** 지탱하다, 찬성하다, 지지하다 **descend** 내려가다, 계통을 잇다, 감소하다, 타락하다 **cite** 인용하다, 언급하다 **in justification of** ~을 정당화하여, ~을 변호하여 **totalitarian** 전체주의 **with regard to** ~에 관해 **unavoidable** 불가피한 **it goes without saying that** ~은 말할 필요조차 없다 **largely** 충분히, 대부분

해설 **39** 마지막 문장은 '가정법 과거(would be proud)'로서, 현재사실과 반대되는 가정을 밝힌 것이다. 따라서 최근 미국의 이라크 공격에 대한 환영은 전제국가에서나 가능하다는 내용이 옳다.

40 첫 문장의 내용이 설문의 단서가 되는데, '～ a world that is truly surreal ～'에서 surreal은 '비현실적인(very strange and difficult to understand, like something from a dream)'이란 뜻을 가지고 있다. 따라서 '이상한'이 옳다.

41 미국의 최근 이라크 공격은 전제주의 국가에서나 일어날 수 있다는 내용일 뿐, 실제로 미국이 전제주의 국가가 되었다는 내용은 아니다.

>>> **다음 글을 읽고 문제의 답을 고르시오.** [42~43]

A recent study reported in the journal Diabetologia may shed some light on one of the causes of type 1 diabetes. Some experts speculate that exposure to certain viruses may trigger type 1 diabetes in people who are genetically susceptible to diabetes. Such viruses may cause the immune system to mistakenly attack the pancreas and destroy cells that produce insulin.

In the largest study of its kind to date, a group of British researchers examined more than 4000 people under age 30 who were diagnosed with type 1 diabetes in Yorkshire, United Kingdom, between 1978 and 2002. The team discovered that new cases of type 1 diabetes occurred in batches within confined sections of Yorkshire, specifically among youths between 10 and 19. The study's findings suggest that perhaps a virus, which people encounter on an irregular basis, may be responsible for this serious autoimmune disease rather than consistent environmental factors such as diet.

42 What's the most appropriate title of this passage?

① Who Is Most Vulnerable to Diabetes Virus?
② Why Is Teens Exposed to Virus?
③ Virus Causing Type 1 Diabetes
④ Protect Your Pancreas from Destroying Insulin.
⑤ Don't be Exposed to Autoimmune Disease.

43 What cannot be inferred as to Type 1 diabetes from the passage?

① Pancreas' damage causes insulin not to be produced.
② Type 1 diabetes may be one of the autoimmune diseases.
③ Type 1 diabetes occurs because of irregular exposure to virus.
④ Type 1 diabetes is due to genetical factors.
⑤ Type 1 diabetes occurs mostly to adults.

해석 다이어비트로지아 저널을 통해 발표된 최근의 연구가 타입 1 당뇨의 원인들 중 하나를 일부 밝혀낸 것 같다. 몇몇 전문가들은 당뇨에 유전적으로 취약한 사람들이 어떤 바이러스에 노출이 되면 타입 1 당뇨에 걸릴 수 있다고 추정한다. 그 바이러스 때문에 면역 체계가 췌장을 공격하거나 인슐린을 만드는 세포를 파괴하는 실수를 범할 수 있다.

바이러스의 종류에 대한 현재까지 가장 폭넓은 연구 내용 중, 영국 연구가들은 영국 요크셔 지역에서 1978년부터 2002년까지 타입 1 당뇨에 걸린 30세 미만의 4,000명 이상의 사람들을 관찰했다. 그들은 새로운 타입 1 당뇨 질병이 요크셔의 제한 지역에 있는 10세에서 19세 사이의 어린아이들에게서 특히나 집단적으로 발생했다. 그 연구 결과는 다이어트와 같은 지속적인 환경 요소라기보다는 사람들이 불규칙적으로 접하게 되는 바이러스로 인해 이 자기 면역 질병이 발생한다고 주장하고 있다.

42 이 글의 제목은 무엇인가?

① 누가 당뇨 바이러스에 가장 취약한가?
② 왜 십대 아이들이 바이러스에 노출되는가?
③ 타입 1 당뇨를 유발하는 바이러스
④ 인슐린 파괴로부터 췌장으로 보호하시오.
⑤ 면역 질병에 노출되지 마시오.

43 타입1 당뇨에 관해 유추할 수 없는 내용은 무엇인가?

① 췌장의 손상으로 인슐린이 만들어지지 않는다.
② 타입 1 당뇨는 면역 질병들 중 하나인 것 같다.
③ 타입 1 당뇨는 바이러스에 불규칙적으로 노출되기 때문에 발생한다.
④ 타입 1 당뇨는 유전적인 요인에 기인한다.
⑤ 타입 1 당뇨는 대체로 성인들에게 발생한다.

어구 **shed light on** ～을 비추다; ～을 명백히 하다　**trigger** 야기하다; 방아쇠를 당기다　**be susceptible to** ～에 취약하다　**mistakenly** 실수로, 부주의하게　**pancreas** 췌장　**to date** 현재까지　**in batches** 여러 묶음으로　**be responsible for** ～의 원인이 되다, ～의 탓이 되다　**autoimmune disease** 자기 면역 질병

해설 **42** 가끔씩 노출되는 바이러스로 인해 당뇨가 어린아이들에게 발생할 수 있다는 내용을 전하는 것이 이 글의 주제가 된다.

43 타입 1 당뇨는 30세 미만의 아동들이 걸린 당뇨를 일컫는다. 윗글의 두 번째 단락에서 연구 대상 연령 또한 10세에서 19세 사이의 아이들이 집단적으로 걸렸다고 언급됐다.

Chapter 08 글의 감상

⇨ 본책 p.119

1 ①	2 ②	3 ④	4 ④	5 ③	6 ③	7 ③	8 ④	9 ②	10 ④
11 ①	12 ②	13 ④	14 ②	15 ③	16 ③	17 ④	18 ②	19 ①	20 ①
21 ②	22 ③	23 ②	24 ②	25 ④					

>>> **다음 글을 읽고 문제의 답을 고르시오.** [1~3]

Religion is an important part of any society's culture and can have a significant impact on business operations. McDonald's and Coca-Cola unfortunately offended Muslims by putting the Saudi Arabian flag on their packaging. The flag's design contains a passage from the Koran, and Muslims feel their Holy Writ should never be wadded up and thrown away. Consider the tragedies in Bosnia and the Middle east, where clashes between religious communities have hurt these economics. In Islamic countries, dawn-to-dusk fasting during the month of Ramadan causes workers' output to drop considerably. Also, the requirement to pray five times daily can affect output. For example, an American manager in Islamic Pakistan toured a new plant under his control in full operation. He went to his office to make some preliminary forecasts of production. As he was working, suddenly all the machinery in the plant stopped. He rushed out expecting a possible power failure and instead found his production workers on their prayer rugs. He returned to his office and proceeded to lower his production estimates.

1 **Why were the Muslims offended?**
① The packaging was thrown away.
② The packaging was kept because of the sacred Holy Writ.
③ The packaging had become worthless.
④ The packaging was too expensive.

2 **How does religion affect business according to the paragraph?**
① The Holy Writ must be commercialized.
② The Holy wars can devastate the economy.
③ The religious practices can affect power outages in plants.
④ Not being familar with the local religion can cause a foreign employer to underestimate production.

3 **Where would you find this paragraph?**
① Travel advisory   ② Tourist brochures
③ Terror watch   ④ Business texts

해석 종교는 어느 사회의 문화에 있어서 중요한 부분이며, 사업 활동에 상당한 영향을 미친다. 맥도날드와 코카콜라는 사우디아라비아 국기를 포장에 인쇄함으로써 불행하게도 회교도들을 화나게 했다. 국기의 디자인에는 코란의 한 문구가 포함되어 있고, 회교도들은 그들의 신성한 경전으로 물건을 포장하거나 버려져서는 안 된다고 느낀다. 종교 공동체들 간의 분쟁이 경제에 타격을 주었던 보스니아와 중동 간의 비극을 생각해 보라. 이슬람 국가에서 라마단의 달에 해가 뜰 때부터 해가 질 때의 금식은 노동자들의 생산량을 상당히 떨어뜨리게 한다. 또한 매일같이 다섯 번 기도해야 하는 의무도 생산에 영향을 미칠 수 있다. 한 예로 이슬람 국가인 파키스탄에 있는 미국인 관리자가 그가 관리하게 된 새 공장을 둘러보았다. 그 미국인은 예비적인 생산 예측을 하기 위해 사무실로 돌아갔다. 그가 일을 하고 있을 때, 갑자기 공장의 모든 기계들이 정지했다. 정전을 예상하고 뛰어 나갔지만 대신에 생산직 근로자들이 기도용 양탄자 위에서 있는 것을 보았다. 그는 사무실로 돌아와 그의 생산 견적의 비율을 낮추었다.

1 회교도들은 왜 화가 났었는가?
① 포장물이 버려졌다.
② 신성한 성서 때문에 포장물이 보관되었다.
③ 포장물이 가치가 없어졌다.
④ 포장물이 너무나 비쌌다.

2 종교가 사업에 어떻게 영향을 미치는가?
① 성서가 상업화될 수밖에 없다.
② 성전이 경제를 망칠 수 있다.
③ 종교적 관행이 공장의 정전에 영향을 미친다.
④ 지역 종교와 친숙하지 못하면 외국 고용주가 생산을 과소평가하게 될 수 있다.

3 이 글을 어디에서 발견할 수 있겠는가?
① 여행안내   ② 관광객 소책자
③ 테러 경계   ④ 사업 기사

어구 **significant** 상당한, 중요한   **unfortunately** 불행히   **offend** 화나게 하다   **flag** 국기   **packaging** 포장   **Holy Writ** 성서(절대적 권위가 있는 서적 또는 발언)   **wad up** 물건을 싸다   **throw away** 버리다   **tragedy** 비극   **clash** 충돌   **dawn-to-dusk** 해 뜰 때부터 해 질 때까지   **fasting** 금식   **considerably** 상당히   **plant** 공장   **preliminary** 예비적인   **forecast** 예상   **power failure** 정전   **prayer rug** 기도에 쓰이는 양탄자   **proceed** 진행되다, 계속되다   **sacred** 신성한(holy)   **worthless** 무가치한   **commercialize** 상업화하다   **devastate** 유린하다, 황폐화시키다   **underestimate** 과소평가하다

해설 **1** 회교도들에게는 사우디아라비아 국기가 신성한 대상인데, 코카콜라와 맥도날드 회사가 자신의 상품에 그 국기 모양을 인쇄하고, 아무렇게나 버려져서 분노를 하게 된 것이다.
2 보스니아와 중동 지역의 종교 전쟁이 경제에 타격을 입혔다고 설명되어 있다. 중동 지역에서 종교적 이유를 바탕으로 벌어지는 전쟁을 흔히 '성전'이라고 한다.
3 종교적인 면이 사업에 미치는 영향을 설명한 글이므로, '경제 관련 사업 기사'에 포함되었으리라 유추가 가능하다.

>>> 다음 글을 읽고 문제의 답을 고르시오. [4~5]

The eye accepted what the mind could not: a sudden burst of white and yellow fire, then white trails streaming up and out from the fireball to form a twisted Y against a pure heaven, and the metal turning to rags, dragging white ribbons into the ocean. A terrible beauty exploded like a primal event of physics—the birth of a universe; the death of a star; a fierce, enigmatic violence out of the blue. The mind recoiled in sheer surprise. Then it filled with horror.

4 The above passage can best be characterized as describing an explosion of ____________.

① a grenade
② a star
③ a cracker
④ a rocket
⑤ a balloon

5 Which is the writer's feeling about the accident?

① anger
② playfulness
③ shock
④ melancholy
⑤ frustration

해석 눈은 마음이 수용할 수 없는 것을 받아들였다. 하얗고 노란 불길의 갑작스러운 폭발이 일어난 후, 맑게 갠 하늘에 뒤틀어진 Y자 모양이 형성된 불덩어리에서 흘러나온 하얀 꼬리가 위로 올라가면서, 금속은 조각으로 변하고, 하얀 리본 모양의 연기를 바다 속으로 끌어갔다. 끔찍한 아름다움이 물리학 최초의 사건인 우주의 탄생, 별의 소멸, 갑작스러운 맹렬하고 불가사의한 격렬함처럼 폭발했다. 마음은 정말 놀라서 위축됐다. 그리고는 공포로 가득 찼다.

4 이 글은 어떠한 물체의 폭발을 묘사하는가?

① 수류탄
② 별
③ 크래커
④ 로켓
⑤ 풍선

5 사고에 대한 작가의 느낌은?

① 분노
② 농담
③ 충격
④ 우울함
⑤ 좌절

어구 **burst** 폭발 **trail** (발)자국, 흔적, 길게 늘어진 것 **stream** 흐르다, 흘러나오다 **fireball** 불덩이 **twisted** 뒤틀린 **drag A into B** A를 B로 끌어가다 **terrible** 무서운, 굉장한, 지독한 **primal** 최초의, 주요한, 근본의 **fierce** 흉포한, 맹렬한 **enigmatic** 수수께끼 같은 **out of the blue** 뜻밖에, 불시에 **recoil** 주춤하다, 되튀다 **sheer** 순전한, 얇은, (섞이지 않고) 순수한 **in sheer surprise** 너무 놀라서

해설 **4** 이 글은 로켓이 폭발하여, 파편 금속이 연기와 함께 바다로 떨어지는 과정을 리본이나 우주, 별에 비유하여 묘사한 글이다. 결정적인 단서는 fireball, the metal 등이 되겠다.
5 마지막 두 문장에서 '마음이 놀라고 공포로 가득 찼다'는 내용을 통해서 작가는 '충격'을 느꼈음을 알 수 있다.

People were sitting on the sidewalk in the dawn. They were like failed sectarian suicides. Others would come to help them. Within a year there were fires on the ridges, deranged chanting, and numberless deaths. The screams of the murdered. By day the dead impaled on spikes along the road. What had they done? Kurtz thought that in the history of the world it might even be that there was more punishment than crime but he took small comfort from it.

6 What is the overall tone of the paragraph?

① analytic
② persuasive
③ pessimistic
④ humorous

7 Which of the following CANNOT be inferred from the passage?

① Kurtz seems to feel sympathetic for the dead.
② Something happened and lots of people died.
③ Some miracle will come to save these people.
④ The world became barren after the accident.

해석 사람들이 새벽에 보도에 앉아 있었다. 그들은 실패한 분리파 자살자들 같았다. 다른 이들이 그들을 돕기 위해 오곤 했다. 1년 내에 산등성의 화재들, 정상이 아닌 외침 그리고 무수히 많은 사망자들이 있었다. 살해당하는 자들의 비명들이 있었다. 낮에는 길을 따라 죽은 자들이 말뚝에 박혔다. 그들은 무슨 짓을 했는가? 쿠르츠는 아마도 세계 역사에 범죄보다는 처벌이 더 많이 있었을 것이라고 생각했지만 그로부터 약간의 위안을 얻었을 뿐이다.

6 이 글의 전체 분위기는 어떠한가?
① 분석적인 ② 납득시키는
③ 비관적인 ④ 유머러스한

7 이 글을 통해 유추할 수 없는 내용은 무엇인가?
① 쿠르츠는 죽은 자들에 대해 동정심을 느끼는 것처럼 보인다.
② 무엇인가 발생하여 많은 사람들이 죽었다.
③ 어떤 기적이 이 사람들을 도울 것이다.
④ 세상이 사고 발생 후 척박해졌다.

어구 sidewalk 보도, 인도 dawn 새벽, 동 틀 녘; 여명 failed 실패로 끝난; 미수로 그친 sectarian 분파의, 종파의; 학파의; 당파심이 강한 ridge 산마루, 산등성이; 능선; 분수선 deranged 혼란된, 미친 chanting 노래, 멜로디, 구호, 성가 numberless 셀 수 없는(innumerable), 무수한 scream 외침 (소리), (공포·고통의) 절규, 비명 impale (뾰족한 것으로) 꿰찌르다, 꿰다; 말뚝에 꿰찌르는 형(刑)에 처하다 spike 긴 못(뾰족한 끝을 위나 밖으로 향하게 담 따위에 박는), 담장 못 it may be that S+V 아마도 ~인 것 같다 punishment 벌, 형벌, 처벌 take comfort from ~에서 위안을 구하다 analytic 분석적[해석적]인 persuasive 납득시킬 수 있는, 이르는 말을 듣는 pessimistic 비관적인, 염세적인 barren (땅이) 불모의, 메마른; 임신을 못하는; 효과가 없는

해설 6 화재와 주검, 비명과 말뚝에 처형당한 사람들 등에 대한 묘사를 통해 이 글의 분위기는 비관적인 것으로 느껴진다.
7 전반적으로 불행한 내용이 묘사됐을 뿐, 기적과 같은 긍정적인 내용은 전혀 등장하지 않았다.

"I didn't realize that we had got so far away," said Gladys, uneasily. "It is growing cooler," said Irma. She looked up at the sky. "I hope it isn't going to get windy now," she murmured. The girls put their strength into paddling, and the canoe skimmed across the darkening water. "There's a squall coming!" cried Gladys. A cold wind blew across the lake, and the waves slapped against the canoe. The girls paddled in strained, tense silence. Just as they rounded a curve in the lake a gust of wind hit the canoe, the waves flung it aside, and as it tipped, the two girls were thrown into the water. The canoe was tossed away from them by the waves.

해석 글래디스가 "나는 우리가 이렇게 멀리까지 온 것을 알지 못했어."라고 불안하게 말했다. "점점 추워지고 있어."라고 얼마가 말했다. 그녀는 하늘을 쳐다보았다. "나는 이제는 바람이 불지 않았으면 좋겠다."고 그녀가 투덜거렸다. 소녀들은 노를 젓는 데 힘을 기울였으며, 카누는 어두워지는 물을 따라 지나갔다. "저기 돌풍이 몰려오고 있어!" 글래디스가 소리쳤다. 차가운 바람이 호수를 따라 불었으며 파도가 카누를 향해 부딪혔다. 긴장되는 침묵이 흐르면서 소녀들은 노를 저었다. 그들이 호수의 굽은 곳을 막 돌았을 때, 거센 바람이 카누를 강타했고, 파도가 카누 옆으로 세게 돌진하여 카누를 뒤집어엎으면서 두 소녀는 물속으로 빠져 버렸다. 카누는 파도에 의해서 그들로부터 멀리 떠내려갔다.

8 윗글의 등장인물들의 심경 변화를 잘 나타낸 것은?

① calm → lonely
② anxious → disappointed
③ angry → regretful
④ worried → horrified
⑤ regretful → horrified

8 윗글의 등장인물들의 심경 변화를 잘 나타낸 것을 고르시오.

① 차분한 → 외로운
② 걱정스러운 → 실망한
③ 화가 난 → 후회하는
④ 걱정하는 → 겁에 질린
⑤ 후회하는 → 겁에 질린

어구 **far away** 멀리 떨어져 **uneasily** 불안하게 **windy** 바람이 센 **murmur** 불평을 하다, 투덜대다 **put strength into -ing** 힘을 써서 ~을 하다 **skim** (수면 등을) 스쳐 지나가다, 미끄러지듯 가다 **darkening** 어두워지는 **squall** 질풍, 돌풍 **paddle** 노를 젓다; 조용히 젓다 **strained** 긴장한, 긴장된 **tense** (신경·감정이) 긴장한; 긴박[절박]한 **round** 일주하다, (커브·모퉁이를) 돌다; 둥글게 하다 **curve** 만곡(부·물(物)) **gust** 돌풍, 일진의 바람, 질풍 **fling A aside** 내던지다; 무시하다, 물리치다 **tip** 기울다; 뒤집히다 **toss away** 내던지다

해설 추워지는 날씨와 카누를 강타하는 파도에 대해 소녀들은 처음에 걱정을 한 후, 파도가 카누를 강타하여 소녀들이 물속으로 빨려 들어갔기 때문에 이것은 비극으로 끝이 났다.

>>> 다음 글을 읽고 문제의 답을 고르시오 [9~10]

My musical director wasn't happy with the performance of one of our percussionists. Repeated attempts to get the drummer to improve failed. Finally, in front of the orchestra, the director said in frustration, "When a musician just can't handle his instrument, they take it away, give him two sticks and make him a drummer!"

A whisper was heard from the percussion section: "And if he can't handle that, they will take away one of his sticks and make him a conductor."

9 The above passage is ____________.

① informative
② funny
③ critical
④ suggestive
⑤ advisory

10 What the director said means ____________.

① he wouldn't conduct any longer
② the orchestra needs more members
③ the drum is the most important musical instrument
④ the drummer is the worst musician
⑤ the conductor is responsible for the orchestra

해석 음악 지휘자는 우리의 타악기 연주자 중 한 사람의 연주 때문에 기분이 나빠졌다. 그 드럼 연주자의 연주 실력을 향상시키려는 반복된 시도를 했으나 실패했다. 마침내, 지휘자는 오케스트라 앞에서 "어떤 연주자가 자신의 악기를 다룰 수 없을 때, 사람들은 그의 악기를 빼앗은 후 두 개의 스틱을 주고 드럼을 연주하게 할 것이다."라고 좌절하여 말했다.
속삭이는 소리가 타악기 섹션에서 들렸다. "그가 그 드럼을 연주할 수 없다면, 사람들은 그의 스틱 하나를 빼앗고 그를 지휘자로 만들 것이다."

9 윗글의 분위기는 어떠한가?

① 정보를 제공하는
② 익살맞은
③ 비평적인
④ 암시하는
⑤ 조언하는

10 지휘자가 의도한 바는 무엇인가?

① 지휘자가 더 이상 지휘할 수 없다.
② 오케스트라가 더 많은 연주자를 필요로 한다.
③ 드럼은 가장 중요한 연주악기이다.
④ 그 드럼 연주자는 최악의 연주가이다.
⑤ 지휘자는 그 오케스트라에 책임을 진다.

어구 **musical director** 음악 지휘자 **percussionist** 타악기 연주자 **get A to R** A에게 ~하도록 시키다 **handle** (손으로) 다루다; 처리하다; 대우하다 **take away** 치우다; 가져가다 **whisper** 속삭임; 속삭이다 **stick** 드럼 연주 스틱; 막대기 **conductor** 지휘자; 안내자; 차장

해설 **9** 지휘자가 지휘하는 오케스트라 연주자 중 드럼 연주자의 실력이 부족하여 앞으로도 계속 그런 부족한 면이 보인다면 다른 사람에게 맡기겠다고 했다. 그러나 연주자들 사이에서 그 실력이 부족한 사람의 실력이 향상되지 않는다면 지휘자를 시키겠다고 하는 것은 익살맞은 내용으로 보아야 한다.
10 드러머의 실력을 향상시키려는 노력이 반복되었어도 실패했다고 했으므로 그 드러머의 실력이 형편없음을 유추할 수 있다.

It is a ① _______________ sensation, this double-consciousness, this sense of always looking at one's self through the eyes of others, of measuring one's soul by the tape of a world that looks on in amused ② _______________ and pity. One ever feels his twoness—an America, a Negro; two souls, two thoughts, two unreconciled strivings.

The history of the American Negro is the history of this strife, this longing to merge his double self into a better and true self. In this merging he wishes neither of the older selves to be lost. He would not Africanize America, for America has too much to teach the world and Africa. He would not bleach his Negro soul in a flood of white Americanism, for he knows that Negro blood has a message for the world. He simply wishes to make it possible for a man to be both a Negro and an American, without being ③ _______________ and spat upon by his fellows, without having the doors of opportunity closed roughly in his face.

11 Which of the following best fits into ①, ②, and ③?

① peculiar - contempt - cursed
② odd - pathetic - disguised
③ obvious - woe - censured
④ appropriate - contempt - disclosed
⑤ naked - indignance - eschewed

12 The author thinks that Negroes should be treated as _______________.

① proteges
② the ordinary
③ the privileged
④ the execrable
⑤ condemned criminals

13 What is the tone of the above passage?

① critical
② depressing
③ informational
④ implying
⑤ ironical

해석 이것은 독특한 감정이다. 이러한 이중적인 의식, 언제나 자기 자신을 다른 사람들의 눈을 통해서 바라보고, 재미있다는 듯이 경멸과 동정 속에서 방관하는 세상의 줄자로 자신의 영혼을 재어 보는 이런 느낌 말이다. 미국 흑인은 항상 이중성을 느낀다. 즉 미국인이자 흑인이라는 의식과 두 개의 영혼, 두 개의 생각, 두 개의 상반되는 투쟁을.

미국 흑인의 역사는 바로 이런 투쟁, 자신의 이중적인 자아를 더 낫고 진실한 자아로 통합하려는 갈망의 역사이다. 이러한 통합에서 들은 과거의 자아들 가운데 그 어느 것도 상실하기를 바라지 않는다. 왜냐하면 미국은 세계와 아프리카에 가르쳐 줄 수 있는 것을 너무도 많이 갖고 있기 때문이다. 또한 그들은 자신의 흑인 영혼을 백인 미국 문화의 홍수 속에 바래게 하고 싶지도 않다. 왜냐하면 흑인의 존재가 세상에 전할 메시지가 있기 때문이다. 다만 그들이 바라는 것은 흑인이면서 미국인이 될 수 있고, 동료인간들로부터 저주와 침 뱉음을 당하지 않고, 기회의 문이 자신의 면전에서 난폭하게 닫히지 않는 것이다.

11 ①, ②, ③에 각각 들어갈 말은?
① 독특한 – 경멸 – 저주받은
② 이상한 – 슬픔 – 변장한
③ 분명한 – 슬픔 – 비난받은
④ 적절한 – 경멸 – 공개된
⑤ 노골적인 – 분노 – 피해진

12 작가는 흑인들이 어떻게 대우받아야 한다고 생각하는가?
① 피보호자
② 평범한 사람들
③ 특권자
④ 저주받은 사람들
⑤ 사형수

13 이 글의 분위기는?
① 비평적인
② 우울한
③ 정보 전달의
④ 함축적인
⑤ 아이러니컬한

어구 double-consciousness 이중의 의식 self 자아 look on 구경하다 amused 재미난 twoness 이중성, 이원성 unreconciled 조화되지 않는, 화해되지 않는 longing 갈망 merge A into B A를 B로 합치다 merging 결합 africanize 아프리카화 하다 bleach 희게 하다, 표백하다 spit 침을 뱉다 peculiar 특이한 contempt 경멸 cursed 저주받은 odd 이상한, 홀수의, 임시의 pathetic 구슬픈; 슬픔 disguised 변장한, 숨긴 woe 슬픔; 슬프다 censure 비난하다 disclose 공개하다 naked 있는 그대로의, 노골적인 indignance 분노 eschew 피하다, 삼가다 protege 피보호자 privileged 특권을 부여받은 execrable 저주스러운, 미운 depressing 우울한 informational 정보 전달의 implying 함축적인, 넌지시 비추는

해설 11 빈칸 ①은 바로 이어서 이중적인 인식이라 했으므로, '특이한'이 적절하며, 빈칸 ②는 앞의 내용을 이어 받아 '동정심'과 더불어서 '경멸감'이 나와야 특이한 감정이 될 것이다. 빈칸 ③은 spit(침을 뱉다)의 과거분사인 spat과 순접으로 and에 의해서 병치되기 위해서는 '저주받은'이란 말이 옳다.

12 작가는 흑인이 미국인이자 흑인으로 대우받고, 침 뱉음을 당하지도 않는 인간다운 그저 평범한 하나의 인격체로 흑인이 대우받기를 소망한다.

13 윗글은 작가가 이중적인 감정을 첫 단락부터 소개하면서 자신의 직접적인 감정을 노출하기보다는 자신의 감정을 은연중에 비추면서, 흑인들의 현실을 간접적으로 묘사한다. 따라서 함축적인 분위기를 띤다.

>>> **다음 글을 읽고 문제의 답을 고르시오.** [14~15]

A melon farmer had noticed that thieves were stealing his crop from the fields at night. Desperate to save what was left to sell at market, he put up a sign with a skull and cross-bones that read, "One of these melons is poisoned." Sure enough, for two nights not one melon was stolen. But after the third night, he noticed that his sign had been altered. It now read, "Two of these melons are poisoned."

14 Which is the best title for the above passage?

① Food Poisoning
② Outwitting
③ Melon Farmer
④ Fruit Stealing
⑤ Melon Harvest

15 In which section of newspapers or magazines do you expect this passage to appear?

① Editorial
② Advertisement
③ Humor
④ Economy
⑤ Domestic

해석 멜론을 재배하는 농부는 도둑들이 밤에 밭에서 멜론을 훔친다는 사실을 알게 되었다. 시장에 팔기 위해 남아 있는 것을 지키기 위해 필사적이었던 그는 "이 멜론 중에 하나에는 독이 들어 있다."라고 적힌 해적 표시를 세웠다. 정말로 이틀 동안 한 개의 멜론도 도둑맞지 않았다. 그러나 사흘 째 밤이 지난 후, 그는 자신이 세워 놓은 표시가 바뀌어 있음을 알았다. 표시판에는 "이 멜론 중 두 개에 독이 들어 있다."라고 쓰여 있었다.

14 이 글의 제목은?

① 식중독
② 의표를 찌르기
③ 멜론 농부
④ 과일 절도
⑤ 멜론 수확

15 어떠한 신문이나 잡지에서 이 글이 보일 수 있을 것이라 예측되는가?

① 신문 사설
② 광고
③ 유머
④ 경제
⑤ 자가 제품

어구 **notice** 알아채다 **steal** 훔치다 **crop** 농작물 **desperate to R** 사적으로 ~을 하는 **put up** 세우다 **skull and cross-bones** 해골 밑에 대퇴골(大腿骨)을 열 자로 짝 지은 그림[죽음의 상징; 해적기나 독약 병의 표지] **read** ~라고 씌어(져) 있다 **poison** 독을 넣다; 독 **sure enough** 정말로, 참으로, 사실상 **alter** 바꾸다 **food poisoning** 식중독 **outwit** ~의 의표를 찌르다, 속이다 **editorial** 신문 사설, 논설 **domestic** 국산품, 자가 제품; 국내의, 가정의, 사육되어 길든

해설 **14** 농부의 거짓 위협에 속지 않고, 오히려 그 농부의 의도를 알고서 농부가 세워 놓은 위협 표시판에 도둑이 장난을 친 것이므로 의표를 찔렀다는 표현이 제목으로서 합당하다.

15 유머 관련 잡지나 책에서 이러한 글이 등장할 것이다.

>>> **다음 글을 읽고 문제의 답을 고르시오.** [16~19]

I once had the misperception that those who are educated in disciplines such as political science, public policy, or pre-law are more likely to be prepared for a graduate education in law than most other students. Now I believe that a student coming from a more (가)nontraditional background can contribute in many ways to society as a lawyer.

In a world where technology is the dominant means of progress and is advancing at such a breakneck pace, it can be a great advantage to society to have knowledgable people working with laws (나)concern technology. I not only believe that I am qualified to perform (다)this service to society as a lawyer, but I am convinced that USC law school possesses the quality of education and diversity in student body that can best help me fulfill these goals.

해석 나는 한때 정치학, 공공 정책, 혹은 법학부와 같은 분야에서 교육받은 사람들이 대부분의 다른 학생들보다 법학 대학원에서 더 교육을 잘 받을 준비가 되어 있다는 잘못된 생각을 한 적이 있었다. 이제 나는 관련 전공 출신이 아닌 학생이 많은 면에 있어서 변호사로서 사회에 더욱 이바지할 수 있다고 믿는다.

기술이 발전의 궁극적인 수단이며 가파른 속도로 발전하고 있는 세상에서, 기술 관련법에 종사하는 유식한 인재들을 보유하고 있다는 것은 사회에 커다란 이익이 될 수 있다. 나는 내가 변호사로서 사회에 이 서비스를 수행할 자격이 있다고 믿을 뿐만 아니라, USC 로스쿨이 내가 이 목표들을 성취하도록 가장 도움을 잘 줄 수 있도록 학생 전체의 교육과 다양성의 가치를 확보하고 있다고 믿는다.

16 The above passage is a part of

____________.

① a chronological report on technological advance
② a critical essay on the law school
③ a graduate admission essay
④ an itinerary column
⑤ jurisdictional statement

17 What field would belong to the "nontraditional background" in (가)?

① political science
② social science
③ public administration
④ computer science
⑤ pre-law

18 Which one is the most appropriate form for "concern" in (나)?

① concern
② concerning
③ concerned
④ to concern
⑤ be concerned

19 What would "this service" in (다) mean?

① to practice legal service in the field of technology
② to take part in scientific progress
③ to help those who need free legal aid
④ to influence the reform of law school
⑤ to assist the lawyers who need technical knowledge

16 이 글은 어떠한 글의 한 부분이 되겠는가?

① 기술 발전에 대한 연대기적 보고서
② 로스쿨에 대한 비평 에세이
③ 대학원 입학 에세이
④ 여행 칼럼
⑤ 판결 성명

17 (가) '비전통 분야'에 속하는 영역은 무엇인가?

① 정치학
② 사회학
③ 공공 행정
④ 컴퓨터 과학
⑤ 법학부

18 (나) 'concern'의 올바른 태 전환은?

19 (다) '이 서비스'가 의미하는 것은 무엇이겠는가?

① 기술 분야의 법률 서비스를 하는 것
② 과학 발전에 참여하는 것
③ 무료 법률 지원을 필요로 하는 이들을 돕는 것
④ 로스쿨의 개혁에 영향을 미치는 것
⑤ 기술적 지식을 필요로 하는 변호사를 조력하는 것

어구 misperception 오해, 잘못된 생각 be educated in ~의 교육을 받다 discipline 학과, 분야, 처벌, 훈련 pre-law 법학부(law school) 입학 준비(의) be prepared for ~의 준비가 되어 있다 graduate education 대학원 교육 come from ~ 출신이다, ~로부터 유래하다 nontraditional 비전통적인 contribute to ~에 기여·이바지하다 breakneck 가파른, 위험한 work with ~에 종사하다 be qualified to R ~할 자격이 있다 fulfill 이행하다, 성취하다 chronological 연대기적 itinerary 여행 jurisdictional 재판의, 사법부의, 판결의 concerning ~에 관하여 free legal aid 무료 법률 지원

해설 **16** 이 글은 대학 학부에서 법학, 정치학, 공공정책을 전공하지 않은 학생이 대학 졸업 후, 로스쿨에 가서 기술 관련법 전문 변호사가 되겠다는 자신의 계획을 대학원 당국에 제출하는 로스쿨 입학 신청 에세이로 볼 수 있다.

17 political science(정치학), social science(사회학), public administration(공공행정), pre-law(법학부)는 모두 law-school에 진학하기 위한 전통적인 분야의 속성을 가진 학문들이지만, '컴퓨터 과학'은 직접적으로 연관된 학문은 아니다. 작가는 본인의 컴퓨터 과학 전공을 살려서 그 분야에 맞는 전문 변호사가 되겠다는 계획이다.

18 concerning은 '~에 관하여'라는 뜻을 가진 '전치사'이다. 따라서 '기술에 관한(기술관련) 법'이라는 내용이 가장 옳다.

19 기술에 관해 전공을 한 필자 자신이 법률가가 될 자격이 있다는 내용은 결국 기술 분야의 법률 서비스를 한다는 내용이 되는 것이다.

>>> 다음 글을 읽고 문제의 답을 고르시오. [20~21]

Compulsory schooling was begun in the United States in the 19th century as a way of transmitting and maintaining Anglo-American culture and language. Educators believed that proficiency in two languages was not passionate, so educational policymakers declared that students should ______________. Also, the ability to speak English was made a condition for American citizenship in 1906, and in 1915 and English-literacy requirement was added. The justification provided for these measures was a peculiar doctrine about the connection between language and political thought, which held that speaking a foreign language was inimical to grasping the fundamental concepts of democratic society.

20 윗글의 어조로 가장 적절한 것은?

① Critical
② Factual
③ Humorous
④ Pessimistic
⑤ Ambitious

21 빈칸에 들어갈 말로 가장 적절한 것은?

① not speak English
② learn English only
③ learn two languages
④ go to public schools
⑤ use their native tongue

해석 의무적으로 받는 학교 교육은 미국 사람들의 문화와 언어를 전하고 유지하고자 19세기 미국에서 시작됐다. 교육자들은 두 언어에 능숙한 것이 가능하지 않다고 생각하며, 교육 정책 입안자들은 학생들이 영어만 공부해야 한다고 공표를 했었다. 게다가 1906년에 영어를 구사하는 능력이 미국 국적을 갖기 위한 조건이 됐으며, 1915년에 영어를 읽고 쓸 수 있는 조건이 추가됐다. 이러한 조치들을 위해 제공된 정당화가 언어와 정치사상 간의 관계에 대한 특이한 사상이었고, 이는 외국어를 구사하는 것이 민주사회의 기본적인 개념들을 이해하는 것에 해로운 것이라고 판단했다.

20 윗글의 어조로 가장 적절한 것은?

① 비평적인   ② 사실적인
③ 유머러스한   ④ 비관적인
⑤ 화려한

21 빈칸에 들어갈 말로 가장 적절한 것은?

① 영어를 구사하지 않아야 한다.
② 영어만 공부해야 한다.
③ 두 개의 언어를 배워야만 한다.
④ 국립 학교로 가야만 한다.
⑤ 모국어를 이용해야만 한다.

어구 compulsory 의무적인 schooling 학교 교육 transmit 전하다, 이송하다, 전파하다 maintain 지키다, 유지하다 Anglo-American 영국계 미국인의 proficiency 능숙함 policymaker 정책 입안자 citizenship 시민권 literacy 읽고 쓰는 능력, 교양 requirement 필요조건, 자격 peculiar 특이한 doctrine 교의, 주의, 사상, 정책 hold 생각하다, 판단하다 inimical 적대적인, 해로운 grasp 이해하다, 잡다 fundamental 근본적인 pessimistic 비관적인 ambitious (문체가) 화려한, 야망이 가득한 native tongue 모국어

해설 20 마지막 문장에서 미국 교육 정책 입안자들의 조치가 '별난 조치'가 '정당화'로 된다고 했으므로 이는 간접적으로 비판한다고 볼 수 있다.

21 앞의 주절에서 두 개 언어의 유창함이 가능하지 못하다고 했으므로 한 개의 언어(영어만)를 공부해야 한다는 논리가 적합하다.

In a large metropolitan airport, that is, an air terminal at the edge of a major city, it is not unusual to have many landings and take-offs during a 24-hour period. The heavy air traffic is under the control of a group of people known as air traffic controllers, who direct the flow of air traffic into and out of the airport. The air traffic control group works in the control tower, which is located at the highest point in the airport terminal complex, permitting the controllers to have maximum vision of all the aircraft arriving and departing the airport. When the weather limits the visibility around the runways, many computerized navigational aids are used to permit a safe landing. All of the procedures used for handling traffic under good and poor weather conditions are established by a governmental aviation administration under the department of transportation.

22 Under poor weather conditions an airport will

_____________.

① postpone all flights
② plan emergency landings only
③ substitute the judgment of machines for that of men and women
④ turn on all lights
⑤ divert all flights

23 The tone of the passage is best described as

_____________.

① argumentative
② factual
③ emotional
④ biased
⑤ sarcastic

해석 대도시 외곽에 있는 공항에서 24시간 계속해서 이착륙이 이루어지는 것은 놀랄 일이 아니다. 복잡한 비행기들은 항공 관제사로 알려진 일련의 사람들이 통제를 하는 것이며 이들은 항공기들의 공항 진입과 퇴장을 하게 해 준다. 항공관제 단체는 관제탑에서 일을 하며 이 탑은 관제사들이 공항에 도착 혹은 출발을 하게 되는 모든 비행기들을 최대한 잘 볼 수 있게끔 하기 위해 공항 터미널의 가장 높은 곳에 위치해 있다. 날씨가 활주로의 시야를 가리게 되면 많은 전산화된 항법 보조장치들이 안전한 착륙을 위해 가동된다. 기상 조건이 좋고 나쁨에 따라서 교통을 통제하기 위해 사용되는 모든 단계들은 수송부의 관리에 의해 정해지게 된다.

22 좋지 못한 기상 조건 하에서 공항은 어떻게 하는가?
① 모든 비행을 연기한다.
② 비상 착륙만을 계획한다.
③ 기계의 판단으로 인간의 판단을 대체시킨다.
④ 모든 전등을 켠다.
⑤ 모든 비행을 전환시킨다.

23 이 글의 분위기는?
① 논쟁적인   ② 사실적인
③ 감정적인   ④ 편견에 치우친
⑤ 냉소적인

어구 that is 즉, 다시 말하자면 air terminal 공항 edge 외각, 테두리, 끝, 가장자리 landing 착륙 take-off 이륙 be under the control of ~을 통제하다 known as ~으로 알려진 air traffic controller 항공관제사 direct A into B A를 B로 안내하다 direct A out of B A를 B로부터 안내하다 control tower 관제탑 complex 단지, 복합건물 aircraft 항공기 runway 활주로 navigation aids 항법 보조장치 aviation administration 항공청 postpone 연기하다 emergency landing 비상착륙 substitute A for B A로 B를 대체하다 turn on ~을 켜다 divert 전환시키다 biased 편견에 사로잡힌 sarcastic 냉소적인

해설 22 기상조건이 악화될 때에는 항법 보조장치를 작동한다고 했으므로 이를 재진술한 ③이 옳다.
23 공항의 비행기 이착륙에 관해서 객관적인 사실을 바탕으로 설명해 준 글이다.

Journalism tends to focus on the poor when the poor make news, usually dramatic news like a tenement fire or a march on Washington. But the poor are poor all the time. It is not journalism's ordinary business to deal with the unstartling normalities of life. Reporters need a story, something shapely and elegant. Poverty is disorderly, anticlimactic and endless. If one wants truth about the poor, one must look ① "where the ball is" not in a ball game.

24 As for the role of journalism in revealing the truth, the author is ___________.

① supportive
② critical
③ enthusiastic
④ neither critical nor supportive
⑤ critical as well as supportive

25 The one that is NOT related to the underlined "where the ball is" in ① is ___________.

① something shapely and elegant
② something climactic
③ celebrities
④ daily routines
⑤ a tenement fire

해석 셋방의 화제나 워싱턴의 시가행진과 같은 극적인 사건의 주인공들이 가난한 사람들일 때, 언론은 (사건보다는) 가난한 사람들에게 초점을 맞추게 되는 경향이 있다. 그러나 가난한 사람들은 언제나 가난하다. 놀랍지 않은 인생사의 평범한 것들을 다루는 것은 언론의 평상 업무가 아니다. 취재 기자는 날카롭고 우아한 것이 될 수 있는 이야기를 필요로 한다. 가난이란 무질서하고 클라이맥스가 없으며, 또 끝이 나지 않는 것이다. 만일 누군가가 가난한 사람들에 대한 진실을 알기 원한다면, 상황이 아니라 그 상황이 어디에 있는지를 보아야만 한다.

24 진실을 알리는 언론의 역할에 관해 필자는 어떠한 견해를 보이는가?

① 지지하는
② 비판하는
③ 열정적인
④ 비평적이지도 지지하지도 않는
⑤ 지지할 뿐만 아니라 비판적인

25 ① "공이 어디에 있는지"라는 표현과 관련 없는 내용은?

① 볼품 있고 우아한 것　　　　② 클라이맥스가 있는 것
③ 저명인사들　　　　　　　　④ 일과들
⑤ 셋방 화제

어구 **focus on** ~에 초점을 맞추다　**dramatic** 극적인　**tenement** 셋방, 집　**deal with** 다루다, 취급하다, 거래하다　**unstartling** 놀랍지 않은　**normality** 평범함　**shapely** 날카롭게　**elegant** 우아한　**poverty** 가난　**disorderly** 무질서한　**anticlimactic** 클라이맥스가 없는, 어처구니없는 결말의, 용두사미의　**ball game** [미국 속어] 상황, 사태, 야구, 소프트볼, 흥미의 중심, 경쟁 활동　**as for** ~에 관해　**reveal** 폭로하다, 공개하다　**enthusiastic** 열정적인　**celebrity** 저명인사　**daily routine** 일과

해설 **24** 마지막 문장에서 '공놀이에서가 아니라(사건이 일어나는 현실이 아니라) 공이 어디 있는지를(언론에서 뉴스거리로 다루는 상황을) 보아야만 한다'는 내용을 통해서, 비유적으로 언론이 알려주는 기사 내용에 대해 간접적으로 비판한다고 유추가 가능하다.

25 이 글에서 ball game은 '상황'이라는 뜻의 미국 속어이다. 이 문장에서 상황이라 함은 언론에서 다루는 주된 내용을 말한다. 그렇다면 상황이 존재하는 장소 또한 언론이 될 것이며, 언론에서 다루는 내용은 '우아하고 볼품 있는 내용, 클라이맥스가 있는 내용, 저명인사, 셋방 화제'는 모두 기삿거리에 해당되지만, 가난한 이들의 그저 평범한 '일상생활'은 해당되지 않는다.

Chapter 09 순서 배열 · 문장 삭제 · 문장 삽입

⇨ 본책 p.130

1 ③ **2** ② **3** ③ **4** ④ **5** ② **6** ⑤ **7** ② **8** ④ **9** ④ **10** ④
11 ② **12** ②

---

1 Rearrange the following sentences to make a coherent paragraph.

> A. One of these was Albert Einstein.
>
> B. There have been only a few scientists whose work has changed man's total view of the world.
>
> C. These theories dealt with everything from the inside of an atom to the farthest regions of the universe.
>
> D. During the first half of this century Einstein set forth a number of theories about the physical world.

① D - C - B - A   ② B - D - C - A
③ B - A - D - C   ④ B - D - A - C
⑤ A - B - D - C

해석 B. 연구를 통해 인간이 세상을 바라보는 관점을 바꾸어 놓은 과학자는 정말 소수였다.
A. 이 중에 아인슈타인이 있었다.
D. 20세기 전반기에 아인슈타인은 물질 세상에 관한 수많은 이론을 정립했다.
C. 이 이론들은 원자의 내면에서부터 우주의 가장 멀리 있는 곳까지 모든 것을 다루었다.

어구 **deal with** 다루다, 취급하다, 처리하다 **atom** 원자 **farthest** 가장 멀리 떨어진 **set forth** 정립하다 **a number of** 수많은

해설 B에서 과학자라는 포괄적인 집단을 설명하고 A로 이어져 그 예로서 아인슈타인을 소개하며 D에서 아인슈타인의 업적을 일반적으로 설명한 후, C에서 그 업적의 구체적인 예를 들어 준다.

---

2 Rearrange the following sentences to make a coherent paragraph.

> A. There is a big difference between a liberal and a reactionary.
>
> B. On the other hand, a person may look back or want to return to the way things used to be.
>
> C. This person doesn't like progress and resents change.
>
> D. The person who favors new ideas, tries to change, and looks for new ways is freer or more liberated.

① D - B - A - C   ② A - D - B - C
③ A - C - B - D   ④ D - C - B - A
⑤ A - C - D - B

해석 A. 자유주의자와 보수주의자 사이에는 큰 차이가 있다.
D. 새로운 생각을 즐기고 변화하기 위해 노력하고 새로운 방법들을 찾는 사람은 더 자유롭거나 더 개방적인 사람이다.
B. 그러나 어떤 이는 뒤를 돌아보거나 예전에 있었던 방법들로 돌아가려 할 수도 있다.
C. 이 사람은 진보를 좋아하지 않으며, 변화에 분노한다.

어구 **liberal** 자유주의자, 자유당원; 자유주의의 **reactionary** 보수주의자, 반동주의자; 반동주의의 **look back** 되돌아보다 **used to R** ～하곤 했었다 **resent** 분노하다 **liberated** 자유로운, 해방된

해설 A에서 자유주의자와 보수주의자 간의 차이점이 있다는 일반화된 설명을 한 이후 D에서 먼저 자유주의자에 관한 특징을 설명한 후, B에서 상반되는 보수주의자에 대한 설명을 하면서, C에서 보수주의자에 대한 특징을 추가적으로 설명하는 내용이다.

3 다음 주어진 문장에 이어질 글의 순서로 가장 적합한 것은?

Although industrial countries have made great advances in health care, today their health care systems are experiencing some serious problems.

가. In the United States, for example, nearly $2 billion is spent every day for healthy care, and this amount is increasing at an annual rate of 12 percent.

나. As a result of these increasing costs, access to good health care is being reduced rather than expanded.

다. By far the most urgent of these problems is financial: medical costs are rising faster than prices in most other areas of the economy.

① 가 – 나 – 다
② 가 – 다 – 나
③ 다 – 가 – 나
④ 다 – 나 – 가

해석 비록 산업(선진)국가들이 의료 분야에서 상당한 진전을 보여 왔을지라도, 오늘날 그들의 의료제도는 몇 가지의 심각한 문제들을 겪고 있다. 다. 이런 문제점들 중 단연 가장 시급한 문제는 재정이다. 즉 의료비용이 국가의 다른 분야들 보다 더 빨리 오르고 있다. 가. 예를 들어 미국에서는 매일 거의 20억 달러가 의료에 쓰이며 이 액수는 연간 12%의 속도로 증가하고 있다. 나. 이러한 증가하는 비용 때문에, 질 좋은 의료를 이용하는 것은 확대되기보다 줄어들고 있다.

어구 **industrial** 산업의   **make a advance** 발전을 하다   **health care system** 의료체계   **as a result of** ~의 결과로서   **by far** 정말로, 단연코   **economy** 경기; 국가; 절약

해설 주어진 문장의 마지막에 나온 some serious problems에 관한 내용이 '다'의 these problems로 이어지고 있으며 '다'의 'medical costs are rising faster than'의 대표적 사례가 '가'에 나오며 그 결과 '나'에서 제시하는 현상이 벌어지고 있다는 순서가 가장 적절하다. 그리고 주로 마지막 단계에서는 'as a result (of), today, however' 등이 많다는 점도 유념하자.

4 글의 흐름상 가장 자연스럽게 배열한 것은?

(1) Knowledge is the stuff from which new ideas are made.

(2) Their knowledge just sat in their crania because they didn't think about what they knew in any new ways.

(3) We've all known people who knew lots of facts and nothing creative happened.

(4) Nonetheless, knowledge alone won't make a person creative.

(5) The real key to being creative lies in what you do with your knowledge.

① (1) - (2) - (3) - (4) - (5)
② (1) - (3) - (4) - (2) - (5)
③ (1) - (3) - (2) - (4) - (5)
④ (1) - (4) - (3) - (2) - (5)
⑤ (1) - (4) - (2) - (3) - (5)

해석 (1) 새로운 생각들이 만들어지면 이를 지식이라고 할 수 있다. (4) 그럼에도 불구하고, 지식만으로는 사람을 창의적이 되게 해 주지는 않는다. (3) 우리는 모두 사실을 많이 알기는 하지만 결코 창의적인 일이 일어난 적이 없던 사람들을 알고 있다. (2) 그들의 지식은 그저 그들의 뇌 속에 자리 잡고 있는데, 그것은 그들이 알고 있던 내용들을 어떤 새로운 방법으로도 생각하지 못했기 때문이다. (5) 창의적이 될 수 있는 진정한 열쇠는 당신이 가진 지식으로 당신이 행하는 일에 달려 있는 것이다.

어구 **crania** cranium(두개, 두개골)의 복수

해설 지식의 의의(일반적 진술문) (1) → 지식 그 자체만으로의 한계 (4) → 그러한 실례 (3) → 그 이유 (2) → 참된 의미에서의 지식 (5). (1)을 가장 먼저 제시한 사항을 이용하되 (4)까지는 대명사, 지시어 등이 전혀 사용되고 있지 않다는 점에 주목한다. (3)에서는 people에 주목하고 이를 받아 주는 대명사(they)와 소유격(their)이 (2)에서 사용되고 있으며 마지막 결론에 해당하는 내용이 (5)가 됨을 확인한다.

5 Which of the following is the most appropriate location for the following sentence?

> Nonetheless, telecommuting could one day be the norm, not the exception.

It seems that more of us will be telecommuting. (A) Some jobs clearly just can't be performed remotely; a hospital nurse, for example, won't ever be able to work from home, while a hospital accountant could. (B) A report by the Reason Foundation found that telecommuters outnumbered actual mass-transit commuters in 27 of the 50 largest U.S. metropolitan areas. (C) Two thirds of Fortune 1,000 companies now have telecommuting programs, while 60 percent of companies that don't have such programs are considering the idea. (D) As wireless and other telecommunications technologies become more sophisticated, the advantages of at-home employment will only grow. (E) It absolutely is the wave of the future.

① (A)　② (B)　③ (C)　④ (D)　⑤ (E)

해석 우리들은 보다 많이 재택근무를 하게 될 것 같다. (A) 일부 직업들은 분명 그저 멀리 떨어져 있어서는 수행할 수 없는 것들이다; 예를 들어, 병원의 간호사는 웬만해선 집에서 일할 수는 없을 것이나, 병원 회계원은 그렇게 하는 것이 가능할 것이다. (B) (그럼에도, 재택근무는 언젠가는 예외가 아닌 표준이 될 수 있다.) 리즌 재단(Reason Foundation)에서 내놓은 한 보고서는 미국의 50대 대도시 권역 중 27개의 지역에서 재택근무자들이 실제 대중교통을 이용하는 통근자들의 수를 앞섰다는 사실을 알아냈다. (C) 포춘(Fortune)지 선정 1000대 기업 중 2/3는 현재 재택근무 프로그램을 두고 있는 한편 그러한 프로그램이 없는 기업들의 60%가 이러한 아이디어를 고려하고 있다. (D) 무선 및 기타 전기통신기술이 더욱 정교해(세련되어)짐에 따라, 재택 고용의 이점들이 늘어날 수밖에 없을 것이다. (E) 이것은 절대적인 미래의 흐름이다.

어구 **remotely** 멀리 떨어져서　**mass-transit** 대량 수송 수단　**outnumber** ~보다 수가 많아지다　**sophisticated** 복잡한, 세련된

해설 현재까지의 상황으로는 일정한 한계가 있지 않을까 할 수 있지만 매우 보편화되어 가고 있는 실상을 (B) 다음에서 열거하고 있다.

---

(1) These might include a house or houses, land, antiques, or other valuable goods.

(2) An interesting historical example of a wealth tax from England is the Window Tax that was in force from 1696 to 1857.

(3) Many countries use wealth tax base. Taxes on wealth can take many forms, but they usually involve taxing a person's possessions.

(4) That is why some old English houses have bricked-up windows, which can still be seen.

(5) A person was taxed if he had over ten windows in his house.

6 Put the above sentences in the best order.

① (2) - (3) - (1) - (5) - (4)　② (2) - (1) - (3) - (5) - (4)
③ (3) - (1) - (2) - (4) - (5)　④ (2) - (5) - (4) - (1) - (3)
⑤ (3) - (1) - (2) - (5) - (4)

7 Why did some English people have their windows bricked-up?

① Because they did not want to pay income tax.
② Because they wanted to pay less tax.
③ Because they wanted to protect their houses from burglary.
④ Because they did not want to allow tax-officials to enter their houses.
⑤ Because their windows were broken.

해석 (3) 많은 나라들이 재산세를 기본적으로 운용하고 있다. 재산세는 많은 형태를 취하고 있지만, 그것들은 대개 개인 소유의 재산에 세금이 부과되는 것과 연관되어져 있다. (1) 이러한 것에는 한 개의 집 혹은 여러 개의 집, 땅, 골동품 혹은 다른 귀중품들이 포함될 수 있다. (2) 영국에서의 재산세에 관한 흥미로운 역사적인 한 예는 1696년부터 1857년까지 시행되었던 창문세이다. (5) 집에 10개 이상의 창문이 있다면 과세가 되었었다. (4) 이 때문에 몇몇 오래된 영국의 집들은 창문을 벽돌로 막아 놓았으며, 이런 집들을 지금도 볼 수 있다.

6 순서가 올바른 것은?

7 영국 사람들이 창문을 벽돌로 막은 이유는 무엇인가?
① 소득세를 지불하기를 원하지 않았기 때문에
② 세금을 적게 지불하기를 원했기 때문에
③ 강도 행위로부터 집을 보호하려 했기 때문에
④ 세무 공무원이 집에 오는 것을 원하지 않았기 때문에
⑤ 창문이 깨지기를 원하지 않았기 때문에

어구 **wealth tax** 재산세　**tax** ~에 세금을 부과하다　**possessions** 재산, 소유물　**antique** 골동품　**in force** 유효하여, 시행 중인　**that is why** 그리하여　**brick up** 벽돌로 막다

해설 **6** 가장 일반적인 내용이 (3), 그것의 세부적인 사항이 (1)이다. (2)는 특수한 예의 시작에 해당되며, (4)는 (5)의 이유이므로 적절한 순서로 배열된 것은 보기 ⑤이다.
7 창문이 많으면 세금 또한 높아졌기 때문에 창문의 개수가 적어 보이게 하기 위해 벽돌로 막았음을 유추가 가능하다.

8 Choose the place that the given sentence is to be inserted to in the following article.

> For example, if the mother eats cabbage or garlic, many babies will refuse her milk.

> Most doctors now agree that mother's milk is better for babies than artificial milk. [A] However, artificial milk has one advantage. It always tastes the same for the baby. [B] Mother's milk, on the other hand, can change flavor. [C] Certain foods may give the milk a strange taste. [D] Doctors have also discovered that babies may also refuse their mothers' milk after she has exercised a lot, After exercise, in fact, the milk may have an unpleasant, sour taste.

① [A]　　　② [B]
③ [C]　　　④ [D]

해석 대부분의 의사들이 모유가 인공 분유보다 더 질이 뛰어나다는 것에 동의를 한다. [A] 그러나 인공 분유는 장점이 한 가지 있다. 아기에게 항상 동일한 맛을 제공한다는 점이다. [B] 반면 모유는 맛이 변할 수 있다. [C] 어떤 음식들은 모유에 이상한 맛을 줄 수 있다. [D] (예컨대 엄마가 양배추나 마늘을 먹는다면 아기들은 모유를 싫어할 것이다.) 또한 의사들은 아이들이 어머니가 운동한 후에 모유를 거부한다는 것을 밝혀냈는데, 실제로 어머니가 운동을 한 이후에 모유의 맛은 불쾌하고 신맛이 날 수도 있기 때문이다.

어구 cabbage 양배추　garlic 마늘　artificial milk 인공 분유　flavor 맛, 향미　a lot 많이　unpleasant 불쾌한

해설 제시문이 '양배추와 마늘이 이유가 되어 아기들이 모유를 싫어하는 예를 든 것'이므로, 그에 합당한 일반화된 지문 뒤에 위치해야 한다.

9 Choose the place that the given sentence is to be inserted to in the following article.

> However, the people who enjoy others' private lives do not always like it when people watch them!

> [A] Most people agree that it is fun to watch people. [B] Many people also enjoy learning about the rich and the famous. They spend millions of dollars yearly on newspapers and magazines that tell about the private lives of rich and famous people. [C] This information makes these famous people real to the readers. [D] In other words, many who enjoy stealing glance at others worry about their right to a private life.

① [A]　　　② [B]
③ [C]　　　④ [D]

해석 [A] 사람들을 지켜보는 일이 재미있다는 데 거의 대부분이 동의를 한다. [B] 많은 사람들은 또한, 부자와 유명 인사들에 대해 아는 것을 즐긴다. 그들은 부유하고 유명한 사람들의 사생활에 대해 말해 주는 신문이나 잡지들에 해마다 수백만 달러를 소비한다. [C] 이러한 정보가 유명한 사람들을 독자들이 좀 더 현실적으로 느낄 수 있도록 만들어 준다. [D] 하지만 타인들의 사생활을 즐기는 사람들도, 다른 사람들이 그들을 지켜볼 때는 그리 즐거워하지 않는다. 다시 말하자면, 다른 사람들을 몰래 훔쳐보는 것을 즐기는 많은 사람들이, 사생활에 대한 자신들의 권리는 도리어 걱정하는 것이다.

어구 in other words 다시 말하자면　steal glance at ~을 슬쩍 훔쳐보다

해설 다른 사람들이 자신을 관찰하는 것을 좋아하지 않는다는 내용과 마지막 문장인 혼자 있을 권리가 있다는 내용과 이어진다.

On the other hand, some scientist argue that the extinction issue is being exaggerated, and that people are "crying wolf" by depicting the loss of species as more alarming than it really is.

[A] In addition, many people point to the fact that the world is already lacking in resources, food, and adequate health care. [B] Concerned more with economic survival, they ask whether it is, in fact, realistic to make a fuss over species that may become extinct many years from now, when people have families to feed tomorrow.

[C] They see saving endangered species as somewhat contradictory as it interferes with of opposes human goals. [D] These people disagree with a law that puts man's own survival above the continuance of lower forms of life.

① [A] 　② [B]
③ [C] 　④ [D]

해석 다른 한편으로는 몇몇 과학자들이 멸종의 문제가 과장되고 있다고 주장하며, 사람들이 실제보다 멸종을 훨씬 더 놀라운 것으로 설명함으로써 거짓 경고를 하고 있다고 주장한다.
[A] 게다가 많은 이들이 세상에는 이미 자원과 식량, 적절한 의료 서비스가 부족한 상태라고 지적한다. [B] 그들은 경제적 생존에 더 관심이 있기 때문에 당장 내일 부양해야 할 가족이 있는 이 시점에 수년 뒤에 멸종할 수 있는 종에 대해 소란을 피우는 것이 현실적이냐고 물어본다.
[C] 그들은 일부 위험에 처해 있는 종을 돕는 것은 어느 정도 인간의 목표를 방해하므로 양립할 수 없다고 간주한다. [D] 이 사람들은 인간의 생존을 하등한 동물의 존속보다 위에 놓는 법에 대해 동의하지 않는다.

어구 extinction 소멸 exaggerate 과장하다 crying wolf 거짓 경고하기 depict 묘사하다 make a fuss 소란을 피우다 contradictory 모순되는 continuance 영속

해설 [A]~[C]까지는 멸종 위기에 처한 종을 구하는 것이 중요하지 않다고 보는 입장인 반면 [D] 문장에서 인간의 생존이 하등 생명체보다 중요하지 않다는 내용이므로 일관되지 못하다.

(가) The genre of literature ranges from personal ones such as poetry, literary essay to impersonal ones like drama, epic and novel.

(나) A literary work therefore possesses greatness by virtue of the power it is able to exert over the imaginative life of attentive readers.

(다) Out of two types, it can be a simple expression of a private emotion. But in many cases its vision is expanded into the common accumulative experience of human being.

(라) But however general and grand in scope a single play, or novel may be, its full realization cannot be achieved without the active and pleasurable participation of the reader.

① (가) – (나) – (다) – (라)
② (가) – (다) – (라) – (나)
③ (가) – (나) – (라) – (다)
④ (가) – (라) – (나) – (다)

해석 (가) 문학 장르는 시나 문학 에세이와 같은 개인적인 것에서부터 드라마, 서사시, 소설과 같은 일반적인 것들까지 있다. (다) 이 두 가지 유형을 통해 문학은 개인 감정의 단순한 표현이 될 수 있다. 그러나 많은 경우에 있어서, 문학의 상상력은 인간의 공통된 누적 경험으로 확대될 수 있다. (라) 그러나 하나의 연극이나 희곡 작품의 범위가 아무리 일반적이고 광범위하더라도, 독자의 능동적이고 유쾌한 참여가 없다면 작품의 충분한 이해는 불가능하다. (나) 그러므로 문학 작품은, 세심한 독자들의 상상력 풍부한 삶을 통하여 발휘될 수 있는 힘에 의해 위대함을 지니게 된다.

어구 range from A to B (범위가) A로부터 B까지 이르다 impersonal 일반적인; 개인감정을 섞지[나타내지] 아니한 epic 서사시 by virtue of ~의 덕택으로 exert A over B B에 대해서 A의 영향력을 발휘하다 imaginative 상상력[창작력, 구상력]이 풍부한 attentive 주의 깊은, 세심한 상상력 accumulative 누적하는, 누적적인 realization 사실로 깨달음, 이해, 실감

해설 (가) 문장에서 등장한 '개인 장르'와 '비개인 장르'를 (다) 문장에서 two types로 이어받아 설명하고 있다. (다) 마지막에서 말한 인간의 공통된 누적 경험으로 확대되어서 그 규모가 (라) 문장에서 아무리 크다 하더라도 독자의 참여가 필수적이라고 말하며, (나) 문장에서 이러한 독자의 상상력이 발휘된 힘에 의해 문학 작품은 위대해질 수 있다고 결론 내린다.

12 윗글의 흐름상 제시문 다음에 이어질 내용을 바른
순서대로 배열한 것은?

One important change that occurs at night time is
increased levels of the 'darkness hormone' melatonin,
which helps us fall asleep. Most adults start to
produce melatonin at about 10 pm.

[I] This delay in melatonin production might be
caused by the behaviour of teenagers.

[II] This stimulates the brain and exposes the
teenagers to bright lights which could cause the
later release of melatonin.

[III] However, researchers discovered that teenagers
usually began to produce the hormone at 1 a.m.

[IV] For instance, when they stay up late, they often
play computer games or watch television.

① [I] – [IV] – [II] – [III]
② [III] – [I] – [IV] – [II]
③ [III] – [IV] – [I] – [II]
④ [I] – [III] – [IV] – [II]

해석 밤에 나타나는 중요한 변화는 잠을 잘 수 있도록 도와주는 멜라토닌(어둠의
호르몬)의 수치가 증가하는 것이다. 대부분의 성인은 대략 저녁 10시쯤
멜라토닌을 생성하기 시작한다. [III] 그러나 연구가들은 십대들이 대개 새벽
1시에 그 호르몬을 만들기 시작한다는 사실을 발견했다. [I] 이러한 멜라토닌
생성의 지연은 십대들의 행동 때문에 발생하는 것 같다. [IV] 예컨대, 십대들이
늦게까지 자지 않고 있을 때, 그들은 종종 컴퓨터 게임을 하거나 TV를 시청한다.
[II] 이것이(이러한 행동이) 두뇌를 자극하고, 십대들을 늦은 멜라토닌의 방출을
야기하는 밝은 빛에 노출시키는 것 같다.

어구 **melatonin** 멜라토닌(망막이 받은 빛의 양에 반비례하여 송과선(松果腺)에서
분비되는 호르몬) **fall asleep** 잠들다 **stay up late** 늦게까지 자지 않다

해설 두 번째 제시문에서 성인들의 멜라토닌 생성 시간을 설명했으며, [III] 문장에서
이와 대조되는 십대들의 멜라토닌 생성 시간을 비교한다. [I] 그 일반적인
이유로서 십대들의 행동을 설명하고, [IV] 구체적으로 그 예를 들어준다. [II] 그
행동에 따른 결과를 추가적으로 말하고 있다.

1 ①　　**2** ④　　**3** ①　　**4** ④　　**5** ①

>>> **다음 글을 읽고 문제의 답을 고르시오. [1~2]**

Although the three currents which have been discussed so far in twentieth century painting may be founded in scupture as well, the parallelism should not be overstressed. Whereas painting has been richer and more adventurous, its leadership as an a form has not remained unchallenged, and scupture has often followed different paths.

1 The paragraphs that preceded the passage most probably deal with ______________.

① movements in modern painting
② nineteenth-century art
③ the development of painting techniques
④ current approaches to art history

2 According to the passage, why are the similarities between painting and sculpture of limited importance?

① The inspiration for painting rarely comes from sculpture.
② Painters are frequently very critical of sculptors.
③ Sculptor's working methods are basically different from those of painters.
④ Trends in sculpture often develop independently of trends in painting.

해석 비록 20세기 회화에서 지금껏 거론되었던 세 가지 경향이 조각에서도 역시 발견될지라도 그 유사한 점이 지나치게 강조되어서는 안 된다. 회화가 더 풍부하고 더 대담했었을지라도, 미술 형태로서의 회화의 지도적 지위가 아무런 도전도 받지 않은 상태로 남아 있었던 것은 아니고, 조각이 종종 다른 경로로 뒤쫓아 왔다.

1 이 글 앞에 등장했을 내용은?

① 현대 미술의 활동
② 19세기 예술
③ 화술의 발전
④ 예술 역사로의 현대적 접근

2 그림과 조각 사이의 중요성이 왜 경시되는가?

① 그림에 대한 열망이 조각으로부터는 거의 유래하지 않는다.
② 화가들이 매우 빈번히 조각가들을 비난한다.
③ 조각가의 작업 방식들이 화가들과는 근본적으로 다르다.
④ 조각의 추세가 그림의 추세와는 독립되어 종종 발전한다.

해설 **1** 첫 문장 종속절인 'Although ~ as well'의 내용이 '20세기 미술의 경향'에 관한 것이므로, 이전 단락의 내용 또한 20세기 그림의 세 가지 경향이었음이 분명하다. 따라서 현대 미술의 활동이 재진술로서 가장 적합하다.
2 조각이 다른 경로를 통해 뒤쫓아 왔다고 했으므로, 회화와 조각이 동일하다고 생각해서는 안 되는 점이 설문의 원인으로서 적합하다.

Today, once more, egos are breaking like eggshells against the wall. Now, however, ______________ is associated with the fracture of the family rather than the economy. As millions of men and women clamber out of the strewn wreckage of their marriages, they, too, suffer agonies of self-blame. And once more, much of ____________ is misplaced. When a tiny minority is involved, the crack-up of their families may reflect individual failures. But when divorce, separation, and other forms of familial disaster overtake millions at once in many countries, it is absurd to think the causes are purely personal.

3 Which of the following topics is most likely to precede this passage?

① Massive Ego's Shattering
② Causes of Ego's Loss
③ Development of Economic System
④ Change of the Status of Men and Women
⑤ Causes of Social Changes

4 The author believes that ____________.

① egos are not fragile unlike eggshells that are easily breakable
② economic depression helps people to maintain their families
③ people belonging to the minority group are not responsible for their failure
④ the causes of family fracture are not only personal but also social
⑤ people need not feel guilty about their economic failure

5 빈칸에 공통적으로 들어갈 단어는?

① the guilt
② the result
③ the benevolence
④ the shivering
⑤ the sibling

해석 오늘날 다시 한번 더 자아가 벽에 계란처럼 부딪혀서 깨지고 있다. 그러나 그 원인이 이제 경제보다 오히려 가족 파탄과 관련되어 있다. 수백만의 남성과 여성들이 엉망진창의 결혼 파탄으로부터 허우적거릴 때, 또한 자책으로부터 오는 괴로움으로 고통 받는다. 그리고 다시 한번 그 원인 중 상당 부분은 잘못된 것이다. 극히 소수가 관련되어 있을 때 가족의 파괴는 개인의 실패를 반영할 수도 있다. 그러나 이혼과 별거, 그리고 다른 형태의 가족 문제가 여러 국가들의 수백만의 사람들에게 직면하게 될 때 그 원인이 단지 개인적인 것에만 있다고 생각하는 것은 터무니없는 것이다.

3 이 글 앞에 등장했을 단락의 내용은?
① 엄청난 자아의 파괴
② 자아 상실의 원인들
③ 경제 체제의 발전
④ 남성과 여성 지위의 변화
⑤ 사회 변화의 원인들

4 작가가 믿는 것은 무엇인가?
① 자아는 쉽게 깨지는 달걀들과 다르게 약하지 않다.
② 경제 침체는 사람들이 자신들의 가족을 지탱할 수 있게끔 도움을 준다.
③ 소수 단체에 소속되어 있는 사람들은 실패에 책임이 없다.
④ 가족 파탄의 원인들은 개인적인 것일 뿐만 아니라 사회적인 부분도 있다.
⑤ 사람들은 경제 파탄에 대한 죄의식을 느낄 요가 없다.

5 빈칸에 들어갈 공통된 단어는?
① 원인   ② 결과
③ 자비심   ④ 전율
⑤ 형제자매

어구 **ego** 자아 **eggshell** 계란 **fracture** 분열, 좌절, 골절 **clamber** 기어오르다 **strewn** 어수선한 **wreckage** 파탄, 난파 **agony** 고뇌 **self-blame** 자기비난 **misplace** 자리를 잘못 지정하다 **crack-up** 파괴, 파멸 **overtake** 따라잡다, 덮치다 **shattering** 파괴 **status** 지위 **guilt** 원인, 책임, 죄, 죄의식 **benevolence** 자비심, 박애 **shivering** 전율 **sibling** 형제자매

해설 **3** 첫 문장에서 '한번 더 자아가 파괴되고 있다'고 했으므로, 앞선 단락에서도 자아 파괴에 관한 일반적인 내용이 진술되었으리라 유추가 가능하다.
4 마지막 문장에서 가족의 문제가 수백만의 사람들이 소속된 사회에까지 영향을 미칠 때 그 원인이 개인적인 문제에만 있다고 생각하는 것은 문제가 있다고 했으므로 그 원인은 개인적인 것뿐만 아니라 사회적인 것도 포함한다고 볼 수 있다.
5 이 글은 자아의 파괴를 야기하는 원인들을 분석하는 글이므로, '잘못된 문제'의 '원인', '책임'이란 뜻을 가진 guilt가 두 개의 문장에 적합하다.

Chapter 11 단락의 구분 ⇒ 본책 p.142

1 ②	2 ①	3 ③	4 ②	5 ①	6 ③	7 ⑤	8 ⑤	9 ③	10 ④
11 ②	12 ⑤	13 ③	14 ①	15 ④	16 ④				

>>> **다음 글을 읽고 문제의 답을 고르시오.** [1~3]

The children scrambled hastily. With prodigious clatter they arranged themselves at table. The babe sat with his feet dangling high from a precarious infant chair and gorged his small stomach. (가) Jimmie forced, with feverish rapidity, the grease-enveloped pieces between his wounded lips. (나) Maggie, with side glances of fear of interruption, ate like a small pursued tigress. (다) The mother sat blinking at them. (라) She delivered reproaches, swallowed potatoes and drank from a yellow-brown bottle. (마) After a time her mood changed and she wept as she carried little Tommie into another room and laid him to sleep with his fists doubled in an old quilt of faded red and green grandeur. Then she came and moaned by the stove. She rocked to and fro upon a chair, shedding tears and crooning miserably to the two children about their "poor mother" and "your father, damn soul."

1 The best title of the passage would be
_____________.

① Maggie: A Girl of the Street
② The Beast-like Family
③ Domestic Violence
④ A Mother's Solitude
⑤ Weighty Meal

2 According to the passage, which of the following is not true?

① It seems that Maggie didn't feel empty.
② The relationship among the family might not be good.
③ The mother's attitude is somewhat hostile.
④ The mother complains to her children about her husband.
⑤ The characters are described as wild beasts.

3 When the above passage can be divided into two paragraphs, which would be the best boundary?

① (가) ② (나)
③ (다) ④ (라)
⑤ (마)

해석 아이들이 허둥지둥 급히 달려 나왔다. 유별나게 타닥거리면서 아이들은 식탁에 자리를 잡았다. 갓난아기는 불안정한 유아용 의자에 높다랗게 앉아서 두 발을 대롱거리며 조그마한 배를 꽉 채웠다. 지미는 기름으로 뒤덮인 감자들을 열날 정도로 빠르게 상처 입은 입술 사이로 밀어 넣지 않을 수 없었다. 매기는 방해받지 않을까 하는 두려움의 곁눈질을 하면서 쫓기는 작은 암호랑이처럼 먹었다. 어머니는 눈을 깜박거리면서 앉아있었다. 그녀는 꾸중을 하고, 감자들을 삼키고 노란 갈색 병에서 술을 마셨다. 얼마 후 그녀는 기분이 변해 어린 토미를 다른 방으로 안고 가면서 울었다. 그녀는 빛바랜 빨갛고 초록의 이불 속에 두 주먹을 포갠 토미를 장엄하게 눕혔다. 그런 다음 그녀는 돌아와서 끙끙거렸다. 그녀는 눈물을 짜고 두 아이에게 그들의 불쌍한 엄마와 저주받은 영혼(이라고 표현한) 아빠에 관해 슬프게 한탄하면서 의자에 앉아 앞뒤로 흔들었다.

1 이 글의 제목은 무엇인가?
① 매기: 길거리의 소녀
② 짐승 같은 가족
③ 가정 폭력
④ 어머니의 독백
⑤ 과식

2 일치하는 않는 내용을 고르시오.
① 매기는 허기를 느끼지 않는 것처럼 보인다.
② 가족의 관계가 좋은 것 같지 않다.
③ 어머니의 태도는 다소 적대적이다.
④ 어머니는 남편에 대해 아이들에게 불평을 늘어놓는다.
⑤ 등장인물들이 야수처럼 묘사된다.

3 윗글을 두 단락으로 나누고자 할 때, 두 번째 단락이 시작되는 문장을 고르시오.

어구 scramble 급히 움직이다, 기어오르다 prodigious 거대한 clatter 시끄러운 소리, 말 dangle 매달리다, 붙어 다니다 precarious 위험한 gorge 게걸스럽게 먹다 with rapidity 서둘러서, 빠르게 grease-enveloped 기름으로 덮인 side glance 곁눈질 tigress 암호랑이, 잔인한 여자 deliver reproach 비난하다 swallow 삼키다 weep 울다 grandeur 웅대함, 장엄함 moan 신음하다 rock 흔들리다, 진동하다 to and fro 이리저리, 앞뒤로 shed tears 눈물을 흘리다 croon 작은 소리로 노래하다, 지껄이다

해설 1 어머니를 비롯해, 지미, 매기, 갓난아기 모두가 무식한 모습으로 식사를 하며, 어머니 또한 자식들 앞에서 상스러운 욕을 하는 모습을 묘사하는 것이 이 글의 내용이다. 따라서 짐승 같은 가족이란 표현이 제목으로서 타당하다.
2 매기 또한 암호랑이처럼 식사를 했다고 했으므로, 배가 고팠음이 유추 가능하다.
3 (나) 문장까지는 아이들의 행동이 묘사되지만, (다) 문장부터 마지막까지 어머니의 행동과 심정이 묘사되고 있기 때문에 두 번째 단락이 시작되는 문장은 (다)가 옳다.

The sheer loathsomeness of nausea and vomiting does seem to serve a biological purpose. The benefit of vomiting after eating something poisonous or tainted is obvious: the toxin is expelled. And the dreadfulness of the accompanying nausea deters you from ever wanting to eat anything like it again. (1) This explains why pills, chemotherapy, and general anesthetics so often cause nausea and vomiting: they are poisonous-albeit controlled onesand the body is designed to reject them. (2) Why other things cause nausea and vomiting is more difficult to explain, but scientists are beginning to see some sense in nature's design. (3) You'd think that pregnancy sickness, for example, would be evolutionarily disadvantageous, since a growing embryo needs nutrition. (4) In a famous 1992 paper, however, the evolutionary biologist Margie Profet made a compelling case that pregnancy sickness is actually protective. (5) She pointed out that natural foods that are safe for adults commonly turn out to be unsafe for embryos. All plants produce toxins, and in order to be able to eat them we have evolved elaborate detoxification systems. But these systems don't eliminate harmful chemicals completely, and embryos can be sensitive to even tiny amounts.

4 When the above passage can be divided into two paragraphs, which would be the best boundary?

① (1) ② (2)
③ (3) ④ (4)
⑤ (4)

5 Which would be the main theme of the passage?

① Positive Effects of Nausea and Vomiting
② Evolutionary Explanation of Nature's Design
③ Several Causes of Nausea and Vomiting
④ Some Merits of Natural Food
⑤ The Birth of Immune System

6 What is the function of pregnancy sickness?

① To prevent the pregnant women from overworking
② To control the weight of the embryos
③ To protect the embryos from the poisons
④ To inform the abnormal status of the body
⑤ To supply the mother with the nutrition she needs

해석 메스꺼움과 구토의 순전한 혐오감은 생물학적 목적을 수행하는 듯 보인다. 독성이 있거나 음식을 먹은 후에 토하는 것의 장점은 분명하다. 즉, 독성이 제거된다. 그리고 수반되는 메스꺼움의 두려움은 당신이 다시는 그와 같은 것을 먹고 싶지 않게끔 해 준다. (1) 이는 알약과 화학 요법, 그리고 일반적인 마취제가 왜 그토록 자주 메스꺼움과 구토를 야기하는지에 대한 이유를 설명해 준다. 통제가 된 것일지라도, 그것들은 독성이 있으며, 신체는 그것들을 거부하도록 고안되어 있다. (2) 왜 다른 것들이 메스꺼움과 구토를 야기하는지 이유를 설명하기는 더욱 힘들지만, 과학자들은 자연의 의도 속에서 어떤 의미를 알아가기 시작하고 있다. (3) 예컨대, 성장하고 있는 태아가 영양분을 필요로 하기 때문에, 당신은 입덧이 진화론적으로 이롭지 못할 것이라 생각할 수 있다. (4) 그러나 1992년 저명한 논문에서 진화 생물학자인 마지 프로펜은 입덧이 실제로 보호 역할을 수행하게 된다고 강력한 주장을 했었다. (5) 그녀는 성인에게 안전한 자연 음식들이라도 태아에게는 안전하지 않다고 지적했다. 모든 식물은 독을 만들어내며, 그것을 먹을 수 있게끔 하기 위해서, 우리는 정교한 독성 제거 시스템을 발전시켜 왔다. 그러나 이 시스템들은 해로운 화학물질을 완전히 제거하지는 못하며, 태아는 심지어 소량에도 민감한 반응을 일으킬 수 있다.

4 두 번째 단락이 시작되는 문장은?

5 이 글의 주제는?
① 메스꺼움과 구토의 긍정적인 효과 ② 자연 의도의 진화론적 설명
③ 메스꺼움과 구토의 여러 원인들 ④ 자연 식품의 몇 가지 장점들
⑤ 면역 시스템의 태동

6 입덧의 기능은 무엇인가?
① 임산부가 과다한 일을 하지 않게끔 해 주는 것
② 태아의 무게를 조절해 주는 것
③ 태아를 독으로부터 보호해 주는 것
④ 신체의 비정상적인 상태를 알려 주는 것
⑤ 산모가 필요로 하는 영양분을 산모에게 공급하는 것

7 성인이 독성을 참을 수 있게 해 주는 것은 무엇인가?
① 일반 마취제 ② 입덧
③ 메스꺼움과 구토 ④ 자연 음식
⑤ 독성 제거 시스템

어구 nausea 메스꺼움 vomiting 구토 serve 봉사하다, 시중들다 tainted 썩은, 더럽혀진 toxin 독소 expel 추방하다, 내몰다 dreadfulness 무서움 accompanying 수반하는, 동반하는 deter A from -ing A가 ~하지 못하게 하다 chemotherapy 화학요법 anesthetic 마취제 albeit ~일지라도(although) see sense 의미를 이해하다 design 의도, 음모, 설계 disadvantageous 득이 될 게 없는 make a case that ~라고 주장하다 compelling 강력한 point out 지적하다 turn out (to be) ~라고 판명되다 detoxification 독성 제거

7 **What makes the grown-ups tolerate the poisons that plants produce?**

① general anesthetics
② pregnancy sickness
③ nausea and vomiting
④ natural foods
⑤ detoxification system

 4 (1)까지는 사람의 구토에 관한 생리적 현상을 설명하고, (2)부터 자연의 의도적 관점으로 그 이유에 관하여 설명하고 있다. 따라서 (2)부터 새 단락이 시작된다고 볼 수 있다.

5 첫 문장이 주제문으로서, 독성이 있는 음식을 먹었을 때 메스꺼움과 구토는 신체의 생리학적 관점에서 분명히 신체에 도움이 된다는 내용이 주제로서 옳다.

6 In a famous ~로 시작되는 (4)에서 입덧은 (태아를) 보호해 주는 기능이 있다고 직접적으로 설명이 됐다.

7 마지막 두 문장을 통해, 산모 배 속의 태아가 독성 제거 시스템에 민감하게 반응한다고 했으므로, 이는 결국 성인(산모)이 독을 토해내지 않고 견디고 참는다는 얘기이다.

>>> **다음 글을 읽고 문제의 답을 고르시오.** [8~13]

The new music was built out of materials already in existence: blues, rock'n'roll, folk music. But although the forms remained, something wholly new and original was made out of these older elements—more original, perhaps, than even (가) the new musicians themselves yet realize. The transformation took place in 1966~68. Up to that time, the blues had been an essentially black medium. As made famous by Elvis Presley, rock'n'roll which was (나) a blues derivative was rhythmic, raunchy, teenage dance music. (1) Folk music, with such singers as Joan Baez, was popular among college students. (2) The three forms remained musically and culturally distinct, and even as late as 1965, none of them were expressing any radically new states of consciousness. (3) In 1966~68 there was a spontaneous transformation. (4) In the U.S., it originated with youthful rock groups playing in the Bay Area. (5) In England, it was led by the Beatles, who were already established as an extremely fine and highly individual rock group. What happened were these. First, the separate musical traditions were brought together. Bob Dylan and the Jefferson Airplane played folk rock, folk ideas with a rock beat. White rock groups began experimenting with the blues. Of course, white musicians had always played the blues, but essentially as imitators of the Negro style; now it began to be the white bands' own music, and all of the groups moved towards a broader synthesis and (다   ).

8 **The main theme of the passage is "__________".**

① How the new music diverged from the existing three forms of music
② The three different forms of music
③ The originality of the new music
④ Difficulties in characterizing the new music
⑤ How the new music came into being

 새로운 음악은 이미 존재했었던 블루스, 로큰롤, 포크송을 바탕으로 만들어졌다. 그러나 비록 그 형태들이 남아 있을지라도 완전히 새롭고 독창적인 것은 이러한 더 오래된 요소들인데, 심지어 새로운 음악가들조차도 그들 스스로가 이미 깨닫고 있는 것보다 아마도 더 독창적인 요소들로 만들어졌다. 변형은 1966~68년에 일어났다. 그때까지 블루스는 본질적으로 흑인의 표현 수단이었다. 엘비스 프레슬리에 의해 유명해진 블루스의 파생물인 로큰롤은 리드미컬하고 누추한 십대의 댄스 음악이었다. (1) 조안 바에즈와 같은 가수와 함께 포크송은 대학생들 사이에서 인기를 얻었다. (2) 그 세 가지 형태는 음악과 문화적으로 두드러지게 남겨졌고, 심지어 바로 1965년까지도 그것들 중 어느 것도 근본적으로 새로운 의식의 상태를 표현하고 있지 않았다. (3) 1966~68년에는 자발적인 변화가 있었다. (4) 미국에서 이것은 베이 에리어(샌프란시스코의 한 지역)에서 연주하는 젊은 록 그룹과 함께 태동했다. (5) 영국에서 그것은 비틀즈에 의해 주도되었는데, 그들은 이미 매우 섬세하고 매우 개인적인 록 그룹으로 결성되었다. 일어났던 사건은 이것들이다. 첫째, 개별적인 음악적 전통들이 결합되었다. 밥 딜런과 제퍼슨 에어플레인은 록 장단을 가진 포크 악상인 포크 록을 연주했다. 백인 록 그룹은 블루스를 가지고 실험하기 시작했다. 물론 백인 음악가들은 항상 블루스를 연주했지만, 본래는 흑인 방식을 흉내내어 연주했고, 이제 그것(블루스)은 백인 밴드들 특유의 음악이 되기 시작했으며, 모든 그룹들은 더 폭넓은 통합과 절충주의를 지향하였다.

8 **이 글의 주제는?**

① 현존하는 세 가지 음악들의 형태가 분리된 방법
② 음악의 세 가지 다른 형태들
③ 새로운 음악의 독창성
④ 새로운 음악의 특징을 설명하는 데 있어서의 어려움
⑤ 새로운 음악이 탄생된 방법

9 **(가) "새로운 음악가"에 속하지 않는 사람은?**

① 베이 에리어 록 그룹들   ② 비틀즈
③ 엘비스 프레슬리   ④ 제퍼슨 에어플레인
⑤ 밥 딜런

10 **이 글 다음에 등장하게 될 단락의 주제는?**

① 음악 통합에 대한 더 정밀한 노력
② 미국과 영국이 음악의 혁명을 야기한 방법
③ 전통적인 음악 형태가 얼마나 빨리 구식이 되었는가
④ 새로운 음악의 또 다른 특징
⑤ 록 비트와 민간의 생각들이 어떻게 합치게 되었는가

9 Who does not belong to "the new musicians" in (가)?

① The Bay Area rock groups
② The Beatles
③ Elvis Presley
④ Jefferson Airplane
⑤ Bob Dylan

10 What is most likely the topic of the paragraph following this one?

① A more detailed elaboration of the synthesis in music.
② How the U.S. and England led to the revolution in music.
③ How quickly the traditional forms of music became out-moded.
④ Another feature of the new music.
⑤ How folk ideas combined with rock beat.

11 "A blues derivative" in (나) is a form of music that is ___________ the blues.

① distinct from
② developed from
③ scornful of
④ similar to
⑤ derogatory to

12 Which of the following is most appropriate for the blank (다)?

① distinctiveness
② ramification
③ divergence
④ eruption
⑤ eclecticism

13 If we divide the passage into two paragraphs, where does the second paragraph begin?

① (1)　　　　② (2)
③ (3)　　　　④ (4)
⑤ (4)

11 (나) "블루스의 파생물"은 블루스와 어떠한 관계에 있는 음악 형태인가?

① 별개의　　　　② 발전된
③ 무시하는　　　④ 유사한
⑤ 가치를 손상시키는

12 (다)에 적절한 것은?

① 특이함　　　　② 분기
③ 차이　　　　　④ 분화, 폭발
⑤ 절충

13 이 글을 두 개의 단락으로 구분하고자 할 때 두 번째 단락이 시작되는 문장은?

어구 **material** 소재, 재료　**in existence** 존재하는　**folk music** 포크송, 민속 음악, 민요　**wholly** 전적으로, 완전히　**make A (out) of B** B를 A로 만들다　**take place** (사건이) 일어나다, (행사가) 개최되다　**up to** (최대) ~까지, ~에 이르기까지　**medium** 중간, 매개물, 매체, 수단, 방법　**derivative** 파생물　**rhythmic** 율동적인, 주기적인, 규칙적으로, 순환하는　**raunchy** 천한, 누추한, 외설스러운　**such A as B** B와 같은　**A as late as** 바로 ~ 만큼 최근에　**radically** 철저히, 근본적으로, 급진적으로, 과격하게　**spontaneous** 자발적인, 임의의　**extremely** 극단적으로, 극도로, 극히　**highly** 매우　**separate** 갈라진, 떨어진, 분리된　**musical** 음악적인　**tradition** 전통, 관습, 관　**bring together** ~을 모으다, 합치다, 결합시키다　**beat** 박자, (심장의) 고동　**imitator** 모방하는(흉내 내는) 사람　**move toward(s)** ~을 지향하다　**synthesis** 통합, 종합, 합성　**diverge** 분기하다　**existing** 존재하는　**originality** 독창성　**come into being** 발생하다, 생겨나다, 태어나다　**elaboration** 노고, 수고　**combined with** ~으로 합쳐진　**scornful** 경멸스러운　**derogatory** 경멸적인, (명예를) 손상시키는　**ramification** 분기, 나뭇가지　**eclecticism** 절충(주의)

해설 **8** '포크 록, 백인이 연주하는 블루스, 퓨전'과 같은 신종 음악이 등장하기까지의 과정을 설명한 것이므로, 그 방법이 제목으로서 합당하다.

9 엘비스 프레슬리는 블루스에서 파생된 (정통) 록 음악을 유명하게 한 사람일 뿐 윗글에서 말하는 새로운 음악가는 아니다.

9 새로운 음악이 통합된 '퓨전의 음악적 성격' 이외의 또 다른 특징 및 성격이 묘사되리라 추유가 가능하다.

10 derivative는 '파생물(something that has developed or been produced from something else)'의 뜻을 가지고 있다. 따라서 블루스에서 발전된 형태임이 유추가 가능하다.

11 '순접-열거'의 논리 정보 장치인 and에 의해서 연결되기 위해서는, 앞서 등장한 synthesis(통합체)와 순접의 논리 관계인 '절충'이 옳다.

12 (2)까지는 새 음악의 기원을 설명하지만, (3)부터 새 음악의 태동을 비롯하여 새 음악의 연주가들을 설명하므로, (3)부터 두 번째 단락이 시작임을 알 수 있다.

The term "hot dog" was <u>coined</u> in 1901 at the New York Polo Grounds. (1) One cold April day, concessionaire Harry Stevens was losing money with ice cream and ice cold soda. (2) He sent his salesmen out to buy up all the dachshund sausages they could find, along with an equal number of rolls. (3) In less than an hour his vendors were hawking hot dogs from portable hot water tanks with "They're red hot! Get your dachshund sausages while they're red hot!" (4) In the press box, sports cartoonist Tad Dorgan was nearing his deadline and desperate for an idea. (5) Hearing the vendors, he hastily drew a cartoon of barking dachshund sausages nestled warmly in rolls. Not sure of how to spell "dachshund" he simply wrote "hot dog"! The cartoon was a sensation. People began to use the term "hot dog".

14 Why did the sports cartoonist write "hot dog" according to the passage?

① Because the name of the sausages was the same as that of a dog.
② Because the sausages were made of dog meat.
③ Because the sausages looked like a dog.
④ Because the vendors were calling the sausages "hot dog".
⑤ Because the sausages were sold in rolls.

15 Which of the following is closest in meaning to the underlined word "coined"?

① cooked   ② moneyed
③ spelled   ④ invented
⑤ used

16 When the above passage can be divided into two paragraphs, which would be the best boundary?

① (1)   ② (2)
③ (3)   ④ (4)
⑤ (5)

해석 "핫도그"라는 단어는 1901년도에 뉴욕 폴로 그라운드에서 생겨났다. (1) 4월의 어느 추운 날 매점 업자인 헤리 스티븐스는 아이스크림과 시원한 얼음 소다로 돈을 벌지 못하고 있었다. (2) 그는 판매원들을 보내 찾을 수 있는 모든 닥스훈트 소시지들과 동일한 수의 롤을 사오게 했다. (3) 30분이 채 되지 않아서 그의 상인들이 휴대용 온수 탱크에서 핫도그를 팔면서, "정말 뜨겁네요! 뜨거울 때 닥스훈트 소시지 드세요."라고 소리쳤다. (4) 기자석에서 스포츠 만화가인 테드 도건은 마감 시간이 다가오면서 한 가지 생각을 떠올리려고 필사적이었다. (5) 상인들의 소리를 들은 그는 롤 빵에 다정하게 안겨서 짖는 닥스훈트 소시지를 급히 그렸다. dachshund(닥스훈트)를 어떻게 써야 할지 확신을 가지지 못한 그는 간단하게 '핫도그'라고 썼다. 그 만화는 센세이션을 일으켰다. 사람들은 '핫도그'라는 말을 쓰기 시작했다.

14 스포츠 만화가는 왜 "핫도그"라고 썼는가?
① 소시지의 이름이 어떤 개의 이름과 같았기 때문에
② 소시지가 개고기로 만들어 졌기 때문에
③ 소시지가 개처럼 생겨서
④ 행상인들이 소시지들을 "핫도그"라고 불러서
⑤ 소시지들이 롤 빵으로 판매됐기 때문에

15 밑줄 친 "coined"의 뜻은?
① 요리된   ② 부유한
③ 표기된   ④ 발명된
⑤ 이용된

16 두 번째 단락이 시작되는 문장은?

어구 **coin** 신조어를 만들다, 주조하다   **concessionaire** 구내매점 업자, 급식업자, 특허권 소유자   **send out** ~을 밖으로 보내다   **buy up** ~을 매점하다, 접수하다   **dachshund** 닥스훈트(짧은 다리에 몸이 긴 독일산 개)   **along with** ~과 함께   **vendor** 행상인   **hawk** 행상하다, 외치면서 팔다   **portable** 휴대 가능한   **red hot** 적열의, 열광적인, 최신의   **press box** 기자석   **cartoonist** 만화가   **near** ~에 근접하다   **deadline** 마감 시한   **be desperate for** ~에 사적이다   **hastily** 급하게, 빨리   **nestle** 편하게 몸을 가누다   **warmly** 다정하게   **be made of** ~으로 만들어지다   **moneyed** 부자의, 부유한

해설 **14** 행상인들의 롤 빵에 다정히 안겨 있는 '닥스훈트'라는 실제 개의 이름에 착안해서 hot dog라는 이름이 지어진 것이다.
15 coin은 '(신조어를) 만들어내다(to invent a new word or expression, especially one that many people start to use)'라는 뜻을 가지고 있다.
16 (3)까지는 매점업자의 일화를 소개한 반면, (4)부터 스포츠 만화가의 일화를 통해서 핫도그라는 단어의 창조를 설명하고 있다. 따라서 새로운 주제로 전환된 단락은 (4)이다.

Chapter 12 재진술

⇒ 본책 p.149

| 01 ② | 02 ① | 03 ② | 04 ② | 05 ① | 06 ② | 07 ① | 08 ③ | 09 ④ | 10 ③ |
| 11 ① | 12 ③ | 13 ② | 14 ① | 15 ③ | | | | | |

1 The student revolt is not only a thorn in the side of the president's newly established government, but has international implications as well.

① This revolt affects the students.
② This revolt affects national and international affairs.
③ This revolt affects the students and international affairs.
④ This revolt affects the side of the president's body.

해석 학생들의 봉기는 새롭게 수립된 대통령의 행정부 입장에서 골칫거리일 뿐만 아니라 국제적인 의미를 가지고 있다.
① 이 봉기가 학생들에게 영향을 미친다.
② 이 봉기는 국내외적 문제에 영향을 미친다.
③ 이 봉기는 학생들과 국제 문제에 영향을 미친다.
④ 이 봉기는 대통령 기구에 영향을 미친다.

어구 revolt 반란, 폭동 thorn 가시, 고통 implication 의미, 관련성

해설 not only A but B as well 구문을 통해서 새로운 행정부(국내적 문제)뿐만 아니라 국제적 의미(국제적 문제)를 모두 갖고 있다고 했기 때문에 '이 봉기는 국내외적 문제에 영향을 미친다.'는 논리가 옳다.

2 It wasn't long before different ideas about how the United States government should be run caused people to take sides.

① Before long people was divided as a result of difference in opinions about the system of government.
② The difference of opinion about the system of government was not serious.
③ People agreed on the system of government unanimously.
④ Soon people took part in the discussion of how the government should be run.

해석 미국 정부가 어떻게 운영되어져야 하는지에 대한 서로 다른 생각들 때문에 사람들이 편을 가르게 되는 데에 얼마 걸리지 않았다.
① 머지않아 미국 정부가 어떻게 운영되는가에 대한 서로 다른 생각이 사람들로 하여금 편을 가르게 만들었다.
② 미국 정부 체계에 대한 의견의 차이는 심각하지 않았었다.
③ 사람들은 정부 체계에 대해서 만장일치로 동의했다.
④ 사람들은 정부가 어떻게 운영되는지에 대한 토론에 참여했었다.

어구 it is not long before ~ 머지않아 ~하게 되다 take sides 편을 가르다 before long 머지않아, 곧

해설 it is not long before S+V는 'before long(부사)'와 같은 뜻이 된다. take sides의 의미를 물어보는 문제로 볼 수 있다.

3 Language is a necessary tool in the sharing transference of ideas, but can also be an impediment to understanding when confused by dialects and localized idioms.

① Language must have its drawbacks.
② Dialects and localized idioms are the main impediment to sharing the transference of ideas.
③ Language is unnecessarily impaired by idiomatic changes.
④ Comprehension can be blurred by local linguistic differences.

해석 언어는 생각의 전달을 공유함에 있어서 필수적인 도구이지만, 방언이나 지방에서 쓰이는 관용어에 의해서 혼란을 느끼게 될 때에는 이해에 지장이 생길 수도 있다.
① 언어는 단점이 있음에 틀림이 없다.
② 방언과 지역 관용어들은 사상의 전달을 공유함에 있어서 중요한 장애 요소가 된다.
③ 언어는 관용적인 변화에 의해 불필요하게 피해를 입는다.
④ 지방적인 차이에 의해서 이해가 되지 않을 수 있다.

어구 transference 이동, 전송 impediment 방해; 신체장애 dialect 방언; 자기 표현법 localized 국지화된 blur (눈·시력·시계 등을) 희미하게 하다

해설 접속사 but을 통해 언어가 방언 및 지방 관용어들에 의해 생각을 전달하는 과정에 있어서 방해받을 수 있다고 했음이 이 글의 논지이다.

4 What is most obvious in this book are all these details of daily living which make Mrs. Richards anything but common.

① Mrs. Richards is quite ordinary.
② Mrs. Richards is an unusual person.
③ Mrs. Richards is very obvious.
④ Mrs. Richards is anything she wants to be.

해석 이 책에서 가장 분명한 것은 리차드 여사를 결코 평범하지 않게 만든 일상생활에 대하여 모든 세부적인 사항을 다루고 있다는 것이다.
① 리차드 여사는 아주 평범한 사람이다.
② 리차드 여사는 비범한 사람이다.
③ 리차드 여사는 매우 노골적인 사람이다.
④ 리차드 여사는 자신이 되고 싶은 바로 그러한 사람이다.

어구 **obvious** 분명한; 명백한 **anything but** 결코 ~이 아닌

해설 anything but(=never)의 뜻을 물어보는 문제이다.

5 He has seen his best days.

① He was once prosperous, but has now declinced.
② He has been quite well up to now.
③ He has never been so well off.
④ He has been living in the memory of his former prosperity.

해석 그에게 한때 전성기가 있었다.
① 그는 한때 잘 나갔지만, 지금은 퇴락했다.
② 그는 지금까지 무사하다.
③ 그는 그토록 잘 살아 본 적이 없다.(지금 가장 잘 살고 있다.)
④ 그는 과거 잘나갔던 기억 속에 살고 있다.

어구 **one's best days** 전성기 **prosperous** 번창한; 번영하는 **be well off** 부유하다

해설 see one's best days(전성기가 있다)의 뜻을 물어보는 문제이다.

6 Long before the genetic basis of heredity was understood, farmers bred animals and plants to enhance desirable traits. In a sense the first genetic engineers, they recognized that selecting superior parents produced improved offspring. Since domestication, cattle have been bred for strength at the plow, for fighting spirit and, as early as 1,700, for more milk or beef.

① Farmers understood the genetic basis of heredity long after the first genetic engineers.
② Farmers are, so to speak, the forerunners of the present-day genetic engineers.
③ Farmers grew animals and plants to get more domesticated ones.
④ Farmers selected superior parents in order to produce more domesticated offspring.

해석 유전학적 기초가 이해되기 오래 전부터, 바람직한 특질을 강화하기 위하여 농부들이 동물과 식물들을 길렀다. 어느 면에서 보면, 우월한 모체를 선택하면 더 뛰어난 새끼들이 태어난다는 사실을 최초의 유전학자들이(농부들이) 인식했던 것이다. 소들은 길들여진 후 쟁기질을 할 수 있는 힘을 위하여, 투혼을 위하여, 그리고 일찍이 1,700년에는 더 많은 우유와 고기를 위하여 키워졌다.
① 최초의 유전학자들보다 이후에 농부들은 유전적 기초를 이해했었다.
② 말하자면 농부들은 현재의 유전 공학의 선구자들이다.
③ 농부들은 더욱 길들여진 동식물을 얻기 위하여 동식물들을 키웠다.
④ 농부들은 더욱 길들여진 새끼들을 얻기 위하여 우수한 어미들을 선택했다.

어구 **heredity** 유전; 전통 **breed** 새끼를 낳다; 품종 **in a sense** 어느 의미에서는 **offspring** 후손 **domestication** 길들임 **fighting spirit** 투혼

해설 유전학자들이 유전 법칙을 깨닫기 전에 농부들이 동식물을 키우는 과정을 통해서 그 유전 법칙을 먼저 알고 있었다는 것이 이 글의 논지이다.

7 Since Einstein didn't begin to talk until he was three years old, no one realized that he was a latent genius.

① Even though he was a genius, it wasn't noticeable because he was late in beginning to talk.
② He talked late, so he must not have been a genius.
③ Geniuses begin talking when they are three years old.
④ No one knows when a genius will begin to talk.

해석 아인슈타인은 3살이 되고서야 비로소 말을 하기 시작했기 때문에 그가 잠재적 천재성을 가지고 있다는 사실을 누구도 깨닫지 못했다.
① 심지어 그가 천재였을지라도, 말을 늦게 시작했었기 때문에 천재라는 사실이 두드러지지는 않았었다.
② 그가 말을 늦게 했으므로 천재가 아니었음에 틀림이 없다.
③ 천재는 세 살의 나이가 됐을 때 말을 시작한다.
④ 누구도 천재가 말을 언제 시작하는지는 알지 못한다.

어구 **latent** 보이지 않는; 잠재적인 **noticeable** 주목할 만한

해설 not ~ until(~하고서야 비로소) 구문의 의미를 물어보는 문제이다.

8 The medical journal reported that heart attack victims who recover are approximately five times as likely as to die within the next five years as those people without a history of heart disease.

① People who have had a heart disease will die in five years.
② People who have had a heart disease are less likely to die than people without a history of heart disease.
③ People who have had a heart disease are more likely to die in the near future than others.
④ People who have had a heart disease are likely to recover soon.

해석 심장 마비에서 회복되는 환자들이 심장 마비 경험이 없는 사람들보다 앞으로 5년 내에 사망할 가능성이 다섯 배는 대략 더 많다는 사실을 그 의학 잡지가 보도했다.
① 심장병을 앓는 사람들은 5년 내에 사망하게 될 것이다.
② 심장병을 앓았던 사람들은 심장병 경력이 없는 사람들보다 사망할 확률이 낮다.
③ 심장병을 앓았던 사람들은 가까운 미래에 다른 사람들보다 사망할 확률이 높다.
④ 심장병을 앓았던 사람들은 곧 회복될 것 같다.

어구 **heart attack** 심장 마비

해설 '배수사(five times) + as ~ as' 구문은 해석상 비교급(more)이 된다.

9 The ancient notion that there is a single, true meaning for a word has been replaced by the concept that words are essentially nothing more than conventional symbols whose use and pronunciation may vary even from person to person.

① The ancients were able to devise fool-proof meanings for words.
② The concept of one single true meaning for a word is unalterable.
③ Language is a tool that is best used by neophytes.
④ The pronunciation of words and their meanings change with the times and usage.

해석 한 단어에는 하나의 진정한 의미만 있다는 낡은 생각은, 단어는 그저 개인이 쓰는 용도와 발음에 따라서 상이해지는 전통적인 상징에 불과하다는 관념에 의해서 대체되었다.
① 고대인들은 단어들에 대한 분명한 의미들을 고안할 수 있었다.
② 하나의 단어에는 하나의 진정한 의미가 있다는 생각이 불변이다.
③ 언어는 초심자들이 가장 잘 이용할 수 있는 도구이다.
④ 단어의 발음과 의미는 시간과 용례에 따라 변화한다.

어구 **nothing more than** ~에 불과한 **conventional** 전통적인 **from person to person** 개인마다

해설 기존의 생각을 대체한 능동의 주체가 has been replaced by 뒤의 concept의 동격 that 절 안에 소개되어 있다. 즉, 대체한 주체가 핵심 내용이 되는 것이다.

10 It must be clearly understood that the "fittest" which survive are not necessarily best or highest on any absolute standard, but simply fittest for the given conditions.

① Only the best survive.
② The best can never be the fittest.
③ On some occasions the best do not survive.
④ The fittest are always the best.

해석 살아남은 "최적자"가 꼭 어떠한 절대적 기준에 따라서 최고이거나 최상의 지위에 있는 것이 아니라, 단지 주어진 상황에서 가장 적합할 뿐이라는 점이 분명히 이해되어야 한다.
① 최고의 자들만이 생존한다.
② 최고인 자는 결코 최적이 될 수 없다.
③ 몇몇 경우에는 최고인 자도 생존할 수 없다.
④ 최적자들은 언제나 최상이다.

어구 **the fittest** 최적자 **absolute** 절대적인 **given** 주어진

해설 but에 의해 '대조' 관계를 이루고 있다. 주어진 상황에 따라 단지 적합해질 수 있다는 논리는 '이따금씩은 최고인 자도 살아남지 못한다.'가 된다.

11 The characters in this book are fictional, and any resemblance to living people is purely coincidental.

① It is only a coincidence if any of the fictitious characters in this book resemble actual people.
② Living persons were used as models for the fictional characters in this book.
③ Coincidences in fiction books are always pure when characters are involved.
④ The people in this book were designed to resemble living persons.

해석 이 책의 주인공들은 허구의 인물이며, 실존하는 사람들과 조금이라도 닮았다면 그것은 순전히 우연의 일치에 불과한 것이다.
① 만일 이 책에 등장하는 인물들이 허구이고 또한 살아 있는 사람들이 약간이라도 닮았다면 그것은 순전히 우연의 일치에 불과한 것이다.
② 이 책에 등장하는 허구의 인물들을 위하여 실존 인물들이 사용됐다.
③ 소설 속의 우연의 일치들은 인물들이 관련을 맺게 될 때 언제나 순수하다.
④ 이 책에 등장하는 사람들은 실존 인물들을 닮도록 고안됐다.

어구 **fictional** 가공의; 허구의   **coincidental** 우연에 불과한   **fictitious** 허위의; 소설의

해설 본문의 해석 그대로 if 부사절을 통해 ①에서 재진술되었다.

---

12 In order to live a religious and moral life worth the name, they feel it is necessary to come out in some degree from the competitive world.

① To live a religious and moral life, they should start from the ordinary routine lives.
② Religion and morality are indispensible for their lives in the world.
③ If being competitive, some people that have a religious belief may deviate from routine lives.
④ Life is so complicated that they cannot catch up with the harsh realities of the world.

해석 그 이름의 가치가 있는 종교적이고 도덕적인 삶을 영위하기 위하여, 경쟁이 치열한 세상으로부터 약간은 일탈해 보는 것이 필요하다고 사람들은 느낀다.
① 종교와 도덕적 삶을 살기 위하여 사람들은 평범한 일상생활로부터 시작해야 한다.
② 종교와 도덕은 세상에서 살기 위하여 필수 불가결한 것이다.
③ 만일 경쟁을 갖추려면 종교적 신념을 가진 몇몇 사람들은 평범한 삶으로부터 벗어날는지 모른다.
④ 인생은 너무나 복잡해서 사람들이 세상의 거친 현실을 따라잡을 수 없다.

어구 **come out** (밖으로) 나가다   **in some degree** 어느 정도는   **indispensible** 없어서는 안 될, 절대 필요한   **deviate** 탈선하다

해설 종교적 삶을 사는 사람들조차도 경쟁이 치열한 세상에서 일탈을 해 본다는 것이 이 글의 논지이다.

---

13 During the periods of physical stress the human body uses up more vitamins than it usually does.

① Only when the human body needs vitamin, is it the periods of physical stress.
② Vitamin's requirement rises when the physical demands on the human body are usually high.
③ Vitamin is very good for the human body.
④ Whenever the human body needs vitamin, he feels physical stress high.

해석 육체적으로 스트레스를 받는 기간에는 인간의 몸이 보통 때보다 비타민을 더 많이 소모한다.
① 인간의 신체가 비타민을 필요할 때만이 육체적인 스트레스를 받는 기간인 것이다.
② 신체에 대한 비타민의 요구량이 대개 높을 때 비타민의 필요성이 증가한다.
③ 비타민은 인간의 몸에 매우 좋다.
④ 인간의 신체가 비타민을 필요로 할 때마다, 인간은 스트레스를 크게 느낀다.

어구 **use up** 다 써 버리다; 소모시키다   **be good for** ~에 이롭다

해설 physical demands on the human body는 결국 본문에서 physical stress를 가리키고 있다.

14 It is unlikely that the results of the elections will be made public until tomorrow morning.

① Tomorrow morning is probably the earliest that anyone will know the results of the elections.
② Before tomorrow morning we will probably know the results of the elections.
③ The results of the elections will most likely be made known before tomorrow morning.
④ We will probably not be told the results of the elections tomorrow morning.

해석 선거 결과는 내일 아침이 되어서야 비로소 공개될 것 같다.
① 내일 아침은 아마도 선거의 결과를 알 수 있는 가장 이른 때일 것이다.
② 내일 아침 전에 우리는 선거 결과를 아마도 알게 될 것이다.
③ 선거 결과가 내일 아침 전에 알려질 가능성이 가장 높을 것이다.
④ 우리는 내일 아침에 선거 결과를 듣지는 못할 것이다.

어구 be made public 공개되다

해설 'it is unlikely(=not likely) that … until ~' 이 구문은 '～하고서야 비로소 …하다'는 뜻이다. 따라서 내일 아침 전까지는 공개되지 않을 것(=내일 아침이 아마도 선거 결과를 알 수 있는 가장 이른 시간)이라는 논리가 옳다.

15 The world seldom asks how a man acquired his property. The only question is, has he got it?

① How a man acquired his money should be nobody's business but his own.
② The world assumes that a rich man must be a good man.
③ A man who has money is usually accepted in any society, even though he may be suspected of dishonesty.
④ The world automatically assumes a rich man to be a crook.

해석 세상 사람들은 그 사람이 재산을 어떻게 취득했는지에 대해서는 거의 질문을 하지 않는다. 유일한 질문은 "그가 과연 돈을 벌었는가?"이다.
① 사람이 돈을 어떻게 벌었느냐는 그 누구도 아닌 자신의 일일 뿐이다.
② 세상은 부유한 사람이 좋은 사람임에 틀림이 없다고 가정한다.
③ 돈이 있는 사람은 비록 그가 부정직하다고 의심받는다 치더라도 어느 사회에서든 보통 인정받는다.
④ 세상은 부유한 사람을 도둑이라고 자동적으로 간주한다.

어구 property 재산; 특성 be suspected of ～의 의심을 받다 crook 사기꾼; 갈고리

해설 돈을 버는 과정이 아니라 돈을 벌었느냐 그 자체가 관심의 대상이므로, 돈을 가진 사람이 비록 부정직함에 대해 의심을 받는다 치더라도 어느 사회에서라도 용납이 된다는 내용이 유추 가능하다.

Chapter 13 문장 완성

⇒ 본책 p.162

01 ②	02 ③	03 ①	04 ②	05 ⑤	06 ②	07 ①	08 ③	09 ④	10 ②
11 ①	12 ③	13 ③	14 ⑤	15 ③	16 ①	17 ⑤	18 ①	19 ③	20 ⑤
21 ②	22 ④	23 ③	24 ⑤	25 ⑤	26 ⑤	27 ③	28 ④	29 ⑤	30 ②
31 ①	32 ④	33 ③	34 ③	35 ②	36 ②	37 ⑤	38 ②	39 ①	40 ③
41 ⑤	42 ②	43 ④	44 ②	45 ②	46 ②	47 ④	48 ②	49 ②	50 ①
51 ③	52 ②	53 ①	54 ④	55 ⑤	56 ④	57 ③	58 ④	59 ⑤	60 ③
61 ④	62 ④	63 ④	64 ⑤	65 ③	66 ⑤	67 ①	68 ①	69 ⑤	70 ①
71 ⑤	72 ④	73 ②	74 ③	75 ④	76 ①	77 ③	78 ①	79 ①	80 ⑤
81 ②									

---

1 "I'd like to open a checking account with this paycheck. Do I have to ___________ it by signing on the back?"

① entitle
② endorse
③ guarantee
④ invalidate

해석 "이 지불 수표를 가지고 당좌 예금 계좌를 하나 만들고 싶어요. 뒷면에 사인을 해서 배서를 해야 합니까?"

어구 **checking account** 당좌 예금 계좌, 수표 계정 **paycheck** 지불 수표, 급료 **sign on the back** 뒷면에 사인을 하다 **entitle** ~의 권리를 주다 **endorse** (어음·증권 등에) 이서하다, 배서하다 **guarantee** ~을 보증하다 **invalidate** ~을 무효로 만들다.

해설 checking account(당좌 예금 계좌), paycheck(지불 수표)과 같은 금융 용어가 등장하는 것으로 보아 '배서하다'라는 단어가 가장 적합하다.

---

2 Far too many people are ___________ the government for help, and steps need to be taken to create jobs to make them independent.

① wiping out
② tearing up
③ relying on
④ stamping out

해석 너무 많은 사람이 정부의 원조에 의존하고 있으므로, 그들이 자립할 수 있도록 일자리를 만들려는 조치가 취해질 필요가 있다.

어구 **step** 수단, 조치, 방법 **independent** 남에게 의존하지 않는, 독자적인 **wipe out** 일소하다, 지우다 **tear up** 뿌리째 뽑다, 잡아 빼다 **stamp out** 진압하다, 박멸하다

해설 and라는 '순접-열거' 논리 정보 장치에 의해 '일자리를 만들려는 조치가 요하다'라는 내용과 순접으로 이어지기 위해서는 '의존하다'라는 논리가 적합하다.

---

3 "Tom, what I told you is so confidential. I want you to keep it under your ___________."

① hat
② eyes
③ nose
④ feet

해석 "톰, 내가 너에게 말한 것은 정말 비밀이야. 비밀을 지켜 주기 바랄게."

어구 **confidential** 비밀의, 은밀한 **under one's hat** 비밀리에, 은밀하게

해설 confidential과 순접으로 이어지기 위해서는 '비밀리에'라는 뜻을 가진 under one's hat이 옳다.

4 Barbara Walters distinguised herself as a journalist by asking famous people the kinds of ___________ questions that other reporters shied away from.

① gentle
② pointed
③ vague
④ indirect
⑤ gross

해석 바바라 워터스는 저명인사들에게 다른 기자들이 주저했었던 신랄한 질문을 함으로써 기자의 명성을 얻게 되었다.

어구 **distinguish oneself** 이름을 떨치다, 유명해지다 **journalist** 기자, 언론인 **shy away from** ~에서 뒷걸음치다, 주춤하다 **pointed** 매서운, 신랄한 **vague** 막연한, 애매한 **indirect** 우회하는, 간접적인 **gross** 조잡한

해설 본인은 명성을 얻을 수 있었지만, 다른 기자들은 주춤거릴 만한 질문이라면 '신랄한' 질문이어야 한다.

5 When one member of the pair is ___________, couples who hope to become parents often seek to adopt a child.

① incapable
② industrious
③ infatuated
④ incisive
⑤ infertile

해석 부부 중 한 사람이 불임일 때, 부모가 되기를 희망하는 부부는 종종 아이를 입양하려고 노력한다.

어구 **pair** 부부, 한 쌍 **seek to R** ~하려고 애쓰다 **incapable** 무능한 **industrious** 성실한, 근면한 **infatuated** 얼빠진, 열중한 **incisive** 예리한, 신랄한 **infertile** 불임의, 생식력이 없는

해설 아이를 입양하려 하는 부모는 '임신이 불가능한' 사람일 경우의 확률이 높다.

6 The management is not responsible for any valuables not ___________ in safety deposit boxes provided at the front office.

① existed
② secured
③ obtained
④ acquired
⑤ achieved

해석 관리팀은 본부에 제공되는 귀중품 보관함에 보관되어 있지 않은 어떠한 귀중품에 대해서도 책임을 지지 않는다.

어구 **the management** 관리부, 관리인 **be responsible for** ~의 책임이 있다, ~의 원인이 되다 **safety deposit box** (귀중품 보관용) 대여 금고 **front office** 본부, 수뇌부 **secured** 안전하게 보관된, 도망칠 염려가 없는

해설 관리팀이 책임을 지지 않을 만한 상태이어야 하면 안전하게 보관되어져 있지 않은 물건이어야 한다.

7 Hyenas have an undeserved reputation as thieves and scavengers that ___________ the leavings of the larger predator.

① subsist on
② succumb to
③ suffer from
④ are subdivided into
⑤ are subsumed under

해석 하이에나는 덩치가 더 큰 육식 동물이 남겨 놓은 것을 먹고 살아가는 도둑이나 청소 동물로 평가절하된 명성을 얻고 있다.

어구 **undeserved** 부당한, 가치가 절하된 **scavenger** 썩은 고기를 먹는 동물, 청소부 **predator** 육식 동물, 약탈자 **subsist on** ~로 연명하다 **succumb to** ~에 항복하다 **subdivide A into B** A를 B로 나누다, 세분화시키다 **be subsumed under** ~의 항목 하에 포함되다

해설 도둑과 썩은 동물을 먹는 동물을 표현하기 위해서는 남이 남겨놓은 먹이로 연명한다는 논리가 적합하다.

8 Bacteria are becoming immune to antibiotics used in farming and may now be ___________ to similar drugs to treat illnesses.

① strange
② tolerant
③ resistant
④ vulnerable

해석 박테리아는 농업에서 사용되는 항생물질에 면역이 되어지고 있으며, 이제는 병을 치료하는 유사한 약에 저항력이 생겼을 수도 있다.

어구 **immune** 면역이 된 **antibiotic** 항생물질 **farming** 농업 **tolerant** 항독력이 있는 **resistant** 저항력이 있는 **vulnerable** 약한, 영향받기 쉬운

해설 항생제에 면역이 생겨나고 있다는 내용과 순접으로 이어지기 위해서는 약물에 저항력이 생긴다는 내용이 옳다.

9 The country saw the number of divorces fall for the first in 16 years last year as Koreans became more ___________ going their separate ways.

① eager in
② satisfied with
③ supportive in
④ cautious about
⑤ enthusiastic about

해석 한국인들이 (이혼하여) 갈라서는 것에 대해 더욱 신중해지면서, 한국은 16년 안에 처음으로 지난 해 이혼한 부부의 수가 줄어들게 되었다.

어구 **eager in** ~에 열정적인 **supportive** 부양하는, 지원하는 **cautious** 신중한 **enthusiastic** 열렬한

해설 이혼하는 부부의 수가 줄어들기 위해서는 이혼에 대해 신중한 태도를 취한다는 원인이 적합하다.

10 The author was too ___________ a figure for us to get any detailed information.

① prominent
② obscure
③ norotious
④ sluggish
⑤ skillful

해석 그 작가는 너무나 무명이었기 때문에 어떤 자세한 정보도 얻을 수가 없었다.

어구 **too A to R** ~할 수 없을 만큼 너무나 A하다 **detailed** 자세한 **prominent** 저명한 **obscure** 모호한, 무명의 **notorious** 악명이 높은 **sluggish** 게으른 **skillful** 실력이 있는

해설 자세한 정보를 알 수 없을 정도의 사람이라면 잘 알려지지 않는 '무명의' 인물이어야 한다.

11 In these days of eco-realism, too many environmentalists, scientists and politicians tend to shift focus swiftly from one issue to another, pronouncing the first solved and considering the second fresher, more mediagenic. ___________. Today, the breakdown of stratospheric ozone—a problem recently declared fixed—is being ignored, while the newer controversy of 'climate change' launches a thousand conferences. But in fact, the peril of ozone depletion, which is caused by humankind's release of chlorofluorocarbons(CFCs) and other chemicals into the atmosphere, is demonstrably worse than conventional environmental wisdom holds.

① Ozone depletion is a case in point
② Depleted ozone may begin recovery
③ Ozone depletion causes climate change
④ The ozone layer is torn worse than ever
⑤ The ozone layer filters out the sun's UV rays

해석 환경 현실주의가 지배하는 오늘날 너무나 많은 환경주의자들과 과학자들, 그리고 정치인들이 한 가지 논쟁에서 다른 논쟁으로 주제를 빠르게 이동시키면서, 첫 번째 논쟁이 해결되었다고 말하고 두 번째 논쟁이 더 새롭고 매스컴에 민감한 것이라고 말한다. 오존 고갈이 하나의 예이다. 오늘날 최근에 정리가 된 것으로 선고받은 문제인 성층권 오존의 붕괴는 간과되고 있는 반면에, 기후 변화에 대한 새로운 논쟁은 1천 개의 회담을 개시하게 했다. 그러나 사실 인간이 방출한 CFC와 기타 화학물질이 대기로 유입되어 야기된 오존 고갈의 위험이 형식적인 환경적 학문이 주장하는 것보다 명백히 더 악화된 상태이다.

어구 **eco-realism** 환경 현실주의 **shift** 이동시키다 **focus** 초점, 주제 **fresh** 신선한, 새로운 **mediagenic** 매스컴을 잘 타는 **breakdown** 고장, 붕괴 **stratospheric** 성층권의 **declare** 선언하다 **peril** 위험 **ozone depletion** 오존 고갈 **chlorofluorocarbon** 클로로 플루오로 카본 (순환성 냉매(冷媒), 발포제, 용제로서 쓰이며 오존 파괴가 문제되고 있음) **conventional** 형식적인, 판에 박힌 **case in point** 예시

해설 다음 문장에서 '오존 고갈'은 간과되고 있는 반면, '기후 변화'에 대해 중시되고 있다는 잘못된 현실을 설명한다. 따라서 앞 문장에서 언급된 '첫 번째' 논쟁은 바로 '오존 고갈'이 된다.

12 It is a paradox that while state-funded child care and extremely long and cushy maternity benefits make it easy to be a working mother in Sweden, such benefits also have the effect of ___________ female employment in the most profitable and powerful jobs.

① punishing ② endorsing ③ dampening ④ augmenting ⑤ guaranteeing

해석 국가의 지원을 받는 아동 양육과 매우 길고도 편하게 돈을 버는 출산 수당으로 스웨덴에서는 직장인 어머니가 되는 것이 쉬운 반면에, 그와 같은 수당이 또 가장 유익하면서도 견실한 직업에서 여성의 고용을 악화시키는 효과 또한 가지고 있다는 것은 모순이다.

어구 paradox 역설, 모순 cushy 편하게 돈을 버는, 쉬운 maternity benefit 출산 수당 poweful 견실한, 강력한 endorse 배서하다, 승인하다 dampen (활기 등을) 꺾다 augment 증강하다

해설 모순적인 사실이 되기 위해서는 '직장인 어머니가 되는 것이 쉽다'는 내용과 '견실한 직장에서 여성의 고용에 악영향'를 미친다는 내용이 어울린다.

13 The Cabinet member's resignation was not a total ___________ : rumors of his imminent departure had been making the rounds in Washington for a week.

① withdrawal ② success ③ shock ④ eclipse ⑤ pretense

해석 고문 단원이 사임한다는 것은 완전히 놀랄 일은 아니다. 그가 곧 떠난다는 소문이 일주일 동안 워싱턴에 퍼졌었다.

어구 Cabinet 고문단[미국], 내각[영국] make the rounds (소문이) 퍼지다 withdrawal 철수, 탈퇴 eclipse 빛의 상실, (명예 등의) 실추 pretense 구실, 핑계

해설 일주일 동안 소문이 퍼져 있었으므로, 사임 내용은 놀랄 일이 아님을 알 수 있다.

14 With similar programs now widely available in inexpensive, easy-to-use consumer versions, just about anyone with ___________ computer skills can cut, paste, erase, combine and retouch photographs.

① solitary ② complimentary ③ snobbish ④ sedentary ⑤ rudimentary

해석 값싸고 사용하기 편리한 소비자 버전으로 오늘날 유사한 프로그램이 널리 활용 가능해지면서, 초보적인 컴퓨터 기술을 갖춘 거의 어떤 사람도 사진을 자르고 붙이고 지우고 합치며 손질(수정)할 수 있다.

어구 available 얻을 수 있는, 이용할 수 있는 just about 그럭저럭 겨우, 거의, 정말로, 아주 solitary 고독한 complimentary 칭찬하는, 무료의, 우대의 sedentary 앉아 있는, 앉아 일하는 rudimentary 기본의, 보적인

해설 사용하기 편리한 소비자 버전이므로, 초보자도 사용할 수 있음을 알 수 있다.

15 Because of the trauma they have experience, survivors of a major catastrophe are likely to exhibit ___________ of behavior and may require the aid of competent therapist.

① concessions ② diminutions ③ aberrations ④ restrictions ⑤ altercations

해석 그들이 겪은 정신적 쇼크 때문에 참사에서 살아난 이들은 정신 이상 증세를 보이며 유능한 심리 치료사의 도움을 필요로 할 것 같다.

어구 trauma 정신적 쇼크 catastrophe 참사, 재앙 competent 유능한 therapist 심리 치료사 concession 양보, 허가 diminution 감소 aberration 정신 이상, 탈선 altercation 언쟁

해설 and라는 '순접-열거' 논리 정보 장치에 의해, 유능한 심리 치료사의 도움을 필요로 한다는 내용과 순접으로 연결되어야 한다.

16 Speciesism is a prejudice or attitude of bias in favor of the interests of members of one's own species and against those of members of other species. Speciesism is wrong for the same reason racism and sexism are wrong—because all beings' interests should count equally. This is often called "the principle of equality." All the arguments to prove human ____________ cannot shatter this hard fact: in suffering, the animals are our equals. For any individual who can suffer, the degree of suffering, not the species of the sufferer is what should count.

① superiority
② genetics
③ nature
④ suffering
⑤ cruelness

해석 종의 차별(편견)은 자기 자신의 종족 구성원들의 이익을 선호하고 다른 종족 구성원들의 그것에는 반대하는 선입견 또는 편견의 태도이다. 종에 대한 편견은 인종차별주의나 성차별주의가 잘못된 이유와 같은 이유로 잘못된 것인데, 그것은 모든 인간들의 이익은 똑같이 중요한 것이어야 하기 때문이다. 이것은 종종 "평등의 원칙"이라 불린다. 인간의 우월성을 증명하려는 모든 주장들은 이러한 엄연한 사실을 산산조각 낼 수 없다. 즉 고통을 겪고 있을 때, 동물들도 우리와 꼭 같은 존재들이다. 고통을 느낄 수 있는 어떤 개인에 있어서도, 고통을 가하는 자의 종이 아닌 고통의 정도가 중요한 것이어야 하는 것이다.

어구 speciesism 종의 차별 in favor of ~은 선호하여 for the same reason 같은 이유로 shatter 파괴하다, 박살내다 genetics 유전학, 유전적 특질 cruelness 잔인함

해설 한 종(족)이 우월하다는 전제에서 다른 종(족)을 차별하거나 편견을 가지게 된 것이다. 하지만 어떤 종족이라 할 것 없이 고통을 느끼는 것은 마찬가지이다.

17 Most Americans are accustomed to thinking of lie detectors as foolproof—as machines that can separate the guilty from the innocent. But in fact, nothing could be further from the truth. Lie detectors can and do ____________.

① keep playing
② get repaired
③ produce the desired results
④ prove successful
⑤ make mistakes

해석 대부분의 미국인들은 거짓말 탐지기를 유죄와 무죄를 구별해 내는 기계로서 절대적으로 안전한 것이라고 간주하는 것에 익숙하다. 그러나 사실은 진실 이상의 것은 없다. 거짓말 탐지기도 실수할 수 있고 실제로도 그러하다.

어구 be accustomed to -ing ~하는 것에 익숙하다 foolproof 고장이 없는, 절대적으로 안전한 separate A from B A와 B를 구분하다 further 그 이상으로

해설 절대 안전하다는 앞의 내용과 but에 의해 반대 개념이 와야 하므로 실수도 있다는 내용이 옳다.

18 Reviews on caffeine and conception ____________. One study of 2,817 women found no effect of caffeine on their chances of conceiving, while another of 1,909 women linked more than 300 milligrams of caffeine daily to a delay in conception

① conflict
② explode
③ step up
④ manifest themselves

해석 카페인과 임신에 대한 평가들이 상충한다. 2,817명의 여성들에 대한 한 연구 결과는 카페인이 그들의 임신 가능성에 어떤 영향도 미치지 않았음을 밝힌 반면 1,909명의 여성들에 대한 또 다른 한 연구는 하루 300밀리그램 이상의 카페인은 임신의 지연과 연관성이 있었다.

어구 conception 임신, 개념 conceive 임신하다, 마음에 품다, 이해하다 link A to B A를 B에 연관시키다 conflict 상충 · 충돌하다 step up 증가하다 manifest 명백하게 하다, 밝혀지다

해설 다음 문장의 주절에서는 카페인이 임신에 아무 영향을 미치지 않는다고 하였으며, while 이하의 종속절에서는 카페인이 임신의 지연을 야기한다고 했으므로, 이는 상충되는 결과 내용임을 알 수 있다.

19 The candidate's speech was filled with empty promises, ____________ and cliches.

① threats
② ingenuity
③ platitudes
④ anger
⑤ candor

해석 그 후보의 연설은 무의미한 공약과 평범한 생각 그리고 진부한 말들로 가득했다.

어구 candidate 후보, 지원자 cliche 진부한 말 · 표현 ingenuity 독창력, 정교함 platitude 단조, 평범(한 의견) candor 솔직함

해설 '순접–열거'를 의미하는 and에 의해서 공허한 약속과 진부한 말이라는 의미와 순접이어야 한다.

20 The ____________ faces of the released prisoners showed how poorly they had been cared for.

① grateful
② exuberant
③ jubilant
④ plump
⑤ haggard

해석 석방된 포로들의 수척한 모습들은 그들이 얼마나 형편없는 처우를 받았었는지를 보여 주었다.

어구 released prisoner 석방된 포로 care for 돌보다, 대우해 주다 grateful 감사의 exuberant 원기 왕성한 jubilant 기뻐하는 plump 살찐 haggard 여윈, 수척한

해설 형편없이 대우받았다는 내용을 가리키기 위해서는 '여윈 모습'이 이유이어야 한다.

21 Though he was theoretically a skilled craftsman, I found his work ____________ and lacking in polish.

① impeccable
② coarse
③ capable
④ functional
⑤ distinguished

해석 그가 비록 이론적으로는 숙련된 장인이었을지라도 나는 그의 작품이 조잡하고 세련미가 없다는 점을 알고 있었다.

어구 skilled 실력 있는 craftsman 장인, 숙련공 lacking in ~이 부족한 polish 세련미, 윤기 impeccable 결점이 없는, 완벽한 coarse 조잡한 functional 기능의, 직무상의 distinguished 저명한

해설 '순접-열거'를 가리키는 등위접속사 and에 의해서 '세련미가 부족한'이란 의미와 순접이 필요하다.

22 ____________ foods may be preserved for a long period of time as they have been freed of moisture.

① Frozen
② Seasoned
③ Jellied
④ Desiccated
⑤ Canned

해석 건조된 식품들은 습기가 없을 때 오랜 시간 동안 보존될 수 있다.

어구 be freed of ~이 없다, ~으로부터 자유롭다 frozen 얼린 seasoned 맛을 낸, 조미가 된 jellied 젤리 형태로 만든 desiccated 건조된 canned 통조림의

해설 습기가 없게 된다면 음식은 건조해지기 마련이다.

23 Our sense of humour is one of our most valuable faculties. Thinkers simple and profound point out that the ability to see the funny side of things and to laugh at ourselves and our troubles is an asset of great importance. It can help us fight off adversity, get greater joy out of living, and ____________.

① believe in what other people say
② fall in love with a charming lady
③ maintain our sanity
④ make a lot of money
⑤ look on the dark side of things

해석 우리의 유머 감각은 가장 소중한 재능 중 하나이다. 단순하면서도 심오한 사상가들은 사물의 즐거운 요소들을 볼 수 있는 능력과 자신과 자신의 역경을 비웃을 수 있는 능력은 매우 중요한 장점이라고 지적한다. 그러한 장점은 우리가 역경을 싸워 물리치도록 도와주고, 생활에서 보다 큰 즐거움을 얻고, 우리의 건전함을 유지하는 데 도움을 줄 수 있다.

어구 faculty 능력, 재능 simple and profound 단순하건 심오하건 laugh at 무시하다, 비웃다 asset 재산, 자산, 장점 fight off 싸워 물리치다 adversity 역경 fall in love with ~와 사랑에 빠지다 charming 매력적인 sanity 제정신, 건전함, 온전함

해설 and라는 '열거'의 논리 정보 장치에 의해서 역경과 싸울 수 있고, 생활에서 즐거움을 얻을 수 있다는 내용과 순접의 내용이 필요하다.

24 Critics who have spoken out on these issues have been jailed or silenced by authoritarian governments, and international investors have been prepared to turn a blind eye to the ______________ violations which have caused political instability.

① animal abuse
② child abuse
③ international trade
④ peace talks
⑤ human right

해석 이들 사안에 대해 솔직한 의견을 밝힌 비평가들은 독재적인 정부에 의해 투옥되거나 침묵을 지키게 되었고, 따라서 국제 투자가들은 정치적 불안을 초래해 온 그런 인권 침해 사례들을 못 본 체할 마음의 준비가 되어 있었다.

어구 **speak out** 주저 않고 말하다 **jail** 수감하다 **silence** 침묵시키다 **authoritarian** 권위주의의, 독재주의의 **turn a blind eye to** ~을 못 본 체하다 **violation** 위반, 침해 **instability** 불안정 **abuse** 학대, 남용

해설 감옥에 갇히거나 침묵을 지킬 수밖에 없는 경우가 정치적 불안을 야기하기 위해서는 '인권의 침해'가 논리상 타당하다.

25 He is most generous about forgiving a slight, an insult, and an injury. Never does he harbor resentment, store up petty grudges, or waste energy or thought on means of revenge or retaliation. He's much too ______________ a person.

① urbane
② intrepid
③ versatile
④ adventurous
⑤ magnanimous

해석 그는 경멸, 모욕 및 무례한 것을 용서하는 것에 대해 관대하다. 그는 결코 원한을 품지 않으며 사소한 유감을 마음에 담아 두지 않으며 보복이나 앙갚음할 수단에 대해 정력이나 생각을 낭비하지 않는다. 그는 너무나도 도량이 큰 사람이다.

어구 **generous** 아끼지 않는, 관대한, 야량 있는 **slight** 경멸, 모욕 **insult** 모욕, 무례 **resentment** 분개, 분노 **store up** 저장하다, 비축하다, 마음에 담아 두다 **petty** 작은, 사소한; 보잘것없는 **grudge** 원한, 악의, 유감 **revenge** 보복, 앙갚음 **retaliation** 보복(복수), 앙갚음 **urbane** 도시풍의, 세련된 **intrepid** 두려움을 모르는, 용감한, 대담한 **versatile** 다재다능한, 다방면의, 다용도의 **adventurous** 모험적인, 모험을 좋아하는 **magnanimous** 도량이 큰, 야량 있는

해설 첫 문장에서 '경멸, 모욕 및 무례한 것을 용서하는 것에 대해 관대하다'고 했으므로 '도량이 큰' 사람이 옳다.

26 Many novels by the Bronte sisters and other nineteenth-century female authors were initially published under masculine ______________ in the belief that works by male authors would meet more favorable reception.

① monikers
② aliases
③ rubrics
④ criteria
⑤ pseudonyms

해석 브론테 자매 소설가와 여타의 19세기 여류 작가들의 많은 소설은 남성 작가들의 작품이 보다 더 호의적인 반응을 도출할 것이라는 믿음에서 처음에는 남성의 필명 하에 출판되었다.

어구 **female authors** 여류 작가들 **initially** 처음에, 시초에 **masculine** 남성의(male), 남자다운 **meet** (희망·요구사항·수요·법률 등을) 충족·만족시키다, 부합하게 하다 **favorable** 호의적인, 찬성하는, 안성맞춤인, 알맞은, 순조로운 **reception** 수취, 수령, 응접 **monikers** 이름, 별명 **alias** 별명, 가명 **rubric** (책 등의) 제명; 항목, 빨간 글씨 **criterion** 표준, 기준, 규범(복수형 criteria) **pseudonym** 가명, 필명

해설 책을 낼 때 작가가 이름 대신 사용하는 것을 'pseudonym(필명)'이라고 한다. 지문의 '남성 작가들의 작품이 보다 더 호의적인 반응을 충족시켜 줄 것이라는 믿음'으로 보아 여류 작가들이 남성의 필명을 사용하여 출간했음을 알 수 있다.

27 Someone once told me I was lucky to be ___________ because I have the best of both worlds. In some ways this is true. I have a huge family that is filled with diversity and is as colorful as a box of Crayons.

① exclusive
② limited
③ biracial
④ cowardly
⑤ arrogant

해석 누군가 한때 나에게 내가 혼혈인인 것은 운이 좋은 것이라고 말했는데, 그 말은 내가 두 세계의 최상의 것을 갖고 있기 때문이라는 것이다. 어떤 면들에 있어서 이것은 사실이다. 나는 다양성으로 가득 차 있고 한 상자의 크레용처럼 다채로운 대가족을 가지고 있다.

어구 **exclusive** 배타적인, 독점적인(sole, unilateral) **limited** 제한된 **biracial** 두 인종의; 혼혈의 **cowardly** 겁이 많은, 비겁한 **arrogant** 거만·교만한, 건방진, 무례한(insolent, impudent, haughty)

해설 문장에서 '두 세계의 최상의 것을 갖고 있기 때문'이라고 했으므로 이에 가장 어울리는 'biracial(혼혈의)'이 답이다.

28 When a couple gets divorced, the court may require the man to pay his former wife a monthly sum of money called ___________. Its amount depends on the husband's income, the wife's needs, and the length of the marriage.

① optimism
② honeymoon
③ elope
④ alimony
⑤ veil

해석 부부가 이혼을 하게 되면, 법정은 남자로 하여금 그의 전 부인에게 이혼 수당이라고 불리는 월정액을 지급하라고 요구할지 모른다. 그 액수는 남편의 수입, 아내의 요구 및 결혼 기간에 달려 있다.

어구 **get divorced** 이혼하다 **needs** 요구 **optimism** 낙관주의 **honeymoon** 신혼여행 **elope** 눈이 맞아 함께 달아나다 **alimony** (이혼시 지급하는) 부양(생활)비 **veil** 베일, 장막

해설 이혼할 때, 남자가 여자에게 월정액으로 지급하는 것을 'aliminy(부양비, 생활비)'라고 한다.

29 Much of the art of being a good teacher or healer consists in staying just one step ahead of your patients or pupils. If you are not ahead, it is unlikely that you will be able to lead them anywhere, but if you are two steps ahead, it is likely that ___________.

① they will be healed without fail
② they will lead you
③ they will love you
④ you will not catch them
⑤ you will lose them

해석 훌륭한 선생님이나 의사가 되는 기술의 상당 부분은 환자나 학생보다 항상 바로 한 걸음 앞에 있는 것에 있다. 만일 앞서 있지 못한다면, 그들을 어떤 곳으로든 인도할 수 없을 것이다. 그러나 만일 두 걸음 앞서 있게 되면 그들을 놓치게 될 것이다.

어구 **art** 기술, 기교, 예술 **healer** 치료사, 의사 **consist in** ～에 존재하다 **ahead of** ～의 앞에서 **unlikely** 가능성이 없는 **without fail** 틀림없이

해설 첫 문장에서 '딱(just) 한 걸음만 앞서 있어야 학생들이나 환자들을 인도할 수 있는 좋은 선생이나 의사가 된다'고 했으므로, 두 걸음이나 앞서 있다면 저 사람들을 놓치게 될 것이라는 논리가 타당하다.

30 다음 빈칸에 공통으로 들어갈 적절한 단어는?

- I'll finish using the computer in a minite. Just keep your ___________ on, and you'll get your turn.
- Jack invested a lot of money in stocks and lost his ___________.
- Mike is such a stuffed ___________ He always wears a tie, and he even eats chicken with a knife and fork.

① hat
② shirt
③ pants
④ socks
⑤ jacket

해석
· 컴퓨터 사용하는 것 금방 끝낼게. 화내지 마, 그러면 (곧) 네 차례가 될 거야.
· 잭은 주식에 많은 돈을 투자했다가 큰 손해를 보았다.
· 마이크는 대단히 얌전 빼는(차리는) 사람이다. 그는 항상 타이를 매고 다니고 심지어 치킨도 나이프와 포크로 먹는다.

어구 **keep one's shirt on** 화를 내지 않다, 냉정을 잃지 않다, 침착성을 유지하다 **lose one's shirt** 무일푼이(알거지가) 되다, 큰 손해를 보다 **a stuffed shirt** 얌전 빼는 사람; 유력자, 명사; 부자

해설 각 숙어의 key word를 물어보는 문제이다.

31 How could high school girls understand their place in American history if their textbooks told them that, from ___________ America to the present, women have had equal opportunity for upward mobility and political participation?

① colonial
② obsolete
③ primitive
④ prehistoric
⑤ savage

해석 식민지 시대부터 여성들의 수직적인 신분 상승과 정치적 참여에 대한 동등한 기회가 주어지는 현재까지의 역사에 대해 교과서를 통해 고등학교 여학생들에게 설명해 준다면, 그 학생들이 미국 역사에서 자신들의 지위가 어떠하다고 생각할 수 있겠는가?

어구 **textbook** 교과서 **upward** 상승의, 위로 향한 **mobility** 이동, 변덕 **colonial** 식민지의 **obsolete** 쓸모없게 된, 폐물의 **primitive** 원시의, 구식의 **prehistoric** 선사 시대의 **savage** 야만의

해설 여성의 지위에 대해 논의가 되기 위해서는 최소한 독립전쟁이 있었던 시기가 적합하다.

32 She accepted his proposal with alarming ___________; she had the "yes" out of her mouth before he finished popping the question.

① enthusiasm
② reserve
③ celerity
④ acerbity
⑤ payola

해석 그녀는 놀라울 정도로 신속히 그의 제안을 수용했다. 그녀는 그가 문제 제기를 끝마치기도 전에 "예"라고 말했다.

어구 **alarming** 놀라운 **pop** 내밀다, (폭죽 · 총을) 터뜨리다 **enthusiasm** 열정 **reserve** 비축, 예비, 자제, 비축하다 **celerity** 신속함 **acerbity** 신랄함, 신맛 **payola** 뇌물

해설 문제를 물어보는 것이 끝나기도 전에 답을 했다는 얘기는 그 정도로 신속한 답변을 했다는 논리가 적합하다.

33 The children were so excited about their vacation trip that they became ___________ and had to be calmed down.

① lanky
② staid
③ boisterous
④ forthright

해석 아이들은 여행에 너무 흥분한 상태라 하도 떠들어 대서 진정을 시켜야만 했다.

어구 **had to be calmed down** 진정해야만 했었다 **lanky** 마르고 키 큰, 호리호리한 **staid** 침착한, 성실한, 안정된 **boisterous** 떠들썩한 **forthright** 솔직한, 거리낌 없는

해설 so … that 구문에 의해 '흥분한 상태'에 따른 결과 표현이 적합하며, 그리하여 진정해야 할 필요가 있었다는 논리로 이어져야 한다.

34 As they helped the community recover from a natural calamity, remarkably ___________ rescue crew worked around the clock with an energy that never seemed to wane.

① chubby
② obsequious
③ indefatigable
④ trenchant
⑤ nominal

해석 자연재해를 입은 지역 사회가 복구되도록 용감한 구조대원들은 힘을 썼는데, 그들은 결코 시들지 않을 것 같은 에너지로 온종일 일을 했다.

어구 **calamity** 참사 **remarkably** 매우 **rescue crew** 구조대원 **around the clock** 쉬지 않고, 하루 종일 **wane** 감소하다 **chubby** (살이) 통통한 **obsequious** 비굴한 **indefatigable** 불굴의, 끈질긴 **trenchant** 비난하는 **nominal** 보잘것없는, 이름의, 명목상의

해설 결코 줄어들지 않는 것 같은 힘을 갖고 있는 사람들은 불굴의 의지를 가진 사람들이라는 논리가 적합하다.

35 Sophists are someone who will win an argument by forcing their adversaries to defend it on the sophists' own ___________.

① qualms
② grounds
③ compromise
④ encouragement

해석 궤변론자들은 자신들이 유리한 상황에서 상대방으로 하여금 방어하게 함으로써 논쟁에서 승리를 거두는 이들을 말한다.

어구 sophist 궤변론자 win an argument 논쟁에서 승리를 거두다 on one's own grounds 자신이 유리한 상황에서 qualm 불안한 마음 compromise 타협 encouragement 격려

해설 상대가 방어를 할 수 있는 상황이라면 논쟁을 벌이는 이는 승리를 거두기 힘들겠지만, 자신이 우선 유리한 상황의 고지에서 논쟁을 이끌어 논쟁의 승리자가 된다는 논리이다.

36 In the 1920s Hollywood became a magnet for men and women on the cutting edge— ___________ artists genuinely excited by the possibilities of the up-and-coming film medium.

① irritable
② innovative
③ untalented
④ sagacious
⑤ coarse

해석 1920년대에 할리우드는 영상 매체의 진취적인 가능성에 진정으로 고무된 최첨단을 걷는 혁신적인 예술가들을 끌어들이는 자석같은 역할을 했다.

어구 magnet 자석, 매력 cutting edge 최신식(의) genuinely 진정으로 up-and-coming 진취적인 irritable 짜증나는 innovative 혁신적인 untalented 재능이 없는 sagacious 영리한 coarse 조잡한

해설 cutting edge라는 표현이 '대쉬(—)'에 의해 순접으로 이어지기 위해서는 '혁신적인'이란 표현이 옳다.

37 I think that having learned our letters we should read the best that is in literature. However, even the college-bred and so-called liberally educated men here and elsewhere have really little or no acquaintance with the recorded wisdom of mankind, ___________.

① the best-sellers
② the novel films
③ the TV documentaries
④ the soap opera
⑤ the ancient classics

해석 나는 우리가 문학을 배웠기 때문에 최고의 문학 작품을 읽어야 한다고 생각한다. 그러나 대학 교육을 받았거나 소위 교양 교육을 받은 이들조차도 실상 기록으로 남겨진 인류의 지혜인 오랜 고전들을 거의 알지 못하거나 전혀 모르고 있다.

어구 letters 문학, 글 college-bred 대학 교육을 받은 so-called 소위, 이른바 liberally educated 교양 과목을 공부한 have acquaintance with ~에 대해 정통하다, 알다 novel 새로운 documentary 기록물, 기록 영화 soap opera (연속) 드라마 ancient classics 오래된 고전작품

해설 첫 문장에서 작가가 주장하는 내용은 '최고의 문학 작품의 독서'이다. 두 번째 문장에서 however라는 '역접-대조'의 접속부사에 의해서 반대 내용인 '고전 작품을 잘 알지 못한다'는 내용이 옳다.

38 Many people, out of anxiety, became unable to contemplate their true situation and with it to plan accordingly. Anxiety, and the wish to ___________ it by clinging to each other, and to reduce its sting by continuing as much as possible with their usual way of life incapacitated many.

① contradict
② counteract
③ frustrate
④ encourage
⑤ deprecate

해석 많은 이들이 불안감 때문에 자신이 처한 실제 상황을 숙고할 수 없고, 그로 인해 상황에 맞게 계획을 세울 수도 없게 되었다. 불안감과 서로에게 매달림으로써 그 불안감을 반감시키고 자신의 일상적인 삶의 방식을 가능한 한 지속함으로써 불안감으로 인한 고통을 줄이고자 하는 소망은 많은 이들을 무력하게 만들었다.

어구 out of anxiety 불안감 때문에 contemplate 심사숙고하다 accordingly 그에 맞게 cling to ~에 매달리다, 집착하다 sting 찌름; 아픔, 고통 incapacitate 무능력하게 하다 contradict 부인 · 반박하다 counteract 방해하다, 중화하다 frustrate 좌절시키다 deprecate 비난 · 반대하다

해설 and라는 '순접-열거' 논리 정보 장치에 의해서 '고통을 줄인다(to reduce it sting)'와 순접으로 이어져야 한다.

39 The hypothesis may explain why college graduates appear less ___________ to memory loss than people with only an elementary school education: Learning strengthens the brain.

① vulnerable
② vigilant
③ indignant
④ pertinent
⑤ unsusceptible

해석 그 가설은 단지 초등학교 교육만 받은 사람들보다 대학 졸업생들이 기억력 상실에 덜 영향을 받는 이유를 설명해 줄 수 있을지 모른다. 즉, 학습은 두뇌를 강화시키는 것이다.

어구 **hypothesis** 가설 **less vulnerable to** ~에 덜 취약한 **memory loss** 기억력 상실 **strengthen** 강화시키다 **vigilant** 주의 깊은, 방심하지 않는 **indignant** 분노한 **pertinent** 적절한 **unsusceptible** 민감하지 못한, ~에 물들지 않는

해설 마지막 문장의 '학습은 두뇌를 강화시킨다'는 내용과 순접으로 이어지기 위해서는 부정어 less와 결합한 또 다른 부정적인 의미인 vulnerable (취약한)이 옳다.

---

40 Peter has a bad habit of making ___________ remarks that wander so far off topic that we forget the gist of what he is saying.

① awkward
② sagacious
③ digressive
④ telling
⑤ tentative

해석 피터는 그가 말하는 골자를 우리가 잊어버릴 정도로 주제에서 너무나 많이 벗어나는 내용을 전하는 나쁜 습관이 있다.

어구 **wander off** 벗어나다, 다른 곳으로 빠지다 **gist** 골자, 요지 **awkward** 서투른 **sagacious** 총명한 **digressive** 주제에서 벗어난 **telling** 효력이 있는, 현저한 **tentative** 주저하는, 임시의

해설 '인과'의 논리 관계를 설명하는 so … that ~ 구문에 의해서 '그가 말하는 골자를 잊어버릴 만한 원인'이 논리상 옳다.

---

41 Increasingly silent and withdrawn, he changed from a fluent, articulate speaker to someone who gave only ___________ answers to any questions asked of him.

① bookish
② effusive
③ idiomatic
④ pretentious
⑤ monosyllabic

해석 점점 조용해지고 수줍어하게 된 그는 유창하고 조리있게 말하는 연설자에서 자신에게 물어본 모든 질문들에 대해서 간결하게 말하는 사람으로 변모했다.

어구 **withdrawn** 수줍은, 인가에서 떨어진 **fluent** 유창한 **articulate** 표현을 잘 하는 **bookish** 학구적인, 독서의 **effusive** 과장된, 감정을 토로하는 **idiomatic** 관용구가 많은 **pretentious** 과장된 **monosyllabic** 간결한

해설 'change A to B(A에서 B로 바뀌다)' 표현에 의해서 A와 B는 상반된 '역접-대조'의 관계가 옳다. 따라서 '유창한(fluent)'과 반의어인 '간결한 (monosyllabic)'이 들어가야 한다.

---

42 Today, birth rates are dropping around the globe, and experts speak darkly of depopulation. ___________? Contraception is more reliable and readily available than ever. In the developed world, large numbers of women are pursuing higher education and careers, delaying marriage and childbirth, and having smaller families. Developed countries have also seen a major migration from the farms to the cities. In urban areas, the high cost of raising children provides economic incentive to keep family size down.

① What is wrong with fewer people
② What is causing the decline
③ What are the implications of the decline
④ How quickly is the birth-rate declining
⑤ What should we do

해석 오늘날, 출산율은 전 세계적으로 떨어지고 있으며 전문가들은 인구 감소에 부정적인 의견을 내놓고 있다. 이러한 감퇴의 원인이 되고 있는 것은 무엇인가? 어느 때보다 피임(법)이 더욱 신뢰할 만하고 쉽게 활용 가능하다. 선진국에서는, 수많은 여성들이 고등교육과 직업을 추구하고 있고, 결혼과 분만(출산)을 미루고 있으며 가족 구성원 수도 적게 두려 하고 있다. 선진국들은 또한 농촌으로부터 도시로의 대규모 이동을 겪어 왔다. 도시 지역에서는 높은 양육비가 가족의 규모를 축소시켜 나가게 하는 경제적 유인책을 제공하고 있다.

어구 **drop** 떨어지다 **speak darkly of** ~에 대해 어둡게 말하다 **depopulation** 인구 감소 **pursue** 추구하다 **childbirth** 분만, 출산 **migration** 이주, 이전 **incentive** 자극, 동기 **implication** 내포, 함축

해설 첫 문장에서 인구 감소에 대한 일반적인 진술을 한 이후, 빈칸 이하에서 그 이유들을 설명하므로, 이유에 대한 문제 제기가 옳다.

43 The Maori ideal in individual behavior was explicit. Generosity was the personal virtue most esteemed. Unless an individual displayed generosity, in all his dealings with people, he __________ attaining social recognition.

① put emphasis on
② made much of
③ took less advantage of
④ stood little chance of
⑤ focused on

해석 개인의 행동에 있어서 마오리족의 이상은 분명했다. 관대함은 가장 존경받는 개인의 덕목이었다. 개인이 사람과의 모든 관계에 있어 관대함을 보이지 못하면, 그가 사회적인 인정을 받을 수 있는 가능성은 거의 없었다.

어구 Maori 마오리족의 explicit 명백한, 뚜렷한 generosity 관대 esteem 존경·존중하다 display 표시하다, 보이다 dealings 관계 social recognition 사회적 인정 put emphasis on ~을 강조하다 make much of ~을 중시하다, 이용하다 stand little chance of ~의 가망성이 거의 없다 focus on ~에 집중하다

해설 관대함이 마오리족의 가장 존경받는 덕목이었으므로, 이를 행하지 못한다면 존경받지 못한다는 논리가 타당하다.

44 Since two-year olds normally express a broad range of emotions, be prepared for everything from delight to rage. However, you should consult your pediatrician if your child seems very passive or withdrawn, perpetually sad or highly demanding and unsatisfied most of the time. These could be signs of depression, caused either by some kind of hidden stress or biological problems. If __________ depression, he'll probably refer your child to a mental health professional for a consultation.

① your child complains
② your doctor suspects
③ you doctor is in
④ you insist on
⑤ you believe in

해석 두 살 먹은 아이들은 일반적으로 다양한 감정을 표현하므로, 즐거움에서부터 분노 표출에 이르기까지 모든 감정에 준비를 하고 있어야 한다. 그러나 만일 당신 아이가 너무 소극적이거나 내향적이고, 계속 기분이 좋지 않거나 요구가 지나치고, 대체적으로 만족해하지 않는다면 소아과 의사의 상담을 받아 봐야 할 것이다. 이런 행동은 모종의 숨겨진 스트레스나 생물학적인 문제에 의해 야기된 우울증의 징후들일 수도 있다. 만일 상담 의사가 우울증을 의심한다면, 아마도 진찰을 위해 당신 아이를 정신건강 전문의에게 보낼 것이다.

어구 rage 격노, 분노 pediatrician 소아과 의사 passive 활기 없는, 소극적인 withdrawn 내향적인 perpetually 끊임없이 demanding 요구가 지나친, 힘든, 벅찬 depression 우울증 refer A to B A를 B에게 보내다, 맡기다 consultation 상담, 진찰 suspect 의심하다

해설 앞의 문장에서 소아과 의사의 상담을 받아 보라고 했으므로, 다른 이의 판단보다는 우선적으로 소아과 의사의 상담을 통해서 우울증이 판명된다면 정신건강 전문의에게 가 볼 것을 권고 받는다는 내용이 타당하다.

45 The whirlwinds of __________ will continue to shake the foundations of our nation until the bright day of justice emerges.

① repose
② revolt
③ amicableness
④ vision
⑤ catalyst

해석 정의로운 밝은 세상이 나타날 때까지 반란의 소용돌이는 우리나라의 기반을 계속하여 뒤흔들 것이다.

어구 whirlwind 회오리 바람, 폭풍 foundation 토대, 기반 repose 휴식, 평화 revolt 반란, 폭동 amicableness 평화 상태, 우호적인 상태 catalyst 기폭제

해설 'whirlwind(폭풍)'이란 단어를 수식하면서, 국가의 토대를 뒤흔들 수 있을 만한 의미는 '폭동', '반란'이 옳다.

46 Pearl's __________ behavior at the party raised some eyebrows; he was certainly the only one who spent the night walking on his hands.

① pliable
② odd
③ adroit
④ buoyant
⑤ ebullient

해석 파티에서 펄의 괴상한 행동은 몇몇 사람들의 눈총을 샀다. 그는 물구나무를 서서 하룻밤을 보냈었던 바로 그 사람이었다.

어구 raise eyebrows 사람들을 놀래키다, 경멸을 초래하다 walk on one's hands 물구나무를 서다 pliable (마음을) 쉽게 바꾸는 odd 이상한, 홀수의, 임시의 adroit 실력이 좋은 buoyant 명랑한 ebullient 원기 왕성한

해설 '사람들의 경멸을 초래했고', '밤새 물구나무를 설 수 있는 사람'은 '괴상한' 사람임이 분명하다.

47 The public health authorities are combatting the claims of ___________ who maintain fraudulently that they have cures for many major ailments.

① salesman
② pharmacists
③ chemists
④ charlatans
⑤ dupe

해석 공중위생 당국은 수많은 주요 질병에 대한 치료제를 가지고 있다고 거짓 주장하는 엉터리 의사들의 주장과 싸우고 있다.

어구 **public health authorities** 공중위생 당국   **fraudulently** 사기를 치며, 속이면서   **ailment** 병, 불쾌, 우환   **salesman** 판매원   **pharmacist** 약사, 조제사   **chemist** 화학자, 약제사   **charlatan** 돌팔이 의사, 잘난 체하는 사람   **dupe** 잘 속는 사람, 얼간이

해설 치료제에 대하여 거짓 주장을 펼치는 사람은 돌팔이 의사가 옳다.

48 The name of the housing developing is a ___________ : although it is called "Forest Hills", it is located in a treeless valley.

① dilution
② misnomer
③ benevolence
④ stalemate
⑤ malediction

해석 그 주택 개발의 명칭은 잘못되었다. 비록 그것이 Forest Hills라고 불리지만, 나무가 하나도 없는 계곡에 위치해 있다.

어구 **housing development** 주택 개발   **treeless** 나무가 없는   **dilution** 희석, 가치 저하   **misnomer** 틀린 이름, 인명 오기   **benevolence** 자비   **stalemate** 교착 상태, 막다름   **malediction** 악담, 저주

해설 명칭은 '숲이 많은 언덕'일지라도, 현실은 나무 한 그루 없는 계곡이므로, 그 명칭은 잘못된 것으로 보아야 한다.

49 Despite strong ___________ from public safety officials, most Californians were inadequately prepared for a moderate preparation to large earthquake.

① calamity
② admonitions
③ observations
④ recovery
⑤ execration

해석 안전 담당 공무원들의 강력한 경고에도 불구하고, 대부분의 캘리포니아 사람들은 대규모 지진에 대해 충분한 준비를 하지 못 했다.

어구 **public safety official** 안전 담당 공무원   **be prepared** 준비가 되어 있다   **calamity** 재난   **admonition** 경고   **execration** 저주

해설 despite라는 '역접-양보' 논리 정보 장치에 의해, '지진에 대해 불충분하게 준비가 되어 있었다'는 표현이 적합하기 위해서는 '경고'가 반의어로서 옳다.

50 Before we spend a lot of money on this project, I would like to see ___________, rather than theoretical, evidence that it is effective.

① empirical
② erroneous
③ conventional
④ deficient
⑤ marvelous

해석 우리가 이 계획에 많은 돈을 쓰기 이전에, 그 계획이 효과가 있다는 점에 대해 이론적이라기보다는 경험에 의한 것이라는 점을 보고 싶다.

어구 **would like to R** ~하고 싶다   **rather than** ~라기보다는   **empirical** 경험의, 경험적인   **erroneous** 잘못된, 틀린   **deficient** 불충분한, 결함이 있는   **marvelous** 기적의, 훌륭한

해설 rather than 이라는 '역접-양보'의 '비교' 연결사에 의해 '이론적인'이라는 의미와 연결되기 위해서는 반의어인 '경험에 의한'이 옳다.

51 Some people like to dream about things that are not possible. They plan wonderful vacations, but they have no money. They think of getting married to someone they do not even know. These people, we say, are ___________.

① building a solid future
② telling telltales
③ building castles in the air
④ making a plain living
⑤ making a new life for themselves

해석 어떤 이들은 가능치 않은 일에 대해 꿈꾸기를 좋아한다. 그들은 굉장한 휴가를 계획하지만 돈이 한푼도 없다. 그들은 알지조차 못하는 누군가와의 결혼을 고려한다. 우리는 이들을 보고 공상을 하고 있다고 말한다.

어구 **solid** 견고한, 확실한   **telltale** 남의 비밀을 폭로하는 것, 고자질   **build castles in the air** 사상누각을 짓다, 공상에 잠기다   **plain** 소박한, 못생긴

해설 가능성 없는 일에 대해 공상하기를 좋아하는 경우에 대해 예를 들어주는 글로서, build castles in the air가 가지고 있는 '공상에 잠기다'의 뜻을 물어보는 문제이다.

52 Many children believe that their parents are ____________ and are shocked to learn that they can make mistakes.

① humble
② flawless
③ insolent
④ indolent
⑤ ludicrous

해석 많은 아이들이 자신들의 부모가 완벽한 존재라고 믿고 있는데, 자신들의 부모도 실수를 할 수 있다는 것을 알면 충격을 받는다.

어구 be shocked to R ~에 충격을 받다 humble 비천한, 겸손한 flawless 완벽한, 흠 잡을 데 없는 insolent 오만한 indolent 게으른 ludicrous 익살스러운

해설 자신들의 부모가 실수를 저질러서 충격을 받기 위해서는, 평소에 아이들은 자신들의 부모가 완벽하다고 믿고 있었다는 논리가 적합하다.

53 While admitting his client's guilt, the lawyer argued that circumstances warranted his plea for ____________ .

① leniency
② innocence
③ conviction
④ confidence

해석 변호사는 그의 의뢰인의 유죄를 인정하긴 했지만, 정황상 그에게 자비를 베풀어도 정당하다고 주장했다.

어구 admit 허락하다, ~을 허용하다, 인정하다 guilt 범죄 사실, 유죄 warrant ~을 정당화하다, ~의 정당한 이유(근거)가 되다 plea 변명, (소송에서의) 진술, 주장 leniency 자비, 관용 innocence 무죄, 천진난만 conviction 유죄 판결, 설득(력) confidence 신뢰, 신임

해설 의뢰인이 죄가 있음은 인정하지만, 자비를 베풀어 줄 것을 부탁했다는 '양보'의 논리가 옳다.

54 Suspicious of too powerful a President, Americans are ____________ when a President does not act decisively.

① unified
② indifferent
③ content
④ uneasy
⑤ adamant

해석 대통령의 권한이 너무 강력한 것을 좋게 보지 않는 미국인들도 대통령이 결단력 있게 행동하지 못할 때에는 불안하다.

어구 suspicious of ~을 수상히 여기는 unify 하나로 통합하다, 단일화하다 uneasy (몸 · 마음의) 거북한, 불안한, 근심스러운 adamant 완고한, 굳센

해설 강력한 대통령을 수상히 여기는 것에 따른 합당한 결과적 논리가 적합하다.

55 In the thirteenth century, Roger Bacon discovered the main substances in gunpowder. The list of substances included charcoal, sulfur and a chemical compound called "saltpeter". But because Bacon ____________, he wrote the list in secret signs the people were not able to understand until 500 years later.

① intended that his discovery should never be known to anyone
② wished that his discovery should be admired all over the world
③ expected that his discovery would be used openly
④ hoped that his discovery could be used immediately
⑤ feared that his discovery might be used harmfully

해석 13세기에 로저 베이컨은 화약의 중요 물질을 발견했다. 물질 리스트는 숯, 유황과 초석이라 불리우는 화합물을 포함했다. 그러나 그는 자기의 발견이 해롭게 이용될까 두려워했기 때문에 500년이 지나서야 비로소 사람들이 이해할 수 있도록 비밀 암호를 기록했다.

어구 substance 물질, 성분 gunpowder 화약 charcoal 숯 sulfur 유황 saltpeter 초석 secret sign 비밀 암호 be known to ~에게 알려지다 openly 공공연히, 솔직히 harmfully 해롭게

해설 비밀 암호를 기록했을 정도라면 그에 합당한 이유가 등장해야 한다. 또한 화약이란 성분은 악용될 수 있는 물질이므로, 논리 관계로 보면 ⑤가 가장 합당하다.

56 Punctuality is important, and people who are consistently late for appointments are thought to be ___________.

① diligent
② friendly
③ practical
④ inconsiderate

해석 시간 엄수는 중요하다. 그래서 시종일관 약속에 늦는 이들은 예의가 없다고 생각되어진다.

어구 punctuality 시간 엄수 consistently 시종일관 appointment 약속, 임명, 지명 diligent 근면한 friendly 우호적인, 친한 inconsiderate 분별력이 없는

해설 시간 엄수는 중요하다고 했으므로, 그와 상반되는 행위를 하는 이들은 당연히 예의가 없는 이들로 간주된다.

57 A foolish consistency is the hobgoblin of little minds, adored by little statesmen and philosophers and divines. With consistency a great soul ___________.

① has surely something to do
② is undoubtedly concerned
③ has simply nothing to do
④ is greatly satisfied
⑤ is well acquainted

해석 어리석은 일관성(고집)이란 소인배들이 도깨비 장난을 치는 것으로, 하찮은 정치인과 철학자 그리고 성직자들이 숭배하는 것이다. 반면 대인은 일관됨에 대해 별다른 신경을 쓸 일이 없다.

어구 consistency 일관성 hobgoblin 개구쟁이, 도깨비 little minds 소인배들 adore 숭배·동경하다 divine 성직자 great soul 큰 인물 have something to do with ~과 관련이 있다 undoubtedly 의심할 바 없이 have nothing to do with ~과 관련이 없다 be acquainted with ~을 잘 알다

해설 소인배들은 어리석게 일관성을 부린다고 했다. 즉, 이 문장에서 consistency는 foolish와 결합되어 '고집'으로 생각하면 되므로, 이하에서 대인들은 저러한 '고집'과 아무 상관이 없다는 내용이 논리적으로 옳다.

58 Our ordinary ways of talking about the world may conceal and ___________ as well as reveal and clarify.

① hinder
② avoid
③ scrutinize
④ obscure
⑤ celebrate

해석 세상에 대해서 우리가 이야기하는 일반적인 방식은 드러내어 분명히 하는 것뿐만 아니라 숨겨서 애매모호하게 하는 것일지도 모른다.

어구 conceal 숨기다 reveal 드러내다, 폭로하다 clarify 분명히 하다, 정화시키다 hinder 방해하다 avoid 회피하다, 막다 scrutinize 정밀 조사하다 obscure 애매모호하게 하다, 어둡게 하다; 애매모호한, 무명의, 비천한 celebrate 축하하다

해설 A as well as B의 관계로서 '드러내다(reveal)'와 반의 관계인 '숨기다(conceal)'의 의미가 등장했으므로, 마찬가지의 '첨가' 논리로서, '분명히 밝히다(clarify)'의 반의 관계인 '모호하게 하다(obscure)'의 의미가 합당하다.

59 A ___________ is a period of time especially at night, when you remain quiet and watchful in one place. You do this, for example, because you are looking after a sick person, praying, or making a political protest.

① fasting
② transition
③ chronicle
④ quarantine
⑤ vigil

해석 밤샘 행위는 특히나 밤 시간 때 있게 되며, 이때 당신은 한 장소에서 말을 삼가고 조심스러워진다. 예컨대, 당신이 아픈 사람을 돌보거나 기도를 드리거나 정치적 시위를 하려 하기 때문에 이런 행동을 하는 것이다.

어구 watchful 조심스러운, 경계하는 look after 돌보다 protest 시위 fasting 단식 transition 변이, 과도기 chronicle 연대기 quarantine 격리, 교통 차단 vigil 밤샘, 철야, 축일 전야, 불침번

해설 밤에 한 장소에서 말을 하지 않고, 누군가를 돌보거나 기도를 드린다는 것은 밤새도록 특정 행위를 하는 것을 의미한다.

60 It is not wise to invent in stocks and shares when shares prices are ___________ so violently.

① moving
② hesitating
③ fluctuating
④ undulating
⑤ exasperating

해석 주가가 맹렬하게 변동하고 있을 때 주식에 투자를 하는 것은 현명하지 못하다.

어구 **stocks** 주식[미국] **shares** 주식[영국] **violently** 격렬하게 **fluctuate** (기준이나 물가 등이) 오르내리다, 변동하다 **undulate** (수면 등에) 물결이 일다, (땅이) 굽이치다 **exasperating** 화나게 하는, 분통 터지는

해설 주어 it은 가주어이며, to invent 이하가 진주어 구실을 하게 된다. 현명하지 못한 행위가 되기 위해서는 '주가의 변동이 심할 때 투자 행위를 하는 것'임을 알 수 있다.

61 The public politician and the private person were ___________ : this mayor was no more and no less than she appeared to be.

① impervious
② invincible
③ inscrutable
④ indivisible
⑤ indiscriminate

해석 공적인 정치가와 사적인 사람은 구분이 되지 않는다. 이 시장은 보이는 것 이상도 그리고 이하도 아니었다.

어구 **no more and no less** 이상도 이하도 아닌 **impervious** 무감동한, 스며들지 않는 **invincible** 무적의, 정복할 수 없는 **inscrutable** 불가사의한, 수수께끼 같은 **indivisible** 불가분의, 나뉘지 않는 **indiscriminate** 무차별의, 난잡한

해설 공적인 정치인을 의미하는 예가 '시장'이 되는데, 그 시장이 (외관상) 보이는 것 이상의 것도 이하도 아니라는 것은 '일반적인 사람'과 다를 것이 없다는 논리이다.

62 Today's children often combine a deceptive ___________ of speech with a shocking lack of firsthand experience, and much of their seemingly sophisticated patter is "tube-talk", a playback of television situation comedies and commercials.

① impediment
② precision
③ impetuosity
④ precocity
⑤ inhibition

해석 오늘날의 어린이들은 직접적인 경험이 부족함에도 불구하고 TV의 코미디 프로들과 상업 광고 방송들로부터 주워들은 세련된 재잘거림을 진실인 것처럼 속여 조숙한 말로서 풀어낸다.

어구 **combine A with B** A와 B를 합치다 **deceptive** 현혹시키는, 사기의 **firsthand** 직접의, 직접적으로 **seemingly** 보기에, 외관상으로 **sophisticated** 순진하지 않은, 복잡한, 세련된, 정교한 **patter** 재잘거림, 은어 **playback** (녹음·녹화한 내용의) 재생 **commercial** 상업 광고 방송; 상업의 **impediment** 방해, 신체장애 **precision** 정확 **impetuosity** 격렬함, 성급함 **precocity** 조숙함 **inhibition** 금지, 억제

해설 순진하지 못한 재잘거림이 상당 부분 있다고 이하에서 설명을 하므로, '(나이보다) 이른 상태'를 설명하는 '조숙함'이 어울린다.

63 A : The pedestrian crossing is too far, why don't we just cross over here?
B : No way! You can be heavily fined for ___________ .

① trespassing
② soliciting
③ speeding
④ jaywalking
⑤ overpassing

해석 A : 보행자 건널목 너무 멀어. 그냥 여기서 무단 횡단 하면 어떨까?
B : 안 돼! 무단 횡단에 대해 크게 벌금을 물 수도 있어.

어구 **cross over** 건너가다 **trespassing** 침입, 침해 **soliciting** 간청, 구걸 **speeding** 속도위반 **jaywalking** 무단 횡단 **overpassing** (시기·경험) 통과, 무시

해설 '건너가다(cross over)'와 '벌금을 크게 물다(be heavily fined)' 표현을 통해 '무단 횡단'임을 알 수 있다.

64 There are some people who believe that the name given to an infant exerts a powerful influence on its later life. But I wonder how many instances they know of a name's being a pointer to the ___________ career of the child who bore it. I have known some Christians in their teens, and I confess I could see few sings that the name had played any part in the molding of their characters.

① malicious
② prodigious
③ frivolous
④ congruent
⑤ subsequent

해석 어떤 사람들은 갓난아이에게 붙여진 이름이 그 아이의 장차 인생에 어떤 강력한 영향력을 끼칠 것이라고 믿고 있다. 내가 알고 싶은 것은 그 이름을 가진 아이의 그 후 인생을 암시한 실례를 그 사람들이 얼마나 알고 있느냐 하는 것이다. 나는 크리스챤이라는 이름을 가진 10대의 아이들을 몇 명 알고 있는데, 솔직히 말해서 이 이름이 그들의 성격 형성에 어떤 영향을 행사했다는 것을 거의 알 수 없다.

어구 **exert an influence on** ~에 영향력을 행사하다 **instance** 예 **pointer** 지침 **bear** 지니다 **play a part in** ~에 역할을 담당하다 **molding** 형성 **malicious** 악의가 있는 **prodigious** 거대한, 놀라운 **frivolous** 경솔한 **congruent** 조화로운 **subsequent** 후에 발생하는, 뒤따르는

해설 장차 인생에 영향을 미치느냐에 관한 글이 핵심이므로, 그에 관한 의미를 가진 어휘가 옳다.

65 You shouldn't listen to other people's private conversations; it isn't polite to ___________.

① earshot
② saunter
③ eavesdrop
④ utter

해석 다른 사람의 개인적인 대화를 들으려 해서는 안 된다. 남의 말을 엿듣는 것은 예의가 아니다.

어구 **earshot** 소리가 들리는 거리 **saunter** 거닐다, 산보하다, 빈둥거리다 **eavesdrop** 엿듣다, 도청하다 **utter** 입 밖에 내다, 발언하다

해설 다른 사람들의 개인적인 대화를 들어서는 안 된다는 당위적 내용과 어울리기 위해서는 도청이 옳다.

66 Your ___________ remarks spoil the effect of your speech; try not to stray from your subject.

① praised
② antique
③ feeble
④ disingenuous
⑤ digressive

해석 주제에서 벗어나는 언급은 당신의 연설 효과를 망친다. 그러니 주제에서 벗어나지 않도록 노력해라.

어구 **spoil** 망치다, 버릇없게 키우다 **stray** (옆길·주제 등에서) 벗어나다 **praised** 찬미의 **feeble** 유순한 **disingenuous** 불성실한 **digressive** 주제에서 벗어난

해설 세미콜론 이하의 '주제에서 벗어나지 않도록 노력하시오.'라는 문장을 통해 주제에서 벗어나는 언급이 연설을 망칠 수 있다는 논리와 적합해진다.

67 Some people argue against capital punishment because there used to be so much racial prejudice against blacks, and it was mostly blacks who were executed. It is no doubt that capital punishment was used unjustly in many cases, but today racial prejudice is not as great. Capital punishment could be given to all those who deserve such a sentence. Only 17 out of 47 men executed since 1947 were black. As a black American, I do not think the racial prejudice argument is ___________ any more.

① valid
② trivial
③ ethical
④ reckless
⑤ irrelevant

해석 과거엔 흑인들에 대한 인종 편견이 너무 많았고, 또 처형당한 이들이 대부분 흑인들이었다는 이유 때문에 어떤 이들은 사형 제도에 반대한다. 물론 사형 제도가 잘못 이용된 경우가 많긴 했지만, 오늘날은 인종 편견이 이전만큼 심하지 않다. 오늘날 사형 제도는 사형 판결을 받아 마땅한 모든 이에게 적용될 수 있다. 1947년 이후에 처형당한 47명 중 17명만이 흑인이었다. 미국에 살고 있는 흑인으로서 나는 인종 편견이라는 주장이 이젠 더 이상 타당하지 않다고 생각한다.

어구 **argue against** ~에 반대하다 **capital punishment** 사형 **execute** 처형하다 **no doubt** 분명, 물론 **unjustly** 부당하게 **sentence** 판결, 선고 **valid** 타당한, 유효한 **trivial** 사소한 **reckless** 무분별한

해설 사형 판결을 받을 이들에게는 그 판결이 적용될 수 있으며, 처형 당한 47명 중 17명이 흑인이었다고 작가가 주장하므로, 그러한 사실이 인종 편견이라는 주장은 타당하지 못하다는 논리가 적합하다.

68 밑줄 친 부분에 공통으로 들어갈 숙어는?

> • Half through the chapter I stopped. I could not ____________ a single word.
> • The people in the neighborhood of the university have difficulty to ____________ students to add to the income.
> • It was really easy to ____________ you ____________. You must be foolish.

① take in
② figure out
③ pick up
④ get through

해석 · 그 장의 절반쯤을 읽다가 나는 멈췄다. 나는 한 마디의 말도 이해할 수 없었다.
· 대학 주변의 사람들은 수입 증대를 위해 하숙할 학생들을 구하는 데 애를 먹고 있다.
· 너를 속이기는 정말 쉬웠어. 넌 멍청한 것이 틀림없어.

어구 **add to** 증가하다, 더하다 **take in** 섭취·흡수하다, 이해하다, 속이다, 숙박시키다, 하숙을 치다 **figure out** 이해하다, 해결하다 **pick up** 우연히 알게 되다, 도중에 태우다, 좋아지다 **get through** 통과하다, 끝내다

해설 각각의 문장에 공통으로 들어갈 수 있는 표현은 '이해하다', '숙박을 시키다', '속이다'라는 모든 뜻을 가지고 있는 take in이 적합하다.

>>> 밑줄 친 곳에 들어갈 알맞은 답을 고르시오. [69~81]

69 The lady got in ____________ with her boss because she didn't finish an important project by the deadline.

① a nutshell
② the dark
③ the same boat
④ the long run
⑤ hot water

해석 그 여자는 마감 시한까지 중요한 계획을 끝마치지 못해서 사장과 함께 곤경에 처하게 되었다.

어구 **in a nutshell** 아주 간결하게 **in the dark** 알지 못하는 **in the same boat** 같은 처지에 있는 **in the long run** 마침내 **in hot water** 곤경에 처한

해설 중요한 계획을 끝내지 못해서 곤경에 처했다는 논리가 가장 적합하다.

---

70 Space scientists view space exploration as a sort of ____________ to future achievements like permanent space stations that could monitor the weather and provide new sources of energy.

① steppingstone
② diversion
③ unexpectedness
④ deadlock
⑤ premium

해석 우주 과학자들은 우주 탐험을 기후를 관찰하고 새로운 에너지 자원을 공급할 수 있는 영구적인 우주 정거장과 같은 미래의 성취물에 대한 발판으로 여긴다.

어구 **view A as B** A를 B로 여기다 **space exploration** 우주 탐험 **space station** 우주 정거장 **steppingstone** 발판 **diversion** (기분) 전환 **unexpectedness** 예기치 못한 일 **deadlock** 난관 **premium** 중요시 여김, 상금

해설 기후를 예측하고 에너지 자원을 공급할 수 있는 역할을 수행한다는 것은 '발판'의 의미가 적합하다.

---

71 Even when his reputation was in ____________, almost everyone was willing to admit that he had genius.

① humidity
② retaliation
③ rebuttal
④ prestige
⑤ eclipse

해석 그의 명성이 쇠퇴 기로에 있었을 때조차도 거의 모든 이들이 그는 천재임을 기꺼이 인정했었다.

어구 **even when ~** 심지어 ~할 때조차도 **be willing to R** 기꺼이 ~하다 **humidity** 습기 **retaliation** 보복, 앙갚음 **rebuttal** 원고의 반박, 항변 **prestige** 위신, 명성, 세력 **eclipse** (명성·영광의) 실추, (해·달의) 식

해설 even when에 의해 주절의 내용과 '역접–양보'의 관계이어야 한다. 천재임을 인정한다는 내용과 역접이 되기 위해서는 '명성의 실추'가 옳다.

72 The text brims with details, but there are no overarching theses to ___________ them.

① specify
② exaggerate
③ confound
④ unify
⑤ modify

해석 그 문서는 자세한 내용으로 가득 차 있다. 그러나 그 내용들을 단일화시킬 중요한 이론은 없다.

어구 **brim with** ～으로 가득 차다　**overarching** 무엇보다 중요한　**theses** 이론들[thesis의 복수 형태]　**specify** 상술하다, 자세히 기입하다　**exaggerate** 과장하다　**confound** 혼동하다, 좌절시키다　**unify** 단일화시키다

해설 자세한 내용으로 가득 차 있다는 앞 문장의 내용이 but에 의해서 '역접–대조'로 이어지기 위해서는 '그 자세한 내용을 단일화시킬 이론이 존재하지 않는다'는 내용이 적합하다.

73 Lovejoy, the hero of Jonathan Gash's mystery novels, is an antique dealer who gives the reader advice on how to tell ___________ antiques from the real thing.

① priceless
② spurious
③ classical
④ authentic
⑤ antiquated

해석 조나단 개쉬의 미스터리 소설에 등장하는 영웅인 인물로서 러브조이는 골동품 상인인데, 독자에게 모조 골동품과 진품을 구별하는 방법에 관한 조언을 해준다.

어구 **tell A from B** A와 B를 구별하다　**priceless** 귀중한　**spurious** 가짜의, 위조의　**authentic** 진짜의　**antiquated** 골동품의

해설 tell A from B 표현에 의해 '진짜(real)'의 반대말이 등장해야 한다.

74 Numerous studies have discovered that people who choose to represent themselves in court on the whole exercise pretty good judgment— they seem to have a ___________ sense of when they need a lawyer and when they don't.

① faulty
② whimsical
③ reliable
④ transient
⑤ drastic

해석 수많은 연구는 법정에서 스스로를 변호하려고 결심하는 사람들이 대체로 매우 뛰어난 판단력을 발휘한다는 사실을 발견했다. 즉 그들은 언제 자신이 변호사를 필요로 하는지 또는 그렇지 않은지에 대한 신뢰성 있는 판단을 발휘한다.

어구 **on the whole** 대체로　**exercise judgment** 판단을 하다　**faulty** 잘못된　**whimsical** 변덕스러운　**reliable** 신뢰할 만한, 의존할 만한　**transient** 변하기 쉬운, 일시적인　**drastic** 급격한

해설 매우 좋은 판단을 한다고 했으므로, 변호사의 선택에 대해서도 신뢰할 만한 올바른 판단을 한다는 내용이 문맥상 옳다.

75 Scientists will discover many subtle genetic factors in the makeup of human beings, and those discoveries will challenge the basic concept of equality on which our society is based. Once we can say that there are differences between people that are easily demonstrable at the genetic level, then society will have to come to grips with understanding ___________—and we are not prepared for that.

① equality
② scientific discoveries
③ science
④ diversity
⑤ competition among human beings

해석 과학자들은 인간을 구성하고 있는 많은 이해하기 어려운 유전 인자들을 발견할 것이며, 그러한 발견들은 우리 사회의 기초가 되고 평등이라는 기본 개념에 의문을 제기할 것이다. 일단 우리가 사람들 사이에 유전적인 차원에서 쉽게 증명할 수 있는 차이가 존재한다고 말할 수 있게 된다면, 사회는 사람들 사이의 차이를 이해하려고 노력해야 할 것이다. 그러나 우리는 그럴 준비가 되어 있지 않다.

어구 **subtle** 미묘한, 이해하기 어려운　**genetic factor** 유전 인자　**makeup** 구성　**challenge** 이의를 제기하다　**equality** 평등　**demonstrable** 논증·논증할 수 있는　**come/get to grips with** ～와 맞붙어 싸우다, ～와 대처하다, 애써 노력하다　**diversity** 상이, 차이

해설 첫 문장에서 이해하기 어렵고 미묘한 유전 인자들을 발견할 것이라고 했으므로, 이해하고 노력해야 할 것은 그만큼 차이가 있고 상이한 의미를 가진 diversity가 옳은 것이다.

76 That is partly why changes in institutional stockholding can make markets highly ___________ and therefore risky for smaller investors.

① volatile
② vociferous
③ mawkish
④ imbecile
⑤ droll

해석 그래서 부분적으로 단체 주주사업에서의 변화가 시장에 매우 심한 변동을 줄 수 있게 된 것이며, 그에 따라 소규모 투자가들은 위험해질 수 있다.

어구 **that is why** 그래서 ~하다 **stockholding** 주주사업 **volatile** (가격 · 가치 등이) 심하게 변동하는, 휘발성의, 변하기 쉬운 **vociferous** 소란스러운 **mawkish** 역겨운, 감상적인 **imbecile** 저능한, 우둔한 **droll** 익살스러운

해설 소규모 투자가들에게 위험이 가해질 수 있는 내용은 '시장의 격심한 변동'이 논리상 적합하다.

77 The point of my keeping a notebook has never been, nor is it now, to have an accurate factual record of what I have been doing or thinking. That would be a different impulse entirely, an instinct for ___________ which I sometimes envy but do not possess.

① severity
② reality
③ punctuality
④ histrionics
⑤ relativity

해석 내가 노트를 기록하는 이유는, 이전에도 또한 지금도, 내가 해 온 일이나 생각해 온 바를 정확하고 사실적으로 기록하기 위해서가 결코 아니다. 그것은 전적으로 다른 욕구로서, 내가 간혹 부러워는 하지만 소유하지 못한 꼼꼼함에 대한 본능일 것이다.

어구 **point** 요점, 논지, 목적 **keep a notebook** 노트를 기록하다 **factual** 사실 · 실제의 **impulse** 충동, 욕구 **instinct** 본능 **severity** 엄함, 심함, 혹독함 **punctuality** 시간 엄수, 정확함 **histrionics** 연극 **relativity** 관련성

해설 노트 기록과 같은 행위를 하지만, 사실적인 기록을 하기 위함이 아니었다는 얘기는 결국 정확성을 필요로 하는 '꼼꼼함'을 시기했다는 내용으로 볼 수 있다.

78 He had no love for Montpelier last time, and it is unkind to require him to make such a ___________ journey.

① strenuous
② insatiable
③ infallible
④ chaste
⑤ platonic

해석 그는 이전에도 몬트필리어(미국 버몬트 주의 주도)지역을 좋아하지 않았으므로, 그와 같이 고된 여행을 가라고 그에게 요구하는 것은 고약한 행위이다.

어구 **had no love for** ~을 좋아하지 않다 **unkind** 고약한, 친절하지 못한 **strenuous** 호된, 힘든 **insatiable** 탐욕스러운 **infallible** 틀림이 없는 **chaste** 정숙한 **platonic** 순정적인

해설 여행을 가라고 요구하는 것 자체가 고약한 행위가 되기 위해서는 그 여행이 고된 일임을 유추할 수 있다.

79 In discussing Rothko's art, Breslin is ___________ in keeping to the facts and resisting the ___________ of fanciful interpretation.

① scrupulous - temptations
② meticulous - integrity
③ ungainly - reward
④ uninterested - echo
⑤ inept - bias

해석 로스코의 예술을 논할 때 브레슬린은 사실들을 고수하고자 하고, 상상에 의존한 해석의 유혹을 뿌리치려고 한다는 점에서 신중했다.

어구 **keep to the facts** 사실을 고수하다 **fanciful** 상상의, 공상의 **interpretation** 해석 **scrupulous** 신중한, 양심적인 **temptation** 유혹 **meticulous** 신중한 **integrity** 완전함, 청렴함 **ungainly** 볼품없는, 어색한 **uninterested** 공평한, 무관심한 **inept** 부적당한, 어리석은

해설 [순접-열거] and resisting

80 This is an age of ___________, with interruptions by telephone, by friends, by noise, by scares and by our own flightiness. Increasingly, work must be done under conditions which are ___________ to concentration.

① concentration - harmful
② concentration - hospitable
③ stress - friendly
④ distraction - favorable
⑤ distraction - hostile

해석 요즘은 전화, 친구, 소음, 공포 그리고 우리 자신의 오두방정에 의한 방해로 주의가 산만한 시대이다. 점차 일은 집중하기에 불리한(부적당한) 여건들 하에서 이루어질 수밖에 없다.

어구 interruption 중단, 방해, 불통 scare 공황; 공포; 협박 flightiness 들뜸, 경솔, 변덕, 오두방정 concentration 집중, 전심전력, 전념 hospitable 손님 대접이 좋은(friendly), 환대하는, 쾌적한 distraction 주의 산만; 기분전환, 오락 hostile 적대적인, 비우호적인(antagonistic, unfriendly), 불리한, 부적당한(unfavorable)

81 Deeply ___________ by the insult to his dignity, he maintained that no true gentleman would accept such an ___________ calmly.

① mortified - opportunity
② incensed - affront
③ puzzled - honor
④ shamed - iconoclasm
⑤ gratified - admonition

해석 그의 존엄함에 대해 모욕을 받자 상당히 분개한 그는 진정한 신사라면 어느 누구도 이와 같은 모욕을 차분히 참을 이는 없을 것이라고 주장했다.

어구 insult 모욕 dignity 존엄함 calmly 차분하게 mortified 굴욕적인 incensed 분노한 affront 모욕 puzzled 당황한 shamed 부끄러운 iconoclasm 인습 타파 gratified 만족한 admonition 훈계, 충고, 경고

해설 존엄함에 대한 분노에 대해 대처할 수 있는 태도는 분노이며, 그에 따른 결과가 두 번째 밑줄에 들어가야 논리상 적합하다.

Part 2
실전편 정답 및 해설

Actual TEST 01 | Actual TEST 02 | Actual TEST 03 | Actual TEST 04 | Actual TEST 05 | Actual TEST 06 | Actual TEST 07 | Actual TEST 08 | Actual TEST 09 | Actual TEST 10

Actual TEST 01

⇨ 본책 p.184

1 ①	2 ③	3 ④	4 ④	5 ①	6 ②	7 ②	8 ②	9 ①	10 ③
11 ①	12 ①	13 ②	14 ⑤	15 ①	16 ③	17 ④	18 ②	19 ⑤	20 ⑤
21 ②	22 ①	23 ③	24 ①	25 ④	26 ①	27 ①	28 ③	29 ④	30 ②

>>> 밑줄 친 곳에 들어갈 알맞은 답을 고르시오. [1~6]

1 If he didn't have ___________ in the decision making, it would be impossible to draw any conclusions.

① initiative
② antipathy
③ malignancy
④ reluctance
⑤ tarnish

해석 만일 그가 의사 결정에서 주도권을 쥐고 있지 않다면 어떠한 결론을 내린다는 것은 불가능할 것이다.

어구 decision making 의사 결정 draw a conclusion 결론을 내리다 initiative 주도(권); 시작의 antipathy 반감 malignancy 악감정, 악의 reluctance 주저함 tarnish 오점, 더러움

해설 결론을 내리기 힘들기 위해서는 주도권을 잡고 있지 못하다는 논리가 적합하다.

2 The crisis is not ___________; it will not affect us for years to come.

① specious
② fleeting
③ imminent
④ meaningless
⑤ venomous

해석 그 위기는 임박한 것이 아니다. 왜냐하면 그것은 다가올 몇 년 안에 우리에게 영향을 미치지 않을 것이기 때문이다.

어구 specious 그럴듯한, 허울 좋은 fleeting 무상한, 빨리 지나가는 imminent 임박한 meaningless 의미 없는 venomous 독이 있는, 원한이 맺힌

해설 세미콜론(;) 이하에서 다가올 몇 년간 우리에게 영향을 미치지 않는다고 했으므로, 이는 시간상 임박한 것이 아님을 알 수 있다.

3 To help her psychology students understand the power of social ___________, Ms. Ewalt had her class participate in an experiment: on a regularly scheduled basis, each member of the class spent two days being shunned by others—no communication, no sharing of a lunchroom table.

① nexus
② mandate
③ mishap
④ ostracism

해석 심리학 수업을 듣는 학생들이 사회적 왕따 현상을 이해하도록 돕기 위하여, 에발트 교수는 학생들을 어떤 실험에 참여시켰다. 예정대로, 그 반의 각각의 학생들은 대화나 구내식당에서의 식사도 함께 하지 못하면서 다른 이들에게 따돌림을 당하며 이틀의 시간을 보냈다.

어구 shun 피하다 lunchroom 구내식당 nexus 연계, 관련, 연쇄 mandate 명령, 지령, 위임 mishap 재난, 사건(accident) ostracism 추방, 배척

해설 다른 이들에게 따돌림을 당하고 함께 식사나 대화도 하지 못하게 된 임상 실험의 예를 통해서 '집단 따돌림'의 힘을 논하고 있다.

4 Despite the poem's archaic and tortuous language, the thrust of the poet's argument is surprisingly ___________.

① vapid
② dated
③ blunted
④ intelligible
⑤ paradoxical

해석 그 시의 고풍스럽게 에두르는 말에도 불구하고, 시인이 주장하고자 하는 요점은 놀랍게도 이해할 수 있다.

어구 archaic 고풍의 tortuous (말이) 에두르는 thrust 요지, 찌르기; 밀어내다, 찌르다 vapid 지루한, 활기가 없는 dated 구식의 blunted 둔감한 intelligible 이해할 수 있는 paradoxical 역설의, 자기모순의

해설 despite라는 '역접'의 논리 정보 장치에 의해서 '에두르는 언어'와 반의 관계가 성립되는 '이해할 수 있다'는 논리가 적합하다.

5 I don't mean to suggest that we should seek to eliminate fear altogether from human life. Were this humanly possible, it would not be practically ___________. Fear is the elemental alarm system of the human organism which warns of approaching dangers and without which man could not have survived in either the primitive or modern world. Fear, moreover, is a powerfully creative force.

① desirable　　② repentable
③ lamentable　　④ potential

해석 우리가 인간의 삶에서 두려움을 완전히 제거하려고 노력해야 한다고 말하는 것은 아니다. 만일 이것이 인간적인 판단으로 가능하다면, 실제로 인생은 바람직하지 못한 것이 될 것이다. 두려움은 위험이 닥칠 때 경고하는 인간 신체의 기본적인 경고 장치이다. 그리고 두려움이 없다면 인간은 원시 세계든 현대 세계든 생존할 수 없을 것이다. 게다가 두려움은 강력한 창조적인 힘이다.

어구 eliminate 제거하다　altogether 완전히　survive 생존하다　repentable 후회할 만한　lamentable 슬퍼할 만한　potential 잠재적인

해설 이 글에서는 두려움을 불가피한 삶의 요소로 바라보고 있으므로 '바람직한'이라는 표현이 적합하다.

---

6 A third revolution was the tremendous growth in industrial chemistry, and in our ability to make chemicals in ___________ quantities, very cheaply, for all kinds of purposes. But these have upset the little understood ___________ balance, and polluted and poisoned our waters.

① adequate - metaphysical
② vast - ecological
③ lucrative - environmental
④ substantial - biological
⑤ excessive - economic

해석 제 3의 혁명은 산업 화학과 여러 목적으로 상당한 양의 저렴한 화학 물질을 만드는 우리의 능력에 있어서의 엄청난 발전이었다. 그러나 이러한 것들은 이해되기 힘든 생태학적 균형을 망쳐 놓았고, 우리의 바다를 오염시키고 독을 퍼뜨렸다.

어구 revolution 혁명　tremendous 상당한　quantity 양　upset 화나게 하다, 망쳐 놓다(spoil)　pollute 오염시키다　poison 독이 들어가게 하다　adequate 충분한　metaphysical 형이상학적인　vast 상당한(stupendous, tremendous, ample, capacious)　ecological 생태학적인　lucrative 수지맞는　substantial 상당한　excessive 과도한

해설 첫 번째 빈칸 – and에 의해 tremendous(상당한)과 순접의 논리가 필요하다. 두 번째 빈칸 – 바다를 오염시켰다는 내용이 나오므로 '생태계'의 균형이 문맥상 옳다.

Most women are employed in traditional fields for females, such as clerical sales, education, and service. However, a growing number choose a career that necessitates spending many hours away from home. These women are engineers, politicians, doctors, lawyers, and scientists, and a few have begun to occupy executive positions in business, government, and banking, breaking through the so-called glass ceiling.

7 What would be the meaning of the expression glass ceiling?

① ceiling made of glass
② invisible barrier to the women promotion
③ invisible helping hand for the promotion
④ ceiling shining too bright to look at with the naked eye

해석 대부분의 여성은 사무직, 교육 및 서비스와 같은 전통적으로 여성들이 많이 일하던 분야에 채용된다. 그러나 점점 여성들이 집에서 멀리 떨어져 많은 시간의 할애를 필요로 하는 직장을 선택하고 있다. 이 여성들 중에는 기술자, 정치가, 의사, 과학자도 있으며, 소수는 사업, 정부 및 은행에서 소위 유리 천장이라고 불리는 승진의 최상한선을 깨뜨리고 중역 간부직을 차지하기 시작했다.

7 '유리 천장'의 의미는 무엇인가?

① 유리로 만든 천장
② 여성 승진을 막는 보이지 않는 장벽
③ 승진을 위한 눈에 보이지 않는 도움의 손길
④ 눈을 뜨고 볼 수 없을 정도로 너무나 밝게 빛나는 천장

어구 clerical 사무원의; 서기의　necessitate 필요로 하다　occupy 점유하다; 점령하다　executive 경영진, 임원; 행정부　break through 깨뜨리다　so-called 소위　glass ceiling (여성·소수파의) 승진의 최상한선(승진을 막는 보이지 않는 장벽)　invisible 보이지 않는　barrier 장벽; 방해 요소

해설 여성들이 승진하기 위하여 깨뜨려야 할 대상이라면 기존에 여성의 승진을 막는 (보이지 않는) 장벽임을 유추할 수 있다.

Indeed, there has been lots of surprisingly good news in general about caffeine and coffee. You would naturally assume that an addictive drug like caffeine must surely be bad for you, and initial studies suggested it might lead to bladder cancer, high blood pressure and other ills. More recent research has not only refuted most of those claims but also come up with some significant benefits. Caffeine appears to have some protective effect against liver damage, Parkinson's disease, diabetes, Alzheimer's, gallstones, depression and maybe even some forms of cancer. The only proven medical downside appears to be a temporary elevation in blood pressure, which is a problem only if you already suffer from hypertension. Some studies have also suggested a higher risk of miscarriage in pregnant women and of benign breast cysts, but those results are highly controversial.

While most of the findings about the effects of caffeine remain open to further testing, caffeine's boosting your brainpower has been proved beyond any reasonable doubt. "As a research psychologist," says Harris Lieberman, "I use the word intelligence as an inherent trait." Caffeine can't change that, Liberman says. But what it can do, he says, is heighten your mental performance.

8 최근 연구에 의해 카페인이 예방할 수 있는 병으로 추정되는 것이 아닌 것은?

① diabetes
② bladder cancer
③ Alzheimer's
④ gallstones
⑤ Parkinson's disease

9 유일하게 입증된 것으로 보이는 카페인의 의학적 문제점은?

① a temporary elevation in blood pressure
② a higher risk of hypertension
③ miscarriage in pregnant women
④ a high risk of benign breast cysts
⑤ leading to bladder cancer

10 신빙성 있게 증명된 카페인의 이로운 점은?

① improving your overall health
② enhancing your intelligence
③ boosting your brainpower
④ cultivating your inherent traits
⑤ having some protective effect against liver damage

해석 실제로 대개는 카페인과 커피에 관한 놀라울 정도로 좋은 소식이 많이 있다. 당신은 카페인과 같은 중독성의 약물이 당연히 당신에게 해로울 것임에 틀림없다고 가정할 것이며, 초기 연구는 카페인성 약물이 방광암과 고혈압, 기타 질병들을 야기할 수 있다고 시사했었다. 보다 최근의 연구는 이와 같은 대부분의 연구들을 반박할 뿐만 아니라 몇 가지 중요한 이점을 제시했다. 카페인은 간 손상과 파킨슨병 및 당뇨, 알츠하이머병, 담석, 우울증 및 심지어 몇몇 암에 대해서 예방 효과를 갖고 있는 것처럼 보인다. 유일하게 입증된 의학적 단점은 혈압의 일시적 상승인데, 이는 단지 당신이 고혈압 환자일 경우에만 문제가 될 뿐이다. 몇몇 연구들은 또한 임신 여성의 경우 낙태와 유방 양성 낭종의 위험이 높다고 주장한다.

카페인의 효과에 관한 연구 결과 중 대부분이 추가 연구에 여지를 남겨 놓았을지라도 당신의 지력을 향상시킬 카페인이 논리적인 의심의 여지가 없음이 증명되었다. 해리스 리버맨은 "실험 심리학자로서, 나는 지능이라는 단어를 타고난 특성으로서 사용한다"고 했다. 리버맨은 카페인이 지능을 변화시킬 수 없다고 했다. 그러나 그의 말에 따르면 카페인이 할 수 있는 것은 당신의 정신 활동을 증대시키는 것이라고 한다.

8 최근 연구에 의해 카페인이 예방할 수 있는 병으로 추정되는 것이 아닌 것은?

① 당뇨병
② 방광암
③ 알츠하이머병
④ 담석
⑤ 파킨슨병

9 유일하게 입증된 것으로 보이는 카페인의 의학적 문제점은?

① 혈압의 일시적 상승
② 고혈압의 높은 위험
③ 임산부의 유산
④ 양성 유방 낭종의 높은 위험
⑤ 방광암을 야기하는 점

10 신빙성 있게 증명된 카페인의 이로운 점은?

① 당신의 건강 전체를 향상시켜 주는 점
② 당신의 사고력을 증대시켜 주는 점
③ 당신의 지력을 증대시켜 주는 점
④ 당신의 타고난 특징을 고양시켜 주는 점
⑤ 간에 손상이 가지 않게끔 몇 가지 예방 효과를 얻게 해 주는 점

어구 lots of 많은 in general 일반적으로 naturally 당연히 addictive 중독성의 initial 초기의 bladder 방광 refute 논박하다 come up with 제안하다(suggest) liver 간 gallstone 담석 downside 단점, 하강부분 temporary 일시적인, 임시의 elevation 높이, 고도 hypertension 고혈압 miscarriage 유산, 조산 benign 양성의; 자비로운, 친절한 cyst 낭종 highly 매우 controversial 논쟁적인 finding 연구 결과 remain open 여지를 남겨놓다 boost 증대시키다, 후원하다 brainpower 지력, 지식인들, 참모단 beyond doubt 의심의 여지가 없는 inherent 타고난 trait 특성 heighten 증대시키다, 고상하게 하다 overall 모든, 종합적인

해설 8 방광암은 초기 연구 결과에 의하여 '카페인에 의해 발생될 수 있는' 악효과였으므로, 예방할 수 있는 병이 아니다.

9 The only proven ~ 문장에서 고혈압의 환자들에게 있어서는 카페인이 혈압을 일시적으로 상승시킨다고 했는데, 이 점이 유일하게 의학적으로 입증된 카페인의 단점이다.

10 두 번째 단락 첫 문장에서 '카페인이 지력을 향상시켜 준다'는 점이 '의심의 여지 없이(beyond ~ doubt)' 입증되었다고 했다.

With 950 million people, India ranks second to China (1.2 billion) among the most populous countries. But since China launched a draconian birth control program in 1971, India has been closing the gap. Indians have reduced their own fertility but not nearly as much as the Chinese have. If current growth rates continue, India's population will pass China's around the year 2028 at about 1.7 billion.

Should that happen, it won't be the fault of the enlightened women of Kerala, a state in southern India. While India as a whole adds almost 20 million people a year, Kerala's population is virtually stable. The reason is no mystery: close to two-thirds of Kerala women practice birth control, compared with about 40% in the entire nation.

The difference lies in the emphasis put on health programs. And an educational tradition and matrilineal customs in parts of Kerala help girls and boys get equally good schooling. While one in three Indian women is literate, 90% of those in Kerala can read and write.

Higher literacy rates foster family planning. "Unlike our parents, we know that we can do more for our children if we have fewer of them," says Laila Cherian. She has limited herself to three children— one below the national average of four. That kind of restraint will keep Kerala from putting added pressure on world food supplies.

11 The best title of this passage is ____________.

① Effects of female education on birth control
② A comparison of the birth control policies between China and India
③ High population growth rates in China and India
④ Population explosion in India
⑤ Learning about birth control

12 According to this passage, which is correct?

① China is implementing more effective birth control policies than India.
② India's population will be reduced around the year 2028.
③ Birth control rates in Kerala is lower than India's average birth control rates.
④ High literacy rates have little bearing on birth control.
⑤ In India, boys and girls have equal educational opportunities.

해석 9억 5천만 명의 인구를 갖고 있는 인도는 12억의 인구를 갖고 있는 중국에 이어서 세계에서 두 번째로 가장 많은 인구를 갖고 있는 국가 중 하나이다. 그러나 중국이 1971년에 엄격한 산아제한 계획에 착수한 이후, 인도가 (인구수를) 따라잡고 있다. 인도인들도 출생률을 감소시켜 왔지만 중국이 해 왔던 것만큼은 아니다. 만일 현재의 인구 성장률이 계속된다면, 인도의 인구는 대략 2028년경에는 약 17억 명으로 중국의 인구수를 넘어서게 될 것이다.

이러한 일이 발생한다면, 그것은 인도 남부에 있는 주인 케랄라(Kerala)의 개화된 여성들의 잘못은 아닐 것이다. 인도 전체에서 1년에 거의 2천만의 인구가 증가한 반면, 케랄라의 인구는 실제로 안정적이다. 그 이유가 미스터리하지 않은데, 케랄라 주의 거의 2/3가 산아제한을 실시하며, 이는 인도 전체의 약 40%의 산아제한 비율과 비교가 된다.

차이점은 건강 프로그램에 대한 비중에서 존재한다. 케랄라의 지역들에서 교육적인 전통과 모계의 풍습들이 소년 · 소녀들에게 평등한 교육을 받을 수 있게끔 도움을 준다. 인도 여성 세 명 중 한 명이 읽고 쓸 수 있는 반면에, 케랄라의 여성들 중 90%가 읽고 쓸 수 있다.

높은 교양 수준들 때문에 가족계획이 장려된다. "우리의 부모님들과는 달리, 우리가 아이를 덜 출산한다면 아이들에게 더 많은 것을 해 줄 수 있다는 점을 압니다."라고 라일라 체리언이 말한다. 그녀는 3명으로 자녀 수를 제한하는데, 이는 전국 평균인 4명보다 한 명이 적은 수이다. 이러한 출산 억제는 케랄라가 지구 식량 공급에 추가 부담을 가하지 않게 해 줄 것이다.

11 가장 적절한 제목을 고르시오.

① 산아제한에 대한 여성 교육의 효과
② 중국과 인도의 산아제한 정책의 비교
③ 중국과 인도의 높은 인구 증가율
④ 인도의 인구 증가
⑤ 산아제한에 대한 학습

12 이 글과 일치하는 것은?

① 중국은 인도보다 효율적인 산아제한 정책을 실시하고 있다.
② 인도의 인구는 대략 2028년도에는 감소될 것이다.
③ 케랄라의 산아제한율이 인도의 평균 산아제한율보다 낮다.
④ 높은 교양 수준이 산아제한과는 관계가 거의 없다.
⑤ 인도에서 소년들은 소녀들은 공평한 교육 기회를 가진다.

어구 rank second to ~ ~에 이어 2등이다 populous 인구가 많은 launch 착수하다, 발사하다, 시작하다 draconian 가혹한, 엄격한 birth control 산아제한 close a gap 간격을 줄이다, 따라잡다 fertility 비옥, 다산, 번식력, 생식력 enlightened 계몽된 as a whole 전체적으로 virtually 실제로 practice 실시하다 compared with ~과 비교되어 put/lay/place emphasis on ~에 비중을 두다 matrilineal 모계의 schooling 학교 교육 literate 읽고 쓸 수 있는, 학식이 있는 foster 장려하다 restraint 억제, 제지, 금지 keep A from -ing A가 ~하지 못하게 하다 put pressure on 압력을 가하다 explosion 폭발, 갑작스러운 증가 implement 이행하다, 권한을 부여하다 have bearing on 관계가 있다

해설 11 인도의 인구수가 급격히 증가하지만, 인도의 주인 케랄라 지역에서는 산아통제가 잘 되는데, 그 이유가 여성들의 교육 수준이 좋기 때문이라는 내용이 주제로서 옳다. 따라서 ①이 이 글의 제목으로서 타당하다.

12 첫 단락 두 번째, 세 번째 문장을 통해서 중국의 산아제한 정책이 효율적으로 시행되어 왔으며 현재도 그렇다고 알 수 있다.

Seldom, if ever, has a highly authoritarian political system, deploying military means sufficient to destroy life on earth, ① dismantle so peacefully. Never has an empire disintegrated with so little bloodshed. Although huge difficulties remained for the successor states, the way Soviet communism came to an end was one of the great success stories of 20th century politics.

13 Why was, according to the above passage, the way Soviet communism came to an end "one of the great success stories of 20th century politics"?

① Because it was a highly authoritarian political system.
② Because it has disintegrated with so little bloodshed.
③ Because there still remained huge difficulties for the successor states.
④ Because it has deployed military means sufficient to destroy life on earth.
⑤ Because it should disappear eventually.

14 Choose the grammatically correct form of the underlined ①.

① has been dismantled
② has dismantled
③ to dismantle
④ to have dismantled
⑤ been dismantled

해석 매우 권위적인 정치체제는 지구상의 생명을 파괴하기에 충분한 군사력을 전개하는데, 설사 그 체계가 붕괴된 적이 있다고 치더라도 평화적으로, 즉 유혈사태가 일어나지 않고 제국이 붕괴된 적은 없었다. 거대한 난제가 후생 국가들에게 남겨졌을지라도 구소련이 종말을 맞게 된 방법은 20세기 정치학의 위대한 성공사 중 하나가 되었다.

13 윗글에 따랐을 때, 구소련 공산주의가 종식된 방식이 왜 "20세기 정치학의 위대한 성공들 중 하나"가 되었는가?
① 매우 권위적인 정치체제였기 때문에
② 매우 적은 유혈사태와 함께 붕괴됐기 때문에
③ 후생 국가들에게는 여전히 거대한 잔재가 남았었기 때문에
④ 지구상의 생명을 파괴할 만큼 충분한 군사력을 전개시켰기 때문에
⑤ 결국에는 사라져야 하기 때문에

14 ①을 문법적으로 맞게 고친 것은?

어구 **seldom, if ever** 설령 ~이라 치더라도 매우 드물게   **highly** 매우   **authoritarian** 권위적인   **deploy** (부대를) 전개시키다, 배치하다   **dismantle** 제거하다, 분해하다   **disintegrate** 분해시키다, 분해하다   **bloodshed** 유혈사태, 학살   **huge** 거대한   **successor state** 후생 국가   **come to an end** 끝나다, 해체하다   **politics** 정치학, 정치

해설 **13** 첫 문장에서 설명하기를 '군사력이 강한 제국이 평화롭게 붕괴된 적이 결코 없었다'고 했는데, 이 말은 즉 '군사 강대국이었던 구소련이 역사에서 드물게 평화로운 붕괴'를 맞이했다는 내용과 같다.
14 seldom이란 부정어가 문두로 위치해서 도치가 발생한 문장이다. 원래 문장은 'A highly authoritarian political system, deploying military means sufficient to destroy life on earth, seldom, if ever, has been dismantled so peacefully.'이다. 주어는 A highly authoritarian political system이며 deploying ~ on earth는 후치 수식하는 분사구문이다. dismantle은 타동사로서 목적어가 필요한데, 이 문장에서는 목적어가 없으며, 문장의 주어인 '매우 권위적인 정치체제'와 '붕괴시키다'의 관계는 수동이므로 수동태가 옳다. 이미 완료시제의 조동사 has가 위치했으므로 been p.p만 필요하다.

James Burton noticed that four times out of five Mary is depicted holding the infant Jesus against her left breast. The Madonna led him to investigate on which side women hold their babies and why. First he noticed that modern mothers, more than 85%, tend to hold their baby on the left. Then (가) <u>an apparently contradictory phenomenon</u> was observed. A large number of mothers who brought their premature babies to follow-up clinic were seen to hold their babies against their right side.

So 115 mothers who had been separated from their babies for 24 hours after birth were observed for (나) <u>holding response</u>. The experimenters presented the baby directly to the midline of the mother's body. 53% of them placed the baby on the left and 47% on the right. Incidentally it was also noted that the mothers of the group who had held their baby on the left had already had a baby from which they had not been separated after birth. The experiment suggests that the time immediately after birth is a critical period when the stimulus of holding the baby releases a certain maternal response, for instance, the feeling that the baby is better off on her left.

Left-handed holding enables the baby to hear the heartbeat. In order to discover whether hearing the heart has a beneficial effect on the baby, the sound of a human heartbeat was played to 102 babies for 4 days in a nursery. A controlled group of babies was not exposed to heartbeats. The babies in the beat group gained markedly more weight and cried far less than the babies in the control group.

15 What is the "apparently contradictory phenomenon" in (가)?

① Mothers of premature babies held their babies differently from other women.
② Mothers of premature babies held their babies on the correct side.
③ Mothers of premature babies took their babies to a follow-up clinic.
④ Mothers who were separated from their babies for 24 hours after birth behaved differently from other women.
⑤ The ways in which Mary and the mothers of premature babies held their babies differed.

해석 제임스 버튼은 다섯 번 중 네 번이 성모 마리아가 아기 예수를 왼쪽 가슴에 안는 것으로 묘사되어 있는 것을 발견했다. 성모 마리아는 그에게 여자들이 어느 쪽으로 아기를 안으며 왜 그런지 조사하게 만들었다. 처음으로 그는 요즘 어머니들 85% 이상이 아기를 왼쪽으로 안는 경향이 있다는 것을 알았다. 그리고 나서 명백히 모순된 현상이 관찰되었다. 조숙아를 부속 병원으로 데려온 많은 어머니들은 아기를 오른쪽으로 안는 것으로 보였다.

분만 후 24시간 동안 아기와 떨어졌던 115명의 어머니들의 안는 반응을 관찰해 보았다. 그 실험자들은 아기를 어머니 몸의 중심선에 똑바로 건네주었다. 그들 중 53%는 아기를 왼쪽에 두었고 47%는 오른쪽에 두었다. 우연히 아기를 왼쪽으로 안았던 그 집단의 어머니들은 분만 후에 아기와 떨어져 있지 않았다. 그 실험은 분만 직후가 아기를 안으려는 자극이 어떤 모성 반응, 예를 들면 아기가 산모의 왼편에서 더 편안하게 느끼게 하는 결정적인 시기라는 것을 암시한다.

왼쪽(왼손)으로 안는 것은 아기가 심장박동을 들을 수 있도록 한다. 심장소리를 듣는 것이 아기에게 이로운 효과를 주는지 아닌지를 알기 위해, 사람의 심장박동 소리를 육아실에서 4일간 102명의 아기들에게 들려주었다. 통제된 집단의 아기들은 심장박동에 노출되지 않았다. 심장박동 집단의 아기들은 현저하게 몸무게가 늘었고, 통제 집단의 아기들보다 훨씬 덜 울었다.

15 (가) "분명히 모순적인 현상"이 가리키는 내용은?
① 조숙아를 가진 엄마들이 다른 여성들과는 다르게 자신들의 아기를 안고 있다.
② 조숙아를 가진 엄마들이 바른 쪽에 아기를 안고 있다.
③ 조숙아를 가진 엄마들이 부속 병원에 아기를 데려 갔었다.
④ 24시간 동안 아기들과 헤어져 있던 엄마들은 다른 여성들과 다르게 행동했었다.
⑤ 성모 마리아와 조숙아들을 가진 엄마들이 아기를 안고 있는 방식들은 다르다.

16 (나) "안고 있는 반응"을 위해서 엄마들이 왜 관찰을 받았는가?
① 조숙아 부모들이 어떻게 아기들을 안고 있는지를 알기 위해
② 아기들과 떨어져 있을 때 엄마들의 반응을 실험하기 위해
③ 출산 후 아기들과 떨어져 있게 되면 아기들을 품에 안는 방식에 영향을 미치는지에 대해 알기 위해
④ 얼마나 많은 엄마들이 첫 출산 후 정상아를 분만하는지 알기 위해
⑤ 부모들이 실험의 질문에 어떻게 답변하는지 알기 위해

17 이 글에 따르면 출산 직후의 시간이 중요하다. 이는 어떠한 시간을 의미하는 것인가?
① 아기들이 엄마와 헤어져 있지 말아야 하는 시간
② 엄마에 대한 아기들의 반응이 나오는 시간
③ 아기가 엄마의 심장소리를 들을 수 있는 시간
④ 엄마가 좌측에 아기를 안으려는 본능적인 경향이 만들어지는 시간
⑤ 아기의 무게가 더 늘어나고 안전한 상태임을 확인하는 시간

18 실험에서 102명의 아기들이 4일의 시간 동안 무엇을 했는가?
① 집에서 엄마의 심장박동 소리를 듣는 것
② 녹음된 심장박동 소리를 듣는 것
③ 실제 소리이든 녹음이 된 것이든 간에 심장박동 소리에 노출되지 않는 것
④ 통제된 그룹 하에 있는 것
⑤ 어머니의 좌측 품에 안겨 있는 것

16 Why were mothers observed for "holding response" in (나)?

① To see how mothers of premature babies held their babies.
② To test their reaction to separation from their babies.
③ To see whether separation from the baby after birth affected the way they held the baby.
④ To see how many of them had delivered a normal baby at her first birth.
⑤ To see how they answered the experimenters' questions.

17 According to the passage, the time just after birth is important. This is when ____________.

① babies must not be separated from their mothers
② the baby's response to the mother is released
③ the baby can hear the mother's heartbeat
④ the mother develops an instinctive tendency to hold the baby on the left
⑤ the baby gains more weight and is assured of safety

18 In one experiment, 102 babies spend four days ____________.

① hearing the heartbeat of their mothers at home
② listening to the recording of heartbeats
③ not being exposed to heartbeats, live or recorded
④ in the control group
⑤ being held on the left side of their mothers

19 According to the passage, which is NOT true?

① Mothers of normal babies tend to hold them on the left.
② Mothers of premature babies do not have the instinct to hold the babies on the left.
③ Babies can hear the heartbeats of their mothers when they are held on the left.
④ Babies who were exposed to the heartbeats were healthier than those who were not.
⑤ Mothers who had a premature baby at her second birth tended to hold their babies on the right.

19 이 글의 내용과 일치하지 않는 것은?

① 정상아를 낳은 엄마들은 아기를 좌측에 안고 있는 경향이 있다.
② 조숙아를 낳은 엄마들은 아기를 좌측에 안으려는 본능을 갖고 있지 않다.
③ 아기들이 좌측에 안겨 있을 때 엄마의 심장박동 소리를 들을 수 있다.
④ 심장박동 소리에 노출된 아기들은 그렇지 못한 아기들보다 더 건강하다.
⑤ 두 번째 출산에서 조숙아를 갖게 되는 엄마들은 아기를 오른쪽에 안는 경향이 있다.

어구 **Mary** 성모 마리아(Madonna) **hold** ~을 (붙)들다, 잡다, 쥐다, (껴)안다 **infant** 유아, 소아, 아기, 미성년자 **breast** 가슴, 유방 **apparently** 겉보기에는, 외관상으로는, 분명히, 명백히 **contradictory** 모순된, 상반된, 정반대의 **observe** 보다, 관찰하다 진술하다, (규칙을) 준수하다 **premature baby** 조산아 **follow-up** 후속의 **separate** 가르다, 떼어놓다, 분리하다, 구별하다 **birth** 출생, 탄생, 출산, 분만 **response** 응답, 대답, 반응 **experimenter** 실험자 **present** ~을 주다, 건네다, 증정하다, 제공하다 **directly** 똑바로 직접, 곧장 **midline** (신체 등의) 중심선 **place** ~에 놓다, 두다, 배치하다 **incidentally** 우연히, 우발적으로, 부수적으로 **note** ~을 적어두다, 주의하다, 주목하다, 알아차리다, (글에서) 언급하다, 주석을 달다 **group** 집단, 모임, 그룹 **experiment** 실험, 시험 **suggest** 암시하다, 시사하다, 제안하다, 제의하다 **immediately** 즉시, 곧 **critical** 중대한, 중요한, 결정적인, 비판적인, 비평적인 **stimulus** 자극, 격려, 고무 **release** 풀어놓다, 해제하다, 방출하다, 해방하다, 개봉하다, 발표하다 **certain** 어떤, 일정한, 확실한 **maternal** 어머니의, 어머니로서의, 모성의 **for instance** 예를 들면, 이를테면 **be better off** 한결 더 잘 살다, 더욱 형편이 좋다, 보다 나은 상태에 있다 **left-handed** 왼손으로, 왼손을 써서, 왼손잡이의, 서투른, 어색한 **enable** ~할 수 있게 하다, 가능하게 하다 **heartbeat** 심장박동, 심장의 고동 **discover** 발견하다, 알다, 깨닫다 **beneficial** 이로운, 유익한, 유리한 **have an effect on** ~에 영향을 미치다, 효과를 나타내다 **effect** 영향, 효과, 결과 **nursery** 육아실, 아이 방 **controlled** 통제된, 억제된 **expose** 보이다, 드러내다, 노출하다, 폭로하다 **beat** 박자, 장단, (심장의) 고동, 맥박 **gain weight** 체중이 늘다 **markedly** 현저하게, 두드러지게, 눈에 띄게

해설 **15** 조숙아 엄마들은 자신의 아기를 다른 부모들과 달리 '우측 가슴' 쪽으로 안고 있는 현상을 의미하는 것이다.
16 출산 후 좌측에 아기를 안으면 출산 경험이 있는 것이고, 우측에 안으면 출산 경험이 없다는 내용이 옳다.
17 두 번째 단락 마지막 문장 when ~ 절에 등장하는 내용이다.
18 세 번째 단락 첫 문장에서 was played가 단서이다. '재생'이 되기 위해서는 사전에 녹음된 소리이어야 하므로, 녹음된 심장박동 소리를 들었다는 내용이 옳다.
19 두 번째 출산에서 조숙아를 가진 어머니들이 우측에 안고 있었다는 설명은 없다.

We had a game in our house called "setting the table" and I was Mother's helper. Forks were to the left of the plate, and knives and spoons were to the right. Placing the cutlery neatly, as I recall, was one of my first duties, and the event was alive with meaning. When a knife or a fork dropped on the floor, that meant a man was unexpectedly coming to dinner. A falling spoon announced the surprise arrival of a female guest. No matter that these visitors never arrived on cue, I had learned a rule of gender identification. Men were straight-edged, ① _______________ pronged and formidable, women were ② _______________ curved and held the food in a rounded well. It made perfect sense, like the division of pink and blue that I saw in babies, an orderly way of viewing the world. Daddy, who was gone all day at work and who loved to putter at home with his pipe, tobacco and tool chest, was knife and fork. Mommy and Grandma, with their ample proportions and pots and pans, were grownup soup spoons, large and capacious. And I was a teaspoon, small and slender, easy to hold and just right for pudding, my favorite dessert.

20 What would be the main topic of this passage?

① Superstition
② Folk myth
③ Setting the table
④ A childhood activity
⑤ Gender identification

21 Which of the following pairs best fits into ① and ②?

① elegantly - bluntly
② sharply - softly
③ delicately - plainly
④ dexterously - poorly
⑤ sufficiently - insufficiently

해석 우리는 집에서 '식탁 차리기'라고 불리는 게임을 했었으며, 나는 어머니를 도와드렸다. 포크는 접시의 왼쪽에, 칼과 수저는 오른편에 놓았다. 생각해 보건대, 칼붙이를 가지런히 놓는 것이 내가 해야 할 첫 번째 임무였으며, 그 일은 의미가 있는 일이었다. 칼이나 포크가 바닥에 떨어졌을 때, 그것은 어떤 남자가 갑자기 저녁 식사에 온다는 의미를 가지고 있었다. 수저가 떨어지는 것은 여자 손님이 갑자기 왕래한다는 것이었다. 신호대로 이 방문자들이 도착을 하는 것에 상관없이 나는 성별을 구별하는 것을 배우게 되었다. 남자는 직선으로 날이 서 있으며, 날카롭게 뾰족하고 무서운 것이었다. 여자는 부드러운 곡선이며 둥근 우물 속에 음식을 담았다. 그것은 내가 아기를 통해서 보았던 분홍과 파란색의 구별처럼 세상을 보는 질서정연한 방법으로서 이치에 닿는 것이었다. 온종일 일하러 나가 있으시고, 파이프, 담배, 도구 상자를 가지고 집에서 어슬렁거리기를 좋아했던 아버지는 칼과 포크였다. 충분한 비율의 항아리와 냄비를 가지고 계셨던 어머니와 할머니는 크고 널찍한 어른용 수프 스푼이었다. 그리고 나는 내가 가장 좋아하는 디저트인 푸딩에 적합한 조그맣고 얇은 티스푼이었다.

20 이 글의 주제는?

① 미신
② 민속 신화
③ 식탁 차리기
④ 유년시절 활동
⑤ 성 구별

21 ①과 ②에 적합한 것은?

① 우아하게 – 무디게
② 날카롭게 – 부드럽게
③ 섬세하게 – 수수하게
④ 능수능란하게 – 형편없이
⑤ 충분히 – 불충분하게

어구 set the table 식탁을 차리다 cutlery 칼붙이 neatly 단정하게, 가지런히 unexpectedly 예기치 않게 dinner 저녁식사 cue 신호 identification 구별 -edged ~하게 날카로운 prong 찌르다, (흙 따위를) 파헤치다; 포크 모양의 물건 formidable 무시무시한, 가공할 만한 curved 휘어진 rounded 둥글린 well 우물 make sense 이치에 닿다 division 구분, 구획 orderly 정돈된, 규율을 지키는 putter 어슬렁거리다, 꾸무럭거리다 tool chest 도구 상자 pot 항아리 pan 냄비 grownup 성숙한, 성장한; 성인 capacious 널찍한 slender 가느다란, 빈약한 pudding 푸딩[밀가루에 우유 · 달걀 · 과일 · 설탕 · 향료를 넣고 찐(구운), 식후에 먹는 과자] elegantly 우아하게 bluntly 무디게 delicately 섬세하게 plainly 수수하게 dexterously 능수능란하게 sufficiently 충분히 insufficiently 불충분하게

해설 20 식탁의 여러 도구들을 통해서 남자 손님과 여자 손님, 여자와 남자, 아버지와 어머니를 구별한 것이므로, 성의 구별이 이 글의 주제로서 옳다.

21 첫 번째 빈칸은 formidable(무서운)이란 단어와 and에 의해서 순접으로 연결되어야 하므로, '날카롭게'라는 뜻을 가진 sharply가 옳다. 두 번째 빈칸은 앞서 나온 내용과 상반되는 성인 '여성'을 말하므로 '날카롭게'와 반대 개념인 '부드럽게'가 옳다.

>>> **다음 글을 읽고 문제의 답을 고르시오.**

A. The idols of today are no longer just war heroes and other male figures, but rather female fashion models and movie stars.

B. And woman now have the right to choose their husbands and obtain jobs outside the home.

C. Therefore Japanese businessmen declare that the surest way to make money nowadays is to produce appliances that will relieve women of work.

D. There are even women executives and business owners who lack time for housework.

E. Housewives demand more automation from their kitchens to liberate them from tiresome household chores.

22 윗글의 흐름상 이어질 내용을 바른 순서대로 배열한 것은?

① A - B - D - E - C
② A - B - C - E - D
③ B - C - A - D - E
④ B - A - C - D - E

해석 A. 오늘날의 우상은 더 이상 전쟁 영웅이나 다른 남자 인물들이 아니라, 오히려 여성 패션모델과 영화배우들이다.
B. 그리고 현재 여성은 남편을 선택하고 집 밖에서 직장을 가질 권리가 있다.
D. 심지어 가사 일을 할 시간이 부족한 여성 경영자와 사업가들도 있다.
E. 주부들은 성가신 집안일로부터 자유롭게 해 줄 수 있는 더 많은 부엌 자동화 기구를 필요로 한다.
C. 따라서 일본 사업가들은 오늘날 돈을 벌 수 있는 가장 확실한 방법은 여성들의 일 부담을 덜어 줄 수 있는 용품을 만드는 것이라고 주장한다.

어구 **idol** 우상, 신상(神像) **no longer** 더 이상 ~ 않다 **female** 여성의 **declare** 선언[언명]하다, 발표[포고, 단언, 성명, 공언]하다 **appliance** 기구, 장치, 설비 **relieve A of B** A에게서 B를 덜어 주다 **executive** 집행권을 갖는; 법률 집행의[에 관한]; 관리직의, 이사[중역, 임원]의; 행정(상)의; 행정부에 속하는 **automation** 오토메이션, (기계·조직의) 자동화, 자동 조작[제어] **liberate A from B** B로부터 A를 해방시키다 **tiresome** 성가신, 귀찮은, 속상한 **household** 가족의, 한 세대의, 가사의 **chore** (일상의, 가정의) 잡일, 허드렛일

해설 A. 오늘날 여성의 지위가 격상됐음을 말하며, B. 그에 대한 추가 설명을 and로 열거하고 있다. D. 부사 even을 통해 특별한 지위에 있는 여성들이 집안일을 할 시간이 부족함을 말하고 있으며, E. 이에 따라 집안일을 대신 해 줄 기계의 자동화 필요성이 언급된다. C. 마지막으로 therefore로 결론을 내린다.

>>> **다음 글을 읽고 문제의 답을 고르시오.** [23~24]

"I am not the first president to take up this cause, but I am determined to be the last." Thus Barack Obama, late in the day, took his quest to reform America's expensive and flawed health-care system to the floor of Congress with a mighty speech that will surely stand as one of the defining moments of his presidency, whether it leads to eventual triumph or disaster. His is a bold ambition indeed; but this week (가) the president looks a bit closer to fulfilling it.

Politics, as everyone knows, is the art of the possible. There have been times over this ill-tempered summer when the idea of tackling a system that costs almost twice as much as any other rich country's, yet yields substandard results and leaves tens of millions of people with no health insurance at all, has seemed simply impossible. Mr Obama has to find a package of policies that is fiscally and politically moderate enough to win over a vital few Republicans to his side (and also prevent the defection of nervous conservative Democrats). But at the same time he has to keep the support of the leftish Democratic Party base, which wants to see a more expansive and costly set of reforms. He may well fail. But on September 9th the president for the first time laid out in some detail what such a plan might look like. Cleverly borrowing good ideas from both sides of the party divide, his proposals at least look like a plausible basis for agreement.

23 The underlined expression in (가) means
______________.

① it appears to be difficult to persuade the opposition party
② his bold ambition may be not convincing but preposterous
③ reforming America's health-care system seems to be not far-fetched
④ reforming America's health-care system seems to be infeasible

24 What is not the key that the writer gives to Obama?

① Keeping conservative Democrats at his arms' length
② Getting over some Republicans to his side
③ Tying up the left-winger of Democrats
④ Not being afraid of failure to reform

해석 "나는 이 소명을 떠안은 최초의 대통령이 아니다. 그러나 내가 마지막이 되기로 결심했다." 따라서 오바마 대통령은 고 비용인 데다 문제점이 많은 건강 보험 제도에 대한 시정 조치를 의회에 요청하면서, 그 시정 조치가 결국 성공하든 실패로 끝나든 간에 자신의 대통령직의 결정적인 순간으로 분명히 남게 될 힘찬 연설을 했다. 그의 요청은 대담한 야망이다. 그러나 이번 주에 오바마는 건강 보험 개혁의 성공에 더 가까워진 것처럼 보인다(자신의 야망을 이룰 것 같다= 건강 보험 개혁이 성공할 것 같다).

모두가 알다시피 정치는 가능성의 예술이다. 다른 어느 부유국보다 거의 두 배의 비용이 들지만 부정적인 결과를 만들어낸 데다가 수천만의 사람들이 누릴 수도 없게 방치한 건강 보험 제도를 폐지하겠다는 생각은, 무더운 여름 동안 수차례에 걸쳐 정말 불가능한 것처럼 보였다. 오바마는 국고와 정치적으로 충분히 적정한 수준의 정견을 모색하여, 절대적으로 필요한 소수의 공화당원들을 자신의 편으로 끌어들여야만 한다(그리고 보수적인 성격을 가진 민주당원들의 탈당 또한 방지해야 한다). 그러나 동시에 그는 더욱 광범위한 고 비용의 대개혁을 원하는 좌파 성향의 민주당을 계속 지지해야만 한다. 실패해도 무방하다. 그러나 9월 9일 오바마는 그 계획에 대한 어느 정도 자세한 내용을 처음으로 밝혔다. 두 당의 좋은 생각을 현명히 받아들인 오바마의 제안은 적어도 의견 합의를 이룰 수 있는 괜찮은 토대를 갖춘 것으로 보인다.

23 밑줄 친 (가)가 의미하는 것은?

① 야당을 설득하기가 힘들 것으로 보인다.
② 그의 대담한 야망이 설득력 있는 것이 아니라 터무니없어 보인다.
③ 미국의 건강 복지 제도를 개혁하는 것이 억지스럽지 않은 것으로 보인다.
④ 미국의 건강 복지 제도를 개혁하는 것이 실행 불가능한 것으로 보인다.

24 작가가 오바마에게 제시하는 해결책이 아닌 것은 무엇인가?

① 보수적인 민주당원들과 거리를 두는 것
② 일부 공화당원들을 자신의 편으로 끌어들이는 것
③ 좌파 성향의 민주당원들을 연합시키는 것
④ 개혁 실패를 두려워하지 않는 것

어구 take up a cause 주의를 받아들이다, 운동에 가담하다 take quest 요청하다 flawed 흠이 많은 floor 회의장, 의원석; (회의장에 있는) 의원, 회원; (의회에서의) 발언권; (연단에 대한) 회장 defining moment 결정적인 시기 a bit 약간 look close to -ing ~할 가능성이 있다 ill-tempered 성마른, 까다로운 tackle 논쟁하다, 맞싸우다 substandard 표준 이하의 win over to (자기편·자기주장에) 끌어들이다 leftish 좌파 성향의 may well R ~해도 무방하다 lay out 펼치다, 진열하다 far-fetched 에두른, 빙 둘러서 말하는; 무리한(forced); 부자연한 keep ~ at one's arm's length ~와 거리를 두다; 가까이 지내지 않다 get over A to side A를 자신의 편으로 끌어들이다 tie up 단단히 묶다; 연합시키다; 구속시키다

해설 **23** look close to -ing는 '~할 가능성이 있다'는 표현으로서, ⑤의 '미국 건강 보험 제도를 수정한다는 것이 억지스럽지 않은 것으로 보인다.'는 내용과 일치한다.

24 at arm's length는 '쌀쌀맞게', '거리를 두고서'라는 뜻으로, ①의 의미는 '거리를 두고서 보수적인 민주당원들을 대하는 것'이 된다. 위에서 작가는 보수적인 민주당원들도 자신의 편으로 끌어들이라고 했기 때문에 상반된 논리가 된다.

>>> **다음 글을 읽고 문제의 답을 고르시오.**

Another mass movement in postwar America was from the cities to the suburbs. Almost as many Americans resided in the suburbs as in the cities by 1960. A combination of motives drew people to the suburbs. Some wanted to leave behind the noise and smells of the city. Some white families moved out of urban neighborhoods because African-American families were moving in. People living in row houses and apartments wanted to move into houses that had yards, family rooms, extra closets, and utility rooms. Many also were looking for a place where they could have a measure of political influence, particularly on the education their children received.

25 윗글의 앞에 들어올 수 있는 내용으로 가장 적합한 것을 고르시오.

① Increase of population of the United States and its geographic distribution
② Change of life style in the United States after World War II
③ Need of housing and highway construction
④ Migrating to the Sunbelt, the southern third of the United States

해석 전후 미국에서 도시로부터 교외로 대규모의 이동이 있었다. 1960년에 이미 도시만큼이나 교외에 많은 사람들이 살았다. (몇 개의) 동기들이 결합하여 사람들을 교외로 끌어들였다. 어떤 사람들은 도시의 소음에서 벗어나기를 원했다. 어떤 백인 가정들은 미국 흑인들이 도시로 이주해 들어오기 때문에 도시에서 이사를 갔다. 연립 주택과 아파트에 살던 사람들은 마당과 거실, 여분의 옷장과 다용도실이 있는 집으로 이주하기를 원했다. 게다가 많은 사람들이 자신의 아이들이 받는 교육에 관해 어느 정도의 정치적 영향력을 가질 수 있는 장소를 찾았다.

25 윗글의 앞에 들어올 수 있는 내용으로 가장 적합한 것을 고르시오.

① 미국의 인구 증가와 지리학적 분포
② 2차 대전 이후 미국인들의 생활 양식 변화
③ 주택 건설 및 고속도로의 필요성
④ 미국 남부의 1/3 크기의 선벨트 지역으로의 이주

어구 **mass** 일반 대중; 다량, 다수 **postwar** 전후의 **reside** 거주하다 **leave behind** (장소 등을) 뒤에 남기고 가다 **row house** 연립 주택 **closet** 옷장 **utility room** 다용도실 **a measure of** 일정량의 **housing** 주택 공급, 주택 건설 **migrate** 이주하다

해설 첫 문장에서 another(또 다른)를 통해 대규모의 이동이 있었다고 했으므로, 앞 단락에서도 또한 사람들이 이주한 사건이 언급되었으리라 유추가 된다.

When I was twenty-eight I started to trip and drop things. What at first seemed my natural clumsiness soon became too pronounced to ① shrug off. I consulted a neurologist, who told me that I had a brain tumor. A battery of tests, increasingly disagreeable, revealed no tumor. About a year and a half later I developed a blurred spot in one eye. I had, at last, the episodes "disseminated in space and time" requisite for a diagnosis: multiple sclerosis. ② I have never been sorry for the doctor's initial misdiagnosis, however. For almost a week, until the negative results of the tests were in, I thought that I was going to die right away. Every day for the past nearly ten years, then, has been a kind of gift. I accept all gifts.

26 Which of the following can be the best title for the passage?

① How I Came to Love My Life
② My Favorite Doctor
③ How I Got Recovered
④ My Anger and Frustration at the Terrible Hospital System
⑤ Different Types of Life-style

27 Which of the following is closest in meaning to the underlined ①?

① regard as trivial
② consider very important
③ worry about
④ repeat the mistakes
⑤ inquire about

28 What does the underlined sentence ② imply?

① I blamed those bad doctors who have misdiagnosed my illness.
② I pities those doctors who have misdiagnosed my illness.
③ I felt relieved when I finally knew what my illness was.
④ I was upset because I didn't know what my illness was.
⑤ I felt I was happier when I had not known what my illness was.

해석 내가 스물여덟의 나이가 되었을 때 넘어지거나 물건을 떨어뜨리기 시작했었다. 처음에는 천성적으로 서툴러서 그랬나 하고 여겼던 것이 너무도 분명해져서 무시할 수가 없게 되었다. 신경 전문의에게 상담을 했는데, 그는 내가 뇌종양에 걸렸다고 말했다. 그러나 점점 불쾌했던 종합 검사 결과는 종양이 아님을 밝혀냈다. 대략 1년 반 정도가 지난 후에 한쪽 눈에 흐릿한 반점이 생겼다. 마침내 '시간과 공간적으로 흩어진' 여러 사건들을 겪게 되었고 그것들은 다발성 경화증이었다. 나는 의사의 초기 오진에 대해서 유감스럽게 느꼈던 적이 없었다. 진단이 음성 결과가 나올 때까지 거의 일주일 동안 나는 곧 죽게 될 거라고 생각했었다. 그러고 나서 지난 거의 10년의 세월이 선물의 일종이었다. 나는 모든 선물을 다 받았다.

26 이 글의 제목은?

① 어떻게 내가 나의 삶을 사랑하게 되었는가?
② 내가 좋아하는 의사
③ 내가 회복된 방법
④ 터무니없는 병원 치료에서 내가 느낀 분노와 좌절
⑤ 다양한 삶의 방식

27 ①의 의미와 가장 비슷한 것은?

① 사소한 것으로 간주하다
② 매우 중요한 것으로 간주하다
③ 걱정하다
④ 실수를 반복하다
⑤ 물어보다

28 ②의 문장이 암시하는 것은?

① 병에 대해서 오진을 범한 나쁜 의사들을 비난했다.
② 병에 대해서 오진을 한 의사들을 가엾이 여긴다.
③ 내 병이 무엇인지를 결국에 알게 되었을 때 안도를 느꼈다.
④ 내 병이 무엇인지를 알지 못했기 때문에 분노했다.
⑤ 내 병이 무엇인지를 알지 못했을 때 더 행복했다고 느꼈다.

어구 trip 넘어지다 drop 떨어뜨리다 clumsiness 서투름 too A to R 너무나 A해서 ~할 수 없다 pronounced 현저한, 명백한 shrug off 무시하다, 과소평가하다 neurologist 신경 전문의사 brain tumor 뇌종양 a battery of tests 종합 검사 increasingly 점점, 더욱더 disagreeable 불쾌한 a year and a half later 1년 반이 지나서 blurred 흐릿한 spot 점, 얼룩, 단편 광고방송 at last 마침내 disseminate 흩뿌리다, 분산시키다 requisite 요물, 수품 multiple sclerosis 다발성 경화증 misdiagnosis 오진 be in 제출되다, 들어오다 right away 즉시, 곧 nearly 거의, 근처에

해설 26 의사의 초기 진단으로 인해 자신이 죽을 수도 있다는 생각에 하루하루 살아가는 것 자체가 소중한 선물이었음을 알게 되었고, 이렇게 느끼게 된 것이 결국 자신의 삶을 사랑하게 되었다는 내용이 이 글의 주제이다.

27 shrug off는 '무시하다, 대단한 것으로 여기지 않다(to treat something as unimportant and not worry about it)'라는 뜻을 가진다.

28 의사의 초기 오진에 대해서 유감을 느끼지 않게 된 원인이 의사의 초기 진단이 잘못된 것이어서, 필자의 생명에 아주 지장이 없게 되었기 때문이다.

>>> **다음 글을 읽고 문제의 답을 고르시오. [29~30]**

When it comes to corporate clichés, fatigued phrases such as "mission critical" or "value added" are among the most annoying. But when it comes to annoying and dangerous, "outside the box" tops the list at least in the opinion of author and consultant Douglas Rushkoff. Rushkoff advises that when companies try to think or act "outside the box" with new packaging, advertising, acquisitions, or even CEOs, that shift in focus often results in a loss of focus. He recalls meeting with the CEO of a home electronics chain who wanted him to help devise a bottoms-up marketing strategy. But Rushkoff quickly realized the company didn't need new marketing as much as it needed better-quality store-brand products. The company had previously outsourced all its design and manufacturing. To some, outsourcing may seem innovative, but in this case, it was cutting the company off from the in-house expertise that built the firm in the first place. "American companies are obsessed with window dressing ... afraid to look at whatever it is they really do and evaluate it from the inside out," says Rushkoff.

29 **"outside the box"에 해당하지 않는 것을 고르시오.**

① new advertising
② window dressing
③ inviting another CEO
④ improving product quality
⑤ devising new marketing strategies

30 **According to Douglas Rushkoff, ___________.**

① "mission critical" is a very annoying cliche among companies
② the companies, above all, should see their reality as it is
③ the companies should develop what are called "value added" methods
④ the CEO of the home electronics chain had better outsource manufacturing
⑤ the CEO of the home electronics chain had better devise a bottoms-up marketing strategy

해석 회사의 상투적 문구라면 "중대한 비평"이나 "부가가치"와 같은 진부한 표현들이 가장 지겨운 것들에 속한다. 그러나 지겹고 위험한 것에 관한 한 작가이자 고문인 더글라스 러시코프의 의견에 따르자면 "혁신적인"이란 표현이 적어도 최상의 위치에 속한다고 한다. 러시코프가 조언하기를 회사들이 새로운 포장, 광고, 인수, 심지어 CEO 등으로 "혁신적인"이란 표현을 생각하거나 행동하려 노력할 때 그런 초점의 변화가 초점의 손실을 종종 야기한다고 한다. 그는 가전제품 체인의 CEO와의 만남을 회고하는데, 그 CEO는 러시코프가 상향식 마케팅 전략 고안을 도와줄 것을 원했다. 그러나 러시코프는 그 회사가 보다 나은 품질의 자가 브랜드 제품을 원하는 것만큼 새로운 마케팅을 원하지는 않는 것을 즉시 알아차렸다. 그 회사는 전에 모든 디자인과 제작을 하청했었다. 어느 면에서는 하청이 혁신적인 것으로 보일 수 있겠지만, 이와 같은 경우에 있어서는 그 회사가 가장 중요시했던 내부 전문가 육성이라는 것과는 단절되고 마는 것이다. "미국 기업들이 겉치레에 신경을 많이 쓰고는 있겠지만, 무엇이든지 간에 정말로 하고 있는 일을 살펴보거나 그 하는 일을 샅샅이 평가하는 것을 두려워한다"고 러시코프는 말한다.

29 **"outside the box"에 해당하지 않는 것을 고르시오.**

① 새로운 광고
② 겉치레
③ 다른 CEO를 초빙하는 것
④ 품질을 향상시키는 것
⑤ 새로운 마케팅 전략을 고안하는 것

30 **더글라스 러시코프의 입장으로 옳은 설명은?**

① 중대한 임무는 회사들 사이에서 매우 진부한 표현이다.
② 무엇보다도 회사는 있는 그대로 자신들의 현실을 직시해야만 한다.
③ 회사들은 부가가치라는 방법으로 불리우는 것을 개발해야만 한다.
④ 가전제품 체인의 CEO는 하청 제작을 하는 편이 더 낫다.
⑤ 가전제품 체인의 CEO는 상향식 마케팅을 고안하는 것이 더 낫다.

어구 **when it comes to** ~에 관한 한, ~에 대해서라면 **corporate** 법인·회사의, 집합적인 **cliché** 진부한 표현 **fatigued** 지친, 피로한 **critical** 중요한, 비평적인 **value added** 부가가치 **annoying** 성가신, 지겨운 **outside the box** 혁신적인, 틀을 벗어나 **top the list** 수위에 오르다, 정상에 오르다 **at least** 적어도 **in the opinion of** ~의 의견에 따르자면 **acquisition** 인수, 습득 **shift in focus** 초점의 이동 **recall** 상기하다 **bottoms-up marketing** 상향식 마케팅 **store brand** 자가 브랜드 **outsource** 하청하다 **innovative** 혁신적인 **cut off from** ~에서 고립시키다 **in-house** 사내의 **in the first place** 첫째로, 애당초 **be obsessed with** ~에 얽매이다 **window dressing** 겉치레 **be afraid to R** ~하기를 두려워하다[from] **the inside out** 샅샅이, 뒤집어서 **as it is** 현재 상태로

해설 **29** 본문에서 인용된 outside the box는 지겨우면서도 위험한 표현이라고 정의 내리면서, 세 번째 문장에서, '새로운 포장, 광고, 인수, 심지어 CEO' 및 '겉치레'는 outside the box의 사항에 포함되지만, 단순히 상품의 질을 향상시키는 것은 이 범주에 포함되지 않았다.
30 러시코프는 초점의 변화가 초점 자체를 손실할 수 있다고 조언하며, 외부에 하청을 주지 말고 자체 브랜드의 철저한 평가를 조언한 점으로 보건대, 결국 회사들은 있는 그대로의 현실을 직시해야 한다는 주장으로서 유추가 가능하다.

Actual TEST 02

⇨ 본책 p.198

1 ②	2 ③	3 ②	4 ④	5 ②	6 ③	7 ④	8 ②	9 ③	10 ②
11 ①	12 ②	13 ①	14 ②	15 ①	16 ④	17 ②	18 ④	19 ①	20 ⑤
21 ②	22 ④	23 ③	24 ④	25 ①	26 ③	27 ②	28 ③	29 ⑤	30 ③

>>> 밑줄 친 곳에 들어갈 알맞은 답을 고르시오. [1~6]

1 His remarks were filled with ____________ which sounded lofty but presented nothing new to the audience.

① aphorism ② platitudes
③ bombast ④ adages
⑤ symbols

해석 그의 언급은 청중들에게는 고상하게 들렸으나 어떠한 새로운 것도 주지 못하는 틀에 박힌 진부한 표현들로 가득 차 있었다.

어구 be filled with ~으로 가득 차다 **lofty** 고상한 **aphorism** 금언, 격언 **platitude** 진부한 말 **bombast** 호언장담 **adage** 격언, 속담

해설 but에 의해 새롭지 못하다는 표현과 반의 관계가 적합하다.

2 Such was Brandon's ____________ that he was frequently described as being honest in all cases.

① vigilance ② munificence
③ probity ④ gravity
⑤ eminence

해석 브랜든 씨는 너무나 성실하여 어느 경우에 있어서라도 정직하다고 종종 묘사되었다.

어구 such 너무나 대단한(so great) in all cases 어느 경우에 있어서라도 **vigilance** 조심, 경계, 불침번 **munificence** 인색하지 않음 **probity** 성실함 **gravity** 진지함, 중대함, 중력 **eminence** 저명함

해설 such that (인과) 구문에 의해 '정직한'이라고 묘사될 만한 이유가 옳다.

3 Power may be compared to a great river. While kept within its due bounds it is both beautiful and useful, but when it overflows its bank, it is then too uncontrolled—it bears down all before it and brings destruction and desolation wherever it comes. ____________.

① Liberty increases the power of men
② Power is like a great river which can do good and bad
③ Liberty is protection against lawless power
④ A great river is powerful
⑤ We should love a great river

해석 권력이란 큰 강에 비유될 수 있다. 그 적당한 범위 내에 유지되는 동안 강은 아름다우며 동시에 유용하지만, 제방을 넘치게 되면 억제할 수 없게 되어, 앞에 있는 모든 것을 집어삼키고 닥치는 대로 파괴와 폐허를 초래한다. 권력이란 이로울 수도 해로울 수도 있는 큰 강과도 같은 것이다.

어구 be compared to ~에 비유되다 **due** 적당; 정당한 **bound** 경계, 범위 **overflow** 범람하다 **bank** 제방 **bear down** 압도하다, 격파하다 **desolation** 황폐화, 폐허

해설 권력을 강에 비유한 첫 문장에 이어서, 강의 이로움과 해를 끼치는 두 특징을 모두 설명하므로 이점과 해로움이 모두 언급되어야 옳다.

4 ____________ is a temporary disruption of one's normal biological rhythms after long-distance travel by airplane through several time zones without sufficient rest en route.

① Motion sickness ② Airsickness
③ Insomnia ④ Jetlag
⑤ Nervous breakdown

해석 시차로 인한 피로는 여행 중 충분한 휴식이 없는 비행기로의 장거리 여행 후에 사람의 정상적인 신체 리듬이 일시적으로 혼란스러워지는 것이다.

어구 disruption 붕괴, 분열; 중단, 두절, 혼란 en route ~ 도중에, 여행 중에 **airsickness** 비행기 멀미 **insomnia** 불면증 **jetlag** (제트기 여행의) 시차로 인한 피로 **breakdown** 고장, 파손

해설 비행기의 장거리 여행에 생기는 신체 리듬의 이상 현상은 '시차로 인한 피로'가 적합하다.

5 The South provides the North with the equipment to remove mines. It is notable that such ___________ spirit has been realized inside the DMZ, where the most acute military ___________ on the earth is taking place.

① strong - attack
② cooperative - standoff
③ friendly - raid
④ fearful - force
⑤ low - zone

해석 남한은 북한에 지뢰를 제거하는 장비를 제공한다. 지구상에서 가장 날카로운 군사적 대립이 일어나는 DMZ에서 그러한 협동 정신이 실현되었다는 것이 주목할 만하다.

어구 **mine** 지뢰, 광산 **notable** 주목할 만한 **acute** 날카로운 **take place** 발생하다 **cooperative** 협동적인 **standoff** 냉담, 고립 **raid** 공습

해설 첫 번째 빈칸 – 남한이 북한에 지뢰 제거 장비를 제공하는 것은 민족 간의 '협력' 정신이다.
두 번째 빈칸 – DMZ는 전쟁 발발 시 가장 먼저 전투가 벌어지는 곳이므로 군사적 대립이 날카롭다는 논리가 옳다.

6 Having lived in the public eye for years, the ex-mayor cannot believe that from now on he will live in ___________.

① adulation
② controversy
③ anonymity
④ agitation
⑤ veneration

해석 여러 해 동안 공인으로 생활했기 때문에, 전직 시장은 지금부터 그가 무명으로 살아갈 것이라는 것을 결코 믿을 수 없다.

어구 **ex-mayor** 전직 시장 **from now** 지금부터 **adulation** 아첨 **anonymity** 익명 **agitation** 선동 **veneration** 존경, 숭배

해설 공공의 시선을 받으며 살았기 때문에 '아무에게도 알려져 있지 않은 무명'으로 산다는 것이 믿기 힘들다는 논리가 적합하다.

7 다음 글의 내용과 일치하지 않는 것은?

Pop art is an art movement that emerged in the mid 1950s in Britain and in the late 1950s in the United States. Pop art challenged tradition by asserting that an artist's use of the mass-produced visual commodities of popular culture is contiguous with the perspective of fine art. Pop removes the material from its context and isolates the object, or combines it with other objects, for contemplation. The concept of pop art refers not so much to the art itself as to the attitudes that led to it. Characterized by themes and techniques drawn from popular mass culture, such as advertising, comic books and mundane cultural objects, pop art is widely interpreted as a reaction to the then-dominant ideas of abstract expressionism, as well as an expansion upon them.

① Pop art is an art movement of the twentieth century.
② Pop art employs images of popular culture which are in use in advertising.
③ Pop art is not a clear separation from the established art.
④ Pop art removes the material from its context because it is associated with art for art's sake.

해석 대중예술은 영국에서 1950년대 중반, 미국에서 1950년대 말에 부상한 예술 운동이다. 대중예술은 예술가가 대중문화의 대량 생산되는 영상 제품을 이용하는 것이 미술의 관점과 유사하다는 주장을 통해 전통에 도전했었다. 대중예술은 사색을 위하여 전체에서 소재를 제거하고 대상물을 격리시키거나 결합한다. 대중예술의 개념은 대중예술 그 자체를 언급하기보다는 그것을 야기한 태도를 언급한다. 대중예술은 광고, 만화, 평범한 문화 대상물과 같은 대량 생산 대중문화로부터 이끌어낸 주제와 기술력의 특징을 갖추었기 때문에, 그때 당시의 주류였던 추상적 표현주의에 기반을 두어 확장된 것뿐만 아니라 그것에 대한 반응으로 해석된다.

7 다음 글의 내용과 일치하지 않는 것은?
① 대중예술은 20세기의 예술 운동이다.
② 대중예술은 광고에서 이용되는 대중문화의 모습을 이용한다.
③ 대중예술은 기존 예술에서 분명히 분리된 것은 아니다.
④ 대중예술은 예술 자체를 위하여 소재가 예술과 관련됐기 때문에, 맥락에서 소재를 제거한다.

어구 **pop art** 대중예술 **mass produce** 대량 생산하다 **commodity** 상품; 필수품 **be contiguous with** ~과 인접하다; ~과 접촉하다 **perspective** 관점; 원근화법 **context** 배경; 상황 **isolate** 격리하다 **contemplation** 숙고, 심사 **attitude** 태도; 의견 **popular mass culture** 대중문화 **mundane** 보통의; 세속적인(earthly) **abstract** 추상적인; 이론적인 **expressionism** 표현주의 **expansion** 확장 **employ** 이용하다; 채용하다

해설 'Pop removes the material ~ for contemplation' 문장을 통해 예술 그 자체를 위해서 소재를 제거한 것이 아니라 사색을 위해서 소재를 제거한 것임을 알 수 있다.

Nearly every major city in the world provides some form of public transportation.

I. The most common form of public transportation is the bus which has been in use in major cities since approximately 1900.

II. Also special busses can be chartered for trips to the mountains, to lakes, and to nearby places of historical interests.

III. This is necessary not only to contribute to visitors to the city, but also to provide citizens with low-cost transportation and to help reduce the traffic on streets and highways.

IV. In some cities, the city bus system offers free "mini-bus" service as a convenience to shoppers in the downtown business district.

① Ⅲ — Ⅱ — Ⅳ — Ⅰ　　② Ⅰ — Ⅲ — Ⅱ — Ⅳ
③ Ⅰ — Ⅳ — Ⅲ — Ⅱ　　④ Ⅲ — Ⅰ — Ⅱ — Ⅳ

해석 세계의 거의 모든 주요 도시가 대중교통 수단을 제공한다.
　Ⅰ. 가장 일반적인 대중교통은 버스이며, 대략 1900년부터 주요 도시에서 사용되어 왔다.
　Ⅲ. 버스는 도시를 방문하는 사람들에게 필요할 뿐 아니라 시민들에게 저비용 교통수단을 제공하고 도로와 고속도로에서의 통행량을 감소하는 데에도 필요하다.
　Ⅱ. 특수 버스는 산으로, 호수로, 역사적 유적지 등으로의 여행을 위해 전세를 낼 수도 있다.
　Ⅳ. 일부 도시에서는 도심 지역 쇼핑객들의 편의를 위하여 무료 "미니버스"를 운행한다.

어구 **public transportation** 대중교통　**be in use** 사용되다　**charter** (비행기·버스·선박 등을) 전세 내다(hire), (비행기·버스·선박 등을) 전세 내다(hire), 특허를 주다

해설 제시문의 public transportation(대중교통)을 받아서 [Ⅰ]에서 가장 일반적인 형태의 대중교통이 버스임을 지적하고, 이 버스를 This로 받아 [Ⅲ]에서 그 용도를 설명하고, 이어 [Ⅱ]에서 특수 버스의 용도를 덧붙이고는 [Ⅳ]에서 일부 도시에 있는 무료 미니버스 운행을 소개한다.

>>> **다음 글을 읽고 문제의 답을 고르시오.** [9~10]

The therapeutic value and healing powers of plants were demonstrated to me when I was a boy of about ten. I had developed an acute, persistent abdominal pain that did not respond readily to hospital medication. My mother had taken me to the city's central hospital on several occasions, where different drugs were tried ① _____________ me. In total desperation, she took me to Egya Mensa, a well-known herbalist in my hometown in the western province of Ghana. This man was no stranger to the medical doctors at the hospital. He had earned the reputation of offering excellent help when they were confronted with difficult cases where Western medicine had failed to effect a cure.

9 What would be the main topic of the passage?

① A life of E. Mensa, a well-known herbalist
② The limitation of Western medicine
③ The healing powers of herbs
④ The healing effects of acupuncture
⑤ The kinds of medical practitioners

10 Which of the following best fits into ①?

① for　　　　　② on
③ at　　　　　④ toward
⑤ to

해석 내가 10살 정도의 소년이었을 때, 치료법으로 식물의 유용성과 치유력 덕분에 나는 치유가 되었다. 나는 병원의 약물치료에 쉽게 치료가 되지 않는 급성, 만성적인 복통에 걸렸었다. 어머니는 여러 번 나를 도시의 중앙병원으로 데리고 갔으며, 그 병원에서는 여러 약을 나에게 시도해 보았다. 완전히 절망하여 어머니는 가나의 서부 지역에 있는 내 고향 마을에서 유명한 본초학자 에그야 멘사에게 나를 데려갔다. 이 사람은 병원의 의사들에게 낯선 이는 아니었다. 그는 서양 의학으로 치료하는 데 실패한 난치병에 걸린 사람들에게 뛰어난 도움을 주어서 명성을 얻은 사람이었다.

9 이 글의 주제는?

① 유명한 본초학자인 멘사의 인생　　② 서구 의학의 한계
③ 식용 식물의 치유력　　　　　　④ 침술의 치유력
⑤ 개업 의사의 종류

10 ①에 알맞은 것은?

어구 **therapeutic** 치료의, 치료법의　**healing power** 치유력　**demonstrate** 증명하다, 시위하다　**develop** (병에) 걸리다　**acute** 날카로운, 급성의　**abdominal** 복부의, 배의　**medication** 약물치료　**try ~ on A** (좋지 않은 짓을) A에게 (시험 삼아) 해 보다　**in desperation** 절망하여　**herbalist** 본초학자　**be confronted with** ~을 직면하다　**case** 병, 경우, 사건, 판

해설 9 일반적인 서구 의학으로 치료가 되지 않던 필자가 본초학자를 우연히 만나서 치료가 되었다는 내용이므로, 본초학자가 수단으로 이용한 식용 식물(herb)의 치유력이 주제로서 옳다.
10 문맥상 치료와 같은 내용이 적용됐다는 속뜻이 필요하므로 be tried on(시험되다)가 옳다.

>>> 다음 글을 읽고 문제의 답을 고르시오. [11~13]

Right now in the U.S. there are almost 3 million students in special-education classes specifically because they can't read. Most of them are probably dyslexic. But there are other slow readers who are simply overlooked—ignored in crowded classrooms or dismissed as discipline problems. Unless corrective action is taken, their self-confidence often crumbles as they see other students progressing. Even worse, their peers might taunt or ostracize them—a situation that Sean Slattery's mother, Judy, remembers all too well. "Sean cried for four hours every day after kindergarten," she says. "He was so unhappy."

In Asia, research on dyslexia suggests its incidence might be significantly lower than in the West due to the differences in how Asian scripts are processed by the brain. The bad news is that Asians with dyslexia are far more likely than Westerners to go undiagnosed, unaided and branded as lifetime losers. Growing up in Malaysia, Ahmad Fitri Isahak was taunted by friends and felt cold-shouldered by teachers because he failed most of his tests. It was only at the age of 25, while studying computer and software engineering at university in England, that a professor told him he was probably dyslexic. "I was devastated and failed that year," he recalls. But he ＿＿＿＿＿＿, finished his degree, and Fitri is now an IT consultant in Kuala Lumpur—a happy ending that he admits is unusual for dyslexics in his homeland. "For now, they are a lost lot," he says.

11 Choose the one that best fills in the blank.

① got back in the saddle
② twisted the knife
③ burned my boat
④ played the fox

12 What is the best title for the passage?

① Serious Problems of the Children Mentality
② Ubiquitous Difficult Condition to Read
③ Bad Effects and Good Effects for Dyslexia
④ Vulnerable Reading Skills

13 What is the author's purpose in the passage?

① To explain several bad effects of dyslexia on readers
② To compare reading ability between the West and the East
③ To inform dyslexics of effective cures
④ To analyze the cause of failure for many children to read well

해석 지금 미국에서는 300만에 가까운 학생들이 글을 읽지 못하기 때문에 특수 교육을 받고 있다. 대부분이 아마도 독서 장애아일 것이다. 그러나 이들 말고도 학생 수가 지나치게 많은 교실에서 도외시되고 있거나 규율 문제아로 가볍게 봐 넘겨짐으로써 그저 간과되고 있는 읽기 속도가 느린 아이들이 있다. 교정 조치가 없을 경우, 이 아이들은 다른 아이들의 진도를 바라보면서 자신감에 상처를 받는 경우가 많다. 설상가상으로 또래 아이들로부터 조롱을 당하거나 따돌림을 당할 수도 있는데, 그것은 숀 슬래터리의 어머니 주디가 너무나 잘 아는 일이다. "숀은 매일 유치원에 다녀와서는 네 시간 동안 울어대는 불행한 처지였지요."라고 그녀는 말한다.

아시아의 독서 장애에 대한 조사를 보면, 그 비율이 서양보다 현저히 낮은 것이 아닌가 하는 생각이 드는데, 이는 아시아 사람들의 뇌가 글을 처리하는 과정이 서양과는 다르기 때문이다. 부정적인 측면은, 아시아의 경우 독서 장애자들이 서양인과는 달리 진단 과정을 거치지 않으며, 그래서 도움을 받지 못한 채 평생 패배자로 낙인찍히는 비율이 서양보다 훨씬 높다는 사실이다. 말레이시아에서 자란 아흐마드 피트리 이사하크는 거의 모든 시험에서 낙제 점수를 받는 바람에 친구들로부터 조롱을 당하고 교사들로부터 냉대를 받는 체험을 했다. 잉글랜드의 대학에서 컴퓨터와 소프트웨어 공학을 공부하던 25세가 되어서야 한 교수로부터 그가 독서 장애자인 것 같다는 이야기를 들었다. "나는 참담한 심정이 되어 그해에는 낙제를 했습니다."라고 그는 당시를 회고한다. 그러나 제 페이스를 되찾아 학위를 딴 피트리는 지금 콸라룸푸르에서 IT 컨설턴트로 일하고 있는데, 이는 그의 나라의 독서 장애자들로서는 보기 드문 해피엔딩의 경우라는 것을 그는 인정한다. "현재로서 그들의 처지는 승산이 없는 것"이라고 그는 말한다.

11 빈칸을 올바르게 채우시오.

① 자기 페이스를 찾다　　　　　② 악화시키다
③ 배수의 진을 치다　　　　　　④ 교활하다

12 이 글의 제목으로 가장 적합한 것은 무엇인가?

① 아동의 심각한 정신 문제　　　② 독서를 하기 힘든 만연한 사태
③ 독서 장애의 악 효과와 긍정 효과　④ 취약한 독서법

13 작가의 목적은 무엇인가?

① 독자에 미치는 독서 장애의 여러 부정적인 영향을 설명하기 위해
② 서양과 동양의 독서 능력을 비교하기 위해
③ 난독증 환자들에게 효과적인 치료법을 알려주기 위해
④ 수많은 아이들이 독서를 잘 하지 못하는 이유를 분석하기 위해

어구 dyslexic 독서 장애(난독증)에 걸린 사람　taunt 비웃다　ostracize 배척하다　dyslexia 독서 장애, 난독증　script 서체　go undiagnosed 진단을 받지 못하다　cold-shoulder 냉대하다　get back in the saddle 자기 페이스를 찾다

해설 **11** 참담한 심정이 되어 낙제했다는 내용이 but에 의해 역접으로 전환되기 위해서는, '제 페이스를 찾다'라는 뜻의 get back in the saddle이 옳다.
12 동양과 서양을 막론하고 독서를 하지 못하는 난독증에 걸린 이들의 폐해에 대해 설명하는 내용이 이 글의 주제이다.
13 이 글은 독서 장애로 인한 여러 폐해들을 설명하기 위함이 목적이 될 수 있다.

This is the reason why it is more correct, as well as more usual, to speak of a University as a place of education than of instruction, though, when knowledge is concerned, instruction would at first sight have seemed the more appropriate work. We are instructed, for instance, in manual exercises, in the fine and useful arts, in trades, and in ways of business; for these are methods, which have little or no effect upon the mind itself, are contained in rules committed to memory, to tradition, or to use, and bear upon an end external to themselves.

But education is a higher word; it implies an action upon our mental nature, and the formation of a character; it is something individual and permanent, and is commonly spoken of in connection with religion and virtue. When, then, we speak of the communication of Knowledge as being Education, we thereby really imply that Knowledge is a state or condition of mind; and since cultivation of mind is surely worth seeking for its own sake, we are thus brought once more to the conclusion, which the word 'Liberal' and the word 'Philosophy' have already suggested, that there is a Knowledge, which is desirable, though nothing come of it, as being of itself a treasure, and a sufficient remuneration of years of labor.

14 When does 'education' gain higher significance?

① When it is based on practical knowledge.
② When it aims at the cultivation of mind.
③ When it loses something individual and permanent.
④ When it combines the merits of education and instruction.
⑤ When it successfully achieves a coexistence of manual skills and Liberal studies.

15 What is the main topic of the above passage?

① Philosophical knowledge as the goal of education
② The relationship between education and occupation
③ Two ways of using knowledge
④ The difference between manual exercises and useful arts
⑤ The history of universities

해석 지식이 관련돼 있어 가르친다는 것이 처음에는 더욱 적절하게 보일 때가 있을지라도 대학을 가르침의 장소라기보다 교육의 장소라고 말하는 것이 더욱 흔할 뿐 아니라 더욱 옳은 것이다. 예컨대, 우리는 손으로 하는 실습, 세련되고 효율적인 기술, 무역 그리고 사업을 하는 방법들에 대해서 학습을 하며, 그 이유는 이러한 것들은 방법이 되어 정신 그 자체에는 거의 또는 전혀 영향을 미치지 않으며, 기억과 전통과 이용에 관계되어 내포되어 있으며, 그리고 부수적인 목적이 된다.
그러나 교육은 더 높은 수준의 단어이다. 왜냐하면 교육은 우리의 정신적 특성과 인격을 형성하는 행위를 암시하기 때문이며 교육은 개인적이고 영원한 것이며, 보통은 종교와 덕성과 연관되어 언급된다. 그래서 우리가 지식의 전달이 곧 교육이 된다고 말할 때, 이러한 말로써 우리는 진정으로 지식이 마음의 상태라는 것을 암시하는 것이다. 그리고 정신 수양은 분명히 그 자신의 목적을 추구할 가치가 있기 때문에, 따라서 우리는 한 번 더 이하와 같은 결론을 내리게 되며, 결론인 즉 '교양'이라는 단어와 '철학'이라는 단어가 이미 제시했던 것인데, 즉 지식이라는 것이 있고, 지식은 바람직한 것이며, 비록 아무것도 생기지 않지만 그 자체가 보물이며, 여러 해 동안의 노력에 대한 충분한 보상이 되는 것이다

14 '교육'은 언제 더 높은 중요성을 가지게 되는가?
① 실용적인 지식에 기반을 두었을 때
② 정신 수양을 목표로 두었을 때
③ 사적이거나 영원한 것을 잃어버릴 때
④ 교육과 가르침의 장점이 합쳐졌을 때
⑤ 손의 솜씨와 교양학습의 공존을 성공적으로 성취했을 때

15 윗글의 주제는?
① 교육의 목표로서 철학적인 지식
② 교육과 직업 사이의 관계
③ 지식을 이용하는 두 가지 방법
④ 손으로 하는 실습과 효율성 있는 기술 사이의 차이
⑤ 대학의 역사

어구 instruction 교훈, 가르침 concern ~에 관계하다, 관여하다 at first sight 첫눈에, 언뜻 보아 appropriate 적당한, 적절한 manual 손의, 손으로 하는 have little effect upon ~ ~에 거의 영향을 미치지 않다 contain (안에) ~을 담고 있다, 포함하다 commit to memory 기억하다, 기억하다 bear upon ~에 영향이 있다 external 외부의, 부수적인 imply 포함하다, 수반하다, 내포하다, 의미하다, 암시하다 formation 형성 character [물건의] 특성, 특색; [사람의] 성격, 품성, 인격; 인물; 문자 individual 개인적인, 개별적인 permanent 영속하는, (반)영구적인, 불변의 commonly 일반적으로 in connection with ~와 관련하여 communication 전달, 통신, 정보 thereby 그것에 의하여, 그 때문에 cultivation 경작, 재배 for one's own sake ~을 위하여 bring ~ to a conclusion ~을 끝맺다 desirable 바람직한 come of ~에 기인하다, ~출신이다 treasure 보물, 보석; 보배; 귀중품; 재산 remuneration 보수, 보상

해설 **14** 교육은 우리의 정신적 특성과 인격을 형성하는 행위를 암시하기 때문에 교육은 더 높은 수준의 단어라고 했다. 정신적 특성과 인격을 형성한다는 내용은 정신 수양이 될 수 있으므로 ②가 옳다.
15 대학은 교육의 장소이긴 하지만, 단순히 가르치는(instruct) 것만이 아니라, liberal하고 philosophical한 knowledge를 이른바 교육하는(educate) 장소라는 것이 이 글의 주제이다.

>>> 다음 글을 읽고 문제의 답을 고르시오. [16~17]

Each night as the sun goes down and the desert darkens, the neon lights of Las Vegas, Nevada, flare into the sky. Beneath the lurid glow of giant casino signs, water splashes in Roman fountains, runs into acres of swimming pools, and overflows into street gutters.

Las Vegas, ① prodigal playground of the West, illustrates the conflict between man and nature in the River basin. Within just ten years the metropolitan area could be using virtually every drop of Nevada's legal share of the Colorado River's flow. City leaders, expecting the population of 800,000 to double in the next 10 years, are searching far and wide for new water supplies.

16 The author calls Las Vegas "prodigal" in ① because of ___________.

① gamblings at casino
② flaring neon lights
③ loose morality
④ an abundant waste of water
⑤ a luxurious mode of living

17 What will put Las Vegas into trouble in a decade?

① floods from Colorado River
② an increase in population
③ booming business
④ an extreme shortage in electricity
⑤ rising crime rate

해석 매일 밤 해가 지고 사막이 어두워질 때 네바다 주의 라스베이거스 네온사인은 하늘로 빛을 쏜다. 거대한 카지노 간판의 번득이는 붉은 빛 밑에서 로마식 분수의 물이 튀어 수많은 수영장으로 흘러들어가며 거리의 배수구에 넘쳐흐른다.

서양의 낭비 놀이터인 라스베이거스는 강 유역에서 인간과 자연의 대립을 보여준다. 10년 내에 그 대도시 지역은 콜로라도 강의 유량 중 네바다 주의 합법적인 지분의 모든 양을 실제로 다 사용할 것이다. 행정가들은 다음 10년 안에 80만의 인구가 두 배까지 증가하리라 예상하면서 새로운 급수법을 위하여 광범위하게 조사하고 있다.

16 필자는 라스베이거스를 왜 "방탕하다"고 하는가?

① 카지노의 도박 때문에
② 빛나는 네온사인 때문에
③ 허술한 도덕성 때문에
④ 물의 많은 낭비 때문에
⑤ 사치스러운 생활방식 때문에

17 무엇이 10년 내에 라스베이거스를 곤경에 빠뜨리겠는가?

① 콜로라도 강의 범람
② 인구의 증가
③ 급등하는 사업
④ 전기의 극단적인 부족 상태
⑤ 증가하는 범죄율

어구 **darken** 어두워지다 **flare** 번쩍번쩍 빛나다 **lurid** 번득이는, 짙게 붉은 **glow** 타다, 빛을 내다, 붉어지다 **splash** (물 등이) 튀기다 **fountain** 분수, 샘, 원천 **acres of** 무수히 많은 **overflow** 넘쳐흐르다 **gutter** 하수도, 배수구, 도랑 **prodigal** 낭비하는, 방탕한 **illustrate** 설명하다, 삽화를 넣다 **virtually** 사실상, 실제적으로 **drop** 하락, 낙하, 방울, 소량 **double** 두 배로 증가하다 **far and wide** 광범위하게 **water supply** 상수도, 급수(법, 량) **gambling** 도박 **loose** 허술한, 흐트러진

해설 **16** 두 번째 단락 이하에서 콜로라도 강의 수량 중 대부분을 차지하고 있으며, 마지막 문장에서 새로운 급수법을 행정가들이 조사하고 있다고 했으므로, 라스베이거스는 물 소비량이 엄청나다고 유추할 수 있다. 따라서 본문에서 사용된 prodigal은 '물 소비가 엄청난'이란 의미 정도로 이해하면 되겠다.

17 마지막 문장에서 10년 내에 80만의 인구가 2배까지 증가하여 새로운 급수법을 찾아야 한다고 했으므로, 라스베이거스가 처한 곤란은 인구의 증가임이 유추가 가능하다.

Perhaps most alarming, says Sharon Levy, a pediatrician and director of the Adolescent Substance Abuse Program at Children's Hospital Boston, is that teens bent on defeating drug tests will sometimes switch their drug of choice to an undetectable (or harder to detect) substance that's considerably more hazardous. Inhalants, for example, include numerous types of chemical vapors that typically produce brief, intoxicating effects. "You don't excrete inhalants in your urine," says Levy, but "inhaling is acutely more dangerous than marijuana." Indeed, inhalants can trigger the lethal heart problem known as "sudden sniffing death" in otherwise healthy adolescents, according to the National Institute on Drug Abuse. The tragic case of young David Manlove is an example.

18 The main theme of the passage ______________.

① A New Finding about the Inhalants
② Medical Vulnerability to Cheating
③ Drug Abuse Affecting Heart
④ Dangers of Escaping Drug Tests by Inhalants
⑤ Way to Check Children's Drug Abuse

19 The above passage is ______________

① expositive ② hostile
③ ambivalent ④ neutral
⑤ chronological

20 Whom is the above passage warning?

① people who already have a heart problem
② the manufacturer that products inhalants
③ a pediatrician
④ the family that has a child
⑤ the younger generation

해석 보스턴 아동 병원의 청소년 약물 중독 연구소 소아과 대표 의사인 샤론 레비는, 십대들이 약물 검사에 걸리지 않으려고 상당히 해로우면서 검사에 발견되지 않거나 감지되기 힘든 해로운 물질로 약물을 바꾼다고 말한다. 예컨대, 흡입제는 단시간에 흥분을 이끌어내는 효과를 발생시키는 화학 기체가 많이 포함되어 있다. "소변에는 흡입제 물질이 배출되지 않지만, 마리화나보다도 더 해롭다."고 레비는 말한다. 게다가 국제 약물 기구에 따르자면, 흡입제를 사용하지 않았을 경우 건강한 청소년들의 "흡입 돌연사 증후군"으로 알려진 치명적인 심장 문제를 야기할 수 있다. 데이비드 맨러브라는 청소년의 비극적인 사건이 그 예이다.

18 가장 적절한 제목을 고르시오.

① 흡입제에 대한 새로운 발견
② 부정행위에 대한 의학적 취약
③ 심장에 영향을 미치는 약물 남용
④ 흡입기를 통해 약물 검사를 모면하려는 위험
⑤ 아동 약물 남용을 억제하기 위한 방법

19 윗글의 분위기는 어떠한가?

① 설명적인 ② 적대적인
③ 모호한 ④ 중립적인
⑤ 연대기적인

20 윗글은 누구에게 경고하고 있는가?

① 이미 심장병에 걸린 사람들
② 흡입기를 만드는 제조업체
③ 소아과 의사
④ 아이가 있는 가족
⑤ 젊은 세대

어구 bent on ～하기로 작정한 undetectable 감지가 되지 않는 hazardous 해로운 inhalant 흡입제, 흡입기 장치 vapor 증기, 수증기, 김, 증발 기체; 공상, 망상 intoxicate 취하게 하다; 도취[흥분]시키다 excrete 배설하다 urine 소변, 오줌 marijuana 마리화나 sudden death 급사; 돌연사 vulnerability 취약성 expositive 설명적인 hostile 적대적인

해설 **18** 약물 검사를 모면하기 위해 흡입기를 사용하다가 오히려 더 큰 신체의 위험을 초래할 수 있다는 내용이 이 글의 주제가 된다.
19 이 글은 청소년에게 흡입기의 위험을 설명하는 글이다.
20 이 글에서 언급되는 약물 중독자는 십대 청소년이다. 따라서 경고 대상 또한 십대 청소년이 옳다.

>>> **다음 글을 읽고 문제의 답을 고르시오. [21~24]**

As much as puppies or pandas or even children, dolphins are universally beloved. They seem to cavort and frolic at the least provocation, their mouths are fixed in what looks like a state of perpetual merriment, and their behavior and enormous brains suggest an intelligent approaching hat of humans-or even, some might argue, surpassing ㉠ it. Dolphins are turning out to be exceedingly clever, but not in the loving, utopian-socialist manner that sentimental dolphin lovers might have hoped.

Researchers who have spent thousands of hours observing the behavior of bottlenose dolphins of the coast of Australia have discovered that the males form social alliances with one another that are far more sophisticated and devious than any seen in animals apart from human beings.

21 The main subject for the passage is the
_____________ of dolphins.

① rare brutality   ② high intelligence
③ beloved nature   ④ living condition

22 Choose the one which might come after this passage.

① What is more, females seem to exert choice over the males that seek to herd them, sometimes swimming alongside them in apparent contentment, but at other times working furiously to escape, and often succeeding.
② Species like the bottlenose dolphins make most of their decisions by consensus, spending hours dawdling in a protected bay, nuzzling each other and generating an eerie nautical symphony of squeaks, whistles, barks, twangs and clicks.
③ The scientists call this effort to control females "herding" but they acknowledge that the word does not convey the aggressiveness of the act.
④ They found that one team of male dolphins will recruit the help of another team of males to gang up against a third group, a sort of multilateral battle plan that requires considerable mental calculus to work out.

23 Which is true about the above passage?

① Dolphins cannot be aggressive.
② Dolphins attack rival groups only for fun.
③ Alliances between groups of male dolphins against others require highly intelligent ability.
④ Dolphins receive even more spotlight due to their aggression.

해석 강아지나 판다 또는 아이들만큼이나 돌고래는 세계적으로 사랑받는다. 최소한의 자극에도 돌고래들은 뛰놀고 장난치는 것으로 보이고, 그들의 입은 언제나 즐거운 것처럼 보이며, 그들의 행동과 거대한 두뇌는 인간의 지능에 접근했다는 점을 암시하고, 몇몇 사람들은 인간의 지능보다 뛰어나다고 한다. 돌고래가 상당히 영리하다고 밝혀지고 있지만, 감상적인 돌고래 애호가들이 희망했을런지도 모르는 사랑스럽고 사회주의적인 태도로 인해 그런 것은 아니다.

수천 시간 동안 호주 해변의 병 모양 코를 가진 돌고래의 행동을 관찰한 연구가들이 밝혀낸 사실은, 수컷 돌고래는 인간을 제외한 동물들에서 나타나는 그 어떠한 것보다도 훨씬 복잡하고 교활하며, 사회적 동맹을 맺는다는 것이다.

21 이 글의 주제는 돌고래의 무엇에 관한 것인가?

① 희귀한 야만성   ② 높은 지능
③ 사랑받는 성격   ④ 생활 상태

22 이 글 이후에 등장할 내용은?

① 더욱이 암컷들은 무리를 지으려고 하는 수컷 이상의 기회를 쓰려는 것으로 보이는데, 때때로 분명한 만족을 하면서 수컷과 헤엄을 치지만, 어떤 때에는 분노하면서 벗어나기도 하며 종종 계속 그런 행위를 한다.
② 병 모양 코를 가진 돌고래와 같은 종들은 합의를 통해서 결정을 내리는 것을 중시하며, 보호만 안에서 빈둥거리며, 서로를 비벼대고, 찍찍거리는 소리와 짖는 소리와 콧소리와 찰칵거리는 소리와 같은 오싹한 항해 연주곡을 들려주는 것에 시간을 들이기도 한다.
③ 과학자들은 암컷을 지배하려는 이러한 노력을 "떼짓기"라고 부르지만, 그 단어는 공격 행위를 의미하지는 않는다는 점을 인정한다.
④ 수컷 돌고래 무리가 다른 수컷 집단의 도움을 요청하여 제3의 돌고래 떼를 공격하려 하는데, 이러한 도움 행위는 문제를 해결하기 위해 상당한 정신적 상관관계를 요구하는 다채로운 전투 계획의 한 유형이라는 점을 알게 되었다.

23 윗글과 일치하는 내용은?

① 돌고래들은 공격적일 수가 없다.
② 돌고래들은 라이벌 집단들을 재미삼아 공격한다.
③ 다른 돌고래들에게 맞선 수컷 돌고래들의 협력은 높은 지적 능력을 필요로 한다.
④ 돌고래들은 그들의 공격성 때문에 더 높은 주목을 받는다.

24 ㉠"it"이 가리키는 내용은?

① 최소한의 자극   ② 영원한 환희의 상태
③ 행동   ④ 인간의 지능

어구 **panda** 판다   **beloved** 사랑하는   **cavort** 날뛰다   **frolic** 소란을 피우다, 장난을 치다   **provocation** 자극, 화나게 함   **merriment** 즐거움   **enormous** 거대한   **surpass** 능가하다   **exceedingly** 지나치게   **sentimental** 감상적인   **bottlenose** 병 모양 코 돌고래; 딸기코의   **alliance** 협력   **sophisticated** 복잡한, 세련된   **devious** 탈선한, 교활한   **apart from** ~은 차치하고서라도   **what is more** 더욱이   **herd** [동물] 떼; 모으다, 무리를 짓게 하다   **dawdle** 빈둥거리다   **bay** 만, 내포   **nuzzle** 달라붙다, 코로 비비다   **nautical** 해상의, 항해하는   **squeak** (양양) 울다, 고자질하다; 찍찍거리는 소리   **gang up against** ~에 단결하여 공격하다   **calculus** 상관관계, 계산법   **for fun** 재미삼아

24 Which does ⑤ "it" refer to?

① the least provocation
② a state of perpetual merriment
③ their behavior
④ the intelligence of humans

해설 **21** 윗글의 주제는 돌고래 지능이 인간만큼이나 뛰어난 지능을 가지고 있다는 것이다.

22 마지막 문장에서 수컷 돌고래들은 모든 동물 중에서 가장 협력·유대관계가 좋다고 했으므로, 외부 무리에 대해 협력하여 공격한다는 내용이 적합하다.

23 이 문제는 22번 문제를 해결할 수 있어야 풀 수 있다. 높은 지능을 가진 돌고래 수컷들이 서로 동맹을 맺어서 다른 수컷 무리를 공격한다고 했으므로, ③이 옳은 내용이다.

24 돌고래의 지능을 인간의 지능과 비교하는 내용이므로, 인간의 지능이 문맥상 적합하다.

>>> 다음 글을 읽고 문제의 답을 고르시오. [25~26]

Human beings no longer thrive under the water from which their ancestors emerged, but their relationship with the sea remains close. Over half the world's people live within 100 kilometers (62 miles) of the coast; a tenth are within 10km. On land at least, the sea delights the senses and excites the imagination. The sight and smell of the sea inspire courage and adventure, fear and romance. Though the waves may be rippling or mountainous, the waters angry or calm, the ocean itself is eternal. Its moods pass. Its tides keep to a rhythm. It is unchanging.

Or so it has long seemed. Appearances (　가　), though. Large parts of the sea may indeed remain unchanged, but in others, especially in the surface and coastal waters where 90% of marine life is to be found, the impact of man's activities is increasingly plain. This should hardly be a surprise. Man has changed the landscape and the atmosphere. It would be odd if the seas, which he has for centuries used for food, for transport, for dumping rubbish and, more recently, for recreation, had not also been affected.

25 What is the main idea of the passage above?

① The sea has been affected greatly by man's activities.
② People like to live in areas close to the sea.
③ We cannot live without the help of the sea.
④ There have been various works of literature on the sea.

26 Which of the following best fills in the blank (가) of the passage above?

① abound　　　　② build
③ deceive　　　　④ lead

해석 인간은 우리 조상이 처음으로 그 모습을 드러냈던 물 아래에서 더 이상 번성하지 못하지만, 바다와 인간의 관계는 여전히 밀접하다. 전 세계 사람들의 반 이상이 해안으로부터 100킬로미터 이내에서 살고 있으며, 10분의 1은 10킬로미터 이내에 살고 있다. 적어도 육지에서, 바다는 감각을 즐겁게 해 주며 상상력을 자극한다. 바다의 풍경과 냄새는 용기와 모험, 두려움과 낭만에 대한 생각을 불어넣는다. 비록 파도에 잔물결이 일거나 산처럼 거대해질 수 있고 바다가 분노하거나 고요할 수도 있지만(모양이나 형태는 계속 변하지만), 바다 자체는 영원하다. 바다의 노여움은 지나간다(오래가지 않는다). 바다의 조수는 규칙적인 반복을 고수한다. 바다는 변하지 않는다.

대체적으로 오랫동안 바다는 변하지 않는 것으로 보인다. 그러나 겉모습은 속인다(변하지 않는 것처럼 속일 뿐이다). 바다의 많은 지역들이 실제로 여전히 변하지 않았겠지만 특히 해양 생명체의 90%가 발견될 수 있는 해수면과 해안과 같은 다른 지역들에서, 인간 활동의 영향은 점점 명백해지고 있다. 이는 결코 놀라운 것이 아니다. 인간이 주변의 풍경과 대기를 변화시켰다. 만약 인간이 수 세기 동안 식량, 운송, 쓰레기 투기, 그리고 더 최근에는 휴양을 위해 이용해 왔던 바다도 또한 (인간의 활동에) 영향을 받지 않았다면 이상할 것이다.

25 윗글의 요지는 무엇인가?

① 바다는 인간의 행동에 상당히 영향을 받았다.
② 사람들은 바다와 가까운 지역에서 살고 싶어 한다.
③ 우리는 바다의 도움 없이는 살 수 없다.
④ 바다와 관련한 다양한 문학 작품이 있다.

26 윗글의 빈칸에 가장 알맞은 것은?

① 풍부하다　　　　② 건설하다
③ 속이다　　　　　④ 인도하다

어구 **no longer** 더 이상 ~하지 않다　**thrive** 번창하다　**ancestor** 조상, 선조　**remain close** 여전히 밀접하다　**coast** 연안, 해안　**at least** 적어도; 최소한　**delight** 매우 기쁘게 하다　**inspire** 고무[격려]하다　**ripple** 잔물결[파문]이 일다　**mountainous** 산더미 같은, 거대한　**eternal** 영구[영원]한, 영원히 변치 않는　**moods** 시무룩함, 우울, 짜증　**keep to** ~을 고수하다　**or so** 대체로, 그 정도로　**indeed** 실로, 참으로; 게다가　**marine** 바다의, 해양의　**plain** 분명한, 명백한; 솔직한, 검소한　**odd** 이상한; 홀수의; 임시의　**dump** (쓰레기 따위를) 내버리다　**rubbish** 쓰레기

해설 **25** 바다와 인간의 관계는 밀접하다는 첫 단락의 주제와 인간에 의해 영향을 받았다는 두 번째 단락의 주제를 합친 내용은 ①이 된다.

26 바다는 변하지 않는 것처럼 보인다는 앞 문장까지의 내용과 해안과 가까운 지역에서 사람들이 살고 있어서 사람들의 영향을 받아 변화한다는 뒷 문장의 내용은 '역접' 관계에 있다. 따라서 겉모습이 속인다는 내용이 옳다.

27 글의 흐름상 필요 없는 문장을 고르시오.

Think of 'weight control' as 'fat control' and it will fit in well with your other good health habits. For most of us, the problem and the solution are personal, not medical. ① Excess weight is very seldom due to thyroid disease or other specific illness. ② It slows you down, makes you less effective in personal encounters, and lowers your self-image. ③ Like the other habits that change your health, management of this problem begins with the recognition that it is a problem. ④ Weight control requires your continued attention and you must have lifelong vigilance about it.

해석 체중 관리를 지방 관리로 생각해 보라. 그러면 당신의 다른 좋은 건강 습관과 조화를 잘 이룰 수 있다. 우리들 대부분의 경우에 있어서, 문제와 해결책은 의학적인 것이 아니라 개인의 몫이다. ①비만은 갑상선 질병이나 다른 특정 질병 때문에 비롯되는 것이 아니다. ②비만은 당신을 느리게 행동하도록 하고, 개인적인 만남에서 덜 인상적인 모습을 갖게 하고, 자신의 이미지를 깎아내리게 한다. ③당신의 건강을 변화시키는 다른 습관들처럼, 체중 문제의 관리가 문제라는 생각과 함께 시작된다. ④체중 관리는 당신의 지속적인 인식을 필요로 하고 평생 경계해야만 한다.

어구 think of A as B A를 B라고 생각하다 fit in with ~과 조화되다 be due to ~에 기인하다 thyroid 갑상선 self-image 자아상 lifelong 평생의 vigilance 경계, 조심; 불침번

해설 다른 문장들의 내용은 질병과 같은 의학적인 문제가 아니라는 것을 논하고 있지만, ②의 내용은 비만으로 인한 단점을 논하고 있기 때문에 ②가 글 전체의 내용에서 어긋난다.

>>> 다음 글을 읽고 문제의 답을 고르시오.

In southern Africa there is a very special snake called the "spitting cobra." This unusual snake is as dangerous as it is beautiful. However, unlike many other dangerous snakes, the spitting cobra usually does not bother to bite its enemies. When an enemy gets near, a spitting cobra raises up its head. Then it seems to spit right at its enemy's eyes. The cobra's deadly venom is squirted through two tiny holes in its fangs, or teeth. If that poison lands in the eyes, it can cause someone to go blind almost immediately. Oddly enough, the poison is completely harmless if it lands on the skin. Even more surprising is the cobra's aim. Spitting cobras have been known to hit an enemy's eyes from as far away as six feet.

28 Which of the following would be useful if you were near spitting cobras?

① mittens
② long pants
③ sunglasses
④ heavy boots

해석 남아프리카에 '침을 뱉는 코브라'라고 불리는 매우 특이한 뱀이 있다. 이 특이한 뱀은 아름다운 것만큼 위험한 존재이다. 그러나 다른 위험한 뱀들과는 달리, 대개 이 침을 뱉는 코브라는 적을 일부러 물지는 않는다. 적이 근처에 있을 때, 침을 뱉는 코브라는 머리를 들어 올린다. 그리고 적의 눈에 바로 침을 뱉는 것처럼 보인다. 코브라의 치명적인 독은 송곳니에 있는 두 개의 작은 구멍을 통해 나온다. 만일 독이 눈에 들어가면, 독은 거의 즉시 실명시킨다. 이상하게도 이 독은 피부에 떨어지면 거의 해를 끼치지 않는다. 코브라의 조준이 훨씬 더 놀랍다. 침을 뱉는 코브라는 멀리 떨어진 6피트에서도 적의 눈에 공격을 가하는 것으로 알려져 있다.

28 만일 당신이 침을 뱉는 코브라 근처에 있다면 유용한 것으로 무엇이 있겠는가?
① 벙어리장갑
② 긴 바지
③ 선글라스
④ 무거운 장화

어구 spit (침 · 음식 · 피 따위를) 뱉다 bother to 일부러 ~ 하다 deadly 치명적인 venom 독액; 원한 squirt 분출하다; 퍼붓다 tiny 작은, 조그마한 fang (육식 동물의) 엄니, 송곳니 land 떨어지다; 상륙하다 go blind 눈이 멀다 oddly enough 묘한 이야기지만, 이상하게도 mitten 벙어리장갑

해설 코브라의 독이 실명을 시킬 수 있다고 했기 때문에 선글라스를 낀다면 눈에 독이 들어가지 않을 수 있다.

Perhaps the greatest discovery that man has ever made, greater than the steam engine, the millstone, the wheel, or the button, was made by the Plato more than twenty-three hundred years ago. It is a perpetual discovery which needs to be made over and over again by generations and by individuals. By means of the analytical method of his master Socrates, Plato discovered the difference between things that are permanent and things which are merely transitory. He called these permanent things Ideas. <u>Never has civilized man forgotten Plato's discovery without disaster, and never has he remembered it without a renaissance of the spirit.</u>

29 Choose the best title of the above passage.

① Disaster which counteracts humans' spirit
② A philosopher's ambition
③ A temporary idea's futility
④ The key to checking disaster
⑤ A lofty ideal: something men should not forget

30 In the passage above, what does the underlined sentence imply?

① Humanistic spirit can be destroyed by civilized men, and it can be aided by civilized men.
② Plato is great, so that men endlessly must be reminded of his philosophy.
③ Ideas can guarantee development, but in our ignoring them, catastrophe can arise.
④ To check disaster, we must remember the Renaissance's philosophy.
⑤ The civilized must ignore Plato's ideas, and disaster must be inevitable.

해석 증기기관이나 맷돌, 또는 바퀴나 단추를 능가하는 인간이 이룩한 가장 위대한 발견은 2,300년 전쯤에 플라톤이 이루었다. 그것은 여러 세대와 여러 개인에 의해 되풀이되어 이루어질 필요가 있는 끊임없는 발견이다. 그의 스승인 소크라테스의 분석적인 방법에 의해서 플라톤은 영원한 것들과 단지 일시적인 것에 불과한 것들 사이의 차이를 발견하였다. 그는 이 영원한 것들을 이데아라 불렀다. 문명인이 이와 같은 플라톤의 발견을 잊을 때마다 반드시 재난이 닥쳤으며, 이를 기억할 때마다 인간정신의 부흥이 일어났던 것이다.

29 윗글의 제목으로 가장 적절한 것을 고르시오.

① 인간의 정신과 역행하는 참사
② 철학자의 야망
③ 순간적인 생각의 무익함
④ 참사를 막을 수 있는 방법
⑤ 사람들이 잊어서는 안 되는 고귀한 이상

30 윗글에서 밑줄 친 문장이 암시하는 것은?

① 문명인들이 인간의 정신을 파괴할 수 있으며, 또한 그들이 인간의 정신을 도와줄 수도 있다.
② 플라톤은 위대하므로 인간들은 끝없이 그의 철학을 명심해야만 한다.
③ 이데아는 발전을 보장하지만 경시하게 될 때 참사가 발생할 수 있다.
④ 재난을 막기 위하여 우리는 르네상스의 철학을 기억해야만 한다.
⑤ 문명인들은 플라톤의 이데아를 무시함에 틀림이 없으므로 재난을 피할 수 없다.

어구 **the steam engine** 증기기관 **millstone** 맷돌 **wheel** 바퀴 **by means of** ~을 수단으로 **analytical** 분석적인 **disaster** 재난 **renaissance** 부흥 **counteract** 역행하다, 방해하다, 좌절시키다 **futility** 무익함 **check** 억제하다, 확인하다 **lofty** 고귀한 **aid** 지원하다 **catastrophe** 재난 **inevitable** 불가피한

해설 29 마지막 문장이 주제문으로서, 플라톤의 이데아는 인류의 흥망성쇠를 결정지을 수 있는 고귀한 것임이 이 글의 주제이다.

30 cannot A without B는 'A하면 반드시 B하다'는 표현이다. 주어진 대로 직역을 한다면, '문명인들이 플라톤의 연구(이데아)를 잊을 때마다 재난이 있었으며, 그것을 기억할 때마다 사상의 부흥이 있었다'는 내용이 된다. 이 내용을 포함하고 있는 보기는 ③이다.

Actual TEST 03

⇒ 본책 p.212

1 ①	2 ②	3 ④	4 ④	5 ①	6 ⑤	7 ③	8 ②	9 ③	10 ①
11 ②	12 ②	13 ①	14 ①	15 ⑤	16 ⑤	17 ①	18 ①	19 ④	20 ②
21 ⑤	22 ④	23 ③	24 ③	25 ④	26 ②	27 ④	28 ④	29 ④	30 ③

>>> 다음 글을 읽고 문제의 답을 고르시오. [1~6]

1 ____________ is the way of walking you can associate with someone who drank too much alcohol.

① Staggering ② Plodding
③ Tramping ④ Prowling

해석 당신이 연상할 수 있는 술 취한 사람의 걸음걸이는 비틀거리며 걷는 것이다.

어구 associate A with B A와 B를 연상·연관시키다 **stagger** 비틀거리다, 망설이다 **plod** 터벅터벅 걷다 **tramp** 쿵쿵거리며 걷다 **prowl** 헤매다, 기웃거리다

해설 술 취한 사람을 연상시킬 수 있는 걸음걸이는 비틀거리며 걷는 것이라고 유추가 가능하다.

2 The servant's attitude was so ____________ that it would have been available to anyone with an appreciation of sincerity.

① natal ② elastic
③ doleful ④ rotund

해석 그 하인의 태도는 너무나 융통성이 있어서 성실하다는 칭찬을 누구에게나 받을 수 있었을 것이다.

어구 natal 출생의 elastic 융통성 있는 doleful 슬픈, 우울한 rotund 토실토실 살이 찐

해설 칭찬받을 만한 태도가 필요하므로 '융통성 있는'이란 표현이 적합하다.

3 I have ____________ in my stomach because I'll take an entrance examination tomorrow.

① worms ② monsters
③ birds ④ butterflies

해석 입학시험을 볼 것이기 때문에 나는 조마조마하다.

어구 have butterflies in one's stomach 조마조마하다 entrance examination 입학시험

해설 have butterflies(조마조마하다)의 표현을 물어보는 문제이다.

4 The theory of evolution suggests that human beings must, like other animals, be entirely selfish in their actions, even when they appear to be self-sacrificing and ____________.

① catastrophic ② evangelistic
③ evolutionary ④ philanthropic

해석 진화론은 인간이 자기희생적이며 이타적인 것으로 보일 때조차도 다른 동물들처럼 자신의 행위를 할 때 완전히 이기적임에 틀림이 없다고 주장한다.

어구 entirely 완전히, 틀림없이 self-sacrificing 자기희생적인 catastrophic 재난의, 비극적인 evangelistic 복음 전도자의 philanthropic 박애적인

해설 and에 의해서 '자기희생적인'이란 단어와 순접의 어휘가 필요하다.

5 The Earth's climate doesn't respond to forcing in a smooth and gradual way. Rather it responds in ___________ which involve large-scale reorganization of the Earth's systems.

① sharp jumps ② regular steps
③ predictable speeds ④ slow ways

해석 지구의 기후는 부드럽고 점진적인 방식의 힘에는 반응하지 않는다. 차라리 대규모 지구 시스템의 재편성과 관련 있는 급격한 변동에 반응한다.

어구 **respond to** ~에 반응하다 **forcing** 강제, 탈취, 촉성 재배 **large-scale** 대규모의 **reorganization** 재조직, 재편성

해설 rather라는 '역접–양보' 접속 부사에 의해 '부드럽고 점진적인'이란 표현의 반대 의미가 필요하다.

6 There seemed to be no spark in American education; no daring, no readiness to engage the individual child's mind as anything other than raw material for statistical reductions. The fear of being ___________ is rooted in the American teacher's soul: you can be fired for treading the path of ___________ enterprise.

① conservative - exceptional
② enthusiastic - traditional
③ mediocre - temporary
④ customary - revolutionary
⑤ unorthodox - experimental

해석 미국 교육에 활기가 전혀 없어 보였다. 즉 통계상의 감소를 위한 원자재를 제외하고서 다른 것에 아이의 마음을 몰두시키려는 어떠한 대담성이나 준비가 없었다. 정통적이지 않다는 것에 대한 두려움이 미국 교사의 영혼 속에 뿌리내려 있으므로 당신은 실험적인 길을 걸어간 것에 대해서 해고될 수 있다.

어구 **spark** 흔적, 불꽃 **daring** 대담함 **readiness** 준비, 용이, 자진 **engage** ~의 마음을 끌다, 약혼시키다, 고용하다 **other than** ~을 제외하고서 **raw material** 원자재 **reduction** 감소, 절감 **fire** 해고하다 **tread** 짓밟다, 걷다 **conservative** 보수적인 **exceptional** 예외적인 **enthusiastic** 열정적인 **mediocre** 보통의 **temporary** 순간의 **customary** 관례의 **unorthodox** 정통이 아닌 **experimental** 실험의, 경험의

해설 순접–유추: There seemed to be no spark ... no daring, no readiness

7 다음 글의 흐름으로 보아 주어진 문장이 들어갈 가장 적절한 곳은?

In addition, take the pictures of the damage to the house and its contents.

When the storm is over, it is natural to want to go home as soon as possible. When it is safe to return, you should take the following steps. First, be careful when you enter your house. (A) There may be snakes or other animals that the flood washed in. Then, open all the windows and doors. You should let the fresh air dry the house. Next, check for gas leaks and electrical system damage. (B) Any of these problems can be very dangerous. If you find anything wrong, you should turn off the power and call the gas company and the electrical company. (C) You will need this proof for the insurance company. Finally, start cleaning your house. (D) This is the hardest job because you must pick up the piece of your life and make it back together.

① (A) ② (B)
③ (C) ④ (D)

해석 폭풍이 그치면, 당연히 가능한 한 빨리 집으로 돌아가고 싶다. 집에 돌아가게 된다면, 여러분은 다음의 단계를 거쳐야 한다. 첫째, 집 안으로 들어갈 때 조심하라. (A) 홍수에 휩쓸려 집 안으로 들어온 뱀이나 다른 동물들이 있을지도 모른다. 그러고 나면 모든 창문과 문을 열어 두어라. 신선한 공기가 집 안을 건조시킬 수 있도록 해야 한다. 그 다음에는 가스 누출이나 전기 시스템에 손상이 없는지를 확인해야 한다. (B) 이런 것들에서 문제가 발생하는 경우에는 매우 위험할 수 있다. 만약 무언가 잘못된 것을 발견한다면 전기를 차단시킨 후 가스 회사와 전기 회사에 연락을 해야 한다. (C) 뿐만 아니라, 집과 가재도구의 피해 상황을 사진으로 찍어 두어라. 이는 나중에 보험 회사에 증거물로 제출하기 위함이다. 마지막으로 집 안 청소를 시작하라. (D) 이 일은 일상의 조각들을 주워다 다시 한데 붙이는 가장 힘든 작업이라 할 수 있다

어구 **take a step** 조치를 취하다 **wash in** 안으로 떠내려 보내다 **pick up** 줍다

해설 피해 상황을 사진으로 찍어둔 것 자체가 보험금을 타기 위한 증거물이 되므로, 보험 회사 내용이 등장하는 문장 앞이 적절하다.

8 다음 글의 흐름으로 보아 주어진 문장이 들어갈 가장 적절한 곳은?

> Of all the voices in nature, the cry of the loon is one of the most haunting.

The common loon is an unforgettable bird of the northern wilderness. The name loon probably comes from the Old English word lumme, meaning a lummox or an awkward person. That description would apply only when the bird is on land or ice. [I] There, the loon is awkward, but in water, it swims faster than a fish, using its wings like flippers. Above all, the most unforgettable thing about the loon is its cry. [II] The loon seems to have four kinds of cries. [III] Its laughter is used in situations of alarm, annoyance, or greeting. Its yodel is used during wide circles of flight and invites other loons to call. [IV] The loon's wail is heard at night in early summer but never during flight. And finally, the loon does a kind of talking—simple one-syllable notes used to communicate with a mate or with the flock. The loon's cries are said to become stronger and more frequent at the approach of storms.

① [I]　　　　② [II]
③ [III]　　　　④ [IV]

해석 일반적인 아비는 북부의 황야에서 잊혀지지 않는 새이다. loon이라는 이름은 아마도 고대 영어 단어인 '멍청이' 혹은 '서투른 사람'을 의미하는 lumme에서 유래한 것 같다. 그런 묘사는 이 새가 육지나 얼음 위에 있을 때만 적용이 될 것이다. [I] 그곳에서 아비는 동작이 서투르지만, 물속에서는 물갈퀴와 유사한 날개를 이용하여 물고기보다 더 빠르게 헤엄을 친다. 무엇보다도, 아비에 대해 가장 잊을 수 없는 것은 그 울음소리이다. 자연에 있는 모든 소리들 중에서 아비의 울음소리는 가장 머릿속을 떠나지 않는 것들 중 하나이다. [II] 아비는 네 가지 종류의 소리가 있는 것 같다. [III] 아비의 웃음소리는 놀람, 불쾌감, 혹은 인사를 전할 때 사용된다. 아비의 노래는(yodel) 장거리 비행을 하는 동안에 사용되고 다른 아비들을 부르도록 유도한다. [IV] 아비의 우는 소리는 초여름의 밤에 들리지만, 결코 비행을 하는 동안에는 울지 않는다. 그리고 마지막으로, 아비는 일종의 대화를 하기도 하는데, 그 대화는 아비가 짝 혹은 무리와 대화를 하기 위해 사용된 한 음절로 된 간단한 울음소리이다. 아비의 울음소리는 폭풍이 다가올 때 더 강해지고 더 빈번하다고 한다.

어구 **haunting** 자주 마음속에 떠오르는, 뇌리를 떠나지 않는　**loon** 아비(북미산 큰 새), 게으름뱅이, 바보, 얼간이　**unforgettable** 잊을 수 없는, (언제까지나) 기억에 남는(memorable)　**lummox** 얼뜨기, 얼간이　**awkward** 섣부른, 서투른　**flipper** 물갈퀴　**annoyance** 성가심, 불쾌감; 괴로움, 곤혹　**wail** 울부짖음, 울부짖는 소리　**syllable** 음절; 음절을 나타내는 문자　**note** (새의) 울음소리

해설 제시문의 단서인 목소리(voices)를 한정사인 the로 수식하고 있으며, 주절의 haunting이라는 '(머리에서) 떠나지 않는'이란 뜻을 가진 단어가 등장하므로, 이 단어와 동의어인 unforgettable이 등장한 다음 문장이 적합하다.

>>> 다음 글을 읽고 문제의 답을 고르시오.

Almost every college student has experienced prefinals terror—the horrible anxiety that puts your stomach on a roller coaster and your brain in a blender. Few escape those final-exam jitters because everyone knows just how much is riding on that one exam, often more than half of the course grade. Yet therein lies the crux of the problem. Infrequent high-stakes exams don't encourage students to do their best work. More frequent tests given—say, every two or three weeks—would be a much more effective method of discovering how well students are or are not mastering course concepts. With more frequent testing, students would be less anxious when they take exams; thus anxiety would no longer interfere with exam performance. More frequent testing also encourages students to review on a regular basis, something that a one-shot final exam does not do. Lots of tests also mean lots of feedback, and students would know early on in the course what terms or concepts required additional explanation and review. They wouldn't have to wait until the end of the semester to find out that they had misunderstood, or missed altogether, a critical point or theory.

해석 거의 모든 대학생들은 기말고사에 앞서 두려움을 경험했으며, 이는 속을 뒤집어 놓고, 머리를 어지럽게 한다. 그 한 번의 시험에 얼마나 많은 것이 달려 있는지를 모두가 알고 있기 때문에 기말고사의 불안감에서 벗어날 학생은 거의 없다. 그러나 거기에 문제의 핵심이 존재한다. 자주 보는 것은 아니지만, 이판사판으로 보는 시험으로는 학생들이 최선을 다해 공부할 수 없게 된다. 이를테면 2～3주에 한 번꼴로 더 자주 보는 시험은 학생들로 하여금 수업에서 배우는 개념들을 얼마나 잘 알고 있는지를 판단하는 훨씬 더 효율적인 방법이 된다. 더 자주 보는 시험을 통해 학생들은 시험을 치를 때 걱정을 덜 하게 된다. 그래서 걱정이 시험 성적을 더 이상 방해하지 않게 될 것이다. 더 자주 보는 시험은 또한 학생들을 규칙적으로 복습하도록 고무시키며, 이것은 단 한 번으로 끝나는 기말고사는 할 수 없는 것이다. 많은 시험은 또한 많은 피드백을 의미하여, 학생들은 그 강의 때 어떠한 용어나 개념들이 추가 설명과 복습이 필요했었는지를 일찍 알게 된다. 학생들은 중요한 요지나 이론을 잘못 이해했는지 혹은 전혀 알지 못하는지 판단하기 위해 학기 마지막까지 기다릴 필요가 없게 된다.

9 이 글의 요지는 무엇인가?
① 학생들은 일찍부터 많은 피드백을 필요로 한다.
② 상담 문제는 학생들의 불안감을 낮추기 위하여 강화되어야만 한다.
③ 자주 보는 시험이 이따금씩 보는 시험보다 더 효과적인 방법이다.
④ 시험이 아닌 새로운 평가 방법이 개발될 필요가 있다.

9 What is the main point of the author's argument?

① Students need lots of feedback early on in the course.
② Counselling programs must be reinforced to lessen students' anxiety.
③ Frequent tests would be a more effective method than infrequent exams.
④ A new evaluation method needs to be developed other than tests or exams.

어구 prefinals 기말 시험 전의   puts one's stomach on a roller coaster ~의 속을 뒤집다   put one's brain in a blender ~를 혼란스럽게 하다   final-exam 기말시험   jitter 대단한 신경과민, 불안감   ride on ~에 의존하다; ~에 달려 있다   therein 그 속에; 거기에; 그 점에서   crux 중요점, 핵심; 십자가; 난문, 난제   high-stakes 이판사판의   say 이를테면, 예를 들면, 글쎄요   take an exam 시험을 보다   interfere 간섭하다; 방해하다   on a regular basis 규칙적으로   one-shot 한 번으로 완전[유효]한, 1회 한의, 단발(로)의   altogether 아주, 전혀   critical 결정적인, 중대한; 비평의   point 목적, 취지; 끝   early on 일찍부터   reinforce 강화시키다   lessen 작게[적게] 하다, 줄이다, 감하다

해설 More frequent tests given ~ 문장이 주제문으로서, 이하부터 이따금씩 치루는 시험보다 자주 치르는 시험이 학생들의 학업에 더 효과적인 방법이 될 수 있다고 주장한다.

One of my friends, a musician, is always upbeat. Nothing gets her down. But when she developed ringing in one ear, I was concerned it might overwhelm even her. When I asked if her condition was especially annoying to a musician, she shook her head. "Not really," she said cheerfully. "The ringing sound is in the key of B flat, so I use it to tune my cello a half-tone lower."

10 윗글의 제목으로서 올바른 것은?

① Optimistic Musician
② Annoying Friend
③ Ringing Ear
④ Troublesome Noise

해석 음악가인 내 친구는 언제나 긍정적이다. 어느 것도 그녀를 우울하게 하지 못한다. 그러나 그녀의 한쪽 귀에 이명이 걸렸을 때 난 이명이 그녀를 격한 감정에 휩싸이게 하는 것은 아닐까 걱정했다. 그녀의 상태가 음악가에게 짜증스럽게 하지는 않은지 물어보았을 때, 그녀는 고개를 저었다. 그녀는 "꼭 그렇지는 않아."라고 발랄하게 말했다. "이명은 B 플랫 키 안에 있어서, 나는 첼로의 음정 반을 낮추기 위해서 (오히려) 그 이명을 이용해."

10 윗글의 제목으로서 올바른 것은?

① 낙관적인 음악가   ② 짜증스러운 친구
③ 이명   ④ 성가신 소음

어구 upbeat 낙관적인, 명랑한; 오름세의   get A down A의 기를 꺾다   develop (병, 습관 등이) 걸리다; 생기다   ringing 울리는 소리   overwhelm (감정이) 휩싸다, 압도하다; 제압하다   annoying 짜증나게 하는   tune A lower A의 (음정을) 낮추다

해설 첫 문장에서 자신의 친구는 언제나 낙관적이라고 했으며, 뒷부분에서도 발랄하게 답변하는 것을 통해 친구의 성격이 낙관적임을 말해 주는 것이 이 글의 주제가 된다.

>>> 다음 글을 읽고 문제의 답을 고르시오.

As used in this book, culture has a different and more specialized meaning. It refers to all the accepted and patterned ways of behavior of a given people. It is a body of common understandings. It is the sum total and the organization or arrangement of all the group's ways of thinking, feeling, and acting. It also includes the physical manifestations of the group as exhibited in the objects they make. In this sense, every people—however primitive—has a culture, and no individual can live without culture.

11 이 글의 목적으로 가장 알맞은 것은?

① To categorize a concept
② To define a concept
③ To give examples for a concept
④ To revise a concept

해석 이 책에 서술된 것처럼 문화는 서로 다르고 조금 더 전문화된 의미를 갖고 있다. 문화는 일정한 사람들에게 수용되고 정형화된 행동 양식들 모두를 일컫는다. 그것은 이해를 같이하는 것들의 총체이다. 이것은 모든 집단의 생각, 감정 그리고 행동 방법들의 총체, 구성 또는 배열이다. 이것은 또한 그들이 만든 사물에서 드러나고 있는 것처럼, 집단의 물리적 표현을 포함하고 있다. 이러한 관점에서 아무리 원시적이어도 모든 사람은 문화를 소유하고 있으며, 어느 개인도 문화 없이 살 수 없다.

11 이 글의 목적으로 가장 알맞은 것은?

① 개념을 분류하기 위하여   ② 개념의 정의를 내리기 위하여
③ 개념의 예를 들기 위하여   ④ 개념을 바꾸기 위하여

어구 specialized 특별한, 전문화된 refer to 언급하다 accepted 일반적으로 인정된 patterned 정렬된; 모방한 given 일정한; 주어진; 정해진 arrangement 배열; 준비; 조정 manifestation 표현; 명시; 데모 in this sense 이와 같은 관점에서 primitive 원시적인 categorize 분류하다 define 정의를 내리다; 밝히다 revise 교정하다, 바꾸다

해설 이 글은 문화의 개념에 대한 정의를 내리고 있다.

>>> 다음 글을 읽고 문제의 답을 고르시오.

Scientists have successfully tested a system that translates brain waves into speech, raising the prospect that people left mute by stroke, Lou Gehrig's disease, and other afflictions will be able to communicate by synthetic voice.

[A] For example, British physicist Stephen Hawking, who is nearly completely paralyzed as a result of Lou Gehrig's disease, takes several minutes to compose a short sentence that is rendered into speech by a computer.

[B] The system was tested on a 26-year-old man left paralyzed by a brain stem stroke, but with his consciousness and cognitive abilities intact.

[C] The condition is known as "locked-in syndrome."

[D] In this condition, communication by eye movement or other limited motion is possible but extremely cumbersome.

12 Choose the best order from [A] through [D] for a paragraph starting with the sentence in the box.

① [B]-[A]-[D]-[C]
② [B]-[C]-[D]-[A]
③ [D]-[A]-[C]-[B]
④ [D]-[B]-[A]-[C]

해석 과학자들은 뇌파를 언어로 해석해 주는 체계를 성공적으로 실험했으며, 뇌졸중, 루게릭병과 다른 고통 때문에 말을 하지 못하는 사람들이 합성 음성을 통해 대화를 할 수 있는 가능성을 높여 주었다. [B] 이 체계는 뇌간 졸중 때문에 마비되었으나 의식과 인지 능력은 멀쩡했던 26세 남성에게 실험되었다. [C] 이 증상은 폐쇄 증후군으로 알려져 있다. [D] 이 상태에서 눈의 행동이나 다른 제한적인 행동을 통해 대화는 가능하지만, 매우 번거롭다. [A] 예컨대, 루게릭병 때문에 거의 완전히 마비된 영국의 물리학자 스테판 호킹은 컴퓨터를 통해 언어로 표현되는 간단한 문장을 만드는 데 몇 분이 소요된다.

12 제시문을 시작으로, 윗글들을 문맥에 맞게 올바른 순서로 연결하시오.

어구 translate A into B A를 B로 해석하다 prospect 가능성; 경치 mute 말을 못하는 affliction 고통 synthetic 합성의; 인위적인 paralyzed 마비된 brain stem stroke 뇌간 졸중 intact 온전한; 멀쩡한 locked-in syndrome 폐쇄 증후군 cumbersome 성가신, 귀찮은

해설 [B] 뇌간 졸중으로 마비됐지만 의식과 인지 능력이 멀쩡한 상태를 [C] 문장에서 폐쇄 증후군이라고 용어 개념을 설명해 준다. [D]에서 그 추가적인 증상을 설명하고, [A] 그 구체적인 예를 들어준다.

Mr. Whitson taught sixth grade science. On the first day of class, he gave us a lecture about a creature called the cattywampus, an ill-adapted nocturnal animal that was wiped out during the Ice Age. He passed around a skull as he talked. We all took notes and later had a quiz.

When he returned my paper, I was shocked. There was a big red X through each of my answers. I had failed. There had to be some mistake! I had written down exactly what Mr. Whitson said. Then I realized that everyone in the class had failed. What had happened?

Very simple, Mr. Whitson explained. He had made up all that stuff about the cattywampus. There had never been any such animal. The information in our notes was, therefore, incorrect. Did we expect credit for incorrect answers?

We should have figured it out, Mr. Whitson said. After all, at the very moment he was passing around the cattywampus skull (in truth, a cat's), hadn't he been telling us that no trace of the animal remained? He had described its amazing night vision, the color of its fur and any number of other facts he couldn't have known. He had given the animal a ridiculous name, and we still hadn't been suspicious. The zeroes on our papers would be recorded in his grade book, he said. And they were.

Mr. Whitson said he hoped we would learn something from this experience. Teachers and textbooks are not infallible. In fact, no one is. He told us not to let our minds go to sleep and to speak up if we ever thought he or the textbook was wrong.

13 Why did all the students fail in the quiz?

① Because they answered exactly as their teacher said.
② Because they didn't study hard enough to pass the quiz.
③ Because the questions were too difficult for them to answer.
④ Because they didn't understand the questions.
⑤ Because they intentionally didn't answer the questions.

14 What did the students actually see when the teacher was passing around a skull?

① a cat's skull
② an extinct animal's skull
③ an owl's skull
④ a cattywampus skull
⑤ a human skull

해석 윗슨 선생님은 6학년 과학을 가르쳤다. 수업이 있던 첫날, 그는 우리에게 cattywampus라 불리는 동물에 대해 강의를 했는데, 그 동물은 빙하시대에 적응을 하지 못했던 멸종된 야행성 동물이었다. 선생님은 설명하시며 그 동물의 두개골을 돌리셨다. 우리 모두는 노트에 적었으며, 후에 퀴즈 시험을 보았다. 그 선생님이 내 시험지를 돌려주었을 때, 나는 충격에 휩싸였다. 내가 표기한 각각의 답에 붉은색으로 큰 X 표시가 있었다. 나는 떨어졌다. 어떤 실수가 있음에 틀림이 없어! 나는 선생님이 설명해 준 그대로 (답안지에) 썼었다. 그때 나는 반 전체 학생이 모두 떨어졌음을 깨달았다. 무슨 일이 발생한 것일까? 선생님은 간단하게 설명해 주었다. cattywampus에 관한 모든 내용은 꾸며낸 것이었다. 그와 같은 동물은 결코 존재하지 않았었다. 우리 노트에 있는 (수업) 정보는 오류가 있는 것이었다. 우리는 틀린 답에 대해 점수를 기대했던 것인가? 우리가 밝혀냈어야 했다고 선생님은 말했다. 결국에 그가 cattywampus의 두개골(사실은, 고양이의 것)을 돌린 바로 그 순간, 우리에게 그 동물의 어떠한 흔적도 남아 있지 않다고 말하지 않았던가? 그는 그것의 놀라운 암시와 그것의 털 색깔과 그가 알 수 없었던 다른 여러 사실들을 설명했었다. 그는 그 동물에 우스꽝스러운 이름을 만들어 주었고, 우리는 그럼에도 의심을 갖지 않았었다. 그는 우리 시험지에 있는 0점 표기들은 성적기록부에 기록될 것이라고 말했었다. 그리고 그렇게 되었다. 선생님은 이번 경험을 통해 우리가 무언가를 배우길 소망한다고 말했다. 선생님들과 교과서는 완벽한 것이 아니다. 사실 어떠한 것도 확실한 것은 없다. 그는 우리의 마음이 잠들게 하지 말고 만일 선생님 자신이나 교과서가 잘못되었다고 생각이 든다면 말을 하라고 전했다.

13 모든 학생들이 왜 시험에서 떨어졌는가?

① 선생님이 말한 대로 정확히 답변을 써서
② 퀴즈 시험을 통과하기에 공부를 열심히 하지 않아서
③ 답을 쓰기에 문제들이 너무 어려워서
④ 문제들을 이해하지 못해서
⑤ 의도적으로 문제에 대한 답을 쓰지 않아서

14 선생님이 두개골을 돌렸을 때 학생들이 실제로 보았던 것은 무엇인가?

① 고양이의 두개골   ② 멸종한 동물의 두개골
③ 올빼미의 두개골   ④ cattywampus 두개골
⑤ 인간의 두개골

15 cattywampus에 관한 설명으로서 옳은 내용은?

① 밤에 대체로 활동적인 동물이다.   ② 빙하기에 멸종했다.
③ 놀라운 암시 능력을 가졌다.   ④ 매우 화려한 털을 가졌다.
⑤ 결코 존재한 적이 없다.

16 윗슨 씨는 학생들이 무엇을 하기를 원하는가?

① 더 세심히 cattywampus의 두개골을 연구하는 것
② 그를 맹목적으로 따르는 것
③ 퀴즈 시험을 통과하기 위해 노트 작성을 잘 하는 것
④ 수학을 공부하는 법을 터득하는 것
⑤ 선생님들이 완벽하지 않을 수 있다는 점을 깨닫는 것

어구 **grade** 학년, 성적, 등급 **ill-adapted** 적응을 하지 못하는 **nocturnal** 야행성의, 야간의 **wipe out** 전멸시키다 **Ice Age** 빙하기 **pass around** 돌리다 **skull** 머리, 두개골 **take notes** 적어두다 **have a quiz** 간단한 시험을 치르다 **return** 돌려주다 **make up** 조작하다, 꾸며내다, 만들어내다, 화장하다 **stuff** 재료, 자료, 내용

15 Which of the following is true of the cattywampus?

① It was an animal active mostly at night.
② It became extinct during the Ice Age.
③ It had an amazing night vision.
④ It had very colorful fur.
⑤ It has never existed.

16 Mr. Whitson hoped that his students
_______________.

① examined the cattywampus skull more closely
② followed him blindly
③ took notes well to pass the quiz
④ learned how to study mathematics
⑤ learned that teachers might not be perfect

해설 13 존재하지도 않는 동물의 두개골을 제시하면서, 답을 작성하라고 했던 것은 교과서나 강사의 강의에만 의존하지 말고 자발적인 연구와 학습을 촉진시키고자 했던 것이다. 잘못된 강의를 그대로 듣고서 잘못된 답변을 했으므로 모두 낙제가 된 것이다.

14 네 번째 단락 두 번째 문장의 괄호에서 사실은 고양이의 두개골이라고 설명했다.

15 실제로는 존재하지 않은 동물이었다고 세 번째 단락 세 번째 문장에 언급됐다.

16 마지막 단락 마지막 문장에서, 선생님이나 교과서의 설명이 완벽하지 않다고 생각이 된다면 질문을 하라고 말한 점을 보아, ⑤의 설명이 옳다.

>>> **다음 글을 읽고 문제의 답을 고르시오.**

Aldous Huxley in his book *Brave New World* painted a picture of a perfectly planned state, from which freedom, difficulty, pain, and insecurity had all disappeared. But too much comfort, too much order, too much pleasure, and a total lack of anxiety had dehumanized the people in it—they had become less than human. Until at last the one rebel in the state cries out to its governor: "I don't want comfort, I want God, I want real danger, I want freedom, I want sin." "In fact," said the governor, "you're claiming the right to be unhappy." Whether or not this is a true picture, there is something in the nature of men which makes them escape from secure situations—e.g., into polar expedition or dangerous mountain climbing.

17 윗글의 요지로서 가장 적절한 것은?

① Material security does not always guarantee happiness to men.
② Human beings prefer, ironically, to be unhappy.
③ Men cannot be made too secure.
④ Men cannot live in a planned state.

해석 알도우스 헉슬리가 자신의 책인 〈Brave New World〉에서 자유, 고난, 고통, 불확실함이 사라진 완벽하게 고안된 국가를 묘사했다. 그러나 과도한 평온, 질서, 즐거움 그리고 열망에 대한 완전한 상실은 그 국민들의 인간성을 빼앗아 버렸다. 즉 그들은 비인간적이었다. 마침내 한 반역자가 그 통치자에게 소리치기를 '나는 안락을 원하지 않으며 신을 원하며 진정한 위험도 원하며 자유도 원하며 죄를 원한다.'라고 했다. 통치자가 말하기를 '사실, 당신은 불행해질 권리를 주장하는 것이다.'라고 했다. 이것이 진정한 상황이든 아니든 간에 안전한 장소에서 북극 탐험이나 위험한 산악 등산을 위해 일상에서 탈출하게끔 하는 인간의 본성에 존재하는 특별한 것이다.

17 윗글의 요지로서 가장 적절한 것은?
① 물질적인 안정이 인간에게 언제나 행복을 보장해 주는 것은 아니다.
② 모순되게도 인간은 불행해지기를 원한다.
③ 인간은 아무리 안정적이어도 지나치지 않다.
④ 인간은 계획된 고안된 국가에서 살 수 없다.

어구 insecurity 불안정, 근심, 불안   dehumanize ~의 인간성을 빼앗다, 비인간화하다   rebel 반역자, 모반자, 배반하다, 모반하다; 반항하다(against)   governor 지배자, 통치자(ruler)   expedition 탐험, 원정; 탐험대   cannot ~ too (much) 아무리 ~해도 지나치지 않다

해설 이 글은 미괄식으로서, 앞서 문학 작품의 줄거리를 간결하게 소개하고 있다. 이렇게 문학 작품의 내용이 앞에서 등장할 때에는 마지막 문장을 읽어 보아야 한다. 그 문장에서 작가가 진정 전하고자 하는 말이 등장하기 때문이다. 본 글은 '인간은 위험한 산악 등산 같은 곳으로 벗어나고자 하는 속성이 있다'는 것이 주제로서, 결국 '물질적 안정만으로 인간의 행복을 보장할 수는 없다'가 요지가 될 수 있다. ③은 '인간은 아무리 안전해도 지나치지 않다'고 해석이 된다. cannot too (much)는 '아무리 ~해도 지나치지 않다'는 뜻이다.

With my brow to the glass, I was thus occupied in scrutinizing the mob, when suddenly there came into view a countenance, that of a decrepit old man, some sixty-five or seventy years of age—a countenance which at once arrested and absorbed my whole attention, on account of the absolute idiosyncrasy of its expression. Any thing even remotely resembling that expression I had never seen before. I well remember that my first thought, upon beholding it, was that Retzsch, had he viewed it, would have greatly preferred it to his own pictural incarnations of the fiend. As I endeavored, during the brief minute of my original survey, to form some analysis of the meaning conveyed, there arose confusedly and paradoxically within my mind, the ideas of vast mental power, of caution, of penuriousness, of avarice, of coolness, of malice, of blood-thirstiness, of triumph, of merriment, of excessive terror, of extreme despair. I felt singularly aroused, startled, fascinated. Then came a craving desire to keep the man in view—to know more of him. Hurriedly putting on an overcoat, and seizing my hat and cane, I made my way into the street, and pushed through the crowd in the direction which I had seen him take; for he had already disappeared.

18 Which of the following CANNOT be inferred from the passage?

① The old man is malicious and fiendish.
② The narrator feels a voyeuristic desire for the old man.
③ Retszch is a painter who is preoccupied with the representation of the devil.
④ When the narrator first sees the old man, he is inside a building looking out the street.

해석 유리창에 이마를 대고서 군중을 유심히 바라보는 것에 몰두하고 있었을 때, 갑자기 한 사람의 모습이 시야에 들어왔는데, 약 65세 혹은 70살의 노쇠한 노인의 모습이었다. 표정이 너무나 특이했기 때문에 그 얼굴은 나의 모든 관심을 사로잡았을 뿐만 아니라 흡수해 버렸다. 나는 그와 조금이라도 비슷한 표정을 결코 본 적이 없었다. 그 모습을 보자마자 처음으로 떠올랐던 생각을 지금까지 기억한다. 레치가 만일 그 모습을 보았더라면 악마를 육체화해 그린 그의 그림들보다 그 표정을 훨씬 더 좋아했을 것이라는 생각 말이다. 처음에 잠깐 조사를 하는 동안 나는 그로부터 전해지는 의미에 대한 약간의 분석을 해보려고 노력했는데, 엄청난 정신적 힘, 경계, 빈곤, 탐욕, 냉담, 악의, 피에 대한 굶주림, 희열, 즐거움, 지나친 공포, 극단적인 절망에 관한 생각들이 나의 마음속에서 혼란스럽고 모순되게 나타났다. 이상할 정도로 나는 흥분, 놀람, 매료됨을 느꼈다. 그때 그 사람을 계속 관찰하며 그에 대해 더 많이 알고 싶은 강렬한 욕구가 나타났다. 나는 급히 외투를 입고 모자와 지팡이를 쥐고서, 그가 가고 있던 방향으로 군중을 헤치고 나갔다. 왜냐하면 그가 이미 사라지고 없었기 때문이었다.

18 이 글을 통해 유추할 수 없는 내용은 무엇인가?

① 노인은 사악하고 잔인하다.
② 작가는 그 노인을 엿보고 싶은 갈망을 느끼고 있다.
③ 레치는 악마의 묘사에 몰두하는 화가이다.
④ 작가가 처음 노인을 보았을 때, 그는 건물 안에서 창밖을 보고 있었다.

어구 brow 이마; 눈썹 be occupied in ~에 몰두하다 scrutinize 유심히 바라보다, 자세히 조사하다, 음미하다 came into view 시야에 들어오다 countenance 생김새, 용모, 안색, 표정; 후원, 장려, 지지 decrepit 노쇠한, 늙어빠진 at once A and B A와 B 모두 arrest attention 관심을 사로잡다 on account of ~ 때문에 idiosyncrasy (어느 개인의) 특이성, 특이한 성격 remotely 희미하게나마, 근소하게나마; 멀리 upon-ing ~하자마자 behold 보다 prefer A to B A를 B보다 더 좋아하다 incarnation 육체를 갖추게 함; 인간의 모습을 취함 fiend 악마; 귀신 endeavor 노력하다 brief 짧은; 간결한 convey 전달하다; 나르다 arise 발생하다 confusedly 혼란스럽게 paradoxically 모순적으로 vast 광대한, 거대한; 방대[막대]한 penuriousness 빈곤, 빈궁 avarice 탐욕, 허욕 coolness 차가움; 침착, 냉담; 무뚝뚝함 malice 악의, 해할 마음, 적의 blood-thirstiness 잔인함; 피에 굶주림 triumph 의기양양한 표정, 환희; 승리 merriment 즐거움 despair 절망 arouse 자극하다 craving 열망 keep A in view A를 계속 보다 put on ~을 입다 seize (붙)잡다, 붙들다 cane 지팡이 make one's way into ~로 (애써) 나아가다, 가다; 성공하다 malicious 사악한 fiendish 귀신[악마] 같은, 마성의; 극악한, 잔인한 voyeuristic 훔쳐보는 취미의, 관음증의 be preoccupied with ~에 몰두하다

해설 그 노인의 얼굴 표정에서 '사악함, 엄청난 정신적 힘, 경계, 빈곤, 즐거움' 등 상이한 다양한 느낌이 풍겨지고 있다고 했을 뿐, 그의 성격 자체가 사악하고 잔인하다고 언급되지는 않았다.

>>> **다음 글을 읽고 문제의 답을 고르시오.**

(A) They are sure that God intends for them to be happy, and they regard any interference with this attainment of happiness as a violation of their rights.

(B) Buying a home, taking vacations in Florida, and driving a new car are promoted as ways to achieve happiness.

(C) The Declaration of Independence includes this pursuit of happiness as a natural right, and the American people are obsessed with this pursuit.

(D) Commercial advertisements proclaim this much more in America than elsewhere.

19 윗글의 흐름상 이어질 내용을 바른 순서대로 배열한 것은?

① (C) - (D) - (A) - (B)　　② (B) - (C) - (A) - (D)
③ (A) - (B) - (C) - (D)　　④ (B) - (D) - (C) - (A)

해석 (B) 집을 사고, 플로리다에서 휴가를 보내고, 새로운 차를 운전하는 것은 행복을 추구하는 방법으로 장려된다.
(D) 상업 광고 방송은 어느 지역보다 미국에서 훨씬 더 많이 이것을 추구한다.
(C) 독립 선언문에는 이러한 행복의 추구가 자연권으로서 포함되어 있으며, 미국인들은 이 추구에 사로잡혀 있다.
(A) 미국인들은 신이 자신들을 행복하게 해 주려 한다는 점을 확신하며, 이 행복 추구에 대해 어느 방해라도 있다면 자신들의 권리에 대한 침해라고 간주한다.

어구 **intend for A to R** A를 ~하도록 의도하다　**regard A as B** A를 B라고 간주하다　**take a vacation** 휴가를 보내다　**promote** 장려하다, 승진시키다　**The Declaration of Independence** 독립 선언문　**be obsessed with** ~에 사로잡히다, 홀리다

해설 this라는 지시 형용사가 등장하는 (C)와 (A)는 첫 문장이 될 수 없으므로, (B) 문장이 첫 문장이 된다. (A) 문장의 they는 (C) 문장의 American People을 가리킨다.

>>> **다음 글을 읽고 문제의 답을 고르시오.** [20~22]

An important development in twentieth-century literary criticism was the growth of the New Criticism. The New Critics assumed that the methods devised for reading long poems could be applied to novels. In practice this meant a new emphasis in the reading of fiction on scrupulous textual analysis as a prerequisite for biographical and ideological comment. A novelist's ideas were now significant mainly as components of his or her writing a novel and concentrated on discerning the development of symbolic patterns. By analyzing symbols in this way, the critic could show how the meaning of a symbol accrued as it was repeated in different passages. This permitted a more complete understanding of the symbol to emerge than that which could be discovered through isolated symbol-hunting. One novelist who benefited from this new emphasis on text was D. H. Lawrence, whose work was rescued from hostile critics who had attacked it as mere ideology.

해석 20세기 문학 비평의 중요한 발전은 신비평의 성장이었다. 신 비평가들은 장문의 시들을 읽기 위해 고안된 방법이 소설에도 적용될 수 있다고 가정했다. 실제로, 이것은 소설을 이해함에 있어서 전기적 및 이념적 논평에 필수 불가결한 요소로서 본문을 꼼꼼하게 분석하는 데 대한 새로운 강조를 의미했다. 소설가의 아이디어들은 이제 주로 그의 창작기법의 구성 요소들로서 의미가 있었다. 본문에 세밀한 관심을 둘 것을 주장하면서, 신 비평가들은 소설의 긴 글귀들을 분석했고 상징적 형태들의 발전을 분별하는 데 집중했다. 이런 식으로 상징들을 분석함으로써, 신 비평가는 다른 글귀들에서 반복된 상징의 의미가 어떻게 생성되었는가를 보여 줄 수 있다. 이것은 고립된 상징의 추적을 통하여 발견될 수 있는 것보다 더 완전한 상징에 대한 이해가 나오게끔 했다. 본문을 분석하고 강조하는 이러한 새로운 사상으로 혜택을 입은 소설가 로렌스의 작품은 오직 이념으로만 공격하는 적대적인 비평가들로부터 인정받았다.

20 신 비평가들은 소설가의 작품에서 나타나는 사상들이 어떻다고 생각하는가?
① 똑같이 시나 소설의 논법에 기여한다고
② 소설가들의 문체의 견지만큼이나 매우 중요하다고
③ 모호하기 때문에 세련된 비평적 판단을 방해한다고
④ 상징 안에서 구현될 때 가장 쉽게 분석되어진다고
⑤ 비평가의 입장에서 전기적 고찰에 개방적이라고

20 According to passage, the New Critics considered the ideas found in a novelist's work to be ___________.

① equally conducive to treatment in poetry or fiction
② important primarily as aspects of the novelist's style
③ ambiguous and therefore stumbling blocks to informed critical judgment
④ most easily analyzed when embodied in a symbol
⑤ open to biographical speculation on the part of a critic

21 The author alludes to D. H. Lawrence in order to give an example of a novelist who ___________.

① sacrificed literary technique to ideology
② wrote both novels and long poems
③ subscribed to the principles of the New Criticism
④ was influenced by New Critical judgment on his work
⑤ was reassessed because of New Critical principles

22 It can be inferred from the passage that the New Critics disliked isolated symbol-hunting because it tended to ___________.

① encourage simplistic critical platitudes
② reduce the role of the critic to that of a literary detective
③ enforce an unnecessary distinction between criticism and symbolism
④ oversimplify the meaning of a symbol
⑤ ignore conventions associated with long poems

21 작가는 어떠한 소설가의 예를 들기 위하여 로렌스를 언급하는가?

① 이데올로기를 위하여 문학적 기술을 희생시켰던
② 소설과 장문의 시를 썼던
③ 신 비평의 원칙에 동의했었던
④ 신 비평에 의해 자신의 작품에 영향을 받았었던
⑤ 신 비평 원칙들 때문에 재평가되었던

22 신 비평가들은 고립된 상징 추적이 어떠한 경향을 보여서 싫어하는 것인가?

① 단순한 형태를 지닌 비평적인 진부한 의견을 조장해서
② 문학에 나오는 형사의 역할에 대한 비평가의 역할을 감소시켜서
③ 비평주의와 상징주의 간의 불필요한 구분을 강요해서
④ 상징의 의미를 지나치게 간소화시켜서
⑤ 장문의 시와 연관된 관습을 무시해서

어구 **scrupulous** 빈틈없는, 신중한　**prerequisite** 수의; 수조건　**symbolic** 상징적인　**accrue** (이익 등이) 저절로 생기다　**isolated-hunting** 고립된 상징의 추적　**hostile** 적대적인　**ambiguous** 애매모호한　**a stumbling block** 장애물, 방해 요소　**sacrifice A to B** A를 B에 희생시키다　**speculation** 사색, 고찰　**reassess** 재평가하다

해설 **20** 'A novelist's ideas were now significant mainly as components of his or her writing a novel'의 문장을 통해서, 작가는 신 비평가들이 소설가의 작품에서 발견되는 사상들이 소설가의 문체의 견지만큼이나 중요하다는 것을 알 수 있다.

21 마지막 문장에서, 이전에는 신 비평가들에게서 혹독한 비판을 받았지만, 상징을 완벽히 이해한 이후에 인정을 받게 되었다는 내용이 등장한다. 즉, 비판을 받다가 인정을 받게 되었으므로 재평가라는 내용이 옳다.

22 마지막에서 두 번째 문장을 살펴보면, '~ than that which could be discovered through isolated symbol-hunting' 문장에서, 신 비평가들의 방법과 비교되는 방법으로서 '고립된 상징의 추적'이라는 표현이 나온다. 즉, 이 고립된 상징의 추적을 신 비평가들이 싫어했다고 유추가 가능하며, 상징이 고립됐다는 내용은 결국 상징의 의미가 지나치게 간소화됐다는 내용으로 재진술이 가능하다.

>>> **다음 글을 읽고 문제의 답을 고르시오.** [23~26]

For the Greeks, beauty was a virtue: a kind of excellence. Persons of beauty were assumed to be what we now have to call—lamely, enviously—whole persons. (1) If it did occur to the Greeks to distinguish between a person's "inside" and "outside", they still expected that inner beauty would be matched by beauty of the other kind. (2) The well-born young Athenians who gathered around Socrates found it quite paradoxical that their hero was so intelligent, so brave, so honorable, so seductive and so ugly. (3) It was principally the influence of Christianity that deprived beauty of the central place it had in classical ideals of human excellence. (4) By limiting excellence to moral virtue only, Christianity set beauty adrift—as an alienated, arbitrary, superficial enchantment. (5) And beauty has continued to lose prestige. For close to two centuries it has become a convention to attribute beauty to only one of the two sexes: the sex which, however fair, is always second. Associating beauty with women had put beauty even further on the defensive, morally.

23 What is the main theme of the passage?

① Beauty and morality: Two sides of the same coin
② The Greeks and Christianity
③ Beauty in the Greek and modern times
④ Beauty and woman
⑤ The paradox of beauty

24 If the passage is divided into two paragraphs, where does the second one begin?

① (1)   ② (2)
③ (3)   ④ (4)
⑤ (5)

25 In modern times, "beauty" is most readily associated with ___________.

① excellence   ② wholeness
③ intelligence   ④ fairness
⑤ bravery

26 Choose the one that is not consistent with the content of the passage.

① In the classical period, beauty was often associated with the male sex.
② While being associated with sex, beauty came to imply a moral defensiveness.
③ The Greeks believed that the person who had the inside beauty should have the outside beauty as well.
④ In the Greek times, intelligence and bravery were an integral part of beauty.
⑤ Christianity contributed to separating the outside beauty from the inside.

해석 그리스인들에게 아름다움은 덕목의 일종으로 빼어남의 또 다른 표현이었다. 당시 아름다운 사람들은 지금 우리가 설득력 없이, 혹은 질투나 하며 칭할 수 있는 완전한 사람들이라는 의미였다. (1) 그리스인들에게 인간의 내면과 외면을 구분해야 한다는 생각이 떠올랐을지라도, 내면의 미는 다른 종류의 미와 일치할 것이라고 예측했었다. (2) 소크라테스 주위에 모여들었던 유복한 젊은 아테네인들은 자신들의 영웅이 너무나 영리하고, 용감하고, 존경받으며, 매력적이며, 동시에 못생겼다는 것이 상당히 모순된다는 점을 알게 되었다. (3) 완벽한 사람들을 아름답다고 칭했던 고대 미의 관점을 바꾼 것은 기독교의 영향이었다. (4) 우수함을 도덕적 미덕에만 제한시킴으로써, 기독교는 외적인 아름다움을 소원하고 독단적이고 피상적인 매력으로 평가절하시켰다. (5) 그리고 미는 계속해서 명성을 잃어갔다. 두 세기 가까이 미를 두 개의 성 중(남녀와 여성) 하나의 성, 즉 아무리 아름다울지라도 남성보다 열등한 위치에 있다고 치부되는 여성에만 국한하는 것은 관습이 됐다. 미를 여성과 연관시키는 것은 미를 심지어 더욱 도덕적으로 불리한 입장에 처하게 했다.

23 이 글의 주제는?

① 같은 동전의 양면인 미와 도덕   ② 그리스인들과 기독교
③ 그리스와 현대 시대의 미   ④ 미와 여성
⑤ 미의 모순

24 이 글의 두 번째 단락이 시작되는 문장은?

25 현대 시대에서 "미"가 가장 분명히 연관되어 있는 것은?

① 탁월함   ② 완전함
③ 지성   ④ 아름다움
⑤ 용기

26 이 글과 일치하지 않는 내용은?

① 고대에 미는 종종 남성과도 관련되어 있었다.
② 미가 성과 연관되는 동안, 미는 도덕적 방어를 의미하게 되었다.
③ 그리스인들은 내면의 미를 갖고 있는 사람은 외면의 미도 가지고 있어야만 한다고 믿었다.
④ 그리스 시대에 지성과 용기는 미의 중요한 부분이었다.
⑤ 기독교는 외면의 미와 내면의 미를 분리시키는 원인을 제공했다.

어구 **be assumed to R** ～이라고 추정되다   **lamely** 절룩거리며, 불완전하게   **enviously** 부러운 듯이, 시기하여   **it occurs to A to R** ～라는 생각이 A에게 떠오르다   **Athenians** 아테네 사람들   **paradoxical** 역설적인, 모순된   **seducive** 유혹하는   **set/get A adrift** A를 표류시키다   **alienated** (관계가) 멀어진   **attribute A to B** A의 탓을 B에게 돌리다   **associate A with B** A를 B와 연관시키다

해설 23 과거 그리스인들이 바라본 '미'는 남성, 여성 구분하지 않고 '완전한 사람들'을 의미한 반면, 현대의 사람들이 바라보는 '미'는 '여성의 미'로 국한시킨다는 내용이 이 글의 주제가 된다.
24 (2) 문장까지는 '그리스인들이 남성, 여성을 구분하지 않고 완전한 사람들을 미인'이라고 보았는데, (3) 문장에서 등장하는 '기독교의 영향력'이 그리스인들의 '미'의 관점을 '현대의 여성으로 국한시키는 미'로 바꾸어 놓았다는 내용이 이어진다. 따라서 미의 관점을 전환시킨 사건이 등장하는 (3)에서 두 번째 단락이 시작된다고 볼 수 있다.
25 마지막 두 개의 문장을 통해서 현대의 '미'는 여성에게만 국한시킴을 알 수 있다.
26 미가 도덕적인 방어를 의미한다는 내용은 결국 마지막 문장에서 말한 것처럼, 미가 불리한 입장에 처하게 됐다는 것이다. 마지막 문장의 주어인 associating~ 동명사구에서 연관되는 대상은 '성'이 아니라 '여성(female)'이었다. 따라서 sex가 아닌 female이 옳다.

(가) Here's a travel guide: if you've had an orthopaedic, chest, abdominal, neurological, ear, nose or throat procedure, wait ten to 14 days before flying, advises lead author Dr Mark Gendreau at Tufts University School of Medicine. An uncomplicated appendectomy or laparoscopic procedure? Schedule your flight at least five days later.

(나) Recent surgery can make air travel a riskier adventure. If you're facing surgery as well as planning a long plane flight, put some time between the two events, says a recent study. Air travel can increase the risk of deep vein thrombosis (potentially lethal blood clots in the deep veins of the legs), and the danger increases if you've recently had an operation—but doctors sometimes fail to warn their patients of the surgery connection, the researchers say.

(다) On board, stay hydrated, avoid caffeine and alcohol, stretch your calves during the flight by walking the aisles or doing seated exercises, and wear compression stockings.

27 Choose the answer that correctly put the above paragraphs into order.

① (다) – (가) – (나)   ② (가) – (나) – (다)
③ (가) – (다) – (나)   ④ (나) – (가) – (다)

28 Which one of the following can be inferred from the passage?

① That who even gets scratch must abstain from getting on a plane.
② The patient who has had a nose operation needs to delay his flight schedule at least three weeks later.
③ If having an operation before long, you had better cancel off your flight schedule.
④ While being in plane, after having an operation, consume much water.

해석 (나) 최근에 수술을 받았다면 비행기 여행은 더욱 위험한 모험이 될 수 있다. 만일 당신이 장거리 비행기 여행을 계획하고 있을 뿐만 아니라 수술을 앞두고 있다면 수술과 비행기 여행 사이에 간격을 두어야 한다고 최근 연구가 밝히고 있다. 비행기 여행은 심정맥 혈전증(다리의 심정맥이 응혈되는 치명적인 증상)의 위험을 증가시킬 수 있으며, 최근에 수술을 받은 경험이 있다면 그 위험은 높아진다. 그러나 의사들은 이따금씩 환자들에게 그 수술과의 연관성을 경고하지 못하는 경우가 있다고 연구가들은 전한다.
(가) 여행에 대한 지침을 살펴보자. 터프츠 의과 대학의 대표 저자인 마크 젠드류 씨에 따르면 만일 당신이 정형외과, 가슴, 복부, 신경, 귀, 코 또는 목 수술을 받았다면 비행기를 타기 전에 10일에서 14일을 기다려야 한다고 한다. 간단한 맹장 수술이나 복강경 수술의 경우 비행 여행을 최소한 5일 후로 연기해야 한다.
(다) 비행기를 타고 가는 동안 물을 충분히 섭취하고, 카페인과 술을 삼가며, 통로를 걷고, 앉아서 운동을 하면서 비행기 여행 기간 동안 종아리 스트레칭 운동을 하고, 압축 양말을 신으면 좋다.

27 윗글들을 차례에 맞게 배열하시오.

28 이 글의 요지로 알맞은 것은?

① 찰과상을 입은 사람조차도 비행기를 타서는 안 된다.
② 코 수술을 받은 환자는 적어도 3주 뒤까지 비행 스케줄을 연기할 필요가 있다.
③ 조만간 수술을 받게 되면 비행 스케줄을 취소하는 편이 좋을 것이다.
④ 수술을 받은 후, 비행기를 타는 동안 물을 많이 섭취하시오.

어구 orthopaedic 정형외과의, 정형술의 chest 흉곽, 가슴; 대형 상자 abdominal 배의, 복부의 neurological 신경학의 uncomplicated 복잡하지 않은 appendectomy 맹장 수술 laparoscopic 복강경 검사[수술](법) air travel 비행기 여행 deep vein thrombosis 심(深)정맥 혈전증 warn A of B A에게 B를 경고하다 hydrate 수화한, 함수(含水)의 calf 장딴지, 종아리; 송아지, 송아지 가죽 aisle (좌석의 사이·건물·열차 내 따위의) 통로; 복도 compression stocking 압축 양말 scratch 찰과상 before long 조만간, 머지않아

해설 **27** (나) 단락을 통해 수술을 받은 직후 비행기 여행을 하게 되면 큰 문제가 생길 수 있다는 문제를 제시한 후, (가) 단락에서 수술을 받았다면 비행 스케줄을 뒤로 미루어야 한다고 조언한다. 마지막 (다) 단락에서 비행기를 탄다면 가벼운 운동을 하라고 조언을 하는 순서가 옳다.
28 마지막 문장의 stay hydrated가 단서이다.

>>> **다음 글을 읽고 문제의 답을 고르시오.** [29~30]

In town for a *shopping spree*, my grandmother parked on a yellow line and was approached by a policeman who wanted to know why she had stopped there. "Well", Grandmother replied, "everybody else has parked here", "If I jumped into that river down there, Madam, would you do the same?" he asked. "My dear, if I thought I could save your life, then I would", was Grandmother's rapid response. At that, the officer ripped up her ticket and allowed her to drive away.

29 Which of the following is closest in meaning to "shopping spree"?

① returning shopped goods for a refund
② shopping contest
③ exhibition where the visitors can make purchases
④ purchasing a large amount of goods in a short time
⑤ getting an advice for shopping

30 What did the policeman really want to say to the writer's grandmother by asking the question?

① She would not save his life.
② She was too fragile to jump into the river.
③ She would not blindly repeat other people's action when it was something she didn't want to.
④ Those who parked their cars on a yellow line should jump into the river.
⑤ Had she jumped into the river, he would have ripped up her ticket and allowed her to drive away.

해석 대규모 쇼핑을 위해 시내로 나가신 할머님께서 주차 금지 구역에 주차를 했는데 경찰관 한 명이 다가와서 할머니가 왜 거기에 차를 세웠는지 알려고 했다. 할머니가 대답하길 "글쎄요. 다른 사람들도 모두 다 여기에 주차를 했었는데요."라고 했다. 경찰이 물어보기를, "제가 저기 강물 속으로 뛰어들면 할머니도 같이 뛰어드실 거예요?"라고 했다. 할머니가 빨리 대답하기를, "경찰관, 만일 내가 당신의 생명을 구할 수 있으리라 생각한다면, 난 뛰어들 수 있어요."라고 했다. 그때 경찰은 위반 딱지를 찢고서 할머니를 그냥 보내 드렸다.

29 밑줄 친 "shopping spree"의 의미와 가장 비슷한 것은?

① 반환을 위해서 구매한 물건을 되돌려 주는 것
② 쇼핑 경쟁
③ 방문객들이 구매할 수 있는 전시회
④ 짧은 시간 내에 상당량의 물건을 구매하는 것
⑤ 쇼핑을 위해 조언을 얻는 것

30 경찰관이 할머니에게 물어보면서 진정으로 말해 주려 했던 것은 무엇인가?

① 할머니는 경찰관의 생명을 구해 줄 수 없었을 것이다.
② 할머니는 너무 약하셔서 강으로 뛰어들 수 없었을 것이다.
③ 그녀가 반복하기를 원하지 않는 무언가가 있을 때, 맹목적으로 다른 이들의 행위를 반복하지 않으려 해야 한다.
④ 노란 선에 주차를 한 사람들은 강으로 뛰어들어야 한다.
⑤ 할머니가 강으로 뛰어들었더라면 경찰은 경찰딱지를 찢어 버리고 그녀가 떠날 수 있게 했었을 것이다.

어구 **shopping spree** 물건을 왕창 사들임, 돈을 물 쓰듯 씀 **rip up** 쪼개다, 찢다 **ticket** 표, 위반 딱지 **shopped goods** 구매한 물건 **refund** 반환 **contest** 경쟁, 경기 **make a purchase** 구매하다 **a large amount of** 상당량의

해설 **29** buying/shopping/spending spree는 돈을 물 쓰듯 씀, '물건을 왕창 사들임'이란 뜻을 가진다.

30 다른 이들도 노란색에 주차를 하는데, 이는 위반 사유이므로, 다른 이가 한다고 해서 그 위반 행위를 따라 해서는 안 된다고 경찰관이 설득하려 했던 것이다.

Actual TEST 04

⇨ 본책 p.228

1 ③	2 ①	3 ④	4 ①	5 ①	6 ①	7 ④	8 ①	9 ④	10 ⑤
11 ①	12 ③	13 ②	14 ④	15 ①	16 ⑤	17 ⑤	18 ②	19 ②	20 ②
21 ①	22 ②	23 ②	24 ③	25 ②	26 ④	27 ①	28 ③	29 ④	30 ④

>>> 밑줄 친 곳에 들어갈 알맞은 답을 고르시오. [1~6]

1 A: Do you mean he rejected your requests for an appointment?
B: Yes, three times he gave me the cold ____________.

① stomach
② ankle
③ shoulder
④ forearm
⑤ engine

해석 A: 그 남자가 너의 약속 요청을 거절했다는 거야?
B: 응. 세 번이나 나를 무시했어.

어구 give A the cold shoulder ~을 냉담히 대하다, 쌀쌀맞게 대하다

해설 give A the cold shoulder = give the cold shoulder to A의 표현을 물어보는 문제이다.

2 Just about everyone is ____________ at some point. What if every time you met a human your hands shook and your forehead sweated?

① timid
② exhausted
③ annoyed
④ injured
⑤ volatile

해석 모든 사람들은 정말로 어떤 때에는 소심해진다. 당신이 사람을 만날 때마다 손이 떨리고 이마에서 땀이 난다면 어쩔까?

어구 just about 정말로　at some point 어떤 때에　what if ~? ~라면 어떨까?　forehead 이마　timid 소심한　exhausted 다 써버린, 지친, 고갈된　annoyed 귀찮아하는　volatile 휘발성의, 변덕스러운, (성격이) 욱하는

해설 손이 떨리고 이마에서 땀이 난다는 것으로 보아 소심한 성격으로 유추가 가능하다.

3 The football team won so many games that it became ____________, and the worst team in the league snuck up and beat it.

① dissolute
② catholic
③ adamant
④ complacent
⑤ rageful

해석 그 축구팀이 너무나 많은 경기에서 승리를 거두어 그 팀은 자기만족에 빠지게 되었는데 이 틈을 타서 리그에서 가장 형편없는 팀이 그 팀을 상대로 승리를 거두었다.

어구 sneak up 살며시 다가가다　dissolute 방탕한, 방종한　catholic 가톨릭의　adamant 강경한, 불굴의　complacent 자기만족의, 만족한　rageful 격분한

해설 so ~ that 구문에 의해 승리를 너무나 많이 거둔 그 결과가 나와야 하며, and에 의해 '다른 팀이 그 승리를 많이 거둔 팀'을 이기게 된 추가 내용을 연결시킬 논리가 필요하므로, 이에 합당한 보기는 '자기만족의'이다.

4 In the Roman circus one of the most popular sports was performed by one who leaps. This "leaper" rode two horses by vaulting expertly from one animal to the other. When people today speak of ___________ conversation, they mean a conversation in which the participants flit from one subject to another.

① desultory
② compensatory
③ inexorable
④ obstinate
⑤ critical

해석 로마시대 서커스에서 가장 인기 있던 스포츠 중 하나는 도약하는 사람의 공연이었다. 이 "도약하는 사람"은 한 동물에서 다른 동물로 노련하게 뛰어 타면서 두 마리의 말을 갈아탔다. 오늘날 사람들이 갈피를 못 잡는 대화라고 말할 때는, 대화 참여자들이 한 주제에서 다른 주제로 왔다갔다 하는 것을 의미하는 것이다.

어구 **leap** 껑충 뛰다, 도약하다　**vault** 뛰다, 도약하다　**expertly** 노련하게　**flit** (획획) 날아다니다, 왔다갔다 하다　**desultory** 일관성 없는　**compensatory** 보상의　**inexorable** 냉혹한　**obstinate** 완고한

해설 도약을 하면서 한 개의 말이 아닌 두 개의 말을 타는 행위를 왔다갔다 한다는 내용을 대화에 비유한다면 하나의 주제로 일관되게 지속하는 것이 아닌 주제에서 벗어난 언급을 자주 한다는 내용이 옳다.

5 The cells at the surface of the outer skin form a tough, waterproof shield which most germs cannot ___________.

① penetrate
② inflect
③ alienate
④ violate
⑤ transplant

해석 표피의 표면에 있는 세포들은 대부분의 세균들이 스며들 수 없는 강한 방수성 보호물들을 만들어 낸다.

어구 **outer skin** 표피　**waterproof** 방수의　**shield** 보호물　**germ** 세균　**penetrate** 관통하다, 스며들다　**inflect** 구부리다, 굴곡시키다　**alienate** 소원하게 하다, 이간하다　**violate** 위반하다　**transplant** 이식하다

해설 강한 방수성 보호물이라면 세균들이 스며들어올 수 없게 한다는 논리가 적합하다.

6 Pat is usually so courteous and ___________ that I was completely taken aback by his unaccountably ___________ and surly reply to my question.

① affable - brusque
② equitable - erudite
③ factious - scurrilous
④ narrow-minded - ingenious

해석 팻은 평소에는 예의가 바르고 상냥한데 별 이유 없이 내 질문에 무뚝뚝하고 퉁명스럽게 답변하는 것에 대해 나는 정말로 당황했었다.

어구 **courteous** 예의가 바른　**take aback** 놀라게 하다, 당황스럽게 하다　**unaccountably** 이유 없이, 설명할 수 없이　**surly** 퉁명스러운　**affable** 상냥한　**brusque** 무뚝뚝한, 퉁명스러운　**equitable** 공정한　**erudite** 박식한　**factious** 당파적인　**scurrilous** 말투가 상스러운　**narrow-minded** 편협한　**ingenious** 독창적인, 영리한

해설 and에 의해서 각각 courteous와 surly와 순접 관계에 있는 어휘들이 옳다.

Human nature does not change, or, at any rate, history is too short for any changes to be perceptible. The earliest known specimens of art and literature are still comprehensible. The fact that we can understand them all and can recognize in some of them an unsurpassed artistic excellence is proof enough (가) ______________ not only men's feelings and instincts, but also their intellectual and imaginative powers, were in the remotest times precisely what they are now. In the fine arts it is only the convention, the form, the incidentals that change: the fundamentals of passion, of intellect and imagination remain unaltered.

7 According to the passage, which of the following is true?

① Human nature doesn't remain rather stationary.
② The ancient works are hard to recognize.
③ Art field's customs are not changeable.
④ Today's intelligence and imagination are similar to those of the past.

8 Which of the following best fits into (가)?

① that
② to
③ for
④ which

해석 인간의 본성은 변하지 않는다. 아니 적어도 역사는 어떠한 변화를 감지하기에 너무나 짧다. 아주 오래된 옛날에 만들어진 예술과 문학의 견본들은 아직도 이해할 수 있다. 우리가 그 본보기들을 모두 이해하고 또 몇몇 견본 속에서 지금까지 능가한 적이 없는 예술적 우수성을 인식할 수 있다는 사실은 인간의 감정이나 본능뿐만 아니라 지적인 힘과 상상력이 옛날에도 오늘날의 모습 그대로였다는 것을 충분히 입증한다는 것이다. 미술 부문에 있어서 변화되는 것은 단지 관례와 형태, 부수적인 내용들뿐이고, 정열과 지성, 상상력의 기본 내용은 변화되지 않고 그대로 남아 있다.

7 이 글의 내용과 일치하는 것은 무엇인가?

① 인간의 본성은 다소 정적으로 유지되지 않는다.
② 고전 작품들은 이해하기 어렵다.
③ 예술 분야의 관습은 변화하지 않는다.
④ 오늘날의 지성과 상상력은 과거의 것과 유사하다.

8 밑줄 친 (가)에 알맞은 것은?

어구 **perceptible** 지각할 수 있는 **specimen** 견본, 실례 **unsurpassed** 탁월한, 유례가 없는 **fine arts** 시각 예술(그림, 건축 등) **convention** 인습, 관행, 전통 **unaltered** 불변의

해설 **7** 인간의 본능뿐만 아니라 상상력이 예전에도 오늘날의 모습 그대로였다는 것이 충분히 입증된다고 했다.
8 앞에 위치한 명사 proof와 동격의 접속사 that이 필요하다. enough는 명사 proof를 뒤에서 수식하는 형용사 역할을 수행할 뿐이다.

>>> **다음 글을 읽고 문제의 답을 고르시오. [9~10]**

In ancient times, clothing was generally not fitted to the body. People wore whole animal skins, and clothes made from woven material usually consisted of rectangular pieces of cloth draped in some way and secured by a tie. In early Europe, people grew flax or raised sheep for wool. They spun their own thread from the flax and wool and wove it into cloth. They then fashioned the uncut cloth into tunics, sometimes stitched up the sides or down the middle, that tied with rope. They used clothing mainly for warmth and protection, not as a fashion statement.

The 1100s saw clothing production undergoing transition. People began to form guilds, and individuals set up shops as shoemakers, weavers, and tailors. Under the guidance of the weaver's guild, the quality of cloth improved. Tailors began to cut and stitch garments into fitted vests, shirts, and trouser for men. Women's shapeless tunics ㉠______________ long dresses that were tightly fitted to the upper body. Clothes went from simple coverings for the body to the beginnings of fashionable apparel.

9 Which one is the most appropriate in the blank ㉠?

① took over
② called off
③ put up with
④ gave way to
⑤ made use of

10 Select the statement which best expresses the main idea of the above passage.

① Clothes have not changed over the centuries.
② The quality of cloth improved before the rise of guilds.
③ Fashion had been an important part of everyone's lives.
④ From its beginning as a simple covering for the body in ancient times, clothing has become a major concern for people.
⑤ Clothing, which for centuries had been loosely draped, began to be fitted and fashionable with the rise of the guild system.

해석 고대에는 옷이 몸에 잘 맞지 않았다. 사람들은 큰 짐승의 가죽을 입었으며, 모직 원자재를 통해 만들어진 옷은 일정 방식으로 늘어지고 끈으로 고정된 직사각형의 옷감으로 만들어졌다. 고대 유럽에서는 아마섬유를 재배하고 양털을 얻으려고 양을 사육했다. 그들은 아마와 양털로부터 실을 만들어냈으며, 그 실을 옷감으로 엮었다. 그러고 나서 그들은 자르지 않은 옷감을 튜닉으로 만들었으며, 때때로 옆쪽이나 가운데를 꿰매어 붙이고 줄로 묶었다. 그들은 패션 표현으로서가 아니라 보온과 보호를 위해서 주로 옷을 입었다.

1,100년대. 의복 제작은 변화를 맞게 되었다. 사람들은 조합을 만들기 시작했으며, 개개인들이 구두 제조업자, 직조공과 재단사와 같이 상점을 운영했다. 직조공 조합의 보호 하에 의복의 질이 향상됐다. 재단사들은 옷을 재단하고 꿰매어 몸에 맞는 남성용 조끼와 셔츠 그리고 바지를 만들기 시작했다. 여자들의 예쁘지 않았던 겉옷도 상체에 꽉 끼는 긴 드레스로 바뀌었다. 옷은 신체를 단순히 가리는 물건에서부터 유행하는 의상으로 변화되었다.

9 ㉠에 들어갈 말은?

① 인계하다　　　　　　　　② 취소하다
③ 견디다　　　　　　　　　④ 대체되다
⑤ 이용하다

10 윗글의 주제를 가장 잘 설명한 것은?

① 옷들은 수세기 동안 변화되지 않았다.
② 의복의 질은 조합이 태동되기 이전에 향상되었다.
③ 유행은 모든 이들의 인생에서 중요한 부분이 되었다.
④ 고대에 신체의 단순한 덮개로서 처음부터, 옷은 사람들의 중요한 관심사였다.
⑤ 수세기 동안 느슨하게 늘어뜨려진 옷은 조합의 태동과 함께 몸에 잘 맞고 유행을 타기 시작했었다.

어구 **woven** 모직의　**consist** ~으로 구성되다　**rectangular** 직각의　**drape** 주름을 피다, 늘어뜨리다　**flax** 아마, 아마섬유　**spin** 실로 만들다　**thread** 실　**fashion** 만들다, 변화시키다　**uncut** 자르지 않은　**tunic** 겉　**stitch up** 꿰매어 붙이다　**fashion statement** 유행 표현　**undergo** 경험하다　**transition** 변화　**guild** 조합, 상인단체　**garment** 의복　**vest** 조끼　**shapeless** 무형의, 못난　**covering** 덮개　**apparel** 의상, 의복　**take over** 인수하다, 점거하다　**call off** 취소하다　**put up with** 참다, 견디다　**give way to** ~으로 대체되다, 양보하다, 굴복하다　**make use of** ~을 이용하다

해설 **9** 고대와 초기 유럽 때 입었던 엉성한 옷이 1,100년대에 긴 드레스로 바뀐 것이므로, '대체되다'의 내용이 적합하다.
10 고대와 초기 유럽에는 단순한 몸의 덮개였던 옷이 1,100년대에 이르러 조합의 태동을 기점으로 하여 유행복의 기원이 시작됐다는 내용이 이 글의 주제이다.

>>> **다음 글을 읽고 문제의 답을 고르시오.** [11~12]

> History, like the drama and the novel, grew out of mythology, a primitive form of apprehension and expression in which—as in fairy tales listened to by children or in dreams dreamt by sophisticated adults—the line between fact and fiction was left undrawn. It has, for example, been said of the *Iliad* that anyone who starts reading it as history will find that it is full of ______________ but, equally, anyone who starts reading it as fiction will find that it is full of ______________ . All histories resemble the *Iliad* to this extent, that they cannot entirely dispense with the fictional element. The mere selection, arrangement and presentation of facts is a technique belonging to the field of fiction, and popular opinion is right in its insistence that no historian can be "great" if he is not also a great artist.

11 The best title of the passage would be

______________ .

① Facts and Fictions of History
② Reading Fiction as History
③ Dispensing with the Fictional Elements
④ The Components of Mythology

12 Which of the following is best for the blanks?

① art - facts
② facts - art
③ fiction - history
④ history - fiction

해석 연극이나 소설처럼 역사는 해석과 표현의 원시적인 형태인 신화로부터 유래되었는데, 그 원시적인 표현 형태에서는 어린이들이 듣는 동화나 세상 물정에 닳고 닳은 어른들이 꾸는 꿈처럼, 사실과 허구의 선이 분명하게 그어지지 않은 채로 남아 있다. 예를 들어 〈일리아드〉에 대하여는, 그것을 한 권의 역사로 읽기 시작하는 사람은 누구나 그것이 허구로 가득 차 있다는 것을 알게 되고, 그것을 허구로 읽기 시작하는 사람은 누구나 그것이 역사로 가득 차 있음을 알게 된다고 이야기되어 왔다. 모든 역사(책)는 그것들에게서 허구적인 요소를 전적으로 없앨 수는 없다는 점에서 〈일리아드〉를 닮았다. 단순히 사실을 선택하고 배열하여 제시하는 것은 허구의 영역에 속하는 기술이며, 역사가가 동시에 위대한 예술가가 될 수 없다면 결코 위대할 수 없다고 주장하는 대중의 의견은 옳다.

11 가장 적합한 제목을 고르시오.

① 역사의 사실과 허구적 요소
② 역사로서 소설을 읽는 것
③ 허구적 요소가 없이 지내는 것
④ 신화의 구성 요소

12 빈칸에 가장 올바른 것은?

① 예술 – 사실　　　　② 사실 – 예술
③ 허구 – 역사　　　　④ 역사 – 허구

어구 **mythology** 신화　**sophisticated** 세련된, 학식이 많은, 궤변의　**Iliad** 일리아드(호메로스가 쓴 트로이의 서사시)　**dispense with** ~ 없이 지내다　**insistence** 주장, 고집

해설 **11** 역사는 신화에서 등장했고, 따라서 사실과 허구의 구별이 쉽지가 않다는 내용이 이 글의 주제가 된다.
12 문맥 전체의 주제로 보건대, 역사라고 읽은 이는 소설적인 요소가 많다고 느껴질 것이며, 소설이라고 읽은 이는 소설에는 역사적 요소가 많다고 느껴야 한다.

>>> **다음 글을 읽고 문제의 답을 고르시오.** [13~15]

In early 1999 Shpend Ahmeti stared anxiously at the televised scenes of destruction left by Serbian troops in Pristina, Kosovo. Sitting alongside him in a university lounge was Emina Hrustic, his friend from the debating team—and a Serb.

"Was that near your home?" she asked. Ahmeti nodded grimly. "How awful", Hrustic said gently. "I'm worried about your home, too." the dark-eyed Albanian replied. And indeed, when military installations around Hrustic's native city of Novi Sad were bombed by NATO planes soon after, it was to Ahmeti that she looked for comfort. He had grown up filled with suspicion towards Serbs. But that changed after he entered the American University in Bulgaria, where the two were students.

"She knew it wasn't my fault that NATO was bombing her country", Ahmeti told me. "And I knew it wasn't her fault what the Serbian special police were doing in Kosovo."

Ahmeti and Hrustic are typical of the young people who have come together in this remarkable young institution, which offers promise of ethnic reconciliation and a new kind of future for these former Soviet bloc countries.

13 Shpend Ahmeti _____________.

① is a student of a university in America
② is an Albanian
③ has always been on good terms with Serbs
④ first met Emina Hrustic in Serbia
⑤ lived in Novi Sad before he came to Bulgaria

14 What did Hrustic do when NATO planes bombed her native city?

① She watched television with Ahmeti.
② She blamed Ahmeti for the bombing.
③ She immediately went back to her country.
④ She sought consolation from Ahmeti.
⑤ She discussed the future of Eastern Europe with Ahmeti.

15 According to the above passage, which of the following statements is NOT true?

① Ahmeti and Hrustic had a debate about the NATO bombing.
② Ahmeti and Hrustic used to belong to the same debating team.
③ Albania and Serbia used to belong to the soviet bloc.
④ Ahmeti and Hrustic went to the same university.
⑤ The American University in Bulgaria was founded not long ago.

해석 1999년 초, 쉬펜드 아메티는 코소보의 프리스티나에서 세르비아 군대의 파괴 TV 장면을 걱정스럽게 응시했다. 대학교 라운지에서 그와 나란히 앉아 있었던 에미나 흐루스틱은 토론 모임의 친구로서 세르비아인이었다.

'(저 폭파 장면에 나오는 장소가) 너희 집과 가까운 곳이니?'라고 그녀(흐루스틱)가 물었다. 아메티는 무서운 듯이 고개를 끄덕였다. '정말 끔찍하다.'라고 흐루스틱은 조용히 말했다. '나는 너희 집도 역시 걱정이 돼.'라며 검은 눈을 가진 알바니아인(아메티)이 대답했다. 그리고 얼마 지나지 않아서, 노비사드에 있는 흐루스틱의 고향 도시 근처에 있는 군사시설들이 나토(NATO) 비행기들에 의해 폭격당했을 때, 그녀(흐루스틱)는 아메티에게서 위안을 찾았다. 그(아메티)는 세르비아인들에 대한 의심을 많이 가진 채 성장했다. 그러나 그러한 의심은 그가 불가리아에 있는 미국 대학에 입학한 후에 변화되었으며, 그곳에서 그 두 사람(아메티와 흐루스틱)은 모두 학생이 되었다.

'그녀(흐루스틱)는 나토가 그녀의 조국을 폭격하고 있는 것이 제(아메티) 잘못이 아니라는 점을 알고 있었어.'라고 아메티는 나에게 말했다. '그리고 나(아메티는)는 세르비아 비밀경찰들이 코소보에서 하고 있었던 것이 그녀(흐루스틱)의 잘못이 아니란 점을 알고 있어.'라고 말했다.

아메티와 흐루스틱은 학교에 함께 모여 있던 이러한 남다른 젊은이들의 일부였는데, 이들로 인해 이 학교는 민족적 화해와 구소련 치하의 국가들을 위한 새로운 유형의 미래를 제공한다.

13 쉬펜드 아메티는 어떠한 인물인가?
① 미국에 있는 대학생이다.
② 알바니아인이다.
③ 세르비아 사람들과 언제나 사이가 좋았다.
④ 세르비아에서 흐루스틱을 처음 만났다.
⑤ 불가리아로 오기 전에 노비 사드에서 살았었다.

14 나토가 고향을 폭격할 때 흐루스틱은 무엇을 했었는가?
① 그녀는 아메티와 TV를 시청하고 있었다.
② 그녀는 폭격 때문에 아메티를 비난했었다.
③ 그녀는 즉시 조국으로 돌아갔다.
④ 그녀는 아메티에게서 위로를 찾았다.
⑤ 그녀는 아메티와 함께 동유럽의 미래에 대해 토의했다.

15 윗글의 내용과 부합하지 않은 내용은?
① 아메티와 흐루스틱은 나토 폭격에 대한 토론을 했었다.
② 아메티와 흐루스틱은 같은 토론 모임에 소속되어 있었다.
③ 알바니아와 세르비아는 구소련 권에 속해 있었다.
④ 아메티와 흐루스틱은 같은 대학에 진학했다.
⑤ 불가리아에 위치한 미국 대학은 얼마 전에 설립됐었다.

어구 televised TV로 중계되는 **leave** (결과적으로) ~한 상태를 만들다 **Serb** 세르비아 사람; 세르비아 사람의 **grimly** 완강히, 무섭게 **military installation** 군사시설 **special police** 특수 경찰 **typical** 특유의, 전형적인, 모범이 되는 **ethnic** 인종의, 민족의 **reconciliation** 화해 **bloc** [정치상·경제상의] 블록, 권(圈) **be on good terms with** ~와 사이가 좋다 **blame A for B** B 때문에 A를 비난하다 **belong to** ~에 속하다

해설 **13** I'm worried ~ . the dark-eyed Albanian replied. 문장을 통해서 '알바니아인'은 쉬펜드 아메티임을 알 수 있다.

14 ~ it was to Ahmeti that she looked for comfort 문장을 통해 흐루스틱은 아메티에게서 위로를 찾았다는 내용이 옳다.

15 나토의 폭격이 있다고 필자가 글을 쓰고 있을 뿐, 아메티와 흐루스틱은 나토 폭격 자체에 대한 토나 논의를 했다고 볼 수는 없다.

There is little agreement concerning the way in which kinds of avalanches should be classified. Some classification systems depend on the kind of snow involved, others are concerned with the type of movement, and once scheme includes both, as well as several other criteria. Existing descriptive terms, most of them German, are deeply rooted in avalanche parlance: they are expressive, but they are often untranslatable into other languages and lack precision in their own. Furthermore, as Dr. Quervain has pointed out, avalanches are not only concrete objects capable of being photographed; they are also events. As events, they include, for example, the development of the avalanches through the influences of weather; the incident that starts the snow moving; and the type of movement. The description of the avalanche as an object includes information about the depth, physical consistency, and stratification of the snow, the features of the terrain, and the type and the dimension of the break.

16 The author suggests that an accurate avalanche classification system would ____________.

① be more useful in theory than in fact
② be useful only for describing avalanches as objects
③ have to be based on existing descriptive terms
④ have to be approved by numerous authorities
⑤ have to take many factors into account

17 The title below that best expresses the ideas of this passage is ____________.

① Why is it important to be able to classify avalanches?
② What are some criteria for classification of avalanches?
③ How did existing avalanche classifications originate?
④ What are some points on which avalanche classification systems agree?
⑤ What has been the most useful criterion used in avalanche classification?

18 It can be inferred that the author mentions the underlined sentence primarily in order to ____________.

① indicate the temporary nature of an avalanche
② illustrate the imprecision of the terms used in avalanche classification
③ introduce his own avalanche classification system
④ avoid complexity of avalanche classification
⑤ further explain why it is important to classify kinds of avalanches

해석 여러 가지 눈사태를 분류하는 방법에 대하여 일치하는 의견은 거의 없다. 몇 가지 분류법은 눈의 종류에 관련된 것이고, 다른 분류법들은 눈의 이동 형태에 관계한다. 그리고 또 한 가지 분류법은 위의 두 가지 경우를 모두 포함하면서 여러 가지 다른 기준들도 더불어 포함한다. 기존 기술용어들은 대부분이 독일어로서 눈사태 관련 용어에 깊이 뿌리를 두고 있다. 그런데 그 용어들은 표현은 다양하지만 종종 다른 언어로 번역될 수 없고, 자기 언어로서의 정확성도 결여돼 있다. 더욱이 퀘베인 박사가 지적했듯이, 눈사태는 사진에 담을 수 있는 구체적인 대상일 뿐만 아니라 사건이기도 하다. 사건으로서의 눈사태는 예를 들면 날씨의 영향을 통한 눈사태의 발전, 눈의 이동을 일으키는 사건, 그리고 이동 형태를 포함한다. 대상으로서의 눈사태에 대한 기술에는 깊이에 관한 지식, 물리적 밀도, 눈의 성층, 지형의 특징, 그리고 갈라진 형태와 크기를 포함한다.

16 필자는 정확한 눈사태 구분 방법은 어떠할 것이라고 주장하는가?

① 실제보다 이론에서 더 중요할 것이다.
② 눈사태를 물체로 묘사하는 점에서만 쓸모가 있을 것이다.
③ 현존하는 묘사 용어에 근거를 두어야만 한다.
④ 수많은 당국들이 승인을 해야만 한다.
⑤ 많은 요소들을 고려해야 한다.

17 가장 적절한 제목을 고르시오.

① 눈사태를 분류하는 것이 왜 중요한가?
② 눈사태의 분류를 위한 몇몇의 기준들은 무엇이 있는가?
③ 현존하는 눈사태 분류법의 어떻게 시작되었는가?
④ 눈사태 체계의 합의가 이루어질 수 있는 몇 가지 목표는 무엇이 있는가?
⑤ 눈사태 분류에서 이용되는 가장 효율적인 분류는 무엇이었는가?

18 필자가 밑줄 친 문장을 언급한 주된 목적은 무엇인가?

① 눈사태의 일시적인 특성을 가리키기 위하여
② 눈사태 분류에서 사용되는 용어의 부정확성을 설명하기 위해서
③ 자신의 눈사태 분류법을 소개하기 위하여
④ 눈사태 분류법의 복잡함을 피하기 위하여
⑤ 눈사태 종류를 분류하는 것이 중요한 이유를 추가적으로 설명하기 위하여

어구 avalanche 눈사태 classification 분류 criteria 기준들 [criterion의 복수] parlance 말투, 어법 expressive 표현하는 untranslatable 번역될 수 없는 precision 정확함, 정밀함 consistency 일관성 stratification 성층, 층화 terrain 지대, 지형 dimension 치수 numerous 많은 take ~ into account ~을 고려하다, 참작하다 temporary 일시적인, 덧없는(fleeting, transient) imprecision 부정확성

해설 16 작가는 이론적인 요소나 사건적인 요소 하나에만 치중하지 않고, 마지막 문장에서 언급한 것처럼 '지식, 물리적 밀도, 눈의 성층, 지형의 특징, 형태와 크기' 모든 것을 복합적으로 고려해야 한다고 간접적으로 내비친다.
17 눈사태 분류 방법에 대해서는 일치된 견해가 없다고 첫 문장에서 언급한 이후, 이하에서 여러 가지 분류 방법에 대해서 소개하며, 결국 그러한 여러 방법들이 골고루 합쳐져야 한다는 내용이 이 글의 주제가 된다.
18 furthermore는 '순접-첨가/강조'에 쓰이는 접속부사이다. 앞서 나온 문장에서 말하기를 '눈사태에 관한 기존의 기술용어들이 다른 언어로 번역되지 않으며, 게다가 부정확하다'고 말했으므로, 이에 대한 추가 설명으로 눈사태 분류에서 이용되는 용어의 부정확성을 설명하기 위해 이 문장을 사용했다고 볼 수 있다.

His servant did not come in on time. Like so many philosophers and poets, Tagore was helpless when it came to the less important things in life: his personal wants, his clothes, his breakfast, and tidying up the place. An hour went by and Tagore was getting madder by the minute. He thought of all sorts of punishments for the man, Three hours later Tagore no longer thought of punishment. He'd discharge the man without any further ado, get rid of him, and turn him out. Finally the man showed up. It was midday. Without a word the servant proceeded with his duties as though nothing had happened. He picked up his master's clothes, set to making breakfast, and started cleaning up. Tagore watched this performance with mounting rage. Finally he said it: "Drop everything, and get out."

However, the man continued sweeping, and after another few moments, with quiet dignity he said: "My little girl died last night."

(가) The show must go on.

19 The best title of the passage would be ____________.

① Work behind Schedule
② Importance of Work
③ Inevitable Sadness: a Daughter's Death
④ A Man's Confidence in His Master

20 The underlined phrase in (가) suggests that ____________.

① don't worry, and we will be happy
② his task will be carried out
③ sweeping and laughing lack harmony
④ his personal matter will continue

해석 그의 하인이 제시간에 오지 않았다. 많은 철학자들과 시인들이 그런 것처럼 일신상의 필요한 것들, 의복, 아침식사, 집안 정돈과 같은 인생에서 덜 중요한 문제들에 관해서, 타고르는 아무것도 할 수 없었다. 한 시간이 지나갔다. 시간이 갈수록 타고르는 화가 점점 더해 갔다. 그는 하인에 대해서 온갖 종류의 처벌을 생각해 보았다. 세 시간이 지나자 타고르는 더 이상 벌에 대하여 생각하지 않았다. 더 이상의 소동을 일으키지 않고 하인을 해고하여 집안에서 쫓아낼 생각이었다. 마침내 하인이 나타났다. 때는 벌써 한낮이었다. 말 한마디 없이 하인은 마치 아무 일도 없었던 것처럼 그가 해야 할 일들을 계속했다. 그는 주인의 옷을 정돈하고, 조반을 짓기 시작하고, 청소를 시작했다. 이와 같은 하인의 행동을 지켜보면서 타고르는 분노가 끓어올랐다. 마침내 그는 마음먹었던 말을 내뱉었다. "손에 들고 있는 것을 다 놓고 여기서 나가시오." 그러나 하인은 비질을 계속했다. 그리고 얼마 후에 무게 있는 태도로 조용히 말했다. "어젯밤에 제 어린 딸이 죽었습니다." 쇼는 계속되어야 한다.

19 이 글의 제목은 무엇인가?

① 예정보다 늦어진 일
② 일의 중요성
③ 타고르에 대한 하인의 분노
④ 주인에 대한 한 남자의 신뢰

20 밑줄 친 (가)가 가리키는 것은?

① 걱정하지 마라. 우리는 행복해질 것이다.
② 그의 임무를 완수할 것이다.
③ 청소와 웃음은 조화가 안 된다.
④ 개인 문제가 계속될 것이다.

어구 come in 도착하다 helpless 쩔쩔매는 personal wants 일신상의 필요한 것들 tidy (up) 깨끗이 정돈하다 discharge 해고하다 ado 야단법석 get rid of 해고하다, 제거하다 turn out 쫓아내다 midday 대낮, 정오 proceed with 계속 ~을 하다 pick up 정돈하다 set to -ing ~하기 시작하다 mount 오르다, 상승하다 dignity 품위, 정중함

해설 19 자신의 딸이 죽었음에도 일을 하러 늦게라도 왔다는 일화를 통해서 자신이 해야 할 일을 해야 한다는 것이 이 글의 주제가 된다.

20 The show must go on.은 '개인의 사정에 관계없이 자신의 직무는 계속되어야 한다.'는 뜻이다.

The popular image of New York conjures up a jungle of muggers, dope addicts, and hustlers creating an obstacle to course for the city's normal citizens. But the tourist will find that the Big Apple threatens only his budget. New York's menacing streets, while not entirely mythical, fortunately do not approach their notoriety. Common sense and an alert eye must insure the safety of all but the most reckless; steer clear of run-down neighborhoods (especially after dark) and keep to the more tourist's parts of the city and trouble will not find you.

21 The underlined expression suggests that

_______________.

① it is expensive to travel around in New York
② tourists are easily cheated over prices in New York
③ tourists should keep an eye open for crime in New York
④ New York police is experiencing financial difficulties
⑤ New York is not a good place for business

22 The main theme of the passage would be that

_______________.

① in New York it is extremely dangerous to hang around
② the violence in New York has been somewhat exaggerated
③ New York needs a new security policy for the safety of tourists and residents
④ the image of New York has recently improved a lot
⑤ New York's security systems have been damaged by financial difficulties

해석 뉴욕에 대한 일반적인 이미지는, 뉴욕 시민들의 하루 생활에 해를 끼치는 노상강도, 어리석은 마약 중독자 및 사기꾼들일 것이다. 그러나 관광을 하다 보면 물가만 높다는 점을 알게 될 것이다. 뉴욕의 거리가 위협적이라는 사실이 전적으로 허구인 것은 아니겠지만, 운이 좋게도 그 악명의 명성에 근접하지는 않는다. 상식과 경계심만 있으면 가장 무모한 경우를 제외하고서는 안전함을 보장할 수 있음에 틀림이 없다. (특히나 어두워진 이후에는) 몹시 황폐한 지역을 삼가고 관광객들이 많은 도심 지역만 다닌다면 어려움을 겪지 않을 것이다.

21 밑줄 친 표현이 주장하는 것은?
① 뉴욕 여행은 비용이 많이 든다.
② 관광객들은 뉴욕에서 쉽게 사기를 당한다.
③ 관광객들이 뉴욕의 범죄에 대해 경계를 해야만 한다.
④ 뉴욕 경찰은 재정난을 겪고 있다.
⑤ 뉴욕은 사업을 하기에 좋은 곳이 아니다.

22 이 글의 주제는 무엇인가?
① 뉴욕에서 어슬렁거리며 돌아다니는 것은 위험하다.
② 뉴욕의 범죄는 다소 과장된 면이 있다.
③ 뉴욕은 관광객들과 거주민들의 안전을 위하여 새로운 치안 정책을 강구할 필요가 있다.
④ 뉴욕의 이미지는 최근에 많이 좋아졌다.
⑤ 뉴욕의 치안 정책은 재정난에 의해 피해를 보았다.

어구 **conjure up** (마음에) 그려내다, 생각해 내다 **mugger** 노상강도 **dope** 멍청한; 진한 액체 **hustler** 거칠게 미는[때리는] 사람; 사기꾼 **Big Apple** 뉴욕시의 애칭 **menacing** 위협적인 **mythical** 가공의; 신화의 **notoriety** 악명 **all but** ~을 제외한 모두; 거의 **steer clear of** ~을 피하다; ~과 관계하지 않다 **run-down** 몹시 황폐한; 몹시 피곤한 **keep to** ~에 계속해 있다; (길, 장소 등을) 벗어나지 않다 **tourist** 관광여행을 하다 **trouble will not find you** 어려움을 겪지 않을 것이다 **keep an eye open for** ~을 똑바로 경계하다 **hang around** 방황하다, 어슬렁[꾸물]거리다

해설 **21** the Big Apple은 '뉴욕'을 가리킨다. 또한 budget이 '예산'의 뜻을 가지기 때문에 뉴욕이 예산을 위협한다는 것은 뉴욕 여행은 돈이 많이 든다는 뜻이다.
22 첫 문장에서 뉴욕에 대한 통념의 잘못된 선입견(마약, 강도 등)과 달리 범죄의 위험은 크지 않다는 내용을 이어서 설명한다. 따라서 뉴욕의 범죄에 대해 과장된 측면이 있다는 내용이 주제이다.

>>> 다음 글을 읽고 문제의 답을 고르시오.

In 1979 when University of Minnesota psychologist Thomas Bouchard read a newspaper account of reuniting of 39-year-old identical twins who had been separated from infancy, he seized the opportunity and flew them to Minneapolis for extensive tests. Bouchard was looking for differences. What "the Jim twins," Jim Lewis and Jim Springer, presented were amazing similarities. Both had married women named Linda, divorced, and married women named Betty. One had a son James Alan, the other a son James Allan. Both had dogs named Toy, chainsmoked Salems, served as sheriff's deputies, drove Chevrolets, chewed their fingernails to the nub, enjoyed stock car racing, had basement workshops, and had built circular white benches around trees in their yards. They also had similar medical histories: Both gained 10 pounds at about the same time and then lost it both suffered what they mistakenly believed were heart attacks, and both began having late-afternoon headaches at age 18. Identical twins Oskar Stohr and Jack Yufe presented equally striking similarities. One was raised by his grandmother in Germany as a Catholic and a Nazi, while the other was raised by his father in the Caribbean as a Jew. Nevertheless, they share traits and habits galore. They like spicy foods and sweet liquors, have a habit of falling asleep in front of the television, flush the toilet before using it, store rubber bands on their wrists, and dip buttered toast in their coffee. Stohr is domineering toward women and yells at his wife, as did Yufe before he was separated.

23 윗글의 요지로 가장 적합한 것을 고르시오.

① Identical twins who were raised separately from infancy provide great opportunities for psychologists to explore differences.

② Identical twins, although separated at birth, have amazing similarities.

③ Religion does not play a significant role in identical twins' traits and habits.

④ Traits and habits of identical twins are influenced by environments to some degree.

해석 1979년 미네소타 대학의 심리학자인 토마스 뷰차드는 유아기 때 헤어진 39살의 일란성 쌍둥이의 재회에 관한 신문 기사를 읽고, 기회를 놓치지 않고 그들을 비행기에 태워서 미니애폴리스로 데려와 광범위한 실험을 진행했다. 뷰차드는 쌍둥이 형제의 차이점을 찾고 있었다. 짐 루이스와 짐 스피링인 '짐 쌍둥이'가 보여준 것은 놀랄 만한 유사성이었다. 두 명 모두 린다란 이름의 여성과 결혼했고, 이혼 후 다시 베티라는 여자와 재혼했다. 한 명은 제임스 앨런(Alan)이란 아들이 있었고, 다른 한 명은 제임스 앨런(Allan)이란 아들이 있었다. 두 사람 모두 토이라는 강아지를 키웠으며, 살램 담배를 즐겨 피웠으며, 보안관 대리로 근무했고, 쉐보레 자동차를 몰았으며, 지칠 때까지 손톱을 물어뜯었고, 일반 승용차 경주를 즐겼으며, 지하실 작업장이 있었고, 정원의 나무 주위에 원형의 하얀색 긴 의자를 지었다. 그들은 또한 비슷한 병력을 갖고 있었다. 둘 다 거의 같은 시기에 10파운드가 늘었다가 같은 시기에 다시 빠졌으며, 둘 모두 심장 발작으로 오인할 만한 증세 때문에 고통을 겪었고, 18세가 되었을 때 오후 늦게 찾아오는 두통을 갖게 됐다. 일란성 쌍둥이인 오스카 스톨과 잭 유페도 똑같이 놀라운 유사성을 나타냈다. 한 명은 독일에서 할머니에 의해 가톨릭 신자이자 나치로 성장했으며, 다른 한 명은 아버지에 의해 카리브 해에서 유대인으로 성장했다. 그럼에도 불구하고 그 둘은 성격과 습관에서 비슷한 점이 많았다. 그들은 매운 음식과 달콤한 술을 즐겼으며, TV를 시청하다가 잠이 드는 버릇이 있었고, 변기를 사용하기 전에 물을 내렸으며, 손목에 고무 밴드를 차고, 버터를 바른 토스트를 커피에 찍어 먹었다. 스톨은 별거하기 전에 그랬던 것처럼 여성들에게 고압적이고 아내에게 고함을 질렀다.

23 윗글의 요지로 가장 적합한 것을 고르시오.

① 신생아 때부터 헤어져 자란 일란성 쌍둥이는 심리학자가 차이점을 연구하는 데 좋은 기회를 제공했다.

② 일란성 쌍둥이는 태어날 때 헤어졌어도 놀라운 유사성을 가지고 있다.

③ 종교는 일란성 쌍둥이의 모습과 습관에 중요한 역할을 담당한다.

④ 일란성 쌍둥이의 모습과 습관은 환경에 의해 어느 정도 영향을 받는다.

어구 newspaper account 신문 기사 reuniting 재결합; 재혼 identical twins 일란성 쌍둥이 seize 붙잡다; 파악하다 chainsmoke 줄담배를 피우다 sheriff 보안관; 주 장관 deputy 대리인; 대표자 chew 씹다; 곰곰이 생각해 보다 fingernail 손톱 to the nub 지칠 때까지 mistakenly 오해하여 striking 현저한 galore 풍부[푸짐]한 spicy 향긋한; 야비한 flush 분출하다; 홍조를 띠다 wrist 손목 dip 담그다; 적시다 domineer 권력을 휘두르다, 뽐내다

해설 이 글은 일란성 쌍둥이가 어렸을 때부터 떨어져 산다 하더라도, 그들의 놀라운 유사성을 예로 들어주는 것이 주제이다.

I. Music is strange stuff. It is clearly different from language. People can, nevertheless, use it to communicate things—especially their emotions. When combined with speech in a song, it is one of most powerful means of communication that humans have. But, biologically speaking, what is it?

II. What are two things that make humans different from all other animals? One is language and the other is music. While other animals can sing— indeed, many birds do so better than a lot of people—birdsong, and the song of animals such as whales, is limited in type. No other animal has developed a musical instrument.

III. If music is truly different from speech, then it ought to come from a distinct part of the brain. That part keeps music separate from other sounds, including language. The evidence suggests that such a part does exist.

24 윗글들을 문맥에 맞게 올바른 순서로 연결한 것은?

① Ⅰ — Ⅱ — Ⅲ   ② Ⅰ — Ⅲ — Ⅱ

③ Ⅱ — Ⅰ — Ⅲ   ④ Ⅱ — Ⅲ — Ⅰ

>>> 다음 글을 읽고 문제의 답을 고르시오.

A study showed that SAT scores for incoming football and basketball players at big-time athletic programs were hundreds of points lower than for the average student admission.

(a) The result is that these athletes find themselves competing in a student body where they are at a considerable disadvantage.

(b) Still, the NCAA insists on using the term "student athlete," claiming that the athlete is and must be treated like all other students.

(c) The leader in this category is The University of Florida, where there is a 346-point gap between its football players and the average student.

(d) This invites the question of transfers. Most students can choose a transfer school.

(e) Not so for student athletes, who do not have this freedom, their current school can prohibit them from enrolling in certain schools.

25 제시문 후에 이어질 내용을 논리 전개 순서대로
나열하시오.

① (a)-(b)-(e)-(c)-(d)   ② (c)-(a)-(b)-(d)-(e)
③ (b)-(c)-(d)-(e)-(a)   ④ (d)-(e)-(c)-(a)-(b)

해석 Ⅱ. 인간을 다른 모든 동물과 구분하게 하는 두 가지는 무엇이 있을까? 하나는 언어이고 다른 하나는 음악이다. 다른 동물들도 노래를 할 수 있지만,(정말 많은 새들이 사람들보다 노래를 더 잘한다) 새의 노래, 그리고 고래와 같은 동물들의 노래는 종류 면에서 제한적이다. 다른 어느 동물도 악기를 개발하지는 않는다.
Ⅰ. 음악은 이상한 것이다. 분명히 언어와는 차이가 있다. 그럼에도 불구하고 사람들은 음악을 이용하여 특히나 그들의 감정을 전달한다. 노래 안에 가사가 결합이 될 때 음악은 인간이 가진 의사 전달의 가장 강력한 방법들 중에 하나가 된다. 그러나 생물학적으로 말하면 음악은 무엇인가?
Ⅲ. 만일 음악이 정말로 언어와 차이가 있다면 그것은 두뇌와는 별개의 부분으로부터 나와야만 한다. 그 부분은 언어를 포함해서 음악을 다른 소리와는 별개가 되게 한다. 그 증거는 그러한 부분이 실제로 존재하고 있다는 것을 암시한다.

어구 **stuff** 재료; 자료; 소질, 재능; 작품; 연출, 연주; (막연히) 물건, 것 **combined with** ~과 결합된 **limited** 제한된, 한정적인, 좁은 **distinct** 별개의 **including** ~을 포함해서

해설 첫 단락에서 인간의 특성을 설명하는 것이 '음악'이라고 설명하고, 두 번째 단락에서 음악에 감정이 담기는 것이 다른 동물들과의 결정적인 차이이며, 세 번째 단락에서 그 생물학적 설명을 하고 있다.

해석 최고의 운동 프로그램에 들어오는 축구와 농구 신입생 선수들의 SAT 점수가 일반 학생의 입학 점수보다 수백 점 낮다는 것을 한 연구가 보여 주었다. (c) 이 범주에 속한 선두는 플로리다 대학교이며, 이 대학에서 축구 선수들과 일반 학생들 간에 점수 차이는 346점이다. (a) 그리하여 이 운동선수(학생)들은 상당히 불리한 입장으로 학생 전체 내에서 경쟁하고 있음을 깨닫게 된다. (b) 그럼에도 미국 대학 체육협회는 '학생 선수'라는 말을 사용해야 한다고 주장하며, 운동선수는 모든 다른 학생들과 같으며 동일 취급받아야 한다고 우겨댄다. (d) 이것은 편입의 문제를 초래한다. 대부분의 학생들은 편입 학교를 선택할 수 있다. (e) 이러한 자유(편입의 자유)가 없는 학생 선수들의 경우에는 그렇지 못하기 때문에(편입의 선택 권한이 없기 때문에), 학생 선수들의 현재 학교는 그 학생들로 하여금 특정 학교에 등록하지 못하게 금지할 수 있다.

어구 **SAT Scholastic Aptitude Test** 대학 진학 적성 검사 **incoming** 들어오는; (이익 등이) 생기는 **big-time** 최고의, 유명한 **admission** 입장(허가), 입학(허가), 입국(허가); 용인 **student body** 학생 전체 **at a disadvantage** 불리한 **category** 범주, 카테고리; 종류, 부류, 부문 **transfer** 편입; 이동, 이전; 운반 **prohibit A from -ing** A가 ~하지 못하게 금지하다 **enroll in** 입회[입학, 입대]하다; 등록하다

해설 제시문에서 학생 선수들의 점수가 일반 학생들보다 낮다는 일반적인 내용의 대한 직접적인 예를 (c) 문장에서 바로 들어주고 있으며, (a) 그에 따른 불리한 학생 선수들의 입장을 설명하고, (b) 문제가 있음에도 문제를 더욱 악화시키는 학교 당국의 입장을 소개한 후, (d) 그에 따른 학생들의 '편입' 문제를 추가적으로 지적한다. (e) 그러나 학생 선수들은 학교 당국의 금지 조치 때문에 편입도 아무렇게나 할 수 없는 내용을 연결한다.

This proverb certainly belongs to one of the most commonly used proverbs in the English language. This should not be surprising since it expresses the only too human idea of discontent, envy, and jealousy in a metaphor which is easily understood. Interestingly enough, the proverb is also literally true, as has been demonstrated in a scientific article based on optical and perceptual laws. Since people are equally dissatisfied with their lot in life, it should not surprise anyone that a modern psychologist has spoken of certain "phenomenon" named after this proverb by which modern individuals continually evaluate supposedly better alternatives for themselves.

26 이 글의 내용을 속담으로 가장 잘 표현한 것은?

① Don't put the cart before the horse.
② An apple a day keeps a doctor away.
③ You can't make an omelet without breaking eggs.
④ The grass is always greener on the other side of the fence.

해석 이 속담은 영어에서 가장 흔하게 쓰이는 속담 중의 하나에 속한다. 이 속담은 불만, 시기, 질투에 대한 아주 인간적인 생각을 쉽게 이해될 수 있는 은유로 표현하기 때문에 놀라운 것이 아니다. 아주 재미있게도, 이 속담은 시각적이고 인지적인 법칙에 근거한 한 과학 기사에서 언급되어 있는 것처럼 문자 그대로도 사실이다. 사람들은 누구나 삶에 있어서 자신의 운명에 불만이기 때문에, 현대의 심리학자가 현대인들이 자신에게 보다 더 좋은 대안들을 계속해서 평가하는 데에 근거가 되는, 이 속담을 따서 이름 붙여진 특정한 현상에 대해서 언급했다는 사실이 그 어떤 사람도 놀라게 하지는 않을 것이다.

26 이 글의 내용을 속담으로 가장 잘 표현한 것은?

① 비논리적인 행동을 피하라.
② 꾸준한 섭취가 건강에 이롭다.
③ 희생 없이는 목적을 이룰 수가 없다.
④ 남의 떡이 더 커 보인다.

어구 **proverb** 속담, 격언(adage) **discontent** (욕구) 불만(의 근원), 불평 **envy** 질투, 부러움, 시기 **jealousy** 질투, 투기, 시샘 **metaphor** 은유, 암유 **interestingly enough** 기묘하게, 참 이상하게도 **literally** 글자 뜻 그대로; 아주, 정말, 사실상 **optical** 눈의, 시각의, 시력의; 시력을 돕는 **perceptual** 지각의; 지각 있는 **lot** 제비뽑기; 몫; 운명 **be named after** ~을 따서 이름 붙여진 **evaluate** 평가하다 **supposedly** 아마, 필경; 소문으로는

해설 마지막 문장 since절 내에서 '사람들은 자신들의 삶의 운명에 대해 불만을 갖고 있다'고 했으며, 주절에서 '자신들을 위한 더 나은 대안들을 계속 평가한다'고 했으므로, 이는 남의 떡이 더 커 보인다는 속담과 더 어울린다.

An angry child will stamp the ground or box the ears of another child even when neither the ground nor the child attacked is remotely connected with the irritation or frustration.

Of course, this kind of behaviour is so common that everyone feels it to be obvious to constitute no serious scientific problem. That a small boy should pull his sister's hair because it is raining does not appear to the ordinary unreflecting person to be an occasion for solemn scientific inquiry. He is, as we should all say, 'in a bad temper.' Yet it is not, in fact, really obvious either why revenge should be taken on entirely innocent objects, since no good to the aggressor can come of it, or why children being miserable should seek to make others miserable also. It is just a fact of human behaviour that cannot really be deduced from any general principle of reason. But it is, as we shall see, of very great importance for our purpose. It shows how (가)it is possible, at the simplest and most primitive level, for aggression and fighting to spring from an entirely irrelevant and partially hidden cause.

해석 화가 난 아이는 화가 난 대상이 땅 또는 다른 아이가 아닐지라도 쾅쾅거리며 발을 구른다거나 다른 아이를 때림으로 화풀이를 한다.
이와 같은 행동은 너무 흔한 것이어서 모든 사람들이 이에 관해 진지한 과학적 문제를 만들어낼 수 없음이 분명하다고 판단한다. 소년이 비가 내린다고 누나의 머리를 잡아당기는 행위에 대해 깊은 고찰을 해 보지 않은 평범한 이에게는 그것이 과학적으로 호기심을 일으키는 행위로 보이지 않을 수 있다. 그 아이는 우리 모두가 말하듯이 성질이 나쁜 아이이다. 그러나 분풀이를 가하는 이에게 어떠한 득도 생기지 않으므로 분풀이가 전적으로 무고한 대상에게 가해져야 하는 이유나 불쌍한 아이가 다른 아이들 또한 불행해지게끔 되어야 하는 이유가 명백히 밝혀지지는 않는다. 그 분풀이는 어떤 일반적인 인과의 법칙에 의해서도 제대로 추론될 수가 없다. 그러나 그 분풀이는 우리가 알 수 있듯이, 우리의 목적(소유욕)을 위해서는 매우 중요한 가치를 가지게 된다. 분풀이는 가장 단순하고도 가장 원시적인 수준에서(미개한 계층에서도) 공격과 싸움이 전혀 무관하고 약간은 숨겨진 명분으로부터 발생하는 것이 어떻게 가능할 수 있는지를 보여준다. 좌절감으로 인해 행복에 대한 장애를 야기함으로써 발생하는 싸움과 비교해 보면, 소망하는 물건을 얻고자 싸우는 행위는 아무리 그 결과가 참담할지라도 상이하고 관련성이 없는 행위를 하게 될 때 직접적이고 합리적인 것이 된다. 그룹 싸움의 이해를 위하여 이러한 사실이 가능하다는 중요성은 이미 분명해진 것임에 틀림이 없다.

Fighting to possess a desired object is straightforward and rational, however disastrous its consequences, compared with fighting that occurs because, in a different and unrelated activity, some frustration has barred the road to pleasure. The importance of (나) <u>this possibility</u> for an understanding of group conflict must already be obvious.

27 Which of the following would be most likely to precede the passage?

① A source of fighting among children is a failure or frustration in their own activity.
② Children end in the complete destruction of the objects of common sense.
③ Aggression closely allied to possessiveness is the tendency for children to resent the intrusion of a stranger.
④ Possessiveness is in all its forms a common cause of fighting.
⑤ The reason for the aggression is fundamentally possessiveness.

28 According to the passage, which of the following is not true?

① A child's resentfulness is not necessarily connected with frustration or irritation.
② People generally don't consider a child's resentfulness as serious.
③ A child's possessiveness has nothing to do with resentfulness.
④ Fighting to possess an desired object is more rational than another fighting.
⑤ When he doesn't acquire an desired object, a child is apt to use violence.

29 The underlined "it" (가) means that

_____________.

① human behaviour
② any general principle of reason
③ very great importance for our purpose
④ to spring from an entirely irrelevant and partially hidden cause
⑤ revenge

30 The underlined "this possibility" (나) means

_____________.

① the fact that some frustration militates against pleasure
② the fact that fighting occurs in an unrelated activity
③ the fact that revenge is surprisingly miserable
④ the fact that fighting for possessiveness may be reasonable
⑤ the fact that group conflict is considerable

27 이 글 앞에 나올 수 있는 내용을 고르시오.
① 아이들 간의 싸움의 원인은 활동을 하지 못하거나 좌절을 느낄 때이다.
② 아이들은 결국 상식적인 물건을 완전히 파괴하는 것으로 끝이 난다.
③ 소유욕과 밀접히 연관된 공격성은 아이들이 낯선 이의 침입에 분개하는 성향이 된다.
④ 소유욕은 모든 형태에 있어서 싸움의 공통된 이유가 된다.
⑤ 공격성의 이유는 근본적으로 소유욕이 된다.

28 이 글의 내용과 일치하지 않는 것을 고르시오.
① 아이의 분노가 좌절이나 짜증과 꼭 연관되어 있는 것은 아니다.
② 사람들은 대개 아이의 분노를 심각한 것으로 간주하지 않는다.
③ 아이의 소유욕은 분노와 아무 상관이 없다.
④ 소망하는 물건을 얻기 위하여 싸우는 것은 다른 싸움보다는 합리적이다.
⑤ 소망하는 물건을 얻지 못할 때 아이는 폭력을 행사하는 경향이 있다.

29 밑줄 친 (가)가 의미하는 것은?
① 인간의 행동
② 일반화된 인과 법칙
③ 우리의 목적을 위한 매우 대단한 중요성
④ 전혀 무관하고 약간은 숨겨진 명분으로부터 발생하는 것
⑤ 보복

30 밑줄 친 (나)가 의미하는 것은?
① 어떤 좌절로 인해 기쁨을 누리지 못하는 것
② 싸움이 관련 없는 행동으로 발생하는 사실
③ 보복이 매우 비참하다는 사실
④ 소유욕 때문에 싸우는 것이 합리적일 수 있다는 사실
⑤ 집단 투쟁이 상당하다는 사실

어구 **stamp** 짓밟다; 날인하다 **box** 때리다 **remotely** 약간이라도 **unreflecting** 깊은 생각을 하지 않는 **in a bad temper** 성질이 더러운 **take revenge** 보복하다 **miserable** 비참한 **aggression** 공격 **straightforward** 솔직한 **bar the road to** ~을 방해하다 **end in** 결국 ~이 되다 **allied to** ~과 연관된 **intrusion** 침입 **have nothing to do with** ~과 연관성이 없다

해설 **27** 첫 문장의 종속절에서 짜증이나 좌절감과 <u>관련 없는</u> 경우에서조차도 아이의 폭력이 나온다고 했으므로, <u>반대 상황</u>이 앞 단락에 나왔을 것이라고 유추할 수 있다.
28 아이의 폭력은 소유욕에서 상당한 이유를 찾을 수 있다고 했으므로, 관련이 없다는 설명은 틀렸다.
29 가주어 it이므로, 진주어 to spring 이하가 옳다.
30 작가는 아이의 소유욕에서 비롯된 폭력성이 기타 폭력들보다 상대적으로 합리적일 수 있다는 견해를 내비치므로, 분명한 가능성을 가진 것 또한 이 설명으로서 타당하다.

Actual TEST 05

⇨ 본책 p.242

1 ③	2 ④	3 ①	4 ②	5 ①	6 ①	7 ①	8 ⑤	9 ④	10 ③
11 ④	12 ⑤	13 ③	14 ②	15 ③	16 ③	17 ④	18 ③	19 ③	20 ③
21 ④	22 ①	23 ①	24 ③	25 ②	26 ②	27 ①	28 ①	29 ②	30 ③

>>> 밑줄 친 곳에 들어갈 알맞은 답을 고르시오. [1~5]

1 Businesses would respond to the sales decrease by reducing their own spending and ____________ their employees.

① giving out
② turning on
③ sack
④ calling forth
⑤ stimulate

해석 회사는 소비를 줄이고 직원들을 해고시킴으로써 판매 감소에 대응할 것이다.

어구 **respond to** 대응하다   **give out** 배포하다, 발표하다   **turn on** 켜다, 틀다   **sack** 해고하다   **stimulate** 자극하다

해설 and에 의해서 판매 감소에 대한 대응책으로서 '소비 감소'와 순접의 내용이 필요하다.

2 One of the American definitions of success is to acquire a high material standard of living. It is not surprising, therefore, that Americans have valued education for its ____________ value.

① reformative
② ethical
③ vocational
④ monetary
⑤ depraved

해석 성공에 대한 미국의 정의들 중 하나는 높은 물질적 생활수준을 성취하는 것이다. 따라서 미국인들이 금전상의 가치를 위해서 교육을 평가해 온 사실은 놀랄 것이 아니다.

어구 **material** 물질의, 중요한; 물질, 내용, 재료   **value** 평가하다   **reformative** 개혁의   **vocational** 직업상의, 업무상의   **monetary** 금전상의   **depraved** 타락의

해설 물질적 생활수준의 성취가 미국인들의 성공에 대한 정의가 되므로, 이와 순접의 내용이 되기 위해서는 금전상의 가치를 위해서 교육의 가치를 평가한다는 내용이 적합하다.

3 The ____________ form looming in the shadows turned out to be a trash can in the light.

① faint
② mischievous
③ identified
④ disagreeable

해석 그림자 속에서 흐릿하게 보였던 형체는 빛 속에 있었던 쓰레기통으로 판명됐다.

어구 **loom** (어렴풋이) 나타나다   **turn out (to be)** ~으로 판명되다   **trash can** 쓰레기통   **faint** 흐릿한   **mischievous** 장난을 치는   **identified** 확인된, 동일한   **disagreeable** 맘에 들지 않는, 불쾌한

해설 그림자 속에서 나타난 형체를 수식할 적절한 어휘는 '희미한 (모습을) 보이는'이 옳다.

4 In some ways, material possessions are seen not only as ____________ evidence of people's work, but also as their abilities to do work successfully.

① invisible
② tangible
③ legitimate
④ invaluable
⑤ of no use

해석 어떤 면에서 물질적인 재산이 사람들의 일에 대한 구체적인 증거일 뿐만 아니라 성공적으로 일을 할 수 있는 그들의 능력으로서 간주되기도 한다.

어구 **possession** 소유물, 소유, 재산   **see A as B** A를 B로 간주하다   **invisible** 보이지 않는   **tangible** 명백한, 실제적인, 손으로 잡을 수 있는   **legitimate** 합당한, 합법적인   **invaluable** 매우 귀중한

해설 not only A but also B 구문에 의해서 '(추상적인 성질이 내포된) 능력'과 상반되는 어구가 필요하다. '(외형적으로) 명백한'이란 뜻이 적합하다.

5 Business will account for 80 percent of Internet use and private users just 20 percent, a well-known technologist attending the economic forum here predicted Tuesday. Michael Dell, who runs Dell Corporation, made the forecast at a session on the "Future of the Internet". Microsoft president Bill Gates on Monday ____________ high expectations about trading and banking in cyber-space. "Is everybody going to be shopping, banking there? It's just not realistic, it takes time for these things to happen", he said.

① dampened
② bolstered
③ illuminated
④ ensnared
⑤ solidified

해석 비즈니스가 인터넷 이용의 80%를 차지하게 될 것이고, 개인 이용자들은 겨우 20%를 차지하게 될 것이라고 경제 포럼에 참석한 한 저명한 공학자가 화요일 예측했다. Dell Corporation사를 운영하고 있는 마이클 델은 "인터넷의 미래"를 주제로 했던 한 회의에서 그러한 예견을 했었다. (반면) Microsoft의 빌 게이츠 회장은 월요일에 가상공간에서의 상거래와 금융에 대한 높은 기대에 찬물을 끼얹었다. 그는 "모든 사람이 그곳에서 쇼핑을 하고 은행 일을 보게 될까요? 현실성이 전혀 없는 일이고, 이런 일들이 벌어지려면 시간이 걸릴 겁니다."라고 말했다.

어구 **account for** ~을 설명하다, ~의 비율을 차지하다 **technologist** 공학자 **cyber-space** 가상공간 **bank** 은행 일을 보다 **dampen** (열기를) 꺾다, 축축하게 하다 **bolster** 지지 · 강화하다 **illuminate** 조명하다, 명백히 하다 **ensnare** 함정에 빠트리다 **solidify** 굳건히 하다

해설 이어서 등장하는 마지막 문장에서 빌 게이츠 회장이 말하기를, 가상 공간에서 쇼핑을 하고 은행 일을 보게 되는 것은 비현실적이라고 했으므로, '높은 기대치의 열기를 꺾다'라는 내용이 논리상 적합하다.

>>> 다음 글을 읽고 문제의 답을 고르시오.

I.   In Florida, people over 60 ____________ for more than 25 percent of the population.

II. Ms. Popper's vacation in Frankfurt had to be cancelled on ____________ of her husband's illness.

III. Salespeople have to take into ____________ the differences between their customers.

6 빈칸에 공통으로 들어갈 가장 알맞은 어휘를 고르시오.

① account
② behalf
③ need
④ regard
⑤ favor

해석 I. 플로리다에 60세 이상의 사람들이 인구의 25퍼센트를 차지한다.
II. 프랑크푸르트에서의 파퍼 부인의 휴가는 남편의 병환 때문에 취소되어야만 했다.
III. 판매원들은 그들 고객들 간의 차이점을 고려해야 한다.

어구 **account for** ~을 차지하다; ~의 원인이 되다; ~을 설명하다 **on account of** ~ 때문에 **take into account** ~을 고려하다, 참작하다

>>> 다음 글을 읽고 문제의 답을 고르시오.

You could find your true reward in teaching.

If you have a desire to help the younger generation, a wish to pass on your specialized knowledge, a way of communication with youth, and the ability to arouse the interest and curiosity of young minds; if you have patience, understanding, tact, a sense of responsibility and preferably a sense of humor, then to you, maths, science or engineering graduates, teaching could be the most rewarding and fulfilling career.

해석   당신은 교사직에서 진정한 보람을 찾을 수 있을 겁니다.
만일 당신이 젊은 세대를 돕고 싶은 욕구와 당신의 전문 지식을 전수하고 싶은 소망, 젊은이들과의 대화 방식, 젊은이들의 마음에 흥미와 호기심을 자극시킬 수 있는 능력을 갖고 있다면, 그리고 만일 당신이 인내, 이해력, 재치, 책임감과 되도록이면 유머감각도 있다면, 수학, 과학, 공학 분야를 졸업할 당신에게는 교사직이 가장 보람 있고 많은 것을 성취하는 직업이 될 수 있을 것입니다.

7 윗글의 종류는 무엇인가?
① 수학과 과학 전공 졸업 예정자들에 대한 광고
② 아이들에게 수학과 과학을 가르치는 보람 있는 경험을 설명하는 신문 기사
③ 교육 목적을 위하여 수학과 과학을 진지하게 가르치라는 충고
④ 성공한 교사에게 필요한 개인특성을 묘사하는 에세이

7. What kind of text is the passage above?

① An advertisement to the prospective graduates of math and science

② A newspaper article which describes the rewarding experience of teaching math and science to children

③ An exhortation to seriously study math and science at college for pedagogical purposes

④ An essay which describes the personal traits required of a successful teacher

어구 **reward** 보람; 보답; 보수 **pass on** 전달하다; 지나가다 **arouse** 자극하다; 깨우다 **tact** 재치 **preferably** 차라리; 즐겨, 오히려, 되도록 **rewarding** 할 보람이 있는, 득이 되는 **fulfilling** 만족스러운 **exhortation** 충고 **pedagogical** 교육학의

해설 마지막 문장에서 졸업 예정자에게 교사직은 보람 있는 직업이라고 얘기하고 있으므로, 교사직 채용을 위한 졸업 예정자들에 대한 구인 광고로 보아야 한다.

>>> **다음 글을 읽고 문제의 답을 고르시오. [8~11]**

One reason that so many people fail is that they lack confidence in themselves. If you think of yourself as being unworthy of great achievement, you will never achieve greatness. If, on the other hand, you know yourself and understand what your abilities are, and if then you determine to accomplish everything of which you are capable, you will certainly stand a much better chance of success. How may one become inspired to realize all his possibilities or to gain confidence in himself? One of the surest ways is for him to associate with persons who have really achieved greatness. It is impossible, however, for most people to come frequently into the actual presence of the great. The next best thing, perhaps, is for him to spend part of his time in reading about great achievers. Biography is a powerful stimulant to action. But these processes will not avail unless one rids himself of a sense of inferiority and determines to do the best that he possibly can. One of our great philosophers expressed the idea in a single sentence when he said that each individual should <u>hitch his wagon to a star</u>.

8 The title that best expresses the main theme or subject of this selection is ____________.

① The value of biography
② Worthy use of time
③ Outstanding persons
④ A sense of superiority
⑤ Ways of becoming successful

9 According to the writer of the selection, a basic cause of failure is lack of ____________.

① perseverance　② pride
③ thoughtfulness　④ self-confidence
⑤ friendliness

해석 많은 사람들이 실패하는 이유는 자기 자신에 대한 확신이 없기 때문이다. 자신이 큰 성공을 거둘 가치가 없다고 생각한다면, 당신은 결코 큰일을 성취할 수 없을 것이다. 만약, 반대로, 당신이 자신을 알고 당신의 능력이 무엇인지를 알고 당신이 할 수 있는 모든 것을 성취하겠다고 결심했다면 당신은 분명히 성공을 거둘 훨씬 더 좋은 가능성을 가지게 된다. 사람이 어떻게 자신의 모든 가능성을 깨닫게 되거나 자신에 대한 확신을 얻을 수 있을까? 가장 확실한 방법 중 하나는 실제로 큰일을 성취한 사람과 교제하는 것이다. 그러나 대부분의 사람들이 위대한 사람들을 실제로 자주 만난다는 것은 불가능하다. 아마도 그 다음으로 가장 좋은 방법은 크게 성취한 사람들에 관하여 독서를 하는 데에 시간을 투자하는 것이다. 자서전은 행동에 대해 강력한 자극이 된다. 그러나 이러한 과정들은 자신에게서 열등감을 없애고 자신이 할 수 있는 최상의 일을 하겠다고 결심하지 않는 한 쓸모가 없을 것이다. 사람들은 각자의 대망을 품어야 한다고 했을 때, 위대한 철학자 중의 한 명이 하나의 문장에 이러한 생각을 표현하였다.

8 이 글의 주제는?

① 자서전의 가치　　　　② 시간의 효율적인 이용
③ 뛰어난 사람들　　　　④ 우월감
⑤ 성공을 거두는 방법들

9 실패의 근본적인 원인은 무엇이 부족해서인가?

① 인내심　　　　　　　② 자존심
③ 깊은 생각　　　　　　④ 자신감
⑤ 우정

10 성공을 향해 출발할 때 사람은 무엇을 해야 하냐고 조언하는가?

① 대학 교육을 받아야 한다고　　② 자신만 생각하라고
③ 자서전을 읽으라고　　　　　　④ 자신을 무가치한 존재로 간주하라고
⑤ 정치에 뛰어들라고

11 밑줄 친 "대망을 품어라"라는 표현은 사람들이 무엇을 하라고 작가가 조언하는 것인가?

① 먼 곳에 여행을 가라고　　　　② 천문학을 공부하라고
③ 세부사항을 무시하라고　　　　④ 큰일을 할 것을 결심하라고
⑤ 뛰어난 책들을 쓰라고

10 The writer advises that, as a start toward greatness, a person should ___________.

① get a college education
② think only of himself
③ read biographies
④ consider himself unworthy
⑤ enter politics

11 The author of the expression "hitch your wagon to a star" was most likely advising people to ___________.

① travel widely
② study astronomy
③ ignore details
④ determine to do big things
⑤ write great books

어구 **confidence** 확신, 자신 **unworthy of** ~의 가치가 없는 **determine to R** 결심하다 **stand a good chance of** ~의 가능성이 충분히 있다 **inspired to R** ~하도록 영감을 얻은 **associate with** ~와 사귀다 **come into presence** 존재하다 **biography** 자서전 **stimulant** 흥분제, 자극(물), 격려 **avail** 도움이 되다, 가치가 있다 **rid A of B** A에게서 B를 제거하다 **inferiority** 하위, 열등 **hitch one's wagon to a star** 대망을 품다 **outstanding** 현저한, 걸출한, 대항하는 **perseverance** 인내 **pride** 자존심 **self-confidence** 자기 확신(자신감), 자기 과잉 **politics** 정치, 정치학, 정견

해설 **8** 사람들이 실패를 거두는 이유에 대해서 먼저 문제를 제기하고, 성공을 거둘 수 있는 해결책들을 열거하면서 '대망을 품는 것'이 최상의 방법이라고 결론을 내린다. 따라서 성공을 거두는 방법들이 주제로서 옳다.

9 사람들이 실패하는 근본적인 원인은 자신감 부족이라고 했다.

10 큰일을 성취한(성공한) 사람을 만나거나 그 사람의 자서전을 읽는 것이 성공을 거둘 수 있는 가장 확실한 방법 중 하나라고 작가가 주장한다.

11 hitch one's wagon to a star 표현은 '대망을 품어라'라는 뜻이다. 따라서 이 표현을 통해 작가는 성공을 거두기 위해서는 큰일을 할 것을 결심하라고 조언하는 것이다.

>>> 다음 글을 읽고 문제의 답을 고르시오. [12~14]

If you have pain, don't suffer in silence. Surveys have shown that many patients don't tell doctors or nurses about their pain for fear of being labeled cranky or difficult or because they assume that their discomfort will go away. However, such reluctance can backfire. Left uncontrolled, the pain you thought was temporary can trigger a long-term chronic condition. It can also interfere with the healing process and lengthen your recovery time. If your current treatment isn't controlling your pain, say so to your doctor. (a) It often helps to have a family member make the case for you. Learn what pain killers can and can't do. Lots of folks fear they will get hooked on strong medications. In fact, though most patients build up a tolerance to pain drugs, they don't become addicted. Others rely solely on pills and ignore lifestyle changes like losing weight that can alleviate pain in the joints and back.

12 What is the main topic of the passage?

① Effective ways to complain about pain
② Prevention of pain medicine addiction
③ Controlling tolerance to medication
④ Interrelation between pain and healing
⑤ Advice for victims of pain

해석 통증이 있다면 침묵으로 참지 마시오. 조사에 따르면 많은 환자들이 괴팍하거나 까다롭다고 낙인찍히기가 두려워서, 혹은 자신들의 불편한 사항들이 곧 사라질 것이라고 간주하기 때문에, 의사나 간호사들에게 자신들의 통증에 대해 얘기를 하지 않는다고 한다. 그러나 그와 같은 주저함은 역효과를 가져올 수 있다. 방치된다면 당신이 일시적일 것이라고 생각했던 통증은 장기간의 만성 상태로 야기될 수 있다. 그것은 또한 치료 과정에 방해가 될 수도 있으며, 회복 기간을 연장시킬 수 있다. 만약 당신의 현재 치료가 통증을 고쳐 주지 못하고 있다면, 의사에게 그렇다고 말하라. 가족이 당신을 위하여 최상의 주장을 해 주는 것도 종종 도움이 된다. 어떤 진통제가 도움이 되고, 어떤 진통제가 도움이 되지 않는지 알아 둬라. 많은 사람들이 강한 약물에 중독될까 봐 두려워하고 있다. 사실, 대부분의 환자들은 진통제에 대해서 내구성이 강화되지만, 중독이 되지는 않는다. 다른 사람들은 알약에만 전적으로 의지하고, 관절과 등의 통증을 감소시켜 줄 수 있는 무게 감량과 같은 생활방식의 변화는 무시한다.

12 이 글의 주제는?
① 고통에 대해 불평하는 효율적인 방법들
② 진통제 중독의 예방
③ 약물 치료 내성의 억제
④ 고통과 회복의 상호관계
⑤ 아파하는 환자들을 위한 조언

13 (a)의 의미와 가장 가까운 것은?
① 가족이 당신의 기분이 언제 좋아지느냐고 물어볼 수 있다.
② 가족이 당신의 고통을 줄여 주기 위해서 베갯잇을 만들어 줄 때 도움을 줄 수 있다.
③ 가족이 당신을 대신해서 의사에게 말해 줄 수 있다.
④ 가족이 당신의 질병과 유사한 질병을 걸린 다른 환자들에 대해서 알아볼 수 있다.
⑤ 가족이 의사에게 치료 과정의 진전 상황을 통보할 수 있다.

13 Which of the following is closest in meaning to (a)?

① A family member can tell the doctor when you feel better.
② A family member can often be helpful in making a pillow case to reduce your pain.
③ A family member can speak to the doctor in your behalf.
④ A family member can find out about other patients whose cases are similar to yours.
⑤ A family member can inform the doctor of your progress in the healing process.

14 From what is stated or implied in the passage, which of the following is NOT true?

① If pain is not treated, it can become a chronic illness.
② Modern pain drugs are so effective that they do not build up a tolerance in patients.
③ Some patients hide their pain from doctors for fear of being considered hypochondriacs.
④ Reduced body weight can reduce the pain in the joints and back.
⑤ For effective pain control patients should take medication and/or make changes in their lifestyle.

14 이 글의 내용과 일치하지 않는 것은?

① 고통이 치료되지 않는다면 만성 질병이 될 수 있다.
② 오늘날의 진통제는 너무나 효과적이어서 환자들의 내구성을 강화시켜 주지 못한다.
③ 몇몇 환자들은 우울증 환자로 간주될까 두려워 고통을 숨긴다.
④ 체중 감량은 관절과 등의 고통을 감소시킬 수 있다.
⑤ 효과적인 통증 억제를 위해서 환자들은 약을 복용하거나 생활패턴을 변화시켜야 한다.

어구 survey 조사, 측량; 조사하다, 측량하다 tell A about B A에게 B에 대해서 얘기하다 for fear of ~을 두려워해서 labelled A A라고 낙인이 찍힌, A라고 딱지가 붙여진 cranky 괴팍한 assume 가장하다 discomfort 불편, 불안 go away 사라지다 reluctance 주저함, 망설임 backfire 역효과를 가져오다 uncontrolled 방치된, 통제되지 않는 temporary 일시적인 trigger 야기하다 long-term 장기간의 chronic 만성의, 상습적인 interfere with 방해하다 lengthen 연장하다 make a case (최상의) 주장·증명을 하다 pain killer 진통제 be/ get hooked 중독되다, 갈고리에 걸리다 build up 강화하다 addicted 중독된 solely 오로지, 혼자서 losing weight 체중 감량 alleviate 경감하다, 완화하다 joint 관절, 이음매 back 등 tolerance [의학] 내성 interrelation 상호관계 pillow case 베갯잇 in one's behalf ~을 대신하여 find out 발견하다, 간파하다 be similar to ~과 유사하다 hypochondriac 우울증 환자 take medication 약을 복용하다

해설 **12** 아프면 참지 말고 진단을 받아서 치료를 받아야 한다는 조언을 전하는 것이 이 글의 주제이다.

13 make a case for는 '(~를 위해서) 주장하다'라는 뜻이다. 문맥상 '본인 스스로 의사에게 현재의 치료가 효과를 보지 못한다고 말하지 못한다면, 가족 구성원 누군가가 대신해서 말해 주겠다'는 내용이 옳다.

14 마지막 두 번째 문장 종속절에서, 대부분의 환자들은 진통제에 대해 내구성이 강화된다고 했으므로, ②의 '내구성을 강화시켜 주지 못한다'는 내용이 틀린 설명이다.

>>> **다음 글을 읽고 문제의 답을 고르시오.**

[1] Not everyone is sold on probiotics. The U.S. Food and Drug Administration is relatively neutral, using the growing popularity of the products as an opportunity to caution manufacturers not to pitch the foods as some sort of panacea for any specific disease. [2] More important, some people should avoid the products altogether. Those with weakened immune systems or who are critically ill would be well advised to stay away from eating live bacteria. [3] The bacteria can battle numerous kinds of allergies—and not just food allergies. [4] Certainly anyone in the hospital would also count.

15 윗글에서 글 전체의 문맥상 어울리지 않는 문장을 고르시오.

① [1]　　　　② [2]
③ [3]　　　　④ [4]

해석 [1] 모두가 바이오유 제품에 열광하는 것은 아니다. 미 식품 의약품국은 비교적 중립적 입장을 취하며, 바이오유 제품의 높아진 인기를 이용하여 제조업체들에게 바이오유 제품이 질병의 만병통치약인 것처럼 홍보하지 말 것을 경고하고 있다. [2] 더 중요한 것은 몇몇 사람들은 그 제품들을 꼭 피해야 한다는 점이다. 면역 체계가 약한 사람이나 매우 아픈 사람은 살아 있는 박테리아를 먹지 말도록 권고받는 것이 현명하다. [3] 이 박테리아는 음식 알레르기뿐만 아니라 다양한 종류의 알레르기와 싸운다. [4] 분명히 병원에 있는 사람들도 또한 포함될 것이다.

어구 be sold on ~에 열광하다 probiotic 생균제; 바이오유 제품 the U.S. Food and Drug Administration 미 식품 의약품국(FDA) relatively 비교적 pitch 던지다; 고정시키다 panacea 만병통치약 altogether 완전히, 모두 합쳐, 대체로 weakened 약화된 critically 비평적으로; 결정적으로 stay away from ~에서 피하다 numerous 무수히 많은

해설 [3] 문장만 알레르기에 대한 내용을 전하고 있으며, 나머지 모든 문장은 바이오유 제품에 관한 설명을 하고 있다.

The website is quick and simple to use. After looking at Goya and Michelangelo, I turned to someone I didn't know much about, to see how useful the site would be.

[A] On the website I soon learned that he spent the latter part of his life in extreme poverty. Among the visionary landscapes is one called The Comedy of Death.

[B] He's an eccentric and unlike anyone else. I've sometimes seen his work in catalogues, but never read about him.

[C] I chose the draughtsman and print-maker Rodolphe Bresdin, 1822-1885, an artist with a distinctive and busy style which tends to cover the whole of a page with detail.

[D] In the picture there is a hut on an island, inhabited by two despairing figures, as the text puts it, surrounded by owls and skeletons and bats and devils.

16 윗글의 박스 안에 있는 제시문과 이어질 순서로 가장 올바른 것은?

① [A]-[D]-[C]-[B] ② [A]-[B]-[C]-[D]
③ [C]-[B]-[A]-[D] ④ [C]-[D]-[A]-[B]

해석 그 웹 사이트는 빠르고 이용하기 편리하다. 고야와 미켈란젤로를 본 후, 나는 이 사이트가 얼마나 유용한지 확인하기 위하여 내가 잘 알지 못하는 다른 사람에게 시선을 돌렸다. [C] 나는 소묘 화가이면서 동시에 판화 제작자였던 루돌프 브레스딘(1822-1885)을 선택했다. 그는 세밀하게 전체 페이지를 채워 나가는 독특하고 복잡한 양식을 갖춘 예술가였다. [B] 그는 특이했으며 어느 누구와도 다른 존재였다. 나는 목록에서 때때로 그의 작품을 보았지만 결코 그에 관하여 글을 읽어 본 적은 없었다. [A] 그 사이트에서 나는 곧 그가 무척 빈곤하게 말년의 삶을 보냈음을 알게 됐다. 그의 환각적인 풍경화 중 '사극(死劇)'이라 불리는 작품이 있다. [D] 그 그림에 두 명의 절망적인 사람이 섬 안의 어떤 오두막에 거주하는데, 이들은 본문의 설명대로 부엉이, 해골, 박쥐 및 악마에 둘러싸여 있다.

어구 **latter** 후자의; 후반부의 **extreme** 극단적인 **poverty** 빈곤 **visionary** 환영의; 실제적이 아닌 **landscape** 풍경화; 풍경 **eccentric** 특이한, 별난 **draughtsman** 도안공; 제도가, 초안하는 사람(draftsman) **print-maker** 판화 제작자 **distinctive** 독특한, 특이한 **hut** 오두막; 임시 막사 **despairing** 절망적인, 가망 없는 **as the text puts it** 본문에서 언급하듯이

해설 제시문에서 다른 누군가에게 시선을 돌렸다고 했다. 이 다른 사람이 [C]에 등장하는 '루돌프 브레스딘'이다. [B] 그에 대해 사전 지식이 전혀 없었음을 경험으로 설명한다. [A] 그의 '사극'이라는 풍경화에 관심을 가지게 되며, [D] 그 풍경화 속 모습을 전달한다.

Our neighbor is an affluent inventor whose latest brainstorm, a feasible umbrella substitute, has been featured in many magazines. As simply as the eye can discern, it is a hard plastic strip, about the size of a ruler, which fits comfortably into a woman's handbag or a man's suit jacket. If a person is caught in a sudden rainstorm, he swings the plastic open in the shape of a cross. Attached to each arm is a clip-like device. Next, he takes the newspaper he is carrying and slides it under each of the four clips. Now, equipped with a rigid head covering he can <u>sally forth to face the elements</u>. To the consternation of the umbrella manufacturers, it has been enjoying a brisk sale, especially among commuters. If it continues to do well, it could have a pernicious effect upon the umbrella industry.

17 이 글에 따랐을 때 올바른 설명은?

① 발명가의 어리석은 생각을 언론이 비난한다.
② 새로운 발명이 초기의 검사 장비들 때문에 복잡한 것으로 증명됐다.
③ 새로운 발명품이 갑작스러운 기후의 변화에서는 무용지물인 것으로 증명됐다.
④ 우산 제조업체는 새로운 발명품의 성공에 놀랐다.
⑤ 새로운 발명품이 우산 사업에 상당한 기여를 할 가능성이 있다.

해석 내 이웃은 부유한 발명가이며 그가 가장 최근에 고안한 실용적인 우산 대용품은 많은 잡지에서 특별 소개 되었다. 간단히 눈으로만 보자면, 그것은 여자의 핸드백이나 남자의 양복 상의에 쉽게 들어갈 수 있는 자 정도 크기의 단단한 플라스틱 조각이다. 만약 그 사람이 갑작스러운 폭우를 맞게 되면, 그는 플라스틱을 십자 모양으로 휙 펼친다. 각 테에는 클립 같은 장치가 부착되어 있다. 다음에는 가지고 있던 신문지를 4개의 클립 밑에 끼워 넣는다. 이제 단단한 머리 덮개로 무장한 사람은 어떤 날씨가 닥치더라도 앞으로 나갈 수 있다. 우산 제조업체들이 깜짝 놀랄 정도로 이 물건은 불티나게 팔렸으며 특히 통근자들에게 많이 팔렸다. 이 물건이 계속해서 잘 팔린다면 우산 업계에 치명적인 영향을 끼칠 수 있다.

17 According to the passage, which of the following is true?

① The inventor has been criticized by the press for his absurd idea.
② The new invention has proved too complicated with initial testers.
③ The new invention has proved useless in a sudden weather change.
④ Umbrella manufacturers have been surprised at the success of the new invention.
⑤ The new invention is likely to make a great contribution to the umbrella industry.

18 The underlined expression means
___________.

① he can easily put the parts together
② he can see each individual part of the product
③ he can venture out in the rain
④ he can finally put the product on the market
⑤ he can lower the production costs

18 밑줄 친 표현이 의미하는 것은?

① 그는 쉽게 부품들을 합칠 수 있다.
② 그는 그 상품의 각각의 개별 부품을 볼 수 있다.
③ 그는 빗속에서 위험을 무릅쓰고 앞으로 나갈 수 있다.
④ 그는 마침내 그 상품을 시장에 내놓았다.
⑤ 그는 생산 비용을 절감시킬 수 있다.

어구 **affluent** 풍부한, 유복한 **brainstorm** 갑자기 떠오른 묘안 **feasible** 실행할 수 있는, 가능한 **ruler** 통치자 **comfortably** 기분 좋게; 마음 놓고 **swing open** ~을 홱 열다 **slide** 슬그머니 넣다 **equipped with** ~한 설비를 갖춘 **rigid** 굳은, 단단한; 완고한 **sally forth** 기운차게 나오다 **the elements** 자연력, (특히) 폭풍우 **consternation** 놀라움; 대경실색 **brisk** 활발한, 기운찬 **pernicious** 해로운; 파괴적인 **absurd** 어리석은 **initial** 처음의; 최초의 **tester** 시험[검사] 장치 **put together** ~을 합치다 **venture out** 위험을 무릅쓰고 가다

해설 **17** To the consternation of the umbrella manufacturers ~표현을 통해 우산 제조업체들이 놀랐다는 사실은 옳은 설명이다.
18 element가 복수 형태를 취하면, 폭풍우와 같은 날씨 환경을 가리킬 수 있다. 따라서 '비'라는 날씨 환경에서 앞을 향해 나갔다는 내용이 옳다.

▶▶▶ **다음 글을 읽고 문제의 답을 고르시오. [19~22]**

A married man and woman, who take no greater excursions outside themselves than an occasional turning-on of the radio or an occasional watching together of a movie, are both likely to feel frustrated and confined, and to express ① these obscurely entertained feelings by an everlasting ② wrangle. It is notorious that the business or professional man, who has confined his whole interest to his business or profession, is likely not to survive his retirement for very long. Ennui, expressing itself via heart or kidneys or arteries, drops him in his tracks. The physical organism has no reason to go on continuing. ③ ____________ men devoted to hobbies and similar interests have a way of continuing into great old age, still lively and alert and inquisitive as chipmunks.

19 The best title of the passage is ____________.

① How to survive the retirement long
② Ennui and health
③ Importance of hobbies
④ How to keep balance between family and work
⑤ How to be as inquisitive as chipmunks

해석 어떤 결혼한 남녀는 이따금씩 라디오를 켜거나 가끔씩 영화를 함께 보지도 않을 뿐더러 바깥으로 소풍을 가는 것조차 하지 않는데, 이는 좌절감을 느끼거나 구속받는다는 느낌을 받기 쉬우며, 모호하게 마음속에 품고 있는 이러한 감정들을 끊임없는 말다툼을 통해 표현하기 쉽다. 자신의 일이나 직업에만 모든 관심을 제한시키는 사업가나 전문가는 매우 오랫동안 은퇴하지 않고 버텨내기 힘들 것이다. 권태는 심장이나 신장, 혹은 동맥을 통해 나타나며, 사람을 인생의 기로에서 떨어뜨린다. 신체 조직이 계속 존재할 이유를 갖지 못한다. 반면에 취미와 유사한 흥밋거리들에 몰두하는 사람은 나이가 지긋할 때까지 (그 흥밋거리들을) 존속시킬 방법들을 갖고 있으며, 여전히 다람쥐처럼 활발하고, 기민하며, 호기심이 많아진다.

19 이 글의 제목은?
① 은퇴로부터 오랫동안 견뎌내는 방법
② 권태와 건강   ③ 취미의 중요성
④ 가족과 일의 균형을 유지하는 방법
⑤ 다람쥐처럼 호기심이 많아지는 방법

20 ① '모호하게 마음속에 품고 있는 이러한 감정들'에 속하지 않는 것은?
① 좌절감   ② 고독해지는 것
③ 열등감   ④ 권태
⑤ 구속감

21 ②를 가장 잘 번역한 것은?
① 칭찬   ② 격려
③ 활기   ④ 불평
⑤ 태만

22 ③에 들어갈 알맞은 것은?
① 대조해 보건대   ② 정반대로
③ 결론적으로   ④ 만일의 경우에 대비하여
⑤ 그렇지 않다면

20 The one that does NOT belong to the underlined ① is ____________.

① frustration
② being forlorn
③ a feeling of inferiority
④ boredom
⑤ a feeling of confinement

21 The one that best interprets the underlined ② is ____________.

① praise
② encouragement
③ vitality
④ complaint
⑤ negligence

22 The expression that is most appropriate for ③ is ____________.

① In contrast
② On the contrary
③ Consequently
④ In case
⑤ Otherwise

어구 take a excursion 소풍을 가다 be likely to R ~하기 쉽다, ~할 것 같다 obscurely 모호하게, 눈에 띄지 않게 entertain 마음속에 품다, 즐겁게 하다 everlasting 영원한 wrangle 논쟁, 말다툼 notorious 극악무도한, 유명한 confine A to B A를 B에 제한하다 ennui 권태 via ~을 거쳐서, ~을 경유하여 kidney 신장 artery 동맥 track (인생의) 행로, 통로, 자국 have no reason to R ~하는 것이 옳지 않다, ~할 이유가 없다 lively 활기찬 alert 기민한, 재빠른 inquisitive 호기심 많은 chipmunk 다람쥐 forlorn 고독한, 버려진 inferiority 열등감 boredom 권태, 따분함 vitality 생명력, 활력, 활기 negligence 태만 in contrast 대조적으로, 비교해 보건대[비교·대조] on the contrary 정반대로[논박·반박] in case 만일에 대비하여 otherwise 그렇지 않다면

해설 19 이 글에서 등장하는 '소풍, 영화, 취미, 흥밋거리, 다람쥐'는 모두 '취미'라는 범주의 핵심어들이다. 즉, 권태에 빠져들지 않고, 나이가 들어서도 마치 동물인 다람쥐처럼 활기차게 살기 위해서는 취미가 중요하다는 것이 주제이다. 따라서 제목 또한 '취미의 중요성'이 옳다.

20 '좌절감과 구속감, 고독'은 앞 문장 ~ feel frustrated and confined에 등장하며, '권태와 고독감'은 이하에서 ennui(권태)를 통해서 유추가 가능하다. 그러나 열등감은 언급된 바 없는 감정이다.

21 wrangle은 '(긴 시간이 소요되는) 논쟁(a long and complicated argument)'이란 뜻을 가진다. 따라서 complaint(불평)이 가장 동의어로서 근접해 있다.

22 앞 문장과 빈칸 이하의 내용은 신체 조직이 계속 존속되느냐 안 되느냐의 상반된 내용을 대조하므로, '역접-대조'의 관계가 옳다. 흔히 on the contrary와 in contrast를 동의어구로 알고 있는데, 이는 잘못된 것이다.

The less expensive ways of going on holidays are to take a camper in which you can stay or to go camping. It is also cheaper when you are travelling abroad to go on a package tour in which your hotel and flight are arranged for you. You can stay in a Bed and Breakfast(also called a B and B) which is usually a private house which takes paying guests and provides them with a room for the night and breakfast for the following morning. In Britain this is usually cheaper than a hotel though in the US it is more expensive. Some people buy timeshares, that is, they become part owners of a holiday home and it is theirs to use a certain time every year.

23 Which of the following is the best title of the passage above?

① Where People Stay on Holidays
② Popular Holiday Entertainments
③ When People Leave for Holidays
④ What People Do on Holidays

해석 당신이 안에서 머무를 수 있는 캠프용 트레일러를 가지고 가거나 캠핑을 가는 것이 저비용으로 휴가를 보내는 방법이 된다. 해외로 여행갈 때 당신의 호텔과 비행이 준비된 패키지로 여행을 가는 것도 또한 더 저렴하다. 당신은 하숙인을 받아서 밤을 보낼 방과 다음날 아침식사를 제공해 주는 개인 주택인 〈베드 앤 브렉퍼스트〉에서 머무를 수도 있다. 비록 미국에서는 호텔보다 더 비싸지만, 영국에서는 이것이 대개 호텔보다 더 저렴하다. 즉, 몇몇 사람들은 휴가용 주택을 부분적으로 구입해 매해 일정한 시간 동안 그것을 사용할 수 있다.

23 윗글의 제목은 무엇인가?

① 사람들이 휴가 때 머무르는 장소
② 휴가 때 인기 있는 오락
③ 사람들이 휴가를 떠나는 시간
④ 사람들이 휴가 때 하는 일

어구 go on holidays 휴가를 가다 camper 캠프용 트레일러; 야영자 arrange A for B B를 위하여 A를 준비하다 take a guest 손님을 받다 a paying guest 하숙인 timeshare 휴가시설의 공동 소유[임차] that is 즉, 달리 말하자면

해설 이 글은 저렴하게 휴가를 즐길 수 있는 장소를 안내해 주고 있다. 따라서 제목 또한 사람들이 휴가 때 머무르는 장소가 적합하다.

>>> 다음 글을 읽고 문제의 답을 고르시오.

However, prevention policies must consider the role that humans play in wildfires, since, for example, only 5% of forest fires in Europe are not related to human involvement.

Wildfire prevention refers to the preemptive methods of reducing the risk of fires as well as lessening its severity and spread. (가) Effective prevention techniques allow supervising agencies to manage air quality, maintain ecological balances, protect resources, and to limit the effects of future uncontrolled fires. (나) North American firefighting policies may permit naturally-caused fires to burn to maintain their ecological role, so long as the risks of escape onto high-value areas are mitigated. (다) Sources of human-caused fire may include arson, accidental ignition, or the uncontrolled use of fire in land-clearing and agriculture such as the slash-and-burn farming in Southeast Asia. (라) Landholders with flammable investments such as orchards and tree crops may encourage neighboring landowners to reduce fire risks.

24 Choose the most appropriate place for the above passage.

① (가) ② (나)
③ (다) ④ (라)

해석 산불 예방책은 화재의 심각성과 확산뿐만 아니라 그 위험도 감소시키는 사전 조치 방법을 말한다. 효과적인 예방책을 통해 감시 기관은 공기의 질을 관리하고, 생태계의 균형을 유지하고, 자원을 보호하며, 미래에 진압되지 않을 수도 있는 화재의 결과를 제한시킨다.(미래에 화재가 발생하지 않도록 사전에 억제한다.) 북미 소방 정책은 자연 발생 화재가 중요한 지역까지 번질 위험성이 낮다면, 생태계의 역할을 유지할 수 있도록 자연 발생 화재는 방치한다. 그러나 예컨대 유럽에서는 인간과 관련되지 않은 화재는 5%가 안 되기 때문에 인간에 의해 화재가 발생하는 경우를 소방 정책은 필히 염두에 두어야 한다. 방화와 우발적인 발화, 혹은 동남아시아에서는 화전 농법과 같은 토지 개간과 농사에서 불을 자유롭게 사용하다가 발생하는 사건이 인간이 일으킨 화재 사건의 원인들로 포함된다. 과수원과 수목 농작물과 같은 가연성 외피물을 소유한 지주들은 이웃 지주들에게 화재의 위험성을 줄여 줄 수 있다.

24 윗글의 흐름으로 보아 주어진 문장이 들어갈 가장 적절한 곳은?

어구 **wildfire** 산불; (천둥이 따르지 않는) 마른번개 **preemptive** 선제의, 우선권이 있는 **arson** 방화 **slash-and-burn farming** 화전 농법 **flammable** 인화성의

해설 제시문의 내용을 미루어 보건대, 95%의 화재 사건이 인간과 관련되어 있음을 알 수 있다. 그런데 however를 통해 그 반대 내용을 가진 문장 뒤에 나와야 한다. (다) 앞에 있는 문장에서 자연 발생 화재를 방치한다고 했는데, 이 문장의 내용은 결국 '인간에 의해 야기되지 않는 화재도 있다'는 내용이 된다. 따라서 제시문과 반의 관계가 되는 것이다.

>>> 다음 글을 읽고 문제의 답을 고르시오.

What I should do everyday is take my dog for a walk. Some days we might go to the park. (1) Other days we might go to the woods and let him chase squirrels. (2) If I'm really busy, some of my roommates may keep the house clean, which I really appreciate. (3) Sometimes I feel bad because I'm unable to do this or no one else is. (4) So my dog has to spend the whole day in the house tied up in the backyard. He can't move around very much in those situations and doesn't get as much exercise as he should.

25 윗글의 흐름과 관계없는 문장을 고르시오.

① (1) ② (2)
③ (3) ④ (4)

해석 내가 매일 해야 하는 한 가지 일은 개를 산책시키는 일이다. 어느 날은 공원에 갈 수도 있을 것이고, 다른 날에는 숲에 가서 내 개가 다람쥐를 쫓게 할 수도 있을 것이다. 정말로 바쁘면 내 룸메이트 중 몇몇이 방을 깨끗이 할 수 있을 것이고, 나는 그것을 참으로 고맙게 여길 것이다. 가끔 나는 나 혹은 다른 누구도 이것을 할 수 없어서 기분이 상한다. 그래서 내 개는 뒤뜰에 매인 채 집 안에서 하루 종일 시간을 보내야 한다. 이런 상황에서 내 개는 많이 움직일 수 없어서 필요한 만큼의 운동을 하지 못한다.

어구 **woods** 숲 **chase** 추적하다, 쫓다 **squirrel** 다람쥐 **tie up** 단단히 묶다, 포장하다, 구속하다

해설 나머지 문장들은 강아지와 산책하는 일에 대한 이야기이지만, (2)만 친구들의 청소 얘기가 나오므로 틀린 문장이다.

> **보어로 쓰인 동사원형**
>
> *What* I should do everyday is (*to*) *take* my dog for a walk.
>
> → 주어가 what절일 경우 be동사의 보어는 to부정사 혹은 동사원형이 가능하다. 이때 동명사는 보어로 올 수 없다.

>>> **다음 글을 읽고 문제의 답을 고르시오.** [26~27]

Pure pursuit of objective truth has been the great ideal and the great faith of science, and it has brought us magnificent technological rewards. The difficulty is that, from Hiroshima on, the most fundamental of sciences seems to have brought some horrible and terrifying rewards as well. All at once, the morality of the science seems to have (가) run colossally afoul of the grand old morality of respect for life, just as the humane men so often predicted it would. Basic scientists have had to face the fact that nuclear weapons were actually made possible by the most basic and pure and detached studies, and that the blame could not be pushed off onto engineers and technologists, as it could be either with dynamite or the machine gun.

26 윗글의 주제는 무엇인가?

① Benefits and disasters of scientific progress
② Conflict of the morality of science with that of humanity
③ Innocence of scientists as to it use
④ Who to blame for unclear disasters?
⑤ How to prevent scientific findings from being misused?

27 (가) 'run colossally afoul of'가 의미하는 것은 무엇인가?

① been extremely at variance with
② secretly conspired with
③ minimally collided with
④ colorfully patched up
⑤ been roughly in harmony with

해석 객관적인 진리에 대한 순수한 추구는 과학의 위대한 이상과 신념이었으며, 우리에게 상당한 기술의 발전을 가져다주었다. 히로시마 이후 줄곧(히로시마 원폭 투하 이후 줄곧) 과학의 가장 기본적인 것이 또한 어떤 끔찍하며 무서운 응보를 가져온 것처럼 보이는 것이 문제이다. 갑자기 과학의 도덕성이, 인도적인 사람들이 그러할 것이라고 너무나 자주 예측하는 것처럼, 생명 존중을 위한 오랜 도덕성과 엄청나게 충돌했던 것처럼 보인다. 기초 과학자들은 핵무기가 실제로는 가장 기본적이고 순수하며 사심이 없는 연구에 의해 가능해졌다는 사실에 직면해야만 했다. 그리고 기초 과학자들은 이전에 다이너마이트나 기관총으로 그러할 수 있었던 것처럼 공학자와 기술자들에게 책임을 떠넘길 수 없다는 사실에 직면해야 했다.

26 윗글의 주제는 무엇인가?

① 과학 발전의 이익과 불행
② 과학의 도덕성과 인간의 도덕성 간의 충돌
③ 과학 이용에 대한 과학자들의 무죄
④ 이해하기 힘든 재난에 대하여 누가 책임을 질 것인가?
⑤ 과학의 발견들이 오용되지 않게끔 어떻게 할 것인가?

27 (가) 'run colossally afoul of'가 의미하는 것은 무엇인가?

① 상당한 차이가 있다   ② 은밀히 공모하다
③ 최소한의 차이가 있다   ④ 화려하게 수습하다
⑤ 대충 조화가 되다

어구 **pure** 순수한; 순결한 **objective** 객관적인; 목표 **magnificent** 상당한; 훌륭한 **reward** 응보; 보답 **horrible** 끔찍한 **terrifying** 겁나게 하는 **as well** 게다가, 또한 **all at once** 갑자기 **run afoul of** ~와 충돌하다 **colossally** 어마어마하게, 굉장히 **grand** 웅대한, 광대한, 장대한 **morality** 도덕성 **just as** ~ 마치 ~처럼 **detached** 초연한, 편견이 없는, 공평한 **blame** 책임, 죄, 허물; 비난 **push off A onto B** A를 B로 떠넘기다, 밀어 버리다 **technologist** 기사 **dynamite** 다이너마이트; 굉장한 **conflict** 충돌, 대립, 불일치 **as to** ~에 관하여 **unclear** 불분명한, 명백하지 않은, 모호한 **collide with** 충돌하다; ~과 차이가 있다 **colorfully** 화려하게 **patch up** (사건·분규를) 수습하다, 가라앉히다; 수선하다 **in harmony with** ~과 조화되어

해설 **26** 과학의 객관적 진실을 탐구한다는 순수 이상과 생명 존중의 도덕성과 모순되게 충돌하는 현상을 묘사한 글이다.

27 run afoul of는 '~과 충돌하다'는 뜻을 가지고 있다. 부사인 colossally가 '거대하게', '어마어마하게'라는 뜻이므로, extremely(극단적으로, 몹시)가 동의어 표현으로서 옳다.

>>> **다음 글을 읽고 문제의 답을 고르시오.** [28~29]

Under the present system of mass education by large classes too much stress is laid on teaching and too little on active learning. The child is not encouraged to discover things on his own account. He learns to rely on outside help, not on his own powers, thus losing intellectual independence and all capacity to judge for himself. The overtaught child is the father of the newspaper-reading, advertisement-believing, propaganda-swallowing, demagogue-led man— the man who makes modern democracy the farce it is. Moreover, lessons in class leave him mainly unoccupied, and therefore bored. He has to be coerced into learning what does not interest him, and the information acquired mechanically and reluctantly, by dint of brute repetition, is rapidly forgotten.

28 윗글에서 현행 교육제도에 대한 저자의 태도는 어떠한가?

① critical
② diffident
③ sarcastic
④ understanding
⑤ optimistic

29 윗글에 따르면, 현행 교육제도 하에서 기대할 수 없는 것은 무엇인가?

① dependence
② creativity
③ sense of balance
④ generosity
⑤ modesty

해석 대량 학급에 의한 집단 교육이 이루어지는 현재 체계 하에서는 교사의 일방적인 가르침에 중점을 두기 때문에 능동적인 학습은 부족한 편이다. 아이는 자신의 힘으로 문제 해결을 하도록 독려받지 못한다. 외부의 힘에 의존하는 법을 배울 뿐, 자신의 힘으로 배우지를 못하여 지적 독립성과 스스로 판단하는 모든 능력을 상실하게 된다. 지나치게 교육을 받은 아이는 신문을 읽고 광고를 믿고 선전 문구를 그대로 받아들이고 선동에 이끌리는 사람이 되어, 현대 민주주의를 보이는 그대로 믿어 버리는 사람이 된다. 더욱이 교실 수업은 그를 집중하지 못하게 해 버리며, 따라서 따분함을 느끼게 한다. 아이가 관심 없어 하는 것을 배우도록 강요받고 야만적인 교수법인 반복 학습을 수단으로 한 기계적이면서 마지못해 습득한 정보는 빠르게 잊혀진다.

28 윗글에서 현행 교육제도에 대한 저자의 태도는 어떠한가?

① 비평적인
② 자신 없는
③ 빈정대는
④ 이해하는
⑤ 낙관적인

29 윗글에 따르면, 현행 교육제도 하에서 기대할 수 없는 것은 무엇인가?

① 독립
② 창조성
③ 균형 감각
④ 관대함
⑤ 겸손

어구 **mass** 대량의, 대형의, 집단의 **lay stress on** ~에 강요하다 **on one's own account** ~을 위하여, ~의 셈으로 **be encouraged to R** ~하도록 격려받다 **overteach** 지나치게 많이 가르치다 **propaganda** (주의 · 신념의) 선전, (선전하는) 주의 · 주장 **demagogue** (민중) 선동자, 선동 정치가 **farce** 어릿광대극, 익살극, 익살 **unoccupied** 할 일이 없는, 한가한, (집 · 토지 따위가) 임자 없는 **be coerced into -ing** ~하도록 강요받다 **be dint of** ~을 수단으로 **brute** 야만적 **diffident** 자신이 없는, 내성적인 **sarcastic** 비꼬는 **generosity** 관대함 **modesty** 겸손, 정숙

해설 **28** 현행 교육제도 때문에 아이들의 능동적인 학습, 지적 독립성 등이 부족해진다고 했으므로, 비평적인 태도를 가지고 있다고 볼 수 있다.

29 첫 문장에서 현행 교육제도 때문에 아이들이 능동적인 학습을 할 수 없으며, 지적 독립성이 부족하다고 했는데, 이는 결국 창조적인 학습과 지적 능력이 부족해진다는 내용이다.

Unjust laws exist: shall we be content to obey them, or shall we endeavor to amend them, and obey them until we have succeeded, or shall we transgress them at once? Men generally, under such a government as this, think that they ought to wait until they have persuaded the majority to alter them. They think that, if they should resist, the remedy would be worse than the evil. But it is the fault of the government itself that the remedy is worse than the evil. It makes it worse. Why is it not more apt to anticipate and provide for reform? Why does it not cherish its wise minority? Why does it cry and resist before it is hurt? Why does it not encourage its citizens to be on the alert to point out its faults, and do better than it would have them? Why does it always crucify Christ, and excommunicate Copernicus and Luther, and pronounce Washington and Franklin rebels?

30 Which of the following is the best title of the passage?

① Reform of Unjust Laws
② Civil Obedience to the Government
③ Injustices of the Government
④ The Government's Struggle to Remove Social Evils

해석 불의한 법률이 존재한다. 그것에 복종하는 것에 만족할 것인가? 아니면 그것들을 수정하려고 노력하고, 성공할 때까지(성공적으로 수정할 때까지) 그것들을 지킬 것인가? 아니면 즉시 위반할 것인가? 그러한 정부 아래에서의 일반적인 사람들은 그것을 바꾸도록 다수를 설득할 때까지 기다려야 한다고 생각한다. 사람들은 만일 저항하면 뿔 고치려다 소 죽이는 꼴이 될 것이라고 생각한다. 그러나 뿔을 고치려다 소 죽인다는 것은 정부 자체의 잘못이다. 정부가 상황을 악화시키는 것이다. 왜 정부는 개혁을 예상하고 준비하는 경향이 더 없는 것일까? 왜 정부는 현명한 소수를 소중히 여기지 않는 것일까? 왜 정부는 피해를 입기 전에 삐걱거리며 저항하는가? 왜 정부는 시민들이 정부의 잘못을 주도면밀히 지적하라고 장려하지 못하고, 이전보다 더 국민들에게 잘하지 못하는 것일까? 왜 정부는 항상 그리스도를 십자가에 못 박으며 코페르니쿠스와 루터를 제명하고, 워싱턴과 프랭클린을 반역자들로 선언하는가?

30 이 글의 제목은 무엇인가?

① 불의한 법률의 개혁 　　② 정부에 대한 시민 불복종
③ 정부의 부정행위들 　　④ 사회의 악을 없애는 정부의 노력

어구 unjust 불공평한, 부당한　be content to R ~하는 것에 만족하다　endeavor to R ~하려고 노력하다　transgress (법률·계율 등을) 어기다, 범하다　at once 즉시　The remedy is worse than the evil. 뿔 고치려다 소 죽인다. (교각살우: 선한 의도가 치명적인 결과를 낳는다.)　be apt to R ~하는 경향이 있다　provide for ~을 준비하다　cherish 소중히 하다　be on the alert to R 경계하며 ~을 하다; 주도면밀히 ~을 하다　crucify 십자가에 못 박다; 처형하다; 괴롭히다　excommunicate 파문하다; 제명[축출]하다　pronounce A (to be) B A를 B라고 선언하다　rebel 반역자; 반역하다

해설 불의한 법률들이 많음에도 정부가 적극적으로 대처하지 못하는 내용을 부정행위로서 비판하는 내용이 이 글의 주제이다. 문제를 제기하는 의문문 및 강력한 주장을 대신 전달하는 수사 의문문을 통해 작가의 의견을 제시하고 있다. ①은 해결책을 말하는 것인데, 글의 대다수 내용이 해결책을 제시하기보다는 정부의 문제점을 지적한다고 보아야 한다.

Actual TEST 06

⇨ 본책 p.256

1 ①	2 ①	3 ②	4 ③	5 ⑤	6 ①	7 ①	8 ①	9 ⑤	10 ①
11 ③	12 ④	13 ①	14 ③	15 ①	16 ①	17 ⑤	18 ④	19 ②	20 ⑤
21 ③	22 ⑤	23 ③	24 ③	25 ①	26 ④	27 ②	28 ⑤	29 ③	30 ②

>>> 밑줄 친 곳에 들어갈 알맞은 답을 고르시오. [1~6]

1 As the reputation of books is raised, not by their freedom from defect, but by the greatness of their beauties, so should that of men be prized, not for their ___________ from fault but the size of those virtues they are possessed of.

① exemption　② bulk
③ goodness　④ hatred
⑤ butts

해석 결점이 없는 것 때문이 아닌 아름다움의 위대함 때문에 책의 평판이 높아지는 것처럼 사람들의 명성도 그와 같이 칭송되어야 한다. 즉 과실이 없다는 이유 때문이 아니고 그들이 몰두하는 미덕의 크기에 의하여 평가되어야 한다.

어구 **freedom** 면제, 해제, 전혀 없음　**freedom from defect** 결점이 없음　**be possessed of** ~에 몰두하다　**exemption** 면제, 공제　**bulk** 크기, 부피　**goodness** 덕　**hatred** 원한　**butt** 목표, 공 , 조롱의 대상

해설 not A but B 구문에 의해 '미덕의 크기'와 반대되는 의미가 필요하다.

2 Convincing arguments for participatory form of democracy were put forward by Rousseau, an eighteenth-century French philosopher. His influential political theory ___________ the direct experience of political participation.

① hinged on　② had nothing to do with
③ called off　④ kept out
⑤ made up for

해석 참여 민주주의에 대한 설득력 있는 주장은 18세기 프랑스 철학자 루소에 의해 제기되었다. 그의 영향력 있는 정치 이론은 정치 참여를 직접 경험하는 것에 달려 있었다.

어구 **convincing** 설득력 있는(assuring)　**argument** 논의, 주장　**participatory form of democracy** 참여민주주의　**put forward** 제언 · 주장하다　**influential** 영향력 있는　**hinge on** ~에 따르다, 달려 있다　**call off** 취소하다; 물러가게 하다　**keep out** 못 들어오게 하다, 막다　**make up for** ~을 벌충 · 만회하다

해설 '참여 민주주의'라는 핵심어는 두 번째 문장에서 '진술–부연'하는 형태이다.

3 The ties that bind us together in common activity are so ___________ that they can disappear at any moment.

① tentative　② tenuous
③ restrictive　④ consistent
⑤ tenacious

해석 공동 활동에서 우리를 묶어 주는 유대란 너무도 빈약해 언제라도 사라질 수 있다.

어구 **ties** 유대(관계)　**bind** 묶다　**tentative** 임시의(temporary)　**tenuous** 얇은, 가는(thin); 희박한, 박약한(weak, ethereal)　**consistent** 일관된　**tenacious** 완강한(persistent)

해설 so ~ that 구문에 의해 '사라지게 한다'는 원인을 택해야 한다.

4 By a strange combination of generosity and greed man protects the weak in asylums and kills the strong in wars. By a strange combination of ingenuity and impotence he multiplies the basic necessities of life far beyond any possible need only to let millions ___________ and unclothed for lack of efficient distribution.

① fall behind　② find shelter
③ go hungry　④ get angry
⑤ be happy

해석 관대함과 탐욕의 이상한 결합으로 인간은 보호시설의 약자를 돕고 전쟁의 강자를 죽인다. 현명함과 무능함의 이상한 결합으로 인간은 가능한 한 필요한 것 이상으로 생활용품을 대량으로 생산하여 효율적인 배분의 부족 때문에 결국에는 수백만의 사람들을 굶주리고 헐벗게 하고 있다.

어구 **combination** 결합　**generosity** 관대　**greed** 탐욕　**asylum** 보호시설, 수용소　**ingenuity** 현명함, 정교함　**impotence** 무능함　**multiply** 증가 · 증식시키다, 대량 생산하다　**unclothed** 발가벗겨진, 밝혀진　**distribution** 분배, 분류　**fall behind** 뒤처지다　**shelter** 피난 장소　**go hungry** 배고파지다

해설 '순접–열거'를 가리키는 접속사 and에 의해서 unclothed와 순접 내용을 가리키는 '굶주리다'가 옳다.

5 The field of American studies began as an amalgam of history and literature during the pre-World War II period. In the post-war period, it gradually incorporated studies of the arts and material culture, expanding later on to encompass popular culture and media, and growing still further with studies that focused on issues of race, ethnicity, and gender. By the end of the 20th century, American studies had also incorporated comparative studies of Canada and Latin America. Indeed a transnational, global perspective on American culture has become one of the leading currents in the filed as we begin the 21st century. Now most scholars agree that the field of American studies ____________, encompassing a wide range of disciplines that, in one way or another, are trying to describe the cultures of the United States.

① began to militate against pluraltiy
② has a shared basis with gender studies
③ is not countenanced
④ is implementing new critical methods
⑤ continues to expand

해석 미국학 분야는 2차 대전 이전에는 역사와 문학을 결합한 형태로 시작됐다. 전후 시대에 이르러 점차 예술과 물질문화에 대한 연구까지 포함하게 되었으며 이후에는 대중문화와 대중매체까지 아우르게 되었다. 이후로도 팽창을 거듭한 미국학 연구는 인종, 민족성, 성에 초점을 둔 연구까지 포괄하게 된다. 20세기 말에는 캐나다, 라틴 아메리카와의 비교 연구까지도 다루게 되었다. 21세기에 들어서면서는 미국 문화를 다국적이고도 광범위한 관점에서 보는 것이 하나의 주도적인 흐름이 되었다. 현재 대부분의 학자들은 미국학 연구가 여러 방식으로 미국 문화를 묘사하려는 넓은 범위의 학문 분야를 포함해 계속 팽창하고 있다는 데 의견을 같이 한다.

어구 **amalgam** 혼합물 **encompass** 망라하다 **ethnicity** 민족성 **transnational** 국적을 초월한, 다국적의 **discipline** 수양, 처벌, 학과; 훈련하다, 징벌을 내리다 **militate** 작용하다, 영향을 미치다 **plurality** 복수, 복수성 **countenance** 지지 · 후원하다(prop up)

해설 〈순접─진술부연〉 encompassing a wide range of discipline

---

6 It is an oft-told story, but it does not get any less horrific on repetition. Fifteen years ago, a pedophile enticed seven-year-old Megan Kanka into his home in New Jersey by offering to show her a puppy. He then raped her, killed her and dumped her body in a nearby park. The murderer, who had recently moved into the house across the street from his victim, had twice before been convicted of sexually assaulting a child. Yet Megan's parents had no idea of this. Had they known he was a sex offender, ____________.

① they would have told their daughter to stay away from him
② they would have ordered their daughter to fight him
③ they would have made their daughter make friends with him
④ they would have let the police catch him

해석 자주 언급되는 사건이지만 여러 번 듣는다고 해서 그 끔찍함이 줄어들지는 않는다. 15년 전, 어떤 소아 성욕자가 7살의 메건 칸카를 강아지로 유인하면서 뉴저지에 있는 자기의 집으로 끌어들였다. 그는 아이를 강간한 후 살해하고 그 시체를 근처의 공원에 유기했다. 이 살인자는 최근에 희생자의 집 건너편으로 이사했었는데, 그 전에 아이들을 두 번이나 성폭행한 혐의로 유죄 판결을 받은 적이 있었다. 그러나 메건의 부모들은 이에 대해 전혀 알지 못했다. 만약 그들이 그가 성범죄자였다는 사실을 알았더라면 그를 가까이 하지 말라고 딸에게 말해 두었을 것이다.

6 ① 그들은 딸에게 그와 가까이 하지 말라고 말했을 것이다.
② 그들은 딸에게 그와 싸우도록 명령했을 것이다.
③ 그들은 딸에게 그와 친구가 되라고 시켰을 것이다.
④ 그들은 경찰이 그를 체포하도록 내버려 두었을 것이다.

어구 **oft-told** 자주 언급되는 **horrific** 끔찍한 **pedophile** 어린이에 대한 이상 성욕자 **entice** 유혹하다 **offer to R** ～하겠다고 말하다 **dump** 버리다, 유기하다 **be convicted of** ～의 유죄 판결을 받다 **assault** (여성에 대하여) 폭행[강간]하다, 습격하다 **stay away from** ～와 멀리하다, ～와 떨어져 있다, ～에 간섭하지 않다

해설 마지막 문장 Had they known he was～는 가정법 과거완료 구문으로서, 그가 이전에 두 번의 아동성범죄 유죄 판결을 받았다는 사실을 알았다면 아이에게 그 사람과 멀리하라고 했을 것이다. ④ 이전에 유죄 판결을 받았다는 이유만으로 별다른 범죄를 저지르지 않은 사람을 또다시 체포할 수는 없으므로 틀린 논리이다.

There is nothing so degrading as the constant anxiety about one's livelihood. I have nothing but contempt for people who despise money. They are hypocrites or fools. Money is like a sixth sense without which you cannot make complete use of the other five. Without an adequate income half the possibilities of life are shut off. The only thing to be careful about is that (가) you do not spend more than a shilling for the shilling you earn. You will hear people say that poverty is the best spur to the artist. Such people have never felt the iron of ① it in their flesh. They do not know how mean ② it makes you. ③ it exposes you to endless humiliation. ④ It is what cuts your wings, and eats into your soul like a cancer. ⑤ It is not wealth one asks for, but just enough to preserve one's dignity, to work unhampered, to be generous, frank, and independent. I pity with all my heart the artist, whether he writes or paints, who is entirely dependent upon his art for subsistence.

7 Which of the following best describes the author's opinion on money?

① Money is important for a decent life.
② Those who love money excessively are hypocrites.
③ Poverty stimulates the sensitivities of artists most effectively.
④ Human nobility lies in overcoming the obstacles of poverty.
⑤ Most people overestimate the power of money in the modern world.

8 Which of the following is closest in meaning to (가)?

① you should stay within your budget
② you should not work solely for money
③ you should spend as little as possible
④ you should not despise doing labor to earn money
⑤ you should strike a balance between poverty and wealth

9 Of the five occurrences of it in ①~⑤, which does NOT refer to the same thing?

① ①   ② ②
③ ③   ④ ④
⑤ ⑤

해석 사람이 생계에 대해 늘 불안해하는 것만큼 품위가 떨어지는 일은 없다. 나는 돈을 경시하는 사람들을 경멸스러워 할 뿐이다. 그들은 위선자이거나 혹은 바보들이다. 돈은 육감과 같으며, 그것이 없다면 당신은 나머지 오감 또한 완전히 이용하지 못할 수 있다. 적절한 수입이 없다면 살면서 기대할 수 있는 가능성들의 절반가량이 차단되고 만다. 신중해야 할 유일한 것은 당신이 벌어들이는 수익 이상으로 소비할 수 없다는 점이다. 빈곤이 예술가들에게 최고의 자극 요소가 된다고 말하는 것을 많이 들었을 것이다. 그와 같은 사람들은 가난이란 족쇄를 결코 느껴 보지 못한 사람들이다. 그들은 가난이 당신을 어떻게 비굴하게 만들어 놓는지 알지 못한다. 가난은 당신을 끝없는 가난으로 접하게끔 한다. 가난은 당신의 날개를 잘라서 암처럼 당신의 영혼을 먹어 삼킨다. 가난은 당신을 끝없는 굴욕으로 내몬다. 품위를 유지하고, 구속받지 않고 일하고, 관대하고, 솔직하고, 남에게 의존하지 않는 것은 사람들이 부탁하는 부가 아니라 그저 충분한 정도이면 되는 것이다. 나는 예술가가 글을 쓰던 그림을 그리건 간에 생계를 위해서 자신의 예술에 전적으로 의존하는 예술가가 진심으로 불쌍하다고 생각한다.

7 돈에 대한 작가의 견해로서 옳은 내용은?
① 돈은 품위 있는 삶을 위해서 중요하다.
② 돈을 과다하게 사랑하는 이들은 위선자이다.
③ 가난은 예술가들의 감성을 가장 효과적으로 자극한다.
④ 인간의 존엄성은 가난이라는 방해물을 극복한다는 점에서 존재하는 것이다.
⑤ 대부분의 사람들은 현대의 세상에서 돈의 힘을 과대평가한다.

8 (가)와 의미가 가까운 것은?
① 예산을 초과하지 않고 생활을 유지해야 한다.
② 돈만을 위해 일해서는 안 된다.
③ 가능한 한 적게 소비해야 한다.
④ 돈을 벌기 위해 노력하는 것을 무시해서는 안 된다.
⑤ 가난과 부의 사이를 비교 검토해야 한다.

9 (1)~(5)의 다섯 개 지칭어 중 다른 의미를 갖고 있는 것은?

어구 **degrading** 품위를 떨어뜨리는 **livelihood** 생계 **contempt** 경멸 **despise** 경멸하다 **hypocrite** 위선자(의) **make use of** ~을 이용하다 **shut off** 차단하다 **shilling** 실링[영국의 화폐 단위] **poverty** 빈곤 **spur** 동기, 자극 **expose A to B** A를 B까지 접하게 하다, 노출시키다 **humiliation** 굴욕, 비굴함 **ask for** 요청 · 부탁하다 **dignity** 존엄, 위품, 명성 **unhampered** 제약받지 않는, 방해받지 않는 **generous** 관대한 **frank** 솔직한, 공공연한 **with all my heart** 진심으로 **subsistence** 생계 **decent** (복장 · 집 등이) 버젓한, (수입 등이) 어지간한, 예의 바른 **stimulate** 자극하다, 흥분시키다 **sensitivity** 감성, 민감도 **nobility** 고귀함, 숭고함 **obstacle** 장애(물) **overestimate** 과대평가하다 **within one's budget** 예산의 범위를 초과하지 않고서 **do labor** 노력하다, 일하다 **strike a balance** 수지를 결산하다, 비교 검토하다

해설 **7** 큰 부는 필요 없을지라도, 품위를 유지하고 구속받지 않으면서 일할 수 있고, 관대해지고 남에게 의존하지 않기 위한(수입이 어지간한) 삶을 위해서는 돈이 중요하다고 작가는 주장한다.
8 shilling은 과거 영국 화폐 단위로서, 이 문장에서는 '부, 재산'의 또 다른 상징적 표현으로 쓰였을 뿐이다. 따라서 해석 그대로 '벌어들이는 재산 이상으로 소비하지 말아야 한다.'는 내용은 결국 '예산의 범위 내에서 생활해야 한다'는 내용으로 재진술이 가능하다.
9 ①~④의 it은 모두 poverty(가난)를 가리키지만, ⑤의 it은 it is ~ that 관계대명사의 it이라는 문법적 기능만 수행할 뿐이다.

If we deduct from nationalism all that (가) it has borrowed or stolen from (나) regionalism, what remains is mostly rubbish. The nation, as distinct from the region, is largely the creation of political manipulators. Almost all nationalist movements are led by ambitious frustrated men determined to hold office. I am not blaming them. I would do the same if I were in their place and wanted power so badly. But nearly always they heavily make use of warm regional feeling, (다) the emotional dynamo of the movement, while being almost untouched by (라) it themselves. Ambition and a love of power can eat like acid into the tissues of (마) regional loyalty.

10 Among (가)~(마), which one differs from the others in its meaning or reference?

① (가) ② (나)
③ (다) ④ (라)
⑤ (마)

11 According to the passage, which of the following is true?

① There is no such thing as regionalism.
② Regionalism is an invention of power-hungry politicians.
③ Nationalism is really a feeling for one's region.
④ Nationalist movements were initiated by loyal regionalists.
⑤ Nationalism is indispensible for the development of one's region.

해석 지역주의에서 빌려왔거나 차용한 모든 것을 민족주의로부터 빼고 나면, 대체로 형편없는 것이 남는다. 지역과는 별개로서, 민족은 주로 정치를 교묘히 다루는 자들의 창작물이다. 거의 모든 민족주의 운동은 공직 자리를 차지하기 위한 불만족스러운 야심가들에 의해 주도된다. 나는 그들을 비난하지 않는다. 내가 그들의 입장에 있어서 권력을 그토록 원한다면, 나도 똑같이 그렇게 할 것이다. 그러나 그들은 민족주의 운동의 감정적인 동력인 열광적인 지역감정을 거의 언제나 지나칠 정도로 이용한다. 그 감정에 거의 영향을 받지 않으면서도 말이다. 야망과 권력에 대한 열망은 산성 물질처럼 지역 충성심의 조직을 갉아 먹을 수 있다.

10 (가)~(마) 중 언급하는 바가 다른 하나는 무엇인가?

11 이 글의 내용과 일치하는 것은 무엇인가?
① 지역주의와 같은 것은 없다.
② 지역주의는 권력을 열망하는 정치인들의 발명품이다.
③ 민족주의는 실제로 지역감정이다.
④ 민족주의 운동은 충성스러운 지역주의자들에 의해 주도된다.
⑤ 민족주의는 지역 발전에 없어서는 안 되는 것이다.

어구 deduct A from B B로부터 A를 공제하다, 빼다 nationalism 민족주의 steal A from B B로부터 A를 무단 차용하다 regionalism 지방(분권)주의 rubbish 하찮은 것, 부질없는 생각; 쓰레기 largely 대부분, 주로 manipulator 손으로 교묘히 다루는 사람; 조종자 hold office 재직하다 badly 대단히; 몹시; 서투르게 make use of ~을 이용하다 dynamo 발전기; 근면[활동]가 untouched 영향을 받지 않은, 손상되지 않은; 재해를 입지 않은 tissue (세포) 조직; 직물 -hungry ~을 열망하는 be indispensable for ~에 없어서는 안 된다

해설 10 (가)의 it은 앞서 나온 nationalism(민족주의)을 가리키는 반면, 나머지 모든 지칭어들은 지역주의를 가리키고 있다.

11 마지막에서 두 번째 문장인 But nearly always ~을 통해 '민족주의 운동은 지나칠 정도로 지역감정을 이용한다.'고 했다. 따라서 민족주의는 실제로 지역감정인 것으로 설명이 가능하다.

>>> **다음 글을 읽고 문제의 답을 고르시오.** [12~14]

Success in producing mental discipline is the chief merit of traditional higher education. I doubt whether it can be achieved except by compelling or persuading active attention to a prescribed task. It is for this reason chiefly that I do not believe methods such as Madame Montessori's applicable when the age of childhood has been passed. The essence of her method consists in giving a choice of occupations, any one of which is interesting to most children, and all of which are instructive. The child's attention is wholly spontaneous, as in play; it enjoys acquiring knowledge in this way, and does not acquire any knowledge which it does not desire. I am convinced that this is the best method of education with young children: the actual results make it almost impossible to think otherwise. But it is difficult to see how this method can lead to control of attention by the will.

12 Mental discipline of the students can successfully be achieved ___________.

① by applying Montessori's method of education
② by allowing students to choose occupations of their own will
③ by teaching students only prescribed subjects
④ by forcing students to pay heed to a prescribed task

13 Traditional higher education ___________.

① is better in producing mental discipline than Montessori's method
② is applicable only to those who are over the age of childhood
③ makes it difficult for students to have control of attention by the will
④ is based on Madame Montessori's educational method

14 According to the author, Madame Montessori's method of teaching ___________.

① will result in creating a lot of occupations
② is very strict and instructive
③ is not likely to achieve its proposed object
④ can be greatly instrumental to students' obtaining of the control of attention

해석 성공적인 정신수양을 성취하는 것이 전통 고등교육의 중요한 장점이다. 규정된 과제에 능동적으로 관심을 가지라고 강요하고 설득하는 것을 제외하고 정신수양을 성취할 수 있을지는 의심스럽다. 주로 이러한 이유 때문에 유년기가 지났을 때 몬테소리식 교육 방법과 같은 방법이 적절하다고 나는 믿지 않는다. 그녀의 교육법의 핵심은 직업의 선택을 주는 데 있다. 그 직업들 중 어느 것이라도 대부분의 아이들에게 흥미를 불어넣으며, 그 직업들 모두가 교훈적이다. 아이의 관심은 놀이에서처럼 대체로 자발적이며, 이와 같은 방식으로 지식을 습득하기를 좋아한다. 그리고 원하지 않는 지식을 어느 것이든 간에 습득하려 하지 않는다. 이것이 어린 아이들에게 가장 최고의 교육 방법이라 확신한다. 즉, 실제 결과들이 그렇지 않았을 경우를 생각하지 못하게끔 하기 때문이다. 그러나 어떻게 이 방법이 의지에 의해서 관심을 통제할 수 있는지를 이해하기는 어렵다.

12 학생들의 정신수양은 어떻게 함으로써 성공적으로 성취될 수 있는가?
① 몬테소리의 교육 방식을 적용함으로써
② 학생들이 자신들의 의지를 가지고서 일을 선택하게 해 줌으로써
③ 학생들에게 단지 규정된 주제들만 가르침으로써
④ 학생들에게 규정된 과제에만 주의를 기울이라고 강요함으로써

13 전통 고등교육은 어떠한가?
① 몬테소리식 방법보다 정신수양의 완성이 더 좋다.
② 아동 시절을 벗어난 이들에게만 단지 적용이 가능하다.
③ 의지로 관심을 통제하는 것이 학생들에게 더 힘들다.
④ 몬테소리 교육 방법에 근거를 두고 있다.

14 필자에 따르자면 몬테소리식 교육 방식은 어떠한가?
① 많은 일을 창출시켜 줄 것이다.
② 매우 엄격하며 교육적이다.
③ 계획된 목표를 성취하기 어렵다.
④ 아이들의 관심을 통제할 수 있게 하는 것에 대단히 유익할 수 있다.

어구 discipline 훈련, 수양, 징계, 학과 **mental discipline** 정신수양 **chief** 중요한, 최고의, 대장 **higher education** 고등교육 **doubt whether** ~인지 의심스럽다 **compel** 강요하다 **prescribed** 정해진, 처방된, 규정된 **chiefly** 주로, 대체로 **applicable** 적용할 수 있는, 적절한 **consist in** ~에 존재하다 **instructive** 교훈적인 **spontaneous** 자발적인, 임의적인, 무의식적인 **lead to** ~의 결과를 초래하다 **will** 의지 **pay heed to** ~에 주의를 기울이다 **strict** 엄격한 **instrumental** 도움이 되는, 쓸모 있는

해설 **12** 두 번째 문장인 '규정된 과제에 능동적으로 관심을 가지라고 강요하고 설득하는 것을 제외하고 정신수양을 성취할 수 있을지는 의심스럽다'는 내용은 결국 규정된 과제만 주의를 기울이라고 강요해야지만 정신수양을 성취할 수 있다고 필자가 확신한다는 내용이다.
13 몬테소리식 교육 방식으로는 정신수양의 완성이 힘들다고 판단했으므로, 우월 비교로 설명한 ①이 옳다. ③, ④는 결국 몬테소리에 관한 설명이므로 전통 고등교육을 물어본 질문과는 맞지 않는 내용이다.
14 몬테소리의 교육 방법은 임의적이고 자발적인 아이들에게 통하므로, 기존에 정해진 틀대로 목표를 성취시키게 하는 것은 어렵다고 할 수 있다. 또한 계획된 목표를 성취하기 수월한 공부 방식은 몬테소리식 방식이 아닌 전통 고등교육이다.

>>> 다음 글을 읽고 문제의 답을 고르시오.

a. It's obvious that people become violent when they are trying to protect someone or something.

b. When a situation is threatening, not only gang members but also average people act violently.

c. Even people who have never shown any violent tendencies might also commit a violent crime if a loved one is in danger.

d. An obvious example of this is when gang members want to protect their neighborhoods from the "invasion" of members of other gangs.

15 윗글을 문맥에 맞게 올바른 순서로 연결한 것은?

① a - d - b - c
② a - c - b - d
③ b - a - d - c
④ b - d - c - a

해석 a. 사람이 누군가 또는 무언가를 보호하려고 할 때 폭력적이 된다는 것은 명백하다.
d. 이것의 확실한 예는 갱단 멤버들이 다른 갱단 멤버의 침입으로부터 그들의 지역을 보호하길 원할 때이다.
b. 상황이 위협적일 때, 갱단의 멤버뿐 아니라 보통의 사람들도 폭력적으로 행동할 수 있다.
c. 심지어 폭력적인 성향을 조금도 보이지 않았던 사람이라도 만약 사랑하는 사람이 위험에 처하게 된다면 폭력적인 범행을 저지를 수 있다.

어구 **obvious** 명백한 **violent** 격렬한, 폭력적인 **tendency** 경향, 성향 **invasion** 침입, 침범

해설 a는 대전제이다. 예시를 들기 시작하는 d가 그 다음에 와야 하며, 그 예시에 이어져 상황이 위협적일 때, 일반 사람들까지 폭력적으로 변할 수 있다는 것을 구체적으로 설명한 b와 c가 이어져야 한다.

>>> 다음 글을 읽고 문제의 답을 고르시오.

[I] Soon after I arrived, I sat on my sunglasses and broke them.

[II] But my worst moments came when I decided to climb up to the high diving tower.

[III] Yesterday at the swimming pool everything seemed to go wrong.

[IV] Later my bathing suit caught on the rough edge of a chair, tearing a hole in the side of the suit.

16 위 문장들을 문맥에 맞도록 가장 잘 배열한 것은?

① [III]-[I]-[II]-[IV]
② [III]-[I]-[IV]-[II]
③ [I]-[IV]-[III]-[II]
④ [I]-[IV]-[II]-[III]

해석 [III] 어제 수영장에서는 모든 것이 엉망이 되었다.
[I] 도착 직후 난 내 선글라스를 깔고 앉아 부러뜨렸다.
[II] 그러나 나의 최악의 순간은 높은 다이빙대를 오르리라 결심했을 때였다.
[IV] 나중에 내 수영복이 의자의 거친 가장자리에 걸려 구멍이 나서 찢어졌다.

어구 **go wrong** 잘못되다 **bathing suit** 수영복 **edge** 가장자리, 칼날, 장점 **tear** 찢다

해설 [III] everything seemed to go wrong이라는 가장 일반적인 사건을 설명하고, [I] 사건 도착지에서 벌어진 첫 사고를 설명한 후, [II] 최악의 사건은 본격적인 수영을 하려고 할 때 벌어진다는 시간 순서의 논리로 이어졌다. [IV] later를 통해 구체적인 사실이 설명된다.

>>> 다음 글을 읽고 문제의 답을 고르시오. [17~18]

Although Socrates did not work out precise rules for definition, he did employ what came to be known as the 'Socratic method'. To get at the true definition of some term, Socrates would engage in conversation with someone who claimed to understand the term. By careful, probing, and persistent questioning, Socrates would _____________ from his opponent all sorts of definitions and show their inadequacy, until finally a correct version was obtained. Naturally this approach tended to be unnerving and humiliating to those with whom the discussion was carried on and who confidently, sometimes arrogantly, thought they knew it all, especially then a crowd gathered around to hear the philosopher destroy their arguments.

17 밑줄 친 부분에 들어갈 가장 알맞은 것은?

① imply   ② condone
③ prevent   ④ alloy
⑤ elicit

18 윗글의 내용과 일치하는 것은?

① Socrates charmed his opponents in public debates.
② The 'Socratic method' is a kind of mind-reading procedure.
③ Socrates experienced many humiliating moments in his conversations.
④ Socrates tried to obtain true definitions of terms through conversations.
⑤ Socrates perfected the rules for definition.

해석 소크라테스가 정의를 내리기 위한 정확한 법칙을 규정하지는 않았을지라도, 그는 '소크라테스식 방법'을 사용했다. 어떤 말의 진정한 정의에 도달하기 위해 소크라테스는 그 말의 의미를 알고 있다고 주장하는 사람과 대화를 한다. 조심스럽고, 정확하게 생각하며, 집요한 질문을 함으로써, 소크라테스는 상대로부터 모든 유형의 정의들을 이끌어내어 그것들의 부적절함을 입증하여 마침내 올바른 정의가 얻어진다. 당연히 이 접근법은 철학자가 그들의 주장을 반박하는 것을 듣기 위해 군중이 운집했을 때 빛을 발하는데, 논의에 참여하는 자신감 넘치고, 모든 것을 알고 있다고 거만한 생각을 하는 사람들로 하여금 불안함과 굴욕을 느끼게 한다.

17 밑줄 친 부분에 들어갈 가장 알맞은 것은?

① 암시하다   ② 용서하다
③ 금지하다   ④ 합치하다
⑤ 이끌어내다

18 윗글의 내용과 일치하는 것은?

① 소크라테스는 공개 토론에서 상대방을 유혹했다.
② 소크라테스식 방법은 일종의 마음을 읽는 과정이다.
③ 소크라테스는 대화를 할 때 많은 굴욕적인 순간들을 경험했다.
④ 소크라테스는 대화를 통해서 용어들의 진정한 의미를 얻으려고 노력했다.
⑤ 소크라테스는 의미의 법칙을 완성했다.

어구 **work out** 이해하다, 성립하다, 총합이 ~가 되다 **be known as** ~로서 알려지다 **term** 기간, 조건, 말, 관계 **engage in** ~을 시작하다, ~에 종사하다 **claim** 주장하다, 강타하다 **probe** 정밀조사하다 **persistent** 집요한 **opponent** 적, 상대방 **inadequacy** 불충분함 **unnerving** 겁주는, 무력화시키는 **humiliating** 굴욕적인 **carry on** 계속 ~하다 **confidently** 확신하여 **arrogantly** 오만하게 **destroy** 파괴하다 **imply** 함축하다, 암시하다 **condone** 용서하다 **alloy** 합금하다, 합치다, (가치를) 떨어뜨리다 **elicit** (사실·논리 등을) 이끌어내다, 유도하다 **charm** 매혹하다; 유혹

해설 **17** 다음 문장에서 상대에게 굴욕을 느끼게 한다는 점으로 미루어 보아, 그 상대의 주장을 끌어내어 그것이 잘못됐음을 입증한다는 내용이 옳다.
18 소크라테스는 어떤 정의를 내리기 위해 상대와 대화를 한 후, 상대가 제시한 논증을 타파함으로써 올바른 정의를 얻어냈다.

>>> 다음 글을 읽고 문제의 답을 고르시오.

One of the most notable features of the Blue Mosque in Istanbul is visible from far away: its six minarets. This is very unique, as most mosques have four, two or just one minaret. According to one account, the Sultan directed his architect to make gold (altin) minarets, which was misunderstood as six (alti) minarets. Whatever the origins of the unique feature, the six minarets caused quite a scandal, as the mosque in Mecca also had six minarets. The problem was solved by adding a seventh minaret to Mecca's mosque.

해석 이스탄불에 있는 블루 모스크의 가장 두드러진 특징은 여섯 개의 첨탑이며, 이것은 멀리 떨어진 곳에서도 잘 보인다. 대부분의 사원이 네 개, 두 개, 혹은 단 한 개의 첨탑을 갖추고 있기 때문에 이는 매우 독특한 형태이다. 이야기에 따르면, 군주가 건축가에게 금 첨탑을 만들라고 명령했는데, 그 건축가는 금(altin)을 여섯 개(alti)로 잘못 이해하여 여섯 개의 첨탑을 만들었다고 한다. 이 독특한 첨탑의 기원이 어찌됐든, 이 여섯 개의 첨탑은 아주 큰 문제를 발생시켰는데, 메카의 사원도 첨탑이 여섯 개였기 때문이다. 이 문제는 메카에 일곱 번째 첨탑을 추가함으로 해결됐다.
서쪽의 주 출입구는 아름답게 꾸며져 있어서 놓쳐서는 안 될 곳이다. 그러나 이 사원의 신성함을 보존하기 위하여 비 숭배자들은(이슬람교가 아닌 사람들, 일반 관광객들) 대 예배당에서 떨어져 있는 북쪽 출입문을 사용하도록 했다. 이 문에 걸려 있는 상징적인 사슬은 말을 탄 군주를 포함한 모든 사람에게 입장하자마자 머리를 조아리도록 종용한다. 실내의 높은 천장에는 이 사원의 대중적인 이름의 기원이기도 한 2만 개의 파란색 타일이 깔려 있다.

The main, west entrance is beautifully decorated and should not be missed. However, to preserve the mosque's sanctity, non-worshippers are required to use the north entrance, off the Hippodrome. Hanging from this gate are symbolic chains that encourage everyone, even the sultan on horseback, to bow his or her head upon entering. The interior's high ceiling is lined with about 20,000 blue tiles that give the mosque its popular name.

19 윗글의 내용과 일치하지 않는 것을 고르시오.

① Only Moslems are allowed to use the west entrance.
② Both entrances have symbolic chains hung low to make people bow upon entering.
③ The decoration of the main entrance is very beautiful.
④ The minarets of the Blue Mosque are visible from far away.

19 윗글의 내용과 일치하지 않는 것을 고르시오.

① 회교 사원만이 서쪽 출입구를 이용하는 것이 허락된다.
② 양쪽 출입구 모두 사람들이 출입하자마자 고개를 숙일 수 있도록 상징적인 사슬을 낮은 곳에 매달아 놓았다.
③ 중앙 입구의 장식이 매우 아름답다.
④ 블루 모스크의 첨탑은 멀리서도 보인다.

어구 **notable** 주목할 만한 **minaret** 첨탑 **account** 이야기; 보고; 계좌 **sultan** 이슬람 국가 군주 **scandal** 추문 **sanctity** 거룩함, 신성 **hippodrome** 대경기장

해설 두 번째 단락 세 번째 문장의 hanging from this gate 표현에서 this gate는 '북문'만을 의미하므로, 북문과 서문 모두를 가리키는 both는 틀렸다.

>>> 다음 글을 읽고 문제의 답을 고르시오. [20~21]

It it possible to check or monitor all sex offenders? It seems not to be necessarily difficult to. It would not be hard to redesign America's sex laws. Instead of lumping (가)them together on the same list for life, states should assess (나)them individually and include only real threats. Instead of posting everything on the internet, names could be held by the police, who would share them only with (다)those, who need to know. Laws that bar (라)them from living in so many places should be repealed, because there is no evidence that they protect anyone: a predator can always travel. The money that a repeal saves could help pay for monitoring compulsive (마)molesters more intrusively—through ankle bracelets and the like.

In America it may take years to unpick this. However practical and just the case for reform, it must overcome political cowardice, the tabloid media and parents'understandable fears. Other countries, though, have no excuse for committing the same error. Sensible sex laws are better than vengeful ones.

해석 모든 성범죄자들을 확인하고 감시하는 것은 가능할까? 그것은 그렇게 어려워 보이지는 않는다. 미국의 성범죄법을 재구성하는 것은 어렵지 않을 것이다. 모든 성범죄자들을 평생 동일한 리스트에서 취급하지 말고, 주에서 개별적으로 평가한 후 진정으로 위협적인 인물들만을 포함시켜야 한다. 인터넷에 모든 것을 올리는 대신, 그 명단을 경찰이 갖도록 하고 그에 대해 알 필요가 있는 사람들과만 공유하도록 해야 한다. 성범죄자들로 하여금 그토록 많은 장소에서 살 수 없도록 금지하는 법률은 반드시 폐지되어야 하는데, 왜냐하면 (공격자는 언제나 이동할 수 있으므로) 그러한 법률이 누군가를 보호할 수 있다는 증거가 없기 때문이다. (이와 같은 법률들의) 폐지로 인해 절약된 자금은 강박적인 공격자들을 보다 강력하게 감시하는 비용(발목 족쇄나 그 비슷한 장치들을 이용하는)에 사용될 수 있을 것이다.

미국에서 이상과 같은 일들이 이루어지려면 수년이 걸릴지도 모른다. 그러나 개선안이 얼마나 실용적이고 공정한 것이건 간에, 이 개선안은 정치가들의 비겁함, 타블로이드 미디어 그리고 충분히 이해될 만한 부모들의 두려움을 극복해야만 한다. 그러나 다른 국가들이 똑같은 실수를 저지르는 데 있어서는 변명의 여지가 없을 것이다. 분별력 있는 성범죄법은 복수하기 위한 법보다 낫다.

20 윗글의 제목을 고르시오.
① 성범죄자에게 가혹한 성범죄 법을 집행하는 것
② 언제 어떻게 범법자들을 감시하느냐
③ 성범죄자들의 신원을 공개하는 것에 대한 불필요성
④ 성범죄자의 감시 비용에 도움을 주는 방법
⑤ 처벌을 성범죄에 적합하게 하라.

21 ①~⑤ 중 가리키는 바가 다른 것은?

20 Choose the title of the above passage.

① Enforcing Rigorous Criminal Law against a Sexual Offense
② When and How to Monitor Law Offenders
③ Unnecessity that Sexual Offenders' Identity be Opened
④ How to Help Pay for Monitoring Sexual Offenders
⑤ Make Punishment Fit the Sexual Crime.

21 Among ①~⑤, which one differs from the others?

① (가)　　② (나)
③ (다)　　④ (라)
⑤ (마)

어구 **lump together** 똑같이 취급하다　**bar A from -ing** A가 ～하지 않게 하다　**repeal** 폐지하다　**predator** 약탈자; 육식 동물　**compulsive** 강박관념에 사로잡힌, 강제적인　**molester** 치한　**bracelet** 팔찌; 수갑　**unpick** (문제를 파악하기 위하여) 조사하다, 검토하다; (솔기 · 자수 · 옷 등을) 실을 빼어 풀다　**tabloid** 요약한, 압축된; 선정적인　**vengeful** 복수심에 불타는

해설 **20** 응보주의에 입각한 형벌을 성범죄자에게 가할 것이 아니라, 성범죄의 강도에 맞추어서 그에 맞는 성범죄법으로 개정해야 한다는 것이 이 글의 주제이다.
21 (다)의 those 뒤에 who need to know 표현을 통해 (다)의 those는 피해자 가족 및 수사기관 당사자들을 가리키는 것으로 유추할 수 있다. 나머지 지칭어는 모두 성범죄자들을 가리킨다.

>>> 다음 글을 읽고 문제의 답을 고르시오. [22~23]

> Suppose you saw somebody being shown a pair of cards. On one of them there is a line, and on the other three lines. Of these three, one is obviously longer than the line on the other card, one is shorter, and one the same length. These cards will be shown to a person and he will be asked to point to the line on the second card which is the same length as the one on the first. The victim, having agreed to this seemingly innocent request, is jointed by about half a dozen people and the experimenter seated in a room. Unknown to our victim, none of the other people in the room is a volunteer like himself; they are all in league with the experimenter. A pair of cards, like those I have described, is introduced; and everyone in turn is asked which of the three lines on the second card is equal to the line on the first. They all, without hesitation, pick—as they have been told to pick—the same wrong line. Last of all comes the turn of our volunteer. In many cases the volunteer, (가) ______, denies the plain evidence of his senses, and agrees.

22 Which of the following would be the best title for this passage?

① Distorted Vision under Pressure
② Length Discrimination
③ The Effect of Anonymity
④ Unreliable Experimental Results
⑤ The Pressure to Conform

23 Which of the following best fits into (가)?

① pretending to be smart
② tired of false judgment
③ faced with this unanimity
④ forgetting the purpose of the experiment
⑤ embarrassed by the number of cards

해석 여러분이 누군가에게 한 벌의 카드를 보여 준다고 가정해 보자. 한 카드에 선이 하나가 있고, 다른 카드엔 선이 세 개가 있다. 세 개의 선 중 하나는 다른 카드의 선보다 분명히 더 길고, 하나는 더 짧고, 하나는 똑같은 길이이다. 이 카드들은 한 사람에게 보여 줄 것이고, 그는 두 번째 카드에서 첫 번째 카드에 있는 선과 똑같은 길이의 선을 골라 보라고 요청받을 것이다. 이런 외관상 단순해 보이는 요구에 동의한 희생자는 방에 앉아 있는 약 여섯 명의 사람들 및 실험자와 실험에 합류한다. 희생자에게는 알려지지 않았지만, 방 안의 다른 사람들 어느 누구도 그처럼 자원한 사람은 없다. 그들은 모두 실험자와 한 패이다. 내가 설명했던 것과 같은 두 장의 카드가 제시되며, 모든 사람들이 차례대로 두 번째 카드에 있는 세 개의 선들 중에서 무엇이 첫 번째 카드에 있는 선과 동일한지 골라 보라는 요구를 받는다. 고르라고 미리 명령받은 대로, 그들 모두 주저하지 않고 똑같이 틀린 선을 고른다. 마지막으로 자원자의 차례가 온다. 대부분의 경우 자원자들은 이러한 만장일치 의견을 보면, 자신의 감각에 입각한 명백한 증거를 부정하고 그들의 생각에 동의한다.

22 이 글의 주제는 무엇인가?
① 길이 측정의 기준　　② 선입견의 가치
③ 익명의 효과　　④ 신뢰할 수 없는 실험의 결과
⑤ 순응하라는 압박

23 (가)에 가장 알맞은 것은?
① 똑똑한 척 하며　　② 잘못된 판단에 지쳐서
③ 만장일치에 직면하여　　④ 실험의 결과를 잊어버리며
⑤ 카드의 숫자에 당황하여

어구 **point to** ～을 가리키다　**victim** 희생자　**seemingly** 외관상; 겉으로 보기에　**innocent** 순진한　**unknown to** ～에게 알려지지 않은　**be all in league with** ～과 한 패이다; ～와 결탁하다　**in turn** 차례대로　**plain** 명백한; 솔직한; 검소한; 평평한; 예쁘지 않은　**distorted vision** 난시　**under pressure** 짓눌리어　**discrimination** 구별; 차별　**anonymity** 익명; 무명

해설 **22** 마지막 문장이 주제문으로서, 매우 단순한 과정을 거치게 되면 자신의 감각의 올바른 판단조차도 오류가 날 수 있다는 내용이 주제이다. 즉, 올바른 판단을 하고 있어도 잘못된 다른 판단을 따르게 된다는 것이다.

23 카드의 선을 고르는 것은 상당히 쉬운 일이다. 그러나 자신을 제외한 나머지 모든 사람들이 결탁하여 다른 선을 고르는 것을 보고 자신도 똑같이 그 선을 선택한 것이다. 따라서 자신을 제외한 나머지 모든 사람의 만장일치에 직면하여 잘못된 판단을 했다는 논리가 옳다.

>>> **다음 글을 읽고 문제의 답을 고르시오.** [24~26]

The theater is one of the richest art forms around. The excitement of opening night can be felt by the people waiting to watch a performance, and by the performance and workers backstage waiting for the curtain to go up. Live theater is thrilling for that reason—no one really knows how well it will go until the play is performed live.

Many people collaborate to bring a play to life. There are playwrights, directors, set designers, costumers, lighting technicians, and, of course, the actors. If the play is a musical, the skills of a songwriter, choreographer, and musicians are also required. The word theater comes from the Greek "theatron", which means "a place for seeing". Although most people think of the theater in terms of a play performed on the stage, theater has taken on much more meaning in the modern world. Theater may come to life on a street corner, or in a classroom. Theater is an art form that changes as it is interpreted in different ways by different people. That is probably why the works of the greatest playwright of all time, William Shakespeare, are still performed and enjoyed today, both in classic and new interpretations.

24 The best title of the passage might be

___________.

① Shakespeare and Theater
② Modern Theater: Adventures in Acting
③ The Excitement of the Theater
④ History of Theatrical Productions

25 According to the above passage, the primary reason that theater is so exciting is that

___________.

① it is performed live
② it is musical
③ it derives from Greek
④ there are so many people waiting for it

26 The author's attitude toward theater can best be described as ___________.

① objective ② apathetic
③ neutral ④ admiring

해석 연극은 주변에서 가장 풍요로운 예술 형태 중 하나이다. 공연이 개최되는 밤의 열기는 이를 보기 위해 기다리는 사람들, 커튼이 올라가기를 기다리는 무대 뒤 스텝들에 의해 느껴질 수 있다. 라이브 공연 극장은 이러한 이유 때문에 스릴이 있으며, 누구도 연극이 라이브로 공연될 때까지 연극이 얼마나 잘 진행될지 알지 못한다.

많은 사람들은 연극에 활력을 불어넣기 위해 공동으로 작업한다. 극작가, 연출가, 무대 디자이너, 의상업자, 조명 기술자와 그리고 물론 배우들이 있다. 만일 연극이 뮤지컬이라면 작사·작곡가, 안무가와 음악가들의 기술이 또한 요구 된다. 극장이라는 단어는 그리스 단어인 "theatron"에서 유래했으며, 그것은 "보기 위한 장소"라는 의미를 가지고 있다. 대부분의 사람들은 무대에서 행해지는 연극의 관점에서 극장을 생각할지라도, 극장은 현대 세상에서 훨씬 더 많은 의미를 띄고 있다. 연극은 거리의 구석에서도 출현할 수 있으며, 또는 교실 안에서도 가능하다. 연극은 여러 사람에 의해 여러 방식으로 해석이 되듯이 변화하는 예술 형태이다. 그리하여 아마도 모든 시대를 통틀어서 가장 위대한 극작가인 윌리엄 셰익스피어의 작품들이 전통적인 해석과 새로운 해석의 두 가지 방법으로 오늘날에도 여전히 공연하고 즐기는 것이다.

24 가장 적절한 제목을 고르시오.

① 셰익스피어와 극장
② 현대 연극: 연기의 뜻하지 않은 경험들
③ 연극에 대한 흥분
④ 연극 작품의 역사

25 연극이 흥분감을 전하게 되는 주된 이유는 무엇인가?

① 연극이 생생하게 공연이 되어서
② 연극이 음악적 성향을 가지고 있어서
③ 그리스에서 유래해서
④ 연극을 기다리는 너무나 많은 사람들이 있어서

26 연극에 대한 필자의 태도는?

① 객관적인 ② 냉담한
③ 중립적인 ④ 찬미하는

어구 **backstage** 무대 뒤에서; 무대 뒤의 **go up** 올라가다, 증가하다, 폭발하다 **thrilling** 스릴 있는 **live** 살아 있는, 생생한, 아직 폭발하지 않은 **go** 진행되다 **collaborate** 협력하다 **bring A to life** A를 소생시키다, 활기를 띄게 하다 **playwright** 각본가, 극작가 **set designer** 무대 디자이너 **lighting technician** 조명 기술자 **songwriter** 작사·작곡가 **come from** 유래하다, ~ 출신이다 **in terms of** ~의 관점에서 **take on** (성질을) 띠다(assume), 고용하다, 떠맡다 **interpretation** 해석

해설 **24** 이 글은 연극이 사람들에게 불어넣은 연극의 매력과 장점을 서술한 글이다.
25 첫 단락 마지막 문장에서 언급되었듯이 '연극이 생생하게' 공연이 되기 때문이다.
26 연극은 가장 풍요롭다고 첫 문장에서 언급됐으며, 필자는 연극에 대해 '흥분, 즐김'과 같은 표현을 자주 썼다. 따라서 필자는 연극을 찬미하고 있다.

>>> 다음 글을 읽고 문제의 답을 고르시오. [27~30]

Something had to replace the threat of communism, and at last a workable substitute is at hand: multiculturalism. (가) The Jacobins of the multiculturalist movement, who are described derisively as P.C., or politically correct, are said to have launched a campus reign of terror against those who slip and innocently say "freshman" instead of "freshperson", "Indian" instead of "Native American". (나) But it's silly to mistake verbal purification for genuine social reform. (다) Even after all women are "Ms." and all people are "he or she", women will still earn only 65¢ for every dollar earned by men. (라) Minorities by any other name, such as "people of color", will still bear a hugely disproportionate burden of poverty and discrimination. (마) Disabilities are not just "different abilities" when there are not enough ramps for wheelchairs, signers for the deaf or special classes for ① the "specially"endowed. With all due respect for the new politeness, ② ________________ .

27 Where can the passage be divided into two parts?

① (가)　　　　　② (나)
③ (다)　　　　　④ (라)
⑤ (마)

28 The underlined the "specially" endowed in ① includes ___________ .

① gifted people
② distinguished scientists
③ talented artists
④ child prodigies
⑤ mentally retarded people

29 The one that is most appropriate for the blank in ② is ___________ .

① the P.C. cause of verbal inoffensiveness should be upheld
② we should keep watching the language on campus
③ action should speak louder than fashionable phrases
④ the P.C. people should be denounced
⑤ the Jacobins of the multiculturalist deserve more attention

해석 공산주의의 위협을 대체할 만한 무언가가 필요했는데, 결국 가까운 곳에서 찾은 실행 가능한 대안은 다문화주의였다. 다문화주의자 운동의 자코뱅 당원들은 '정치적으로 올바르다(차별적 편견이 없다)'고 비아냥거리듯 묘사되는데, freshperson 대신 freshman, Native American 대신 Indian이라고 무심코 말하거나, 악의 없이 말하는 사람들에 대항해 대학 구내에서 공포정치를 펼쳤다고 전해진다. 그러나 언어 정화를 진정한 사회 개혁으로 오해하는 것은 어리석은 짓이다. 심지어 모든 여성이 'Ms.'이고 모든 사람들은 'he 또는 she'가 된 이후에도, 남자가 1달러를 벌 때, 여성은 아직도 65센트밖에 벌지 못한다. '유색인'을 포함한 기타 소수 집단은 여전히 가난과 차별이라는 엄청나게 불균형적인 무거운 짐을 안고 있다. 휠체어를 위한 충분한 경사로가 없고, 청각 장애인들을 위한 수화 구사자도 없으며, '특별한' 능력을 부여받은 사람들(특이하게 타고난 장애인들)을 위한 특수 수업이 없을 때. 장애인들은 단지 '다른 능력자'가 아니다. 소수 집단에 대한 새로운 친절함(언어의 선택에 대한 예의)도 좋지만, 표면적으로 그럴듯해 보이는 말보다는 행동이 더 필요하다.

27 두 번째 단락으로 나누어지는 문장은?

28 ①"특별히 타고난" 사람들의 범주에는 누가 포함되는가?
① 타고난 재능이 있는 사람들　　② 유명한 과학자들
③ 재능 있는 예술가들　　　　　　④ 아동 천재들
⑤ 정신 지체인들

29 ②에 적절한 문장은?
① 언어적으로 불쾌감을 주지 않는 차별적 편견이 없는 사람들의 명분은 유지되어야 한다
② 우리는 학교에서 언어를 계속 관찰하여야 한다
③ 인기를 얻는 문구들보다 행동이 더 크게 외쳐져야 한다
④ 차별적 편견이 없는 사람들은 비난받아야만 한다
⑤ 다문화주의자 운동의 자코뱅 당원들은 관심을 받을 가치가 있다

30 차별적 편견이 없는 사람들이 다른 이름으로 부르기를 좋아하는 유형에 속하지 않는 그룹은 누구인가?
① 여성　　　　　　　　　② 동성애를 혐오하는 사람들
③ 소수 단체들　　　　　　④ 인디언들
⑤ 장애인들

어구 **threat** 위협　**communism** 공산주의　**at last** 마침내, 결국　**workable** 실행 가능한　**substitute** 대리인, 대체물　**be at hand** 가까이에 있다　**multiculturalism** 다문화주의　**Jacobin** 자코뱅당원(프랑스 혁명 때의 과격 공화주의자), 과격혁명가　**derisively** 조롱하듯이　**launch** 착수 · 시작하다, 발진시키다　**reign** 통치　**slip** 무심코 말하다, 미끄러지다　**innocently** 악의 없이, 순진하게　**freshman** 신입생, 신입사원　**silly** 어리석은　**mistake A for B** A를 B로 오해하다　**verbal** 말의, 말에 관한　**purification** 청결히 하기, 몸을 정화하는 의식　**genuine** 진정한, 진짜의　**minority** 소수파, 소수무리　**bear** 나르다, (몸에) 지니다.　**hugely** 대단히, 거대하게　**disproportionate** 불균형적인　**discrimination** 구별, 식별, 차별　**disability** 불구, 무능력　**ramp** 경사로　**signer** 수화자　**endowed** 타고난　**with all due respect for** ~은 지당하지만, 송구하지만　**gifted** 타고난 재능이 있는　**distinguished** 유명한, 현저한, 특출한　**talented** 재능 있는　**prodigy** 신동　**retarded** (정신 등이) 지체된　**inoffensiveness** 악의가 없는 행위, 불쾌하지 않음　**uphold** 지지하다, 떠받치다　**denounce** 비난하다, 고발하다　**homophobic** 동성애를 혐오하는　**handicapped** 신체장애가 있는

30 Who does not belong to the group that the P.C. people prefer to call by another name?

① women
② homophobic people
③ minorities
④ Indians
⑤ handicapped people

해설 **27** (가) 문장까지는 '학교 구내'의 실정을 설명하지만, (나) 문장부터 작가의 의견이 담긴 내용들이 등장하므로, 두 번째 단락의 시작은 (나) 문장이 옳다.

28 앞서 열거되는 대상들이 '휠체어가 필요한 이들', '청각 장애인들'이 등장했으므로, 마찬가지로 '장애인'인 '정신 지체인'들을 의미한다고 볼 수 있다.

29 예의를 갖춘 언어를 선택해 봤자 여전히 장애인들에 대한 편의시설 및 제도가 확보되어 있지 않으므로, 말과 반대되는 '행위 · 조치'가 우선되어야 한다는 내용을 담고 있는 ③이 옳다.

30 women은 Ms.로, minorities는 people of color로, Indians는 Native American으로, handicapped people은 different abilities로 차별적 편견이 없는 사람들은 부르지만, '동성애를 혐오하는 이들'에 대한 설명은 언급되지 않았다.

Actual TEST 07

⇒ 본책 p.268

1 ①	2 ⑤	3 ②	4 ⑤	5 ①	6 ⑤	7 ④	8 ④	9 ③	10 ④
11 ④	12 ②	13 ③	14 ④	15 ③	16 ①	17 ①	18 ④	19 ③	20 ①
21 ①	22 ②	23 ④	24 ③	25 ④	26 ③	27 ②	28 ②	29 ②	30 ⑤

>>> 밑줄 친 곳에 들어갈 알맞은 답을 고르시오. [1~5]

1 There is a class of businessmen in the US known as corporate raiders because their business is that of ___________ large corporations.

① taking over ② sneaking into
③ fooling around with ④ infiltrating
⑤ turning down

해석 미국에는 기업 사냥꾼이라고 알려진 기업가 부류가 있는데 그렇게 불리는 이유는 대기업들을 인수하는 일을 하기 때문이다.

어구 **corporate raider** 기업 인수가 **take over** 인계받다, 인수하다 **sneak** 살금살금 다가오다 **fool around with** 빈둥대며 시간을 낭비하다 **infiltrate** 침투시키다, 스며들다 **turn down** 거절하다, 각하하다

해설 기업 인수가들이 하는 일은 회사를 인수하는 일임을 통해 유추가 가능하다.

2 Many westerners find quite ___________ the Korean use of different terms of address when Koreans speak to a superior or an inferior.

① embezzled ② pedantic
③ inquisitive ④ perfunctory
⑤ bewildering

해석 한국인들이 연장자와 연하에게 말을 할 때 다른 형태의 말을 한다는 점에 대해 많은 서양인들이 당혹스러워 한다.

어구 **term** 용어, 기간, 조건 **superior** 연장자 **inferior** 연하 **embezzled** 횡령한 **pedantic** 아는 척하는, 현학적인 **inquisitive** 호기심 있는 **perfunctory** 형식적인 **bewildering** 당혹스러운

해설 나이가 많고 적음에 따라 다른 말을 사용하지 않는 서양 사람들에게는 연장자와 연하에 따라 구분하여 구사하는 한국인의 말이 당혹스러울 것이라는 점이 유추가 가능하다.

3 We won't let you work shorter hours and get more money. You can't eat your ___________ and have it, too.

① bread ② cake
③ apple ④ pudding
⑤ bread and salt

해석 우리는 당신이 더 적게 일하면서 더 많은 돈을 벌게 해 줄 수 없다. 꿩 먹고 알 먹고 할 수는 없는 노릇이다.

어구 **You can't eat your cake and have it, too.** 꿩 먹고 알 먹고 할 수는 없다.

해설 두 가지를 한 번에 다 가질 수는 없다는 논리가 적합하다.

4 We are far less ready to contemplate our own historical aberrations. Instead, we prefer to project our repressed awareness of wrongdoing on to others, as sacrificial victims or whipping boys. We are markedly reluctant to admit, and work on, our own shortcomings. ___________ is in short supply.

① Power ② Reluctance
③ Resistance ④ Persistence
⑤ Honesty

해석 우리는 우리 과거에 저질렀던 탈선 행동에 대해 생각해 볼 준비가 되어 있지 않다. 대신에 우리는 희생자를 만들거나 아이들을 때리는 잘못된 행동을 함으로 이런 억압되어 있는 의식을 투영하기를 선호한다. 우리 자신의 부족한 점들에 대해 인정하고 반응하기를 꺼려한다. 솔직함이 부족한 것이다.

어구 **be ready to R** ~할 준비가 되어 있다 **aberration** 탈선 **repressed** 억압된 **wrongdoing** 나쁜 행위, 비행 **sacrificial** 희생의 **whipping** 매를 맞는 **markedly** 분명히 **be reluctant to R** ~하기를 주저하다 **work on** 작용하다, 종사하다 **shortcoming** 결점, 단점 **in short supply** 부족한

해설 앞 문장에서 우리의 단점에 대해 인정하기를 주저한다는 내용으로 보아, 솔직함이 부족하다는 내용으로 유추가 가능하다.

5 To find their ______________ in the desert landscape during Operation Desert Storm, soldiers relied on hand-held electronic gadgets called Global Positioning System receivers, which can pinpoint a location instantly anywhere on the earth.

① bearings ② groups
③ belongings ④ orders
⑤ routines

어구 **landscape** 풍경, 방향, 조망 **Operation Desert Storm** 사막의 폭풍 작전 **rely on** 의존하다 **hand-held** 손바닥 크기의, 휴대 가능한 **gadget** 장비, 장치 **pinpoint** 위치를 정확히 가리키다 **bearing** 자신의 위치 · 입장, 태도, 관계 **belonging** 소유물, 재산 **routine** 일과, 일상의 일

해설 위성항법 장치를 통해 위치를 정확히 알려준다고 했으므로, 자신의 위치가 어느 곳인지 알기 위함이라는 내용으로 유추가 가능하다.

>>> **다음 글을 읽고 문제의 답을 고르시오.**

I. Certainly there are plans in ______________ for a response to an attack.

II. The tree-lined streets of this city wouldn't be out of ______________ in a small town.

III. Not all engineering failures take ______________ suddenly and dramatically.

6 빈칸에 공통으로 들어갈 가장 알맞은 어휘를 고르시오.

① use ② order
③ turn ④ charge
⑤ place

해석 I. 공격에 대한 반응을 위한 적절한 계획들이 분명히 있다.
II. 나무가 늘어선 도시의 거리가 작은 마을에서는 부적절하지 않을 것이다.
III. 모든 공학기술의 실패가 갑자기 그리고 극적으로 발생하는 것은 아니다.

어구 **in place** 적절한, 적소에 **out of place** 부적절한 **take place** 발생하다

>>> **다음 글을 읽고 문제의 답을 고르시오.**

A. Their democratic ideals and system of justice have spread over the world to become the foundation for the laws and government of many nations.

B. Yet no one can fully understand the modern world without knowing some English history.

C. England is a very small country, not much bigger than the state of New York.

D. The English worked out ideas of justice and obedience to law.

해석 C. 영국은 매우 작은 나라이며, 뉴욕 주보다 훨씬 크지 않다.
B. 그러나 어느 누구도 영국 역사의 일부를 알지 않고서는 현재를 완전히 이해할 수는 없다.
D. 영국인들은 이상적인 사법제도와 법률에 대한 복종을 만들어냈다.
A. 그들의 민주주의 이상과 사법제도는 세계로 뻗어나가서 많은 국가의 법과 정부의 기반이 되었다.

7 순서에 맞게 문장을 배열하시오.

어구 **system of justice** 사법제도 **foundation** 기반, 토대 **fully** 충분히, 완전히 **the English** 영국인들 **work out** 수행하다, 만들어 내다 **justice** 정의, 재판 **obedience** 복종

7 Rearrange the following sentences to make a coherent paragraph.

① A - B - C - D ② C - D - A - B
③ C - A - D - B ④ C - B - D - A
⑤ D - B - C - A

해설 C 문장에서 국가의 영토는 그리 크지 않다는 상대적 단점 뒤에 B의 yet을 통해 장점을 설명하게 된다. D 문장에서 법을 만들어 내어 A 문장에서 전 세계로 확산시켰다는 논리가 적합하다.

>>> 다음 글을 읽고 문제의 답을 고르시오.

One factor that has affected the price of gold has been the increasingly difficulty in acquiring it. Today, most of the gold left in the ground is in microscopic pieces mixed with rock. To get it, miners must dig up tons of rock to separate the gold. For one ounce of gold—a wedding ring, for example—the mine processes about 30 tons of rock. This is already a costly operation. But the missing and processing of gold is also ruinous to the environment and to the health of people living nearby. Most mines are in poor regions where the people have had little voice in whether there should be mines and how the mines should be run. Large multinational mining companies simply bought the land and opened the mines. However, as people and governments begin to realize the extent of the damage caused by the mines, the situation might change. If the mining companies ever have to pay the full environmental and social costs of mining gold, the price of gold is likely to climb higher.

8 윗글의 내용과 일치하지 않는 것은?

① The health of people in mining areas is threatened by the mines today.

② People are starting to be aware of the damages caused by the mines.

③ About 30 tons of rock has to be dug up to acquire an ounce of gold.

④ Mining companies have paid for the environmental damages they caused.

해석 금의 가격에 영향을 미친 것은 금을 얻기가 점점 힘들어진다는 점이었다. 현재 땅속에 남아 있는 대부분의 금은 큰 돌에 섞인 미세한 크기의 조각들 안에 있다. 이 약간의 금 조각을 얻기 위하여 광부들은 수천 톤의 바위를 파내고 금을 분리해야만 한다. 결혼반지를 통해 예를 들 수 있는 1온스의 금을 얻기 위해서는, 광산에서 약 30톤의 바위를 처리해야만 한다. 이것 자체가 이미 비용이 상당히 들어가는 작업이다. 그러나 또한 금의 채굴과 처리 과정은 근처 환경과 주변에 사는 사람들의 건강에 매우 해롭다. 대부분의 광산은 꼭 그 지역에 있어야만 하는지에 대한 문제와 금광이 어떻게 운영되어야 하느냐에 있어서 거의 발언권을 가지지 못하는 사람들이 사는 가난한 지역에 있다. 큰 다국적 금광 기업들은 간단히 땅을 사서 금광을 열었다. 그러나 사람들과 정부가 금광에 의한 피해 정도를 인식하기 시작하면서 상황은 변화할 것이다. 만일 광산 회사가 금광으로 인한 환경 및 사회적 비용 모두를 지불해야 한다면, 금값은 더 높아질 것이다.

8 윗글의 내용과 일치하지 않는 것은?

① 광산 지역에 사는 사람들의 건강은 현재 광산에 의해 위협을 받는다.

② 사람들은 광산에 의해 야기된 피해를 인식하기 시작하고 있다.

③ 1온스의 금을 얻기 위하여 대략 30톤의 바위가 채굴됐다.

④ 광산회사들은 자신들이 야기했던 환경 피해에 대해 비용 지불을 했다.

어구 **microscopic** 극히 작은; 현미경에 의한　**dig up** 파내다, 발굴하다　**separate** 분리하다; 떼어놓다　**mine** 광산, 채굴하다　**process** 가공 처리[저장]하다　**ruinous** 파괴적인, 파멸을 초래하는　**value** 평가하다, 값을 치다; 소중히 하다

해설 ④의 시제가 현재완료이므로 이미 지불을 했다는 의미이다. 그러나 본문 마지막에서 if절을 통해 '조건'으로 가정할 뿐이기 때문에 틀린 설명이다.

Thousands of years ago, people in Egypt preserved the bodies of their dead and wrapped them in cloth called linen. Today, these mummies can tell scientists about how the Egyptian lived. However, scientists have always had a big problem when they tried to study mummies. If they unwrapped a mummy, they would damage it. Now, scientists have a way to study mummies without unwrapping them. An X-ray machine called a CAT scanner takes pictures of mummies right through their wraps. The first mummies that scientists scanned was a female Egyptian mummy. The scanner took pictures of her from different angles. Then, a computer put all the pictures together to form a complete image.

9 Which of the following would come after the passage?

① Additional ways of unwrapping the mummy
② revenge of Egyptian mummies
③ things scientists learned by scanning
④ other machines used by scientists which study mummy

해석 수천 년 전에 이집트 사람들은 사체를 보존하여 삼베라고 일컫는 천 속에 그 사체를 감쌌다. 오늘날 이 미라들은 과학자들에게 이집트인들이 어떻게 살았는지에 대해 알려준다. 그러나 과학자들이 미라를 연구할 때에는 언제나 고생을 했다. 그들이 미라의 천을 풀려고 하면 미라가 손상을 입었다. 현재 과학자들은 미라를 풀지 않고서도 연구할 수 있는 방법을 갖추었다. CAT로 불리는 엑스레이 장비가 천을 통과하여 미라의 사진을 찍는다. 과학자들이 처음 스캔한 미라는 이집트 여성의 것이었다. 스캐너가 여러 각도로 그녀의 사진을 찍었다. 그러고 나면, 컴퓨터가 완전한 영상을 얻기 위하여 모든 사진을 합친다.

9 이 글 다음으로 나올 내용은?

① 미라를 감싸는 추가적인 방법
② 이집트 미라의 보복
③ 스캔을 통해 과학자들이 알게 된 것들
④ 미라를 연구하는 과학자들이 이용하는 다른 장비들

어구 wrap 싸다, 싸다; 포장하다   linen 아마포, 리넨, 아마사   mummy 미라; 바싹 마른 시체[물건]   have a big problem 고생하다   unwrap 포장을 풀다, (꾸러미 따위를) 끄르다, 열다   take a picture of ~의 사진을 찍다

해설 엑스레이의 스캔 기술을 통해 미라의 사진을 촬영하여 종합한 다음의 내용이 필요하므로, 이 방법을 통해 알게 되는 내용들이 후 단락의 주제로 적합하다.

Become the hero or heroine of your own story. Don't feel sad that your favorite show has ended. This city preserves the sets on which popular TV shows and movies had been shot. The beautiful landscapes captured in your favorite movies and TV shows make the romantic plots even more beautiful. Plan a trip to these shooting locations this week and book the right to become the main character of your favorite story!

10 Which of the following is the main purpose of the passage?

① to warn   ② to complain
③ to argue   ④ to advertise

해석 이야기 속 주인공이 되어 보세요. 여러분이 좋아하는 쇼가 끝났다고 해서 슬퍼하지 마세요. 이 도시는 인기 방송 프로그램이나 영화가 촬영된 곳의 세팅을 보존해 두고 있습니다. 여러분이 좋아하는 영화와 방송 프로그램에 있던 아름다운 풍경은 낭만적인 이야기를 더욱 아름답게 만들어 줍니다. 이번 주에 이 촬영 장소로 여행을 떠날 계획을 세우고, 여러분이 좋아하는 이야기의 주인공이 될 수 있는 권리를 예약하세요.

10 이 글의 목적은 무엇인가?

① 경고   ② 불평   ③ 주장   ④ 광고

어구 heroine 여주인공   capture 획득하다; 체포하다   plot 이야기; 음모   shooting location 촬영 현장

해설 방송 등에서 인기 있었던 장소를 그대로 보존하여 관광 장소로 사용하고 있는데, 그것을 광고하는 글이다.

>>> **다음 글을 읽고 문제의 답을 고르시오.** [11~18]

Iona sees a hall porter with some sacking, and decides to talk to him.

"Friend, what sort of time is it?" he asks.

"Past nine. What are you standing here for? Move on."

Iona moves on a few steps, doubles up, and abandons himself to his grief. In less than five minutes he straightens himself, holds his head up as if he felt some sharp pain, and gives a tug at the reins he can bear it no longer. "The stables", he thinks, and the little horse, as if it understood, starts off at a trot.

About an hour and a half later Iona is seated by a large dirty stove. Around the stove, on the floor, on the benches people are snoring; the air is thick and suffocatingly hot. Iona looks at the sleepers, scratches himself, and regrets having returned so early.

One of the cabdrivers half gets up, grunts sleepily, and stretches toward a bucket of water.

"Do you want a drink?" Iona asks him.

"Don't I want a drink!"

"That's so? Your good health! But listen, mate— you know, my son is dead... Did you hear? This week, in the hospital... It's a long story."

Iona looks to see what effect his words have, but sees none—the young man has hidden his face and is fast asleep again. The old man sighs and scratches his head. Just as much as the young one wants to drink, the old man wants to talk. Is it nothing to tell?

"I'll go and look after my horse", thinks Iona; "there's always time to sleep. No fear of that!"

He puts on his coat, and goes to the stables to his horse; he thinks of the corn, the hay, the weather. When he is alone, he dares not think of his son; he can speak about him to anyone, but to think of him, and picture him to himself, is unbearably painful.

"Are you tucking in?" Iona asks his horse, looking at its bright eyes, "Go on, tuck in. Though we've not earned our corn, we can eat hay."

Iona is silent for a moment, then continues:

"That's how it is, my old horse. There's no more Kuzma Ionitch. Now let's say, you had a foal, you were the foal's mother, and suddenly, let's say, that foal went and left you to live after him. It would be sad, wouldn't it?"

The little horse munches, listens, and breathes over its master's hand... Iona's feelings are too much for him, and he tells the little horse the whole story.

해석 아이오나는 자루를 갖고 있는 호텔 짐꾼을 보고서 대화를 나누려고 한다.

"여기요, 지금 몇 시나 되었죠?"라고 그가 묻는다.

"9시가 넘었어요. 여기 왜 서 계시죠? 가세요."

아이오나는 몇 걸음 지나가다가 몸을 구부리고는 비탄에 잠겼다. 5분이 채 못 지나 그는 심한 고통을 느낀 듯이 머리를 꼿꼿이 세운 뒤 더 이상 견디지 못하고는 고삐를 잡아당긴다. "마구간"이라고 그는 생각한다. 그리고 덩치가 작은 말이 마부의 마음을 알기라도 한 듯이 빨리 달려 나간다.

1시간 반 가량 지난 지금 아이오나는 크고 지저분한 난로 옆에 앉아 있다. 마루 위와 난로 주위의 긴 의자 위에서는 사람들이 코를 골고 있다. 공기가 탁하고 질식할 정도로 덥다. 아이오나는 자고 있는 사람들을 보고 몸을 긁적이고, 너무 일찍 돌아온 것을 후회한다.

마부 중 한 명이 몸을 반쯤 일으켜서 졸린 목소리로 투덜대면서 물 양동이쪽으로 팔을 뻗는다.

"물 마시고 싶니?" 아이오나가 그에게 묻는다.

"물 마시고 싶지 않아."

"그래? 자네는 건강하군. 이보게나 친구, 자네가 알듯이 내 아들이 죽었어. 들었나? 이번 주에 병원에서……. 얘기하자면 긴 이야기야."

아이오나는 자신의 말이 어떤 반응이 일어나는지 주목해 보지만 아무 반응도 없다. 그 젊은 사람은 얼굴을 파묻고서 곧 다시 깊은 잠에 빠진다. 노인은 한숨을 쉬며 머리를 긁적인다. 젊은 사람이 술을 마시고 싶은 만큼 노인은 이야기를 하고 싶다. 이야기를 해봤자 무슨 소용이 있겠어.

"가서 내 말을 돌봐야겠어."라고 아이오나는 생각한다. "잠잘 시간은 항상 있는 거야. 문제될 게 없어."

그는 옷을 입고는 마구간에 말을 보러 간다. 그는 낟알갱이와 건초와 날씨에 대해 생각한다. 혼자 있을 때면 그는 자신의 아들을 생각할 엄두가 나지 않았다. 누구에게도 아들에 대해 이야기할 수 있지만 아들을 생각하면서 마음에 그리는 것은 견딜 수 없을 만큼 괴로운 일이다.

"많이 먹고 있니?" 아이오나는 말의 빛나는 눈을 들여다보면서 말에게 물어본다. "계속 먹어. 낟알갱이는 구하지 못했지만 건초는 먹여 줄 수 있을 거야."

아이오나는 잠시 동안 말을 하지 않다가 계속 말을 한다. "내 오랜 친구야. 얘기인 즉 이런 거야. 구즈마 아이오니치는 이제 존재하지 않는다. 너는 망아지가 한 마리 있고 너는 걔의 어미지. 그런데 갑자기 걔가 구즈마와 살기 위해 네 곁을 떠나 버린 거야. 그렇다면 매우 슬플 거야. 그렇지 않니?"

작은 말은 건초를 씹어 먹으며 듣는다. 그리고 주인의 손길 위에 김을 내뿜는다. 아이노나의 감정은 자신에게 너무 벅찬 것이어서, 그는 자신의 작은 말에게 모든 이야기를 다 말하고 있는 것이다.

11 아이오나가 난로가 있는 방에 들어간 것을 가장 후회하는 이유로 적절한 것은?
① 말이 충분히 먹지를 못해서
② 자신이 있을 만한 자리가 없어서
③ 잠을 자는 이들이 그에게 불친절해서
④ 그의 이야기를 경청해 줄 사람이 없어서

12 아이오나가 마차 운전수와 만났을 때 어떠한 모습을 보였는가?
① 애국심　　　② 체념　　　③ 의심　　　④ 심술

13 이 이야기에서 어떠한 점이 아이러니컬한가?
① 마차 운전수가 물을 마시고 싶어하는 점
② 호텔 짐꾼이 아이오나에게 떠나라고 말한 점
③ 아이오나가 자신의 얘기를 말에게 한 점
④ 아이오나가 말에게 줄 음식이 바닥이 났다는 점

11 Iona most probably regrets going to the room with the stove because ____________.

① his horse has not been fed
② there is no room for him
③ the sleepers are unfriendly to him
④ there is no one who will listen to him

12 In his encounter with the cabdriver Iona shows ____________.

① patriotism
② resignation
③ suspicion
④ ill will

13 In this story it is ironic that ____________.

① the cabdriver wants a drink
② the hall porter tells Iona to move on
③ Iona tells his story to his horse
④ Iona has run out of food for his horse

14 Iona's grief is strongest when he ____________.

① is seated by the stove
② realizes that he is dying
③ speaks with the cabdrive
④ is alone

15 The author's purpose in using the present tense is most probably to ____________.

① make the story seem modern
② increase the length of the story
③ heighten the reader's sense of immediacy
④ reinforce the first person point of view

16 The title that best expresses the main idea of the passage is ____________.

① "A Father's Grief"
② "A Horse and Its Master"
③ "A Day in the Life of a Groom"
④ "A Senile Old Man"

17 Iona goes to take care of his horse. He does so most probably to ____________.

① have something to do
② show his great love for his horse
③ remove his feelings of guilt
④ prove that he does not resent the cabdriver's action

18 The tone of the passage is one of ____________.

① gaiety
② impartiality
③ destruction
④ sadness

14 아이오나의 슬픔은 언제 가장 깊어지는가?
① 난로 옆에 앉았을 때
② 자신이 죽을 것이라는 점을 깨달았을 때
③ 마차 운전수와 얘기를 나누었을 때
④ 혼자 있을 때

15 필자가 현재시제를 이용하는 목적은 아마도 무엇 때문이겠는가?
① 이야기를 현대적인 것으로 만들게끔 하기 위해
② 이야기의 길이를 늘이기 위해서
③ 독자의 현장감을 강화시키기 위해서
④ 일인칭 시점을 강화시키기 위해서

16 가장 적절한 제목을 고르시오.
① 아버지의 슬픔
② 말과 주인
③ 마부의 일생에서 하루
④ 노쇠한 사람

17 아이오나는 말을 돌보러 간다. 그 주된 목적이 무엇이겠는가?
① 무언가 해야 할 일을 구하기 위해서
② 말에 대한 깊은 사랑을 보여 주려고
③ 죄의식을 없애기 위해서
④ 마차 운전수의 행동에 대해 유감스러워하지 않는다는 점을 증명하기 위해서

18 이 글의 분위기는?
① 유쾌함
② 공평함
③ 파괴적임
④ 슬픔

어구 **porter** 운반인, 짐꾼, 사환; 운반기　**sacking** 굵은 삼베, 약탈　**double up** 몸을 굽히다　**abandon oneself to grief** 비탄에 빠지다　**straighten** 몸을 바로 하다　**give a tug at ~** ~의 끈을 잡아당기다　**rein** 고삐　**stable** 마굿간, 외양간; 안정된　**start off** 시작하다, 출발하다　**trot** 빠른 걸음, 속보　**at a trot** 빠른 걸음으로　**suffocatingly** 숨 막힐 듯이　**sleeper** 자는 사람; 잠꾸러기　**regret** ~을 후회하다, 뉘우치다; 한탄하다　**cabdriver** 마차의 마부, 택시 운전사　**grunt** ~을 툴툴거리다, 불평하다　**stretch** ~을 내뻗치다, 쭉 펴다　**hay** 건초, 꼴　**foal** 망아지　**munch** ~을 우적우적 씹어먹다　**patriotism** 애국심　**resignation** 체념, 포기, 단념　**immediacy** 직접, 즉시　**reinforce** ~을 강화하다　**groom** 마부, 신랑　**senile** 노쇠한, 노망난; 고령의　**resent** ~을 분개하다, 원망하다

해설 11 난로가 있는 방에서 어떤 사람에게 자신의 아들이 죽은 얘기를 해도 들은 척하지 않자 말이 있는 마구간으로 갔다. 따라서 자신의 아들 이야기를 들어줄 사람이 없어서 후회했다고 유추할 수 있다.
12 Iona moves on a few steps, doubles up, and abandons himself to his grief. 문장을 통해서 체념을 보였음을 알 수 있다.
13 이야기를 해도 알아듣지 못할 말에게 자신의 상심을 털어놓은 점이 아이러니하다고 볼 수 있다.
14 When he is alone, he dares not think of his son 문장을 통해서 혼자 있을 때 슬픔이 깊어짐을 알 수 있다.
15 문학 작품에서 현재시제를 사용하는 주된 이유는 독자로 하여금 공간이나 시간, 관계 등이 가깝고 직접적인 느낌을 갖게 하기 위해서이다.
16 죽은 아들을 잊지 못하고 비통해하는 아버지의 슬픔을 다룬 내용이 주제가 된다.
17 죽은 아들에 대한 슬픔 때문에 무언가라도 하면서 잊기 위해서 무작정 말에게 간 것이므로, (막연히) 해야 할 무언가를 찾기 위해서 말에게 갔다고 볼 수 있다.
18 아들의 죽음에 대해 슬퍼하는 아버지의 상심을 다루었으므로 슬픈 분위기이다.

>>> 다음 글을 읽고 문제의 답을 고르시오. [19~20]

Writing these novels helped prepare Melville for Moby-Dick(1851), perhaps the greatest novel of American literature. Equally important was the encouragement Hawthorne gave Melville while he was writing it. From the beginning, it is clear that the voyage of the whaling ship Pequod will be a symbolic voyage. It is also clear that Moby-Dick, the great white whale, represents God or fate, _______________ Melville gives the reader a great deal of factual information about whale-hunting in order to make the world of Moby-Dick seem real. Captain Ahab, the central character, is "a grand, ungodly, God-like man". He is torn between his humanity and his desire to destroy the white whale. These two sides—the light and the dark—fight each other in Ahab. The dark side wins. To Ahab, Moby-Dick is part of a "universal mystery" which he hates, because he cannot understand it. When Ahab finds the whale and attacks him, his ship is destroyed. Ahab himself is pulled down into the sea to his death. Melville seems to say that personal identity is only an illusion.

19 **Choose the main idea of the above passage.**

① Men cannot hold sway Nature.
② Men cannot defy God.
③ Evil cannot help repelling good.
④ It is vain that he himself judges his identity.
⑤ Good and evil are inevitably opposite.

20 **Which one is most appropriate for the blank?**

① whereas
② otherwise
③ for
④ as though
⑤ meanwhile

해석 이 소설들을 쓴 것은 멜빌이 아마도 미국 문학 상 가장 위대한 소설인 '모비 딕(1851)'을 준비하는 데 도움이 되었다. 멜빌이 이 소설을 쓰는 동안에 호손이 해 준 격려 또한 중요했다. 처음부터 포경선 피쿼드의 항해가 상징적인 항해가 될 것이라는 점은 분명하다. '모비 딕'의 세계를 사실적으로 보이게 하기 위해서 멜빌이 독자에게 고래 사냥에 관한 많은 사실적인 정보를 제공하고 있지만, 큰 백고래인 모비 딕이 신이나 운명을 상징한다는 것도 분명하다. 중심인물인 아합 선장은 '위엄 있고 신을 믿지 않는 신 같은 인간'이다. 그는 그의 인간미와 백고래를 죽이고자 하는 욕망 사이에서 분열된다. 아합의 내면에서는 밝고 어두운 이 두 면이 서로 충돌하는데 결국 어두운 면이 이긴다. 아합에게 모비 딕은 그가 이해할 수 없는 존재이므로 증오할 수밖에 없는 "세계의 신비"이다. 아합이 그 백고래를 발견하여 공격할 때 그의 배는 파선되며 아합 자신도 바다 속으로 끌려 들어가 죽는다. 개인 스스로 가지는 주체성은 환상에 불과하다.

19 **가장 적절한 제목을 고르시오.**

① 인간은 자연을 지배할 수 없다.
② 인간은 신에게 저항할 수 없다.
③ 악은 선을 물리치지 않을 수 없다.
④ 인간 스스로 자신의 자아를 판단하는 것은 헛된 일이다.
⑤ 선과 악은 어쩔 수 없이 상반되는 존재이다.

20 **빈칸에 알맞은 것은?**

① ~임에 반해
② 그러하지 않다면
③ ~이기 때문에
④ 마치 ~처럼
⑤ 반면에

어구 **whaling ship** 포경선 **symbolic** 상징적인 **grand** 거대한 **ungodly** 신앙심이 없는 **god-like** 신과 같은 **tear** 찢다, 눈물을 흘리다; 눈물, 찢어진 곳 **identity** 정체, 동일함 **cannot help -ing** ~하지 않을 수 없다 **vain** 헛된 **hold sway** 지배하다 **defy** 도전하다 **inevitably** 불가피하게 **as though** 마치 ~처럼

해설 **19** 마지막 문장이 주제문으로서, '개인의 주체성을 스스로 판단한다'는 것은 허망한 것임을 나타낸다. 신이나 고래, 자연 등은 이 주제를 설명하기 위해 등장하는 도구들이다.
20 that절 안에서 완전한 문장을 이을 수 있으려면 빈칸에 접속사가 와야 한다. 고래 사냥에 관한 많은 정보를 제공하면서, 반면에 그 고래는 신이나 운명을 상징한다는 것은 역접의 관계이다. 또한 완전한 문장을 이끌 접속사가 필요하므로 '역접-양보'의 whereas가 옳다.

The word "hacker" is widely misused. Among hackers themselves, it refers to someone who enjoys tinkering with technology, exploring its boundaries and getting it to do unexpected or unintended tricks, though in general use the word refers to individuals who break into computers for nefarious ends (for whom hackers prefer the terms "malicious hacker" or "cracker"). But a hacker is not necessarily bad and is not necessarily just someone who messes around with computers. Thomas Edison was arguably a hacker, back in the 19th century. Today's technological tinkerers, however, have a far wider range of household gizmos to play with and modify, from cars to cameras. Getting them to do new things, and not merely what the manufacturer had in mind, is an increasingly popular pastime. It even has its own magazine, MAKE, which is filled with projects for the technologically intrepid.

21 Choose the best topic of the above passage.

① Misapplication of the term hacker
② The comparison between a hacker of the past and a hacker of the present
③ The ends of contemporary hackers
④ The household goods which is made by hackers
⑤ How hackers break to pieces household goods

22 According to the passage, which of the following statements is true?

① Thomas Edison was a malicious hacker.
② Hackers are individuals that not only break computers but rebuild other equipment as well.
③ The magazine, MAKE, lets persons know the information that they can illegally rebuild various machines.
④ The hackers of the past is not much similar to those of the present.
⑤ Hackers resort to tricks within the limits of possible supposition.

해석 hacker라는 단어는 널리 오용되고 있다. 해커 사이에서는 그 해커란 단어가 기술력으로 어설프게 만지작거리고, 다양한 기술의 영역들을 탐구하며 갑작스럽고 의도되지 않은 함정을 파는 것을 즐기는 사람을 가리킨다. 비록 일반적으로는 그 해커란 단어가 사악한 목적을 가지고서 컴퓨터를 망가뜨리는 자를 가리킬지라도 말이다. (해커들은 사악한 해커 혹은 거짓말쟁이라고 불리우는 것을 좋아한다). 그러나 해커가 꼭 나쁘거나 컴퓨터를 가지고 허송세월을 보내는 것만은 아니다. 19세기로 돌아가 보면 토마스 에디슨도 틀림없이 해커였다. 그러나 오늘날의 기술공들은 자동차에서 카메라에 이르기까지 만지작거리며 개조를 할 수 있는 가정용 장비들을 갖고 있다. 일반 제품의 제작업체들이 의도했던 바는 아닐지라도 이들을 새로운 것으로 개조하는 것은 점차 인기있는 오락거리가 되고 있다. 이 분야에 관한 MAKE라는 잡지도 있는데, 이는 과학적으로 도전적인 것들을 위한 계획들로 가득 차 있다.

21 가장 적절한 제목을 고르시오.

① 해커라는 단어의 오용
② 과거의 해커와 현재의 해커의 비교
③ 현재 시대 해커들의 목표
④ 해커들이 만드는 가정용 장비들
⑤ 해커들이 가정용 장비들을 망가뜨리는 방법

22 이 글의 내용과 일치하는 것은?

① 토마스 에디슨은 사악한 해커이다.
② 해커들은 컴퓨터를 망가뜨릴 뿐만 아니라 다른 장비들도 개조하는 이들을 말한다.
③ MAKE라는 잡지는 사람들로 하여금 불법적으로 여러 기계들을 개조할 수 있는 정보를 알 수 있게끔 한다.
④ 과거의 해커는 현재의 해커와 매우 유사하지는 않다.
⑤ 해커는 추측이 가능한 범위 내의 함정을 이용한다.

어구 misuse 오용하다, 남용하다 tinker ~을 (서투르게) 수선하다, 개조하다 unexpected 예기치 못한 unintended 의도하지 않은 in general 일반적으로 nefarious 사악한 malicious 사악한 cracker 거짓말쟁이 mess around with ~와 빈둥거리다, 시간을 허송하다, ~을 가지고 놀다 household gizmo 가정용 장비 pastime 오락거리 intrepid 용감한 misapplication 오용, 남용 break to pieces 부수다, 파손하다 malicious 사악한 rebuild 재건하다, 개조하다 resort to 의지하다, 호소하다 supposition 상상, 가설

해설 21 이 글은 hacker란 단어를 잘못 쓰고 있다는 것이 주제이다. 이하에서 그 예로 실제 hacker들은 컴퓨터들을 망가뜨리는 사람들만이 아니라 과거에도 단순히 장비를 바꾸거나, 현시대에서도 가정용 장비를 개조하는 이들을 가리켜 hacker라고 설명함으로써, 그 범위를 확장시키고 있다.

22 이 글은 hacker라는 단어를 쓸 수 있는 사람들의 범위를 확장시키고 있다. 따라서 hacker는 통념상 컴퓨터를 망가뜨리는 사람들일 뿐만 아니라 일반 제품을 개조하는 이들을 가리킨다.

>>> 다음 글을 읽고 문제의 답을 고르시오. [23~24]

The way we parent our children is undergoing a rapid and profound transformation. Where once mothers did virtually all the caring, today there is greater sharing of that task by dads. Typically, where a mother is working outside the home, fathers now do a third of parental childcare—an eightfold increase in a generation for fathers of pre-school children, according to the Equal Opportunities Commission. This revolution from one-parent to two-parent care in the UK is a direct consequence of women taking a greater role in the workplace and the falling away of gendered roles in our society. These social changes pose important questions. If fathers are now looking after children—including small babies—for lengthy periods of time, fathers need the same skills and knowledge that we have traditionally expected mothers to have. And this means services which support parents should ① _______________ to support fathers as well as mothers. The task now for these family services is to modernize—to support other significant carers in the family, notably fathers, who have, or want to have, a more active role in day-to-day care of their children.

23 Choose the statement that the above passage does not say or imply.

① Nowadays in the UK fathers' participation in childcare has greatly increased.

② The revolution from one-parent to two-parent care is taking place in the UK.

③ Fathers nowadays have, or want to have, a more active role in day-to-day care of their children.

④ All fathers in the UK should play a more active role in day-to-day care of their children.

⑤ Once mothers did virtually all the parental childcare.

24 Choose the most appropriate expression for the underlined blank ①.

① satisfy
② enlighten
③ be geared up
④ be helped
⑤ be focus

해석 우리가 아이들을 양육하는 방법은 빠르고 엄청난 변화를 겪고 있다. 이전에는 어머니들이 거의 모든 양육을 했었지만, 오늘날에는 아버지들의 역할 분담이 커졌다. 일반적으로 어머니가 집 밖에서 일을 하던 곳에서 현재 아버지들은 자녀 양육의 1/3을 돕고 있는데, 이러한 사실은 교육평등위원회에 따르자면 취학 이전의 아이들을 가진 아버지들의 세대에서 8배가 증가한 것이라 한다. 영국에서는 한 명의 부모에서 두 명의 부모가 양육을 담당하게 된 이러한 혁신은 직장에서 여성이 더 큰 역할을 담당하게 된 것과 우리 사회에서의 성 역할이 붕괴된 직접적인 결과를 낳았다. 이러한 사회적 변화들은 중요한 문제를 제기한다. 만일 아버지들이 유아를 포함한 어린 자녀들의 양육에 장기간 참여하게 된다면, 전통적으로 어머니들이 갖추리라 기대했던 기술들과 지식이 아버지들도 필요하게 된다. 그리고 이것은 부모들을 지원하는 서비스들이 어머니들뿐만 아니라 아버지들을 지원하는 것으로 확산되어야 함을 의미한다. 이러한 부모 지원 서비스는 양육에 능동적인 참여를 하고자 하는 보호자, 특히 매일 자녀 양육을 하고 있거나 하기를 희망하는 아버지들도 지원해야 하는 것이다.

23 윗글에서 암시하거나 언급하지 않은 것은?

① 오늘날 영국에서 아버지들의 자녀 양육에 대한 참여도가 매우 증가했다.

② 한 명의 부모에서 두 명의 부모가 양육을 하는 발전이 영국에서 발생되고 있다.

③ 오늘날 아버지들은 아이들을 돌보는 능동적인 역할을 갖고 있거나 갖기를 원한다.

④ 영국의 모든 아버지들은 아이들을 돌보는 더 능동적인 역할을 담당해야만 한다.

⑤ 이전에 어머니들은 실제로 모든 부모의 자녀 양육을 했었다.

24 ①에 들어갈 가장 적절한 것은?

① 만족시키다
② 계몽시키다
③ 준비가 되다
④ 도움을 받다
⑤ 점이 되다

어구 **parent** 양육하다 **undergo** 경험하다, 겪다 **profound** 심오한, 엄청난 **virtually** 실제로, 거의 **caring** 양육, 돌봄 **childcare** 자녀 양육 **eightfold** 8배의 **Equal Opportunities Opportunity** 교육평등위원회 **take/have a role in** ~의 역할을 담당하다 **workplace** 직장, 일터 **gendered** 성별의 **pose a question** 문제를 제기하다 **look after** 돌보다 **including** ~을 포함하여 **lengthy** 긴, 장황한 **task** 일, 임무, 과업 **notably** (그중에서도) 특히 **day-to-day** 나날의, 하루살이의 **be geared up to R** ~하도록 준비가 되다

해설 **23** 아이들을 돌보는 능동적인 역할을 갖고 있거나 그러기를 원하는 아버지들을 후원해 주고 지원해야 한다고 했을 뿐, 모든 아버지들에게 그래야 한다는 당위적 의무를 제시한 것은 아니다.

24 다음 문장에서 자녀 양육을 하고 있거나 하기를 희망하는 이들을 위해서 도움을 주어야 한다고 했으므로, 그에 맞는 서비스들이 '준비가 되어 있어야 한다'는 내용이 적합하다. gear up은 '준비하다, 확대하다'는 뜻을 가지고 있다. be geared up to R로 수동태 전환시 '(특정 목적을 위해서) 준비 · 조직되다(to be organized in a way that is suitable for a particular purpose or situation)'의 뜻을 가지므로, 의미상의 주어인 서비스가 '준비되다'는 수동태의 관계가 옳다.

Still and her husband, Ed, who has lost nearly 100 pounds, get most of their exercise at work. They visit an onsite fitness center almost daily, meet co-workers outside to walk through beautifully landscaped grounds and take wide, airy stairs instead of elevators. That's exactly what their employer, Sprint Corp, intended when it moved its thousands of employees to a 200-acre campus in suburban Johnson County. Sprint is part of a small but growing movement that encourages business owners to construct or renovate buildings in ways that motivate—or require—employees to get more exercise. The premise is simple: Happier, healthier employees are more productive and reduce health care costs for their companies.

25 이 글의 내용과 일치하는 것을 고르시오.

① Still and Ed are frequent users of elevators at work.
② Sprint Corp. is located in the center of Johnson County.
③ Sprint Corp. put parking garages next to its buildings.
④ Sprint Corp. induces its workers to exercise.

해석 스틸과 거의 100파운드의 체량 감량에 성공한 그녀의 남편 에드는 직장에서 대부분의 운동을 한다. 그들은 거의 매일 직장에 있는 헬스클럽을 찾으며, 헬스클럽에서 나와 동료들을 만나고, 아름답게 조경을 갖춘 운동장을 가로질러 걷고, 엘리베이터 대신 바람이 잘 통하는 계단을 이용한다. 이것이 바로 그들을 고용한 스프린트 회사가 수천 명에 이르는 종업원들을 수용하는 사옥을 200에이커의 넓은 근교 존슨 카운티로 옮겼을 때 의도했던 것이다. 스프린트 회사는, 사업주들이 직원들로 하여금 보다 많은 운동을 할 수 있도록 건물들을 짓거나 리모델링하는, 사회적인 동향에 참여하고 있는 것이다. 이 운동이 전제로 삼고 있는 것은 간단하다. 보다 행복하고, 건강한 근로자들이 보다 생산적이 되며, 그리고 회사로서는 근로자 건강 관리 비용을 줄일 수 있다는 것이다.

25 이 글의 내용과 일치하는 것을 고르시오.

① 스틸과 에드는 직장에서 엘리베이터를 종종 이용한다.
② 스프린트 회사는 존슨 카운티의 중심부에 위치해 있다.
③ 스프린트 회사는 건물 옆에 주차장을 두었다.
④ 스프린트 회사는 직원들에게 운동하도록 유도한다.

어구 onsite 현지의[에서], 현장의[에서] fitness center 헬스클럽 landscaped 전망이 좋은 airy 바람이 잘 통하는 motivate A to R A가 ～할 동기를 부여하다 induce A to R A에게 ～하도록 설득하다, 꾐에 빠뜨리다

해설 스프린트 회사는 직원들에게 엘리베이터 이용 대신 걷기를 유도하는 것처럼, 운동할 수 있는 근무 환경을 조성했다.

Sociologists reserve the term small group to refer to a group small enough for all members to interact simultaneously, that is, to talk with each other or at least be acquainted with each other. Small groups such as work groups and families are the intermediate link between the individual and the larger society. The intermediate position defines their importance in terms of attitudes, values, and behaviors. For this reason, sociologists are interested in what happens when people get together in small groups, whether it is to share gossip, reach a decision, or even play card games.

26 윗글의 내용과 일치하는 것을 고르시오.

① Sociologists reserve the place for small groups to interact one another.
② Small groups function as a link between the family and the society.
③ Sociologists are interested in attitudes, values, behaviors of small groups.
④ Gossiping and playing games are the best ways to make the members of small groups acquainted with each other.

해석 사회학자들은 모든 구성원들이 동시에 상호 작용할 수 있을 정도로 충분히 소규모의 집단을 일컫기 위하여 소집단이라는 단어를 마련해 놓는다. 즉 달리 말하자면, 서로 대화를 나누거나 혹은 적어도 서로 잘 알고 지내는 것을 말한다. 노동 집단과 가족과 같은 소규모 집단은 개인과 더 큰 단체 사이의 매개체 역할을 한다. 그러한 중간적 위치가 태도, 가치관과 행동이라는 관점에서 소집단의 중요성을 분명히 밝힌다. 이러한 이유 때문에 사회학자들은 소집단 안에서 사람들이 모일 때 무슨 일이 발생하며, 잡담을 나누든 결정에 도달하든 또는 심지어 카드게임을 하는 것이든 간에 흥미를 가진다.

26 윗글의 내용과 일치하는 것을 고르시오.

① 사회학자들은 서로 상호 작용을 하기 위하여 소집단을 위한 공간을 마련해 놓는다.
② 소집단은 가족과 사회의 중간적 위치로서 기능을 수행한다.
③ 사회학자들은 소집단의 태도, 가치관 및 행동에 흥미를 가진다.
④ 잡담을 나누고 게임을 하는 것은 소집단 구성원들이 서로를 잘 알 수 있게 하는 최고의 방법이 된다.

어구 reserve 준비[마련]해 두다; 예정해 두다 interact 상호 작용하다, 서로 영향을 주다 simultaneously 동시에; 일제히 that is 즉, 달리 말하자면 intermediate 중간의; 중등학교의 link 연결하는 사람[물건]; 유대(bond); 연결부, 연쇄부 in terms of ～의 관점에서 get together 함께 모이다 gossip 한담, 세상 이야기 reach a decision 결정을 내리다

해설 마지막 문장에서 사회학자들은 소집단 내에 사람들이 모였을 때 발생하는 일, 잡담 이야기, 결정, 카드 게임과 같은 '태도, 가치관, 행동'에 흥미를 가진다고 했다.

The authority of government, even such as I am willing to submit to, is still an impure one: to be strictly just, it must have the sanction and consent of the governed. It can have no pure right over my person and property but what I concede to it. The progress from an absolute to a limited monarchy, from a limited monarchy to a democracy, is a progress toward a true respect for the individual. Even the Chinese philosopher was wise enough to regard the individual as the basis of the empire. There will never be a really free and enlightened State until the State comes to recognize the individual as a higher and independent power, from which all its own power and authority are derived, and treats him accordingly. I please myself with imagining a State at least which can afford to be just to all men, and to treat the individual with respect as a neighbor; which even would not think it inconsistent with its own repose if a few were to live aloof from it, not meddling with it, nor embraced by it, who fulfilled all the duties of neighbors and fellow-men.

27 윗글의 요지를 고르시오.

① Individual's challenge to their government is always legitimate.
② The best government is one which esteems the individual's right.
③ The power of government can be justified by democratic leaders.
④ Individuals can hardly be alienated from society.

해석 비록 내가 기꺼이 복종할 의지가 있다 하더라도, 정부의 권위는 여전히 불순하다. 엄밀히 말하자면 피통치자들의 허락과 동의가 필요한 것이다. 정부는 내가 허용한 것 이외의 신체나 재산에 대하여 온전한 권리를 가질 수 없다. 전제 군주제에서 입헌 군주제로, 입헌 군주제에서 민주주의로 발전한 것은 개인에 대한 진정한 존중을 향한 발전인 것이다. 심지어 중국의 철학자조차도 개인을 제국의 근본으로 간주할 만큼 충분히 현명했다. 국가가 개인을 더욱 큰 독립된 힘으로 인식하고, 국가의 권력과 권위는 이 개인의 힘이 원천이라고 인정하고, 그에 맞는 대우를 개인에게 해 주고서야 비로소 자유롭고 계몽화된 국가가 될 것이다. 모든 사람들을 공정할 수 있고 개인을 한 이웃으로 존경할 수 있는 국가를 상상하는 기쁨을 가져 본다. 그러한 국가는 소수의 사람들이 국가에 초연한 태도를 갖고 국가에 대해 간섭을 하지 않고 살더라도 동포에 대한 의무를 다하며 국가의 안녕을 해치는 자들이라고 생각하지 않을 것이다.

27 윗글의 요지를 고르시오.

① 정부에 대한 개인의 도전은 언제나 정당하다.
② 최고의 정부는 개인의 권리를 존중해 주는 정부이다.
③ 정부의 힘은 민주주의 지도자들에 의해 정당화가 이루어진다.
④ 개인들은 사회로부터 소외되는 경우가 거의 없다.

어구 **authority** 권위; 권한 **be willing to R** 기꺼이 ~을 하다 **submit to** ~에 굴복하다 **impure** 불결한; 부도덕의 **to be strictly just** 엄밀히 말하자면 **sanction** 제재; 상벌; 인가 **consent** 동의; 허가(하다) **monarchy** 군주국; 군주제 **enlightened** 문명화한; 진보한 **recognize A as B** A를 B라고 인식하다 **derive** 기원을[유래를] 찾다 **accordingly** 따라서, 그에 맞게 **please oneself** 만족하다 **afford to R** ~할 여유가 있다 **treat A as B** A를 B라고 간주하다 **inconsistent** 일치하지 않는, 조화되지 않는 **repose** 침착, 휴식 **aloof** 멀리 떨어진; 무관심한 **meddle with** 참견하다, 간섭하다 **fellow-man** 같은 인간, 동포

해설 첫 문장이 주제문으로서, 정부가 권위를 가지기 위해서는 피통치자들(국민들)의 허락과 동의를 얻어야 함이 이 글의 요지가 된다. 이를 달리 말하면 '최고의 정부는 개인의 권리를 존중해 주는 정부이다.'라고 할 수 있다.

---

28 다음 글의 흐름상 필요 없는 문장을 고르시오.

The diversity of ethnic and racial backgrounds of Americans today is the living legacy of immigration. The social forces that cause people to emigrate are complex. ① The most important have been economic: expectations of higher incomes and standards of living in the new land. ② Many come legally, applying for immigrant visas, but others enter illegally. ③ Other factors include dislike of new regimes in their native lands and a desire to reunite families. ④ All these factors push people from their homelands and pull them to other nations such as the United States.

해석 오늘날 미국인들의 민족적, 인종적인 배경의 다양성은 이민이라는 현존하는 유산 때문이다. 사람들이 이민을 가도록 야기하는 이유는 복잡하다. ① 경제적인 이유가 가장 중요하다. 새로운 곳에서의 더 높은 수입과 생활 수준에 대한 기대치들이 바로 그것이다. ② 많은 사람들이 이민 비자를 신청하여 합법적으로 이민을 오지만, 불법적으로 건너오는 이민자들도 상당하다. ③ 이민을 유발하는 다른 요인들에는 조국의 새로운 정권에 대한 반감과 떨어져 사는 가족들과의 재결합에 대한 열망도 포함된다. ④ 이러한 모든 요인들이 미국과 같은 다른 나라로 이민을 가도록 사람들에게 영향을 미친다.

어구 **diversity** 다양성, 차이 **legacy** 유산 **emigrate** 이민을 가다 **immigrant visa** 이민 비자 **dislike** 반감, 혐오 **regime** 정권; 제도 **reunite** 재결합하다 **push** 밀다, 영향을 미치다

해설 이 글의 전체 내용은 사람들이 이민을 떠나는 이유의 다양성을 예를 들어 주고 있는데, ②문장의 내용만 이민 방식의 법적 절차의 위배 여부를 논하고 있기 때문에 틀린 표현이 된다.

Alternative medicine is not available under the national health service in some countries, such as Britain.

Medical treatments which are used instead of drugs, surgery, and other officially accepted methods of treatment are known as alternative medicine, or complementary medicine. (가) These more natural methods of treating illness include acupuncture, chiropractic and aromatherapy. (나) Therefore, in such countries, people who use it have to pay for it when they receive their treatment. (다) Since the beginning of the 1980s, alternative medicine has become more and more popular with people. (라) Although it is not officially accepted by the medical profession, some doctors do accept that such methods can be effective in treating some types of illness.

29 제시문이 위치하기에 가장 적합한 곳을 고르시오.

① (가) ② (나)
③ (다) ④ (라)

해석 약물, 수술 및 다른 공식적으로 인정된 치료 방법들 대신에 사용되는 의학 치료법들은 대체 의학이라고 알려져 있다. 이러한 더욱 자연스러운 질병 치료법에는 침술, 척추 교정 지압법과 방향 요법들이 포함되어 있다. 대체 의학은 영국과 같은 일부 국가들에서는 국가 건강 보험의 혜택을 받지 못한다. 따라서 이러한 나라들에서 대체 의학을 이용하는 사람들은 치료를 받을 때 돈을 지불해야 한다. 1980년대 초반 이후 대체 의학은 사람들에게 더욱 인기를 얻게 됐다. 비록 대체 의학이 의학 전문가들에게서 공식적으로 인정받고 있지는 못할지라도, 몇몇 의사들은 그런 방법들이 일부 종류의 질병을 치료할 때 효과적일 수 있다는 사실을 인정한다.

어구 **healthy service** 건강 보험, 공공 의료 **instead of** ~대신에 **surgery** 외과 (의술), 수술 **alternative medicine** 대체 의학 (complementary medicine) **chiropractic** 척추 조정[지압] 요법 **aromatherapy** 방향 요법

해설 대체 의학이 건강 보험의 혜택을 받지 못하면 치료를 받을 때 돈을 지불해야 한다. 따라서 제시문은 (나)에 위치해야 한다.

Travel at its best is a solitary experience: to see, to examine, to assess, you have to be alone and unencumbered. Other people can mislead you; they crowd your meandering impressions with their own; if they are companionable they obstruct your view, and if they are boring they corrupt the silence with non-sequiturs, shattering your concentration with "Oh look, it's raining. And You see a lot of trees here." The gist of travelling is not understood by Japanese who, coming across you smiling wistfully at an acre of Mexican buttercups, tend to say things like "Where is the rest of your team?" It is hard to see clearly or to think straight in the company with other people. Not only do I feel self-conscious, but the perceptions that are necessary to writing are difficult to manage when someone close by is thinking out aloud.

30 According to the passage, Japanese travellers considered the author ___________.

① indifferent ② courageous
③ unreliable ④ cynical
⑤ odd

해석 최고의 여행은 고독한 경험을 할 때이다. 보고, 연구하고, 평가하기 위해서 당신은 혼자 있어야 하고 방해받지 않아야 한다. 다른 사람들은 당신의 판단력에 영향을 줄 수 있다. 그들은 그들의 언어로 당신을 정신없게 할 수도 있고, 동행해도 괜찮을 듯한 사람과 여행을 할 때라도 그들은 당신의 시야를 방해할 수 있다. 만일 그들이 지루하다면 그들은 상관없는 말로 고요한 분위기를 깨뜨리며, "오! 비가 오네." "여기에 나무가 많이 보인다."라는 말로 당신의 집중력을 분산시킨다. 넓게 펼쳐진 멕시코 미나리아재비를 넋을 놓고서 바라보는 당신을 우연히 만나 "나머지 일행은 어디 있나요?"라고 말하는 성향이 있는 일본인들은 여행의 근본을 이해하지 못한다. 다른 사람과 함께 있으면서 정확하게 생각하는 것은 어렵다. 가까이 있는 누군가가 소리 내어 생각을 말할 때, 나는 의식적이 될 뿐만 아니라 글을 쓰기 위하여 필요한 지각을 조절하기가 힘들어진다.

30 이 글에 따르면, 일본 여행객들은 작가를 어떻게 생각했는가?

① 무관심한 ② 예의 바른
③ 신뢰할 수 없는 ④ 빈정대는
⑤ 이상한

어구 **Mexican buttercup** 멕시코 미나리아재비 **self-conscious** 스스로 인식하는 **close by** 바로 옆에 **courageous** 예의 바른 **unreliable** 신뢰할 수 없는 **cynical** 빈정대는 **odd** 이상한; 임시의; 홀수의

해설 홀로 여행하는 것이 참된 여행이라고 작가는 판단한다. 그러나 이러한 작가를 일본인들이 이해하지 못한다고 했기 때문에 결국 일본 사람들은 홀로 여행하는 작가를 이상하게 생각한다고 볼 수 있다.

Actual TEST 08

⇨ 본책 p.284

1 ④	2 ④	3 ④	4 ④	5 ⑤	6 ③	7 ②	8 ③	9 ③	10 ③
11 ④	12 ②	13 ⑤	14 ②	15 ⑤	16 ④	17 ②	18 ③	19 ①	20 ③
21 ②	22 ①	23 ①	24 ④	25 ③	26 ①	27 ③	28 ②	29 ④	30 ③

>>> 밑줄 친 곳에 들어갈 알맞은 답을 고르시오. [1~6]

1 He has had three jobs in the last two years; he never ___________ anything for long.

① sticks down
② thinks over
③ goes with
④ sticks to
⑤ takes after

해석 지난 2년 동안 그는 세 곳의 직장을 전전했다. 왜냐하면 그는 어떤 일이든 오랫동안 끈기 있게 배겨내지 못했기 때문이다.

어구 **stick down** 아래에 놓다, 적어두다   **stick to** 고수하다, 끈기 있게 하다   **take after** 닮다, 흉내내다

해설 지난 2년간 직장을 세 곳이나 옮겼다는 얘기는 한 가지 일에 대한 끈기가 부족함을 알 수 있다.

2 Since the detective believed her to be candid and trustworthy, he refused to consider the possibility that her explanation had been ___________.

① irrelevant
② facetious
③ mistaken
④ insincere
⑤ critical

해석 그 형사는 그녀가 솔직하고 확실한 사람이라고 믿었기 때문에 그녀의 설명이 거짓된 것이라고 생각하지 않았다.

어구 **detective** 형사   **candid** 솔직한   **irrelevant** 부적절한   **facetious** 익살스러운   **insincere** 정직하지 못한

해설 since는 '인과'를 나타내는 접속사이므로, 정직하다고 믿은 내용에 따른 결과가 필요하다.

3 The world of nature is free for our enjoyment, from the glory of a sunrise to the quaintness of a cricket. It is all here, around us, for taking. There is no ___________. Not only free, nature has the priceless advantage of being everywhere.

① serious planning
② danger
③ hurry
④ charge
⑤ obligation whatsoever

해석 우리는 일출의 모습에서부터 귀뚜라미의 특이함에 이르기까지 자연 세계를 마음껏 즐길 수 있다. 취할 모든 것이 우리 주변에 있다. 요금은 없다. 공짜일 뿐만 아니라 자연은 모든 곳에 존재한다는 값으로 매길 수 없는 이점을 가지고 있다.

어구 **sunrise** 일출   **quaintness** 기이함   **cricket** 귀뚜라미   **charge** 요금, 부담, 비난, 책임   **priceless** 매우 소중한

해설 자연 세계를 누릴 수 있는 장점이 무료라고 다음 문장에서 제시되므로, 요금을 내지 않는다는 논리가 적합하다.

4 She was usually a model of ___________, so her sudden burst of temper was atypical.

① veracity
② lucidity
③ facility
④ equanimity
⑤ wrath

해석 그녀는 평상시 침착함의 전형이어서 그녀의 갑작스런 분노는 이상해 보였다.

어구 **atypical** 정형에 맞지 않는, 불규칙한, 이상한   **veracity** 정직   **lucidity** 맑음, 투명, 선명   **equanimity** 침착함, 평정   **wrath** 분노

해설 분노의 표출이 이상해 보였다는 논리는 원인에 해당되는 주절의 반대 의미가 등장해야 옳다.

224

5 Legal ___________ initiated by the government necessitate that manufacturers use ___________ in choosing food additives.

① entanglements - knowledge
② devices - intensification
③ talents - decretion
④ proclivities - moderation
⑤ restraints - caution

해석 정부에 의해 제안된 법적 조치들은 생산자들이 식품첨가제를 선택하는 데 있어 주의를 기울일 것을 필수화시켰다.

어구 initiate 제안하다, 시작하다　necessitate 필요하게 하다, 강요하다　additive 첨가제, 부가물　entanglement 분류, 연루, 혼란　intensification 격화, 강화　decretion 법령　proclivity 경향, 성향　restraint 억제, 자제

해설 법률의 내용과 적합한 어휘 차제가 '제한'이 되며, 이러한 법령의 내용이 식품첨가제의 선택에 주의를 기울이게 한다는 내용으로 유추가 가능하다.

6 The term stork indicates that the fact that a woman sees a bird of stork is that she will be pregnant. The fact that Caroline saw a stork the week before she became pregnant is merely a coincidence; it should not imply any ___________ whatsoever.

① fortuity　　　② catastrophe
③ causality　　　④ nemesis

해석 황새라는 단어는 한 여성이 황새를 보게 되면 그녀가 임신하게 될 것이라는 내용을 가리키기도 한다. 캐롤라인이 임신하기 전에 황새를 보았다는 것은 단순히 우연의 일치일 뿐이다. 그 사실은 조금도 (인과 관계가 분명한) 사건이 전혀 될 수 없다.

어구 stork 황새(아이들에게 갓난아기는 이 새가 갖다 주는 것이라고 가르침)　coincidence (우연의) 일치, 부합; 동시 발생　whatsoever (부정문에서) 조금도　fortuity 우연; (뜻밖의) 사건　catastrophe 재난　causality 인과 관계　nemesis 좌절과 곤란을 안겨주는 것

해설 여자가 황새를 보면 임신할 수 있다는 사실은 분명히 우연의 일치일 뿐, 일종의 사건이 될 수 없음을 부연 설명하는 글이다.

>>> **다음 글을 읽고 문제의 답을 고르시오.**

When I overheard one of my cashiers tell a customer, "We haven't had it for a while, and I doubt we'll be getting it soon," I quickly assured the customer that we would have whatever she wanted by next week. After she left, I read the cashier the riot act. "Never tell the customer that we're out of anything. Tell them we'll have it next week," I instructed her. "Now, what did she want?" The cashier said, "She wanted rain."

7 What would be the writer's occupation?

① customer
② supervisor
③ teacher
④ lawyer

해석 나의 출납원 중 한 명이 고객에게 "우리는 현금이 한동안 없었으며, 곧 보유할 것 같지 않습니다."라고 말하는 것을 우연히 들었다. 나는 고객에게 다음 주까지 고객이 원하는 것이 무엇이든 우리가 갖추어 놓을 것이라고 재빨리 안심시켜 주었다. 고객이 떠난 후, 나는 출납원을 엄하게 나무랐다. "우리가 아무것도 없다는 사실을 고객에게 절대로 말하지 마시오. 고객에게 다음 주면 우리가 갖추어 놓을 것이라고 말하시오."라고 그녀에게 가르쳤다. "그런데 고객이 무엇을 원하신 거죠?" 출납원은 "그녀는 비가 오기를 원했습니다."라고 말했다.

7 작가의 직업은 무엇인가?
① 고객　　② 관리인　　③ 교사　　④ 변호사

어구 overhear 우연히 듣다; 도청하다　cashier 출납원; 회계원　read A the riot act A를 호되게 나무라다　be out of ~이 바닥나다

해설 출납원이 고객에게 말한 것을 나무랄 수 있고, 그 출납원 대신에 고객에게 확신을 시킬 수 있는 사람은 관리인이다.

>>> 다음 글을 읽고 문제의 답을 고르시오.

It's noon on a sweltering June day, a perfect time for a teenager to listen to tunes and work on a tan. So Hanna Forest, 16, blond and blue-eyed, is trying to brown. But she's not worshiping the sun. She lies on a glass bed in the Coral Reef tanning salon in a suburban strip mall, basking under the ultraviolet. "It takes too long to lay out," says Hanna, a high-school cheerleader in Sycamore, Illinois. "I don't want to be pale. This makes me feel as if I look healthy." But it's the health of so many tanning-bed teens that worries dermatologists, who say the UV rays increase the risk of skin cancer. Now a bill proposed in California would prohibit youths under 18 from using tanning salons without a doctor's prescription. It would be the first such ban in the nation. For now, 27 states, including California, require parental consent for tanners 15 to 17, and turn away those 14 and under. The tanning industry says a ban could do more harm than good because people who tan indoors are less likely to burn outside.

8 이 글의 내용과 가장 일치하는 것을 고르시오.

① Tanning has the same risk of skin disease as burning.
② Tanners under the age of 14 need their parents' consent for using tanning salons.
③ California would be the first state to ban using tanning salons for those under the age of 18.
④ The tanning industry in the US argues that people obsessed with tanning are most at risk.

해석 무척 더운 6월의 어느 날 오후, 십대 소녀가 음악을 들으며 선탠을 하기 위한 완벽한 시간이었다. 그래서 금발에 푸른 눈을 가진 16살의 한나 포레스트는 갈색 피부를 만들고자 했다. 하지만 그녀는 햇빛을 좋아하지 않는다. 그녀는 시외 번화가에 위치한 코랄 리프라는 선탠 미용실의 유리 침대에 누워 자외선을 쐬고 있었다. "외출하여 태우려면 시간이 너무 많이 걸려요."라고 한나가 말했다. 그녀는 일리노이 주, 사이카모어에 있는 고등학교에서 치어 리더로 활동 중이다. "나는 창백해 보이기를 원하지 않아요. 선탠은 내가 건강한 것처럼 느끼게 해줘요." 그러나 피부과 전문의들은 인공적인 선탠을 많이 받은 십대들에 대한 우려의 목소리를 내고 있는데, 그들에 따르면 자외선이 피부암에 걸릴 위험을 증가시킨다고 한다. 이제 캘리포니아에서 제출된 법안에 따르자면 의사의 처방 없는 18세 미만의 청소년들이 선탠 미용실을 이용하지 못하게 된다. 이 법안이 통과되면 미국에서 최초로 시행되는 선탠 미용실 이용 금지법이 될 것이다. 현재 캘리포니아를 포함하여 27개의 주가 15살에서 17살 사이의 선탠을 원하는 이들에게 부모의 동의를 요구하고 있으며, 14살 이하의 아이들은 돌려보내고 있다. 실내에서 선탠을 하는 사람들은 야외에서처럼 피부에 화상을 입을 가능성이 적기 때문에 선탠 업계는 이 금지 조치가 좋은 것보다는 해를 끼칠 것이라고 한다.

8 이 글의 내용과 가장 일치하는 것을 고르시오.
① 선탠은 화상과 유사한 피부 질병에 걸릴 위험이 있다.
② 14세 미만의 선탠을 하는 아이들이 선탠 미용실을 이용하기 위해서는 부모의 허락을 필요로 한다.
③ 캘리포니아는 18세 미만의 아이들이 선탠 미용실을 이용하는 것을 금지하는 최초의 주가 될 것이다.
④ 미국의 선탠 업계는 선탠의 강박 관념에 빠진 사람들이 가장 위험하다고 주장한다.

어구 sweltering 찌는 듯이 더운 work on 일을 계속하다 tan (피부를) 햇볕에 태우다; 때리다 blond 금발의 brown 갈색으로 하다; 갈색 worship 숭배[존경]하다; 예배 bask 몸을 녹이다, 햇볕을 쬐다 ultraviolet 자외(선)의 take long 시간이 오래 걸리다 lay out 펼치다, 진열하다; 설계하다 dermatologist 피부과 (전문) 의사 prohibit A from -ing A가 ~하지 못하게 하다 ban 금지; 금지하다 parental 부모의 consent 동의, 허가; 동의하다, 허가하다 turn away 쫓아 버리다 do harm 해치다 do good 도움을 주다

해설 'It would be the first such ban in the nation.'에서 it은 앞 문장 전체를 가리킨다. 따라서 캘리포니아 주가 미국에서 최초로 18세 미만의 아이들이 부모의 허락 없는 선탠 미용실에 가지 못하게 조치를 취하는 최초의 주가 된다는 설명이 옳다.

>>> 다음 글을 읽고 문제의 답을 고르시오.

(가) Although your resume looks impressive, we have no plans to hire new staff in the immediate future.

(나) Allow me to begin by thanking you for your interest in joining our firm.

(다) Your resume, however, will be duly filed for future reference.

(라) Thanks again, and I wish you every success.

9 윗글들을 문맥에 맞게 올바른 순서로 연결한 것은?

① (가) – (다) – (나) – (라)

② (가) – (나) – (라) – (다)

③ (나) – (가) – (다) – (라)

④ (나) – (라) – (가) – (다)

해석 (나) 먼저 저희 회사에 입사하고 싶다는 관심을 보여 주신 데 대해 감사드립니다. (가) 당신의 이력서는 분명히 인상적이지만, 가까운 미래에 신규 채용의 계획이 없습니다. (다) 하지만, 당신의 이력서는 앞으로 참조하기 위해 정식으로 보관해 두겠습니다. (라) 다시 한번 감사드리며, 하시는 일 모두 잘 되기 기원합니다.

어구 begin by ~으로 시작하다 duly 정식으로 file 보관하다

해설 (나) 문장을 통해 입사 지원서에 대한 답변을 정중하게 한 후, (가) 문장에서 신규 채용이 없는 것에 대한 양해를 구하고 있다. (다) 문장에서 차후 신규 채용을 할 경우 검토를 위해 보관을 할 것이며, (라) 문장에서 마지막 인사를 통해 맺음을 하고 있다.

>>> 다음 글을 읽고 문제의 답을 고르시오.

Undeterred by this scientific pronouncement, a few weeks later the Wright brothers took their "flyer" to Kitty Hawk, North Carolina, and changed the world.

The idea of a heavier-than-air flying machine was roundly ridiculed by the scientific establishment in the early 1900s. [A] In 1902, the year before Wilbur and Orville Wright took their famous flight, the U.S. Navy's chief engineer declared the very idea to be "absurd." [B] The following year, an eminent professor of mathematics and astronomy at Johns Hopkins University proved to the world that a heavier-than-air craft was "scientifically impossible." [C] Even after photographs circulated of the historic flight, the Wright brothers's hometown newspaper refused to print anything about their revolutionary contraption because, as the editor admitted, "We didn't believe it." [D]

10 윗글의 흐름으로 보아 주어진 문장이 들어갈 가장 적절한 곳은?

① [A] ② [B]

③ [C] ④ [D]

해석 1900년대 초에는 중항공기에 대한 생각은 과학계 전반에 걸쳐 가차 없는 조롱거리였다. [A] 1902년 윌버와 오빌 라이트 형제가 유명한 비행을 시도하기 전에 미 해군의 수석 엔지니어는 하늘을 비행하는 장비에 대한 생각을 "터무니없는" 것이라고 단언했다. [B] 그 다음 해 존스 홉킨스 대학의 저명한 수학 및 천문학 교수는 중항공기가 "과학적으로 불가능한" 것이라고 세상에 증명했다. 이 과학적 선언에 용기가 꺾이지 않고 몇 주가 지난 후 라이트 형제는 자신들의 "비행기"를 노스캘로라이나 주의 키티 호크로 가져가서 역사를 바꾸어 놓았다. [C] 심지어 그 역사적 비행에 대한 사진이 유포된 후에도 라이트 형제의 고향 신문은 그 형제의 혁명적인 고안물에 관해 개제하는 것을 거절했다. 왜냐하면 편집장이 시인했던 것처럼 그 비행을 믿을 수 없었기 때문이었다. [D]

어구 heavier-than-air flying machine 중(重)항공기 roundly 가차 없이; 충분히; 둥글게 ridicule 비웃다; 조롱거리 take a flight 비행하다 chief engineer 수석 엔지니어 the very 바로 그 absurd 터무니없는 circulate 유포하다; 배포하다; 유통시키다 contraption 기묘한 장치; 새로운 고안, 신안

해설 제시문에 this scientific pronouncement가 있다. 따라서 앞에 과학적 선언이 있었음을 유추할 수 있다. 그 과학적 선언이 [B] 문장에서 말한 중항공기가 '과학적으로 불가능하다'라고 단언한 내용임을 알 수 있다.

The kind of people who send their kids to Bible camp are appalled. Answers in Genesis, a Christian fundamentalist group, berates Camp Quest for drumming a "hopeless" world view into young minds. But a humanist camp is about indoctrination less than about reassurance that it is all right not to be religious; that it is possible to be moral without believing in the supernatural. (가) Nearly all the kids at Camp Quest say they find it comforting to be surrounded by others who share their lack of belief. Many attend schools where Christianity is taken for granted. (나) Many keep quiet about their atheism. (다) Those who don't are sometimes taunted or told they will burn in hell. (라) Atheists are broadly disliked in America. Only 5% of Americans admit that they would not vote for an otherwise qualified black presidential candidate, but 53% say they would shun an atheist. That makes the godless less popular than Muslims, Mormons or gays. Granted, the proportion of Americans who say they might vote for an atheist has doubled in the past half-century, and the polls are muddied by those who do not know what an atheist is.

11 두 번째 단락이 시작되는 문장을 고르시오.

① (가)   ② (나)

③ (다)   ④ (라)

12 밑줄 친 부분이 가리키는 것은 무엇인가?

① people who don't preach Christianity

② people who suggest that they don't believe in God

③ people who dislike atheists

④ people who vote for black presidential candidates

해석 자녀들을 성경 캠프로 보낸 부모들은 깜짝 놀란다. 기독교 근본주의 단체인 '창세기 시대의 답변'은 퀘스트 캠프가 어린 아이들에게 절망적인 세계관을 심어 주고 있다고 비난한다. 그러나 인문주의자(비종교주의자) 캠프는 주입식 교육이라기보다는 종교를 믿지 않아도 좋다는 점을 안심시키는 것과 관련이 있는 것이다. 즉, 초자연을 믿지 않고서도(눈에 보이지 않는 것을 믿지 않아도 = 신을 믿지 않아도) 도덕성을 가질 수 있다는 것이다. 퀘스트 캠프의 거의 모든 아이들은 종교를 믿지 않는다는 공통점이 있는 다른 아이들과 함께 있다는 것(신을 믿지 않는 아이들과 함께 어울리는 것)이 위안이 된다고 말한다. 많은 아이들은 기독교를 당연하게 여기는 학교(기독교 학교)를 다닌다. 많은 아이들은 자신들의 무신론에 대해 침묵한다. 침묵하지 못하는 아이들(신을 믿지 않는다고 말하는 아이들)은 가끔씩 조롱을 받거나 지옥에서 불타 죽을 것이라는 말을 듣는다. 미국 상당 지역에서 무신론자들은 반감을 산다. 5%의 미국인들만이 그렇지 않은 자격을 갖춘 흑인 대통령 후보(무신론이 아닌 대통령 후보= 종교가 있는 대통령 후보)에게 투표하지 않을 것이라고 시인하지만, 53%의 미국인들은 무신론자를 기피할 것이라고 말한다. 그래서 이슬람교인, 모르몬교인 혹은 게이보다 무신론자들이 더 인기가 없다. 그렇다 치더라도 무신론자에게 투표할 수 있다고 말하는 미국인들의 수는 지난 반세기 동안 두 배나 증가했으며, 여론 조사는 무신론자의 정체를 알지 못하는 사람들에 의해 모호해졌다(여론 조사가 유명무실해졌다).

12 밑줄 친 표현이 가리키는 것은 무엇인가?

① 기독교를 설파하지 않는 사람들

② 신을 믿지 않는다고 주장하는 사람들

③ 무신론자를 싫어하는 사람들

④ 흑인 대통령 후보자에게 투표한 사람들

어구 **berate** 호되게 꾸짖다   **drum** 모집하다, 선전하다, 쿵쿵 치다   **supernatural** 초자연의, 불가사의한   **comforting** 위안이 되는   **atheism** 무신론, 무신앙 생활   **taunt** 조롱하다   **vote for** 투표하다   **qualified** 자격 있는, 적임의   **Mormon** 모르몬교도; 일부 다처주의자   **granted** 그렇다 치더라도   **muddy** 혼잡해지다

해설 **19** (라) 단락 앞까지 성경 캠프에서의 무신론에 대해 논하고 있으며, (라) 단락부터 미국 전역의 무신론자 비율에 대해 논하고 있다. 이렇게 장소, 시간적으로 전환되는 전체의 내용이 바뀔 경우 새로운 단락으로 바꿔 말하게 된다.

20 do동사는 앞서 나온 일반동사의 대동사로 활용된다. 즉, 앞서 등장한 keep quiet를 대신했으며, 부정문이 된 것이다. 따라서 침묵하지 않는 사람들이 직역 표현이 되며, 의역을 해 본다면 '자신이 무신론이라고 침묵하지 않는 = 자신은 신을 믿지 않는다고 주장하는'의 의미를 가지게 된다.

Judge Richard Posner, the most prolific federal judge, quotes the Austrian-born economist Joseph Schumpeter. Schumpeter—hardly a sympathetic figure—was an elitist who believed the achievements of capitalism were threatened by the greed and ignorance of the masses. "Democracy", as Posner describes Schumpeter's view, "is conceived of as a method by which members of a self-interested political elite compete for the votes of a basically ignorant and apathetic, as well as determinedly self-interested, electorate".

Is our democracy, then, entirely squalid? Not really, or not so it should bother us. Judge Posner brings to mind Winston Churchill's quip that democracy is the worst system of government except all the others that have been tried over the years. As most people believe, "American democracy", writes Posner, "enables the adult population to punish at least the flagrant mistakes of officialdom, to assure an orderly succession of at least minimally competent officials, to generate feedback to the officials concerning the consequences of their policies, to prevent officials from entirely ignoring the interests of the governed, and to prevent serious misalignments between the government action and public opinion".

13 Winston Churchill implies that democracy is ＿＿＿＿＿ tried over the years.

① an ideal system of government
② as bad as any other system of government
③ as good as any other system of government
④ worse than any other system of government
⑤ better than any other system of government

14 According to Richard Posner, democracy can ＿＿＿＿＿.

① stop the mistakes of bureaucracy
② make the officials more responsible for their policies
③ make the officials do their best for the interests of the governed
④ bring about an ideal cooperation between the government and the people
⑤ guarantee the succession of the social system by the ablest officials possible

15 Concerning democracy, who differ in opinion?

① the writer　　　　② most people
③ Richard Posner　④ Winston Churchill
⑤ Joseph Schumpeter

해석 가장 재판 경험이 많은 연방판사인 리처드 포스너가 오스트리아 출신의 경제학자 조지프 슘페터를 예로 들어 설명한다. 동정적인 인물이 결코 아닌 슘페터는 대중의 탐욕과 무지가 자본주의의 업적을 위협한다고 믿었던 엘리트였다. 포스너 판사가 슘페터의 견해를 설명하기를, 민주주의란 이기적인 정치 집단의 구성원들이 분명히 이기적일 뿐만 아니라 본래 무지하고 냉담한 유권자들의 표를 얻기 위하여 경쟁하는 한 가지 방식이라고 간주되는 것이다. 그렇다면 우리의 민주주의는 정말로 지저분한 상태가 되어 버렸는가? 사실 그렇지는 않으며, 우리를 괴롭히는 것도 아닌 것이다. 포스너 판사는 '민족주의는 수년간 시도되어 온 다른 모든 것들을 제외하고서 최악의 정부 체계'라고 윈스턴 처칠이 빈정대는 투로 말을 했던 것을 생각해 본다. 대부분의 이들이 믿듯이, 포스너는 "미국의 민주주의는 성인들로 하여금 적어도 공무원들의 분명한 과실들에 대하여 처벌하고, 적어도 약간이나마 유능한 공무원이라면 조직 체계에 따른 지위 계승을 보장하여 주며, 정책의 결과에 관하여 공무원들에게 반응을 만들어 주며, 공무원들로 하여금 국민들의 권익을 완전히 무시하지 못하게 하며, 정부의 조치와 국민 여론 사이의 심각한 괴리를 막아 주는 것"이라고 하였다.

13 윈스턴 처칠은 민주주의가 수년간 어떠한 체계였다고 암시하는가?
① 이상적인 정부 체계였다.
② 어느 다른 정부 체계만큼이나 나빴다.
③ 어느 다른 정부 체계만큼이나 좋았다.
④ 어느 다른 정부 체계보다 나빴다.
⑤ 어느 다른 정부 체계보다 좋았다.

14 포스너 판사에 따르자면 민주주의는 어떠한가?
① 관료주의의 과오들을 막을 수 있다.
② 공무원들로 하여금 자신들의 정책에 대하여 보다 더 책임을 질 수 있게끔 할 수 있다.
③ 공무원들로 하여금 국민들의 이해를 위하여 최선을 다하게 한다.
④ 정부와 국민들 사이의 이상적인 협력을 야기할 수 있다.
⑤ 가장 유능한 공무원들에 의한 사회제도의 계승을 보장해 줄 수 있다.

15 민주주의에 대하여 다른 견해를 갖고 있는 사람을 고르시오.
① 작가　　　　　② 대부분의 사람들
③ 포스너 판사　④ 윈스턴 처칠　⑤ 조셉 슘페터

어구 **quote** 인용하다, 예시하다　**figure** 인물　**ignorance** 무지　**the masses** 일반 대중　**A is conceived of as B** A가 B로 간주되다　**self-interested** 이기적인　**apathetic** 무감각한, 냉담한　**determinedly** 결연히, 단호히　**electorate** 유권자, 선거인들　**squalid** 더러운, 비열한　**bother** 괴롭히다　**bring to mind** 생각이 나다　**quip** 경구, 빈정대는 말, 신랄한 말　**flagrant** 명백한, 사악한　**officialdom** 공무원, 관리, 관료주의　**competent** 유능한, 적임의　**concerning** ～에 관하여　**misalignment** 괴리, 조정 불량　**the governed** 국민들, 피통치자　**bureaucracy** 관료주의

해설 **13** 민주주의가 이상적인 체계는 아닐지언정 다른 제도들보다는 상대적으로 우월하다는 내용이다. 따라서 우월 비교가 옳다.
14 민주주의는 지위 계승을 보장하여 주며, 정책의 결과에 관하여 공무원들에게 반응을 만들어 준다는 내용은 공무원들이 그들의 정책에 책임감을 가질 수 있도록 한다는 내용으로 이해가 가능하다.
15 리처드 포스너 판사와 처칠은 민주주의가 최고의 이상적인 정부 체계는 아닐지라도 상대적으로 우월한 위치에 있어서 대중 민주주의를 지향하지만, 슘페터는 첫 단락 마지막 문장에서 밝혔듯이 탐욕과 무지에 의해서 민주주의가 위협을 받는다는 비판적인 시각을 보였다.

>>> **다음 글을 읽고 문제의 답을 고르시오.**

[A] "I'm just waiting around so I can put away the chairs," he added.

[B] After pounding out more songs, one of the tired musicians finally suggested to the music lover that if he left, they could all go home.

[C] "Do whatever you want," said the man.

[D] A colleague's band performed in a park before an audience that gradually dwindled down to one lone man.

16 윗글들을 문맥에 맞게 올바른 순서로 연결한 것은?

① B - A - C - D　　　② B - D - A - C
③ D - A - C - B　　　④ D - B - C - A

해석 [D] 동료 악단이 공원에서 공연을 했는데, 청중은 점점 줄어들어 단 한 명만 남았다.
[B] 노래 몇 곡을 더 연주한 후에 지친 연주자들 중 하나가 마침내 마지막 남은 그 음악 애호가에게 만약 그가 떠난다면 자기들도 모두 집에 갈 수 있을 것이라고 말했다.
[C] "원하는 대로 하시오."라고 그 남자가 말했다.
[A] "의자를 치우기 위해서 주변에 그냥 기다리고 있다."라고 그가 덧붙여 말했다.

어구 **put away** 치우다　**pound out** (매우 시끄럽게) 연주하다　**dwindle down to** 줄어들어서 ~이 되다

해설 [D] 한 명 앞에서 공연을 하다가 인원이 감소한 사건이 발생했고, [B] 그 남은 한 사람마저 떠난다면 공연을 그만하고 집에 가겠다고 제안을 한다. [C] 그에 대한 답변을 하며, [A] 의자를 치우려고 기다리고 있다는 것은 결국 더 이상 공연을 할 의지가 전혀 없음을 말하는 것이다.

>>> **다음 글을 읽고 문제의 답을 고르시오.**

In June the high court of the secular government of Turkey upheld a long-standing ban on religious headscarves at universities. Hundreds of women took to the streets. But the controversy isn't new. A former member of the Turkish parliament, Merve Kavakci, was stripped of her citizenship for wearing a hijab to work in 1999 and is now living in the United States. Writing in Foreign Policy, she challenged Westerners and feminists who, like her former government, denounce the hijab: "They're better off honoring a woman's right to choose than trying to impose their prejudices on Muslims."

17 Which is NOT true of Ms. Kavakci?

① She used to be a Turkish.
② She is now an active feminist.
③ She was a member of the Turkish parliament.
④ She was kicked out of Turkey for wearing a hijab.
⑤ She is currently staying in the USA as a Muslim.

해석 6월에 세속주의 성향인 터키 정부의 고등 법원이 대학에서 종교적 성향을 띠는 두건을 쓰지 못하게 하는 오랫동안 존속된 금지령에 대하여 합헌 판결을 내렸다. 수백 명의 여성이 길거리로 나갔다. 그러나 그 논쟁이 새로운 것은 아니다. 전직 터키 국회 의원이었던 메르베 카바키 여사는 1999년에 히잡을 착용했다는 이유로 시민권을 빼앗겼으며, 현재 미국에서 생활 중이다. 외국 정책이란 책을 저술한 그녀는 이전 정부(터키 정부)처럼 히잡을 비난하는 서양인들과 페미니스트에게 맞섰다. "이슬람인들에게 자신들의 편견을 강요하기보다 여성의 결정권을 존중하는 편이 더 좋을 것이다."

17 카바키 여사에 대해 틀린 것은?

① 그녀는 터키 사람이었다.
② 그녀는 현재 적극적인 페미니스트이다.
③ 그녀는 터키 국회 의원이었다.
④ 그녀는 히잡을 착용했다는 이유로 터키에서 쫓겨났다.
⑤ 그녀는 이슬람인으로서 미국에서 현재 거주 중이다.

어구 **high court** 고등 법원　**secular** 세속의; 비종교적인　**uphold** 지지하다; 떠받치다　**long-standing** 오래 계속되는　**ban** 금지(하다)　**headscarf** (모자 대용의) 머리 스카프　**take to the street** 거리로 나가다, 거리를 점령하다　**strip A of B** A에게서 B를 빼앗다　**hijab** 히잡(이슬람 여성들의 얼굴 가리개)　**challenge** 이의를 제기하다; 도전하다　**feminist** 페미니스트, 여성 해방론자　**denounce** 비난하다　**be better off** ~하는 편이 더 좋다　**be kicked out of** ~에서 쫓겨나다

해설 'she challenged Westerners and feminists.' 문장을 통해 본인이 페미니스트가 아님을 알 수 있다.

In reading, one should notice and fondle details. There is nothing wrong about the moonshine of generalization when it comes after the sunny trifles of the book have been lovingly collected. If one begins with a ready-made generalization, it means that he begins at the wrong end and travels away from the book before he has started to understand it. Nothing is more boring or more unfair to the author than starting to read, say, *Madame Bovary*, with the preconceived notion that it is a denunciation of the bourgeoisie. We should always remember that a literary work is invariably the creation of a new world, so that the first thing we should do is to study that new world as closely as possible, approaching it as something brand new, having no obvious connection with the worlds we already know.

18 Which of the following best expresses the main idea of the passage?

① Generalization is based upon what we already know of the world.
② Reading always provides us with the practical information about the world.
③ A close reading is essential in understanding a literary work.
④ *Madame Bovary* deals with the condemnation of the bourgeoisie.

해석 글을 읽을 때 세부 내용을 주목하고 소중히 여겨야 한다. 책의 세부 내용을 정성껏 수집한 후 일반화를 해야 한다. 기존의 일반화를 가지고 (독서를) 시작한다면, 그것은 잘못된 목표를 향해 독서를 시작하는 것이고 책을 이해하기 전부터 헤매는 것을 의미한다. 예컨대, 〈보바리 부인〉은 유산자 계급을 비난한 책이라는 선입관을 가지고 그 책을 읽기 시작하는 것보다 더 지루하고 저자에게 더 부당한 것은 없다. 문학 작품은 변함없이 새로운 세계를 창조한다는 것을 언제나 기억해야 하며, 따라서 우리가 해야 할 첫 번째 일은 저 새로운 세계를 가능한 상세히 연구하여 이미 우리가 알고 있는 세계와는 분명한 관련성이 없는 완전히 새로운 것으로서 접근해야 한다.

18 이 글의 요지를 고르시오.

① 일반화는 우리가 세상에 대해 이미 알고 있는 것을 근거로 한다.
② 독서는 언제나 우리에게 세상에 대한 실용적인 정보를 제공한다.
③ 주도면밀한 독서는 문학을 이해하는 데 있어서 필수적이다.
④ 〈보바리 부인〉은 유산자들의 비난을 다룬다.

어구 fondle 소중히 여기다; 귀여워하다, 애무하다 detail 세부, 세부 묘사 moonshine 상상; 달빛 generalization 일반화, 보편화 sunny 명랑한, 쾌활한, 밝은 trifle 변두리 내용; 하찮은 것 lovingly 애정을 기울여 ready-made 기존의; 기성품의 travels away from ~에서 헤매다 boring 지겨운 unfair 부당한, 불공평한 preconceived 선입견에 치우친 denunciation 위협; 탄핵; 고발 bourgeoisie 중산계급의 시민, 부르주아 invariably 변함없이, 일정불변하게 as ~ as possible 가능한 ~하게 brand new 아주 새로운, 신품의, 갓 만들어진 have connection with ~과 관련이 있다

해설 일반화된 내용만 가지고서 독서를 할 것이 아니라 세부 내용에 대한 독서가 문학 작품을 이해하는 필수 요소가 된다는 것이 이 글의 주제가 된다.

The same nonverbal behavior may have a totally different meaning when it occurs in another context.

Like verbal communication, nonverbal communication exists in a context, and that context determines to a large extent the meanings of any nonverbal behaviors. (1) A wink of the eye to an attractive person on a bus means something completely different from a wink of an eye to signify a lie. (2) Similarly, the meaning of a given bit of nonverbal behavior depends on the verbal behavior it accompanies or is close to in time. (3) Pounding the fist on a table during a speech in support of a politician means something quite different from the same fist pounding in response to news of a friends' death. Of course, even if we know the context in detail, we still might not be able to decipher the meaning of the nonverbal behavior. (4) In attempting

해석 비언어적 대화도 언어적 대화처럼 문맥 속에 존재하며 문맥은 어떤 비언어적 행위들의 의미라도 상당한 정도로 결정한다. 동일한 비언어적 행위도 다른 문맥에서 발생할 때 완전히 다른 의미를 가질 수 있다. 버스를 탔을 때 매력적인 사람에게 윙크하는 것은 거짓말임을 나타내기 위해 눈을 깜빡거리는 것과는 완전히 다른 것을 의미한다. 마찬가지로 주어진 소량의 비언어적 행위의 의미는 비언어적 행위가 수반하거나 곧 근접하게 되는 언어적 행동에 좌우된다. 어떤 정치인을 지지하는 연설을 할 때 연단을 주먹으로 치는 것은 친구의 사망 소식을 듣고 똑같이 주먹을 치는 것과 완전히 다른 것을 의미한다. 물론 우리가 문맥을 자세히 알고 있다 치더라도 그 비언어적 행위의 의미를 여전히 파악할 수 없을 수도 있다. 그러나 비언어적 대화를 이해하고 분석하려고 시도할 때, 그 문맥에 대한 충분한 인식이 꼭 필요하다.

어구 nonverbal behavior 비언어적 행위 occur 발생하다, 생기다 context (사건 등에 대한) 경위, 배경; 상황 determine 결정하다 to a large extent 상당한 정도까지 attractive 매력적인 signify 의미하다, 뜻하다 accompany 수반하다, 동반하다 in time 조만간 pound 탕탕 치다, 사정없이 치다 fist 주먹 in detail 상세히 decipher (암호문 등을) 해독하다(decode) recognition 인식

to understand and analyze nonverbal communication, however, it is essential that full recognition be taken of the context.

해설 눈을 깜빡거리고, 주먹을 내려치는 행위가 다른 맥락 하에서는 다른 의미를 가지게 된다는 구체적 예가 제시되는 (1) 문장 앞에 위치해야 한다. 왜냐하면 제시문은 그 예를 가리키고 있는 일반화된 문장이기 때문이다.

19 윗글의 흐름으로 보아 주어진 문장이 들어갈 가장 적절한 곳은?

① (1)　　　　② (2)
③ (3)　　　　④ (4)

>>> 다음 글을 읽고 문제의 답을 고르시오.

A common pattern in many societies provides for a periodic relaxation of the rules of conventional behavior. In some societies this goes to the length of letting down all sex barriers, even to the relaxing of incest taboos. In other societies there may simply be feasting, drinking, or dancing along with some other forms of entertainment. We find a counterpart of such activities in our Halloween parties, masked balls, costume parties, and Mardi Gras. Some societies make provision for ritual teasing and joking, or occasions when buffoonery, ribald tricks or tales, and other such activities are permitted or even encouraged. The jester and the clown are stock characters in many societies. By their uninhibited behavior they provide a vicarious outlet for socially restrained resentments and hostilities.

20 Which one of the following best summarizes the above passage?

① People in many societies enjoy life by relaxing rules.
② In some societies sex taboos are relaxed from time to time.
③ People in many societies relax their rules of behavior periodically.
④ Relaxation of morality is not dangerous in some cases.

해석 많은 사회에서는 전통적인 행동 규칙을 주기적으로 완화시키기 위해 공통된 패턴을 가지고 있다. 몇몇 사회에서는 이것이 모든 성(性) 장벽을 낮추어 놓고, 심지어는 근친상간의 금기까지 허용할 정도이다. 다른 사회에서는, 몇 가지 다른 형태의 오락과 더불어 축제를 하고, 술을 마시고, 춤을 추기까지 한다. 우리는 핼러윈 파티, 가면무도회, 변장 파티, 그리고 참회의 화요일에서 그 활동들과 대응하는 것들을 발견한다. 어떤 사회는 의식적인 괴롭힘과 놀리기를 준비하고, 아니면 해학이나, 상스러운 짓이나 이야기, 그리고 다른 활동들이 허용되거나 심지어 장려되는 행사들도 준비한다. 농담하는 사람과 광대는 많은 사회에서 전형적인 인물들이다. 그들의 구속되지 않은 행동들을 통해, 그들은 사회적으로 제약된 분노와 적대감을 대신하여 배출해 준다.

20 윗글의 요지는 무엇인가?

① 많은 사회에서 사람들은 규칙을 완화시켜서 삶을 즐긴다.
② 몇몇 사회에서 성적 금기 사항들이 때때로 완화가 된다.
③ 많은 사회에서 사람들은 간헐적으로 행동 규칙을 완화한다.
④ 도덕의 완화는 몇몇의 경우에 위험하지 않다.

어구 **common pattern** 공통 양식　**provide for** 준비하다, 대비하다; 규정하다　**periodic** 정기적인; 간헐적인　**relaxation** (의무 · 부담 따위의) 경감, 완화; 오락　**let down** (명예 · 체면 · 위신 등을) 떨어뜨리다, 낮추다, 내리다; (사람을) 낙심시키다, 실망시키다　**barrier** 장벽, 장애(물); 울타리　**feasting** 축제　**along with** ~과 함께　**counterpart** 상대물[인], 대응물[자]; 부본, 사본　**masked ball** 가면무도회　**costume party** 변장 파티　**Mardi Gras** 참회의 화요일　**make provision for** ~에 대비하다　**ritual** 의식의; 관습의　**tease** 괴롭히다; 희롱하다, 놀리다　**occasion** 행사; (특정한) 경우, 때; 기회　**buffoonery** 익살, 해학　**ribald** 상스러운; 음란한　**jester** 농담을 하는 사람; 어릿광대　**clown** 어릿광대; 천한 사람　**stock** 표준의; 평범한, 보통의; 재고의　**uninhibited** 금지되지 않은, 제약받지 않은　**vicarious** 대신하는; 대리의　**restrained** 삼가는, 자제하는　**hostility** 적대감

해설 첫 문장이 주제문으로서, '많은 사회는 전통적인 행동 규칙을 주기적으로 완화시키기 위한 공통된 패턴을 갖고 있다.'는 내용이 주제가 된다. 그 다음 문장부터는 지역에 따른 예를 구체적으로 상술하고 있다.

>>> 다음 글을 읽고 문제의 답을 고르시오.

The absence of risk produces a type of boredom which paralyses in a different way from fear, but almost as much. Risk is a form of danger which provokes a deliberate reaction; that is to say, it doesn't go beyond the soul's resources to the point of crushing the soul beneath a load of fear. The protection of mankind from fear and terror doesn't imply the abolition of risk; it implies, on the contrary, the permanent presence of a certain amount of risk in all aspects of social life; for the absence of risk weakens courage to the point of leaving the soul, if the need should arise, without the slightest inner protection against fear. All that is wanted is for risk to offer itself under such conditions that it is not transformed into a sensation of fatality.

21 윗글의 내용과 일치하지 않는 것은?

① A certain amount of risk always exists in all aspects of social life.
② We must protect mankind not only from fear and terror, but also from risk.
③ A type of boredom produced by the absence of risk paralyses nearly as much as fear does.
④ If risk is entirely absent, our courage will become so weak that the soul will not be properly protected against fear.

해석 두려움과는 다르지만, 리스크의 부재는 두려움만큼이나 무기력하게 만드는 일종의 권태를 만들어 낸다. 리스크는 신중한 반응을 유발하는 일종의 위험이다. 달리 말하자면, 그것은 상당한 두려움으로 정신을 망가뜨릴 정도까지, 정신의 능력을 넘어서지는 않는다. 인류를 두려움과 공포로부터 지켜내는 것이 위험을 없애는 것을 암시하지는 않는다. 반대로, 그것은 모든 사회적 측면에 있어서 어느 정도의 위험이 영원히 존재하는 것을 의미한다. 왜냐하면 위험의 부재가 필요하다면, 정신이 두려움에 대한 내적인 보호를 약간이라도 받을 수 없을 정도까지 용기를 약하게 하기 때문이다. 리스크로 인해 죽음을 느끼게 되지는 않는 그러한 상황에서 위험이 제공되는 것이 바람직하다.

21 윗글의 내용과 일치하지 않는 것은?

① 어느 정도의 위험은 모든 사회 생활 측면에서 언제나 존재한다.
② 우리는 두려움과 공포뿐만 아니라 위험으로부터 인간을 보호해야만 한다.
③ 위험이 없어져서 생겨난 일종의 권태는 두려움만큼이나 거의 그 정도로 많은 것을 무력화시킨다.
④ 만일 위험이 정말 사라진다면, 우리의 용기는 너무나 약해져서 공포로부터 영혼은 제대로 보호받지 못할 것이다.

어구 **absence** 없음, 결여; 부재 **boredom** 권태; 지루함 **paralyze** 마비시키다, 무기력하게 하다 **provoke** (감정 따위를) 일으키다, 일으키게 하다 **deliberate** 생각이 깊은, 신중한 **that is to say** 즉; 달리 말하자면 **crush** 눌러서 뭉개다, 짓밟다. 으깨다 **a load of** 상당한, 부담이 되는 **abolition** (법률·습관 등의) 폐지, 철폐, 전폐 **to the point of** ~의 정도까지 **slightest** 가장 미비한 **inner** 내부의 **transform A into B** A를 B로 변형시키다 **fatality** 불운, 불행; 죽음; 치사성

해설 위험은 목숨을 앗아갈 정도가 아니라면 일상생활 속에서 존재하게 되는 것은 당연한 것이 이 글의 주제가 된다. 따라서 두려움과 공포뿐만 아니라 위험으로부터 인간을 보호해야 한다는 설명은 틀렸다.

>>> 다음 글을 읽고 문제의 답을 고르시오. [22~23]

The idea that work is good for teenagers, no matter how miserable or time-consuming their jobs, is held with a deep moral conviction comparable to that surrounding the joys of motherhood or the benefits of apple pie. The idea has its origins in images of diligent adolescent apprentices working side by side with caring adult mentors.

Although the workplace has changed, it is still widely held that paid work is a character-building enterprise for young people—even more so than schooling. ______________ studies indicate that the sorts of characters work builds in the current workplace are not exactly what most of us have in mind.

해석 십대들이 일을 하는 것이 얼마나 절망적이고 시간을 낭비하는 것일지라도 십대들이 일을 하는 것이 좋다는 생각은 모성애의 기쁨이나 애플파이의 이점을 에워싸고 있는 것에 필적할 만한 깊은 도덕적 확신을 유지한다. 이러한 생각은 십대들을 돌보아 주는 성인 지도자와 협력하여 일하는 근면한 청소년 수습공들의 모습에 기원한다.

일터의 모습이 변했을지라도 임금 노동은 심지어는 교육보다 더 젊은이들의 인격을 형성하는 일이라고 아직도 널리 알려져 있다. 그러나 연구들에 따르자면 그것은 우리가 생각하는 것만큼 청소년들의 인격 형성에 기여하지 않는다고 한다.

22 윗글의 내용과 일치하는 것을 고르시오.

① 임금 노동이 십대들의 인격을 형성하는 데 도움이 된다는 사실은 꾸며낸 이야기이다.
② 학교 교육은 지금으로서는 바람직한 게 없다.
③ 십대들은 대체적으로 쾌적한 상태에서 일을 한다.
④ 젊은 학생들은 생각이 깊은 성인 지도자들과 함께 일하도록 권고받는다.
⑤ 십대들은 대개는 어머니들로부터 대단히 득을 본다.

22 윗글의 내용과 일치하는 것을 고르시오.

① It is a myth that paid work is instrumental in teenagers' character-building.
② Education in school now has nothing to be desired.
③ Teenagers in general work under favorable conditions.
④ Young students are recommended to work together with thoughtful adult supervisors.
⑤ Teens usually benefit a lot from their mothers.

23 빈칸에 들어갈 가장 적절한 것을 고르시오.

① Yet
② No doubt
③ In addition
④ Indeed
⑤ Otherwise

23 빈칸에 들어갈 가장 적절한 것을 고르시오.

① 하지만   ② 의심할 바 없이
③ 게다가   ④ 참으로
⑤ 그렇지 않다면

어구 be good for ~에 유익하다   no matter how 아무리 ~할지라도   miserable 가련한   time-consuming 시간을 낭비하는   be held with ~에 편들다, ~에 찬성하다   comparable to ~에 필적할 만한   motherhood 모성애, 어머니 구실   have one's origin in ~에 기원을 두다   diligent 근면한   adolescent 청춘기의   apprentice 견습공; 견습공으로 삼다   side by side 협력하여, 나란히   caring 돌보는   mentor 스승   workplace 직장, 작업장   character-building 인격을 형성하는   schooling 학교교육   not exactly 반드시 그런 것은 아니다[부분 부정]   have ~ in mind ~을 고려하다   myth 꾸며낸 이야기, 신화   be instrumental in ~에 도움이 되다   be recommended to R ~하도록 권고받다   a lot 대단히, 종종[부사]

해설 22 임금 노동이 젊은이들에게 학습보다 더 좋다는 생각이 잘못되었음을 마지막 문장에서 현실과 상반된다는 내용으로 결론을 내리고 있다. 즉, 임금 노동이 젊은이들에게 학습보다 더 중요하다는 내용은 일종의 '꾸며낸 이야기'라고 볼 수 있다.
23 앞 문제의 내용을 참조하건대, 현실이 반영된 내용이 마지막 문장에서 나오므로 '역접'의 관계가 옳다.

>>> 다음 글을 읽고 문제의 답을 고르시오. [24~25]

Pigeons have been taught to recognize human facial expressions, upsetting long-held beliefs that only humans had evolved the sophisticated nervous systems to perform such a feat. In recent experiments at the University of Iowa, eight trained pigeons were shown photographs of people displaying emotions of happiness, anger, surprise, and disgust. The birds learned to distinguish between these expressions. Not only that, but they were able to correctly identify the same expressions on photographs of unfamiliar faces. Their achievement does not suggest, of course, that the pigeons had any idea what the human expressions meant.

24 From the passage, which of the following can be inferred about pigeons?

① They can understand the same emotions humans can.
② They can always recognize human emotions.
③ They can only identify the expressions of people they are familiar with.
④ They have more sophisticated nervous systems than was once thought.

해석 비둘기들은 사람의 얼굴 표정을 인식할 수 있도록 길들여져서 단지 인간들만이 그와 같은 것을 할 만한 정교한 신경 체계를 발전시켰다는 오랜 믿음을 뒤집어 버렸다. 아이오와 대학의 최근 연구에서 8마리의 훈육된 비둘기들에게 행복, 분노, 놀라움과 혐오감을 드러내는 사람들의 사진을 보여 주었다. 그 새들은 이 감정들을 구별하도록 훈육되었다. 이것뿐만 아니라 익숙치 않은 얼굴의 사진들에 나오는 같은 표정들도 올바르게 구분해낼 수 있었다. 물론 그러한 결과는 비둘기가 인간의 표정이 의미하는 바가 무엇인지 모두 이해할 수 있다는 사실을 시사하는 것은 아니다.

24 비둘기에 대한 설명으로서 유추할 수 있는 내용은?
① 비둘기는 인간이 이해할 수 있는 감정을 역시 이해할 수 있다.
② 비둘기는 언제나 인간의 감정을 인식할 수 있다.
③ 비둘기는 익숙한 사람들의 표정만 단지 이해할 수 있다.
④ 비둘기는 예전에 생각했던 것보다 더 정교한 신경 체계를 갖고 있다.

25 윗글의 내용과 일치하는 것은?
① 비둘기들은 인간의 표정이 의미하는 바가 무엇인지를 안다.
② 비둘기들은 익숙하지 않은 얼굴이 찍힌 사진에 보이는 같은 감정들을 식별할 수 없다.
③ 비둘기는 교육받은 후에 인간의 얼굴 표정에 나타나는 감정을 구분하게 되었다.
④ 비둘기들은 교육받기 전에도 인간의 얼굴 표정에 나타나는 감정을 구분할 수 있었다.

25 Choose the one which is corresponding to the meaning of the above passage.

① Pigeons had an idea what the humans beings' expressions meant.

② Pigeons could not identify the same expressions on photographs of unfamiliar faces.

③ Pigeons became to distinguish emotions of human beings' facial expressions after they were taught to.

④ Pigeons were able to distinguish emotions of human beings' facial expressions before they learned to.

어구 **recognize** 인식하다, 인지하다 **upset** 뒤집다 **long-held** 오래 지속된 **sophisticated** 복잡한, 세련된 **feat** 공적, 위업, 기술 **be shown A** A가 보여지다 **disgust** 혐오 **identify** 감정하다, 확인하다, 동일시하다 **unfamiliar** 익숙하지 않은

해설 **24** 비둘기들이 인간의 감정을 이해할 수 있어서, 단지 인간들만이 그와 같은 것을 할 만한 정교한 신경 체계를 발전시켰다는 오랜 믿음을 뒤집어 버렸다는 첫 문장을 통해서 ④의 내용은 유추가 가능하다.

25 첫 문장에서 비둘기가 길들여져서 인간의 표정을 통해 감정을 인식할 수 있다는 것이므로, ③이 옳은 설명이다.

Robert had just moved into the neighborhood where he felt strange and unwanted. He realized that the other boys were probably sizing him up. He could not blame them for their lukewarm reception. He knew that he had to be tested, but proving himself would not be all that easy. (1) He did not want to run with the gangs or get into a legal hassle in order to prove that he was tough. (2) No! He must show what he was made of in (가) <u>a more constructive way</u>. (3) The next day was Sunday. (4) He knew that most of the guys would be down at the schoolyard choosing up sides for the weekly game. (5) Robert knew he could play well and that just might be enough to gain their approval. He arrived early and went through his places.

He wheeled around for a reverse layup, dribbled to the top of the key for a long jumper; and ran through his sky hook. Then the guys came. No one said a word. Everyone just stared and mulled it over. Then the biggest of the group just grinned and shook his head. Robert knew he had made it.

26 The best theme of the passage is
"______".

① How to gain friendship

② How to test courage

③ How to beat out tough guys on the street

④ How to be admitted into a sports team

⑤ How to mull over a tough situation

해석 로버트는 이사한 이웃 동네에서 자신이 낯설고 불필요한 존재라고 느끼게 되었다. 그는 다른 소년들이 아마도 그를 평가하고 있음을 인식했다. 그는 그들이 미온적인 태도를 보인다고 해서 비난하지 않았다. 그는 자신이 시험 받아야 한다는 것을 알기는 했지만 자신을 증명한다는 것이 그렇게 쉽지는 않았다. 그는 자신이 강하다는 것을 입증하기 위해 불량배들과 어울리거나 법적 싸움에 말려들고 싶지 않았다. 아니다! 그는 더 건설적인 방법으로 자신의 존재를 보여 줘야 했었다. 다음날은 일요일이었다. 그는 대부분의 아이들이 주간 경기를 위해 팀을 나누기 위해서 학교 운동장에 내려올 것이라는 것을 알았다. 로버트는 자신이 경기를 잘하고, 인정받기에 충분하다는 것을 깨달았다. 그는 일찍 도착해서 그 장소를 지나갔다.

그는 역레이업슛을 위해 회전했고, 긴 점프슛을 위해 자유투 지역 끝까지 드리블했으며, 공중 슛을 연습했다. 그때 그 아이들이 왔다. 어느 누구도 말을 하지 않았다. 모두 그저 응시했고 단지 곰곰이 생각하는 듯했다. 그때 그 아이들 중 가장 덩치가 큰 아이가 웃으면서 고개를 끄덕였다. 로버트는 그가 해냈음을 알았다.

26 이 글의 주제는?

① 친구를 사귀는 법

② 용기를 시험하는 법

③ 거리의 거친 아이들을 물리치는 법

④ 스포츠 팀에 가입하는 법

⑤ 힘든 상황을 숙고하는 법

27 로버트에 따르면 "건설적인 방법"은 무엇인가?

① 아이들에 동조하는 것

② 아이들과 친구가 되는 것

③ 자신이 운동을 잘하는 사람임을 보여 주는 것

④ 무리의 가장 거친 아이를 제압하는 것

⑤ 법적 투쟁으로 빠져 드는 것

28 이 글에 따랐을 때 로버트가 보여 준 스포츠는 무엇인가?

① 권투　　　　　　② 농구

③ 테니스　　　　　④ 축구

⑤ 야구

27 According to Robert, what is "a more constructive way" in (가)?

① To run with the guys
② To make friends with the guys
③ To show that he is a good athletic player
④ To subdue the toughest guy of the group
⑤ To get into a legal hassle

28 According to the passage, what game did Robert play?

① Boxing
② Basketball
③ Tennis
④ Football
⑤ Baseball

29 The attitude of the guys toward Robert was _____________.

① rather friendly
② quite hostile
③ quite indifferent
④ rather inhospitable
⑤ extremely antagonistic

30 If we divide the passage into three paragraphs, where does the second paragraph begin?

① (1)
② (2)
③ (3)
④ (4)
⑤ (5)

29 로버트에 대한 아이들의 태도는 어떠했는가?

① 우호적인
② 매우 적대적인
③ 매우 무관심한
④ 대접이 나쁜
⑤ 매우 적대적인

30 윗글을 세 개의 단락으로 나누고자 할 때 두 번째 단락이 시작되는 문장은?

어구 unwanted 불필요한 size up 평가하다 blame A for B B를 이유로 A를 비난하다, B의 탓을 A에게 돌리다 lukewarm 미지근한, 미온스러운 reception 반응 all that 그렇게나 run with 동조하다 legal hassle 법적 투쟁 be made of ~으로 구성되다 choose up sides 틈을 가르다, 선수를 뽑다 wheel around 방향을 바꾸다 layup 농구 슛, 휴식 long jumper 긴 점프슛 run through 연습하다, 통독하다, 낭비하다 stare 응시하다 mull over 숙고하다 make it 해내다 gain friendship 친구를 사귀다 beat out 물리치다, 입증하다 subdue 제압하다 get into ~으로 빠져들다, 착수하다 hostile 적대적인 friendly 우호적인 inhospitable 대접이 나쁜, 황량한 antagonistic 적대적인

해설 **26** 자신이 이사를 간 동네의 아이들이 환대를 해 주지 않자, 스스로 먼저 그 아이들과 친구가 되기 위해서 운동을 잘하는 자신의 모습을 보여 주려고 노력한 점은 결국 친구가 되기 위해서였다. 따라서 이 글의 주제는 친구를 사귀는 법이 옳다.

27 (가) 이하에서 친구가 되기 위해 그들 앞에서 농구 연습을 한 것으로 보아 ③의 내용이 가장 옳다.

28 레이업(layup), 긴 점프 슛(long jumper) 등으로 보아 농구임을 유추할 수 있다.

29 세 번째 문장에서 '미온적인 태도'를 보였다고 했는데, 이는 결국 이사 온 본인에게는 '대접이 나쁘거나 냉대한' 태도라고 볼 수 있다.

30 (2) 문장까지는 본인의 처한 상황과 마음가짐만 설명이 되지만, (3) 문장에서부터 행동으로 이어지므로 (3)에서 새로운 단락이 시작임을 알 수 있다.

Actual TEST 09

⇨ 본책 p.300

1 ②	2 ⑤	3 ③	4 ③	5 ②	6 ①	7 ④	8 ③	9 ③	10 ④
11 ①	12 ⑤	13 ②	14 ③	15 ②	16 ②	17 ②	18 ⑤	19 ②	20 ⑤
21 ④	22 ③	23 ④	24 ③	25 ③	26 ④	27 ①	28 ④	29 ⑤	30 ⑤

>>> 밑줄 친 곳에 들어갈 알맞은 답을 고르시오. [1~6]

1 Although all of the guests at the dinner party were ____________, the food was so poorly prepared that no one ate more than a small portion.

① elegant
② ravenous
③ invited
④ forewarned
⑤ surly

해석 저녁 파티에 참석한 모든 손님들은 배가 너무 고팠지만 준비된 음식이 너무나 형편없어서 아무도 한 입 이상 먹지 않았다.

어구 portion 일부, 소량, 조각 elegant 우아한 ravenous 몹시 굶주린, 게걸스러운 forewarn 미리 경고하다 surly 퉁명스러운, 무뚝뚝한

해설 although 양보 부사절이므로 '한 입 이상 먹지 않았다'는 내용과 역접의 관계가 옳다.

2 Judging from the ____________ of new talent on Broadway and the large number of revivals, we may assume that the era of the American musical is over.

① temerity
② versatility
③ laxity
④ verbosity
⑤ paucity

해석 브로드웨이에 재능을 가진 새로운 인재가 부족하다는 점과 재공연이 많다는 점을 고려해 보건대, 미국 뮤지컬의 시대가 끝이 났음을 우리는 가정할 수 있다.

어구 judging from ~을 고려해 보건대 revival 재공연 era 시대 temerity 무모함, 만용 versatility 다재다능함 laxity 느슨함 verbosity 장황함, 말이 많음 paucity 소량, 결핍

해설 '미국 뮤지컬의 시대가 끝이 났다'는 내용과 순접으로 이어지기 위해서는 새로운 인재의 부족이 옳다.

3 Again his speech was ____________. He just rattled away, boring everybody to death.

① to the point
② off the record
③ run-of-the-mill
④ straight from the horse's mouth
⑤ off the air

해석 또다시 그의 연설은 지극히 평범했다. 그는 그저 떠들어댈 뿐이었고 모든 사람들이 지루해 죽으려 했다.

어구 rattle away (시 · 이야기 · 선서 따위를) 줄줄 외다 bore A to death A를 지루하게 하다 to the point 요령 있는, 적절한 off the record 비공식적인 run-of-the-mill 통상적인, 평범한 straight from the horse's mouth 가장 확실한 계통에서 들은 off the air 일이 벗어나, 방송이 중단된

해설 줄줄 읊어대기만 했다는 얘기는 기존의 얘기들과 뻔하다는 내용을 의미한다.

4 Hot milk has long been a standard cure for insomnia because of its ____________ quality.

① malevolent
② amorphous
③ soporific
④ plaintive
⑤ desultory

해석 뜨거운 우유는 졸리게 하는 성질이 있기 때문에 오랫동안 불면증에 대한 기본적인 요법이 되어 왔다.

어구 insomnia 불면증 malevolent 악의가 있는 amorphous 무형의 soporific 최면의, 졸린 plaintive 애처로운, 슬픈 desultory 산만한, 일관성이 없는

해설 불면증에 대한 처방이 되기 위해서는 잠을 오게 하는 성향이 있어야 한다.

5 Her acceptance speech was ___________, eliciting thunderous applause at several points.

① tedious ② well-received
③ cowardly ④ uninteresting
⑤ poorly written

해석 그녀의 수락 연설이 매우 반응이 좋아서 여러 곳에서 우레와 같은 박수갈채를 이끌어 냈다.

어구 acceptance speech 수락 연설 thunderous 우레와 같은 elicit 이끌어 내다 tedious 지루한 well-received 반응이 좋은 cowardly 비겁한 uninteresting 재미가 없는

해설 우레와 같은 박수갈채를 얻어 낼 만한 좋은 뜻을 가진 어휘이어야 한다.

6 When interest rates fall as quickly as the retired have in recent months, their income falls, and they will be forced to spend less. ___________. They are too old to work, or companies may not consider them employable. They could take more risk by moving into corporate bonds or equities. But that strategy incurs the danger of a permanent loss of capital.

① They do not have the option of making up lost income
② They must build a castle in the air
③ They can find a change of occupation
④ They have no choice but to return to a former business
⑤ They should plan to get rich at a single bound

해석 금리가 최근 몇 달처럼 급격하게 하락할 경우 그들의 수입도 떨어지게 되며 따라서 소비를 줄일 수밖에 없는 압박을 받게 된다. 이 고령의 은퇴자들은 손실된 수익을 메울 만한 옵션을 갖고 있지 않다. 그들은 일하기에 너무 늙었거나 혹은 회사들이 그들을 고용할 만한 대상으로 여기지 않는다. 그들은 회사채나 주식으로 옮겨가는 위험을 감수할 수도 있을 것이다. 그러나 그러한 전략은 자본의 영원한 손실이라는 위험을 초래할 수 있다.

6 ① 그들은 손실을 만회할 대안을 갖고 있지 못하다.
② 그들은 공상에 잠김에 틀림이 없다
③ 그들은 이직을 구할 수 있다
④ 그들은 이전 회사로 돌아가지 않을 수 없다
⑤ 그들은 일확천금을 노려야 한다

어구 corporate bond 회사채 build a castle in the air 공상에 잠기다 plan to get rich at a single bound 일확천금을 노리다

해설 다음 문장에서 나이가 너무 많아서 채용되기 힘들다고 했기 때문에, 하락한 금리로 인해 손해를 번 돈을 메울 수 없다는 논리가 적합하다.

>>> **다음 글을 읽고 문제의 답을 고르시오.**

Although Malthus was disciple of Smith and on a number of basic issues sided with the Classical school, he nevertheless holds a special place as the consistent defender of the interests of the landed aristocracy, in opposition to the Classics(Smith, Ricardo, and their followers), who expressed the interests of the industrial bourgeoisie.

7 윗글의 내용과 일치하는 것은?

① Malthus mainly defended the interests of the bourgeoisie.
② Ricardo theoretically represented the views of the landed aristocracy.
③ Smith was one of Malthus' pupils.
④ Malthus learned a lot from Smith.
⑤ Malthus was one of the chief exponents of the Classical school.

해석 맬더스는 스미스의 제자였고, 많은 기본적인 문제에서 고전학파와 입장이 같았지만, 그럼에도 불구하고 그는 지주 귀족 계급의 이익을 일관되게 옹호하는 사람으로서 특별한 위치를 차지하고 있다. 이러한 사실은 산업 자본가 계급의 이익을 나타내는 스미스나 리카도나 그들의 추종자들이 속하는 고전파와는 대립되는 것이다.

7 윗글의 내용과 일치하는 것은?
① 맬더스는 주로 자본가 계급의 이익을 옹호했다.
② 라카도는 이론적으로 지주 귀족 계급의 관점을 대표하였다.
③ 스미스는 맬더스의 문하생 중 한 명이었다.
④ 맬더스는 스미스로부터 많은 것을 배웠다.
⑤ 맬더스는 고전학파의 대표 옹호자 중 한 명이었다.

어구 disciple 제자, 문하생 side with ~에 찬성하다, 편들다 the Classical school 고전학파 consistent defender 일관된 옹호자 landed aristocracy 지주 귀족 계급 industrial bourgeoisie 산업 자본가 계급 landed 토지를 가지고 있는 exponent 설명자, 대표자

해설 맬리스는 스미스의 제자였으므로 그로부터 많은 것을 배웠다는 내용이 유추 가능하다.

Brains in middle age, which, with life spans increased, now stretches from the 40s to late 60s, also get more easily distracted. Start boiling water for pasta, go answer the doorbell and—whoosh—all thoughts of boiling water disappear. Indeed, aging brains, even in the middle years, fall into what's called the default mode, during which period the mind wanders off and begin daydreaming. Given all this, the question arises, can an old brain learn, and then remember what it learns? Put another way, is this a brain that should be in school?

As it happens, yes. While it's tempting to focus on the flaws in older brains, that inducement overlooks how capable they've become. Over the past several years, scientists have looked deeper into how brains age and confirmed that they continue to develop through and beyond middle age.

8 According to the passage, brains in middle age

______________.

① are hopeless
② deteriorate rapidly
③ need to be trained
④ start producing new cells
⑤ cease to evolve

해석 수명이 증가하면서 현재 40대에서 60대 후반대의 중년층의 두뇌는 집중하기 어려워진다. 파스타를 만들기 위해서 물을 끓이다가, 초인종이 울려서 누구인지 알아보러 가다 보면 중간에 물을 끓이고 있었다는 것을 잊어버리게 된다. 게다가 노화되는 두뇌는 중년의 나이에서조차도 소위 불이행 형태라고 불리는 것으로 빠져들며, 그동안에 정신이 산만해지며 백일몽을 꾸기 시작한다. 이 모든 것을 고려해 보건대, 노화되는 두뇌가 학습을 할 수 있을까, 그리고 배운 것을 기억할 수 있을까라는 의문이 발생한다. 달리 말하자면, 이러한 두뇌는 배울 능력이 있는가라는 의문이다.

그런 의문에 대한 답은 "그렇다"이다. 노화된 두뇌가 일으키는 결점들에 집중해 연구하는 것이 더 흥미롭겠지만, 그러면 노화된 뇌가 얼마만큼의 능력을 갖게 되는지를 간과하게 된다. 지난 수년 동안, 과학자들은 어떻게 뇌가 노화되는지를 더 심도 있게 조사하여 두뇌가 중년 기간 내내, 그리고 중년의 나이를 지나서도 계속해서 발전한다는 것을 확인했다.

8 이 글에 따르면 중년의 두뇌는 어떠한가?

① 절망적이다
② 빠르게 감퇴하고 있다
③ 교육받을 필요가 있다
④ 새로운 세포를 만들 필요가 있다
⑤ 진화가 중단되고 있다

어구 **life spans** 수명 **distracted** 괴로운, 마음이 산란한 **whoosh** 휙[쉭]하고 움직이다 **default mode** 불이행 형태 **wander off** 옆길로 빗나가다, 탈선하다 **put another way** 달리 말하자면 **tempting** 유혹하는, 부추기는, 사람의 마음을 끄는 **inducement** 유도, 권유, 장려

해설 첫 단락 마지막 문장을 통해 '두뇌가 교육을 받아야만 하는가?'라는 문제가 제기되고, 두 번째 단락 첫 문장에서 '그렇다'라고 답했다. 따라서 중년의 두뇌는 교육받을 필요가 있다는 설명이 옳다.

Unfortunately, the guarantee is often also a lie.

How can you recognize a quack? Sometimes it's easy because he or she offers something that we know is impossible. (1) A drink to keep you young is an example of this. But many times, these people lie, saying that their product was made because of a recent scientific discovery. (2) This makes it more difficult to know if the person is real or a fraud. Another way to recognize quackery is that many quacks will say their product is good for many different illnesses, not just for one thing. They usually like to offer money-back promises if their treatment doesn't work. (3) Finally, the fraudulent clinic will often be in another country. (4) Laws in the United States will not allow a quack to have a clinic in the United States because the quack doesn't have the proper medical training.

해석 어떻게 당신은 돌팔이 의사를 알아낼 수 있을까? 때로 돌팔이 의사는 우리가 아는 바로는 불가능한 어떤 것들을 제시하기 때문에 그들을 알아보는 것은 어렵지 않다. (1) 당신을 젊게 해 준다는 음료수가 이것의 예가 된다. 그러나 이런 사람들은 그들의 상품이 최근의 과학적인 발견으로 만들어졌다고 말하면서 거짓말을 한다. (2) 이 때문에 그 사람이 진짜인지 사기꾼인지를 아는 것이 더 어려워진다. 엉터리 치료를 알아낼 수 있는 또 다른 방법은 많은 돌팔이 의사들은 그들의 상품이 단지 하나의 질병을 위해서가 아니라 많은 다른 질병에도 좋다고 말할 것이라는 점이다. 대개 그들은 그들의 치료약이 효과가 없으면 환불을 보장한다고 한다. 불행하게도 보장한다는 그 말도 또한 거짓말이다. (3) 결국, 무허가 진료소도 종종 다른 나라에 있을 것이다. (4) 미국 법에서는 돌팔이 의사들은 정규 의료 교육을 받지 않았기 때문에 미국 내에 진료소를 열 수 없도록 하고 있다.

어구 **guarantee** 보증, 담보 **quack** 돌팔이 의사, 사기꾼 **keep ~ young** ~의 젊음을 유지시키다 **fraud** 사기 행위 **quackery** 엉터리 치료; 사기꾼 같은 짓 **money-back** 환불 **fraudulent** 사기의, 부정의

해설 also라는 '첨가'의 논리 때문에 (1)은 부적절하며, '환불 약속'은 '환불해 주겠다는 보증'이 된다. 따라서 (3)이 옳다.

9 윗글의 흐름으로 보아 주어진 문장이 들어갈 가장 적절한 곳은?

① (1)　　② (2)　　③ (3)　　④ (4)

>>> 다음 글을 읽고 문제의 답을 고르시오. [10~11]

I have lived through most of this century and I have traveled to the four corners of the globe. I do not think I am stuck in a white U.S.-European viewpoint: I know how it feels to be an ① underdog. I have been in various jails as a political protester, and during those five medieval years when the Germans occupied the country of my youth, Holland, and most of Europe, I was a fugitive and a "terrorist."

10 Which of the following statements is NOT true?

① The writer is quite old.
② The writer has traveled various places of the world.
③ The writer was in Holland when he was young.
④ The writer was a runaway in the Middle Ages.
⑤ The writer spent some part of his life in jail.

11 Which of the following is closest in meaning to ①?

① loser　　　　　② tyrant
③ undergrounder　④ runaway
⑤ pervert

해석 나는 이번 세기 대부분을 살았으며 지구의 구석구석을 여행 다녔었다. 나는 나 자신이 백인인 미국과 유럽 중심적 관점으로 고정되어 있다고 생각하지 않는다. 나는 그것이 얼마나 패배자 같은 느낌이 드는지를 안다. 나는 정치범으로서 여러 감옥살이를 했으며 독일이 내 젊은 시절에 조국인 네덜란드와 유럽 대부분을 점령한 5년의 중간 기간 동안 도망자이자 테러리스트였다.

10 이 글과 일치하지 않는 내용은?

① 작가는 꽤 나이가 먹었다.
② 작가는 세계 여러 지역에 여행을 다녀왔다.
③ 작가는 젊었을 때 네덜란드에 있었다.
④ 작가는 중세 시대 도망자였다.
⑤ 작가는 약간의 삶을 감옥에서 보냈다.

11 밑줄 친 단어와 뜻이 가장 유사한 것은?

① 패배자　② 폭군　③ 지하에서 일하는 사람　④ 도망자　⑤ 변태

어구 **four corners** 구석구석　**the globe** 지구　**stick** 고정시키다, 찌르다, **viewpoint** 관점　**underdog** (생존 경쟁 따위의) 패배자, 낙오자, (사회적 부정·박해 등에 의한) 희생자, 약자　**occupy** 점령하다, 차지하다, 거주하다　**fugitive** 도망자; 도망치는, 즉흥적인, 일시적인　**pervert** 성욕 도착자, 변태

해설 **10** 마지막 문장의 during those five medieval years는 '중세 시대'가 아닌 독일 침공 시기 중, '중간 시기'를 의미하므로, the Middle Ages(중세 시대)는 틀린 설명이다.

11 underdog은 '패배자, 낙오자, 약자(a person, team etc that is weaker than the others, is always expected to be unsuccessful, and that is often treated badly)'의 의미를 가진다.

>>> 다음 글을 읽고 문제의 답을 고르시오. [12~15]

Maps don't just pinpoint sites and attractions; they influence how their readers experience a region. "They are generalizations," says geographer Mark Monmonier, "that often depict only what those who make them want you to see." In Asia and beyond, a good map—current or historical—can serve ① ______________ both an essential travelers tool and a rich portrait of the region's past. Early Western explorers, like Macro Polo and Christopher Columbus, used maps derived ② ______________ incredible tales about Asia that were accepted as facts. A widely used 1626 map of China drawn by the Englishman John Speed was based on the writings of Marco Polo, who some historians contend never actually laid ③ ______________ on the place. ④ In Speed's map, China is drawn in the shape of a horse's head, the South China Sea is infested with monsters and the region north of the Great Wall (present-day Mongolia) is noted as a place where "men are seduced by wonderful illusions." The earliest Chinese-made world maps usually portrayed the country as a large, smooth circle surrounded by several smaller satellites.

해석 지도는 위치와 매력적인 장소들만 나타내는 것이 아니라, 지도를 보는 사람들이 그 지역을 어떤 방식으로 경험하는지에도 영향을 미친다. 지리학자인 마크 몰모니어는 "지도를 만드는 사람들이 당신(일반인들)이 보고 싶어하는 것만을 묘사해 일반화한 것이 지도이다."라고 말한다. 현재 또는 과거의 아시아와 그 이외 지역에 관한 훌륭한 지도는 여행자의 필수 도구이자 그 지역의 과거를 풍부하게 알 수 있게 도와준다. 마르코 폴로와 크리스토퍼 콜럼버스와 같은 초기 서양 탐험가들이 아시아에 관한 믿을 수 없는 이야기들을 사실로 받아들였던 이유는 지도였다. 영국인인 존 스피드가 편찬한 1626년도의 널리 사용된 중국 지도는 마르코 폴로의 작품에 근거를 둔 것이었는데, 몇몇 역사가들은 마르코 폴로가 실제로 그 지역을 결코 본 적도 없었다고 주장한다. 스피드의 지도에서 중국은 말의 머리 모양으로 그려져 있었고, 남지나해는 괴물들이 몰려다니고 있으며, 만리장성 북쪽 지역(현재의 몽골)은 '놀라운 환영에 의해 사람들이 매혹되는' 장소라고 주석이 표기되어 있다. 가장 초기의 중국이 제작한 세계 지도들은 보통 중국을 아주 크고 몇 개의 위성국가가 에워싼 부드러운 원형으로 묘사하였다.

12 Which of the following is true?

① Map-making has been one of the most empirical businesses from the beginning.
② In Speed's map, the South China Sea is noted as a place where men are seduced by wonderful illusions.
③ Speed's 1626 map of China was based on the actual drawings by Marco Polo of the regions of the country.
④ The maps which explorers like Marco Polo and Christopher Columbus used in their adventures were based on unreliable tales about Asia which no one believed to be true.
⑤ According to Mark Monmonier, the configuration of a map is often decided by what the maker wants the user to see on it.

13 Which of the following best fits into ① and ②?

① as - by   ② as - from
③ by - to   ④ before - to
⑤ for - from

14 Which of the following best fits into ③?

① hands   ② imagination
③ eyes   ④ emphasis
⑤ arms

15 The underlined part ④ implies ______________.

① The South China Sea was a very dangerous place for travelers because of monsters.
② Speed's map cannot be said to have been the result of first-hand experience.
③ The earliest Chinese map drawers were very interested in the realistic depiction of countries other than China.
④ Northern China was a strange place where men were seduced by wonderful illusions.
⑤ None of the above.

12 다음 중 옳은 것은?

① 지도 제작은 시작부터 가장 경험이 필요한 사업 중 하나였었다.
② 스피드의 지도에서 남지나해는 인간들이 놀라운 환영에 의해 매혹됐었던 지역이라고 주석이 달렸었다.
③ 스피드의 1626년도 중국 지도는 마르코 폴로가 그린 국가의 지역의 실제 그림에 근거를 두었다.
④ 마르코 폴로와 크리스토퍼 콜럼버스 같은 개척자들이 신대륙 탐험에서 사용했었던 지도들은 어느 누구도 사실이라고 믿지 않았었던 믿을 수 없는 이야기에 근거를 두고 있었다.
⑤ 마크 몰모니어에 따르자면 사용자가 지도에서 보기 원했던 정보가 무엇이냐에 의해 지도의 형태가 종종 결정이 됐었다.

13 ①과 ②에 알맞은 것은?

14 ③에 들어갈 말은?

① 손   ② 상상
③ 눈   ④ 강조
⑤ 팔

15 ④가 암시하는 것은?

① 남지나해는 괴물들 때문에 여행자들에게는 매우 위험한 장소였다.
② 스피드의 지도는 직접적인 경험의 산물이라고 전해질 수 없다.
③ 가장 초기의 중국 지도 편찬가들은 중국이 아닌 다른 국가들의 실제 묘사에 매우 관심을 가졌었다.
④ 중국의 북쪽은 인간들이 황홀한 환영에 의해서 매혹됐었던 이상한 장소였다.
⑤ 유추할 수 있는 내용이 없음.

어구 **pinpoint** 정확히 위치를 지적하다 **attraction** 매력, 매력거리 **generalization** 일반화, 보편화 **essential** 긴요한, 수적인 **portrait** 상세한 묘사, 초상화 **explorer** 탐험가 **derive from** (다른 것, 근원에서) ～을 끌어내다, 얻다; 추론하다 **incredible** 믿을 수 없는, 믿어지지 않는 **contend** ～을 주장하다 **lay/set/clap eyes on** ～을 주시하다 **be infested with** ～이 만연하다, 들끓다 **seduce** 유혹하다, 매혹하다 **illusion** 환상, 환영 **satellite** 위성국, 위성, 위성도시 **map-making** 지도 제작 **empirical** 경험의, 경험적인 **configuration** 배치, 형태 **first-hand** 직접적인 **other than** ～을 제외하고서

해설 12 두 번째 문장에서 '지리학자인 마크 몰모니어는 "지도는 보통 지도를 만드는 사람들이 당신이 보고 싶은 것을 그림으로 나타내는 일반화된 것이다"라고 말한다'고 했으므로 ⑤가 옳은 문장이다.
13 serve는 전치사 as와 결합하여, '도움이 되다, 봉사하다'는 뜻을 가지게 된다. derive는 자·타동사 기능이 모두 있는데 전치사 from과 결합하여 '유래하다, ～에서 시작되다'는 뜻을 가지게 된다.
14 lay eyes on은 '～을 주시하다'는 뜻을 가진 표현이다. 문맥상 중국을 방문한 마르코 폴로가 중국의 실제 풍경을 보았느냐 또는 못 보았느냐는 논점이 옳다.
15 스피드의 지도에는 중국이 괴상한 모습으로 묘사됐음이 단서이다.

>>> 다음 글을 읽고 문제의 답을 고르시오. [16~19]

For a week or so after the Storm, when (1) New Orleans wallowed in its filth and misery without help from (2) the United States of America, which (3) it had mistakenly believed (4) it was part of, people helped one another drag the taped-up fridges outside. Rows and rows of white metal boxes cradling generations of maggots began to fill the narrow byways of one of America's oldest cities. Waves of putrefaction rolled over the streets. New Orleans sank into the ① _______________ like a corpse into the embrace of the earth. New Orleans music and art had always been inspired by ① _______________ : rotting vegetation, blooming night jasmine, the faint smell of the dead wafting from the city's above-ground cemeteries, rotting crustaceans, transpiration and sex. Now (5) here was all this ① _______________ , magnified a thousand times. And here were ② all these metal tombs stretching as far as the eye could see, more numerous than the graves they resembled.

16 Choose one word most appropriate for the three underlined blank ①.

① inspiration　　② funk
③ integrity　　④ felicity
⑤ bliss

17 What does the underlined ② refer to?

① the city's graves　　② the taped-up fridges
③ rotting crustaceans　　④ blooming night jasmine
⑤ rotting vegetation

18 Which of the following cannot be inferred from the above passage?

① The administration might not be concerned about New Orleans' disaster.
② New Orleans was a slum for a long time.
③ Under the condition that there were no supports, the dwellers laid corpses in refrigerators.
④ New Orleans' music presented a gore atmosphere as well as no animation.
⑤ New Orleans didn't yearn for active support of the administration.

19 Among (1), (2), (3), (4) and (5), which one differs from the others in what they refer to?

① (1)　　② (2)
③ (3)　　④ (4)
⑤ (5)

해석 폭풍우가 지난 후 대략 일주일 동안 뉴올리언스는 참사에 관심을 갖지 않았던 미국 정부 때문에 오물과 고통으로 몸부림쳤는데, 사람들은 서로를 도와서 테이프로 봉한 냉장고를 밖으로 끌어냈다. 구더기들이 내장된 하얀색 금속 상자의 행렬이 미국에서 가장 오래된 도시 중 하나의 좁은 옆길에 채워지기 시작했다. 부패물의 물결이 거리 전체로 요동쳤다. 뉴올리언스는 지구의 품 안으로 시체와 같은 악취로 빠져들었다. 뉴올리언스의 음악과 예술은 계속해서 악취에서 영감을 얻었는데, 그 악취는 썩은 채소, 밤에 만개하는 재스민, 도시의 공동묘지의 시체들에서 둥둥 떠다니는 희미한 냄새, 썩은 갑각류, 땀과 섹스로부터 온 것이었다. 바야흐로 이 모든 악취가 여기에 있으며, 악취의 정도가 천 배나 심해졌다. 그리고 여기에 눈으로 볼 수 있는 곳까지 멀리 펼쳐져 있는 모든 금속 무덤들이 있으며, 그 금속 무덤들이 닮은 실제 무덤보다 더 숫자가 많아졌다.

16 ①에 들어갈 말은?

① 영감　　② 악취　　③ 완전함
④ 행복　　⑤ 행복

17 ②가 가리키는 것은?

① 도시의 무덤들　　② 테이프로 봉인된 냉장고들
③ 부패한 갑각류들　　④ 만개한 밤 재스민
⑤ 부패한 채소

18 윗글을 통해서 유추할 수 없는 내용은?

① 미국 정부는 뉴올리언스의 참사에 관심을 갖지 않았다.
② 뉴올리언스는 이전부터 빈민가였다.
③ 지원이 없는 상태에서 주민들이 시체를 냉장고에 안치했다.
④ 뉴올리언스의 음악은 생동감이 없으며 끔찍한 분위기를 띤다.
⑤ 뉴올리언스 주민들은 정부의 지원조차 바라지도 않았다.

19 보기항 (1)~(5) 중 다른 하나를 가리키는 보기는?

어구 or so 대략　wallow 뒹굴다, 허우적거리다　filth 오물　misery 불행, 고통　mistakenly 오해하여, 잘못하여　taped-up 테이프로 봉해진　fridge 냉장고(refrigerator)　rows and rows 끝없는 행렬　cradle 보호하다, 요람에 넣다; 요람　maggot 구더기　narrow 협소한　byway 샛길, 옆길　putrefaction 부패(물)　roll over 구르다, 자빠뜨리다　sink into 가라앉다, 침몰하다　corpse 시체　be inspired by ~에 영감을 얻다　rotting 썩은　blooming (꽃이) 만개한　faint 희미한, 미세한　waft (물체·소리·냄새 따위가) 감돌다　above-ground 지상의　cemetery (공동)묘지　crustacean 갑각류　transpiration 땀, 증발, 발산　tomb 무덤　stretch 뻗치다　as far as ~하는 한 (멀리까지)　numerous 수많은　funk 악취, 공포, 겁쟁이　integrity 완전한 상태, 성실　felicity 행복　bliss 행복　administration 정부　disaster 참사, 재난　slum 빈민가　for a long time 오랫동안　under the condition that ~ ~라는 상태 하에서　dweller 주민　lay a corpse in 시체를 안치하다　present a atmosphere 분위기를 띠다　gore atmosphere 끔찍한 분위기　animation 활기　yearn for 갈망하다

해설 16 뉴올리언스의 참사에 따른 시체 부패의 악취에 의해서 지역 전체가 잠식을 당하므로, 썩은 채소와 공동묘지의 시체에서 나올 수 있는 것은 악취가 옳다.

17 이 글에서 시체를 안치한 냉장고는 taped-up fridges(테이프로 봉인된 냉장고) → whiter metal boxes(흰 금속 상자) → all these metal tombs(이 모든 금속 무덤)으로 비유적으로 재진술되고 있다.

18 ~ the United States of America, which it had mistakenly believed it was part of ~ 지문을 통해서 '뉴올리언스 지역이 미국의 영토라고 잘못 믿었다'는 해석이 가능하다. '잘못 믿었다'는 내용은 '본래 뉴올리언스 지역이 미국의 영토이니 지원을 받을 수 있다'고 착각했음을 알 수 있으므로, 지원조차 바라지 않았다는 내용은 틀린 설명이다.

19 (3)~(5)는 모두 뉴올리언스라는 지역을 가리키므로 국가를 나타내는 (2)는 틀렸다.

>>> 다음 글을 읽고 문제의 답을 고르시오. [20~22]

Bill Smith said the most common form of HIV worldwide evolved from simian immunodeficiency virus, or SIV, that was in the chimpanzee. SIV genetically converted to HIV either while it was in the chimp or after a human (A) contracted SIV.

The disease did not become a worldwide menace, he said, until people left the isolated areas of Africa and carried the virus around the globe.

The findings are consistent with earlier studies that suggested that HIV originated early in 20th century and then was spread when Africa became less isolated. Bill Smith said the date when SIV first evolved to HIV makes it "very unlikely" that a polio vaccination campaign in the late 1950s can be blamed for the rise of AIDS. Some researchers have suggested that a polio vaccine made using chimpanzee kidney cells could have transferred HIV into humans between 1957 and 1960.

Although the new research could not eliminate that possibility entirely, Bill Smith said, the fact that HIV originated before the polio vaccine means "you can probably discount (B) the scenario".

20 The best title of this passage is ____________.

① Spreading of HIV
② A Polio Vaccine as the source of HIV
③ Africa as the Origin of HIV
④ HIV vs. SIV   ⑤ Origin of HIV

21 The underlined "contracted" in (A) is closest in meaning to ____________.

① was immunized against
② discovered   ③ inherited
④ became infected with   ⑤ detected

22 밑줄 친 (B) the scenario가 일컫는 것은?

① HIV가 소아마비 백신을 사용하기 전에 인간에게 전염되었다는 것
② HIV가 아프리카의 개방과 더불어 인간에게 급속히 퍼졌다는 것
③ HIV가 침팬지를 이용한 소아마비 백신을 통해서 인간에게 전염되었다는 것
④ HIV가 침팬지 몸에 있는 SIV를 통해 인간에게 퍼졌다는 것
⑤ HIV가 20세기에 원숭이의 바이러스를 통해 인간에게 발생했다는 것

해석 빌 스미스는 세계에 퍼진 HIV의 가장 공통된 형태는 유인원 면역결핍 바이러스, 즉 다시 말하자면 SIV로부터 발전된 것이며, 침팬지의 몸 속에 있었다고 전했다. SIV는 침팬지의 몸 안에 있는 동안, 또는 후에 사람이 SIV에 감염된 이후에 유전적으로 HIV로 바뀌게 된다.

그가 말하길, 그 병은 사람들이 아프리카의 고립된 지역을 떠나서 세계 곳곳에 그 바이러스를 옮겨 놓고서야 비로소 세계를 위협하는 존재가 되었다고 한다.

그 발견들은 HIV가 20세기 초기에 시작되었으며 그런 후에 아프리카가 덜 고립되었을 때 확산되었다고 주장하는 초기 연구들과 일치한다. 빌 스미스는 SIV가 처음 HIV로 발전한 시기가 1950년대 후반에 있었던 소아마비 백신 캠페인이 AIDS 증가의 원인이 될 수 있다는 사실을 매우 가능성이 없게끔 만들어 버린다고 말했다. 몇몇 연구가들은 침팬지의 신장세포를 이용하여 만들어진 소아마비 백신은 1957년과 1960년 사이에 HIV를 인간에게 옮겨 놓았다고 주장해 왔다.

또한 비록 새 연구가 가능성을 완전히 배제할 수는 없을지라도, 소아마비 백신이 생기기 전에 HIV가 생겼다는 사실은 "당신이 아마도 그 시나리오를 무시할 수 있다"는 점을 의미한다고 전한다.

20 이 글의 제목은?

① HIV의 확산   ② HIV의 원인이 된 소아마비 백신
③ HIV의 근원이 된 아프리카   ④ HIV vs. SIV
⑤ HIV의 기원

21 (A) contracted의 의미로서 유사한 것은?

① 면역이 되다   ② 발견되다
③ 상속하다   ④ 병에 걸리다
⑤ 감지하다

22 밑줄 친 (B) the scenario가 일컫는 것은?

어구 HIV 에이즈 바이러스 worldwide 세계적인, 세계에 퍼진 simian 유인원(의), 원숭이(의) immunodeficiency 면역결핍 contract 병에 걸리다, 계약하다, 축소하다 menace 위협(하다) isolated 고립된 finding 발견, 조사 결과 originate in ~에 기원을 두다 unlikely 가능성이 없는 be blamed for ~의 원인이 되다, ~ 때문에 비난받다 kidney cell 신장세포 eliminate 제거하다 discount 무시하다 immunize 면역이 되게 하다, 면역성을 주다 inherit 타고나다, 내재하다

해설 **20** 이 글은 에이즈 바이러스인 HIV의 생성 과정과 기원에 대해 빌 스미스의 의견을 중심으로 설명하고 있다.

21 contract는 '축소되다, 병에 걸리다, 계약하다'는 뜻이 있는데, 본문에서는 '(병에) 걸리다' 뜻으로 쓰였다.

22 마지막 문장의 입장을 밝히는 이는 빌 스미스이다. 그의 입장에서 무시받게 된다는 '시나리오'라 함은, 결국 앞 단락에서 자신의 견해와 다른 입장을 밝힌 '소아마비 백신이 에이즈의 원인이 될 수 있다.'고 주장한 Some researchers의 시나리오가 되겠다.

>>> 다음 글을 읽고 문제의 답을 고르시오.

It is estimated that there are nearly 5,000 gangs in the United States with a total of almost 250,000 members.

a. In my opinion, gangs are a direct result of the breakdown of the traditional family.

b. Why are all these young adults choosing to be gang members?

c. In fact, in inner cities, where gangs are most common, 7 percent of all teenagers are gang members.

23 제시문 이후 문장들이 올바른 순서로 배열된 것은?

① a - b - c 　　② b - c - a
③ a - c - b 　　④ c - b - a

해석 미국에는 거의 총 25만 명으로 이루어진 대략 5,000개의 조직폭력단이 있다고 추정된다.
c. 사실, 폭력배가 많은 도심 지역에는 전체 십대의 7퍼센트가 조직폭력단의 멤버이다.
b. 왜 이 모든 젊은이들이 조직폭력단의 멤버가 되는 것을 택할까?
a. 내 생각으로는, 조직폭력단은 전통적인 가정 붕괴의 직접적인 결과이다.

어구 **estimate** 어림잡다, 예측하다　**gang** 일당, 한 떼, 갱단　**breakdown** 고장; 몰락, 붕괴

해설 대략 5,000개의 조폭이 있다는 수치와 이어질 수 있는 비율 표현인 c 문장이 바로 이어지게 되며, 많은 젊은이들이 왜 조직폭력단의 멤버가 되기를 원하는지 문제점을 제시한 b와 원인을 밝힌 a가 차례로 연결되어야 한다.

>>> 다음 글을 읽고 문제의 답을 고르시오.

In the very old time, there lived a king who was a man of exuberant fancy and of an authority so irresistible that, at his will, he turned his varied fancies into facts. He was greatly given to self-communing, and when he and himself agreed upon anything, the thing was done. When everything moved smoothly, his nature was bland and genial; but whenever there was a little hitch, he was blander and more genial still, for nothing pleased him so much as to make the crooked straight, and crush down uneven places.

24 According to the above passage, which of the following is true about the king?

① He was generous but incompetent.
② He was so keen to construct new buildings.
③ He was determined and autocratic.
④ He dedicated himself to forgiving wrongdoers.

해석 아주 오래 전에, 풍부한 상상력과 이 상상력을 자신의 의지대로 현실로 바꿀 정도의 거부할 수 없는 권위를 가진 왕이 살았다. 그는 몹시 자기 생각에 몰두하였고, 그와 자신이(내면의 생각이) 어느 것이라도 합의를 하게 되면(맞아 떨어지면), 그 일은 완수되었다. 모든 일이 순조롭게 진행될 때, 그의 성격은 온화했고 상냥했다. 그러나 약간의 문제가 생길지라도, 그는 더욱 온화하고 상냥했다. 왜냐하면 그 어떤 것도 비뚤어진 것을 바로잡고 울퉁불퉁한 곳을 눌러 펴는 것만큼 그를 즐겁게 해 주지 못했기 때문이다.

24 윗글에 따르면, 왕에 대해 맞는 것은?

① 그는 관대하지만 무능했다.
② 그는 새로운 건물들을 건설하는 것에 열중했다.
③ 그는 단호했고 독재적이었다.
④ 그는 잘못을 저지른 사람들을 용서하는 것에 헌신을 다했다.

어구 **exuberant** (상상력·재능 등이) 넘치게 풍부한　**fancy** 공상, 상상　**be given to** ~에 몰두하다　**self-communing** 자기 성찰, 깊은 생각, 심사숙고　**bland** (기후가) 온화한; 부드러운; 침착한　**genial** (봄 날씨 따위가) 온화한; 다정한　**hitch** 지장, 장애; 급격히 잡아당김[움직임]; 급정지　**crooked** 꼬부라진, 비뚤어진　**crush down** 뭉개다; 바수다, 가루로 만들다; 진압하다　**uneven** 평탄하지 않은, 울퉁불퉁한　**generous** 관대한　**incompetent** 무능한

해설 자신이 상상하는 것을 반드시 현실로 바꿔 놓는 것은 '결단력'이 있다는 것이며, 마음에 안 드는 것을 펴 버린다는 것은 그만큼 독재적이라는 특성으로 설명이 가능하다.

>>> **다음 글을 읽고 문제의 답을 고르시오.**

I am passionate about the game of golf. I have played it most of my life and have spent more time than I should try to figure out what I find so intriguing about getting a small white ball into a small dark hole. I'm sure that part of the reason is the range of emotion a round of golf can bring out and the complex array of personality traits it reveals.

I have often said that I can tell more about how someone is likely to react in a business situation from one round of golf than I can from a hundred hours of meetings. Maybe golf cuts more directly to the psyche than other games and situations. Or maybe it's the venue itself—green grass and rolling hills. It's astonishing how so simple a game can reveal so much.

25 윗글의 요지로서 가장 적절한 것은?

① Most businessmen are passionate about the game of golf.
② A golf course is often used for important business meetings.
③ You can get much insight about people from a round of golf.
④ You need lots of mental training to become a good golf player.

해석 나는 골프에 빠져 있다. 나는 인생 대부분 골프를 쳤으며, 작고 하얀 공을 작고 어두운 구멍 속에 들어가게 하는 것에 대하여 무엇이 그토록 흥미롭게 하는지를 알아내려고 노력한 것보다 더 많은 시간을 소비했다. 확신하건대, 그 이유의 일부는 골프 한 라운드가 드러낼 수 있는 감정의 범위와 그 라운드가 드러내는 연이은 복잡한 성격의 특성 때문이다.
나는 사업의 상황에서 누군가가 어떻게 반응할지에 대해 수백 시간의 모임을 통해 할 수 있는 것보다 골프 한 라운드를 통해 더 많이 알 수 있다고 말하곤 했다. 골프는 다른 어떤 운동이나 상황보다 정신과 직접 연결되어 있다. 또는 푸른 들판과 굽이치는 언덕 자체가 현장이 된다. 그렇게 간단한 경기가 그토록 많은 것을 드러내 보일 수 있다는 것이 놀라울 뿐이다.

25 윗글의 요지로서 가장 적절한 것은?

① 대부분의 사업가들은 골프 경기에 빠져 있다.
② 골프 경기는 중요한 사업 모임을 위해서 종종 이용된다.
③ 골프 한 경기를 통해 사람들에 대한 많은 통찰력을 가질 수 있다.
④ 당신은 뛰어난 골프 선수가 되기 위하여 많은 정신 훈련을 필요로 한다.

어구 **be passionate about** ~에 푹 빠져 있다 **figure out** 파악하다; 이해하다 **intriguing** 흥미로운 **a round of** ~의 한 게임 **bring out** (빛깔·성질을) 드러나게 하다; (의미를) 분명히 하다; (재능을) 발휘하다 **cut to psyche** 정신과 연결되다 **venue** 행위[사건]의 현장, (경기·회의 따위의) 개최(지정)지; (의론의) 입장, 논거

해설 골프 경기는 인간의 감정이나 성격의 특성과 같은 정신적 상태와 밀접한 관련을 맺고 있음이 이 글의 주제이다.

>>> **다음 글을 읽고 문제의 답을 고르시오.**

TV watching not only contributes to making us more violent, primarily by modelling violence as a conflict resolution strategy of first resort—it also serves to make us more frightened of the society we live in. Studies conducted by George Gerbner, founder of the Cultural Environment Movement, show that the more TV one watches, the more violent they believe the world around them to be, and hence, the less likely they are to leave their homes or interact with other people. He calls this the "Mean World Syndrome." Of course, the less people leave their homes, the more they watch TV. Hence, as they become trapped and isolated in front of their TV sets, the meaner they believe the world they no longer interact with to be.

해석 TV 시청은 폭력을 처음부터 의존할 만한 갈등 해결의 방법으로 인식하도록 하고 우리를 더욱 폭력적으로 만들 뿐만 아니라, 우리로 하여금 우리가 살고 있는 사회를 더 두려워하게 만드는 데 일조한다. 문화 환경 운동이라는 단체의 설립자인 조지 거브너가 실시한 연구에서는, TV 시청이 많아질수록 사람들은 자신의 주변 세상이 더 폭력적이라고 믿게 되며, 따라서 사람들은 가정을 떠날 가능성이 적어지고 다른 사람들과의 상호 작용을 할 가능성도 더 적어진다고 한다(따라서 사람들이 집에 더 많이 머무르려 하고, 혹은 타인과의 상호 작용 또한 더 감소된다고 한다). 그는 이것을 '비열한 세계 증후군'이라고 부른다. 물론 사람들이 집을 덜 비울수록, 사람들은 TV를 더 많이 시청하게 된다. 따라서 사람들이 TV 앞에서 꼼짝 못한 채 고립되기 때문에, 사람들이 더 이상 상호 작용을 하지 않는 세상이(더 이상 서로 접촉하지 않는 세상이) 그만큼 더 비열하다고 믿는다.

26 윗글에서 말하는 Mean World Syndrome이란 무엇인가?

① 사람들이 TV를 많이 볼수록 더욱 폭력적이 될 경향이 있으며, 세상을 더욱 비열한 곳으로 믿게 된다.
② 점점 더 많은 사람들이 폭력적인 세상을 싫어하는 경향을 보인다.
③ 사람들이 집에 더 많이 머물수록, TV를 더 많이 시청하게 되고 세상과 더욱 고립되게 된다.
④ 사람들이 TV를 많이 볼수록 세상을 더욱 폭력적인 곳으로 믿게 되고 세상과 접촉을 덜 하게 된다.

26 윗글에서 말하는 Mean World Syndrome이란 무엇인가?

① The more TV people watch, the more violent they tend to become and the meaner they believe the world to be.
② More and more people show the tendency of hating their violent world.
③ The more people stay home, the more they watch TV and the more isolated they are form the world.
④ The more people watch TV, the more violent they believe the world to be and the less they interact with it.

어구 contribute to -ing ~에 이바지하다 primarily 주로; 근본적으로; 첫째로 model 모방하다; ~의 모형을 만들다 strategy 전략; 작전; 책략 resort 의지, 의뢰; 번화가 serve to R ~에 도움이 되다 believe A to be B A를 B라고 믿다 hence 그러므로 be likely to R ~할 것 같다 interact with 상호 작용하다 trap 덫으로 잡다, 덫을 놓다; 곤궁에 빠뜨리다 isolate 고립시키다, 분리[격리]하다 mean 비열한; 평균; 의미하다

해설 Studies ~ show that ~ 문장을 통해 '사람들의 TV 시청이 많아질수록 사람들은 자신의 주변 세상이 더 폭력적이라고 믿게 되고, 따라서 사람들이 집에 더 많이 머무르려 하고, 혹은 타인과의 상호 작용 또한 더 감소된다고 한다.'는 것이 Mean World Syndrome임을 알 수 있으며, 이를 재진술한 것이 ④이다.

>>> **다음 글을 읽고 문제의 답을 고르시오.**

> "If I were to die first, would you remarry?" the wife asks. "Well," says the husband, "I'm in good health, so why not?" "Would she live in my house?" "It's all paid up, so yes." "Would she drive my car?" "It's new, so yes." "Would she use my golf clubs?" "No, she's left-handed."

27 Which of the following CANNOT be inferred from the passage?

① The wife will die soon.
② The wife is right-handed.
③ The husband is having an affair.
④ The husband is healthy.

해석 "혹시라도 내가 먼저 죽는다면 당신은 재혼할 건가요?"라고 아내가 물었다. 남편은, "글쎄, 난 건강하니까 왜 안 되겠어?"라고 말했다. "그 여자가 우리 집에서 살게 될까요?" "돈을 다 지불했으니까 아마도 가능하겠지?" "그 여자가 저의 차를 운전하게 될까요?" "새로 구입한 차니까 그러겠지." "그 여자가 내 골프채들을 사용할까요?" "아니, 그녀는 왼손잡이거든."

27 윗글에서 유추할 수 없는 내용은 무엇인가?

① 부인은 곧 죽을 것이다.　　② 부인은 오른손잡이이다.
③ 남편은 바람을 피우고 있다.　　④ 남편은 건강하다.

어구 if S were to R 혹시라도 ~한다면 remarry 재혼하다 in good health 건강한 pay up 지불하다 golf club 골프용 타봉; 골프 클럽(조직 또는 건물·부지) left-handed 왼손잡이의 have an affair 바람을 피우다

해설 첫 문장에서 if ~ were to R 구문을 통해 '가정법 미래'로 물어보고 있다. 이는 즉 부인이 죽지 않을 것임에도 완전 반대되는 가정법으로 물어보는 것이다. 따라서 그녀가 곧 죽지는 않을 것임이 분명히 유추가 된다. 마지막에서 가정법으로 묘사되던 그녀가 갑자기 왼손잡이라고 답변한 것으로 보아 남편이 누군가와 내연 관계에 있음을 유추할 수 있다.

---

28 다음 글의 흐름상 필요 없는 문장을 고르시오.

> What makes college such a vital force in shaping lives? For us, college not only can prepare you for a career, but also can broaden your horizons in other ways. ① From history classes, you may develop an interest in the French Revolution. ② You may become a regular concert-goer due to a music course. ③ A literature course may help discover the authors you will be reading for most of your life. ④ In many courses, most professors share information primarily via lecture and the text.

해석 인생을 살아가면서 대학을 필수적인 것으로 만드는 것은 무엇인가? 우리에게 있어서, 대학은 당신이 직업을 가질 수 있도록 준비시킬 수 있을 뿐만 아니라 다른 방법들로 당신의 시야를 넓혀 줄 수 있다. ①역사 수업에서 당신은 프랑스 혁명에 대한 관심을 발전시켜 나갈 수도 있다. ②당신은 음악 수업 때문에 정기적으로 음악회에 갈 수도 있다. ③문학 수업은 살면서 읽게 될 책의 작가들을 찾을 수 있도록 도와줄 수도 있다. ④많은 수업에서 대부분의 교수들은 주로 강의와 교재를 통하여 정보를 공유한다.

어구 vital 필수적인 broaden 넓히다 horizon 지평선; 시야 concert-goer 음악회에 자주 가는 사람; 음악 애호가 via ~을 거쳐 (by way of)

해설 나머지 글에서는 대학에서 직·간접적으로 배우는 내용을 설명하지만, ④만이 대학 교수의 수업 방식을 말하기 때문에 틀린 표현이 된다.

A form of diabetes common in overweight adults is increasingly striking overweight children, says a panel convened by the American Diabetes Association. In the past, nearly all cases of childhood diabetes were Type 1, in which the body fails to make insulin. But Type 2, an obesity-related disease in which the body can't respond well to insulin, has surged in children.

The panel recommends: children aged ten or older, more than 20 percent overweight and with a family history of Type 2 diabetes should see a doctor to determine if they need testing.

Overweight children of Asian, African, South Pacific or Hispanic ancestry are at greater risk. The best Prevention: (A) an active lifestyle and healthy weight, says Dr. Alan Moses of Boston's Joslin Diabetes center. "Tell your kids to go and run around."

29 What does the author imply by (A) "an active lifestyle"?

① Participating in every event actively
② Going everywhere to listen to ideas about treating Type 1 diabetes
③ Searching for good medical care for Type 2 diabetes
④ Encouraging people with incurable diseases like diabetes
⑤ Getting plenty of exercise and going out for many activities

30 According to the passage, which of the following statements is true?

① Type 1 diabetes has not appeared so far in children.
② Type 1 diabetes has increased in children due to the failure of making insulin.
③ Children with Type 2 diabetes are responsive to insulin.
④ Children with Type 2 diabetes are mostly age ten or younger.
⑤ Type 2 diabetes is closely linked to weight problems.

해석 비만인 성인들에게서 흔한 당뇨병의 형태가 비만 어린이들에게도 점점 두드러진다고 미국 당뇨병 협회에 의해 소집된 조사단이 말한다. 과거에는 거의 모든 아동 당뇨병의 경우 유형 1이었는데, 그 상태 하에서는 몸이 인슐린을 만들어 내지 못한다. 그러나 유형 2는 몸이 인슐린에 잘 반응할 수 없는 비만과 관련된 질병으로서, 아이들 사이에서 증가했다.

조사단은 20% 이상 몸무게가 더 나가고 유형 2의 당뇨병에 걸린 가족력이 있는 십대 혹은 그 이상의 나이가 된 아이들은 치료가 필요한지 확인하기 위해서 의사를 만나보아야 한다고 권고한다.

아시아, 아프리카, 남태평양 또는 히스패닉 계통의 비만 어린이들은 더 위험한 상태에 있다. 가장 좋은 치료책은 활동적인 생활 방식과 건강을 지킬 수 있는 체중이라고 보스턴의 조슬린 당뇨병 센터의 앨런 모지스 박사는 말한다. "아이들에게 밖에 나가 놀라고 하시오."

29 (A) "능동적인 생활 방식"을 통해 작가가 암시하는 내용은?
① 모든 행사에 능동적으로 참여하는 것
② 유형 1의 당뇨 치료에 관한 생각들을 들어보기 위해 모든 곳에 가 보는 것
③ 유형 2의 당뇨에 대한 좋은 치료법을 찾는 것
④ 당뇨병과 같은 불치병에 걸린 사람들을 격려하는 것
⑤ 많은 운동을 하고 많은 활동을 위해 외출하는 것

30 이 글의 내용과 맞는 것은?
① 유형 1의 당뇨병은 아직까지 아이들에게 나타나지 않았다.
② 유형 1의 당뇨병은 인슐린을 만들 수가 없었기 때문에 증가했었다.
③ 유형 2의 당뇨병에 걸린 아이들은 인슐린에 반응한다.
④ 유형 2의 당뇨병에 걸린 아이들은 대체로 십대 또는 그보다 어리다.
⑤ 유형 2의 당뇨병은 체중 문제와 밀접히 연관되어 있다.

어구 **diabetes** 당뇨병 **overweight** 비만의, 너무 살찐 **adult** 어른, 성인 **increasingly** 점점 더, 더욱 더 **strike** (병·죽음 등이) 덮치다, 발생하다 **panel** 토론자단, 강사단; 심사원단, 조사원단 **convene** 소집하다, 소환하다 **American Diabetes Association** 미국 당뇨병 협회 **obesity-related** 비만과 관련된 **respond** (자극에) 반응하다, 대답하다 **surge** 밀어닥치다, 급등하다 **family history** 가족력 **determine** 결정하다, 결심시키다 **testing** 치료, 실험 **ancestry** 계통, 조상 **be at risk** 위험하다 **run around** 돌아다니다 **encourage** 격려하다 **incurable** 불치의 **plenty of** 많은 **so far** 지금까지는 **due to** ~ 때문에 **responsive** 대답하는, 응하는, 감응하기 쉬운 **be linked to** ~과 연결·결부되다

해설 **29** 다음 문장에서 '아이들에게 나가서 놀라고 하시오.'라는 문장을 통해서 아이들이 외출을 통해 운동을 하고 활동을 해서 몸무게 관리를 하라는 내용이 유추 가능하다.

30 두 번째 단락에서 유형 2의 당뇨병의 가족력이 있고 몸무게가 20% 이상 더 나간다면 진단이 필요하다고 했으므로, 유형 2의 당뇨병은 체중과 관련이 있다고 볼 수 있다.

Actual TEST 10

⇨ 본책 p.314

1 ②	2 ⑤	3 ③	4 ①	5 ①	6 ①	7 ⑤	8 ④	9 ⑤	10 ②
11 ③	12 ④	13 ②	14 ①	15 ②	16 ③	17 ②	18 ④	19 ③	20 ⑤
21 ②	22 ②	23 ④	24 ③	25 ④	26 ④	27 ⑤	28 ③	29 ③	30 ⑤

>>> 밑줄 친 곳에 들어갈 알맞은 답을 고르시오. [1~6]

1 Looting is wrong and looters have no legal title to the things they ___________.

① buy
② steal
③ sell
④ give
⑤ seek

해석 약탈은 나쁜 행동이며, 따라서 약탈자에겐 자신이 훔친 물건에 대한 법적 권리가 전혀 없다.

어구 **looting** 약탈, 강탈(plunder) **looter** 약탈 · 강탈자 **have a title to** ~에 대한 권리 · 자격을 갖다

해설 법적 권리가 없는 행위라는 것이 단서이다.

2 The society was not ___________ and required much help from outside.

① self-centered
② self-indulgent
③ self-absorbed
④ self-conscious
⑤ self-sufficient

해석 그 사회는 자급자족을 하지 못하며, 외부로부터 많은 도움을 필요로 했다.

어구 **self-centered** 자기중심적인 **self-indulgent** 방종한 **self-absorbed** 제 생각 · 이익에 여념이 없는 **self-conscious** 자의식이 강한 **self-sufficient** 자급자족의, 제 힘으로 해나갈 수 있는

해설 많은 도움을 필요로 한다는 내용과 순접이어야 한다.

3 At first I was blamed for damaging Dad's typewriter, but when my sister said she was responsible, I was ___________.

① expiated
② exonerated
③ amended
④ set free
⑤ encroached

해석 처음엔 아버지의 타자기를 망가뜨려 비난을 받았지만, 여동생이 자신의 책임이라고 말하자 나는 잘못이 없어졌다.

어구 **damage** 손해 · 피해를 입히다 **expiate** 속죄하다 **exonerate** 무죄임을 밝히다 **amend** 수정하다 **set free** 석방하다, 놓아주다 **encroach** 침입 · 침해하다

해설 일반적으로 행위의 잘못이 없음을 밝힌다는 표현에는 amend를 쓴다.

4 The economic stability of nations and continents is often affected by the abundance or ___________ of precipitation.

① dearth
② allusion
③ force
④ condensation
⑤ rainfall

해석 국가와 대륙의 경제적 안정성은 강우량이 충분한지 아니면 부족한지에 의해 종종 영향을 받는다.

어구 **abundance** 풍부 **precipitation** 강수 · 강우(량) **dearth** 부족, 결핍 **allusion** 암시 **condensation** 응축, 응결; 요약

5 Knowledge of language results from the interplay of initially given structures of mind, maturational processes, and interaction with the environment. Thus there is no reason to expect that there will be ___________ properties of the knowledge that is acquired.

① invariant ② minimal
③ pointless ④ imaginative
⑤ unanimous

해석 언어에 대한 지식은 타고난 정신 구조, 성장 과정, 환경과의 상호작용 이 세 요소의 복합 작용의 결과이다. 따라서 후천적으로 습득되는 지식이 똑같은 특성을 보이리라 기대할 만한 이유가 전혀 없는 것이다.

어구 **interplay** 상호작용(interaction) **initially given** 타고난 **maturational process** 성장 과정 **properties** 특질, 특성 **acquired** 후천적인; 획득한 **invariant** 불변의 **minimal** 최소·극소의 **pointless** 무단; 무의미한 **imaginative** 상상력이 풍부한 **unanimous** 만장일치의(agreed)

6 Johnnie ___________ for his girlfriend the entire time she was away at camp; he didn't eat or sleep and just stared at her picture all day.

① pined ② apologize
③ precipitate ④ distill
⑤ vie

해석 자니는 여자 친구가 캠프에 없을 때 그리워하며 지냈다. 먹지도 자지도 않고 하루 종일 그녀의 사진만 보았다.

어구 **pine for/away** 연모하다. (너무 사랑하여) 그리워하며 지내다 **apologize for** ~에 대해 사죄하다. **precipitate** 마구 재촉하다 **distill** (불순물을) 제거하다(purify), (요점 등을 책에서) 뽑다(extract) **vie** 경쟁하다, 다투다

해설 먹지도 자지도 않으면서 여자 친구의 사진만 보았다는 논리는 연모하여 한탄한다는 내용이다.

>>> **다음 글을 읽고 문제의 답을 고르시오.** [7~9]

Chimps and children, gulls and Greeks—the ethologists go their merry way, comparing bits of human cultural behavior with bits of genetically programmed animal behavior. True, humans are animals; they share certain anatomical features with other animals, and some items of human behavior may seem analogous to the behavior of other animals. But such analogies can seriously mislead if we fail to look at the context of a particular item of behavior. Thus one ethologist compares the presentation of a twig by a cormorant with gift-giving in humans. Yet the cormorant's twig-presentation simply inhibits attack and is comparable to other appeasement rituals found in many species. Human gift-giving differs in form and purpose not only from culture, but within the same culture in various social contexts. Everything significant about it derives from its social context. Thus, ethologists can accomplish little beyond reminding us that we are animals—until they study humans as cultural beings.

해석 침팬지와 아이들, 갈매기와 희랍인들 등 인성학자들은 마음대로 인간의 문화행위 일부와 유전적으로 짜여진 동물의 행위 일부를 비교한다. 인간이 동물이라는 것은 맞는 말이다. 인간은 다른 동물과 특정 해부학적 특징을 공유한다. 인간 행위의 어떤 것은 다른 동물의 행위와 유사해 보일 수도 있다. 그러나 그런 유추들은 우리가 특수한 어떤 행위와 상황을 보지 않으면 심각하게 오해할 수 있다. 한 인성학자는 가마우지가 식물의 가는 가지를 주는 것을 사람들이 선물을 주는 행위와 비교한다. 그러나 가마우지가 가는 가지를 주는 것은 단지 공격을 억제하게 하며 여러 종에게서 찾아볼 수 있는 다른 유사 행위들과 비교될 수 있다. 선물을 주는 인간의 행위는 다양한 사회 상황 속에서 다른 문화권에서뿐만 아니라 같은 문화권 내에서도 형식과 목적에 있어서도 다르다. 그에 대한 의미 있는 모든 것은 사회적 상황에서 유래한다. 이리하여 인성학자들은 우리가 동물이라는 것을 우리에게 상기시켜 주는 것 이상의 일은 거의 할 수 없게 되는 것이다. 그들이 인간들을 문화적 존재로 연구할 때까지는 말이다.

7 The author is primarily concerned with

_____________.

① demonstrating the usefulness of ethology in discovering the behavioral limits within which humans operate

② objecting to the degradation of humanity implicit in the ethologists' equation of humans and animals

③ pointing out the dangers inherent in comparing highly dissimilar species, such as humans and cormorants, rather than similar ones, such as humans and apes

④ refuting the idea that the appeasement rituals in human cultural behavior can be profitably subjected to ethological analysis

⑤ arguing that the ethologists' assumption that human behavior can be straight forwardly compared with animal behavior is invalid

8 The author believes that gift-giving in humans

_____________.

① is instinctive behavior

② is analogous to appeasement rituals in other animals

③ is not an appropriate subject of study for ethologists

④ must be considered within its social context to be properly understood

⑤ may be a cultural remnant of behavior originally designed to inhibit attack

9 The author's attitude toward contemporary ethologists can best be described as

_____________.

① puzzled ② conciliatory
③ defensive ④ amused
⑤ disparaging

7 필자의 주된 관심사는 무엇인가?

① 인간이 운영하는 행위적 한계들을 연구하는 데 있어서 인성학의 효율성을 증명하는 것

② 인성학자들의 인간과 동물의 동일화에 내제된 인간의 타락을 반대하는 것

③ 인간과 유인원과 같은 유사한 종 대신에 매우 상이한 종들을 비교할 때 내재된 위험 요소들을 지적하는 것

④ 인간의 문화적 행동의 타협적 풍습들이 인성학자들의 분석에 대해 유리하게끔 제시될 수 있다는 생각을 반박하는 것

⑤ 인간의 행동이 잇달아서 동물의 행위와 비교될 수 있다는 인성학자들의 가정이 타당하지 못하다고 주장하는 것

8 필자는 인간의 선물 증정이 어떻다고 믿는가?

① 본능적인 행동이다.

② 다른 동물들의 타협적 풍습과 유사하다.

③ 인성학자의 적절한 연구 주제가 아니다.

④ 사회적 맥락에서 옳게 이해되어지게끔 고려되어야만 한다.

⑤ 원래는 공격을 막기 위해 고안된 행동의 문화적 잔존물일 수도 있다.

9 필자의 현대 인성학자에 대한 태도는 어떠한가?

① 당황한 ② 타협적인
③ 보호하는 ④ 즐거운
⑤ 비난하는

어구 gull 갈매기 ethologist 인성학자 anatomical 해부학적인 analogous 유사한 mislead 잘못 인도하다 cormorant 가마우지 inhibit 억제하다 appeasement 진정, 완화 ritual 의식, 제식 usefulness 유용성 implicit 함축적인, 은연중의 refute 논박하다 instinctive 본능적인 puzzled 당황한 conciliatory 회유적인, 타협적인 defensive 방어·변호의 amused 즐거운 disparaging 비난하는, 깔보는

해설 7 필자는 이 글에서 '식물 및 동물과 사람의 비교를 대등선상에서 하고 있는 인성학자들의 가정'을 비판하고 있다.

8 마지막에서 세 번째 문장을 통해 필자는 '인간의 선물 증정 행위는 형식과 목적의 차이가 다양한 사회적 측면에서 존재한다'고 했다.

9 마지막 문장에서 필자는 '인성학자들이 우리가 동물이라는 점을 상기시켜 주는 것 이상의 일을 할 수 있는 것은 거의 없다'고 표현한 점을 착안하여, 비난하는 태도로 볼 수 있다.

Today even the most incorrigible junk food addicts know that fats in any form are bad for their health and girth, but (1) trans fats are doubly bad for the heart. Formed when (2) liquid oils are solidified by adding hydrogen, trans fats boost bad-cholesterol (LDL) and depress good-cholesterol (HDL) levels in the blood. A recent study estimates that processed food and oils account for 80% of Americans' intake of trans fats. Researchers recommend people cut down as much as possible on (3) the fats. Another study concluded that eliminating (4) hydrogenated oils could prevent up to 100,000 premature coronary deaths a year.

10 밑줄 친 (1)∼(4) 중 가리키는 대상이 나머지 셋과 다른 것은?

① (1) ② (2)
③ (3) ④ (4)

해석 오늘날 구제할 수 없을 정도로 즉석 식품에 중독된 사람들조차도 어떤 형태의 지방이라도 그들의 건강과 허리둘레에 해롭다는 것을 알고 있다. 그러나 전이 지방은 그들의 심장에 두 배는 더 해롭다. 수소가 첨가되어 액체 기름이 고체화될 때 형성되는 전이 지방은 혈액 안에서 해로운 콜레스테롤을 증가시키고 이로운 콜레스테롤을 감소시킨다. 최근의 연구에 따르자면 가공식품과 기름이 미국인의 전이 지방 섭취의 80%를 차지한다고 보고한다. 연구가들은 사람들이 전이 지방을 가능한 한 많이 줄여야 한다고 권고한다. 또 다른 연구는 경화유를 없앰으로써 조기 관상 동맥 질환 사망자를 연간 10만 명까지 예방할 수 있다고 결론을 내렸다.

어구 incorrigible 제멋대로의; 교정할 수 없는 junk food 즉석 음식 be bad for ~에 해롭다 trans fat 전이 지방 liquid oil 액체 기름 solidify 응고시키다; 단결시키다 hydrogen 수소 boost 증가시키다 depress 약화시키다; 불경기로 만들다 processed 가공된 account for ~을 차지하다; ~을 설명하다 intake 섭취량, 흡입량 cut down 감소시키다; 삭감하다 as ~ as possible 가능한 eliminate 제거하다; 무시하다 hydrogenated oil 경화유 premature 시기상조의; 조숙한 coronary 관상 동맥의

해설 (2)의 액체 기름은 수소와 결합하여 전이 지방으로 만들어지는 객체일 뿐 전이 지방 그 자체는 아니다. 나머지 모든 표현은 몸에 해로운 전이 지방을 일컫고 있다.

The bird dipped again slanting his wings for the dive and then swinging them wildly and ineffectually as he followed the flying fish. The old man could see the slight bulge in the water that the big dolphins raised as they followed the escaping fish. The dolphins were cutting through the water below the flight of the fish and would be in the water, driving at speed, when the fish dropped.

"It is a big school of dolphins," he thought. "They are widespread and the flying fish have little chance. The bird has no chance."

11 Which of the following is most likely to be discussed afterwards?

① The bird will catch the flying fish.
② The dolphins will attack the old man.
③ The flying fish will be caught by the dolphins.
④ The wings of the bird will be hurt by the old man.

해석 그 새가 물에 살짝 몸을 다시 닿게 하고서, 다이빙을 하기 위해서 날개를 기울였다. 그리고는 날치의 뒤를 맹렬히 쫓아갔지만, 비효율적으로 날갯짓을 했다. 노인은 바다에서 커다란 돌고래들이 물 위로 살짝 올라와서 도망가는 물고기를 쫓아가는 모습을 보았다. 돌고래는 날아가는 물고기 아래에서 물살을 가르고 있었고, 날치가 물속으로 떨어질 때 빠른 속도로 물속을 헤엄쳤다. "커다란 돌고래 무리가 있네."라고 노인은 생각했다. "돌고래는 바다에 퍼져 있고, 날치들은 거의 가능성이 없어. 그리고 새들도 가능성이 없겠다."

11 이 글에 이어서 논의될 내용은 무엇인가?

① 그 새가 날치를 잡을 것이다.
② 돌고래가 노인을 공격할 것이다.
③ 돌고래가 날치를 잡을 것이다.
④ 노인이 새의 날개에 상처를 입힐 것이다.

어구 dip 담그다, 살짝 담그다 slant 기울이다; 기대게 하다 dive 다이빙, 잠수; 전념 bulge 부풀어 오름, 팽창 cut through 가르고 나가다 flying fish 날치 have no chance 가능성이 없다

해설 마지막 문장에서, 노인이 돌고래가 바다에 퍼져 있고, 날치들과 새들이 가능성이 없다고 얘기한 것은 돌고래의 공격을 날치들과 새들이 피할 수 없을 것임을 예측한 것이다.

>>> **다음 글을 읽고 문제의 답을 고르시오.**

Life moves in circles of power and of vividness, and each circle of life only maintains its orbit upon the subjection of some lower circle. If the lower circles of life are not mastered, there can be no higher circles. In nature, one creature devours another, and this is an essential part of all existence and of all being. It is not something to try to reform, nor something to lament over.

12 다음 글의 제목으로 가장 적절한 것은?

① The ladder of power and vividness in life
② The perpetual motion of life
③ Sacrifice; a tragedy of life
④ The stronger preying on the weak

해석 생명은 강하고 활기찬 집단들 내에서 움직인다. 각각의 생명체 집단은 몇몇 하위 집단의 종속 하에 궤도를 유지한다. 만일 하위 생명체들이 정복당하지 않는다면 상위 집단들도 존재할 수 없다. 사실상 한 동물이 다른 동물을 잡아먹으며, 이는 모든 실제, 존재와 생명체의 필수 요소가 된다. 바꾸려고 노력하거나 슬퍼할 것이 아니다.

12 ① 생명의 힘과 활기의 사다리
② 생명의 영속적인 이동
③ 희생: 삶의 비극
④ 약자를 잡아먹는 강자

어구 **circle** 집단, 사회; 원; 범위　**vividness** 원기 왕성; 활기　**upon the subjection of** ~의 종속 하에　**master** 정복하다; 터득하다　**in nature** 사실상　**devour** 게걸스럽게 먹다; 탐독하다　**being** 존재; 생존; 생명　**lament over** 슬퍼하다, 비탄하다; 애도하다　**prey on** ~을 잡아먹다

해설 이 글은 집단 내에서 상위 집단이 하등 집단을 정복하는 '양육강식'에 관해 논하고 있다. 따라서 그 제목 또한 '약자를 잡아먹는 강자'라는 제목이 옳다.

>>> **다음 글을 읽고 문제의 답을 고르시오.** [13~14]

What is good literature, what has educational value, what is refined public information, what is good art, varies with individuals as it does from one generation to another. There doubtlessly would be a contrariety of views concerning Cervantes' *Don Quixote*, Shakespeare's *Venus and Adonis*, or Zola's *Nana*. But a requirement that literature or art conform to some norm prescribed by an official smacks of an ideology foreign to our system.

13 The writer above is discussing ___________ .

① how literature is created
② censorship
③ limits of literature
④ the importance of literature
⑤ vicissitudes of literature

14 The writer above introduces Shakespeare's *Venus and Adonis* to make the point that ___________ .

① people differ on what is considered obscene in literature
② people should not be exposed to obscene literature
③ modern literature is better written
④ what was obscene in the past is obscene now
⑤ he introduces the importance of literature

해석 훌륭한 문학이란 무엇이고, 교육적 가치가 있는 것은 무엇이며, 세련된 대중적인 정보는 무엇이고, 또는 훌륭한 예술인은 누구냐 하는 것은 한 세대에서 다른 세대로 옮겨 가면서 변화하는 것처럼 개인들에 따라 변화한다. 의심할 바 없이 세르반테스의 〈돈키호테〉와 셰익스피어의 〈비너스와 아도니스〉, 또는 졸라의 〈나나〉에 관한 의견들의 차이가 존재할 것이다. 그러나 문학이나 예술이 한 공직자에 의해 규정된 어떤 규칙에 따라야 한다는 요구사항은 우리의 체계와 이질적인 이데올로기와 같은 성질을 띠게 된다.

13 윗글에서 작가가 논하고 있는 것은?
① 문학이 창조되는 방법　　　② 검열
③ 문학의 한계　　　　　　　④ 문학의 중요성
⑤ 문학의 흥망성쇠

14 작가가 윗글에서 셰익스피어의 〈비너스와 아도니스〉를 소개한 것은 무엇을 가리키기 위해서인가?
① 사람들은 문학에서 외설스럽다고 여겨지는 것에 대해 다른 입장을 취한다.
② 사람들이 외설스러운 문학에 노출되어서는 안 된다.
③ 현대문학이 더 훌륭히 저술된다.
④ 과거에 외설스러웠던 것은 지금도 외설스럽다.
⑤ 문학의 중요성을 소개한다.

어구 **contrariety** 상반된 사실, 모순, 불일치　**smack of** ~의 기미가 보이다　**foreign to** ~과 이질적인　**vicissitude** 흥망성쇠

해설 13 공직자의 판단에 따라 내려진 규범은 검열이다.
14 문학의 평가는 시대가 변함에 따라 변화할 수 있다는 설명의 예로, 셰익스피어의 작품을 소개한 것이므로, 입장 차이가 있다는 내용의 범주에 포함되는 ①이 가장 합당하다.

>>> 다음 글을 읽고 문제의 답을 고르시오.

At the age of eighty my mother had her last bad fall, and after that her mind wandered freely through time. Some days she went to weddings and funerals that had taken place half a century earlier. On others, she presided over family dinners cooked on Sunday afternoons for children who were now gray with age.

"Where's Russell?" she asked one day when I came to visit at the nursing home.

"I'm Russell," I said.

"Russell's only this big," she said, holding her hand, palm down, two feet from the floor. That day she was a young country wife with chickens in the backyard and I was a stranger old enough to be her father.

15 Which of the following is NOT true regarding Russell's mother?

① She is at the nursing home.

② She remembers her father as a stranger.

③ She has some problem to recognize her son.

④ She wanders free through time after her fall.

해석 어머니의 연세가 여든이 됐을 때, 어머니는 마지막으로 심하게 넘어지셨고, 그 후 어머니의 정신은 세월을 자유로이 넘나들었다. 어떤 기간에는 반세기 전에 있었던 결혼식이나 장례식에 가셨다. 다른 날에는 지금은 나이가 들어 백발인 우리들을 위해서 일요일 오후마다 가족 식사를 주도하셨다.

"러셀이 어디 있나요?"라고 어느 날 내가 요양원에 방문했을 때 물어보셨다.

"제가 러셀이에요."라고 나는 말했다.

"러셀은 겨우 이 정도 크기밖에 되지 않아요."라고 말하시면서, 손바닥을 아래로 하여 손을 바닥에서 60센티미터 가량 높이에서 잡고 계셨다. 그날 어머니는 뒤뜰에서 닭과 함께 있는 젊은 시골 여성이셨으며, 나는 어머니의 아버지가 될 정도로 나이가 많은 낯선 사람이 되었다.

15 러셀의 어머니에 관한 설명으로 옳지 못한 것은?

① 그녀는 요양원에 있다.

② 그녀는 아버지를 낯선 사람으로 기억한다.

③ 그녀는 아들을 알아보는 데 약간의 애를 먹고 있다.

④ 그녀는 넘어진 사고를 당한 후 오랜 시간 동안 정신이 오락가락한다.

어구 have/get a fall 넘어지다 **wander** (마음이) 종잡을 수 없게 이리저리 변하다; (정신이) 오락가락하다 **take place** 나타나다, 발생하다 **preside over** (식탁에서) 주인 역을 맡아 보다; 의장 역을 맡다 **backyard** 뒤뜰; 세력 범위 **through time** 오랜 시간 동안

해설 마지막 문장인 'I was a stranger old enough to be her father.'을 통해, 어머니가 필자인 자식을 자신의 아버지로 잘못 알아보고 있음을 말하고 있다. 따라서 '어머니가 자신의 아버지를 낯선 사람으로 기억한다.'는 틀린 설명이다.

>>> 다음 글을 읽고 문제의 답을 고르시오.

In most areas of the world, both the physical landscape and the maps of it are relatively stable. Map revision is usually concerned with man-made features, such as buildings and roads. This is not true of Antarctica. The Antarctic ice sheet is a dynamic entity and cartographers have to contend with big and rapid changes in the physical geography of the continent. For example, earlier this year they faced the dramatic break-up of the Larsen ice shelves in the Antarctic region, which is where the British Antarctic Survey concentrates its mapping activity. Topographic maps are probably changing faster in Antarctica than anywhere else in the world.

16 What does the break-up of the Larsen ice shelves illustrate?

① The errors that occur on maps of the Antarctic

② The difficulties in reaching areas in the Antarctic

③ The sort of changes that can occur in the Antarctic

④ The regularity with which map-makers visit the Antarctic

해석 지구상의 많은 지역은 물리적 풍경과 그에 관한 지도가 비교적 고정되어 있다. 지도 수정은 보통 건물이나 길처럼 사람이 만든 지형과 연관성이 있다. 그러나 남극 대륙에서는 그렇지 않다. 남극의 빙하는 역동적인 것이기 때문에 지도 제작자들은 대륙의 물리적인 지형에 일어나는 크고 빠른 변화들과 경쟁해야 한다. 예컨대, 올해 초에 지도 제작자들은 남극 대륙에 있는 라센 빙붕의 극적인 붕괴를 보았다. 그곳에서 영국 남극 조사단은 지도 제작 작업에 열중하고 있었던 것이다. 지형상의 지도는 이 세상의 어느 곳보다 남극 대륙에서 가장 빠르게 변하고 있다.

16 라센 빙붕의 붕괴는 무엇을 묘사하는 것인가?

① 남극 대륙에서 나타나는 오류들

② 남극 대륙 지역에 도착하는 어려움들

③ 남극 대륙에서 발생할 수 있는 변화의 종류들

④ 지도 제작자들이 남극 대륙에 규칙적으로 방문하는 것

어구 ladnscape 풍경 **stable** 고정된, 안정된 **be concerned with** ~과 관련이 있다 **man-made** 인간이 만든 **be true of** ~의 경우에도 그렇다 **ice sheet** 빙하 **dynamic** 활발한; 동력의 **cartographer** 지도 제작자 **contend with** ~과 다투다, 경쟁하다 **dramatic** 극적인 **break-up** 분산, 붕괴, 파괴 **shelf** 지층; 대륙붕; 선반 **Topographic** (시·그림 따위) 일정 지역의 예술적 표현의, 지지적(地誌的)인 **occur** 발생하다 **regularity** 규칙, 정규

해설 마지막에서 세 번째 문장인 For example ~에서 라센 빙붕의 극적인 붕괴를 보았다고 했으며, 이하에서 이는 가장 빠른 변화라고 설명하고 있다.

>>> **다음 글을 읽고 문제의 답을 고르시오.**

To what use does a kangaroo put its great heavy tail? It leans back and props itself on it, a man does on a shooting stick. Many lizards use their tails that way too. The original monster lizards, almost certainly, swung their tails as weapons, in a carry-over from the tail-swinging technique of fish. And today? Is it true that a crocodile uses its tail as a weapon? Yes. It can knock a man over with one wallop. Do any warm blooded animals do the same sort of thing? Yes again. Take an ant bear. It thwacks with its tail as powerfully as a bear with its forepaw.

※참고 shooting stick 수렵용 지팡이 | ant bear 개미핥기

17 윗글의 내용과 일치하는 것을 고르시오.

① A lizard is the only animal which can use its tail as a shooting stick.
② A kangaroo uses its tail as a tool to recline itself.
③ A monster lizard is good at the technique of transportation.
④ An ant bear like the warm blooded animals uses its tail more than a forepaw.

해석 캥거루는 크고 무거운 꼬리를 어떤 용도로 사용할까? 캥거루는 마치 사람이 수렵용 지팡이에 기대는 것처럼, 몸을 기대고 자신의 몸을 꼬리로 버틴다. 많은 도마뱀들도 또한 그렇게 꼬리를 이용한다. 원시 괴물 도마뱀은 물고기의 꼬리를 흔드는 기술을 유전 받아, 꼬리를 무기로 휘둘렀던 것이 거의 분명하다. 그리고 현재는 어떠한가? 악어가 꼬리를 무기로 이용하는 것이 사실일까? 맞다. 악어는 한 번의 타격으로 인간을 쓰러뜨릴 수 있다. 어떤 온혈 동물이라도 똑같이 그럴 수 있을까? 그렇다. 개미핥기는 곰의 앞발만큼 강력하게 꼬리로 때릴 수 있다.

17 윗글의 내용과 일치하는 것을 고르시오.

① 도마뱀은 수렵용 지팡이로 꼬리를 이용할 수 있는 유일한 동물이다.
② 캥거루는 자신의 몸을 지탱하기 위한 수단으로 꼬리를 이용한다.
③ 원시 괴물 도마뱀은 운송 능력이 뛰어나다.
④ 온혈 동물과 같은 개미핥기는 앞발보다 꼬리를 더 많이 이용한다.

어구 **lean back** 상체를 굽히다; 뒤로 젖히다   **prop** 버티다, ~에 버팀목(木)을 대다(up); 기대 놓다   **original monster lizards** 원시 괴물 도마뱀   **carry-over** 이월(移越), 잔품(殘品); 이월 거래; 나머지   **in a carry-over from** ~로부터 건네받아, ~로부터 물려받아   **tail-swinging** 꼬리를 휘두르는   **knock** 치다, 두드리다   **wallop** 패다, 강타하다   **warm blooded animals** 온혈 동물   **thwack** 찰싹 때리다, 강타하다, 두들기다   **forepaw** 앞발   **be good at** ~에 능숙하다   **transportation** 운송, 수송

해설 두 번째 문장에서, 사람이 몸을 기대기 위하여 수렵용 지팡이를 사용하듯이, 캥거루는 자신의 꼬리를 이용하여 몸을 기댄다고 했다.

>>> **다음 글을 읽고 문제의 답을 고르시오.**

[I]   Taboos are associated with behavior that is considered undesirable or immoral.

[II]   One clear example of this is the way in which languages reflect cultural taboos.

[III]   We have already seen that language often mirrors its own society's values and beliefs.

[IV]   Consequently, these acts are forbidden and to be avoided.

18 위 문장들을 의미가 가장 잘 통하도록 배열한 것은?

① [I] — [III] — [IV] — [II]
② [I] — [II] — [III] — [IV]
③ [III] — [I] — [IV] — [II]
④ [III] — [II] — [I] — [IV]

해석 [III] 우리는 이미 언어가 사회의 가치와 신념을 종종 반영한다는 사실을 알고 있다.
[II] 이것에 대한 분명한 예는 언어가 문화적 금기를 반영하는 방식이다.
[I] 금기는 바람직하지 않거나 도덕에 어긋나는 것으로 간주되는 행동과 관련이 있다.
[IV] 결과적으로 이러한 행위들은 금지되고 피해야만 한다.

어구 **be associated with** ~과 관련되어 있다   **undesirable** 바람직하지 못한   **immoral** 비도덕적인   **taboo** (종교상의) 터부, 금기   **mirror** 반영하다   **forbid** 금지하다

해설 [III] 언어의 사회의 가치 및 믿음을 반영한다는 일반적인 진술이 나오고, [II] 이에 대한 예로 언어가 문화의 금기를 반영한다는 내용으로 들어준다. [I] 금기와 연관된 세부 내용을 전달하며, [IV] consequently라는 접속 부사로 결론을 내린다.

The complete science of 'politics' falls into two parts which may for convenience be called ethics and politics. Aristotle's ethics, no doubt, are social, and his politics are ethical; he does not forget in the Ethics that the individual man is essentially a member of society, nor in the Politics that the good life of the state exists only in the good lives of its citizens. Still, he has no doubt that there is a difference between the two enquiries. About the nature of the relationship between them he is not so clear. At the outset of the Ethics he describes the good of the state as 'greater and more perfect' than that of the individual, and the latter as merely something _______________ which we may have to put up if we cannot attain the former. But his sense of value of the individual life appears to grow as he discusses it, and at the end of the work he speaks as if the state were merely ancillary to the moral life of the individual, supplying the element of compulsion which is needed if man's desires are to be made subservient to his reason.

19 According to the passage, which of the following statements is true?

① Aristotle wrote the Ethics, but not the Politics.
② Aristotle didn't distinguish between ethics and politics which constitute social science.
③ Aristotle didn't lucidly specify the nature of the relationship between ethics and politics.
④ Aristotle criticized politicians, in the Politics, for pursuing a policy of conciliation.
⑤ Aristotle was the only scholar who considered ethics and politics are both social.

20 According to the passage, what does Aristotle think at the end of the Ethics about the relationship between the state and the individual?

① Man's desires are more important than the state's future.
② The individual must work hard to build up the power of the state.
③ The state must provide the individual with wealth and power.
④ The moral life of the individual is secondary to the good of the state.
⑤ The state is subsidiary to the moral life of the individual.

21 밑줄 친 부분에 들어갈 가장 알맞은 것은?

① for   ② with
③ of   ④ under
⑤ to

해석 정치에 대한 완전한 학문은 편의를 위하여 윤리학과 정치학으로 일컬어지는 두 분류로 구분된다. 의심할 여지 없이 아리스토텔레스의 윤리학은 사회적이고 그의 정치학은 윤리적이다. 그는 '윤리학'에서 개인은 사회의 구성원이라는 점을 잊지 않으며, '정치학'에서는 국가의 안녕은 시민의 행복한 삶에서 존재한다는 점을 잊지 않는다. 그럼에도 불구하고 그는 이 두 과제 사이의 차이점이 있다는 점을 의심하지 않았다. 이들 사이의 관계의 본질에 관해 그는 분명한 태도를 보이지 않는다. '윤리학'의 초두에서 그는 국가의 이익을 개인의 이익보다 '더 크고 더 완벽한' 것으로 묘사하며 전자를 달성할 수 없다면 후자는 견뎌야 할 것으로 설명한다. 그러나 개인의 삶의 가치에 관한 그의 감각은 논의를 진행하면서 더 커지는 것처럼 보이며, 그 작품의 마지막에서는 국가가 인간의 욕망이 그의 이성에 봉사하도록 하기 위해 필요한 의무 요소를 제공해 주는 개인의 도덕적 인생에 대해 단지 부속품에 불과한 것처럼 말한다.

19 윗글의 내용과 일치하는 내용은?
① 아리스토텔레스는 윤리학을 썼지만 정치학은 쓰지 않았다.
② 아리스토텔레스는 사회과학을 구성하는 윤리학과 정치학을 구분하지 않았다.
③ 아리스토텔레스는 윤리학과 정치학의 성질을 투명하게 설명하지 못했다.
④ 아리스토텔레스는 정치학에서 정치인들이 타협의 정치를 추구한다는 이유로 비평했다.
⑤ 아리스토텔레스는 윤리학과 정치학 모두 사회적이라고 간주했었던 유일한 철학자이다.

20 이 글에 따르자면, 윤리학의 끝부분에서 국가와 개인의 관계에 관해 아리스토텔레스는 무엇이라 생각했겠는가?
① 개인의 소망이 국가의 미래보다 더 중요하다.
② 개인이 국가의 힘을 증강시키기 위해 열심히 일을 해야 한다.
③ 국가는 개인에게 부와 힘을 제공해야만 한다.
④ 인간의 도덕적인 삶은 국가의 이익에 종속되는 존재이다.
⑤ 국가는 개인의 도덕적인 삶에 종속되는 존재이다.

어구 **fall into** 분류되다 **for convenience** 편의상 **ethics** 윤리학, 도덕 **politics** 정치학, 정치 **no doubt** 의심할 바 없이 **enquiry** 문의, 조사(inquiry) **outset** 착수, 시작, 최초 **put up with** 견디다, 참다 **attain** 획득하다, 달성하다, 이루다 **ancillary** 보조물, 보조자, 조력자; 보조의 **compulsion** 강요, 강제, 충동 **subservient** 도움이 되는, 비굴한 **lucidly** 투명하게 **specify** 상술하다, 자세히 쓰다 **conciliation** 회유, 화해, 달램 **build up** 증강하다 **secondary** 종속적인, 제2의

해설 **19** 'About the nature of the relationship between them he is not so clear.' 문장을 통해 아리스토텔레스는 윤리학과 정치학의 성질을 명백히 구분했다고 볼 수는 없다는 내용이 유추가 가능하다.
20 마지막 문장에서 '국가가 … 개인의 도덕적 인생에 대해 단지 부속품에 불과한 것처럼 말한다.'라고 말했으므로, 국가가 개인의 도덕적인 삶에 종속된다고 볼 수 있다.
21 put up with는 '견디다'는 뜻을 가진 구동사이다.

>>> 다음 글을 읽고 문제의 답을 고르시오. [22~24]

The common good is a term that can refer to several different concepts. In the popular meaning, the common good describes a specific "good" that is shared and beneficial for all (or most) members of a given community. This is also how the common good is broadly defined in philosophy, ethics, and political science.

However there is no strict definition of the common good for each situation. The good that is common between person A and person B may not be the same as between person A and person C. (가) ______________, although there are some things such as the basic requirements for staying alive: food, water, and shelter—that are always good for all people.

The common good is often regarded as a utilitarian ideal, thus representing "the greatest possible good for the greatest possible number of individuals". In the best case scenario, the "greatest possible number of individuals" would mean all sentient beings. This definition of the common good presents it as a quality which is convertible, or reducible, to the sum total of all the private interests of the individual members of a society and interchangeable with them.

22 Choose the main theme of the above passage.

① The basic requirement for the utilitarian ideal
② The common good's relativity
③ How to tell the difference between private and common good
④ The absolute quality of the private interests

23 Which of the following is best for the blank (가)?

① Paradoxically the good may be unuseful.
② The common good can always be absolute.
③ Each group's opinion can be objective.
④ Thus the common good can often change.

24 According to the passage, which of the following is characteristic of common good?

① either absolute or subjective
② either objective or subjective
③ either relative or adaptable
④ neither absolute nor adaptable

해석 공익은 여러 다양한 의미를 가리킬 수 있는 용어이다. 보편적인 의미로서 공익은 일정한 단체의 모든 (혹은 대다수의) 구성원들이 공유하거나 그들에게 이로운 구체적인 '이익'을 말한다. 게다가 공익은 철학, 윤리학 및 정치 과학의 분야에서도 광범위하게 정의 내려진다.

그러나 각각의 상황에 맞는 공익의 엄격한 개념은 존재하지 않는다. A와 B의 공통된 공익이 A와 C 간의 공익과 동일한 것이 아닐 수 있다. 언제나 모든 사람들에게 도움이 되는 식량, 물, 대피소와 같이 생존을 위한 필수품과 같은 것이 있더라도, 공익은 종종 변화할 수도 있다.

공익은 때로는 공리주의적 이상이라고 간주가 되기 때문에, "최상의 잠재력을 가진 자들을 위한 최상의 잠재력을 가진 이득"이라고 묘사가 된다. 최상의 시나리오로 "최상의 잠재력을 가진 자들"은 지각이 있는 모든 개인들을 의미할 것이다. 공익에 대한 이 묘사는 공익을 어느 사회 구성원들의 모든 전체 사적 이익으로 변화할 수 있거나 환원할 수 있으며, 이 공익이 사적 이익과 교체가 가능한 가치라고 느끼게 한다.

22 이 글의 주제를 고르시오.

① 공리주의적 이상의 기본이 되는 필수 조건
② 공익의 상대성
③ 사익과 공익을 구별하는 방법
④ 사익의 절대적인 가치

23 (가)에 가장 알맞은 것은?

① 모순적으로 공익은 쓸모없는 것이 될 수 있다.
② 공익은 언제나 절대적일 수 있다.
③ 각 단체의 의견은 객관적일 수 있다.
④ 따라서 공익은 종종 변화할 수 있다.

24 이 글에 따랐을 때, 공익의 특징은 무엇인가?

① 절대적이거나 주관적인
② 객관적이거나 주관적인
③ 상대적이거나 융통성이 있는
④ 절대적이지도 않고 융통성도 없는

어구 beneficial 유익한, 이익을 가져오는 given 일정한; 주어진 utilitarian 공리주의; 실용주의 present A as B A를 B라고 느끼게 하다 sum total 전체, 총체적 결과; 요지

해설 22 공익의 절대적인 개념은 존재하지 않으며, 공익은 각각의 상황과 분야에서 상이하고도 상대적인 성질을 갖추고 있다는 것이 이 글의 주제가 된다.

23 앞 문장에서 개인마다 공익의 개념이 상이할 수 있다고 했기 때문에, 그 성질이 종종 변화할 수 있다는 내용으로 연결되어야 한다.

24 앞서 설명한 두 문제의 해설 참조

A lot of experimental work is being done to increase our knowledge about insomnia and other sleep-related problems in order to help people who are deprived of sleep. Some of these studies have shown that, although some people have trouble falling asleep, others have an equally difficult time waking up. It is believed that there is a natural cycle which regulates man's body temperature. During the night a person's temperature may drop one or two degrees, and it can be difficult to arouse him in the morning if his body hasn't become hot enough yet. In addition, a person awakened during a period of heavy sleep is irritable and can not think clearly. Finally, some people don't want to get up simply because they don't like the activity that awaits them.

25 According to the passage, which of the following is NOT true?

① In our falling asleep, our temperature may fall.
② For men to get up from bed well, some temperature will be needed.
③ Heavy sleep can cause people to be nervous.
④ Potential daily work can cause men to suffer from insomnia.
⑤ Natural phenomenon can affect men's sleeping cycle.

26 이 글의 주제를 고르시오.

① Our Increased Knowledge about Insomnia
② Men's Body Temperature
③ The Reasons for Insomnia
④ The Contents of Sleep Research
⑤ The Interrelation between Insomnia and Oversleeping

해석 잠을 자지 못하는 사람들을 돕기 위해서, 불면증과 수면과 관련된 다른 문제들에 대한 지식을 증가시키기 위해서 많은 실험이 행해지고 있다. 이런 연구 중의 몇몇에 의해 밝혀진 바에 의하면, 잠이 드는 것에 어려움을 겪는 사람들도 있지만, 잠에서 깨어나는 데 마찬가지의 어려움을 겪고 있는 사람들도 있다. 사람의 체온을 조절하는 자연의 사이클이 있다고 믿어진다. 밤 동안에는 사람의 체온이 1~2도 떨어질 수 있으며, 몸이 아직 충분히 더워지지 않을 때에는 아침에 깨우는 것이 어려울 수도 있다. 게다가, 깊은 잠에서 깬 사람은 신경질적이며 생각을 또렷하게 할 수가 없다. 마지막으로, 단지 그들을 기다리고 있는 활동이 싫기 때문에 일어나고 싶어 하지 않는 사람들도 있다.

25 불일치하는 내용은?

① 우리가 잠이 들 때 체온이 떨어질 수 있다.
② 사람들이 기상을 잘 하기 위해서는 약간의 온도가 필요할 것이다.
③ 깊은 잠은 사람들이 짜증감을 느낄 수 있게 할 수 있다.
④ 하루 동안 있게 될 일이 불면증에 걸리게 할 수 있다.
⑤ 자연현상이 인간의 수면 사이클에 영향을 미칠 수 있다.

26 이 글의 주제를 고르시오.

① 불면증에 대한 우리의 증가하는 지식
② 체온
③ 불면증의 이유들
④ 수면연구의 내용들
⑤ 불면증과 잠의 상호관계

어구 insomnia 불면증　deprive A of B A에게서 B를 빼앗다　have trouble (in) -ing ～에 어려움을 겪다　fall asleep 잠들다　regulate 규제하다　arouse 자극하다, 깨우다　irritable 신경질적인

해설 25 하루 동안 있게 될 일이 불면증에 걸리게 하는 것이 아니라, 깊은 잠에서 깨지 못하게 하는 결과를 야기할 수 있다고 했다.
26 이 글은 불면증과 잠과 같은 수면과 관련된 이유들 및 영향들 연구들에 의해 밝혀지고 있음을 설명하고 있다.

>>> **다음 글을 읽고 문제의 답을 고르시오.** [27~30]

Christopher Finch, in his semiofficial pictorial history of Disney's work, comments: "The Mickey Mouse who hit the movie houses in the late twenties was not quite the ⓐ ______________ character most of us are familiar with today. He was mischievous, to say the least, and even displayed a ⓑ streak of cruelty." ⓒ ______________ Mickey soon cleaned up his act, leaving to gossip and speculation only his unresolved relationship with Minnie and the status of Morty and Ferdie. Finch continued: "Mickey ... had become virtually a national symbol, and as such he was expected to behave properly at all times."

27 Choose the most appropriate word for blank ⓐ.

① well-known　　② well-trained
③ well-to-do　　④ well-dressed
⑤ well-behaved

28 Choose the word closest in meaning to the underlined word ⓑ.

① steak　　② stream
③ tendency　　④ strength
⑤ toughness

29 Choose the most appropriate transition word for blank ⓒ.

① Additionally　　② Therefore
③ But　　④ First
⑤ Moreover

30 According to the passage, Mickey ______________.

① has not been shown until the thirties
② has shown no change in character from the beginning
③ has developed its mischievousness later
④ has shown no cruelty in the beginning
⑤ has been influenced by the public opinion

해석 크리스토퍼 핀치는 디즈니 작품에 대한 비공식적인 그림 역사 이야기에서 이렇게 논평했다. "20세기 후반에 영화에서 히트를 한 미키 마우스는 현재 우리에게 익숙한 착한 캐릭터라고 보기 어렵습니다. 미키 마우스는 최소한 장난스러우며 심지어 일종의 잔인함까지도 갖고 있었죠." 그러나 미키 마우스는 곧 이런 결함을 개선하고 미니와의 관계와, 모티와 퍼티의 관계만을 사람들의 관심에 오르내리게 한다. 핀치는 이어서 "미키는 사실상 국민적인 상징이 되었고 그런 상징으로서 계속해서 바르게 행동하리라 기대가 되었습니다."라고 했다.

27 ⓐ에 적합한 보기는?

① 잘 알려진　　② 훈련이 잘된
③ 유복한　　④ 차려입은
⑤ 행동이 바른

28 ⓑ와 유사한 의미는?

① 스테이크　　② 흐름
③ 경향　　④ 힘
⑤ 강인함

29 ⓒ에 적합한 보기는?

① 게다가　　② 따라서
③ 그러나　　④ 첫째로
⑤ 더욱이

30 이 글에 따르자면 미키 마우스는 어떠한가?

① 30년대가 되어서야 비로소 모습을 드러냈다.
② 처음부터 캐릭터의 변화를 나타내지 않았다.
③ 장난기가 나중에 개발되었다.
④ 처음에는 잔인성을 나타내지 않았다.
⑤ 여론에 영향을 받았다.

어구 semiofficial 반관적인[보도 · 성명 따위], 반공식적인　pictorial 그림의, 그림이 들어간　mischievous 장난스러운　to say the least 최소한, 아무리 줄여 말해도　streak 경향, 줄, 선, 기간, 단기간　clean up 깨끗이 치우다, 해결하다　speculation 추측, 추정　virtually 실제로　well-known 잘 알려진　well-to-do 유복한

해설 27 다음 문장에서 mischievous(장난스러운)란 단어가 등장하므로, 빈칸 앞에 위치한 부정어 not과 결합하기 위해서는 '행동이 바른'이 적합하다. 그래야만 순접으로 이어지기 때문이다.
28 streak는 '(다른 이와 구분될 만한) 경향, 성질(a part of someone's character that is different from the rest of their character)'을 의미한다.
29 미키 마우스의 초기 모습은 장난스러워 보였지만, 이후에는 미니 마우스 등과 관계를 맺기 시작하면서 초기의 모습에서 발전했다고 했으므로, 역접의 but이 옳다.
30 마지막 문장에서 미키 마우스가 미국의 국민 상징이 되면서부터 이에 상응할 만한 행동을 하게 되었다고 했으므로 여론에 영향을 받았다는 내용이 옳다.

MEMO